FROM FOREST TO STEPPE

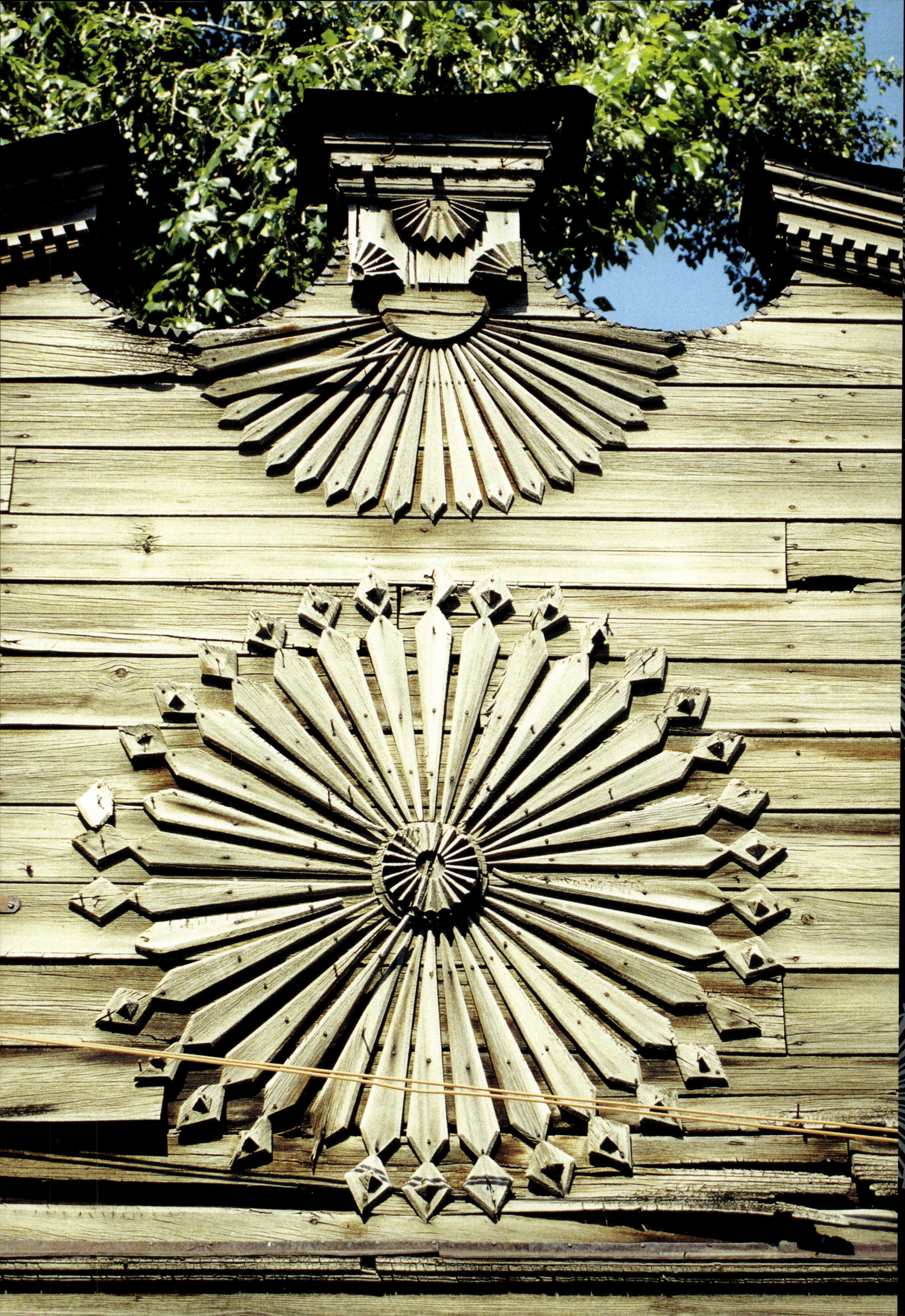

From Forest to Steppe

THE RUSSIAN ART OF BUILDING IN WOOD

Text and photographs by

William Craft Brumfield

DUKE UNIVERSITY PRESS   DURHAM AND LONDON   2025

Printed in the United States of America on acid-free paper ∞
Project Editor: Livia Tenzer
Designed by Matthew Tauch
Typeset in Alegreya and Degular by Westchester Publishing Services

Library of Congress Cataloging-in-Publication Data
Names: Brumfield, William Craft, [date] author, photographer.
Title: From forest to steppe : the Russian art of building in wood / text and photographs by William Craft Brumfield.
Description: Durham : Duke University Press, 2025. | Includes bibliographical references and index.
Identifiers: LCCN 2024033060 (print)
LCCN 2024033061 (ebook)
ISBN 9781478028246 (hardcover)
ISBN 9781478060451 (ebook)
Subjects: LCSH: Building, Wooden—Russia (Federation)—History. | Architecture—Russia (Federation)—History. | Vernacular architecture—Russia (Federation)—History. | Building, Wooden—Russia (Federation)—Pictorial works. | Architecture—Russia (Federation)—Pictorial works. | Vernacular architecture—Russia (Federation)—Pictorial works.
Classification: LCC NA4110 .B78 2025 (print) | LCC NA4110 (ebook) | DDC 721/.04480947—dc23/eng/20250122
LC record available at https://lccn.loc.gov/2024033060
LC ebook record available at https://lccn.loc.gov/2024033061

Cover art: (*front*) Church of the Transfiguration of the Savior, (*back*) Church of the Intercession, bell tower, Khizhi Island. Photo: William Craft Brumfield, July 13, 2007.

Duke University Press gratefully acknowledges the generous support of Richard Hedreen, who provided funds toward the publication of this book.

Frontispiece: Pediment, wooden house, Khmelnitsky Street 38, Blagoveshchensk. Photo: William Craft Brumfield, June 14, 2002.

TO THE MEMORY OF ELIZABETH HEDREEN (1936–2022), whose devotion to the fine arts was amplified by her compassionate, sustaining generosity.

Contents

Acknowledgments

FOR A BOOK COVERING SO MUCH TIME AND SPACE, acknowledgments can only occur on the most general level, yet there are certain colleagues who moved beyond the essential to the existential in supporting my Russian work: the late James Billington, Librarian of Congress; Dan Davidson, former president of American Councils for International Education; Blair Ruble, former director of the Kennan Institute for Advanced Russian Studies; and David Godine, publisher nonpareil, and the only person on the planet who would have published my first, magnificent book, *Gold in Azure: One Thousand Years of Russian Architecture*. In one way or another, they enabled my work on Russia and provided the means to bring that work to a global public. I am also indebted to students and colleagues at Tulane University who have assisted my archival project over the decades. Students have been my lifeblood, and certain of them contributed far more than they perhaps realized to the arduous work of archiving my photographic collection, which is the basis of this book. The main part of that archive is housed in the Department of Image Collections (formerly the Photographic Archive) at the National Gallery of Art in Washington, DC, which began acquiring my photographs in the spring of 1985. Colleagues at the National Gallery have played a fundamental role in preserving my documentation of architecture in Russia and the former Soviet Union. I am again delighted to acknowledge the collaboration of Miriam Angress, who has edited two of my recent books for Duke University Press. Her judgment and professionalism have worked miracles. And I am again deeply grateful to the generosity of Richard and Elizabeth Hedreen, whose enlightened patronage has done so much to support the publication of my work. This book is dedicated to the memory of Elizabeth (Betty) Hedreen. As for the Russian friends and colleagues who contributed so much to my work in that vast Eurasian space, I call out to them in the Exordium.

Author's Note

THIS BOOK IS A PERSONAL VIEW OF THE BROADEST possible topic in Russian architecture: building in wood. In the most literal sense, it is a view of wooden structures through photographs spanning five decades (beginning in 1970), seven time zones, and latitudes from 47° (Rostov-on-Don) to 70° (Norilsk). It is also a personal view in its selection. Those readers who have already delved into the topic might wonder why this or that favorite building or town was not included. The process of selecting the photographs (slightly more than four hundred out of many thousands) was a special form of agony. Others might ask why the geographic range was so broad or the sites so numerous. Would it not have been preferable to focus on fewer places in greater detail? In a sense I did that in my book *Architecture at the End of the Earth: Photographing the Russian North* (2015), half the length of this one but also including ancient cathedrals of brick and stone. In this book I intend to show both variety and continuity across many places (authentic examples are often situated in little-known backwoods), including outdoor museums of wooden architecture. The choice was mine and the details were difficult. Not everything could be included, much less discussed.

The book is also personal in its approach. There are countless volumes on Russian wooden architecture, exhaustively examining variations on the form of the traditional log house (*izba*) or the wooden church. Although there is a general bibliography at the end, the book does not pretend to explore the topic at the same level of detail as many of its predecessors—nor should it. There is no point in reinventing the wooden wheel. In the introductory sections I give an overview of construction practices, but my hope is that many of the specifics are best shown in the photographs. As for sources of information, most of them are from decades of field notes, conversations with museum specialists, and Russian guidebooks for general audiences, as well as scholarly sources. I should repeat that this volume takes a view as wide as Russia itself. Detailed analysis can be instructive, yet my primary goal is to show the sweep of what I have seen.

One of the unique features of the book is the precision of the image dates (day, month, year) based on concise daily records that I have been keeping since the late 1960s, well before the first trip to the Soviet Union in the summer of 1970. I have placed the date of the photograph at the end of each caption, information that is particularly important because many of the buildings photographed no longer exist. I have tried to note these vanished structures in the captions, but I cannot keep up with the pace of destruction, particularly in urban areas. At least the photographs, preserved in my archival collection at the National Gallery of Art, record their existence and as such have gained a life of their own: It is my wish to share them as broadly as possible. Speaking of that collection, I should add that before switching to digital cameras, I often photographed on black-and-white film, a medium that I greatly admire aesthetically. My first major exhibit in Russia (in 2001) was in black-and-white. But color photography adds valuable information, particularly with decorative detail, and for the sake of consistency it is used throughout this book.

Books on Russia often begin with a note on transliteration from the Cyrillic to the Latin alphabet. In this work I decided to use a system easily accessible to the nonspecialist public. I trust that any minor inconsistencies will not impede an understanding. In a few cases, I have given a pronunciation guide.

Exordium

HOW SHALL I BEGIN? LET ME NAME THEIR NAMES, the friends and colleagues, the drivers who got me through some of the worst roads on earth, the friends and strangers who gave me shelter, a shot of vodka, a warm meal, a jar of cloudberries (*moroshka*): Tomochka, Vanya, Olya, Lyuba, Tanya, Ira, Misha, Vasya, Alyosha, Andrusha, Dima, Masha, Galya, Nadya, Sasha, Boris, Vera, Tamara; Oleg Samusenko, Olga Bakhareva, Mikhail Karachev, Valery Esipov, Irina Samsonova, Mikhail Dmitriev, Irina Velieva, Nelli Belova, Irma Komladze, Arkady Levin, Alexey Komech, Sergey Miturich, Father Andrei Kozlov, Rafael Khakimov, Oleg Glushchenko, Dmitry Shvidkovsky, Igor Shurgin, Alexander Popov, David Sarkisiyan, Tatiana Shchepetkova.

Two of you in particular represent the polarities of our Russian-American intersection. Oleg (Samusenko), your boundless generosity led to the most insanely improbable trips through the Vologda and Kostroma territories—trips usually in third-hand white Volgas. Any one of those cars could have killed us: faulty brakes, clogged carburetors, broken fan belts, shot ignitions, worn tires. And yet we made it from Cherepovets to ancient Soligalich in the Kostroma forests; Ustiuzhna to the west; and Vytegra and Saminsky Pogost in the north. You were neither a careerist nor "a pillar of the community," and your broad historical knowledge was, I felt, often ignored. But there were those who understood your deep wisdom and would help when you asked on my behalf. Your wife, Olga—by profession a librarian and by character the soul of endurance—sustained us and kept our spirits up.

Ghena, I am forever grateful for your generosity in bringing me to places that I would not otherwise have seen. In July 2012, your small, bright-green Zhiguli got us to distant Yurevets on the Volga River. And we saw so much in between. But at other moments, over a late dinner, you made no secret of your animosity toward America as a global power and resentment at the collapse of the Soviet Union. You were a believer in alternative approaches to medicine and every morning religiously prepared a blender cocktail of vegetables fresh from the summer garden for your wife, Sveta, who was living with advanced-stage cancer. Sveta, I remember sitting next to you at the train station in Kineshma, a brief conversation, then touching your emaciated arm in parting, your wan smile and glittering, tired eyes hungry to know health. We stayed in touch a few more months when both of you returned to Moscow for the winter, but then Ghena sent a message saying that he could no longer associate with me, an American. Sveta, unfailingly kind and gentle, passed away soon thereafter.

Will I see any of you again? The tragedy of war separates us, but what we did remains, on my film and in memory.

Introduction
Getting There

During more than five decades of study and documentation of Russian architecture, my primary focus has been stone and brick, from eleventh-century churches to twenty-first century office towers. Yet wooden structures have always been in my field of view, and their story has played a part in several of my books. The time has now come to place them in the center, to recapitulate the experience of years of fieldwork and thousands of photographed sites, to trace a path linking barns and windmills, and houses and churches in the Far North with Buddhist shrines in the Trans-baikal region and elegant eighteenth-century palaces on the outskirts of Moscow—all underneath log constructions. Although the identity of the builders is rarely known, their ingenuity and creativity have formed an essential component of the country's heritage.

Russia's wooden architecture is a creation at war with itself. The myth of wooden architecture as the purest expression of the Russian national genius—a myth that I accept—collides with a reality of flight and neglect. For centuries Russians lived in a wooden environment, from the smallest hamlets to the largest cities. Even in the middle of the twentieth century, a large part of the population in Russia—including Tatars, Buriats, Yakuts, Evenks, and many other ethnic groups in a territory roughly equivalent to the contemporary Russian Federation—lived in wooden dwellings.

Yet, during the half century that I traveled and photographed in an area extending from the White Sea to the Sea of Japan, vast swaths of wooden buildings have been demolished (in towns and cities) or abandoned (in villages). For this, there are many reasons—demographic, economic, social, political, cultural, lack of ownership, lack of conveniences, lack of financial resources, fear of fire, urban regulations, and reconstruction. This book is not based on data sets, but throughout the photographs and text illustrate a simple fact—given a choice, most Russians cannot leave the wooden habitat fast enough. With few exceptions, the commitment to preserving a viable form of wooden habitat in urban areas rings hollow. It is far easier—particularly for families—to move to a masonry (brick, stone, reinforced concrete) building, however faceless, with the conveniences that modern life demands.

As for the persistent myth of wooden Russia, those who pine can visit the open-air museums of wooden architecture that have been assembled on the outskirts of so many Russian cities, from Arkhangelsk to Ulan-Ude. There they will see not only superbly crafted log homesteads with barns, bathhouses, and mills but also log shrines ranging from small forest chapels to soaring multidomed churches—a fraction, however, of those existing even a century ago. Those churches, like log dwellings, have often been abandoned by the communities they once served in rural areas. A few have been reopened for service at museum sites, many new log churches have been built in suburban areas—a relatively inexpensive way of expanding church presence and at the same time summoning the aura of cultural traditions. But the sources of those traditions are rapidly disappearing at their original sites.

Must it be that way? Wood is a durable, natural material, and the threat from fire can be managed and contained. I live in a city whose neighborhoods consist largely of wooden houses, thousands of them—shotguns, bungalows, Victorian mansions, Carpenter Gothic caprices. Although New Orleans is unique in the scale and cultural significance of its wooden housing, many American cities have neighborhoods with wooden houses from a century or more ago. However, they are frame (post-and-beam) constructions whose weight is balanced on masonry supports, in some cases despite the treacherous local subsoil (quickly recognized by anyone traversing New Orleans streets, for example). They are not massive log structures.

Let it be emphasized at the outset that wooden architecture in Russia means a log structure. It can be covered with plank siding or plaster over lathing, but the buildings are underneath constructions of solid logs tightly fitted and laid in horizonal courses. The reasons for this centuries-old practice are several, including a severe continental climate demanding a reliable self-insulating material. Logs were readily available (the territory of Russia being the largest forested zone on the planet) and could often be purchased precut for market sale in urban areas. Furthermore, equipment for milling timber was rare until the latter part of the nineteenth century,

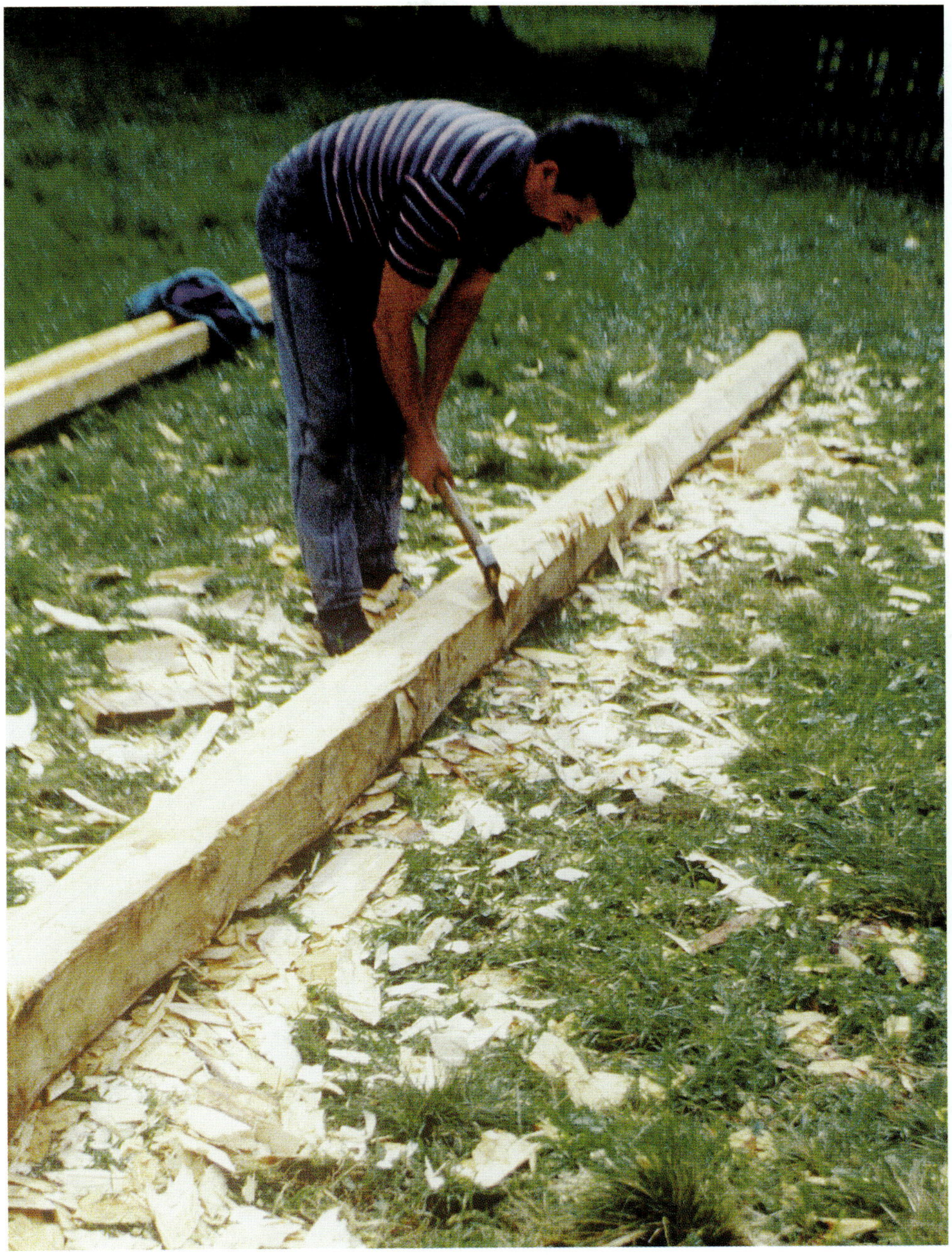

VITOSLAVLITSY (Novgorod region). Master carpenter working pine log with an ax. Note hewn roof gutter at upper left. He told me: "Pines don't grow the way they used to." May 27, 1996.

and even then, sawmill production was used for finishing details such as floor planks, roofing, and decorative details. Hence the ubiquity in Russia of the log house, whether the *izba* (pronounced eez-BAH) in the countryside or simply the "wooden house" (*derevyanny dom*) in towns. Wood was also commonly used by the gentry for their estate houses in the eighteenth and nineteenth centuries, as well as for the suburban dachas (cottages) that began to proliferate later in the nineteenth century. All these types will be illustrated in the chapters that follow, but regardless of external appearance (with or without plank siding), they were all solid log structures.

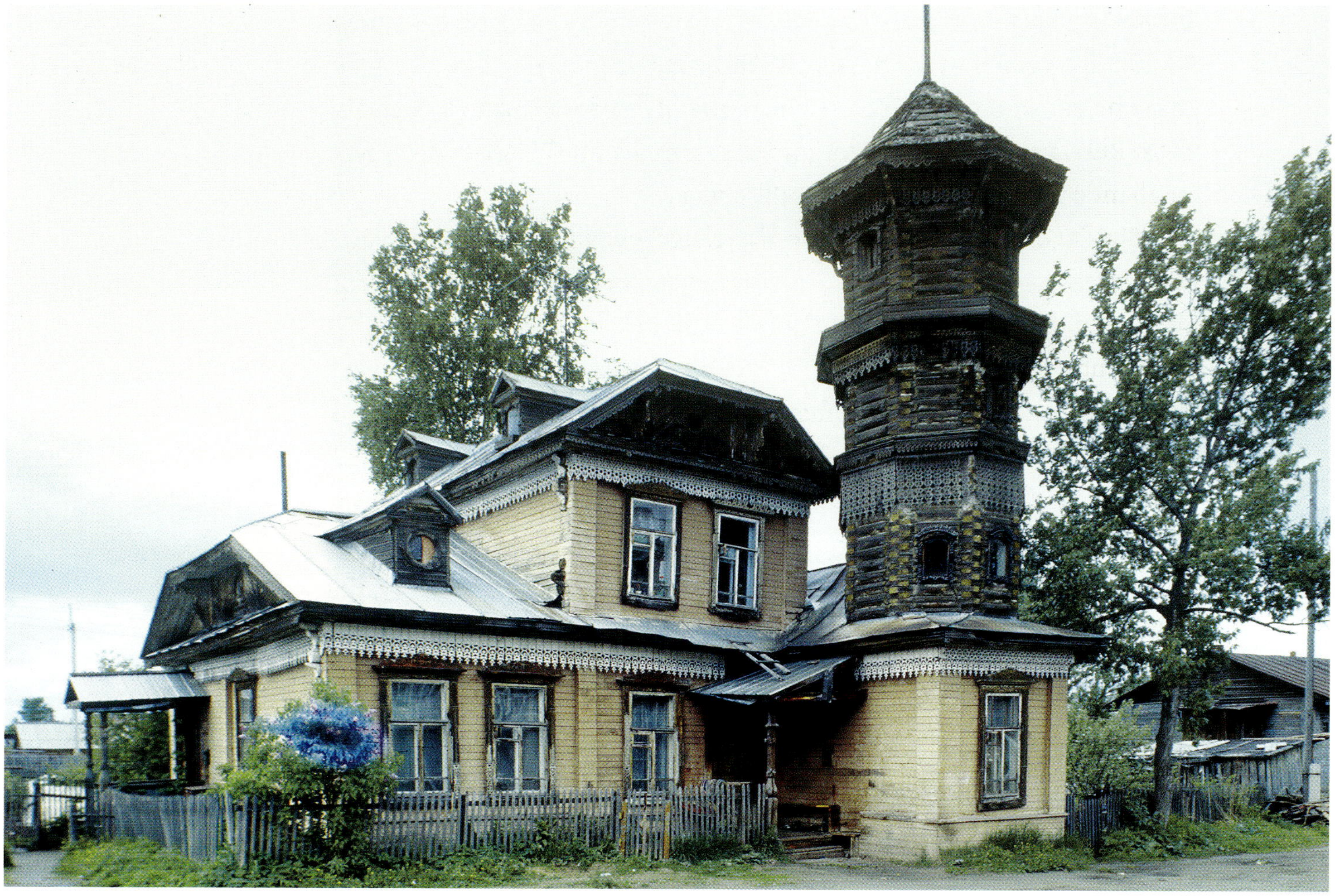

USTIUZHNA (Vologda region). House of the merchant Nikolay Kurbatov, Ustiuzhna Lane 4. Built in the late nineteenth century by a true enthusiast of log construction, the richly decorated house included a three-tiered tower visible in the photograph. In 2009, the upper two tiers were dismantled. The house is now in critical condition. May 22, 2001.

The *izba* has been praised by many for its "authentic" rough-hewn materiality, but such buildings weigh heavily on the surface in a literal sense. In towns, wooden houses were typically supported by brick foundations, or even a masonry ground floor. In the countryside, larger structures (log churches, in particular) rested on fieldstone foundations, but wooden dwellings often were built directly on the ground, especially for impoverished households. Lower logs were subject to decay, and the ground itself might shift with freezing and thawing. Before the late nineteenth century, milled lumber (including planks) was relatively expensive and labor intensive, and therefore the basic *izba* known to generations of peasant serfs often had a floor of tamped clay mixed with manure as a hardener.

Whether the *izba* or a wooden house, these structures were generally not expected to last more than a few generations—rarely more than a century. Depending on the area (climate), size of the structure, and socioeconomic factors, log dwellings were regularly replaced. With the spread of limited prosperity in the nineteenth century, families came to expect new dwellings as generations passed. To this natural process of regeneration must be added the fires that not infrequently swept Russian towns. For most Russians, logs were as common as air or water. What was destroyed or abandoned could always be rebuilt quickly.

Similar conditions also affected log churches, which were both a common, everyday fact of life and a crowning glory of native Russian culture, particularly in the Russian North. Log churches, of vastly different sizes and structural complexity, were everywhere—in monasteries, in towns of all sizes, and in villages. In fact, there are two basic terms for "village" in Russian—*derevnya* and *selo*. The former generally referred to any small group of rural households designated with a toponym (for example, Ivanovka). In distinction, *selo* referred to a household grouping sufficiently significant to have a church—almost always of logs. Frequently, log churches—like log houses—could be disassembled and taken to another location, whether by purchase by another village or because a community moved to another location.

Log churches could be expected to exist for a longer period than houses, but like any log structure, such churches had to be maintained if they were to survive; decaying logs had to be replaced. Perhaps the greatest threat to log churches was fire. Because of their height, they could be destroyed by lightning strikes; their interiors had votive candles; or a fire could spread from a nearby structure. Fires took (and still take) a heavy toll on log churches, whether in villages or towns, and if the village survived, the church was rebuilt either of logs or, in many cases, as a masonry (brick) structure if local resources permitted. With the demographic and sociopolitical upheavals of the twentieth century, village churches were abandoned on a massive scale. In urban areas, log churches had long since disappeared because of the fire hazard that they posed. Ironically, there has recently been a surge of log church construction in large urban housing developments, both for their relatively lower cost and for their appeal to Russian tradition.

The widespread twentieth-century impulse to preserve traditional wooden buildings as cultural objects had two points of origin. As Russian nationalism assumed prominence in Stalinist ideology during and immediately after the Second World War (known in Russia as the Great Fatherland War), the state on various levels began to promulgate the concept of preserving wooden architectural monuments, whether secular or sacred, as a worthy expression of Russian identity. One of the earliest examples was the 1945 designation of the original church ensemble on the Karelian Island of Kizhi (under Finnish occupation for much of the war) as a state preserve. The establishment of outdoor museums dedicated to wooden architecture gathered strength with the adoption, on January 30, 1964, of the state decree "Concerning Measures for the Improvement of the Preservation of Monuments of Wooden Architecture." More will be said of Kizhi and other outdoor museums throughout part 2 of this book.

Yet the movement to create these museum preserves focused almost entirely on rural structures. In urban areas, a second impulse, less statist in its origins, gathered strength in the post-Stalinist era when wooden buildings were rapidly becoming less essential for providing basic housing stock. If in the middle of the twentieth century provincial towns and cities still had extensive areas of wooden houses (log structures), the trend was inexorably in another direction. Alternatives—primarily mass-produced apartment buildings—became increasingly available after the 1940s at a time when people were beginning to leave the countryside in droves. To take one example from a site that will appear later in this book: the Bolsheboldinsky *raion* (county), which contained an estate belonging to the family of Russia's greatest poet, Alexander Pushkin (1799–1837). In 1939 the population was some 38,000; in 1959, 29,000; in 1989, 14,000.

This trend was not exceptional, and those who left rural areas often abandoned wooden houses for which there was little or no demand. I have photographed villages that consisted entirely of abandoned log houses. Furthermore, those who moved to towns and cities were generally not inclined to move into another wooden dwelling with a privy in the yard. Most anyone who could angled for an apartment with at least minimal conveniences in a brick (or, increasingly, prefabricated concrete-panel) building. From being an object of local pride, the log house acquired for many the stigma of backwardness, its darkened walls a point of shame.

Within many rapidly changing provincial towns, however, there were those who, as a matter of local pride, wanted to preserve wooden houses for what they represented to Russian history and culture. There are numerous reasons for the urban preservation of traditional wooden buildings, which are often marvels of construction ingenuity and superb design. I have not only photographed beautifully maintained wooden (log) houses but have in some cases followed the painstaking process of historically accurate restoration. But restoration requires, in the first place, clear title to the property (by no means a given after seven decades of Soviet power) followed by commitment, skill, knowledge, and substantial financial resources just to maintain the structure. Modern amenities require still further resources. Unfortunately, those who live in large wooden houses in charming provincial cities such as Vologda are often those with few means and less *blat* (clout).Multiple tenants are crammed into dwellings that either were not designed for this use or can no longer bear the weight of prolonged neglect. There are few incentives to maintain such houses, whether on an individual or municipal level, and cases of arson are not uncommon. Municipalities can adopt zoning regulations that include preservation of areas with wooden dwellings, but enforcement measures are weak and widely flouted.

In a context of dilapidated and unsightly buildings, city planning agencies, contractors, and local boosters have every reason to level swaths of wooden houses and replace them with office or apartment buildings with a modicum of stylistic trappings that say "postmodernist," "neoconstructivist," or simply "jemenfoutiste" (a piquant French-derived term perfectly suited to bland confusion). Isolated wooden buildings remain, often wedged between much larger structures that deform drainage and other properties of the ground on which the wooden structure rests. Street expansion pushes against the house frontage, increasing noise, pollution, and degrading vulnerable foundations. If not placed in a special preservation zone or street (such as one in the center of Arkhangelsk), the fate of isolated survivors is destruction. I have witnessed this process directly in cities such as Kazan (the capital of Tatarstan on the Volga River) and have confirmed it more recently in street-level views provided through Yandex, the Russian counterpart to Google. Many of the wooden houses that I photographed in the 1980s, 1990s, and 2000s no longer exist. In isolated cases, losses will be noted in the captions, but I cannot pretend to keep pace.

Getting There

This book is unique for its photographs, archivally recorded over a period of five decades, and it seems appropriate to provide readers with certain information about this process. Field research and photography in Russia is an arduous undertaking that often requires access to remote areas where even a graveled road is considered a highway. Such areas are reachable only by rugged vehicles operated by experienced drivers. I have never driven a car in Russia; it is too hazardous. I was also concerned about how to keep the cameras operative and deciding where to go. Basic research determines the reasons and the directions. Vehicles for my fieldwork have been provided either by local administrations (often at the recommendation of the Ministry of Culture) or by others—usually friends but also generous strangers—who were intrigued by the peculiarities of my work. I am endlessly grateful for their knowledge of the territory and the conditions, which for professional drivers is an ordinary working day. In the winter there is less light, but in many areas—whether the North or Siberia—packed, ice-hardened snow makes a better travel surface in areas served by boggy tracks.

For difficult terrain the four-wheel drive Uazik is the ubiquitous vehicle of choice, Russia's closest equivalent to the classic Jeep. The name derives from the acronym for Ulyanovsk Auto Factory, located in the city of Ulyanovsk on the Volga River. The version that I knew had two gear sticks, two gas tanks (left and right), taut suspension, high clearance, and four-wheel drive, but the front axis could only be engaged from outside. Seat belts? Don't ask. The top speed was one hundred kilometers an hour, but only on regional asphalt, not the rutted tracks and potholed back roads for which it was designed. Comfortable it is not, but an experienced driver can take this machine over rutted ice tracks in the middle of a snowstorm and not miss a beat. No place in Russia has more of such roads than Arkhangelsk Province, a vast territory that extends from the White and Barents Seas in the north to its boundary with Vologda Province to the south. A combination of poverty, government default on both the local and national levels, and distances that exceed those of most western European countries have created some of the worst roads in European Russia. Yet, as part 2 will show, this area contains the greatest concentration of traditional wooden architecture.

For regional fieldwork, a sturdy vehicle in whatever form (including motorized quadricycle) is indispensable, but for longer distances between regions, there is the Russian rail system, massive and reliable. In the Russian North (northwestern part of the country) and Siberia, this network covers hundreds of kilometers between launching points to the "backcountry." (The favored term in Russian is *gloosh*, a word whose very sound evokes oblivion.) Yet, rail travel can be exhausting, not only for travel in a rattling third-class open-bunk sleeper known as *platskart* (why pay

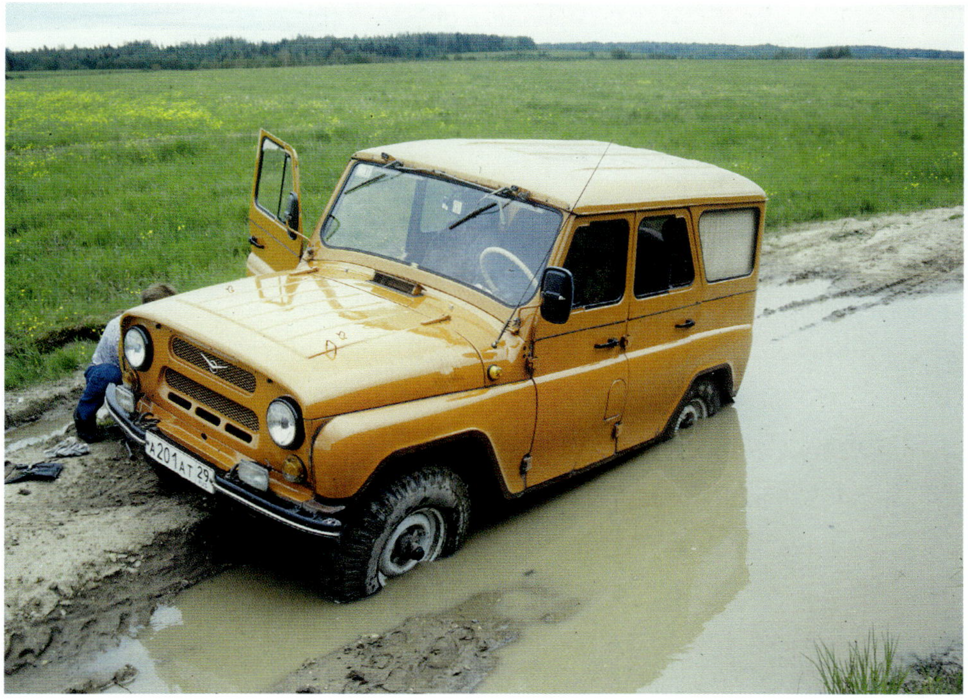

FEDKOVO (Velsk region). Driver engaging front wheel drive of Uazik. June 14, 2000.

more to be cooped in a sleeping coupe with a snorer?) but also the waiting for long-distance trains arriving in the middle of the night.

Consider, for example, Nyandoma Station, serving a nondescript railroad town (population about 18,000) settled in the late 1890s and once known for its poultry-processing plant. Located some five hundred kilometers south of Arkhangelsk on the mainline to Moscow and Saint Petersburg, Nyandoma is the portal to one of the richest areas of Russian traditional culture and wooden architecture, centered around the medieval town of Kargopol, sixty kilometers to the west; yet the station has little to distinguish it—a brick box with a plate glass wall facing the tracks. I passed through it many times—the first during a snowstorm in late February 1998—and paid little attention. Get in, get out.

But there was one episode that provided in the most prosaic of settings an unexpected insight into the mysteries of human communication, an experience both ordinary and surreal. The antiquated, straining evening bus from Kargopol (standing room only) arrived at the Nyandoma Station on a late Monday evening (August 9, 2010), and a few of us stumbled into the gray-blue-green waiting hall. The Saint Petersburg train (009A) was not due for another six hours. I found a row of empty plastic seats and attempted to stretch out, but the glare of the florescent light, the seat contours, and the background noise made anything resembling sleep

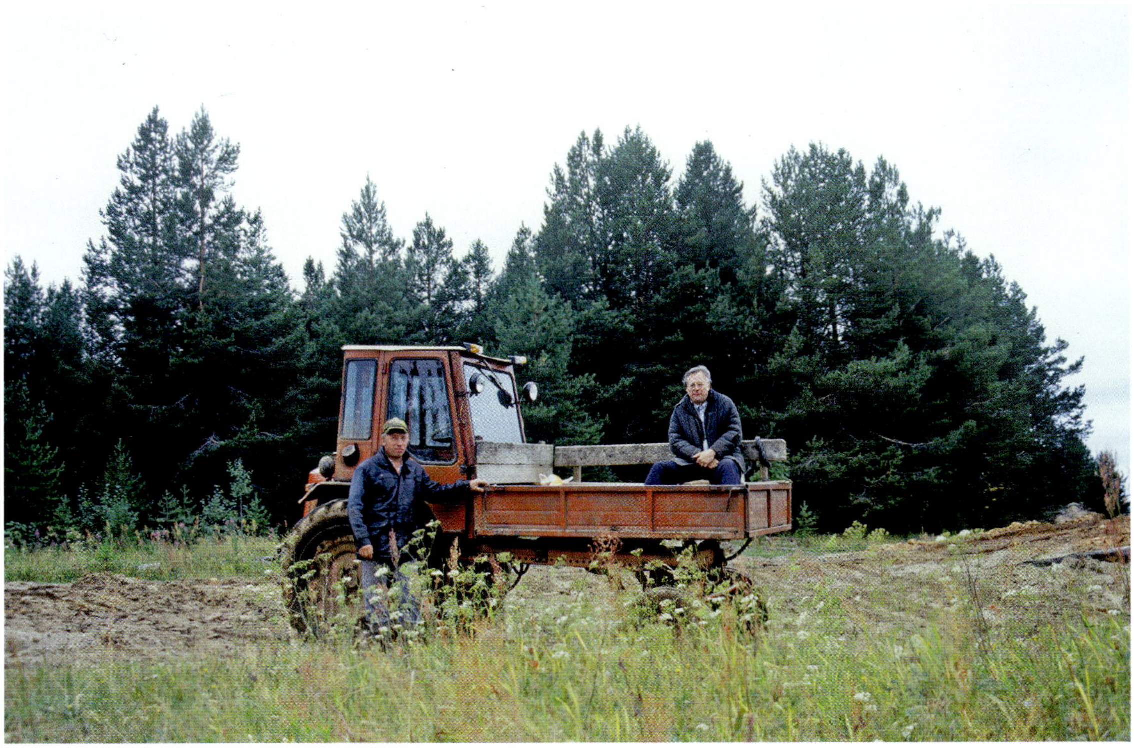

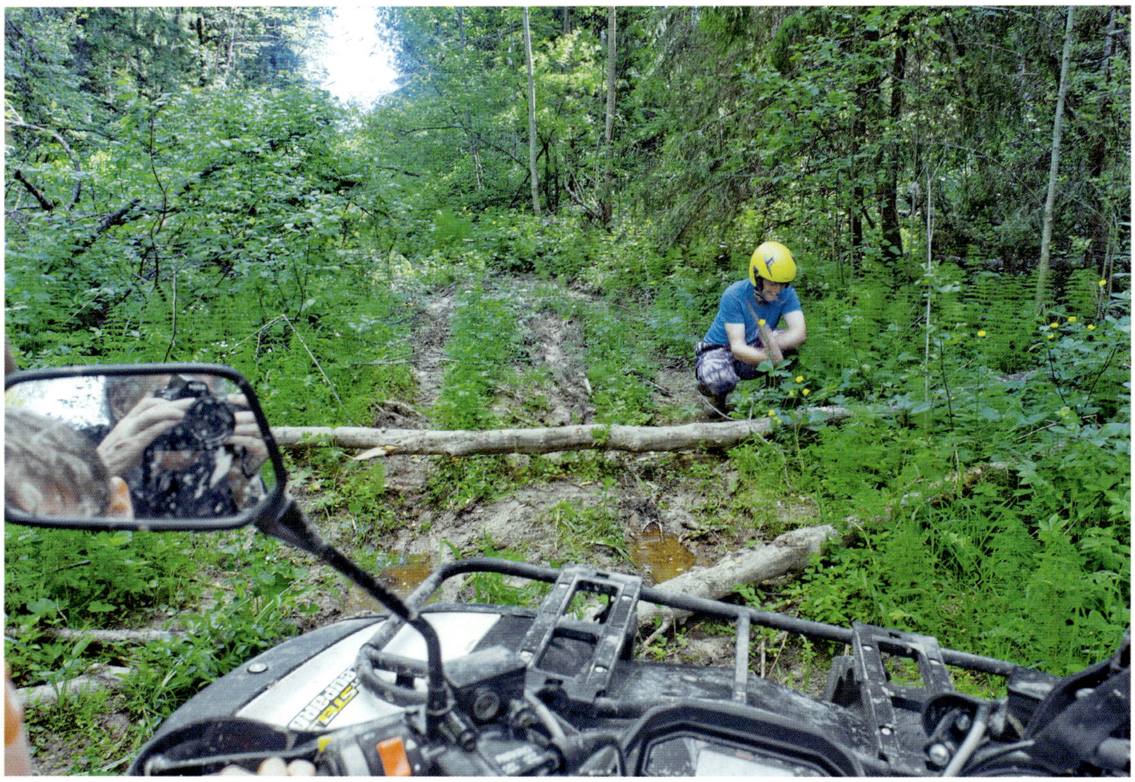

MEZEN RIVER BANK (Arkhangelsk Province). Author in tractor adapted for human conveyance. August 3, 2000.

NEAR POGORELOVO (Kostroma Province). Clearing forest track for quadricycle. Author with camera in mirror. May 31, 2016.

impossible. I thought of the friends, Olga and Oleg Samusenko, who would meet me just after noon at the steel town of Cherepovets. I thought of the fieldwork we would do in this underexplored area of the Russian North. The hours dragged, the florescent light turned every face ashen.

Around midnight, two women—struggling with travel bags and dressed in the no-nonsense slacks and pullover attire that Russians adopt for train travel—entered the waiting room. Each had a small girl, a two-year old and a four-year-old. The two-year-old was tired, cross, and let everyone know it. Trying to placate the infant, her mother went to the trinket booth and bought a small green plastic music box (for want of a better word), undoubtedly made in China. It played one thing, a single line of notes from the beginning of "Ode to Joy" in Beethoven's Ninth Symphony. Everybody knows it: "Freude, schöner Götterfunken, Tochter aus Elysium." What could be more appropriate in the Nyandoma Station waiting room in the middle of the night? FREUDE! JOY!

But the two-year-old was not pleased; the green plastic box regularly hit the cement floor and erupted in a series of tinkly Beethoven notes, endlessly repeated. The two mothers tried to communicate with the whining child, to no effect. She was clearly asking for something and frustrated that she could not be understood. Soon, the four-year-old came to the fore. She had a rapport with her playmate, and both mothers, exasperated and leaning over in anticipation, asked the four-year-old what the two-year-old was saying. She turned to the two-year-old, posed a question, received a reply (incomprehensible to adults), and confidently relayed the message to the mothers. Situation resolved (temporarily). The little drama was absorbing, yet toddlers frequently talk among themselves. The greatest delight in the unfolding transaction—repeated until the infant dozed off—was the two-year-old's appreciation of her companion's linguistic skill, the eager nod of approval when her syllables were processed. "Yes! That's it!"

At 4:03 a.m., the Saint Petersburg train rumbled in from Arkhangelsk, and dawn had already appeared in the northern summer sky. Groggy with fatigue, we clambered aboard *platskart* sleeping cars. No rush, Nyandoma is a crew change, and we had half an hour to find our places, step across snoring bodies, and spread out the bunk bedding. I never saw them again, those tiny, energetic daughters of Elysium. They should be in their late teens now, and I wish them whatever joy life can bring. For my part, I still pause over the mystery of comprehension when one small child transformed the words of another—anagogical, indeed.

Upon arrival at the research sites in the Russian regions—whether the Kola Peninsula in the north or the Urals or Siberia—successful implementation of field photography depends on an additional critical factor: the ability to defend against the mosquito (*komar*) and other biting, sucking plagues related to the general category *gnus* (gnat). Indeed, their presence is so detested that the common Russian word for "repulsive" (applied to people or situations) is *gnusno*. There are, of course, synonyms, but none is quite so succinct and emphatic an expression of disgust as *gnusno* (for example, *gnusnoe povedenie*—depraved, intolerable behavior).

In the Russian North, with its innumerable lakes and bogs, the plague is compounded by the *moshka*, a biting midge similar to a no-see-um. Small and difficult to see, the female of the species requires warm blood (usually mammalian) for propagation. Physically more damaging than a mosquito insertion, the abrasion of the *moshka* not only itches but can pustulate and become infected. This is particularly a problem for rural pensioners in the North who depend on vegetable gardens and are exposed to the *moshka* on hot summer days while working in the garden. Not wanting to use a lotion (or to buy one), they typically wrap their face and neck in cloth and protect their hands with old gloves. Nonetheless, the *moshka* gets through, and I remember one elderly woman showing me splotched traces of bites on her hands. A genuine bedevilment.

I have encountered those who say mosquitoes do not affect them, and no doubt there are those who develop natural resistance or are less susceptible to allergic reactions. After all, communities have endured this environment for centuries. One monk at the Monastery of Saint Antony of Siya near the Northern Dvina River told me that the eponymous Saint Antony did not kill mosquitoes and proclaimed, "They, too, are God's creatures." And there are folk remedies, such as the one I saw in the Krasnoyarsk region of Siberia: strips of birch bark were heated in an open pot over a fire. The extruding moisture was gathered and mixed with a paste of what seemed to me rotten fish. The resulting salve works not only for humans but also for household animals such as dogs, who suffer from bites during the worst of summer.

One might assume that as a long-time resident of southern Louisiana, I would be used to the mosquito. Nothing of the sort. Although New Orleans controls the breeding habitat and sprays if infestation reaches a certain level, they remain omnipresent. Furthermore, there are many varieties of mosquito (more than 3,500 species), and the severity of reaction

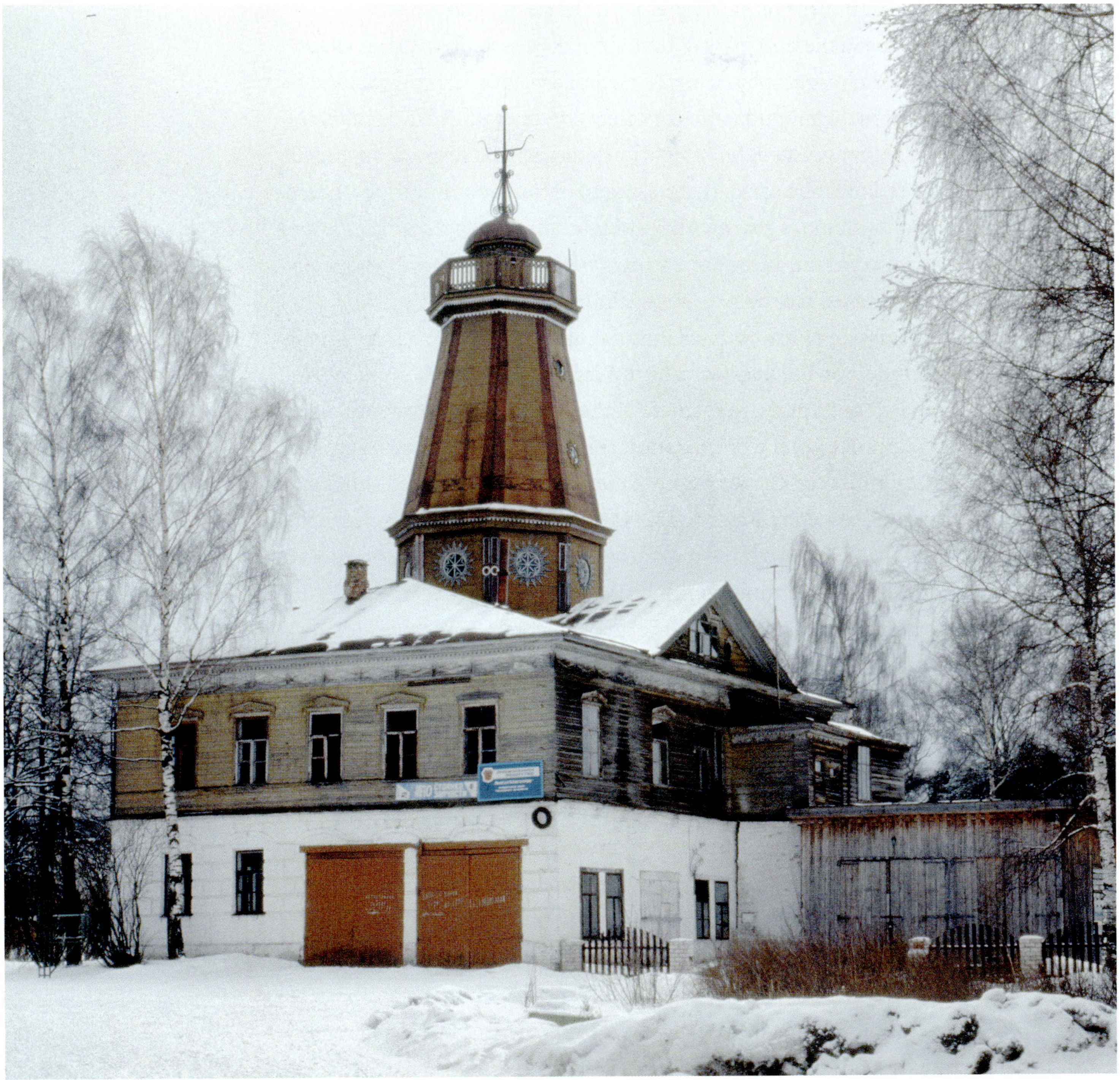

USTIUZHNA. Former City Council (*Duma*) building with fire watch tower. The entire wooden structure of this national landmark, built in 1887, burned at the end of 2000. March 10, 1998.

to the bite (swelling, itching) can depend on the type of mosquito as well as prior exposure (or lack thereof) to a specific type. Mosquitoes have been remarkably successful in occupying their evolutionary, ecological niche, and they are an essential food source for other fauna. I still remember the delight in seeing swallows and nightingales dart into the open passageway of a large log house in the Kostroma region to feed on mosquitoes in mid-flight. Attempts to control them by chemical means in the United States led to alarm—notably in Rachel Carson's 1962 book *Silent Spring*—over the widespread use of DDT in eradication campaigns. Such considerations, however, are quickly forgotten during fieldwork in Russia. The overriding task is to repel, by whatever means, the swarming hordes.

And they swarm, indeed. The one genuine panic attack I have experienced occurred a half century ago during an early period of my work in the northern forests. I had forgotten to carry repellent and returning in the late afternoon from a sunlit site into the forest shade, I was attacked by a cloud that had not even begun to bite. (I was moving and waving my hands furiously.) Their intense humming and hitting my face propelled me in total panic toward a small lake with an old, blackened rowboat at the edge. Jumping into the boat, I grabbed the half-rotted oars and pushed away with such force that one of the oars snapped. With the remaining oar I managed to maneuver out a short distance (the mosquitoes did not follow over the fresh, rippled water) and stayed there until friends arrived at the shore with salve. I paddled back, left the oars (one broken) in the boat, and made it out of the forest. Some three decades later, in the late 1990s, I experienced similar swarms while working on Large Solovetsky Island, but at that time I was prepared and took pleasure in the sound of mosquitoes veering from my DEET-slathered head.

Whatever the local circumstances (and there have been moments of transcendent beauty), the photographs in this book and the field notes that underly the text span half a century of work throughout Russia. In presenting this vast range, which includes thousands of photographs of wooden structures, I have defined two parts. The first, "Wooden Architecture as Cultural Environment," begins with the chapter "From Palace to Dacha," which illustrates the place of wooden architecture in high culture. The grand eighteenth-century summer pleasure palaces of the elite, such as Kuskovo and Ostankino, built for the fabulously wealthy Sheremetevs in the northern suburbs of Moscow, were basically sturdy log constructions, skillfully crafted to resemble neoclassical masonry structures. Although they are not usually thought of as log constructions, these imposing monuments are among the earliest log dwellings to survive in Russia. I have also included—if only as a telling cultural curiosity—the recent re-creation of the grand, rambling wooden palace originally built in the seventeenth century for Tsar Alexey Mikhailovich at the royal estate of Kolomenskoe.

Evidence as early as the twelfth century indicates that Russia's potentates had long preferred to live in wooden dwellings, although none of them has survived. Wood was readily available, as were master carpenters, while stonework was costly, rare, and reserved primarily for a few major religious buildings. Bricks were produced, but not until the late fifteenth century were brick production and technology brought to the advanced level visible in the Moscow Kremlin and its walls (designed primarily by Italian engineers). Logs also possessed material properties that mitigated the effects of extreme cold. There is something reassuring in the aroma, the touch of a warm log interior in the middle of a snowstorm.

The first chapter further explores two seminal country estates—Abramtsevo and Talashkino—that became cultural laboratories for exploring, preserving, and extending Russian folk traditions in artistic culture, both high and low, secular and sacred. Here irony rests upon irony. Both estates were supported by fortunes made from Russia's fitful industrialization, which threatened the economic viability of crafts workshops. Furthermore, local villagers who had been compelled to abandon the rural folkways were encouraged—even taught—to maintain the folk crafts traditionally associated with a rural way of life. And at Talashkino, a notable attempt was made to reimagine the traditional design of a Russian log dwelling. Such conceptions were formed by a sophisticated, Westernized, wealthy elite who defined the authentic as originating in rural (peasant) culture.

Striving to preserve traditional crafts and then transferring them to *haute culture* (with its commercial ramifications) became a major force in nineteenth-century Russian design and cultural history. The result is a wondrous interchange in a search for the authentic, an interchange that could involve entrepreneurs of peasant origins assimilating urban intellectual conceptions of how peasant culture (in architecture and design) should look. Who, then, is authenticating whom? In a further irony, one must also mention the profound influence of a non-Russian, Eugène Viollet-le-Duc, the renowned French architect, medievalist, and theoretician who in 1877 published his book *L'art russe: Ses origines, ses elements constitutifs, son apogee, son avenir* (Russian art: Its origins, its constituent elements, its apogee, its future). This seminal work shocked by elevating the value of traditional Russian art, notably expressed in wood, as the basis of an authentic national culture for architectural design.

A splendid illustration of the creativity emanating from an urbane reinterpretation of traditional design, the first chapter includes two magnificent log mansions built at the villages of Astashovo (Ostashovo) and Pogorelovo in the Kostroma forests near Chukhloma. Improbable both in their construction and preservation, they were built by peasants—peasant master craftsmen—who were permitted to go to Saint Petersburg in the mid-nineteenth century to work in the urban building boom. Both then acquired substantial wealth as contractors and returned to their native countryside to build large houses that reflected not only their acquired status but also urbane conceptions of the "authentic" in the design of a Russian dwelling. The first chapter concludes with a survey of landmark wooden dachas built in the northern suburbs of Saint Petersburg.

The second chapter, "The Wooden Ambience of Russian Literature," explores telling examples of wooden dwellings as they appeared in the lives of some of Russia's greatest writers, from Alexander Pushkin to Vladimir Nabokov. These houses varied widely in form, but all had some form of classicizing elements, whether a portico, a pediment (the Russian word is derived from the French *fronton*), or a rotunda. Sadly, many of these sites were destroyed in the twentieth century, from the chaos in the countryside leading to the Revolution of 1905 (called by some the First Russian Revolution) to the destructive frenzy of the Russian Civil War and its aftermath to World War Two. Some houses photographed in this chapter were rebuilt from the ground up as cultural shrines. Are they "authentic"? I decided to include certain rebuilt structures because they give a reasonably accurate view of the original, and they demonstrate a willingness to expend significant resources on the reconstruction of wooden landmarks when cultural circumstances are favorable.

Part 2, "Where the Folk Live: From Forest to Steppe," encompasses a broad survey, arranged in a geographical progression, of traditional vernacular architectures that housed most of Russia's population. In exploring intriguing intersections of rural traditions and urban(e) interpretation, there will be noticeable differences in design between the village *izba* and urban wooden housing, which acquired a certain standardization of form beginning with the reforms of Peter the Great. Peter and his imperial successors periodically undertook campaigns to give Russian towns something like an ordered, "civilized" appearance, primarily with the application of certain minimal features of neoclassical architecture. To that end they encouraged construction in brick (in part to mitigate the devastation of fires that periodically swept Russian towns) and promulgated plans for the standardized design of urban buildings.

Yet, with such notable exceptions as Saint Petersburg, the drive to increase the tempo of masonry construction had limited success. It was so much easier and quicker to build in wood, yet at least for urban dwellings, the standardized plans seem to have had an influence. If the house was not built of brick, it could resemble one that was. At a minimum the house would be clad in plank siding, which obscured the "primitive," village connotations of a log structure. In many cases, particularly in Moscow, log walls were covered with lathing to support stucco, thus making the structure indistinguishable from a masonry building. This increasing tendency to obscure the log structure is evident in all chapters in part 2. By the middle of the twentieth century, however, the wooden ambience of Russian towns yielded to demographic, economic, and planning pressures that accelerated the demolition of wooden housing, whether in the Russian North or the Far East.

All the developments described above appear throughout part 2, beginning with chapter 3, which surveys the log houses and churches of the Russian North (Arkhangelsk Province, Vologda Province, and Karelia). The distinctive feature of northern wooden architecture—secular and sacred—is the size that dwellings and churches often achieved. This unrivaled scale can be traced to the relative prosperity of peasant free holdings in the north (where serfdom was uncommon) and to an exceptionally harsh winter climate that led to the creation of structures large enough to accommodate everything under one roof—large families, livestock, forage, food supplies, and implements. The growth of provincial towns such as Vologda and Arkhangelsk created its own form of wooden habitat for merchants, craftsmen, and officials of all ranks (*chinovniki*); but underneath, these houses, too, were log structures.

The second chapter in part 2—chapter 4, on the heartland, or central part of European Russia—covers a territory extending from Novgorod in the northwest to Kazan and Samara on the Volga. Throughout this enormous, diverse space, there is a general diminution in size of the rural *izba* in comparison with the North. The more densely populated urban areas

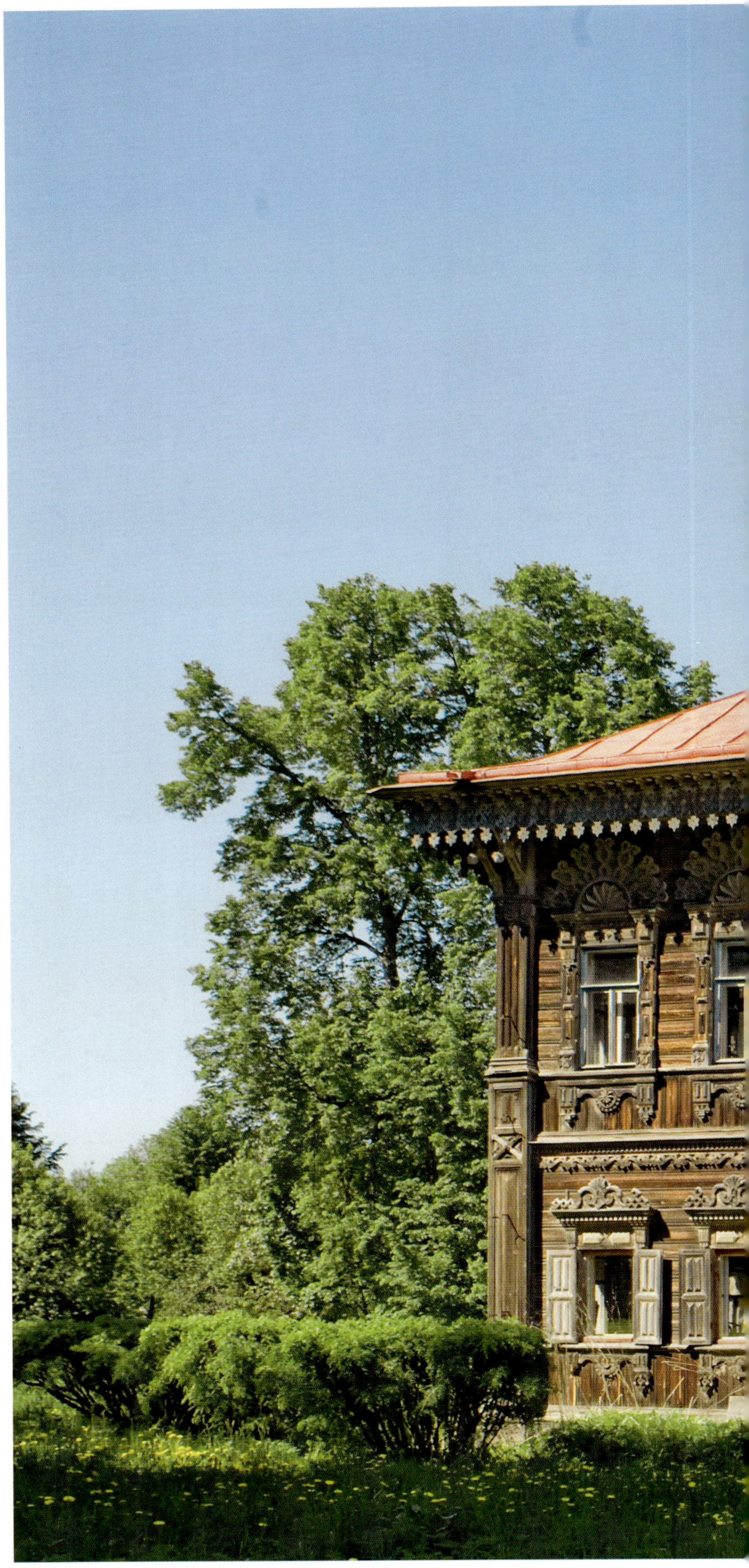

POGORELOVO (Kostroma Province). Poliashov mansion. May 29, 2016.

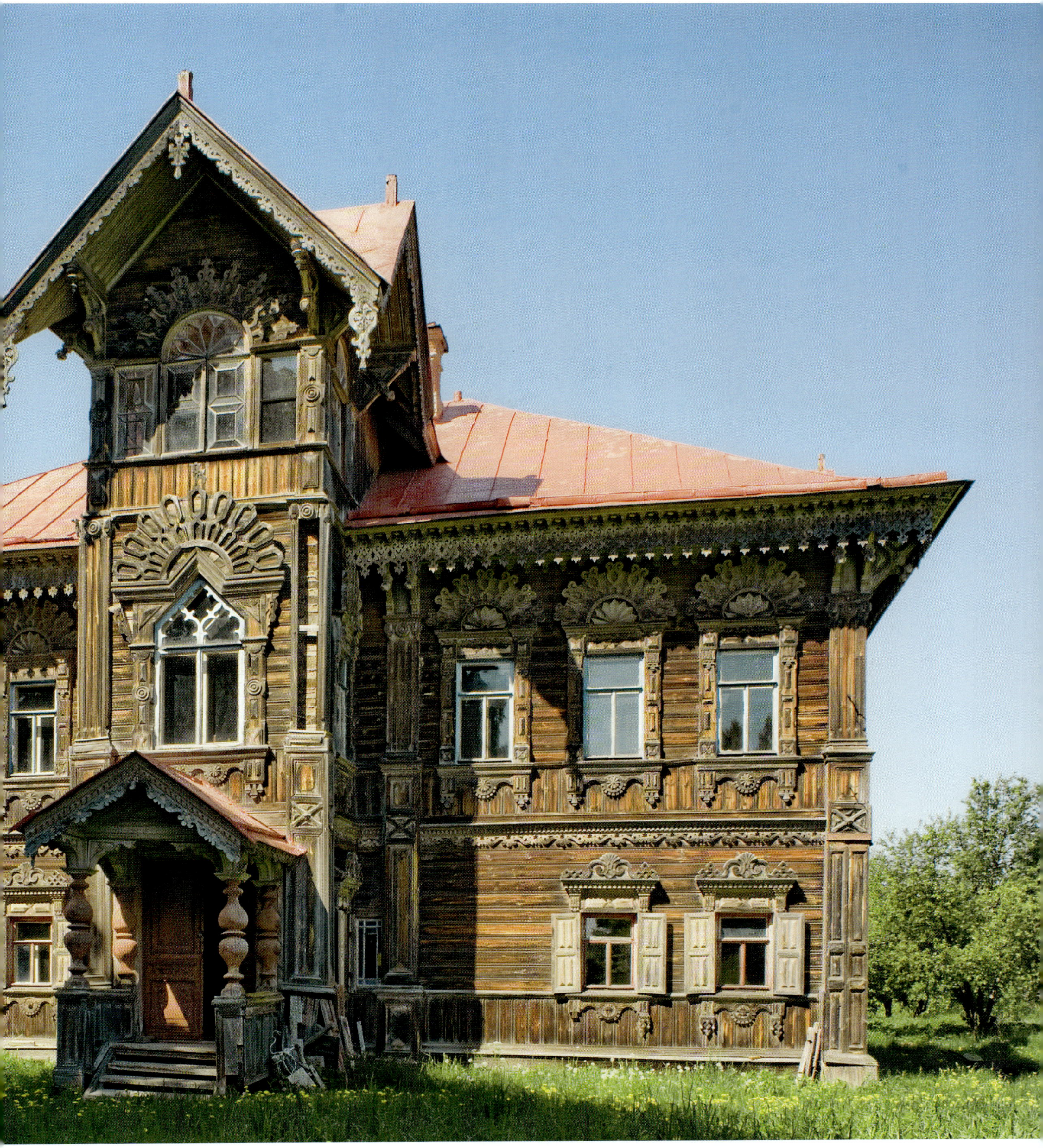

created new variations on urban wooden houses for individual household and multifamily dwellings. Chapter 5 crosses the Ural Mountains from Europe to Asia and moves longitudinally from the northern areas of the enormous Perm region to the southern reaches of the Chelyabinsk territory, which borders on Kazakhstan.

The greatest span geographically is chapter 6, on Siberia, extending from the first Russian settlements in the Irtysh River basin to the remarkable merchant houses of Tomsk and Irkutsk that give new meaning to the term "Carpenter Gothic." Several of the Tomsk mansions belonged to Siberian Tatar merchants, thus illustrating the multicultural range of wooden architecture in Russia. Beyond Lake Baikal, the survey moves into the Far East (loosely considered by some to be a part of Siberia) with chapter 7. Prerevolutionary merchant culture is reflected in the *style moderne* mansions of distant Chita and Barnaul. The multicultural aspect of wooden architecture reappears in my documentation of wooden shrines within Buddhist lamaseries in the Transbaikal territory and of preserved Indigenous log yurts in the same area.

Of special interest are the challenges faced by wooden buildings in the permafrost zone of Sakha-Yakutia, whose capital—Yakutsk on the Lena River—still had many prerevolutionary wooden buildings at the time of my visit in late May 2002. But climate change has not been the only threat to the preservation in Yakutsk and many other sites in the Russian Federation. On May 26 I was able to photograph the last remaining log tower of the late seventeenth-century Yakutsk fortress (*ostrog*). Three months later, on August 22, the tower burned to the ground during an unusually hot summer. Possible causes include arson by disgruntled former employees or simply carelessness with fire in an open public space. My photographs are the last recorded documentation of that major, uniquely surviving monument to the history of Russia's expansion to the Pacific Ocean. And this is far from the only case of historic wooden structures that now exist only in my photographs. Much that I have photographed no longer exists, and in some cases, the caption will indicate a destroyed building; but I cannot answer for the current condition in every case.

In addition to houses of diverse configurations, the survey will present utilitarian log structures, such as barns, sheds, barracks, schools, and several windmills, their forms delighting the eye. During the lifetimes of these buildings, Russia has witnessed profound social change and every possible tragedy. I dare say this is the only book—at least in English—that

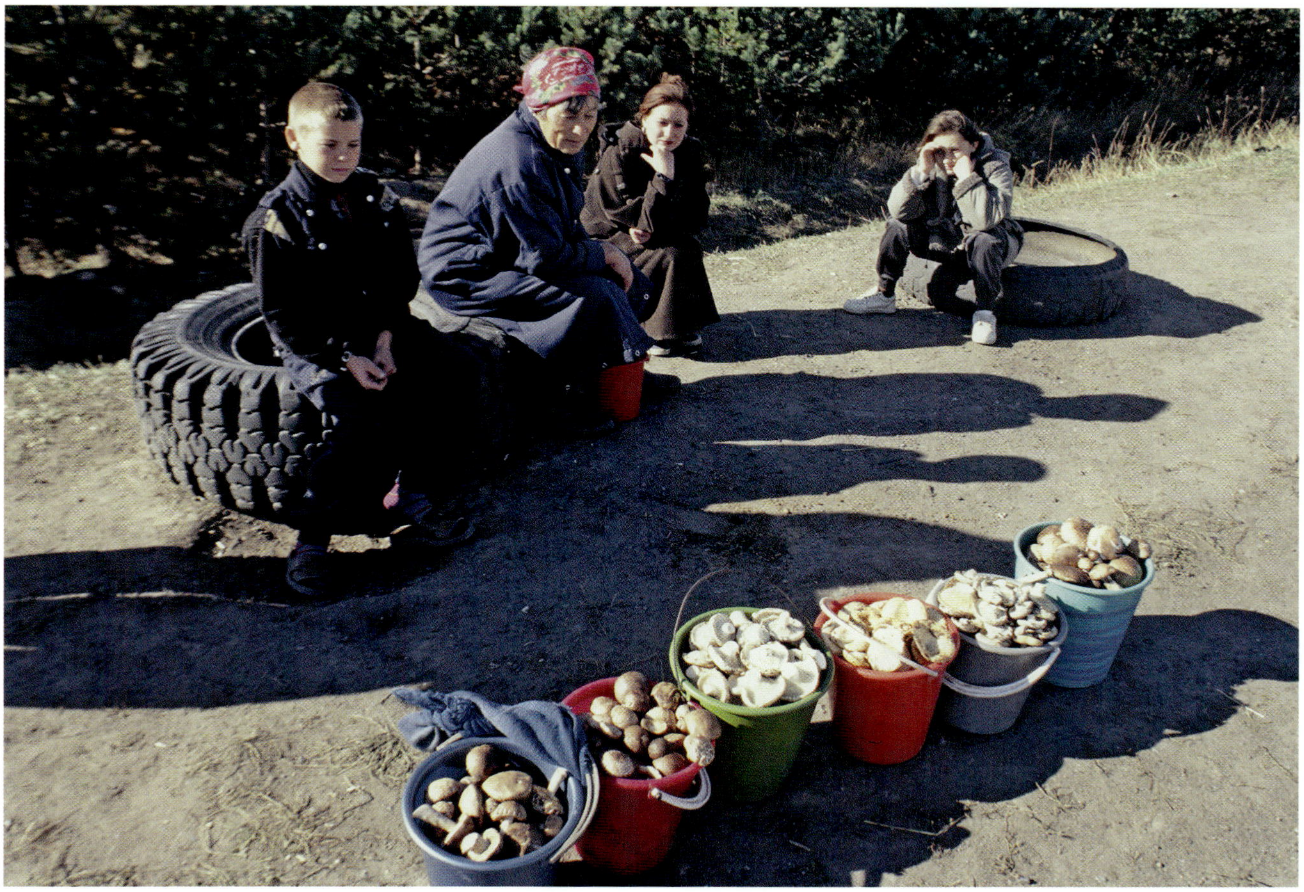

contains photographs of wooden houses that served as places of exile for both Vladimir Lenin (at Shushenskoe, in the Russian Far East) and Joseph Stalin (Solvychegodsk, in the Russian North). And at the end of the book, in Arctic Norilsk, there are wooden echoes of the Gulag, echoes of the wooden Cross. Throughout all, the wooden house and the wooden shrine have provided a refuge, like the forests that surround them.

SARGATSKOE (Omsk Province). Family selling forest mushrooms on a Siberian roadside. September 17, 1999.

PART I Wooden Architecture as Cultural Environment

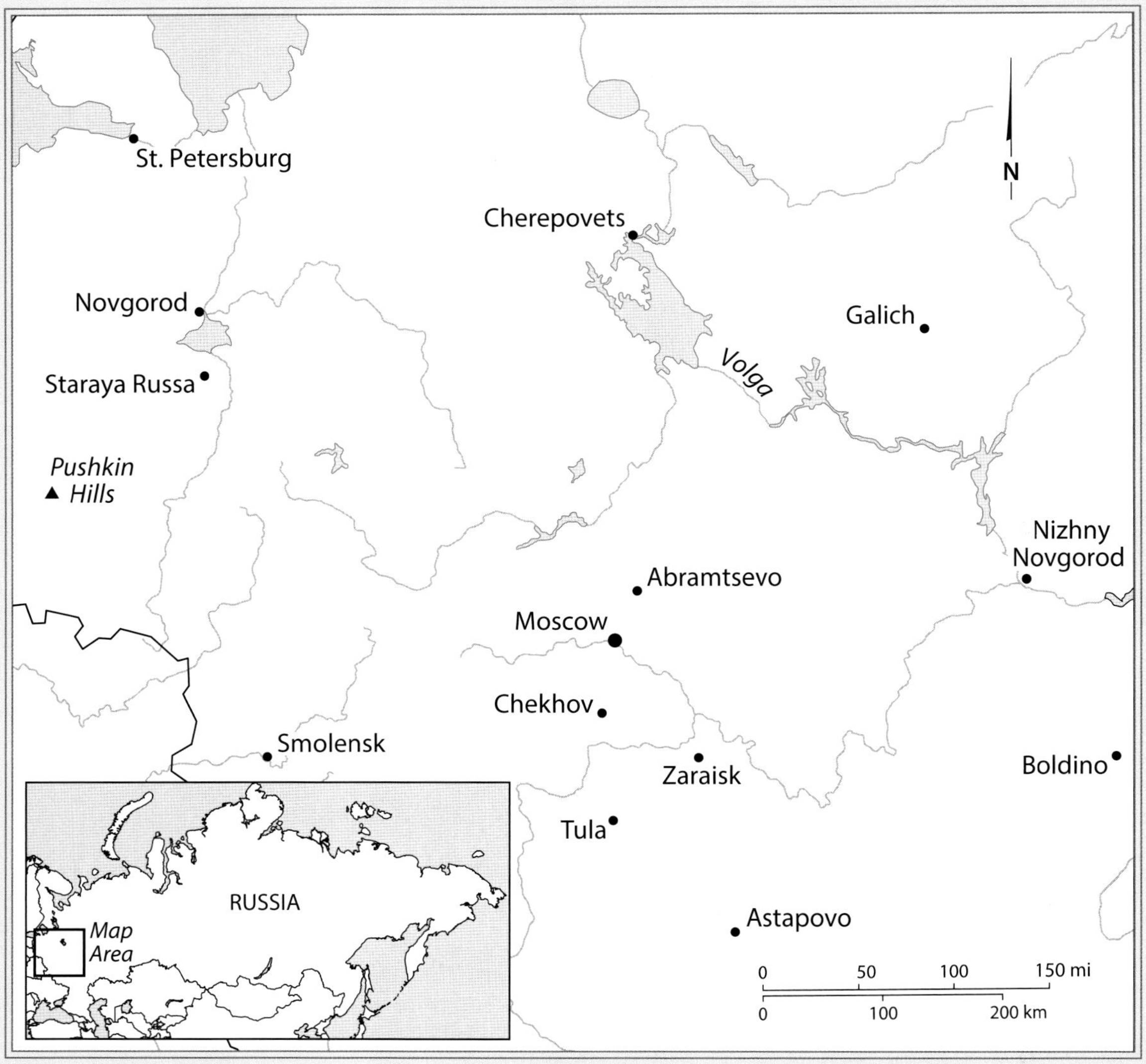

Landmarks of Estate Culture.

CHAPTER ONE

From Palace to Dacha
High Art Revisits Folk Traditions

Wooden Pleasure Palaces on the Fringes of Moscow

For much of Russia's history the built environment was defined by wooden structures, occasionally punctuated by a masonry church or the brick walls of a monastery. Even the dwellings of the rich and powerful were usually log structures, including the rambling, picturesque royal palace at Kolomenskoe, built in 1666–71 during the reign of Tsar Alexey Mikhailovich and demolished in 1762 by order of Catherine the Great.[1] In 2008–10 the palace of Tsar Mikhailovich was rebuilt at another part of Kolomenskoe as a park attraction with wooden walls supported by modern, reinforced concrete elements.

With the rapid assimilation of Western architectural styles during the reign of Peter the Great, wooden architecture was relegated to the ubiquitous background. While remaining an integral part of the Russian experience, its anonymity reflected its status as an awkward relic belonging to a period before the civilized European enlightenment brought by Peter, with its commitment to masonry structures at least superficially resembling those in the West. Nonetheless, building in wood remained an indispensable, if anonymous, part of life for the Russian elite. Although few remain, many neoclassical houses of the Moscow nobility were, in fact, log structures encased in lathing and plaster with neoclassical decorative details. Many were lost in the 1812 fire, but they were quickly rebuilt, with the same Western stylistic flourishes, in the time-honored Moscow practice after catastrophic fires. (For centuries Muscovites could acquire ready-to-assemble log houses at trading squares.)

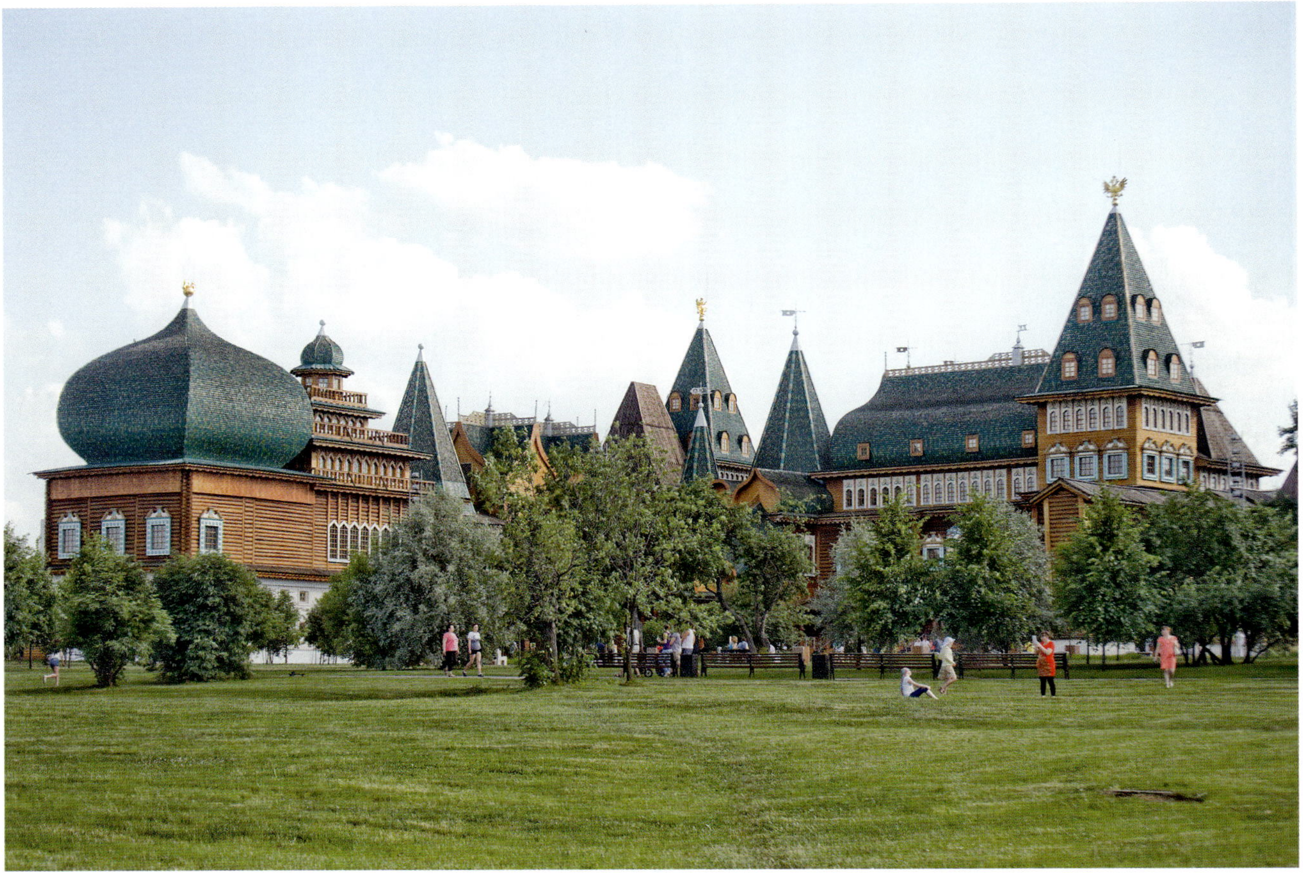

MOSCOW. Kolomenskoe royal estate. Modern replica of seventeenth-century wooden palace built for Tsar Alexey Mikhailovich. June 18, 2014.

Stylistically, much the same could be said of innumerable country manor houses for the gentry, essentially log structures with plank siding, porticoes, and neoclassical plans. The design of estate houses in the Western manner begins in Moscow with the Petrine era, yet it is difficult to define with precision the evolution of this form, since the few extant examples have been so frequently remodeled. By the 1760s, however, the vocabulary of neoclassicism had been introduced to Moscow and the surrounding area by architects such as Karl Blank, whose late baroque churches and other structures showed greater restraint in the application of surface ornament than did contemporary work in Petersburg. Soon thereafter Blank was involved in the creation of Kuskovo, one of the first major neoclassical estate ensembles in the Moscow area—and still the best preserved.

Located to the north of the historic center of Moscow, the village of Kuskovo was acquired in 1715 by Boris Sheremetev—a close associate of Peter I (the Great) and commanding general at the Battle of Poltava—who

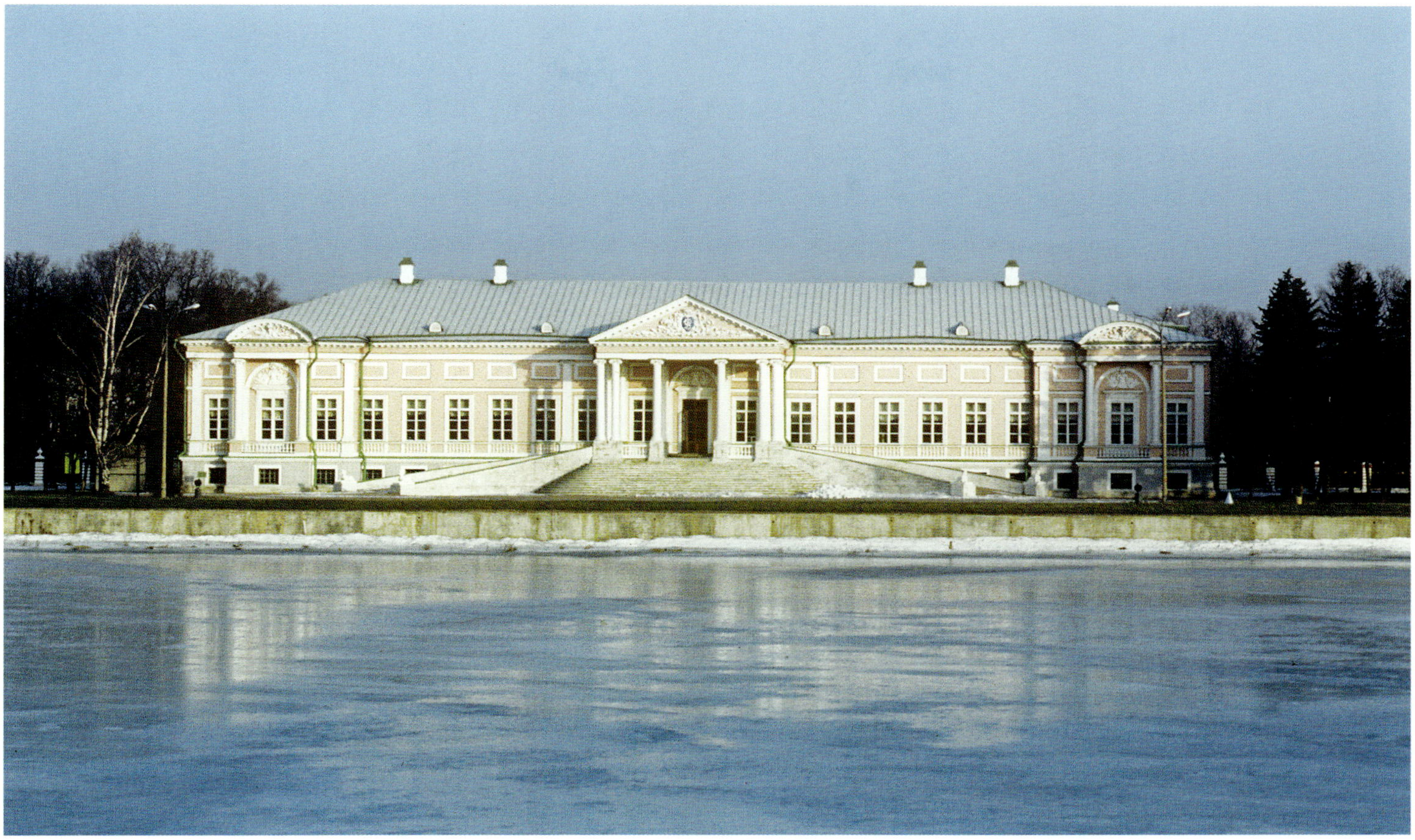

MOSCOW. Kuskovo estate, Sheremetev Palace, main facade. View across large palace pond. December 9, 1983.

built there a wooden summer residence. Kuskovo's accession to magnificence began soon after the marriage of his son Peter Borisovich Sheremetev to Varvara Cherkasskaya in 1743; for not only did the union produce one of the greatest private fortunes in Russia, but the dowry also included serf architects and painters who played the major role in implementing Sheremetev's expansive plans for the estate.[2] The enhancement of the estate grounds, located next to the Cherkassky estate of Veshniaki, was no doubt further stimulated by the proximity of Bartolomeo Francesco Rastrelli's palace for Empress Elizabeth at Perovo—in the same area to the northeast of Moscow.

In 1765 Karl Blank assumed the duties of architect at Kuskovo, where he remained until 1780.[3] The main enterprise at Kuskovo during the late eighteenth century was the creation of the imposing Sheremetev summer residence. Modifications to the original structure had begun by the 1750s, and in 1755 a large pond was excavated in front of the house. Yet the grand design of the mansion took shape only in the late 1760s under the supervision of Blank. The final plan of the main facade and much of the interior followed designs commissioned from Charles de Wailly, who had worked for Catherine the Great. The structure rested on a limestone and brick foundation, but the structural, load-bearing walls consisted of horizontal courses of pine logs. Although the texture of the plank facing is clearly visible on close inspection, the articulation of the facade conveyed the impression of masonry, with balusters beneath the windows and simply etched panels above. Framed by flanking projections with a curved pediment over ionic columns and classical motifs carved in wood, the main portico is reached by curving ramps and culminates in a pediment with an elaborately carved Sheremetev crest.

The interior is defined by two parallel enfilades—one overlooking the pond (containing the "state," or formal rooms) and the other facing the formal park, with the living rooms on a more intimate scale. Despite its lavish decor, Kuskovo was not intended as a major palace, which would have required masonry construction. Much of the interior decoration was derived either from existing Sheremetev palaces in Saint Petersburg or from standard patterns, as in the design of the parquet floors (another example of the skills of Russian master carpenters). The molding is of papier-maché or plaster, while the larger, architectural details are of faux marble. Despite this illusionistic use of material (suited to the theatrical nature of the house, with the rooms like stage sets, distinct in character and decor), the design and its implementation represent the most accomplished example of French-inspired neoclassical decor in Moscow.

The main entry space—the vestibule—was decorated with vases of alabaster, grisaille murals of scenes from classical mythology, scagliola pilasters, and capitals of papier-maché and plaster. It opens on either side to a view of the main enfilade of drawing rooms (including the Tapestry Room, with its Chippendale chairs, Flemish tapestries, and busts of Peter and Vavara Sheremetev by Fedot Shubin), which concludes with a blaze of color in the mauve drawing room of the southwest corner. The color themes of each room—stated primarily by fabrics such as silk damask, satin, and brocatelle—are coordinated not only in relation to the adjoining rooms but also in regard to the exterior setting and the quality of the natural light through the large windows.[4] The perpendicular turn at the mauve drawing room leads to the State Bedroom, a replica of the same room in the Sheremetev Palace on the Fontanka in Saint Petersburg. Adjoining the State Bedroom is the suite used by the family and connected to the enfilade on the

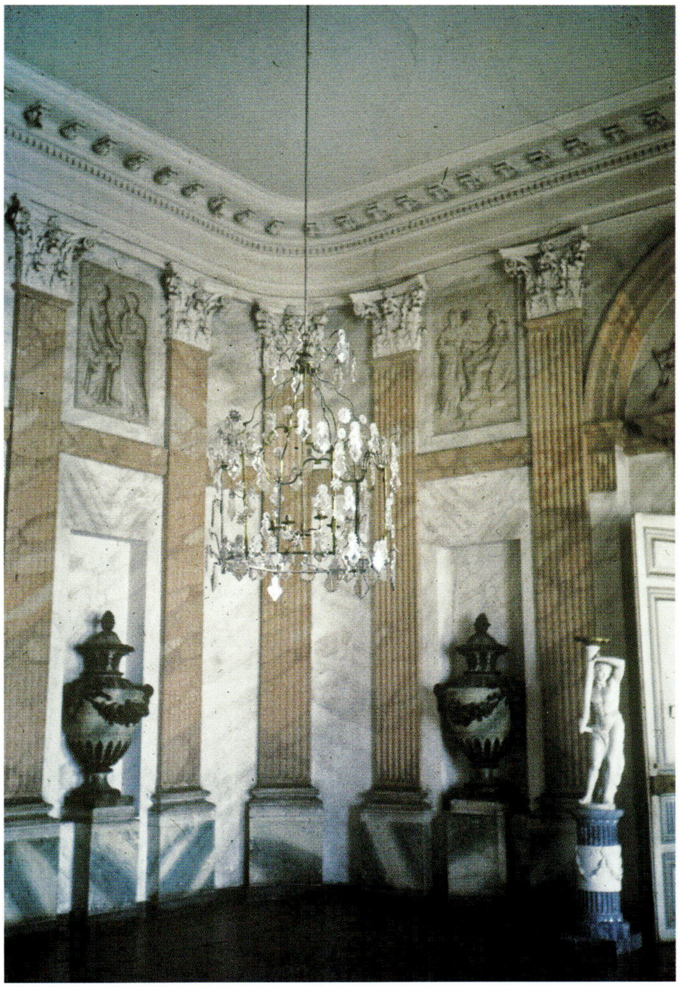

Kuskovo estate, Sheremetev Palace. Vestibule with faux marble walls and papier-maché urns. March 8, 1972.

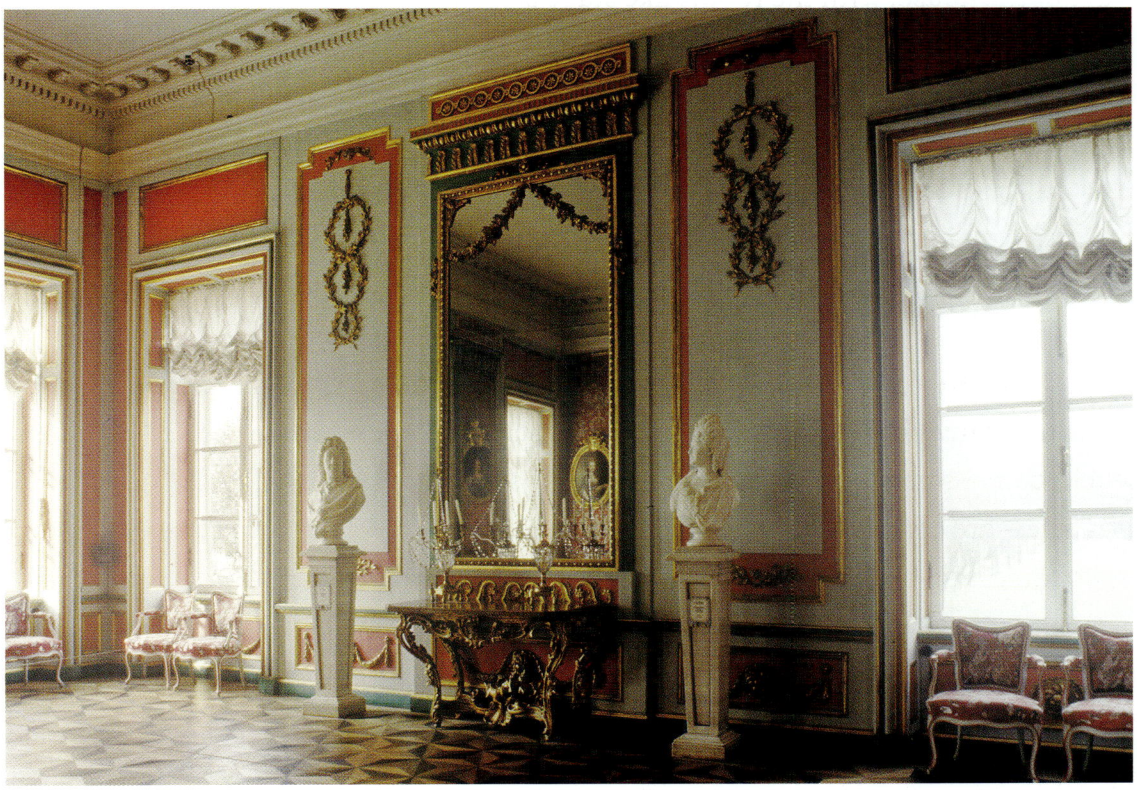

Kuskovo estate, Sheremetev Palace. Crimson Drawing Room, third (end) room of south enfilade. Marble busts, by Fedot Shubin, of Field Marshal Boris Sheremetev and his wife Anna. October 21, 1992.

park facade. This suite contains such Russian elements as the ceramic stove with decorative motifs that combine the traditional and the neoclassical.

The references to heroic classicism culminate in the ballroom, or Mirror Gallery, located at the center of the park enfilade and named for the mirrored inset French windows of the interior wall that reflect the light admitted by their counterparts overlooking the formal park. Mirrors are frequently used in the major rooms at Kuskovo to enlarge the impression of space and to enhance the luster provided by natural light, torchères, and gilded candelabras—a technique that had been explored by Rastrelli and his predecessors in the design of the imperial palaces of Saint Petersburg. The decoration of the ballroom displays the iconography of estate culture, particularly in the ceiling painting. Executed by Lagrenée and renovated in the 1880s, it represents the apotheosis of Peter Sheremetev surrounded by various muses. The borders of the ceiling are decorated with paintings of his various orders, including the crosses of Saint Andrew and Saint Anne. The heroic values proclaimed by classical iconography are further evident in a series of gilded relief panels—designed by Johann Just for the ends of the ballroom—that depict the exploits of Gaius Mucius Scaevola, the mythic Roman hero of the sixth century BC who, having failed to assassinate the Etruscan king Porsenna, held his right hand to the fire as a sign of indifference to physical pain. The Mucius Scaevola legend acquired great resonance in Russia at the time of the Napoleonic invasion when it can be said to have penetrated the popular consciousness as a symbol of self-sacrifice and patriotic devotion. For Peter Sheremetev and his contemporaries, the panels would have served as further expressions of the standards of antiquity upheld by the elite of the Russian nobility.

Although the ballroom extends to the full height of the interior, the other rooms along the park enfilade comprise living suites and have lower ceilings than the state rooms. The additional space above forms an entresol composed of servants' rooms with low ceilings (slightly above human height) illuminated by a second level of small windows extending the length of the park facade.[5] The skillful distribution of space within the floor plan and the means of circulation between the enfilades create an unusual variety of perspectives as one moves through the house and out to the steps leading to the parterre of the formal garden.[6] Within the parterre are two monuments to Catherine the Great, including a column with an allegorical statue of Minerva. The empress visited Kuskovo in 1783,

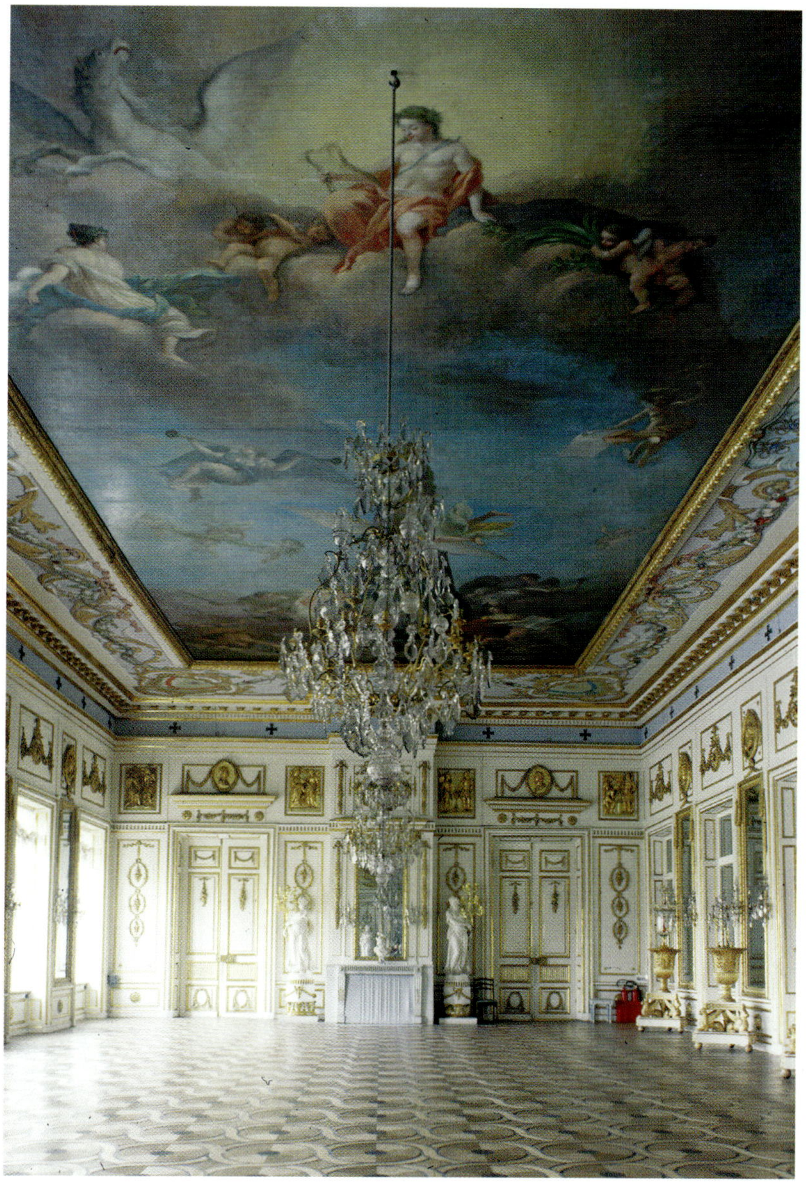

Kuskovo estate, Sheremetev Palace. Ball room, modeled on the Hall of Mirrors at Versaille. Ceiling painting by Louis Jean François Lagrenée, "The Glory of the Sheremetev Clan." October 21, 1992.

the year of Peter Sheremetev's election to the honorific post as head of the Moscow nobility.

In the 1790s, however, Sheremetev's son Nikolay tired of the scale of entertainment and perhaps also of the style of Kuskovo. He had passed much of his youth in Holland and France, was familiar with recent developments in Western art, and—typically for third generation fortunes—preferred to devote himself to the pursuit of the arts, with a special interest in theater. Having formed at Kuskovo the leading serf theatrical troupe in Russia, Nicholas Sheremetev in 1792 undertook the construction of a palace-theater at his neighboring estate of Ostankino, a former Cherkassky

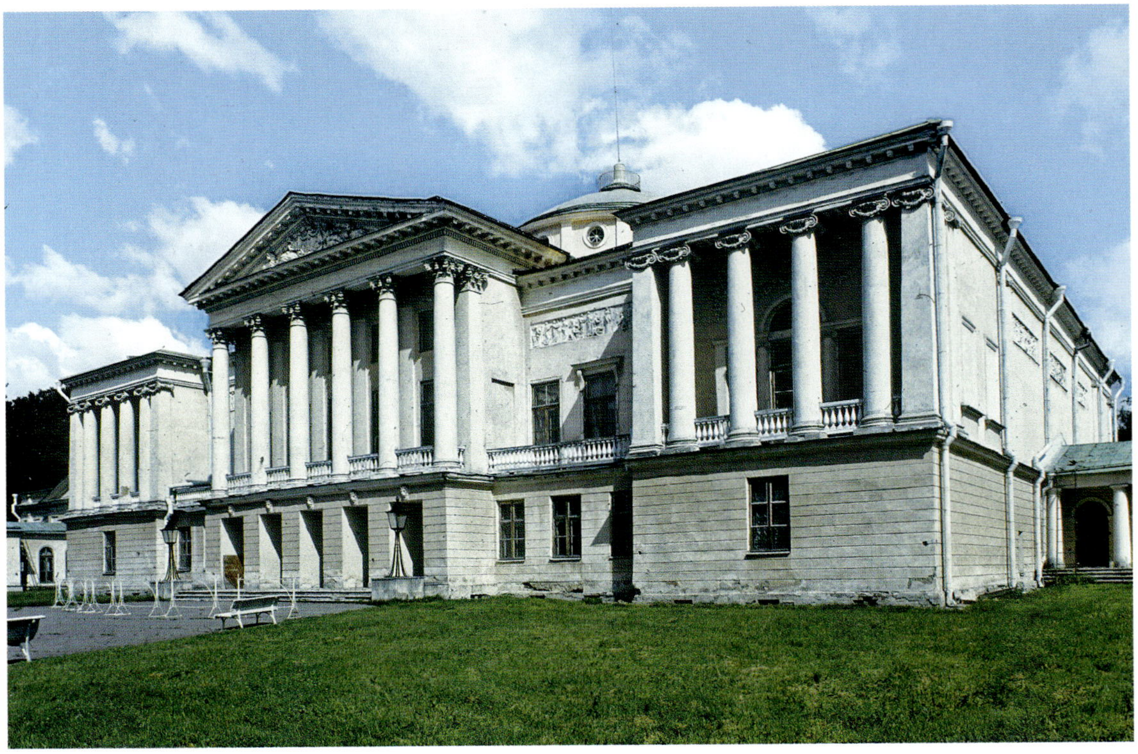

MOSCOW. Ostankino estate. Sheremetev Palace, southeast view. June 29, 1994.

village whose church, built by the serf Pavel Potekhin, so brilliantly exemplifies the late seventeenth-century ornamental style.[7] Sheremetev, the owner of 210,000 serfs and vast land holdings, could well afford to build an entire estate around a theater, and the dimensions of the central structure, culminating in a rotunda, are much larger than those of the Kuskovo mansion. Several architects submitted proposals, including Giacomo Quarenghi, author of major projects in Moscow. The basic plan for the structure, its facades, and the adjoining park is attributed to Francesco Camporesi, although during the next six years, Sheremetev turned to Quarenghi, Karl Blank, and even Vincenzo Brenna for modifications as well as additions to the wings. The construction was supervised by Sheremetev's serf architects Alexey Mironov, Grigorii Dikushin, and Pavel Argunov (son of the painter Ivan Argunov), who had apprenticed with Bazhenov in Petersburg.

The entire monumental ensemble of palace and attached pavilions at Ostankino was built, within the space of a decade, of Siberian pine covered with stucco. The core structure has an elevated portico of six Corinthian columns and culminates in a rotunda with Palladian overtones. This establishes a center for a ramifying series of wings and attached pavilions that were used for living space. The interior is dominated by the

Ostankino estate. Sheremetev Palace. Blue Hall, loggia with faux marble columns. October 20, 1992.

Ostankino estate. Sheremetev Palace. Theater, view from stage toward loges and entrance. Papier-maché columns. October 20, 1992.

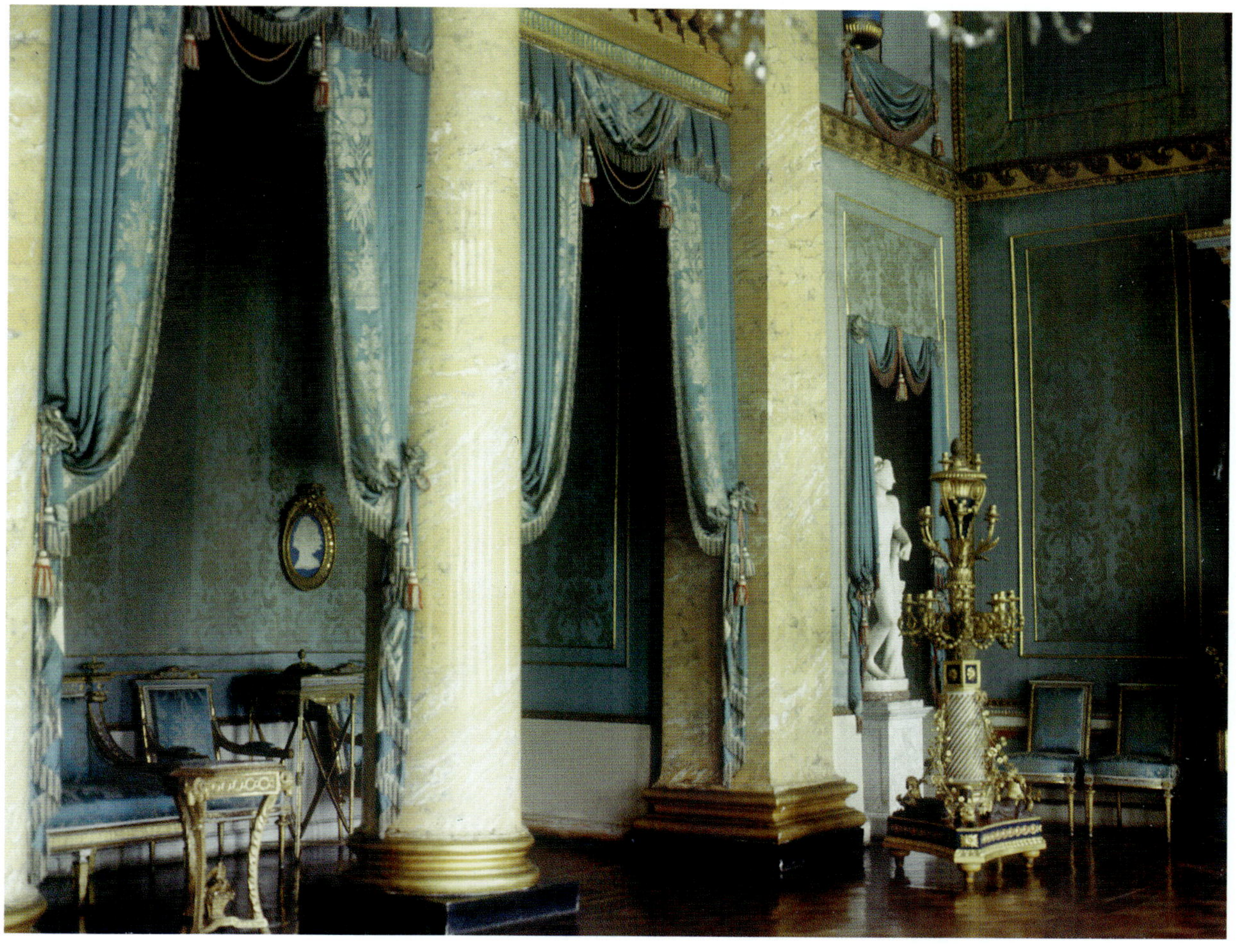

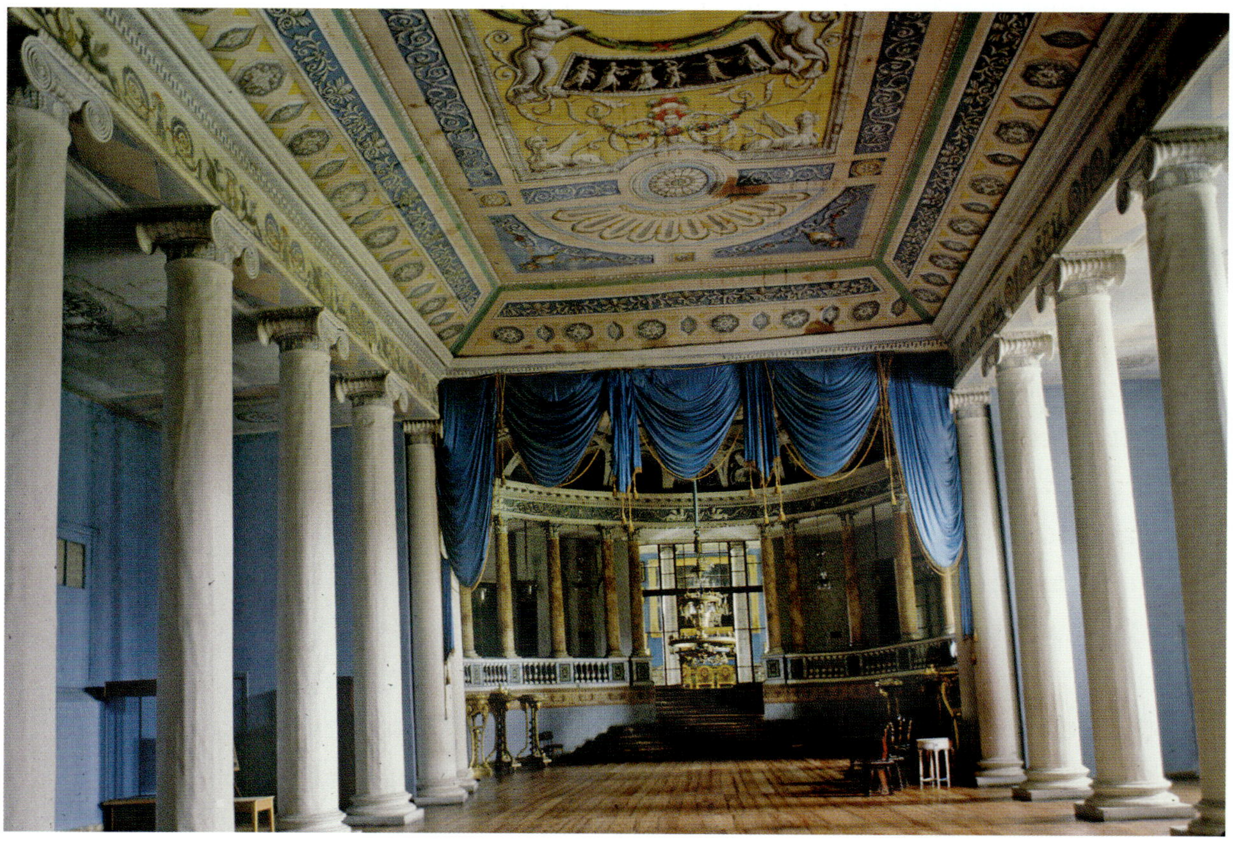

theater, which is two stories high and extends across much of the central block. Its floor was ingeniously designed to serve also as a grand ballroom. The upper floor, or bel étage, consists of an enfilade of state rooms that open onto the portico and a picture gallery.

On the ground floor, galleries extend from either side of the central structure to the two main pavilions: the Italian (west), with a sculpture gallery; and the Egyptian (east), containing a concert hall. The facades of the palace and its pavilions are, like the park, liberally decorated with statuary placed in niches, as well as friezes composed of abstract patterns and classical tableaux (of special note are the bas reliefs of sacrifice to Jupiter and Demeter by Fyodor Gordeev and Gavriil Zamaraev). In 1801 Alexander I visited Ostankino as a part of his coronation ceremonies; but soon thereafter, the theater waned, no doubt in response to the illness and death, in 1803, of Zhemchugova, the leading actress of the troop and Nikolay Sheremetev's wife. After Sheremetev's own premature death in 1809, the palace remained in the family as a little-used monument to the culture fostered by the Russian nobility at its zenith.

The third relatively well-preserved estate mansion in Moscow is located at the opposite, southwestern side of the city in what was once the village of Uzkoe. Located on open land along the Old Kaluga Road, the estate was bought from the state in 1629 by Maksim Streshnev, a prominent figure at the royal court in the first half of the seventeenth century. In the early 1690s, the boyar Tikhon Streshnev erected the magnificent four-lobed Church of the Kazan Icon of the Virgin. The estate remained in the hands of various branches of the Streshnev clan until 1726, when it was acquired through marriage by Prince Boris Golitsyn. At that time, the manor house was built of brick. The Uzkoe mansion passed to his son, Prince Alexey Golitsyn (1732–92), who made substantial changes to the estate, including the replacement of the brick main house with a grand wooden mansion around 1780.[8]

Remarkably, that house, repaired and modified over the decades, still stands, in no small measure due to its acquisition in 1922 by a state commission as a sanatorium for scholars and eventually (1937) transferred to the powerful Academy of Sciences, which in the Russian system includes the arts. The sprawling neoclassical structure has at its center a two-storied portico framed by entrance ramps and situated over a grotto, elements that apparently have survived from the original design. Carved garland panels decorate the plank facade, which is marked by large French windows.

MOSCOW. Uzkoe estate house. Main portico. June 22, 2019.

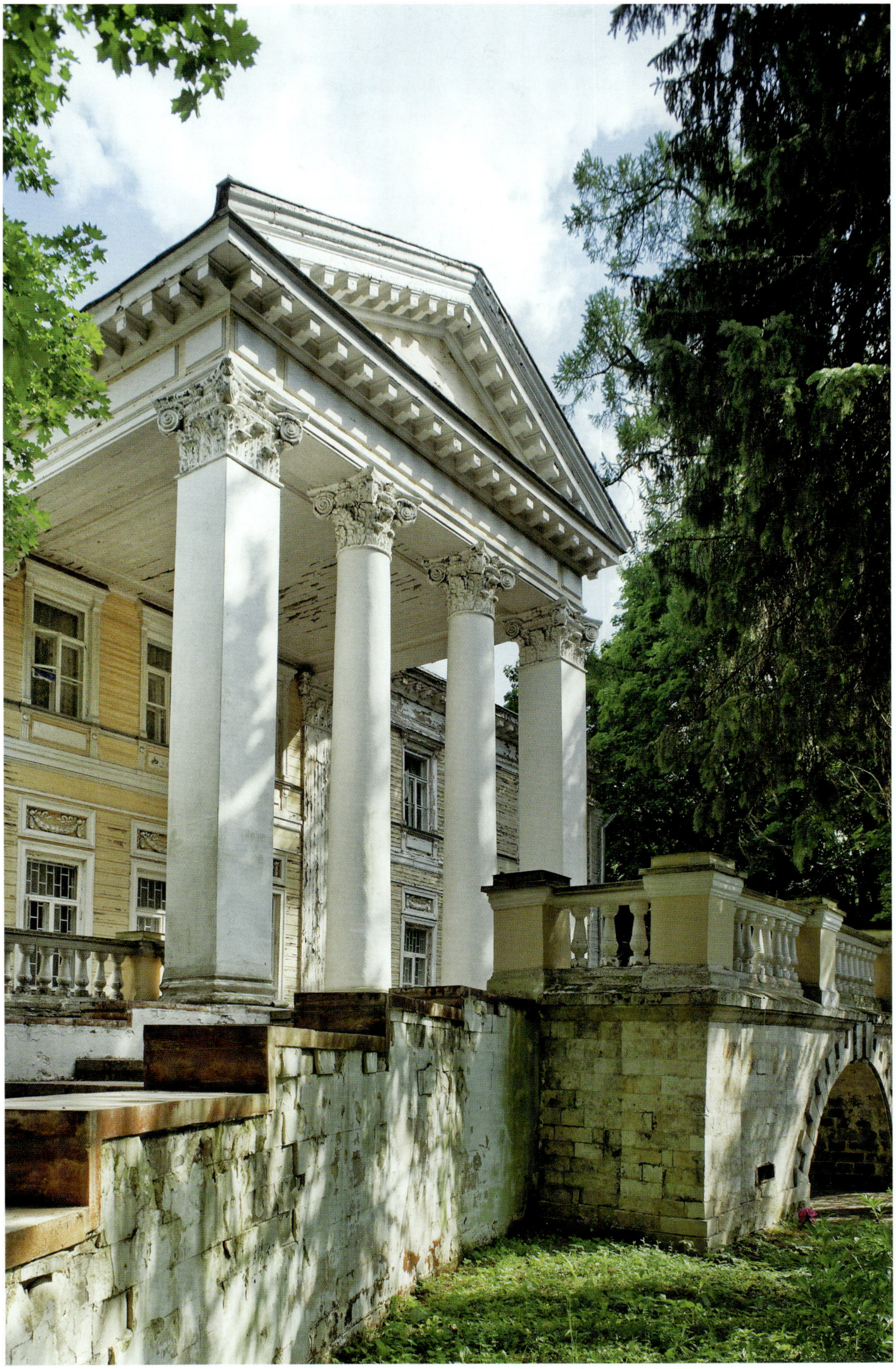

After the sudden death of Alexey Golitsyn's unmarried son Egor Golitsyn in 1811, the estate was inherited by his sister Maria Tolstaya, a prominent grande dame who was married to the eccentric Count Peter Alexandrovich Tolstoy, general of the infantry, diplomat, and a member of the upper stratum of the Russian nobility. After the death of his wife in 1826, Tolstoy spent his final years at Uskoe occupied by the only thing he considered important in life—flowers. Interestingly, in 1822 the hospitable Tolstoys were visited by a distant relative, Count Nicholas Tolstoy (1794–1837), who had recently married Princess Maria Volkonskaya (1790–1830). After a brief visit, the couple made their way to one of Princess Maria's estates, Yasnaya Polyana, where the great writer and thinker Leo Tolstoy was born in 1828. More will be said of that Tolstoy in the next chapter.

Following the death of Peter Tolstoy in 1844, Uzkoe was inherited by his son Vladimir, after whose death in 1875 the estate became the property of his widow, who transferred it in 1883 to her nephew Prince Peter Trubetskoy (1858–1911), who revived the estate's agricultural enterprises and in 1885–89 had the main house renovated in a neoclassical revival style by the architect Sergey Rodionov. After the Bolshevik Revolution, the Trubetskoys left Russia, except for Vladimir Trubetskoy, who fell victim to the savage purge of 1937. For all its former patronage, the mansion is now desperately in need of repair.

Idyll on the Sheksna River: Gorka

Readers of the Russian classics, from Pushkin to Turgenev and Tolstoy, know that the country estate was a special cultural and social environment. Despite the problems of Russia's social and economic system in the countryside, the estate possessed an enchanted ambiance—at least in the literary imagination. The revolutionary cataclysm following 1917 destroyed most of the estates and dispersed the nobility. The fraction of estate houses remaining were converted to a variety of uses, usually with poor maintenance, yet there have been remarkably successful examples of preservation and restoration. None is more unexpected than the Galskoy estate of Gorka ("little hill"), located on the sloping left bank of the Sheksna River opposite Cherepovets in the western part of Vologda Province. Known for the giant Severstal (NorthSteel) plant and other industrial behemoths, Cherepovets (population 316,000) seems remote from the typical image of the gentry estate. But in the mid-nineteenth century, when the Galskoy family came into possession of the estate, Cherepovets was a modest town of only a few thousand inhabitants on the Sheksna.[9]

The Gorka estate house is itself a curiosity, imposingly designed in the early 1830s in a neoclassical style befitting a brick mansion. In fact, only the shallow foundation is brick, while the house itself is constructed of stout logs surfaced in painted plank siding. The interior walls of the main rooms were plastered and covered with wallpaper. Thus, the structure combined the warmth of wood with the appearance of a grand masonry residence. The original owner of the house was Andrey Kudryavy (1792–1848), who achieved noble status and the rank of colonel for his military service, which included the War of 1812. His daughter Alexandra—one of five children—married Lev Galskoy (1814–75), of a noble family known in the area since the early eighteenth century. In 1856 Alexandra inherited the Gorka estate, thus linking it to the Galskoy family. Lev and Alexandra had four children, including three sons.

The Gorka estate prospered, and in 1896 it passed into the hands of the third son, Nicholas (1855–1920). He and his wife Maria had four children—two sons who died in infancy and two daughters. A frequent guest at the estate was Nicholas's sister Maria Yanish, who had five sons, all of whom entered military service. Although life on the estate maintained its tranquility in 1914, war touched the Galskoy clan. One of Maria Yanish's sons had already perished as a test pilot in 1912. The disastrous campaigns on the eastern front undermined the Romanov dynasty, which had just celebrated its tercentenary in 1913. Nicholas II abdicated the throne on March 2 (15), 1917. (For pre-1918 events, Old Style dates from the then-in-use Julian calendar are given, with today's Gregorian-calendar dates in parentheses.)

The four years of civil war that followed the Bolshevik seizure of power in Petrograd on November 7, 1917, fundamentally altered Russia's economic and social situation. In a story repeated throughout the country, the Galskoy family was driven from its estate and reduced to penury. Nikolay, the father, died in 1920. Of the two daughters, Anastasia (1904–67) resorted to menial labor to support her ailing mother and her small sister Maria (1914–92). In 1930 Maria Galskaya was arrested and sent with her younger daughter, Maria, to the distant Siberian town of Yeniseisk. After her

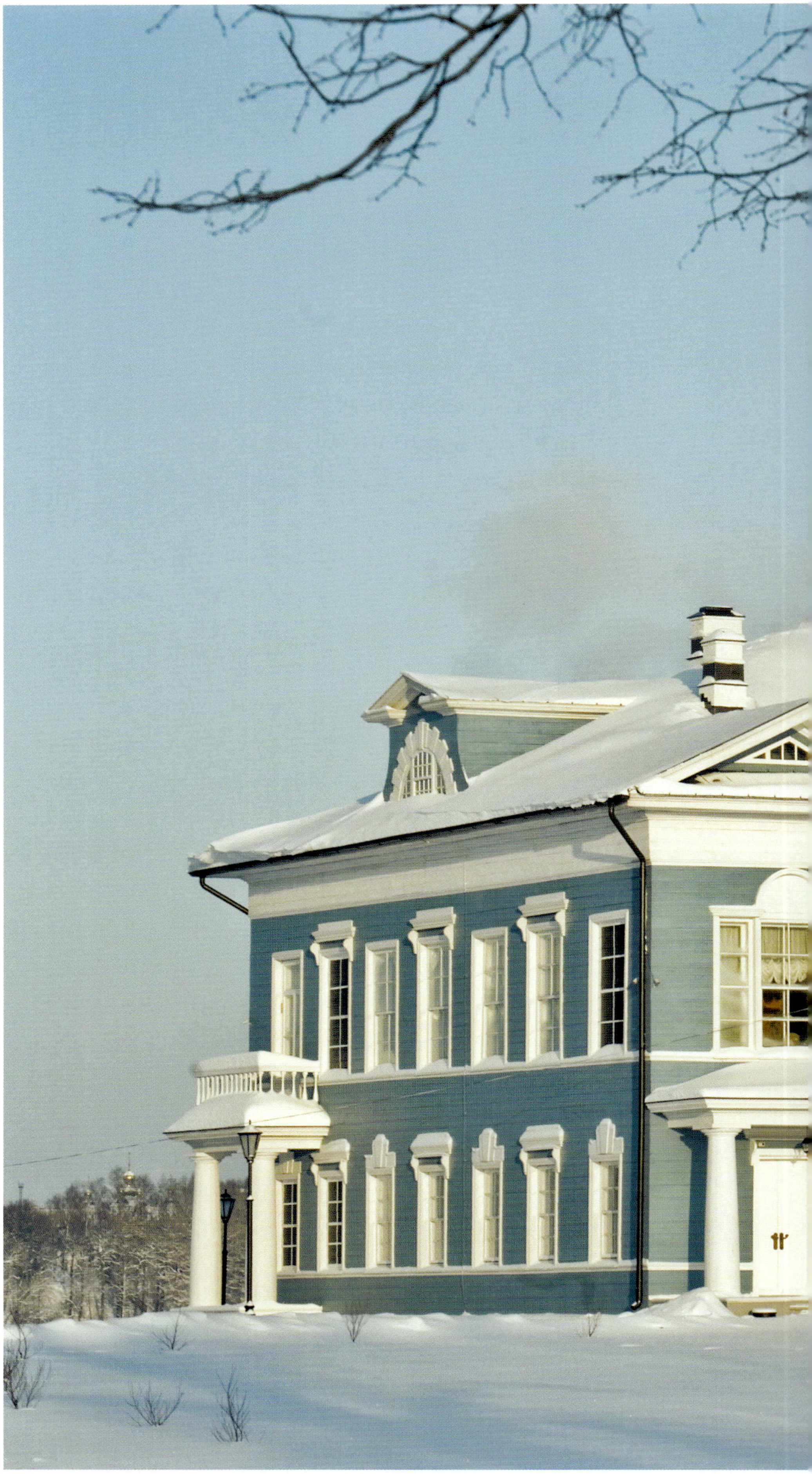

CHEREPOVETS. Galskoy estate house, view across courtyard. January 2, 2010.

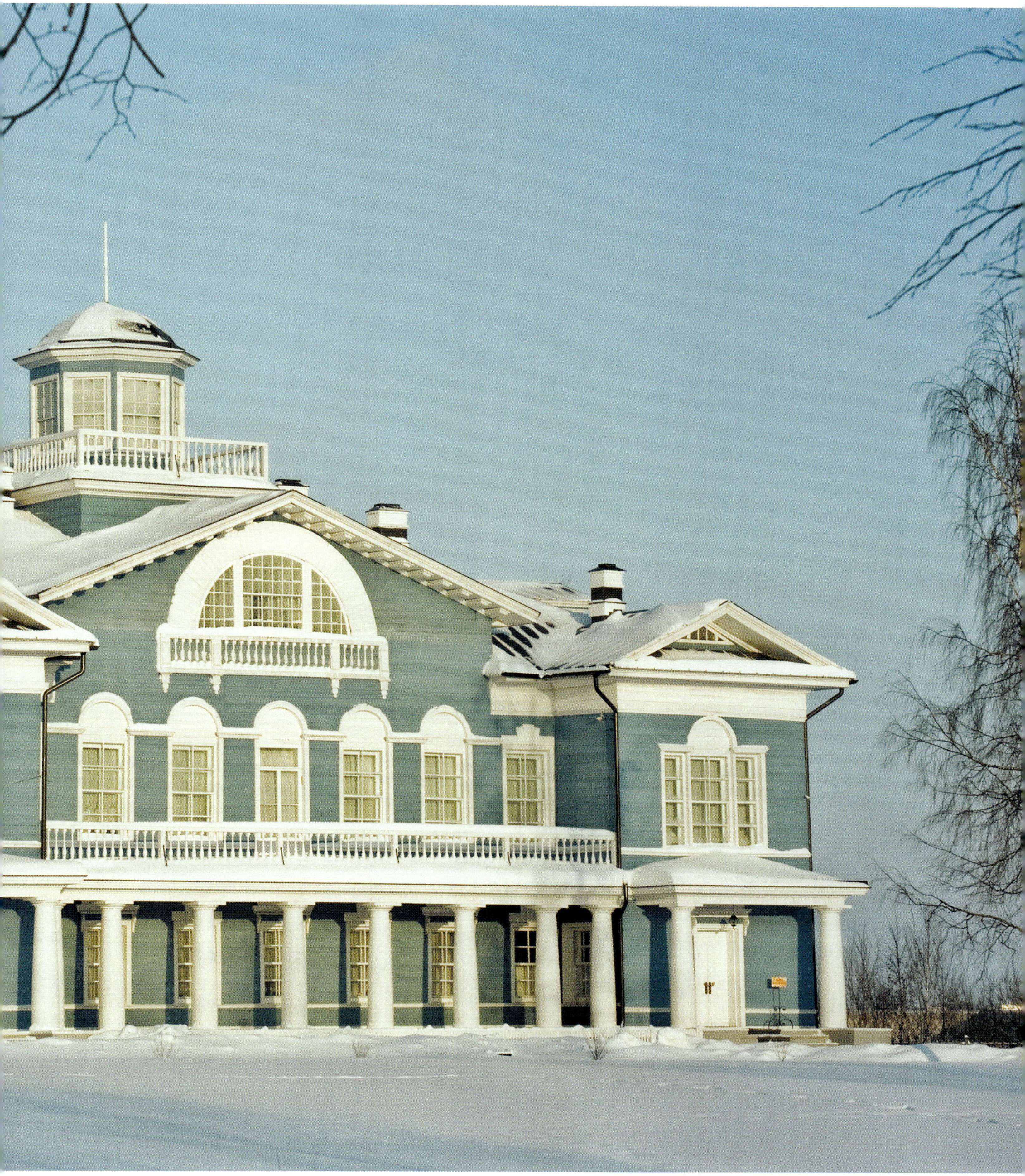

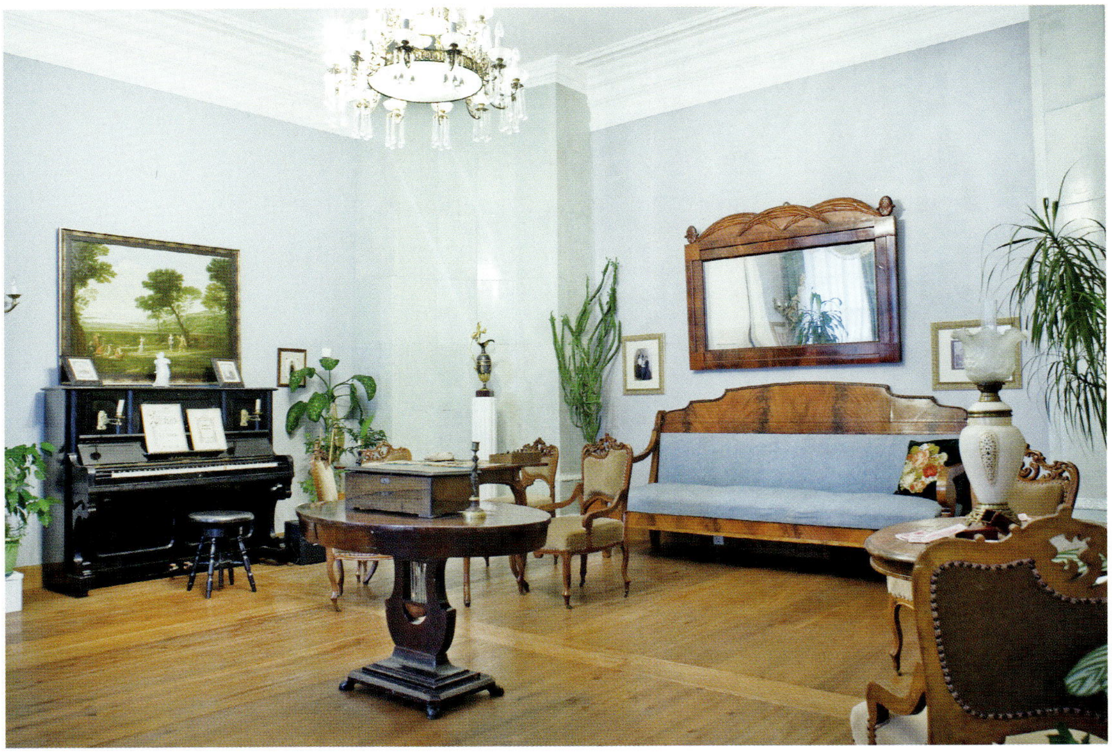

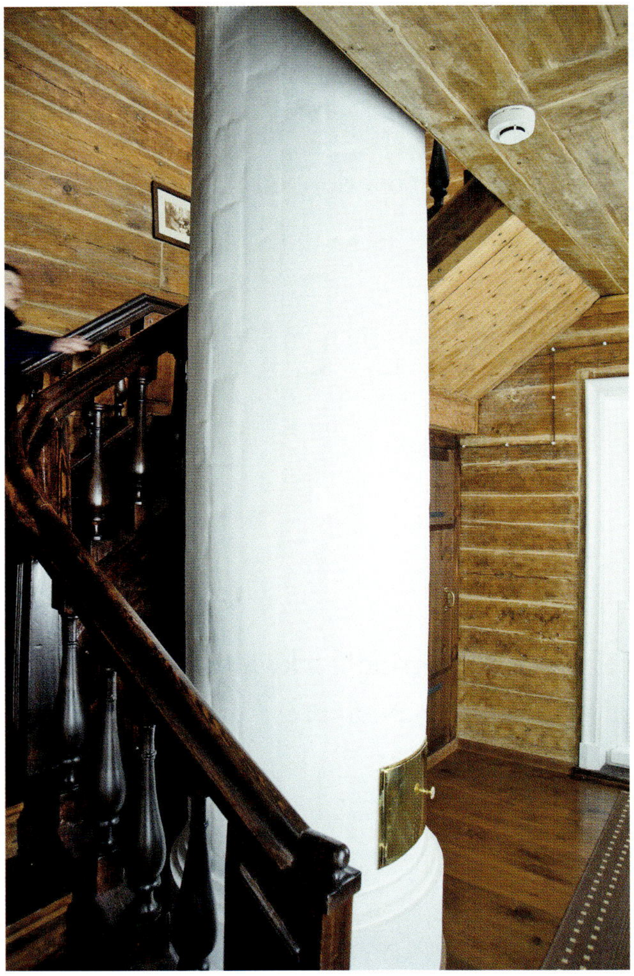

Galskoy estate house. Reconstructed main living room. December 29, 2013.

Galskoy estate house. Central stairway with a view of log walls. Foreground: brick support column with heating stove. December 29, 2013.

mother's death, in 1933, Maria made her way back to her sister Anastasia, then living in Leningrad. Other family tragedies ensued, but fortunately, both daughters and their progeny survived the war. In 1956 the daughters obtained the formal rehabilitation of their mother, an admission that she, like so many others, had been unjustly arrested. Descendants of the family now live in Saint Petersburg and Moscow. (Another, "southern" branch of the family resettled in the United States.)

The estate house has survived. During the Soviet period its various uses included an agricultural school, a dormitory, and a state farm named "Red Gorka." In 1960 the house—still housing farm workers—gained landmark status. In 1989 the Gorka estate territory was declared a historical museum, and the process of restoration slowly began. Twenty years later, in 2009, the house opened to visitors, even as the restoration of rooms continued. Descendants of the Galskoy family have donated original items to the superb restoration effort.

Visitors to the house today enter the slightly elevated ground floor of the house, which originally included vestibules, living and dining rooms, rooms for servants, a wine cellar, and perhaps a kitchen. (Many country houses in Russia had the kitchen in a separate nearby structure.) The upper floor has higher ceilings and contains the main rooms for the family, including the master bedroom, separate studies for husband and wife, a library, and children's room. A large living room overlooked the portico on one facade of the house, and a ballroom occupied the center of the other side. Above the main floor is a spacious attic that was sparsely outfitted for family use, particularly in the summer. A few service buildings have been preserved on the territory, including a two-story barn with an exterior gallery.

From Abramtsevo to Talashkino

In the cyclical manner of style and history, the very pre-Petrine "backwardness" of Russia's wooden architecture would become a point of interest in the nineteenth century, as Russian intellectuals and artists began to search for origins, antecedents, and authenticity in the native culture. Engravings of traditional structures began to be distributed and published. One of the early signals of this process of reaffirmation can be found in the *izba* designed by Nikolay Nikitin for the noted historian and Moscow University

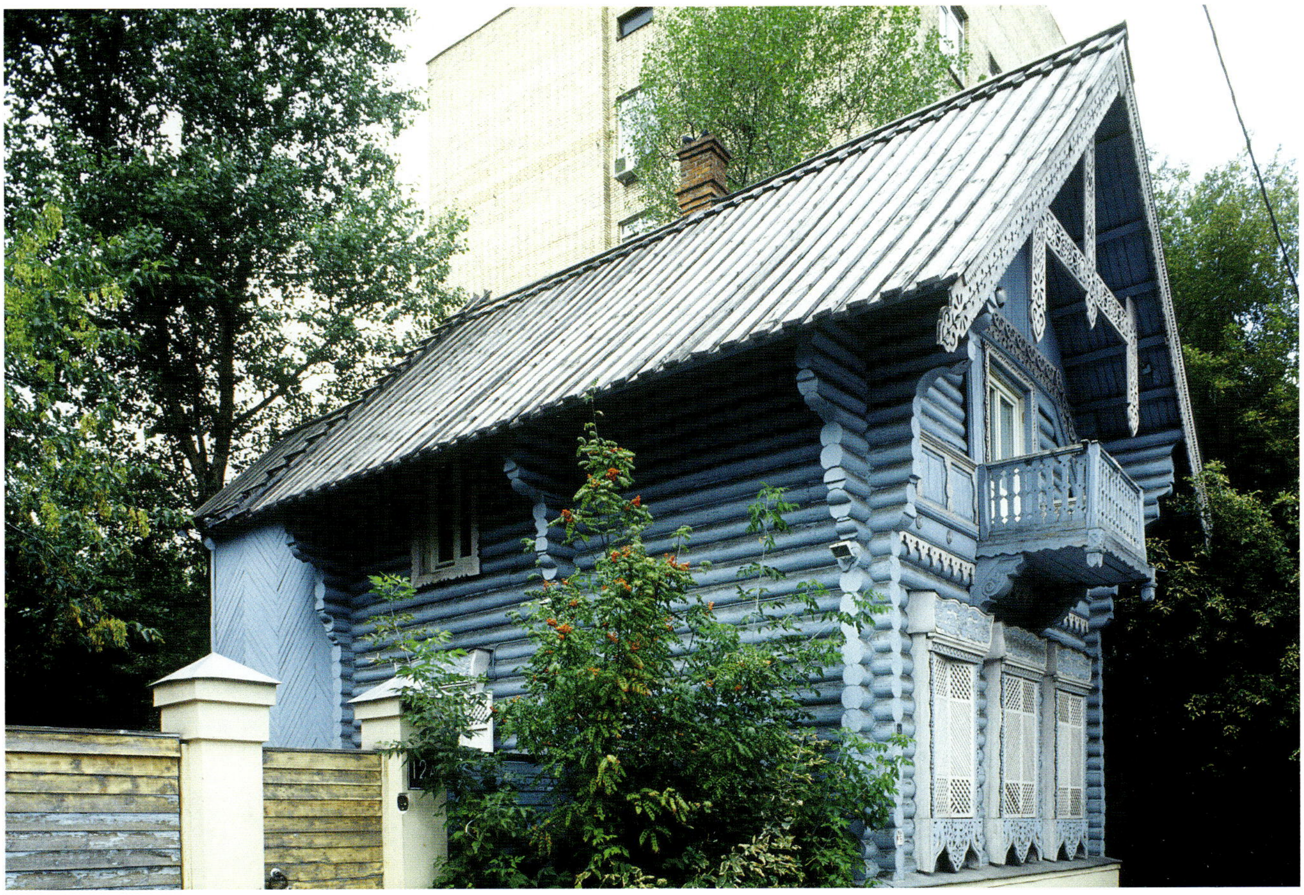

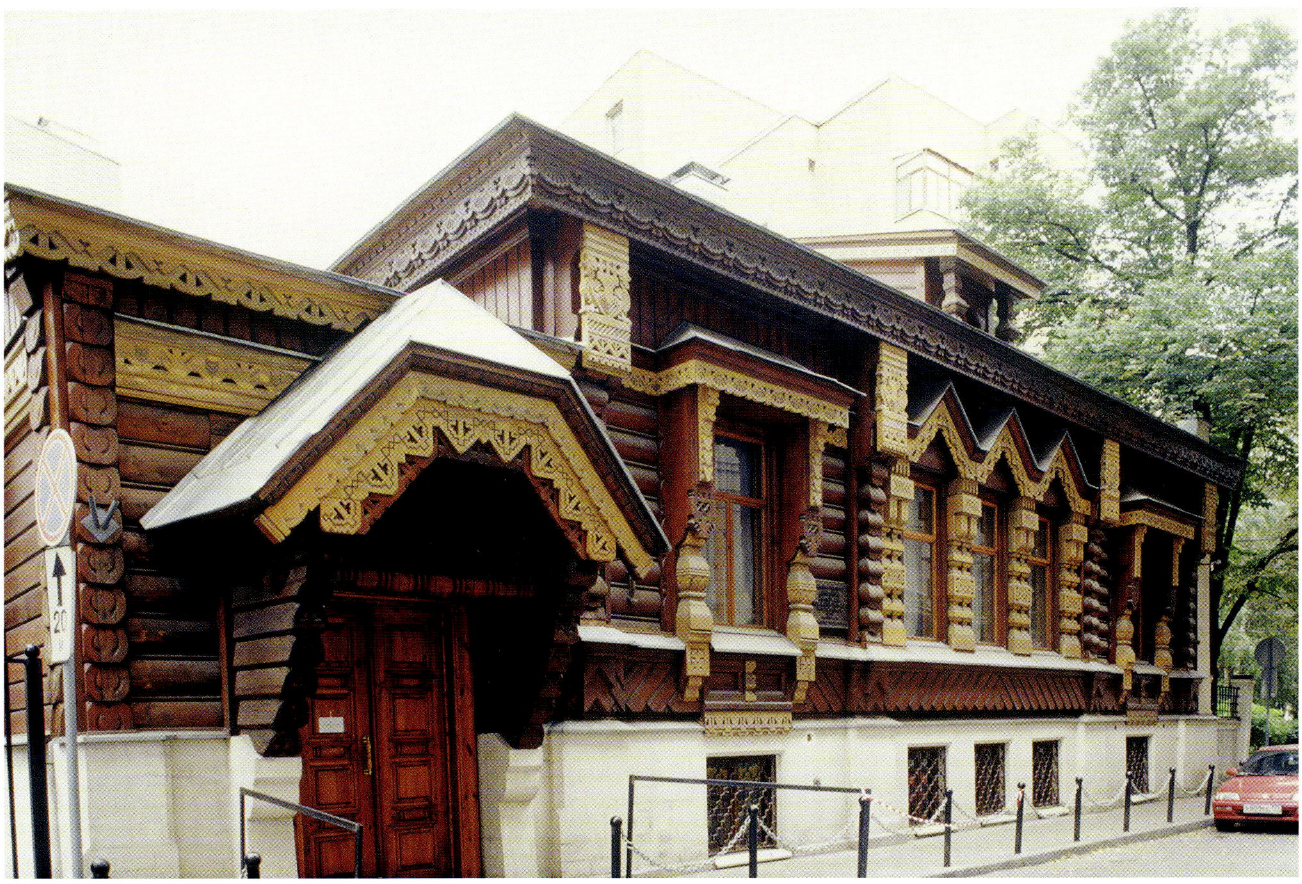

professor Mikhail Pogodin.[10] The use of a traditionalist, "folk" style for the house of a prominent intellectual was intended to elevate the anonymous quality of vernacular architecture to the virtue of national authenticity. Other such houses followed as a reflection of the owners' allegiance to various nationalist, Pan-Slavic programs. Architects such as Andrey Huhn (designer of a log house in the center of Moscow for the entrepreneur and Slavophile Alexander Porokhovshchikov), Nikolay Pozdeev, and Viktor Vasnetsov began to adapt the asymmetrical and three-dimensional characteristics of old Russian architecture to their work in both wood and brick.[11]

MOSCOW. Pogodin *izba*. The exterior color has changed with repainting over the decades. August 26, 2007.

MOSCOW. Alexander Porokhovshchikov house. August 26, 2007.

A consciously aestheticized interpretation of the wooden vernacular appeared in the 1870s and was associated particularly with the estate of Abramtsevo, whose artistic community received substantial support from the entrepreneur Savva Mamontov. Although inhabited as early as the seventeenth century, its intellectual significance dates from 1843, when the estate was acquired by Sergey Aksakov (1791–1859), a leading figure in an intellectual group known as the Slavophiles. During the mid-nineteenth century, Aksakov's legendary hospitality was extended to a circle of cultural luminaries, including the writers Nikolay Gogol and Ivan Turgenev. The main house, a long log structure covered with plank siding, has preserved its general form much as Aksakov acquired it.

MOSCOW. Viktor Vasnetsov house. Completed in 1894 by peasant builders from Vladimir Province, the house was designed by Vasnetsov, a leading proponent of the Russian Revival style, which valued traditional Russian wooden architecture. Although the entire structure was built of logs, the ground floor (containing the main living space) was clad in stucco. August 9, 1988.

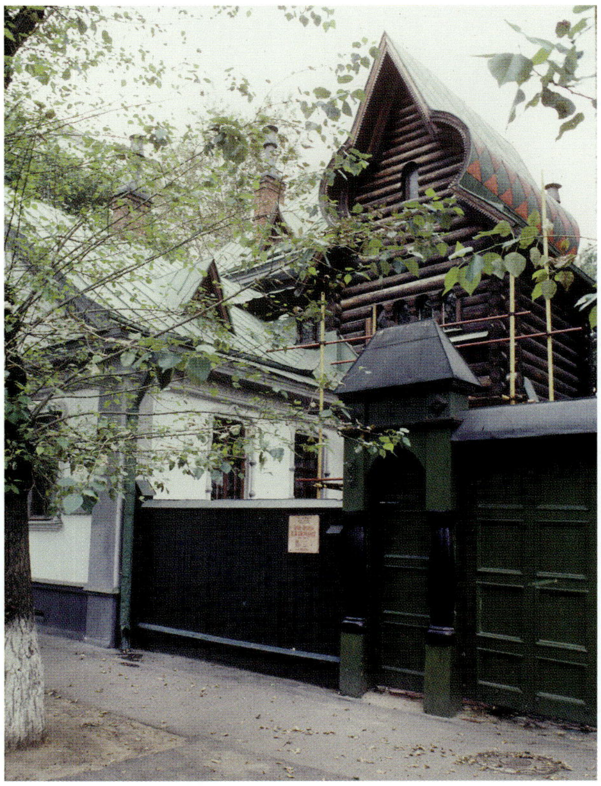

In 1870 Abramtsevo was sold to Savva Mamontov (1841–1918) the year after the death of his father, the pioneering Moscow industrialist Ivan Mamontov. Savva Mamontov enlarged the considerable inherited fortune and emerged as one of Russia's most energetic railway developers. At the same time, he discovered an interest in the arts and in traditional Russian culture. With the purchase of Abramtsevo—then in dilapidated condition—Mamontov and his wife Elizabeth, a descendent of the Sapozhnikov silk and fabrics dynasty, not only had a bucolic retreat from Moscow but also a setting in which they could gather a group dedicated to the revival of the arts and crafts. Mamontov's "colony" at Abramtsevo provides a quintessential example of the productive relation between

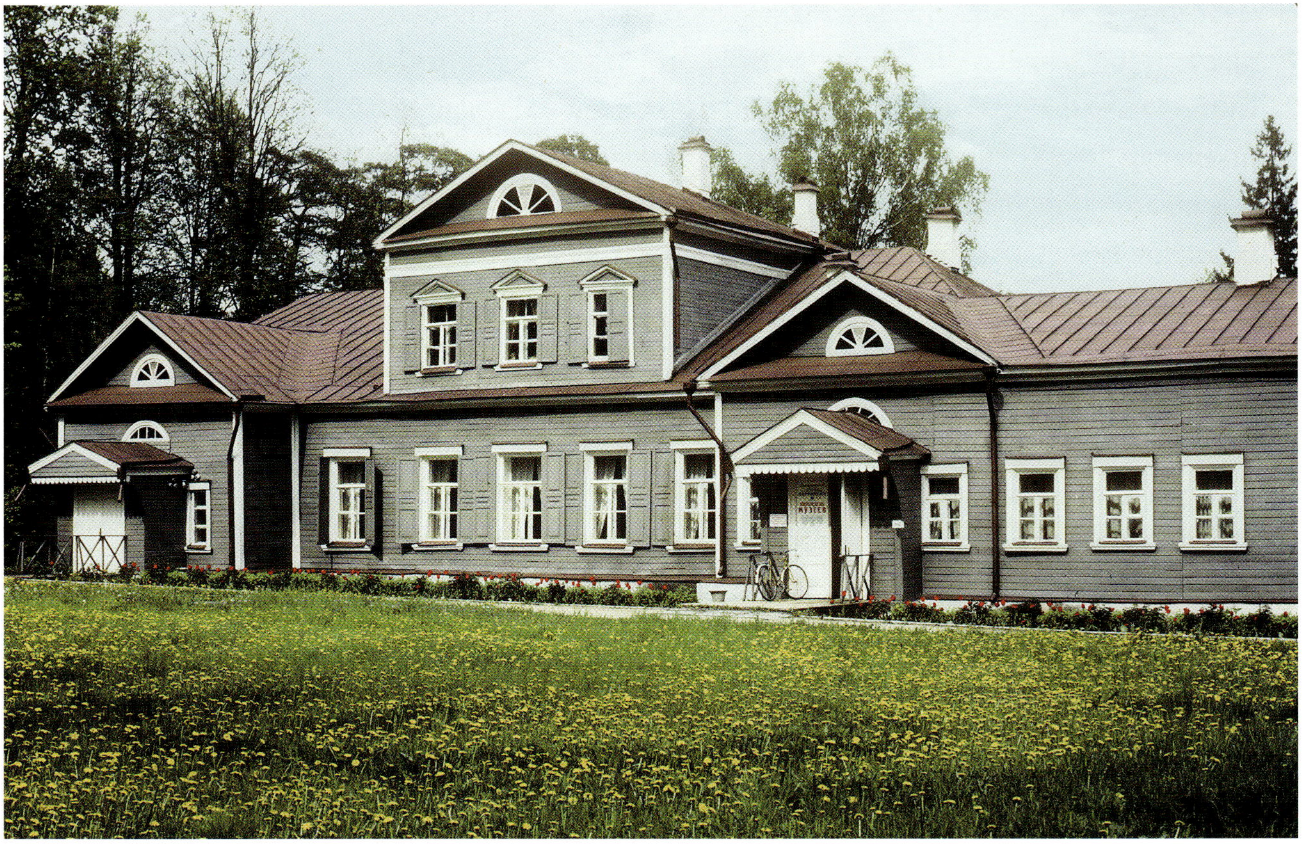

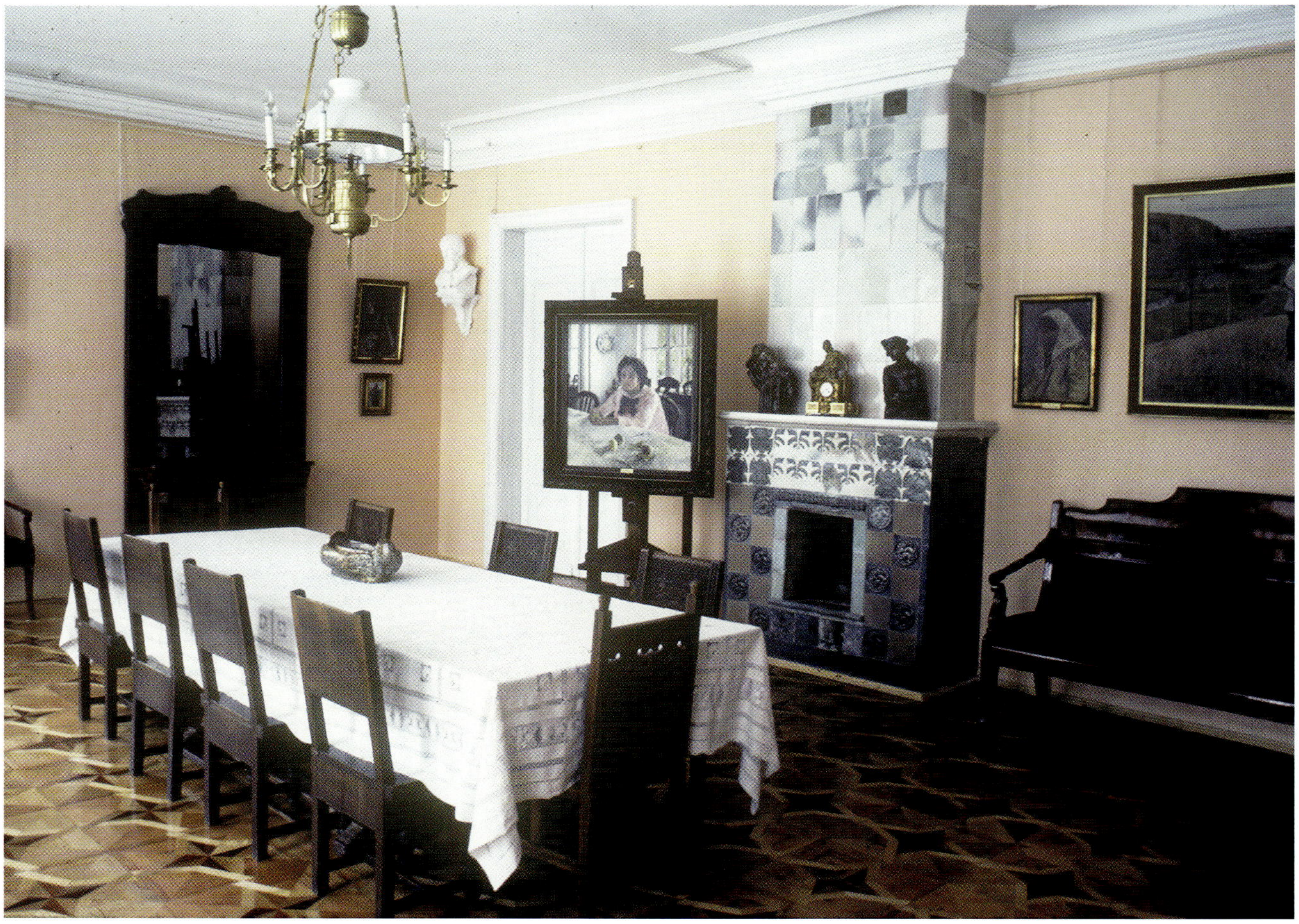

industrial entrepreneur and artist in the post-reform period.[12] Although Abramtsevo would soon be rivaled by another center of vernacular revivalism at the Talashkino estate of Princess Maria Tenisheva, Mamontov's Abramtsevo group was unique in its breadth of artistic interests and its influence on architecture and design at the turn of the century.

Among the first artists to define the wooden vernacular as a stylistic inspiration were Viktor Hartmann and Ivan Ropet, leading proponents of the Russian Revival style in architectural design, both of whom worked at the Abramtsevo estate in the early 1870s. Hartmann, shortly before his death in 1873, built a studio at Abramtsevo, with richly carved wooden decorations typical of the crafts revival. Today the studio serves as a museum of the innovative ceramic designs created at Abramtsevo. Ropet's *teremok* bathhouse nearby is more interesting structurally than Hartmann's work, united asymmetrical shapes under a steep trapezoidal roof that serves as a backdrop for the window and porch gables.[13] The fanciful manner of the *teremok* gave a foretaste of freestyle, sculpted architecture of the new style (*style moderne*) at the turn of the twentieth century.

ABRAMTSEVO ESTATE. Main house, view across courtyard. May 18, 1990.

ABRAMTSEVO ESTATE. Main house. Dining room with copy of *Girl with Peaches*, portrait by Valentin Serov of Savva Mamontov's daughter Vera. Background: tile fireplace created by Abramtsevo Ceramics Workshop to a design by Mikhail Vrubel. March 25, 1984.

ABRAMTSEVO ESTATE. Main house. Sitting room with tile stove created by Abramtsevo Ceramics Workshop. March 25, 1984.

ABRAMTSEVO ESTATE. Bathhouse (*teremok*). Porch with decorative carving. March 25, 1984.

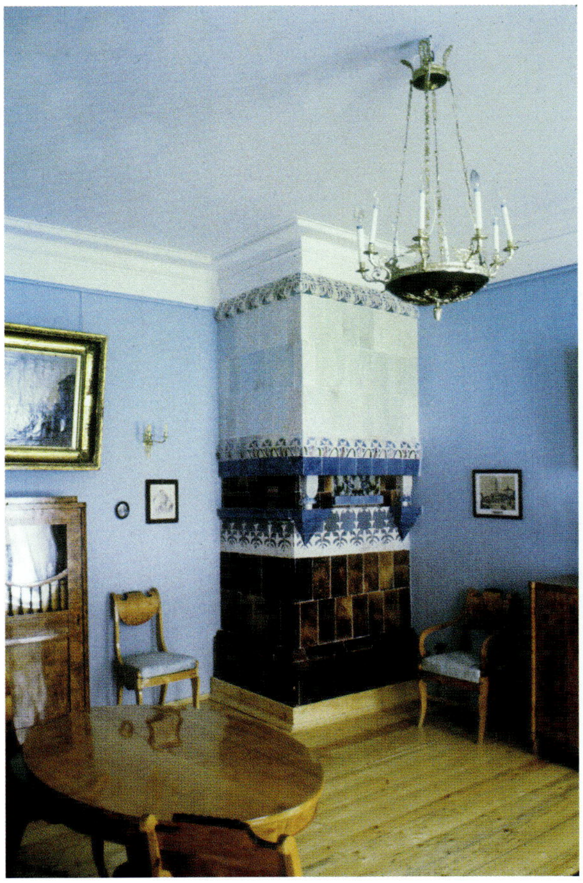

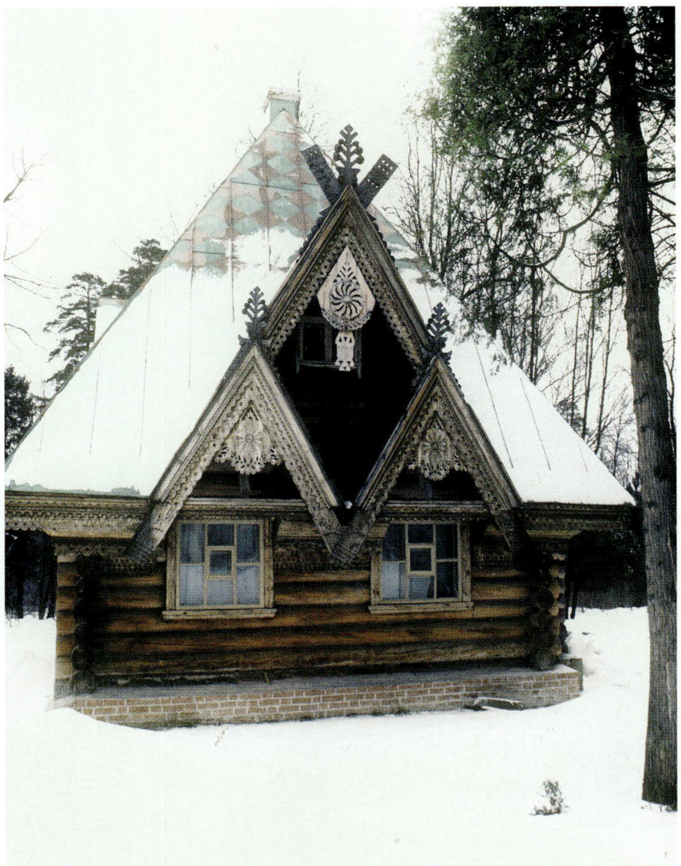

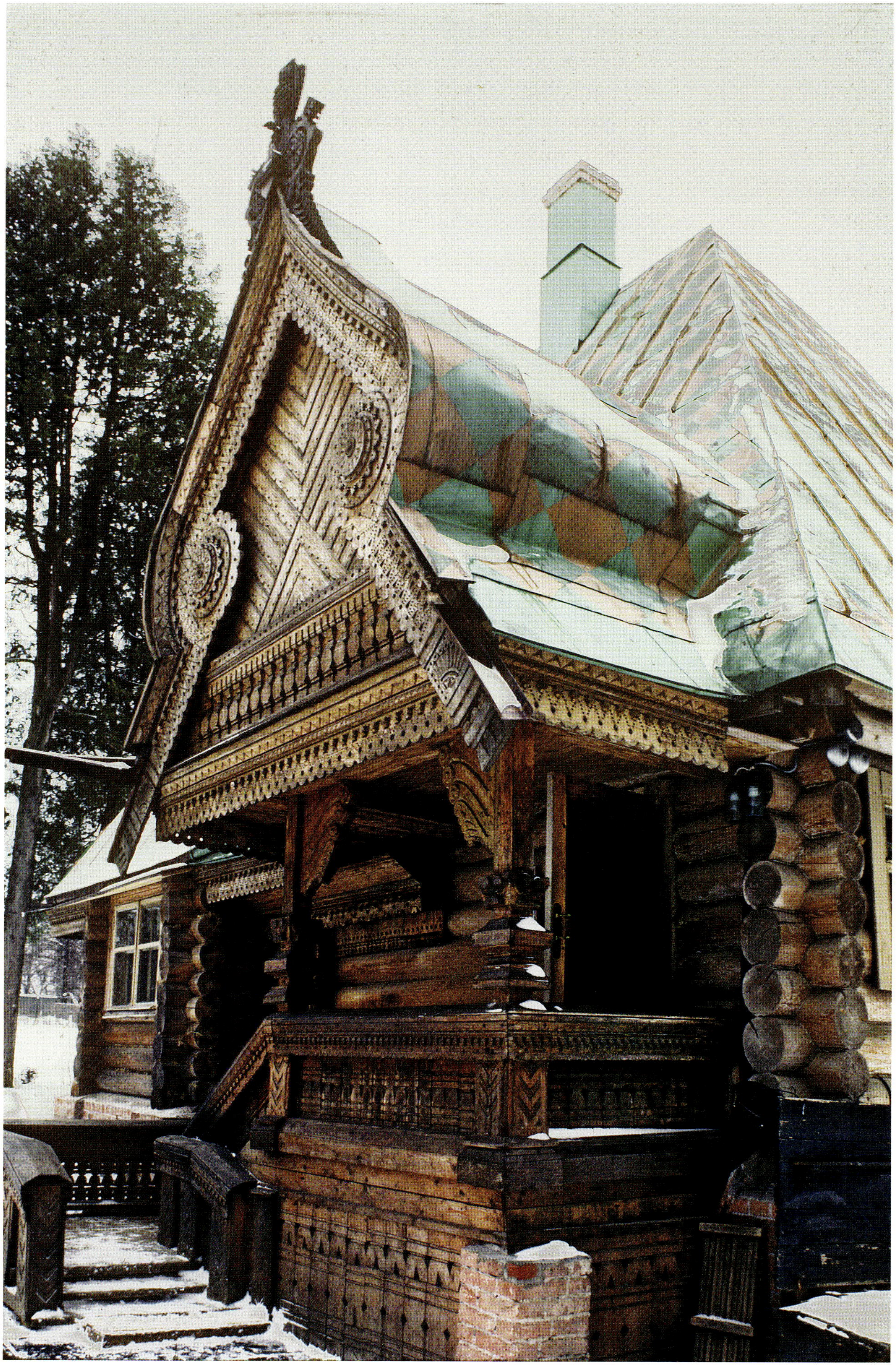

The creative artists of the Abramtsevo group also included Elena Polenova (1850–98), sister of the painter Vasily Polenov. In 1882 she established a furniture and woodworking shop, which used peasant crafts traditions and encouraged the continuation of those traditions in the education of village children. Polenova's most productive enterprise was the ceramics workshop, which started modestly but after 1889 became a remarkable force in design and architecture in Moscow. For example, Polenova was able to draw on the talent of the visionary artist Mikhail Vrubel, whose ceramic designs are preserved in tile stoves inside the estate house at Abramtsevo as well as in the Hartmann studio.

The prominence of the crafts revival and the use of folk motifs—however stagy—demonstrate a remarkable confluence of purpose and understanding among a group of artists, set designers, and architects at the turn of the century. The Vasnetsov brothers as well as Golovin, Korovin, Vrubel, Maliutin, Shekhtel, Polenov, and others had each explored the connection between architecture and decorative art. As Elena Borisova has noted, in architecture the Abramtsevo painters "could satisfy that tendency to the plastic that professional architects felt somewhat later, for which painters still had not found a place on their canvases."[14] The logical bond between material and structure in the medieval or folk traditions of pre-Petrine Russian architecture was given an aesthetic interpretation in the neo-Russian variant of the *style moderne*. Maliutin, for example, gained a reputation for his work in the arts and crafts community at Talashkino—the estate of Princess Maria Tenisheva, a benefactor of the community.

Interested in the arts at an early age, Maria Klavdievna Tenisheva (1858–1928) studied voice and painting in Paris in the 1880s. Her first marriage, which produced a daughter, Maria, ended in divorce. In 1892 she married Prince Viacheslav Tenishev (1843–1903), who combined noble ancestry with entrepreneurial success in railroads and banking. Tenishev was also interested in the arts, and in 1898 he founded the renowned Tenishev School in Saint Petersburg, one of the most distinguished and progressive high schools in Russia. (Its alumni included two of Russia's greatest writers, Vladimir Nabokov and Osip Mandelstam.) The couple first settled near a factory owned by Tenishev in the Briansk area. Here she established a school for the workers' children and engaged in other philanthropic activities for the local community. In 1896 Tenishev purchased the estate of Talashkino, owned by Princess Ekaterina Sviatopolk-Chetvertinskaia, who continued to manage the estate. (The two women had been friends

ABRAMTSEVO ESTATE. Bathhouse (*teremok*). Side facade with decorative end boards. March 25, 1984.

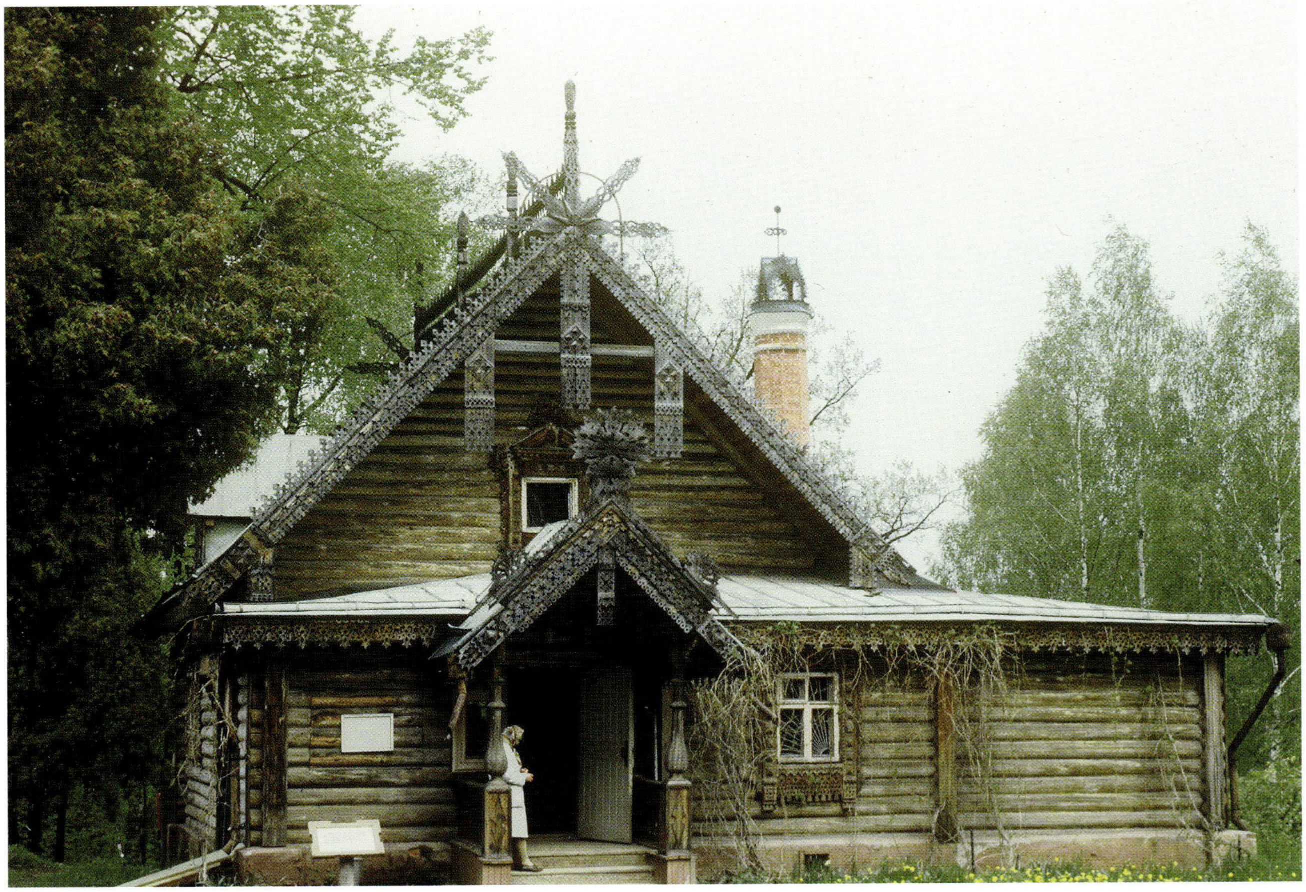

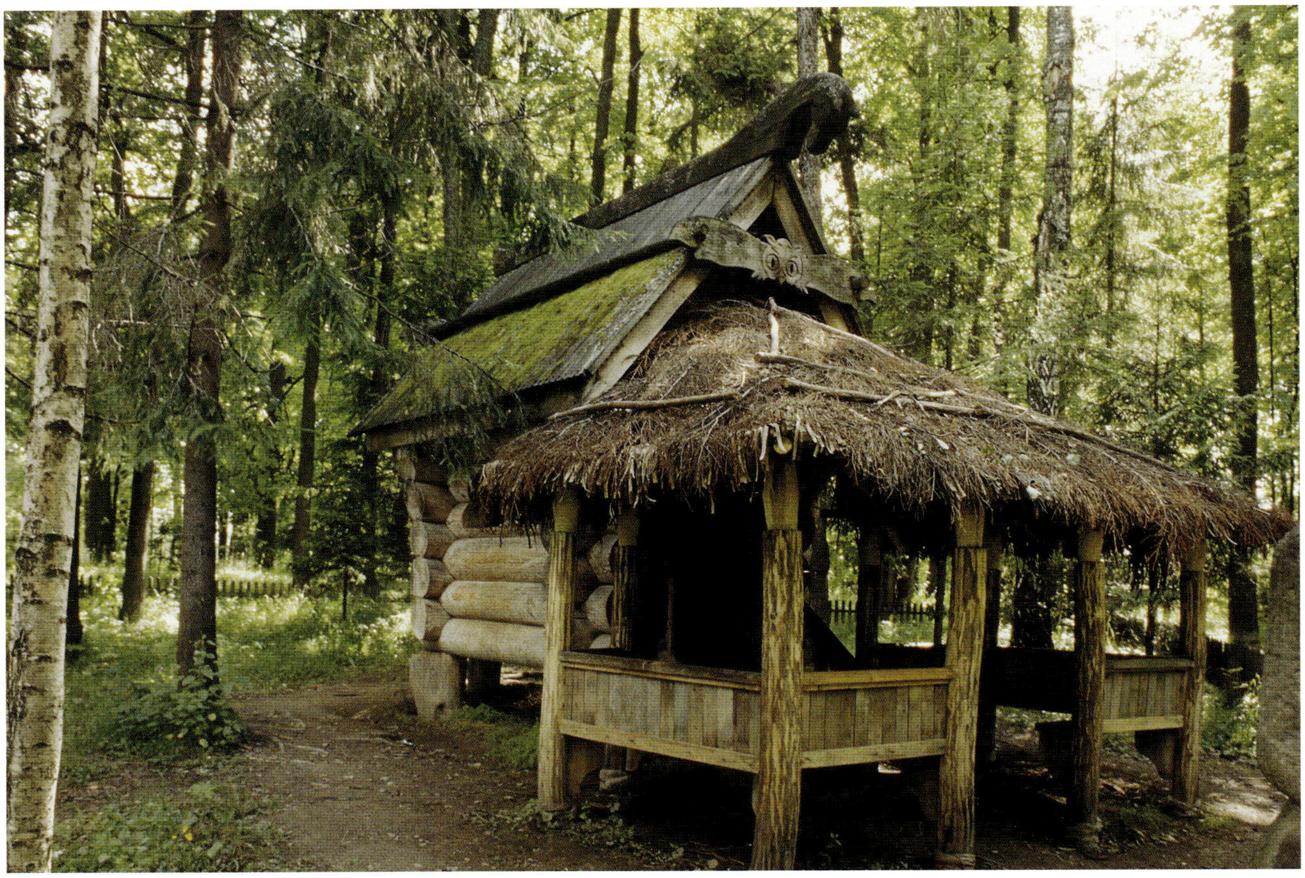

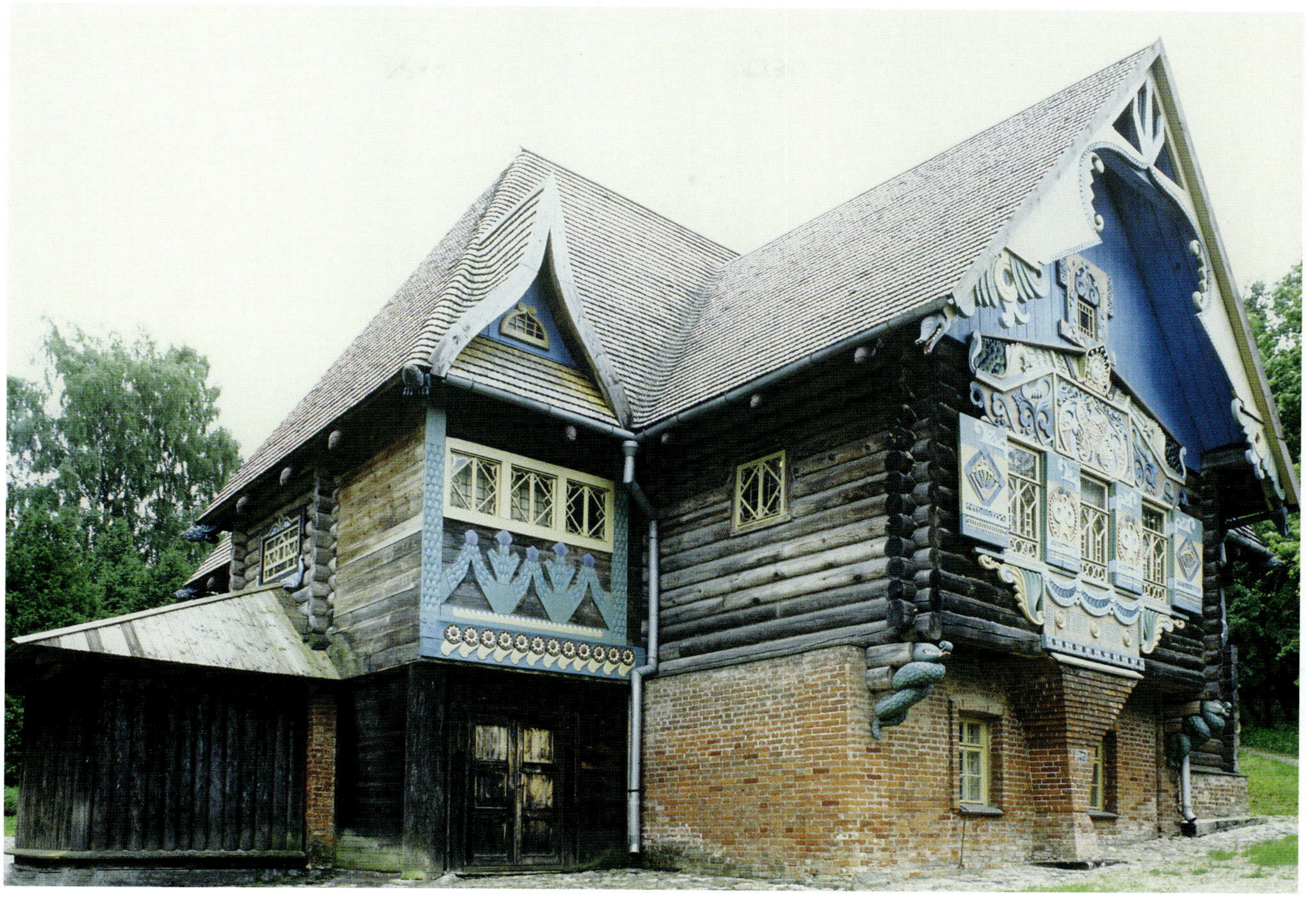

from childhood.) Talashkino gave Maria Tenisheva the opportunity and resources to combine her interests in the arts with philanthropic and educational projects.[15]

Talashkino, a functioning agricultural estate with a manor house, also included the adjacent farmstead of Flyonovo (Flenovo). It was here, away from the bustle of the main estate, that most of Tenisheva's projects took shape. As at Abramtsevo, an important goal was to train local peasant children in craft traditions that seemed on the brink of extinction in an age of industrial growth and standardization. Agronomy was also emphasized. The earliest surviving structure at Flyonovo is the agricultural school that she launched in the late 1890s, and at the same time she built a small boarding school for orphans. In addition to the educational projects for young people, Tenisheva intended to integrate her interests and abilities in the decorative arts with an authentically Russian artistic revival. Her ambition was to move beyond Abramtsevo's production of crafted items into the realm of artistic inspiration. Her hospitality and connections with Sergey (Serge) Diaghilev's World of Art movement made Talashkino a summer

ABRAMTSEVO ESTATE. Studio building, entrance facade. May 18, 1990.

ABRAMTSEVO ESTATE. "Hut on Hen's Legs" house. July 8, 1994.

FLYONOVO. Talashkino estate. *Teremok* house, facade with decorative folk motifs and ceramic elements. August 16, 2006.

destination for such prominent artists as Ilya Repin and Mikhail Vrubel. Yet to realize her larger goals of an artistic revival, she needed a resident artist.

In 1900 Tenisheva invited Sergey Maliutin and his large family to move to Talashkino from Moscow. Maliutin (1859–1937), who had made a name for himself in Savva Mamontov's artistic circle, was commissioned to build a church at Flyonovo. His design, with its exuberant form drawn from late medieval Russian traditions, won Tenisheva's support. But before work began on the church, Maliutin created another fantasy structure at Flyonovo, the so-called *teremok* ("little tower"); this log structure on a high brick base combined ideas of late medieval design and Russian folk architecture. Built in 1901 to house a library for the Talashkino school, it soon served as the premises for a workshop devoted to natural dyes, one of Tenisheva's passions. (Tenisheva was herself a highly accomplished fabric and furniture designer.) The *teremok* at Talashkino was decorated with fanciful interpretations of Russian folk art and resembled the Russian pavilion designed by Konstantin Korovin and Alexander Golovin for the 1900 Paris Exposition.

As Grigorii Sternin notes regarding the Russian decorative arts displayed at the Paris Exposition: "National exotica served here as a means of theatricalization, and spectacle proved to be one of the most important inner properties of the 'neo-Russian style.' The handicrafts from Talashkino demonstrated how completely the 'neo-Russian' style had been incorporated into the *style moderne*." Sternin argues that although Golovin and Maliutin were dilettantes in their imitations of folk crafts, their purpose was to express the "magic" of folk creativity. "The deliberate conditionality [*uslovnost*] of the decorative image was the very basis on which the 'new style' affirmed itself."[16]

Maliutin continued to explore the idea of the *teremok* as a union of theater, architecture, and interior design—all devoted to a revived awareness of Russian traditions. Many Russian artists, such as Ivan Ropet, had elaborated upon the *teremok* theme, in art, architecture, and stage design. By the beginning of the century, both Viktor and Apollonary Vasnetsov, as well as Golovin and Maliutin, had published or displayed (in some cases, built) variants on the *teremok*. The noted impresario Sergey Diaghilev was ecstatic in his praise of Maliutin's *teremok* at Talashkino, which he considered the expression of a national, non-Western architectural form.[17]

Talashkino estate. *Teremok* house, facade with decorative folk motifs to a design by Sergey Maliutin. August 16, 2006.

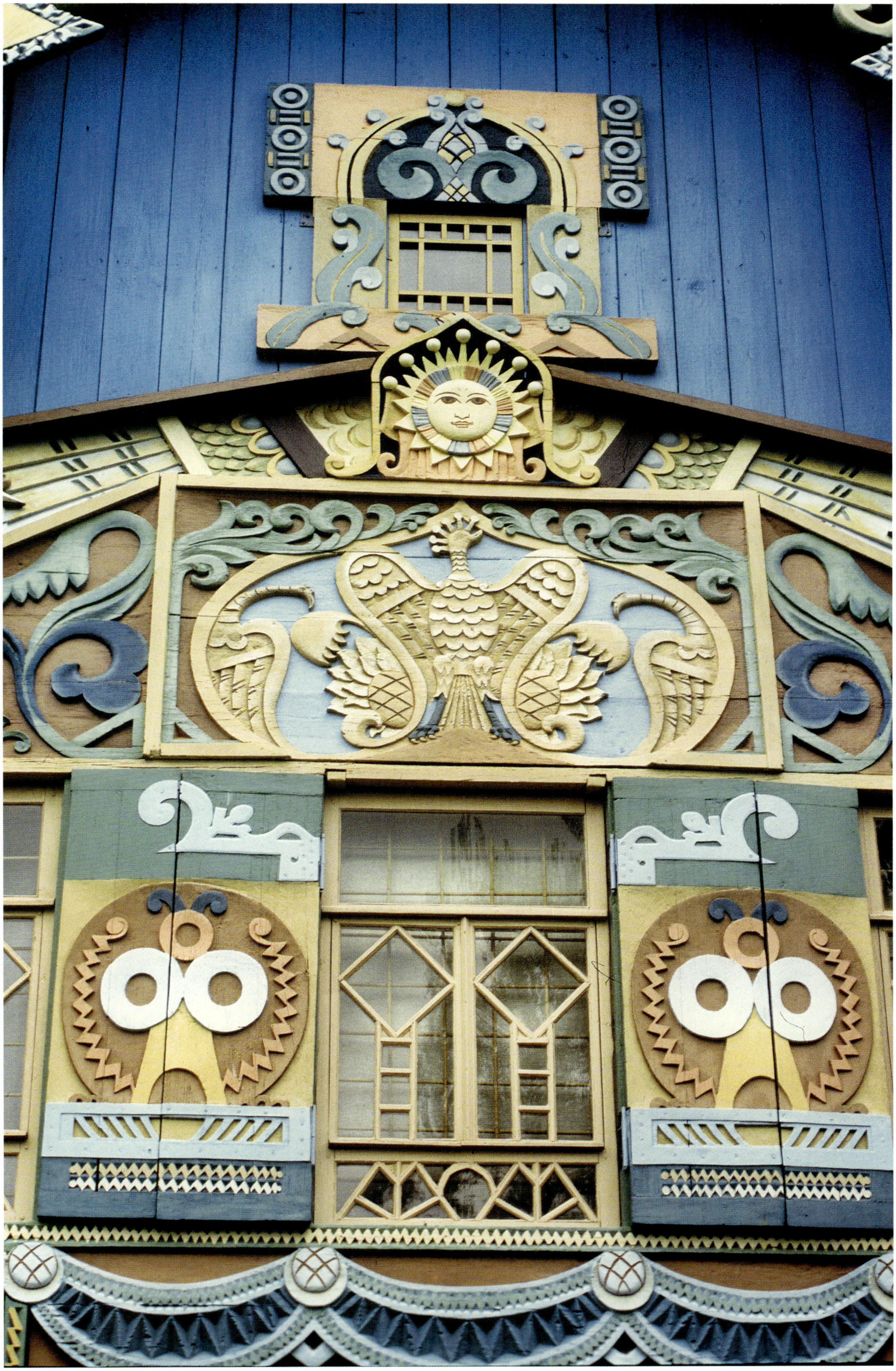

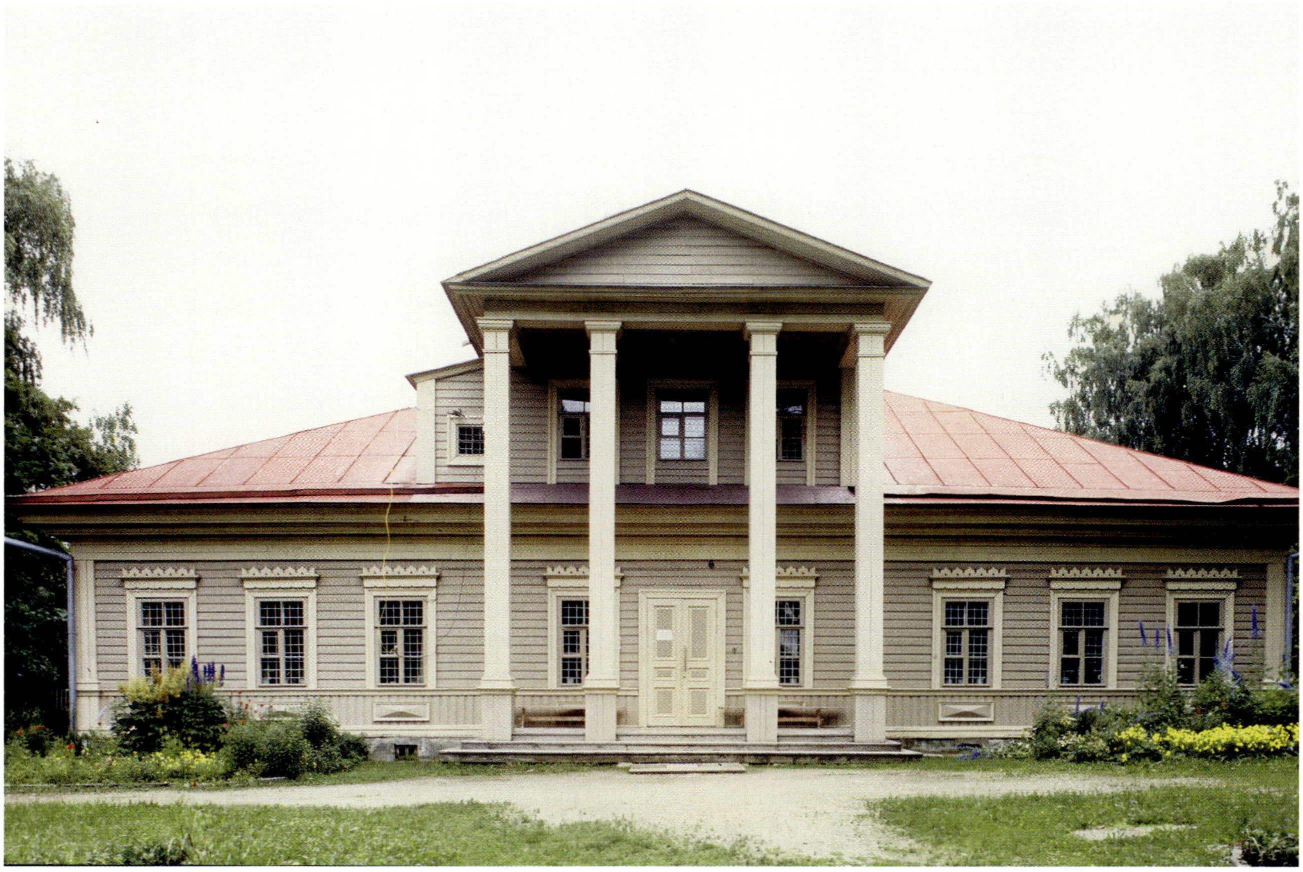

Talashkino estate. Wooden building of Agricultural School for Peasant Children, opened by Princess Maria Tenisheva in 1895. August 16, 2006.

Forest Fantasies: Astashovo and Pogorelovo

Bounded in the west by the Volga River and to the north by Yaroslavl, an important medieval center of art and commerce, Kostroma Province has a rich array of cultural landmarks accumulated over the past half millennium. Among the most interesting regions from a historical and ecological perspective is an area of lakes situated more than one hundred kilometers to the northeast of the city of Kostroma. The main natural features of this region are Lakes Galich and Chukhloma, each of which supports a town of the same name. The primary administrative center is the town of Galich (current population nearly 17,000), located on the eastern shore of Lake Galich and connected to Moscow by one of Russia's main lateral rail lines. The historic centers of both Galich and Chukhloma comprise a mixture of brick and wooden buildings from the nineteenth and early twentieth centuries.[18] The wooden buildings are primarily log structures (often on a high masonry base) with plank siding and relatively simple ornamentation. Such decorative austerity seems paradoxical in a region that produced so many master carpenters, yet this paucity of ornamentation is common among small provincial backwaters with limited economic resources. In these circumstances, the most enterprising carpenters would have made their way to the vastly more profitable zone of Saint Petersburg.

There is no better example of this economic logic than the career of Martyan Sazonovich Sazonov, builder of the extraordinary wooden mansion, or *terem*, at the village of Astashovo (also spelled Ostashevo) near Chukhloma. The biography of Sazonov exposes common assumptions about the peasantry in nineteenth-century Russia.[19] Although the mass of peasants had little land and less money, there were many exceptions, who by dint of hard work and good fortune amassed considerable wealth. In the Kostroma and Yaroslavl areas this wealth typically came from Saint Petersburg, where enterprising youths would go as seasonal laborers. Born in 1842 at Ostashevo village, Sazonov came from a prosperous family of state peasants. As a youth, when the time came to submit documents allowing him to work in Saint Petersburg, he decided to take the first name of his father (Sozon Markov) as his family name—Sozonov, pronounced and subsequently written as Sazonov.

According to the regional practice, young men between the ages of twelve and fourteen would be sent for a four-year apprenticeship in the capital's building trades, after which they would be placed according to their specific skills. Martyan gained the profitable designation as a master carpenter and woodworker with a special ability in furniture making (*krasnoderevshchik*). At the same time, he, like most of his peers, maintained close ties with his native region—in his case Ostashevo. Clear evidence of this is provided by his marriage in 1862 to a woman, Anna Andreevna, from the neighboring village of Faleleevo.

Having become a successful contractor with his own laborers and workshops in Saint Petersburg, Sazonov brought some of his profits back to the Chukhloma region. He not only built houses in the town itself but also apparently made local charitable donations. However, it appears that after the 1860s Sazonov's successful business kept him in Saint Petersburg for most of the year. In the mid-1890s his first wife died, and he remarried to Ekaterina Dobrovolskaya, the twenty-one-year-old daughter of a deacon at the neighboring Church of Elijah the Prophet. Shortly thereafter (apparently in 1897) he built the grand wooden mansion at Ostashevo (Astashovo), near the village of Ilinskoe.

The house that Sazonov built—referred to variously as *terem* and "dacha"—follows a complex, sophisticated design.[20] The two-story main

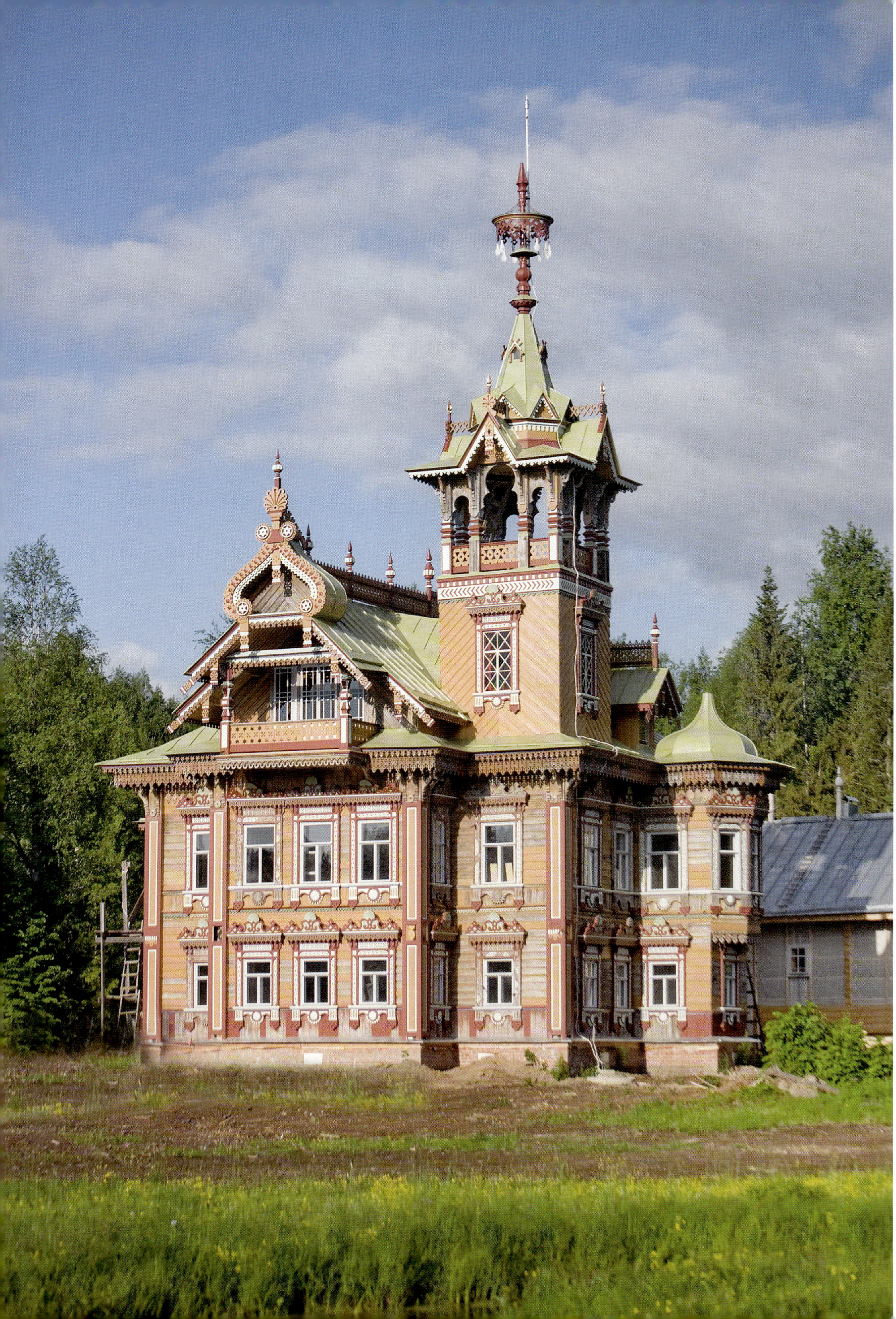

structure of stout fir logs supports a third floor with projecting balconies and summer rooms. The skillfully integrated components culminate in the visual accent of a soaring observation tower. This upper structure reflects a nineteenth-century interpretation of traditional chambers known as a *terem* (or the diminutive term *teremok*), of which more below. The facades of painted plank siding provide a background for decorative window surrounds (*nalichniki*) in bright colors.

Although suggestive of traditional carved surrounds prevalent in traditional wooden architecture (particularly the *izba*), their bold abstracted design is more of an urban stylization characteristic of the nineteenth-century national revival aesthetic. The stylized urban influence is especially evident in such details as shell cartouches, triglyphs, metopes, and even acroteria. These elements bear little relation to folk traditions in decorative carving, although it should be emphasized that those traditions were also being transformed in the nineteenth century, as master carpenters who flooded into urban centers such as Saint Petersburg returned to their villages with a new repertoire of decorative motifs. The cornices of the intricate roof are profusely decorated with patterned end boards. On sunlit days these sawn and cut motifs cast patterns on the facades.

The Sazonov mansion is an urbane work of art that owes as much to national revival aesthetic programs as to borrowings from traditional crafts. Ivan Ropet, so instrumental in the Abramtsevo group, was one of the main proponents of this movement, and his work figured prominently in the popular publication *Motivy russkoi arkhitektury*, widely distributed and probably known to Sazonov and the architects with whom he worked. Through this conduit, the Sazonov forest house in remote Astashovo is connected with a major aesthetic movement in the Russian capitals. With his knowledge of fashionable building trends (essential to the success of his profession), Sazonov would have known the designs for suburban or country houses (*zagorodnyi dom*) presented in *Motivy russkoi arkhitektury*, which in turn were heavily influenced by the Ropet style. It is even possible that Sazonov knew Ropet, who was active in the creation of Russian style for such residences. The fanciful ornamental flourishes of the Sazonov *terem* exuberantly proclaimed the success of a master contractor who brought a neo-Russian style back to the Russian heartland that had produced him.

Sazonov lived in his mansion for not quite two decades. He died in September 1914, a few weeks after the beginning of the First World War. There is a sense of the appropriate in the timing of his departure. The war

ASTASHOVO. Sazonov mansion (*terem*). Main facade. May 28, 2016.

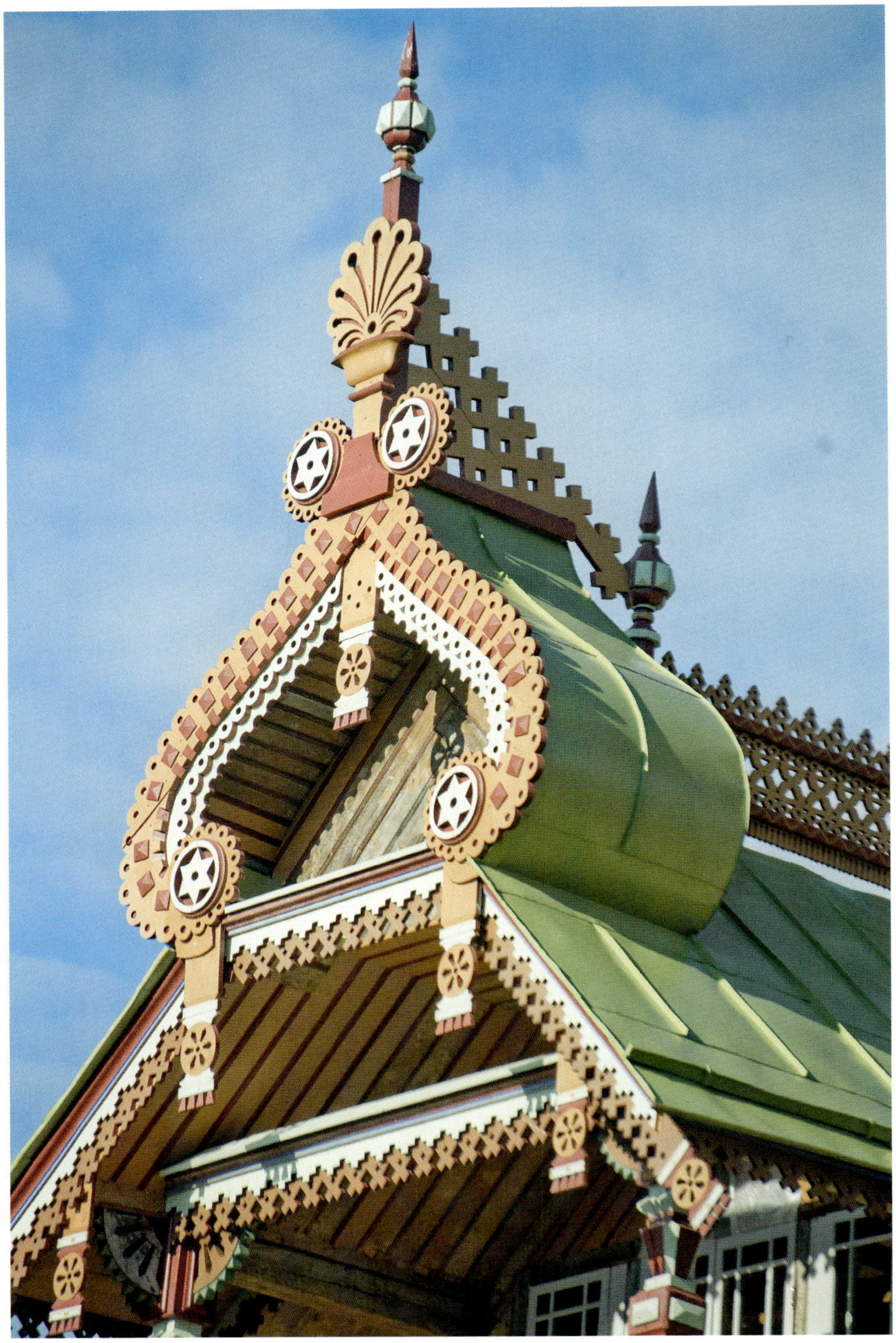

ASTASHOVO. Sazonov mansion (*terem*). Main facade, decorative gable. May 28, 2016.

proved a catastrophe that ended the way of life represented in such displays of personal fortune. In the wake of the Bolshevik Revolution, Sazonov's widow was deprived of the house, which was locked and uninhabited until 1942, when the interior—intact but devoid of furniture—was converted for use by the local village administration. With the cessation of these functions in the early 1970s, the house was again abandoned in a depopulated village. (The last inhabitant of Astashovo left in the early 1990s.)

Without maintenance, the superbly built structure receded into the forest growth that increased with every passing year. In the early twenty-first century alarms were raised about the fate of the *terem*, which in its dilapidated state resembled nothing so much as a stereotypical haunted mansion. As is often the case with such treasures, no viable plans for rescue seemed available. However, publicity brought the house to the attention of a young investment specialist, Andrey Pavlichenkov and his wife Olga Golovicher, who turned the decaying landmark into a personal project.[21]

Knowledgeable in Russian culture and preservation, Pavlichenkov enlisted the services of Alexander Popov, the most experienced specialist in the restoration of historic wooden structures. The first task was to clear the site of new forest growth. In 2011 Popov's brigade of workers disassembled the entire remaining structure and transported it to the Popov workshops at the Saint Kirill Belozerskii Monastery in the town of Kirillov (Vologda oblast'), where the wooden components were carefully analyzed. Restoration methods were applied to serviceable components, and the rest (particularly the decorative details) were replicated. In 2013 work began on reassembling the *terem* at its original site on a new brick foundation that reproduced the original. This process also entailed the rebuilding of the annex (*pristroika*), a wooden service structure that extended from the back of the mansion. In 2016 the exterior work was completed.

Work on restoring and furnishing the interior proved more complicated. Pavlichenkov acquired the shell of a house that had been thoroughly depleted. Nonetheless, the original arrangement of the rooms was clear and was restored by 2017. The restoration of the *terem* at Astashovo also includes the reconfiguration of the ponds that lay in front of the mansion. (Water for the household came from a deep artesian well in this swampy area.) As a magnet for cultural tourism, the *terem* at Astashovo became a display of enlightened architectural preservation.

If the *terem* mansion at Astashovo is an exemplar of the late nineteenth-century reinterpretation of the aesthetic possibilities of wooden architecture, there is another log mansion in the area that is no less remarkable. Located at the village of Pogorelovo near the Viga River, this log edifice was built at the turn of the twentieth century (perhaps 1902) by Ivan Poliashov, another local who acquired wealth in the Saint Petersburg building boom. And like Sazonov he displayed this wealth exuberantly in the design of

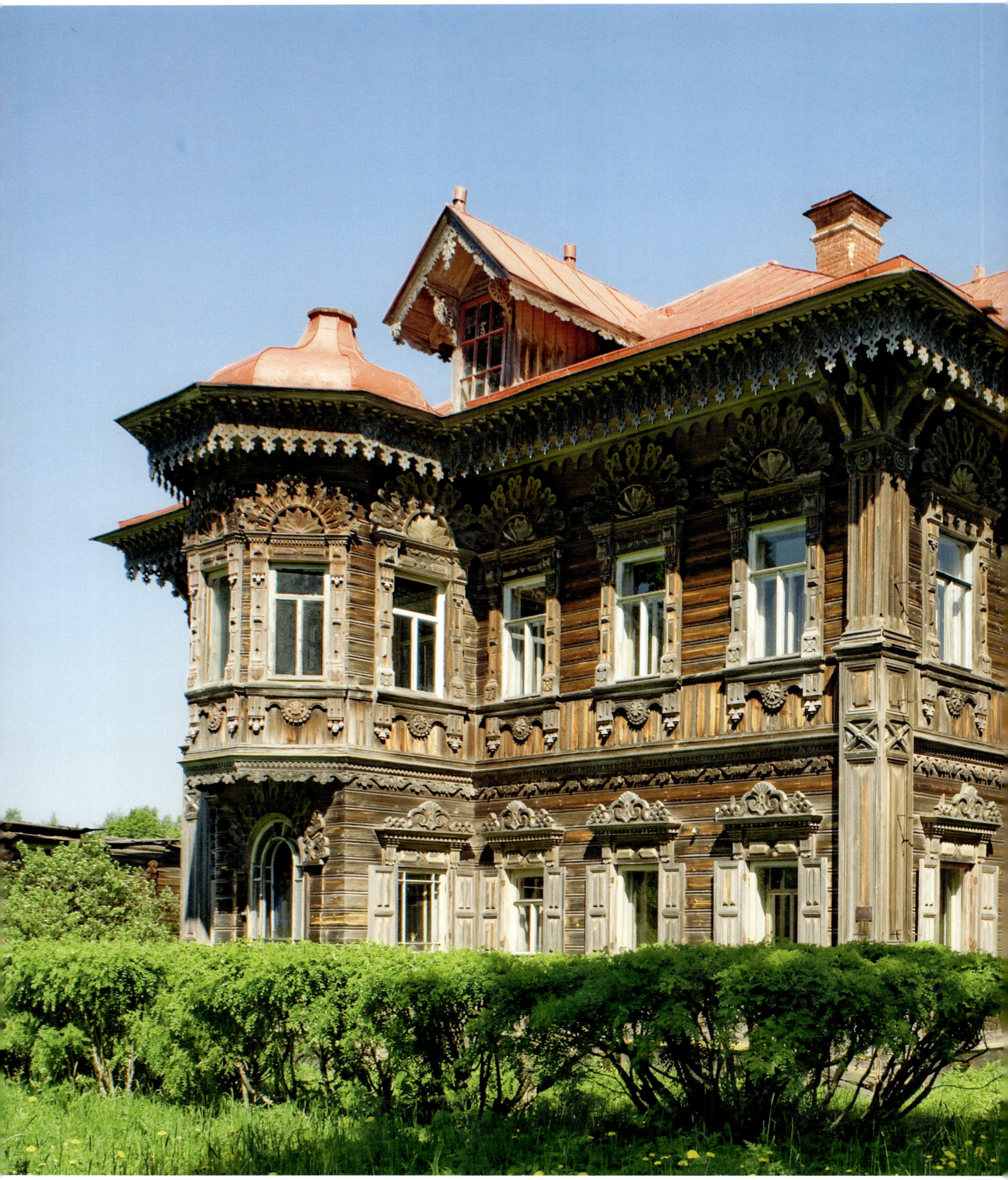

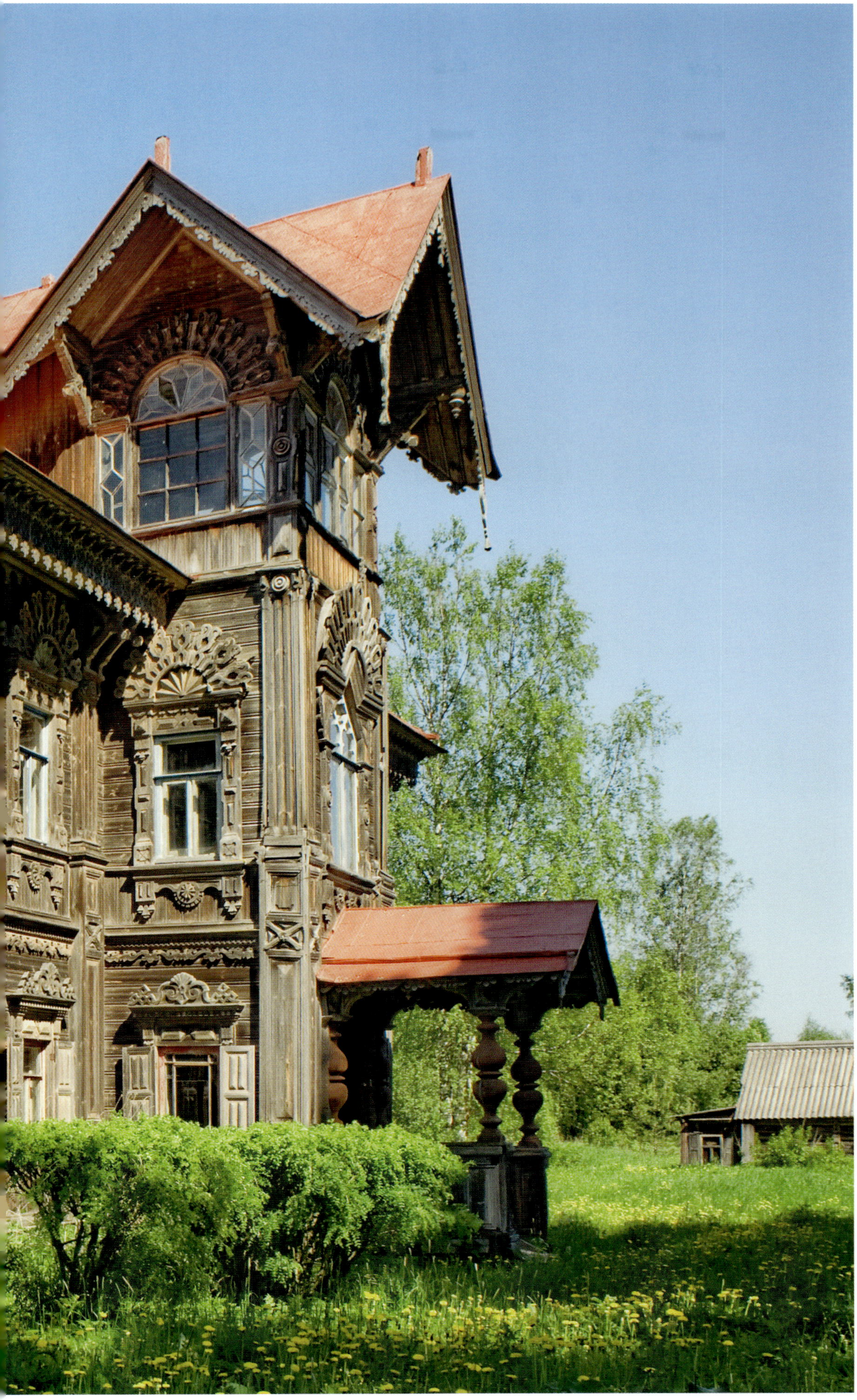

POGORELOVO. Poliashov mansion. May 29, 2016.

a wooden house back in his native village. Fortunately, the Pogorelovo house—a durable log edifice with plank siding—has largely withstood the ravages of time, both on the exterior and on much of the interior.[22] This happy fate is due partly to differences in design and partly to the exceptional story of an artist who lives to preserve the house.

Ivan Poliashov was born presumably in 1850 as the son of the peasant Ivan Dmitrev. Known as Ivan Ivanov, he assumed the family name Poliashov for work in Saint Petersburg. In 1868 he married Evdokiya Egorova with whom he had two sons and two daughters. His work in the construction trade flourished in Saint Petersburg, but he also developed enterprises back in Pogorelovo, including a profitable water mill and selling timber. In a situation similar to that of Sazonov, Poliashov's first wife died at the end of the nineteenth century, and in April 1904 he took a second wife, Maria Suvorova, the twenty-six-year-old daughter of a priest from the village of Vvedenskoe. The second marriage produced three sons and three daughters. After the establishment of Soviet power, Poliashov's property was expropriated, but he continued to live in one room of the house and even played a managerial role in the sawmill that he built. He died in 1935 and was buried in the cemetery of the Church of Saint Nicholas at Dorok.

Although more rustic in its exterior appearance than the *terem* at Astashovo, the Pogorelovo country house (*zagorodnyi dom*) also demonstrates the influence of urban design in such details as the window surrounds with baroque flourishes. Particularly notable are the elaborately carved semicircular ornaments that crown the windows of the second story, which serves in the classical manner as a bel étage or story containing the main living space. These ornamental window pediments—which can be said to resemble sun bursts, or a woman's festive headdress (*kokoshnik*), or even a display of peacock feathers—proclaim the prosperity of the house's owner and builder. The second story culminates in an exuberant decorative cornice. The structure is crowned with a half story whose components function as a belvedere. The plasticity of the structure is emphasized by projecting bays, verandas, and loggia on three of its facades.

The plan of the house represents a skillful combination of neoclassical and modern approaches to the arrangement of interior space—neoclassical in the exterior symmetry and balance, modern in the arrangement of rooms around a central stairway. At the same time the house contains ample storage areas that correspond to the attached barn of a large *izba*. The interior of the house still preserves spaces decorated in an urbane

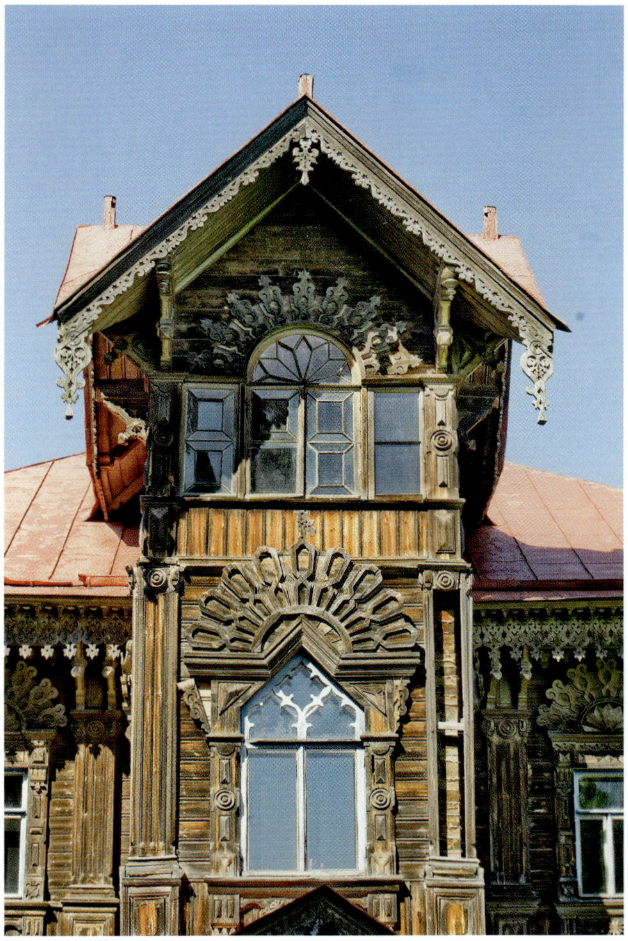

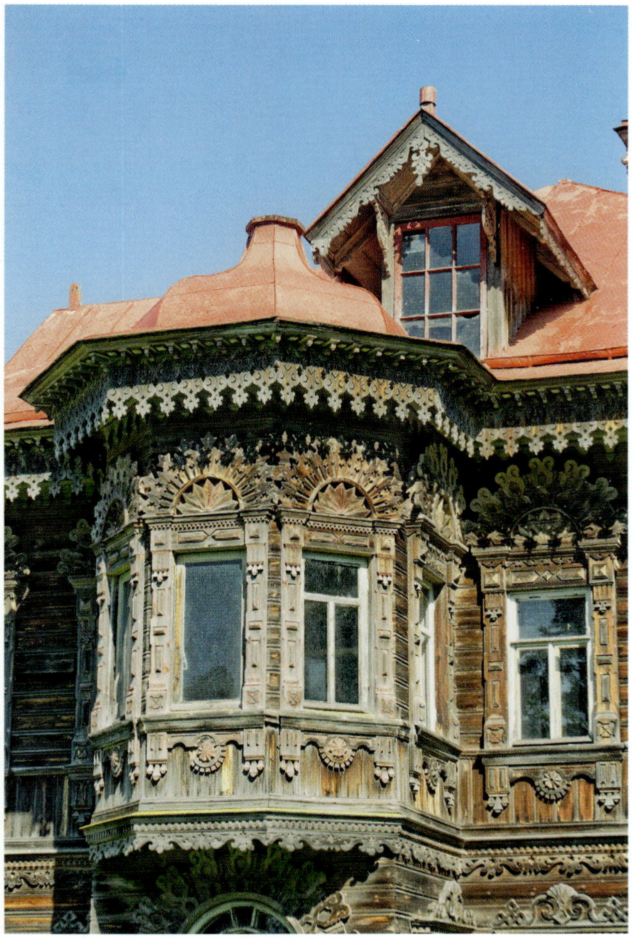

POGORELOVO. Poliashov mansion. Decorative carving over main entrance. May 29, 2016.

POGORELOVO. Poliashov mansion. Side facade, window bay. May 29, 2016.

manner that is particularly impressive on the upper landing of the main stairway. Carved woodwork and the strict geometry of ceiling caissons alternate with graceful wall paintings of floral motifs and arabesques.

The preservation of so much of the interior decoration has depended on constant maintenance, especially of the roof, to prevent rapid decay and collapse from moisture seepage. Many country houses continued to be lost to such neglect from the 1960s to 1980s, as villages were abandoned. This might have been the fate of the Poliashov house, yet its remarkable appearance appealed to an unlikely savior who has played a crucial role in maintaining the structure. Anatoly Zhigalev, an artist active in the Moscow movement of nonconformist art, was so taken by the house on first sight in 1971 that he decided to settle there in 1972. Since that time, he has lived there (except winters) and with limited assistance has managed to preserve one of Russia's most remarkable houses, a worthy companion of the *terem* at Astashovo.

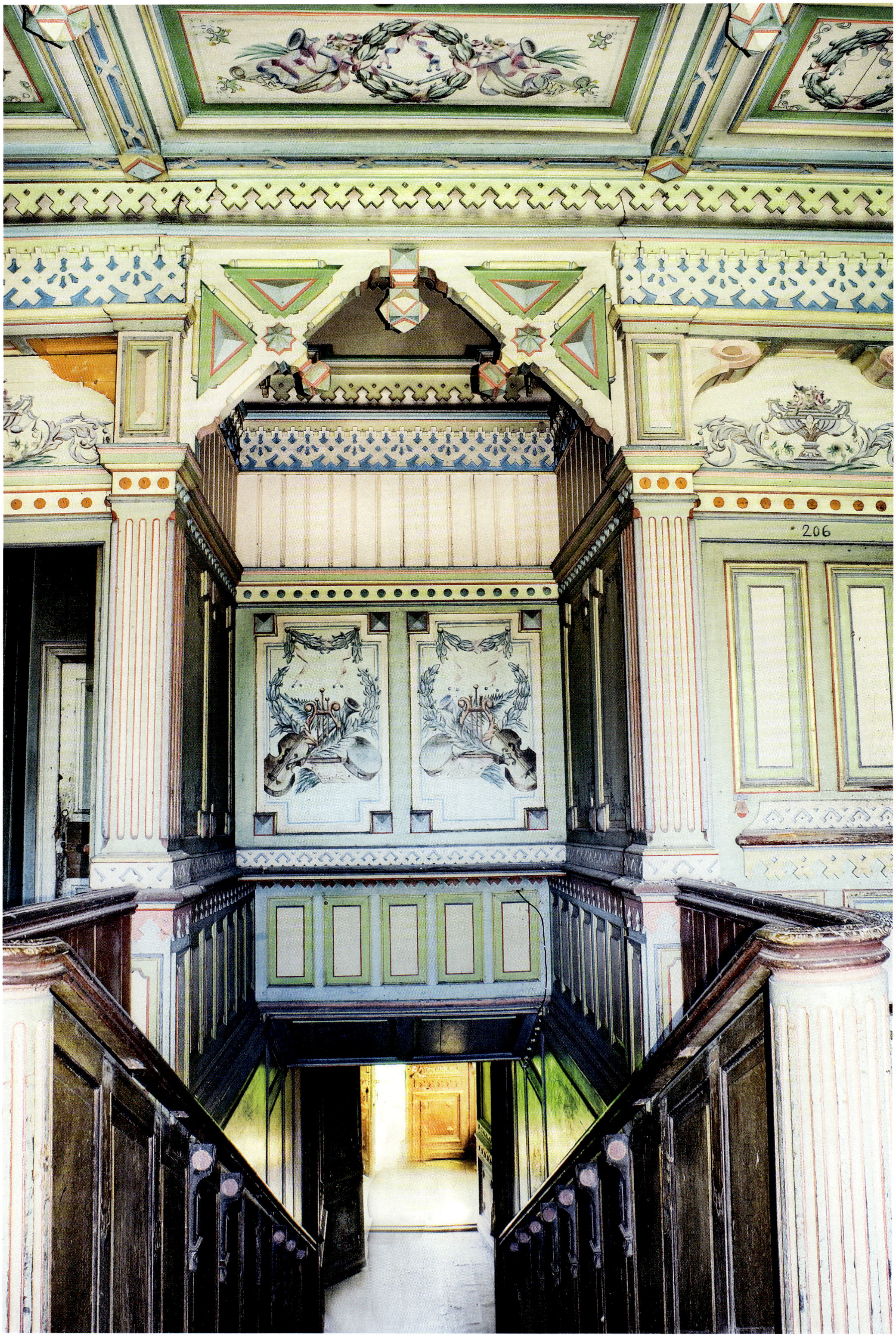
206

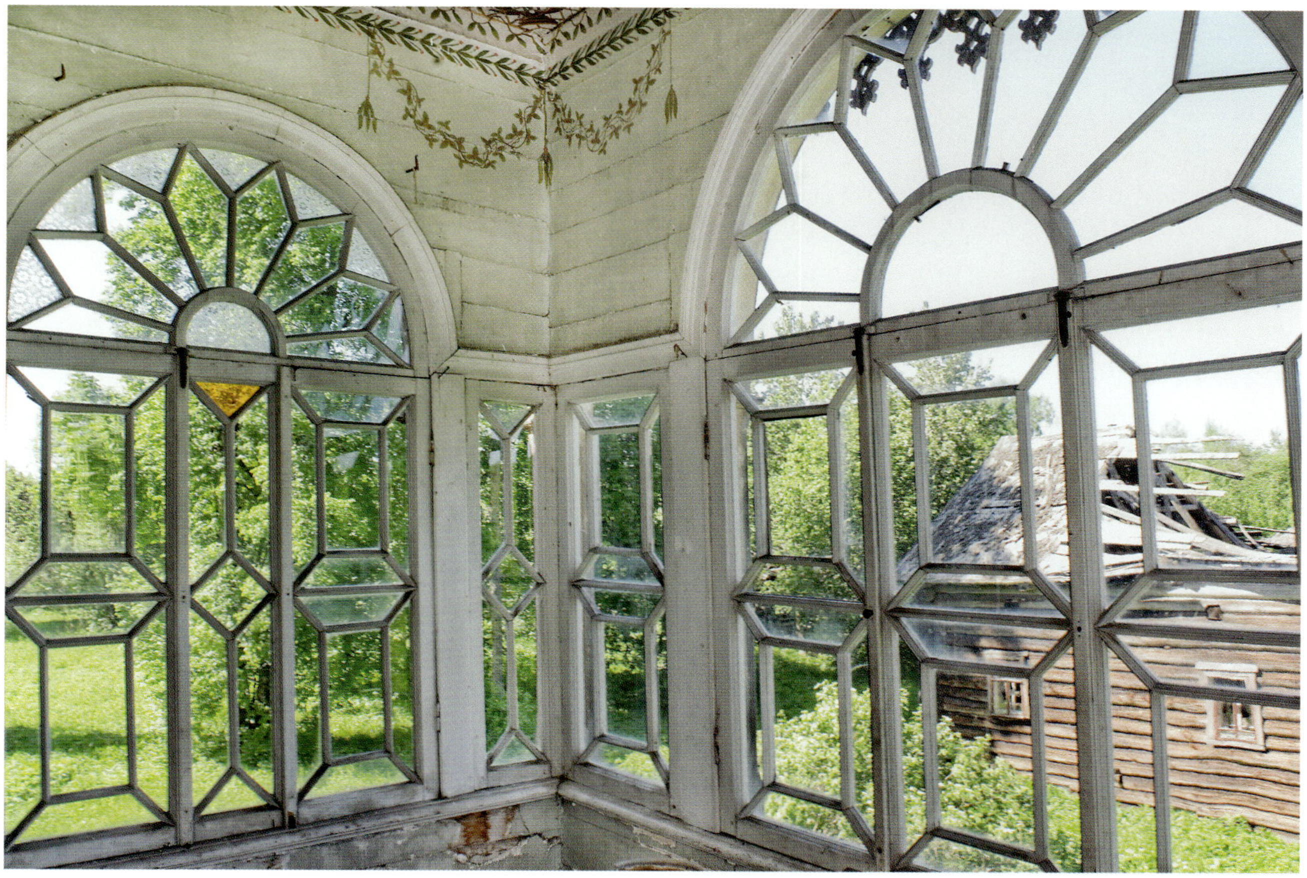

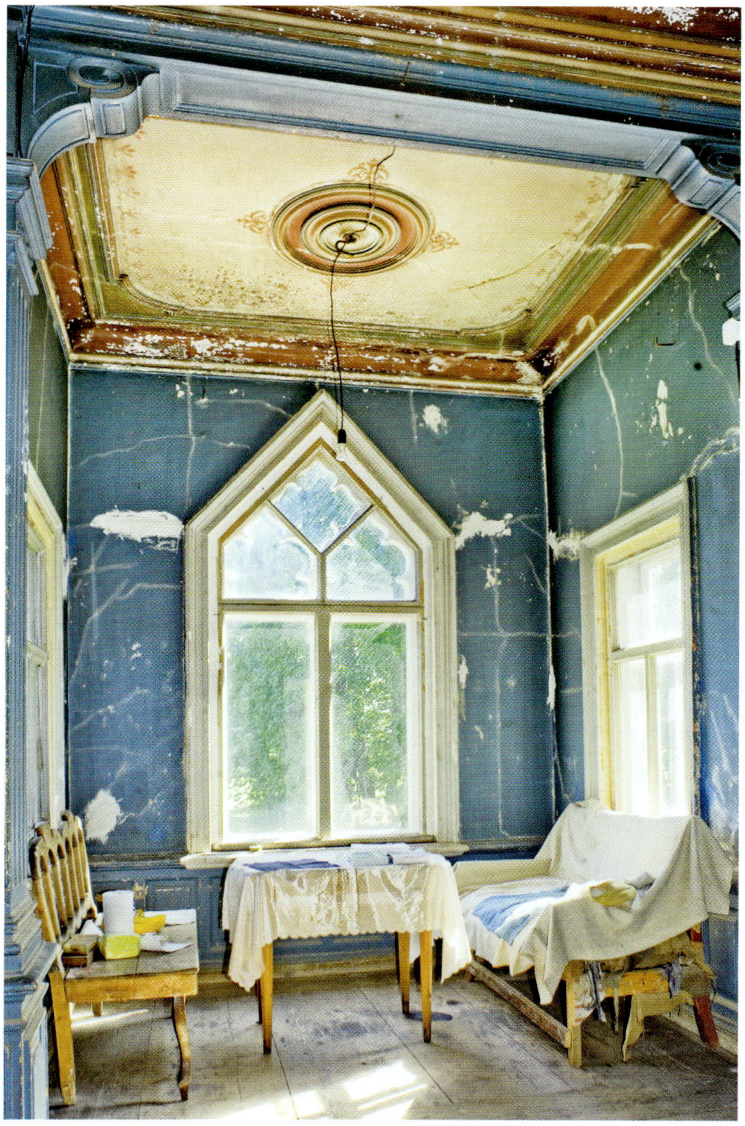

POGORELOVO. Poliashov mansion. Main staircase and upper landing with stenciled wall patterns. May 29, 2016.

POGORELOVO. Poliashov mansion. North loggia windows with view toward collapsed neighboring log house. One photograph captures opposing fates of large wooden houses in the backwoods. May 29, 2016.

POGORELOVO. Poliashov mansion. Upper floor drawing room. May 29, 2016.

The Brief Flourishing of Saint Petersburg's Suburban Dachas

With the growth—albeit uneven—of Saint Petersburg at the turn of the twentieth century, demand rapidly increased for summer cottages (dachas), most of which were built of wood and some of which could be called mansions for their size and decorative opulence. Many were built on newly subdivided lots in the vicinity of imperial palaces, such as Tsarskoe Selo, to the south of the city and easily accessible by rail. However, the northern suburbs in the direction of the Karelian Isthmus remained relatively undeveloped, although the area's fresh air, (primarily) pine forests, and mineral springs had come to the attention of none other than Peter the Great, who in 1714 intended to complete a palace complex on the Gulf of Finland near the Sestra River. Plans changed, and the Sestroretsk area became known for its arms factory. The completion of a rail line to Sestroretsk in 1894 led to the opening in 1900 of the sanatorium Sestroretsk Resort, which increased the area's popularity. Lots were subdivided, and dachas—mostly built of wood—proliferated. Among its seasonal visitors was the poet Alexander Blok, who alluded to the nearby dacha community of Ozerki in one of his greatest poems, "Neznakomka" (Unknown woman), composed in 1906. The war and 1917 revolutions brought this short-lived development to a halt, but the area remained a popular, accessible suburban resort throughout the Soviet period.[23]

Unfortunately, maintenance of the large wooden dachas with multiple tenants became unsustainable, and many of the best examples in Sestroretsk (as elsewhere) decayed, despite the quality of the original construction. Inevitably some were lost, others continue to decay, and still others were renovated or essentially rebuilt in a similar style. The designs of surviving examples resemble Carpenter Gothic or picturesque variants of the *style moderne*, rather than the Russian Revival or Ropet style that had been so actively promulgated in fashionable design publications. The tastes of the Petersburg bourgeoisie had taken a turn against the mythologizing of the *izba*. The same tendency is evident in other dacha communities, such as the one that developed in the late nineteenth century at Tsarskoe Selo near the grand Catherine Palace, completed in the mid-eighteenth century by Bartolomeo Francesco Rastrelli. Here, as elsewhere in the Saint Petersburg suburbs, the essential component was the development of a rail network for convenient access to the sylvan paradise.

SESTRORETSK. Kliachko dacha, built in 1907 by architect Sergey Ghingher on the territory of the sanatorium Sestroretsk Resort. Sold in 1908 to noted Doctor Lev Kliachko. A fine example of *style moderne* applied to an asymmetrical, picturesque log dwelling. August 12, 2003.

SESTRORETSK. Krechev dacha, built in 1906–9 for Doctor Ivan Krechev, who served in a local military hospital. *Style moderne* design with towers and inventive fenestration. August 12, 2003.

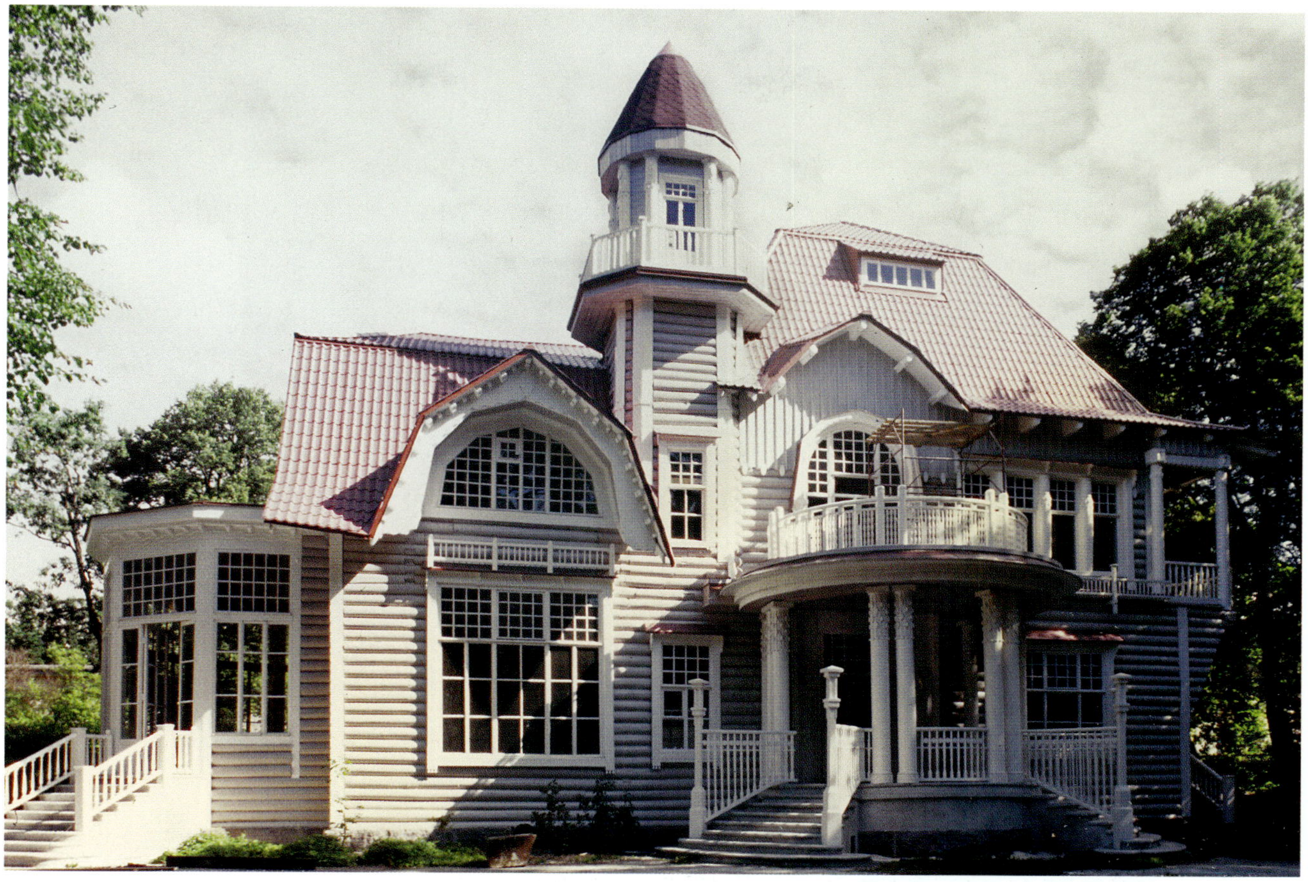

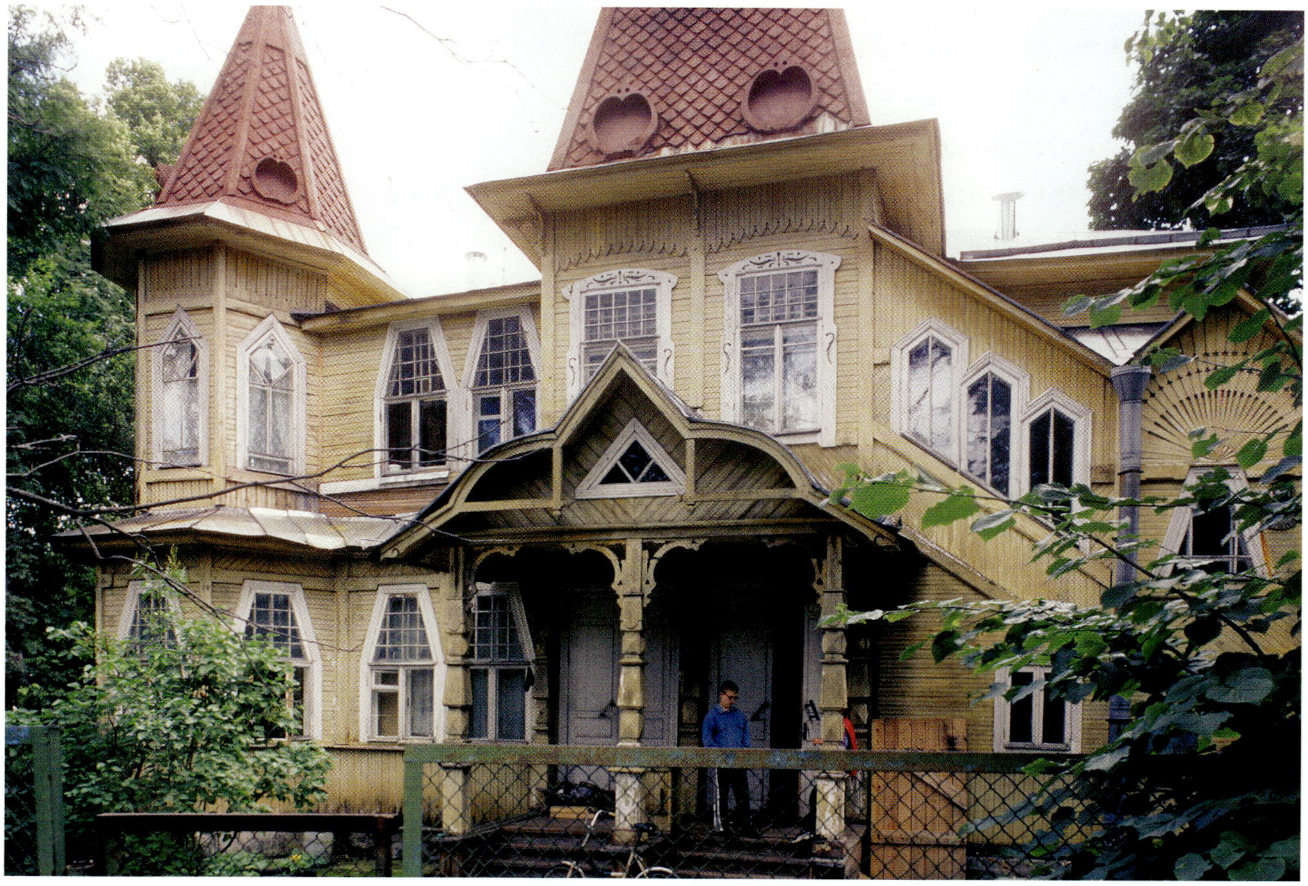

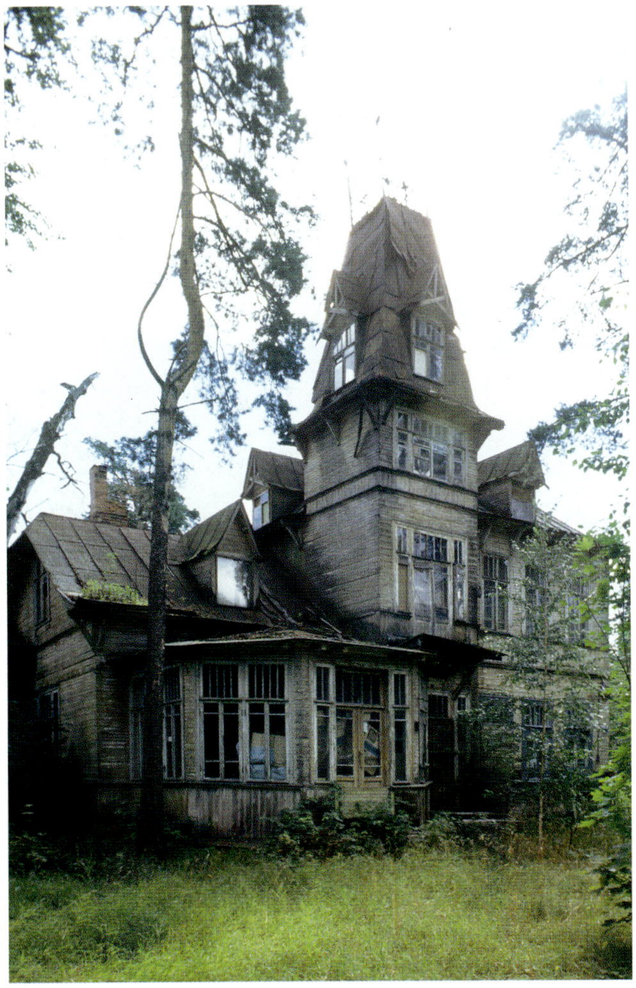

SESTRORETSK. Dacha built in 1906–7 for Valentina Krivdina, a noblewoman and teacher. In need of major repair at the time of my photograph, this *style moderne* masterpiece has continued toward inevitable collapse. August 12, 2003.

SESTRORETSK. Dacha built in 1903 for the entrepreneur V. G. Likhachev. Restored and recently converted to a boutique hotel. August 12, 2003.

KOMAROVO (before 1948 known by the Finnish name Kellomäki). Soviet-era dacha near the grave of the poet Anna Akhmatova, who frequently stayed at Komarovo. August 27, 1971.

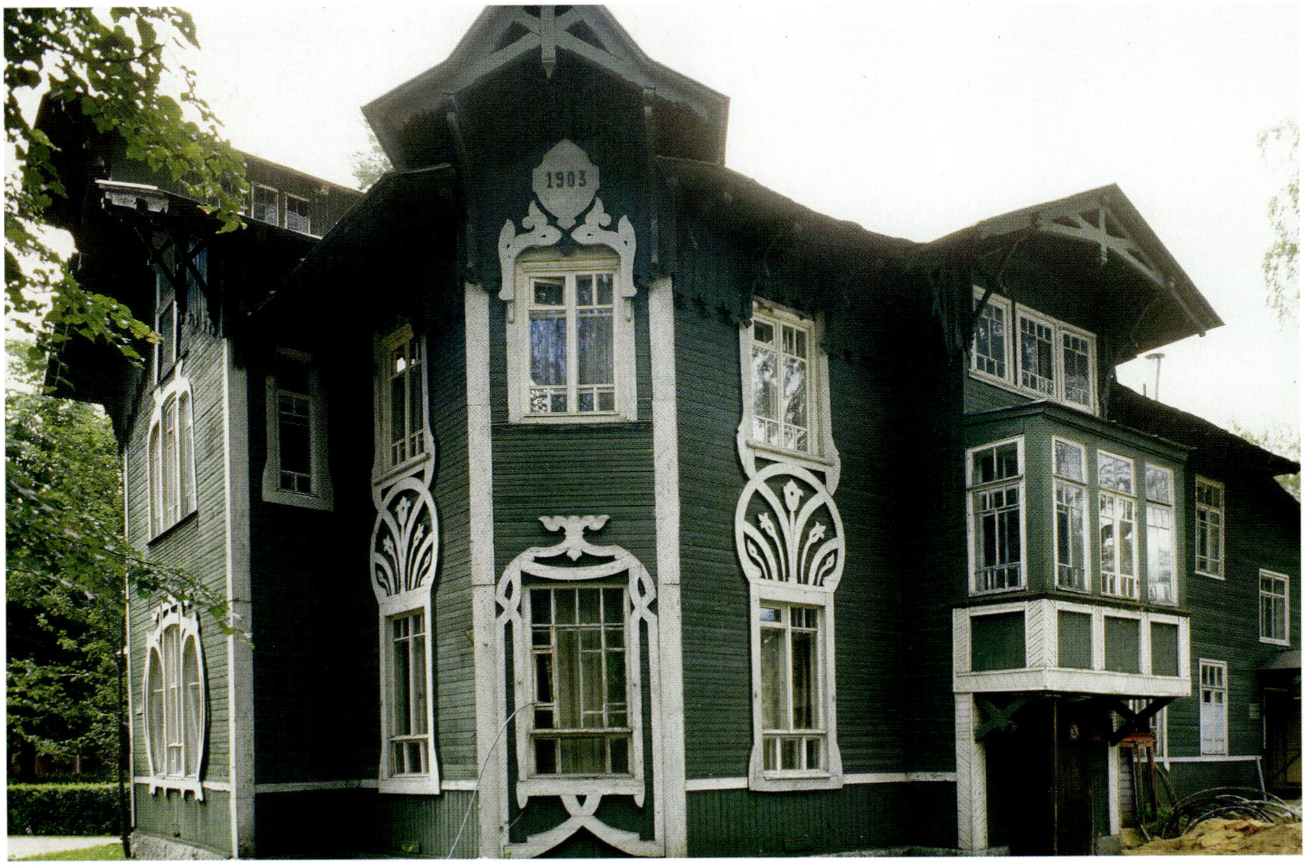

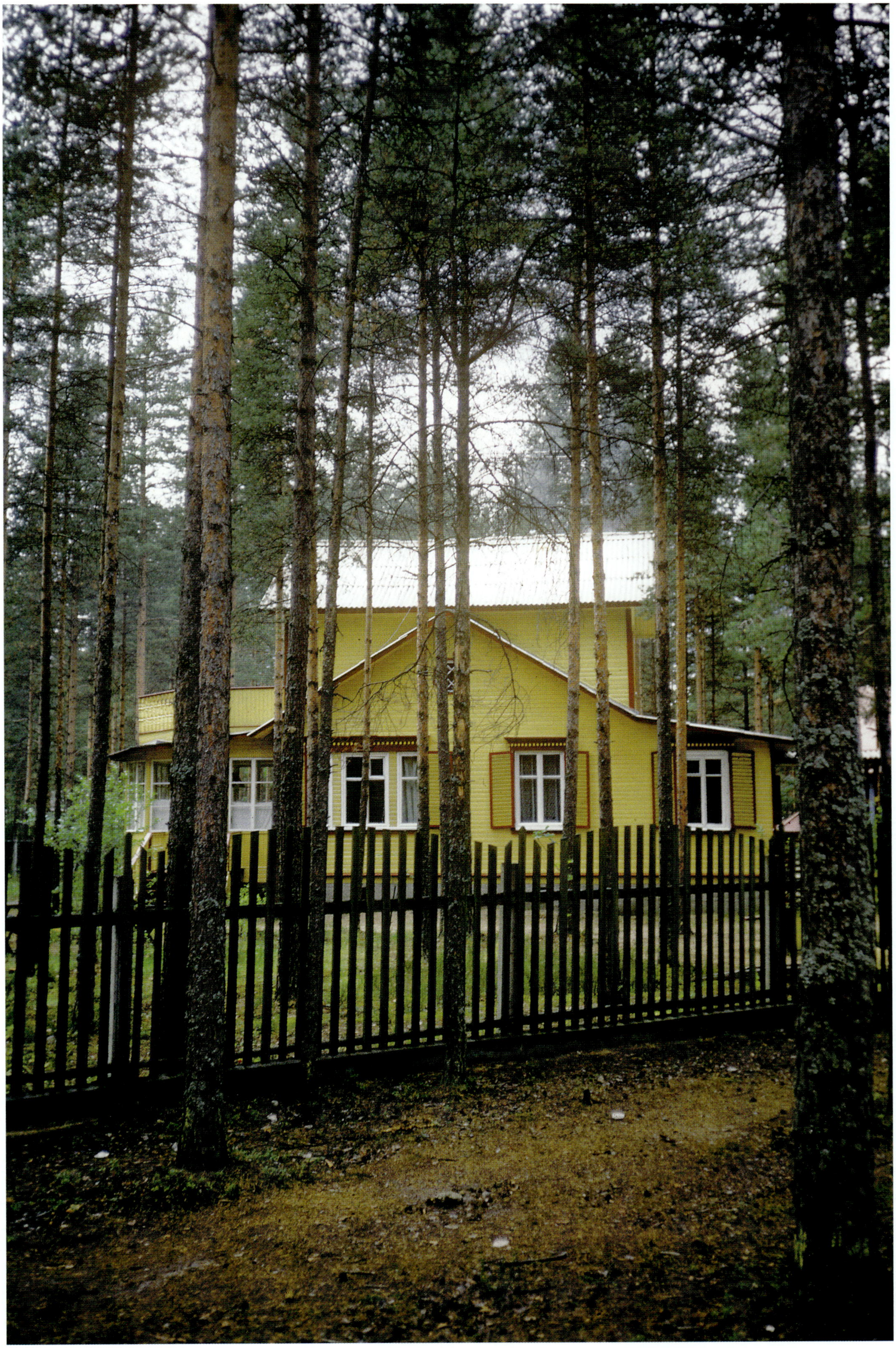

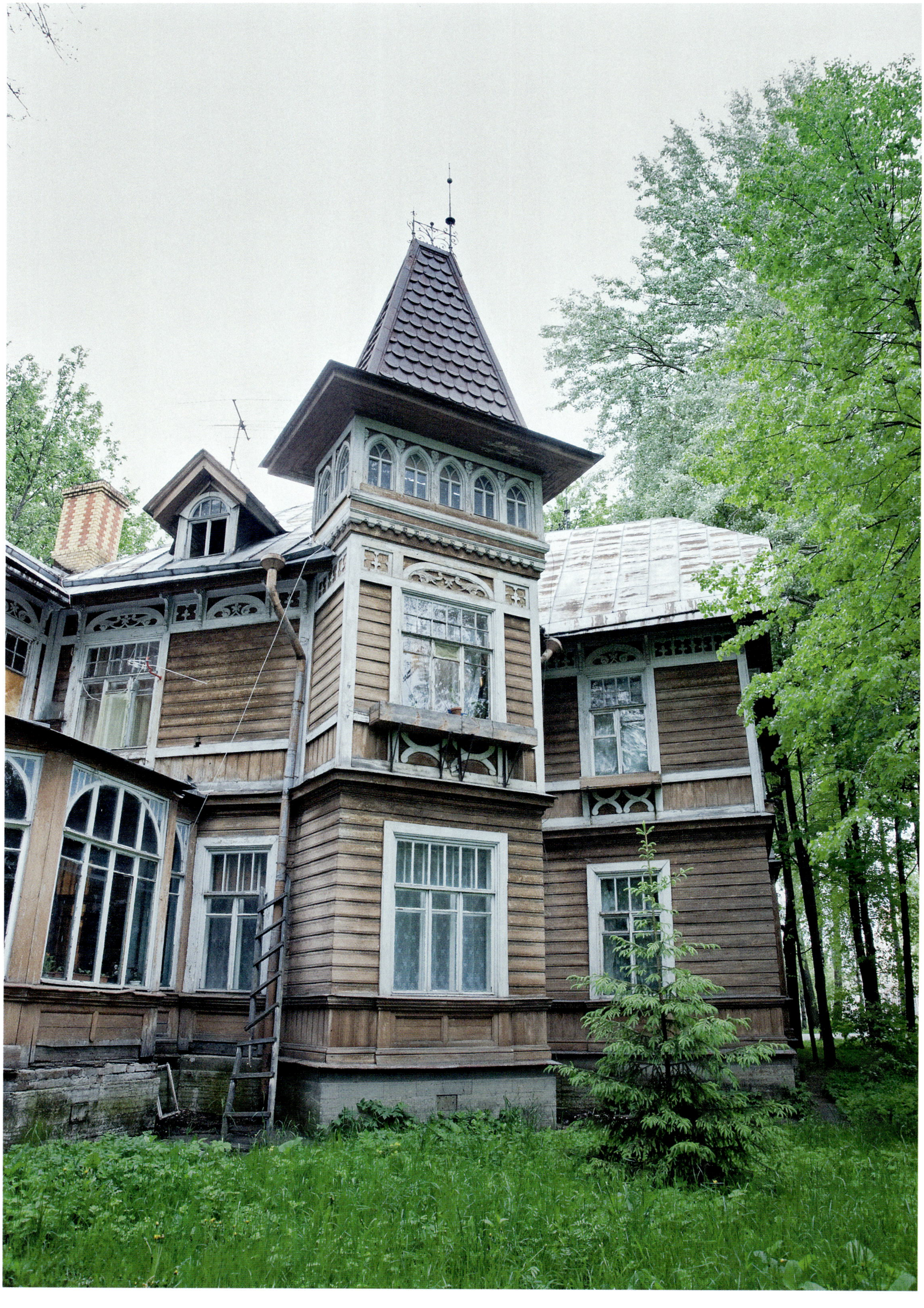

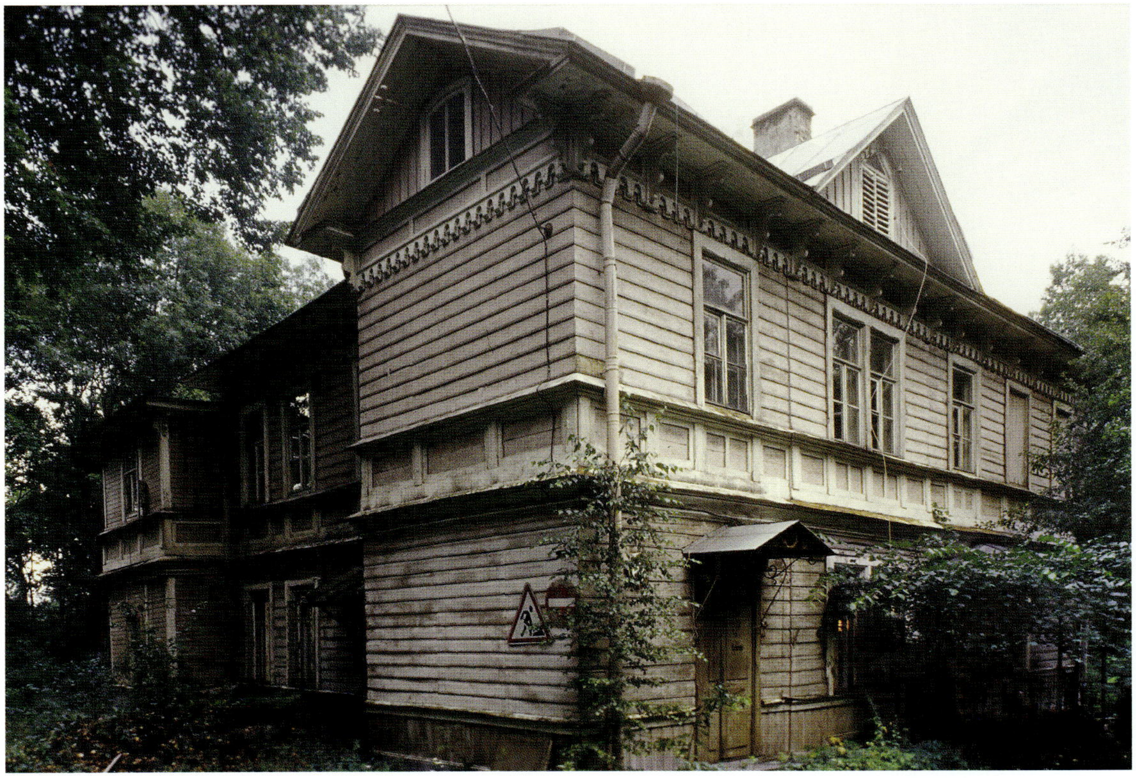

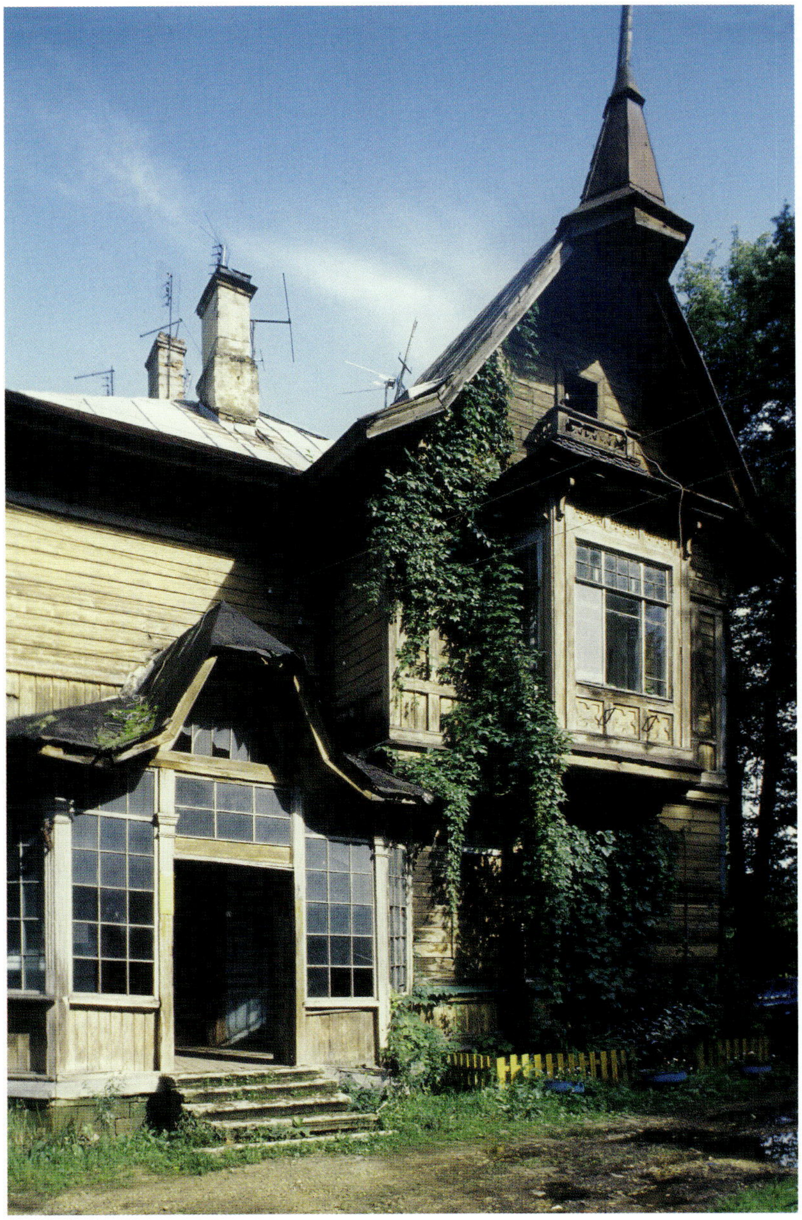

PUSHKIN (Tsarskoe Selo). Deriker dacha. Originally built in 1876 for Vasily Deriker (doctor to the imperial court), the house was rebuilt around 1905 by court architect Silvio Danina for Anna Sinyova, wife of Alexander Sinyov, purveyor of live fish to the imperial court. May 24, 2010.

PUSHKIN (Tsarskoe Selo). Sverchkov dacha, originally built in 1866 for the artist Nikolay Sverchkov. After Sverchkov's death in 1898, the lot was acquired by Sofya Tami, who had the dacha rebuilt in 1900 by her brother-in-law, Silvio Danini. Destroyed by fire in 2011; copy rebuilt by 2015. August 22, 2008.

PUSHKIN (Tsarskoe Selo). Silvio Danini dacha, built for rental purposes in 1899–1900 by the imperial court architect. In a state of rapid decay, the structure was purchased by a private restoration company in 2023. August 22, 2008.

NOTES

1 A detailed description of the palace at Kolomenskoe is contained in L. Beliaev and T. Panova, *Dvorets Tsaria Alekseia Mikhailovicha XVII veka: Iistoriko-khudozhestvennaia rekonstruktsiia* (Moscow: MGOMZ, 2011).

2 An architectural survey of the Kuskovo ensemble is provided by L. V. Tydman, "Kuskovo," in *Kuskovo; Ostankino; Arkhangel'skoe*, ed. I. M. Glozman (Moscow: Iskusstvo, 1976), 15–74. See also A. P. Vergunov, V. A. Gorokhov, P. I. Lapin, and L. N. Andreev, *Russkie sady i parky* (Moscow: Nauka, 1988), 178–85.

3 On the legacy of Karl Blank at Kuskovo, see L. V. Tydman, "Rabota arkhitektora K. I. Blanka v Kuskove (Zakazchik i arkhitektor v XVIII v.)," in *Russkoe iskusstvo barokko*, ed. T. V. Alekseeva (Moscow: Nauka, 1977), 216–25. Peter Sheremetev involved himself in all aspects of the design of the house and kept copious records, which document the involvement of serf architects and artisans in the project until its completion in 1775.

4 The use of color and light as organizing principles within the enfilades of state rooms is analyzed in Vergunov et al., *Russkie sady*, 179.

5 Tydman analyzes the relation of the entresol rooms, with their contrasting simplicity, to the rooms of the enfilade below. See Tydman, "Kuskovo," 46–47.

6 The example of Kuskovo in the evolving design of large state rooms in the Russian country house is examined in R. M. Baiburova, "Zal i gostinaia usadebnogo doma russkogo klassitsizma," in *Pamiatniki russkoi arkhitektury i monumental'nogo iskusstva*, ed. V. P. Vygolov et al. (Moscow: Nauka, 1983), 113–14.

7 An authoritative study of the Ostankino estate and its architecture is L. A. Lepskaia et al., *Ostankinskii dvorets-muzei: Tvorchestvo krepostnykh* (Leningrad: Khudozhnik RSFSR, 1982). There were several, related considerations behind the move from Kuskovo to Ostankino, in particular Sheremetev's decision to marry the troupe's lead actress and his former serf Praskovia Kovaleva (stage name Zhemchugova).

8 For a detailed study of the Uzkoe estate, see M. Iu. Korobko, *Usad'ba Uzkoe* (Moscow: Veche, 2013).

9 On the Galskoy estate of Gorka, see William Craft Brumfield, *Cherepovets: Arkhitekturnoe nasledie cherepovetskogo kraia/Cherepovets: Architectural Heritage of the Cherepovets Region* (Moscow: Tri kvadrata, 2017), 16–18, 97–108.

10 On the Pogodin *izba* and subsequent Russian revival buildings in wood, see William Craft Brumfield, *The Origins of Modernism in Russian Architecture* (Berkeley: University of California Press, 1991), 9–11.

11 For a description of the Porokhovshchikov house, see D. Liushin, "Dereviannyi dom g-na Porokhovshchikova," *Zodchii* 2 (1872): 16. This volume also contains a plan and architectural drawings of the structure.

12 For commentary on Mamontov's transformation of Abramtsevo, see G. Iu. Sternin, "Abramtsevo: ot 'usad'by' k 'dacha,'" in Sternin's *Russkaia khudozhestvennaia kul'tura vtoroi poloviny XIX-nachala XX veka* (Moscow: Sovetskii khudozhnik, 1984), 187–88. See also E. R. Arenzon, "Ot Kireeva do Abramtseva. K biografii Savvy Ivanovicha Mamontova," *Panorama iskusstv* 6 (1986): 359–82.

13 A survey of Ropet's work and his view of the role of historical interpretation in architecture is provided in E. I. Kirichenko, "Arkhitektor I. P. Ropet," *Arkhitekturnoe nasledstvo* 20 (1972): 85–93. Despite Ropet's attempt to incorporate stylistic features of Russian vernacular architecture into his work, Kirichenko notes that his use of the "Russian style" was not the antithesis to eclecticism, but rather another eclectic manifestation (87). Reproductions of the designs of both Hartman and Ropet were included in a series of illustrated volumes entitled *Motivy russkoi arkhitektury*, ed. A. Reinbot (Saint Petersburg: A. Reinbot, 1874–80.). See particularly volume 2, for the year 1875.

14 Elena Borisova, *Russkaia arkhitektura vtoroi poloviny XIX veka* (Moscow: Nauka, 1979), 264.

15 On the Talashkino estate, see William Craft Brumfield, *Smolensk: Arkhitekturnoe nasledie v fotografiiakh/Smolensk: Architectural Heritage in Photographs* (Moscow: Tri kvadrata, 2014).

16 Sternin, *Russkaia khudozhestvennaia kul'tura*, 179.

17 Maliutin was the subject of a brief but informative article by Sergey Diaghilev, "Neskol'ko slov o S. V. Maliutine," *Mir Iskusstva* 4 (1903): 157–60. The article is accompanied by a series of photographs of Maliutin's work, primarily at Talashkino.

18 For a historical and architectural survey of the Chukhloma region, see the bilingual volume William Craft Brumfield, *Chukhlomskii krai: Arkhitekturnoe nasledie v fotografiiakh/Chukhlomskii Region: Architectural Heritage in Photographs* (Moscow: Tri kvadrata, 2016). This is the only comprehensive study in English.

19 On the biography of Sazonov, see T. N. Baikova, *Na zemle blagoslovennoi: Istoriko-kraevedcheskoe izdanie* (Kostroma: Kostromaizdat, 2014), 194–98.

20 A detailed description of the Sazonov estate and the *terem* is provided in V. M. Rudchenko, G. K. Smirnov, P. N. Sharmin and E. G. Shcheboleva, *Pamiatniki arkhitektury Kostromskoi oblasti: Katalog*, vol. 6 (Kostroma: Komitet po delam kul'tury i iskusstva Administratsii Kostromskoi oblasti, 2004), 186–88.

21 On Pavlichenkov's project, see Iurii Snegirev, "Kto v tereme zhivet?," *Rossiiskaia Gazeta Nedelia*, March 24, 2016, 8–9.

22 An analysis with floor plan of the Poliashov house at Pogorelovo is contained in Rudchenko et al., *Pamiatniki arkhitektury Kostromskoi oblasti*, 194–97.

23 The most detailed study of Sestroretsk is L. I. Amirkhanov, E. A. Balashov, and V. A. Dorogin, *Istoriia Sestroretska i ego okrestnostei* (Saint Petersburg: Ostrov, 2006).

CHAPTER TWO

The Wooden Ambience of Russian Literature

The great Russian writers of the nineteenth century are often associated with their place of origin, with the environment that nurtured their early years or served as a refuge (sometimes involuntary) during times of trouble. The most famous example is the Tolstoy estate. Though the manor house at Yasnaya Polyana was built of brick, most of the surviving ancillary buildings are log structures (see below). At many other notable estates, however, the manor house was built of wood, and fate did not treat them kindly. The survey below will reveal that several of the most notable examples have been painstakingly reconstructed in the interests of preserving cultural memory. The manor houses associated with Russia's most revered writer, Alexander Pushkin, illustrate this complicated legacy.

Alexander Pushkin: Mikhailovskoe, Petrovskoe, and Trigorskoe

Of the many sites connected with Alexander Pushkin—Russian literature's free spirit and founding genius—none is more lyrically evocative and biographically rich than the cluster of estates collectively known as "Pushkin Hills." Mikhailovskoe, Trigorskoe, and Petrovskoe are located some 120 kilometers to the southeast of the ancient city of Pskov, and nearby is the Sviatogorsky Monastery, where Pushkin is buried. In this picturesque region of Pskov Province, pine forests and birch groves are interspersed with fields, small lakes, and gentle hills.

From a biographical perspective, the most important of these estates is Mikhailovskoe, which Pushkin's great-grandfather, Abraham Petrovich Hannibal (or Gannibal, of African descent), received from Empress Elizabeth in 1742 for his services to her father, Peter the Great. After Abraham's death in 1781, the estate went to his son Osip, who built the main house and

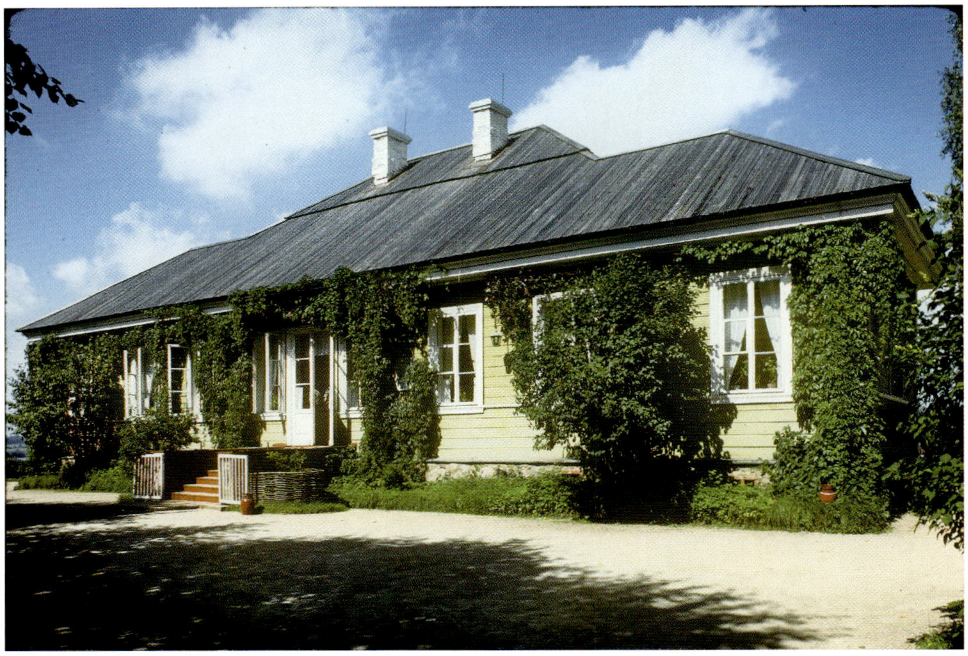

PUSHKINSKIE GORY. Mikhailovskoe estate house (reconstruction). August 13, 1988.

laid out a park. Following Osip's death, in 1806, the house remained in the hands of his widow, Maria, and daughter, Nadezhda, who was Pushkin's mother. In 1866 this original house was dismantled by Pushkin's younger son Grigory and rebuilt in a different style on the same foundation. That house in turn burned twice, in 1908 and 1918, yet each time it was rebuilt because of the association with Pushkin. Severe fighting during World War II caused further damage. In 1949 architects used the original foundation and old memoirs to reconstruct the house in a form closer to that of Pushkin's time. Although the present house and most of the adjacent service buildings are twentieth-century reconstructions, the ambience of the estate is so evocative that visitors can imagine the modest existence Pushkin led here.

In fact, the poet rarely lived on this remote estate. His first visit was in the summer of 1817, just after graduation from the Alexander Lycée at Tsarskoe Selo. He would later write of these six weeks as a delightful time in which he discovered the pleasures of village life. Yet he was perceptive enough to realize that not all was idyllic in this serf society. His sentiments of protest appeared so clearly in certain poems that Alexander I sent him in lenient exile to the south of the Russian Empire, where he spent almost five years. Pushkin's continued expression of free thought led to a return from Odessa to Mikhailovskoe in August 1824 as an extension of his exile.

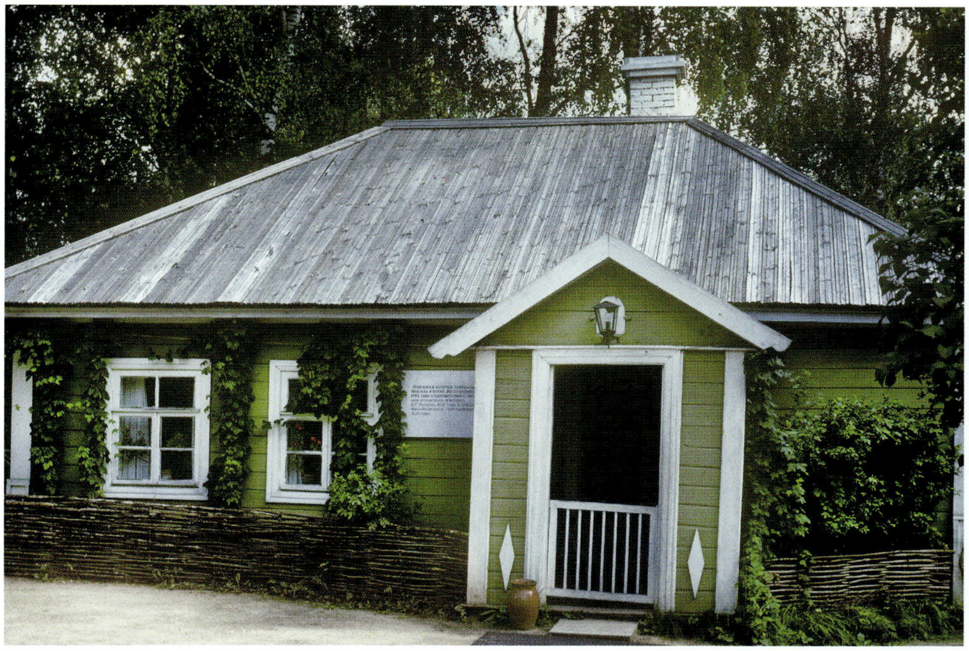

PUSHKINSKIE GORY. Mikhailovskoe estate, servants' wing and kitchen. Restored in 1955. August 13, 1988.

He was not alone: His parents, as well as his sister Olga and his brother Lev, were there. Pushkin had a difficult relationship with his father, and he must have been relieved when the family left for Saint Petersburg in November. For the next two years Pushkin was left largely to himself. The enforced idleness proved productive. At Mikhailovskoe he continued writing his novel in verse, *Eugene Onegin*, as well as the dramatic tragedy *Boris Godunov*. During this period, he also wrote some of the greatest lyrics in the Russian language. Despite the languor of provincial exile, Pushkin was not a recluse. He came to a more profound appreciation of the folk culture embodied in his former nanny, the elderly Arina Rodionovna, with whom he had frequent talks.

His primary antidote to boredom, however, was at the neighboring estate of Trigorskoe, where Pushkin visited the family of Praskovya Osipova (Vulf by her first marriage). Like the Mikhailovskoe manor, the Trigorskoe house burned in 1918 because of the implacable violence that swept the Pskov region during the civil war. After World War II it was rebuilt on the original foundation. The elongated, barn-like structure had earlier been used for weaving linen, and the family moved there temporarily in 1820 as major repairs were being made to the main house. When the latter burned to the ground, Madame Osipova decided to remain in the temporary residence and added porches on either end.

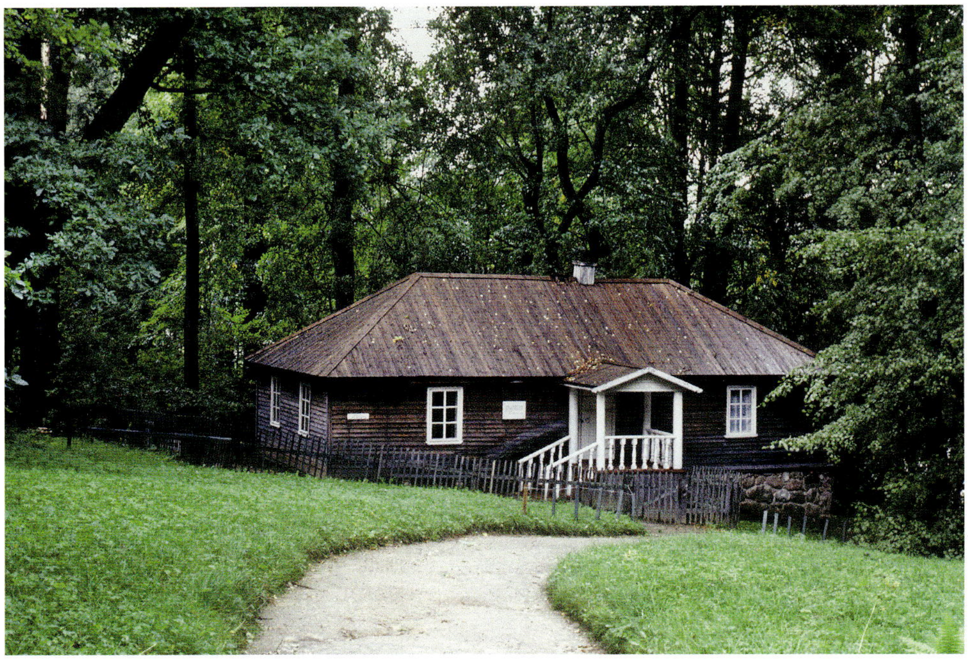

PUSHKINSKIE GORY.
Trigorskoe estate, bathhouse.
August 14, 1988.

The Osipova family included the twice-widowed Praskovya, her four daughters and one son (Alexey Vulf), as well as assorted relatives. The matriarch was enamored of Pushkin, and he was pleasantly spoiled during his visits to their house; but the poet's attentions were directed to Osipova's niece, Anna Petrovna Kern, who visited Trigorskoe in the summer of 1825. Pushkin had met Kern previously in Saint Petersburg, and this unexpected reacquaintance stimulated his desire for her. He wrote for her one of his

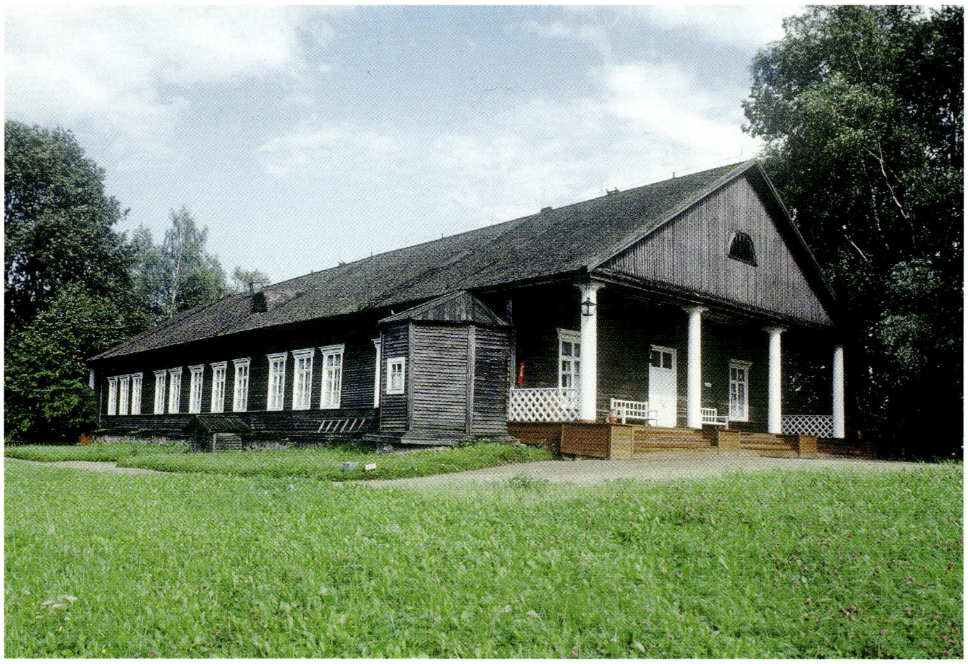

PUSHKINSKIE GORY.
Petrovskoe estate house (reconstruction).
August 12, 1988.

most passionate love lyrics: "I remember the miraculous moment." When Osipova got wind of this romance, she spirited Kern back to her husband in Riga. In September 1826, Pushkin was allowed to return to the great world of Moscow and Saint Petersburg, albeit under the supervision of Nicholas I and his gendarmerie.

The third in this ensemble of estates, Petrovskoe, is the one most closely connected with Pushkin's Hannibal ancestors. In 1781 it was deeded to the first of Abraham Hannibal's sons, Peter, who made it his home. Pushkin was several times visited by his great-uncle, who reminisced about the era of the illustrious Abraham Hannibal. Although smaller, Petrovskoe was the most impressive among the three Pushkin estates. It, too, was burned in 1918. After the Second World War archival documents were used in its reconstruction, completed in 1976. The house was surrounded by a natural park leading to Lake Petrovskoe (or Kuchane), with a network of paths, bowers, and pavilions.

In the opposite direction from Mikhailovskoe, the village of Boldino, in the southeastern part of Nizhny Novgorod Province, is equally associated with the genius of Alexander Pushkin. Having journeyed to the family estate at Boldino on business in the late summer of 1830, Pushkin was forced to stay there in the fall because of a severe cholera outbreak in the territory around Moscow. This unexpected conjunction of events led to a surge of creativity known as the "Boldino autumn." The several master-

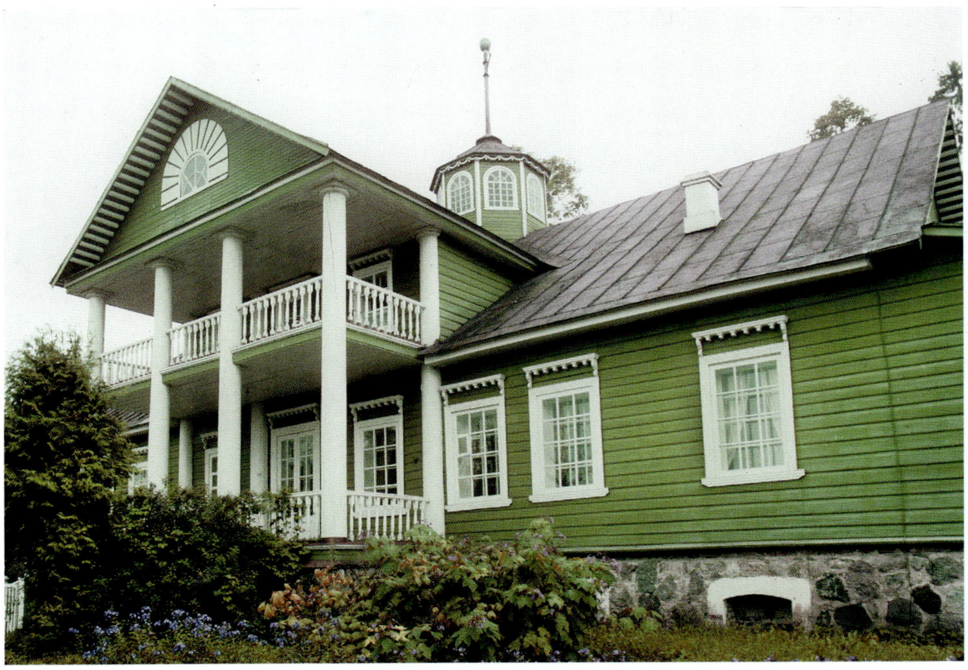

PUSHKINSKIE GORY. Trigorskoe estate house (reconstruction). August 14, 1988.

pieces completed during that brief period include the final chapters of his epochal novel in verse, *Eugene Onegin*, one of the most influential works in Russian culture.

Boldino, however, is not a literary abstraction. Bolshoe Boldino (the official name of the small town) and its surrounding region have a rich history that has been witness to such dramatic events as Ivan the Terrible's campaign against Kazan in 1552 and the Pugachev Rebellion in 1774. In the nineteenth century the region experienced the difficulties of famine and the transition from serfdom to an underdeveloped form of agriculture. The cultural center of Boldino is the Pushkin estate on the small Azanka River. The Boldino estate had been associated with the Pushkin family since the end of the sixteenth century and was formally granted to Pushkin's ancestor Fedor Pushkin for his services in the recapture of Moscow from the Poles in 1612. There is no information about the appearance of the earlier family houses, but the general outline of the present house, with its gabled center, follows a typical pattern for wooden manor houses whose log walls were usually clad in plank siding to create a more imposing appearance. The Boldino house is now painted a bright yellow, although the more usual color for such houses was gray or green.

Opinions vary on the age of the present Boldino house, which was substantially modified throughout the nineteenth century. Recent dendrological tests suggest that the lower log courses of the main structure date at least to the early nineteenth century and thus would have existed during

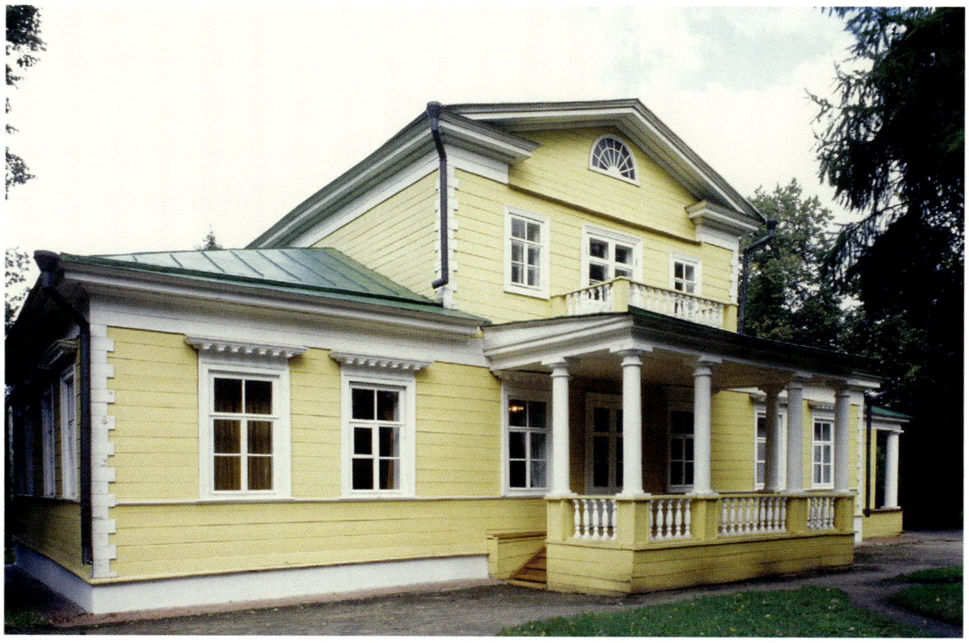

BOLSHOE BOLDINO. Boldino estate house (partial reconstruction). September 12, 2007.

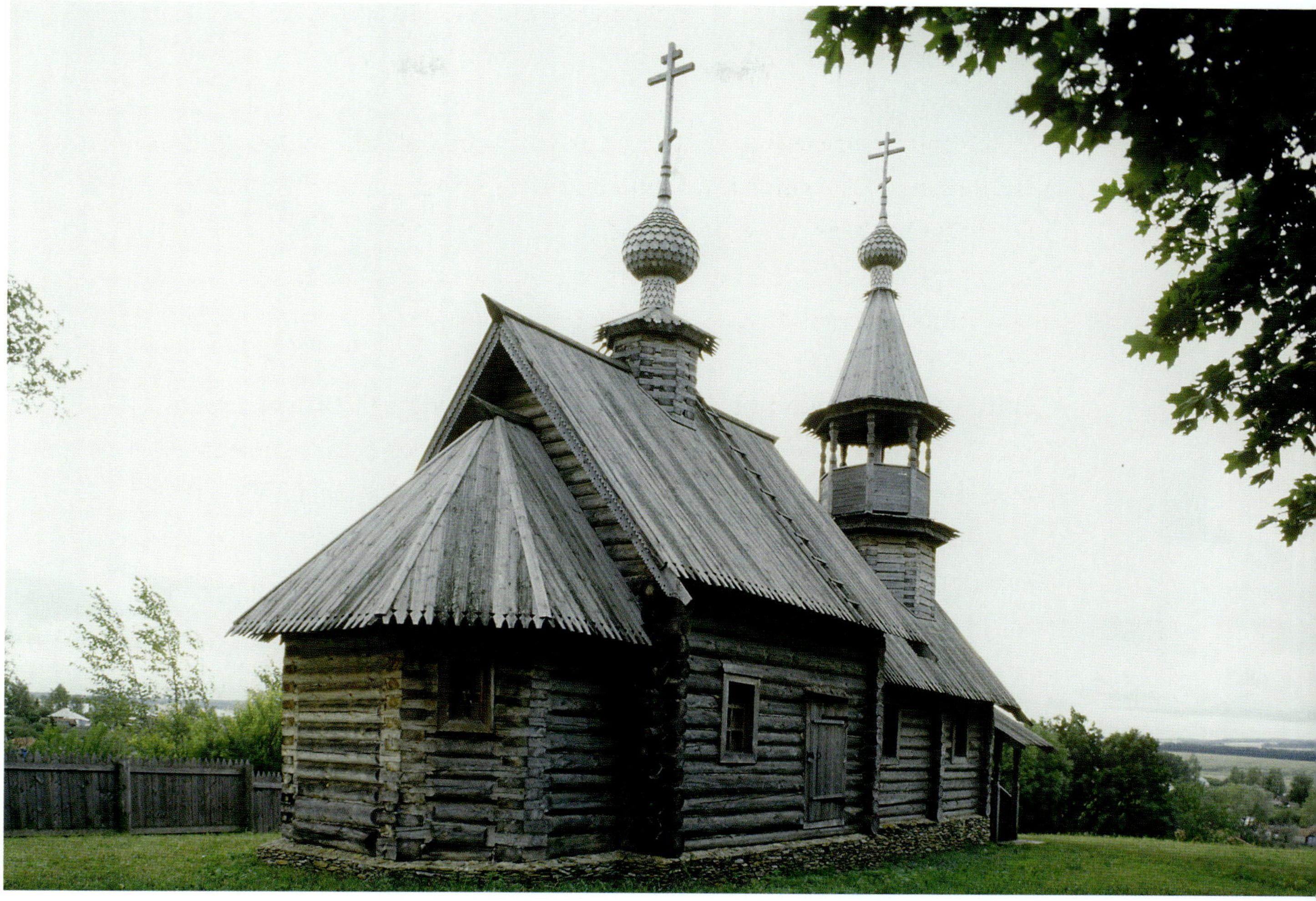

BOLSHOE BOLDINO. Chapel of Archangel Michael, northeast view. Built in 1999 on site of the former Boldino estate cemetery. September 11, 2007.

Pushkin's visits to the house in the 1830s. The back wing of the house was added in the 1870s. The interior of the house adheres to a nineteenth-century enfilade plan, with ceramic tile stoves in most rooms and furnishings based on an inventory of 1849. The appearance of his corner study—sacred to all lovers of Russian culture—has been restored on the basis of a sketch by Pushkin himself. From its large windows he could look directly to the Church of the Dormition, whose neoclassical form rises above the main square.

The territory of the museum park includes several smaller structures, such as the separate kitchen wing, the stables and carriage shed, the house for domestics, and the estate office—all of them log structures. A recent addition to the park is the traditional log Chapel of Archangel Michael, located on the site of the ancient estate cemetery and completed in 1999 as part of the bicentennial of the poet's birth. Although the chapel is not used for worship, its location provides an inspiring view of the surrounding landscape.

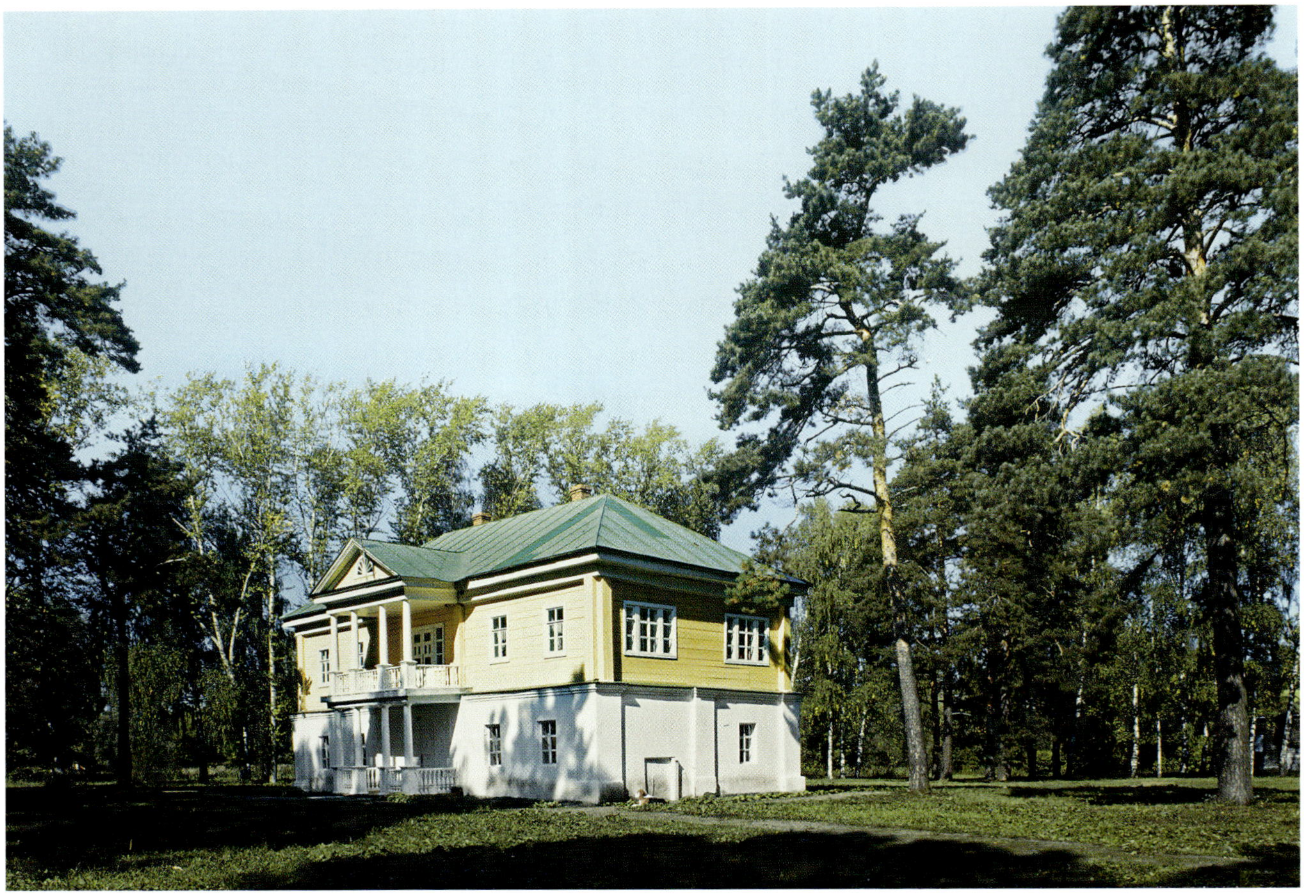

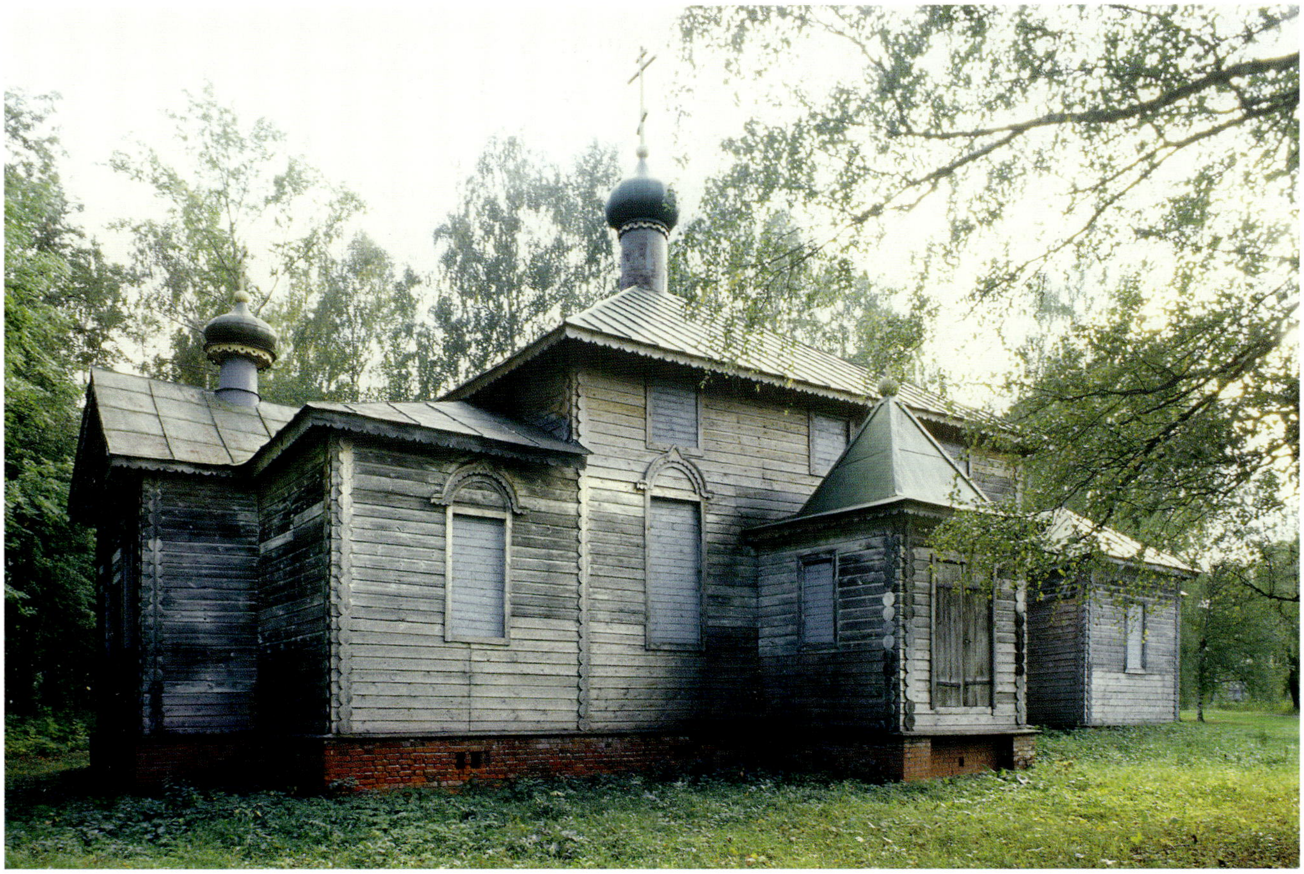

The Boldino region is dotted with other villages that preserve fragments of nineteenth-century estate culture. Foremost among them is Lvovka, created in the late eighteenth century by Pushkin's grandfather, Lev Alexandrovich, as a secondary estate to Boldino. At first the estate languished, but its fortunes improved in the 1840s, and in 1856 it became the residence of Pushkin's son Alexander. The main house, with its masonry ground floor, has been handsomely restored. Nearby is the late nineteenth-century wooden church dedicated to Saint Alexander Nevsky. Recently restored, the church is a reflection of the former size of the village of Lvovo, now almost entirely abandoned. The manor house at Lvovka is graced with tall pines, some of which were apparently planted during the time of the younger Alexander Pushkin.

BOLSHOE BOLDINO REGION. Lvovka estate house. September 13, 2007.

BOLSHOE BOLDINO REGION. Lvovka estate. Church of Saint Alexander Nevsky, northeast view. Substantially rebuilt in 2005. September 13, 2007.

Moscow Estate Houses

The Russian term *usadba*, is usually interpreted as "country estate" for the landed gentry. However, the *usadba* concept could also exist within an urban context, particularly in Moscow, where prosperous noble families maintained a residence for the fashionable social season. The "urban estate" (*gorodskaya usadba*) typically consisted of a main house, facing the street, on a lot enclosed by a fence and containing service buildings grouped around an interior courtyard. Despite the vicissitudes of Moscow's history during the past two centuries, a few classic wooden houses still stand, although demands on urban property have eliminated most of the service buildings.

One of the rare examples of a wooden neoclassical mansion from post-1812 Moscow was built in 1823 for Lieutenant (Heavy Cavalry Guards) Alexander Polivanov (1784–1845), descendant of a noble clan of Tatar origins. Denezhny Lane (Khamovniki District) completely burned in the 1812 fire, but Polivanov was able to erect the house on a surviving seventeenth-century foundation of limestone blocks. Apart from its imposing portico, the rusticated facade lacks ornamentation. Over the past century the house has been damaged by fire, and after a fire caused by a short circuit in 2001, there was a threat of demolition. Fortunately, public opinion and private donors managed to save the landmark.

The most appealing of the post-fire wooden houses was built in 1816 by Baron Vladimir Shteingeil (1783–1862) on Gagarin Lane. Shteingeil,

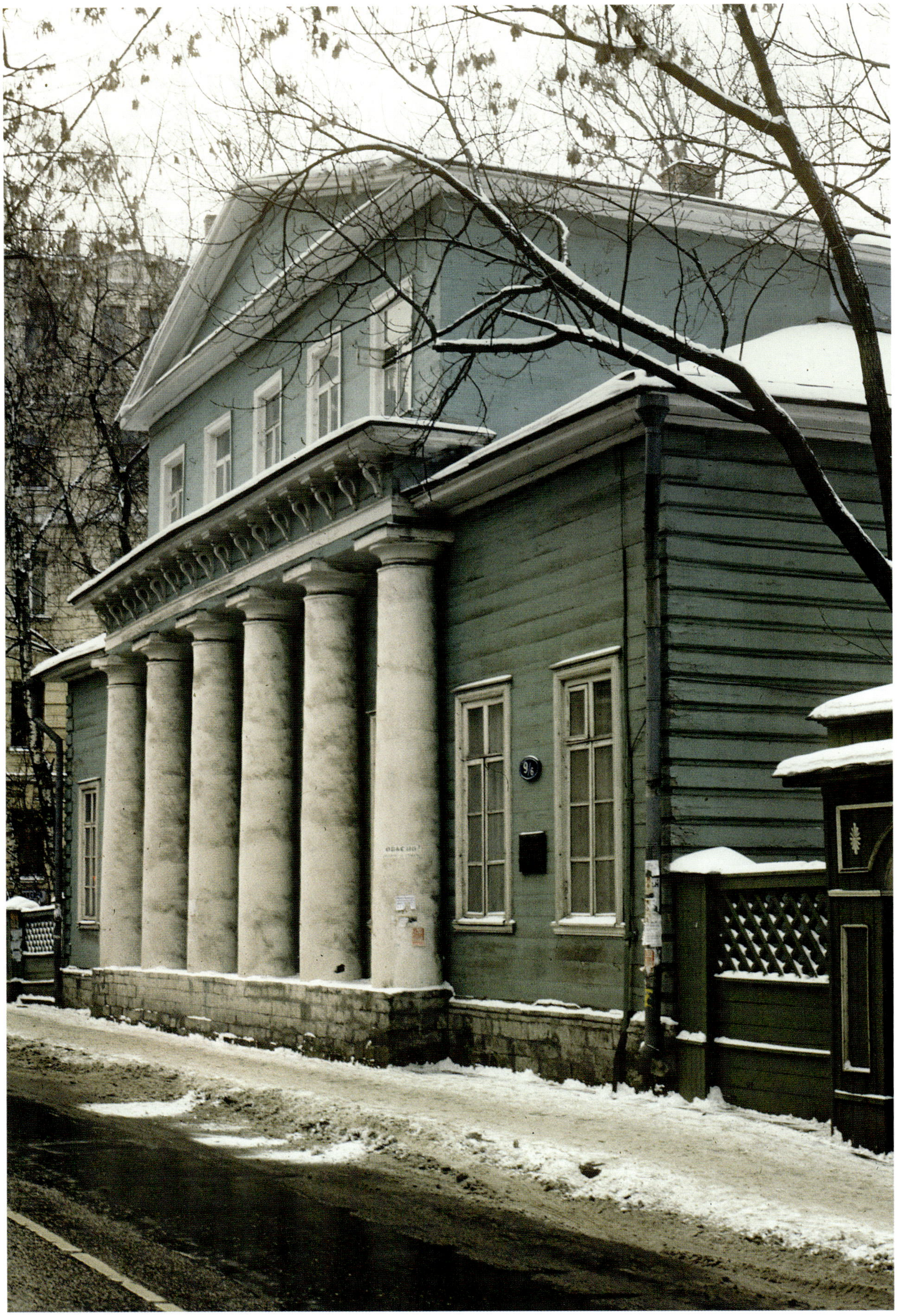

who played a major role in the rebuilding of Moscow, sold the house in 1819 and moved elsewhere in Moscow. He belonged to a Masonic lodge and by 1824 had become involved with the Northern Secret Society, which attempted to prevent the accession of Nicholas to the throne in December 1825 (the Decembrist Uprising, whose participants will appear in subsequent chapters). His charming house, with its tetrastyle portico, passed through several owners, most notably Lev Lopatin (1855–1920), a renowned philosopher and professor at Moscow University, whose family owned the house from 1821 to 1917. By the turn of the twentieth century, the Lopatin house had become a gathering place for the cream of Moscow's literary and intellectual society (the so-called Lopatin Wednesdays). The house is now maintained by the Russian Academy of the Arts.

The connection between the wooden urban estate ambience and classic Russian literature is perhaps best illustrated by the house at Ostozhenka Street 37/7. Like most of Moscow, Ostozhenka was raked by fire in the fall of 1812, but in the following decade burned-over lots were sold and new houses built. In 1819 General Karl Knorring sold his parcel to the nobleman Dmitry Fyodorov, who built a large wooden house for rental purposes. Well located, with a portico and crowned with a large *mezonin* (gabled half-story), it saw a succession of owners and renters from the nobility, including relatives and acquaintances of Alexander Pushkin, although there is no evidence that the great writer visited this address. In 1840 the home became the residence of Varvara Turgeneva (1787–1850), mother

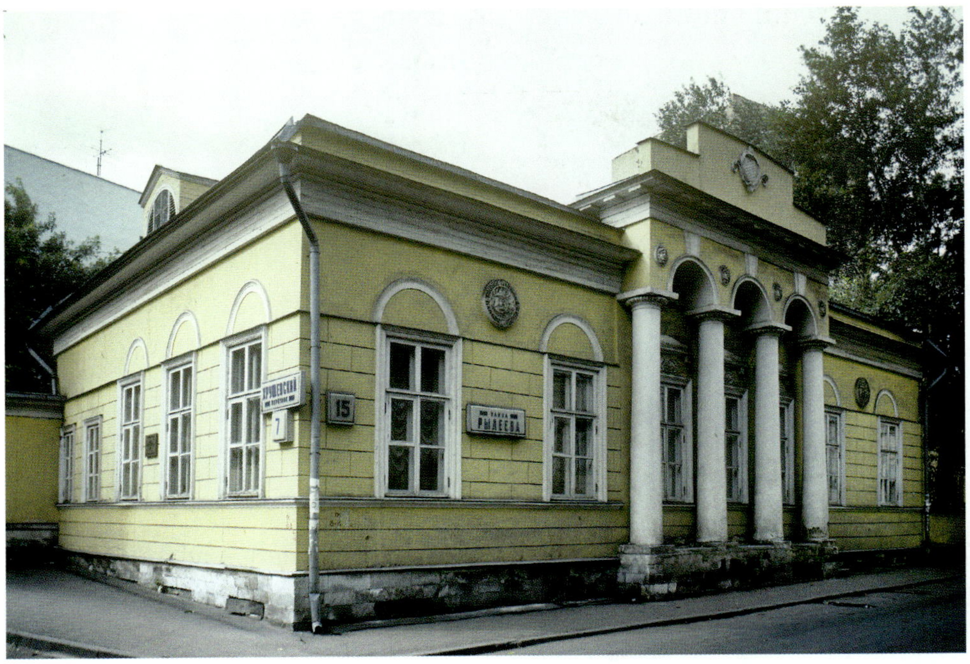

MOSCOW. Alexander Polivanov house, Denezhny Lane 9/6. December 31, 1996.

MOSCOW. Vladimir Shteingeil house, Gagarin Lane 15/7. June 7, 1993.

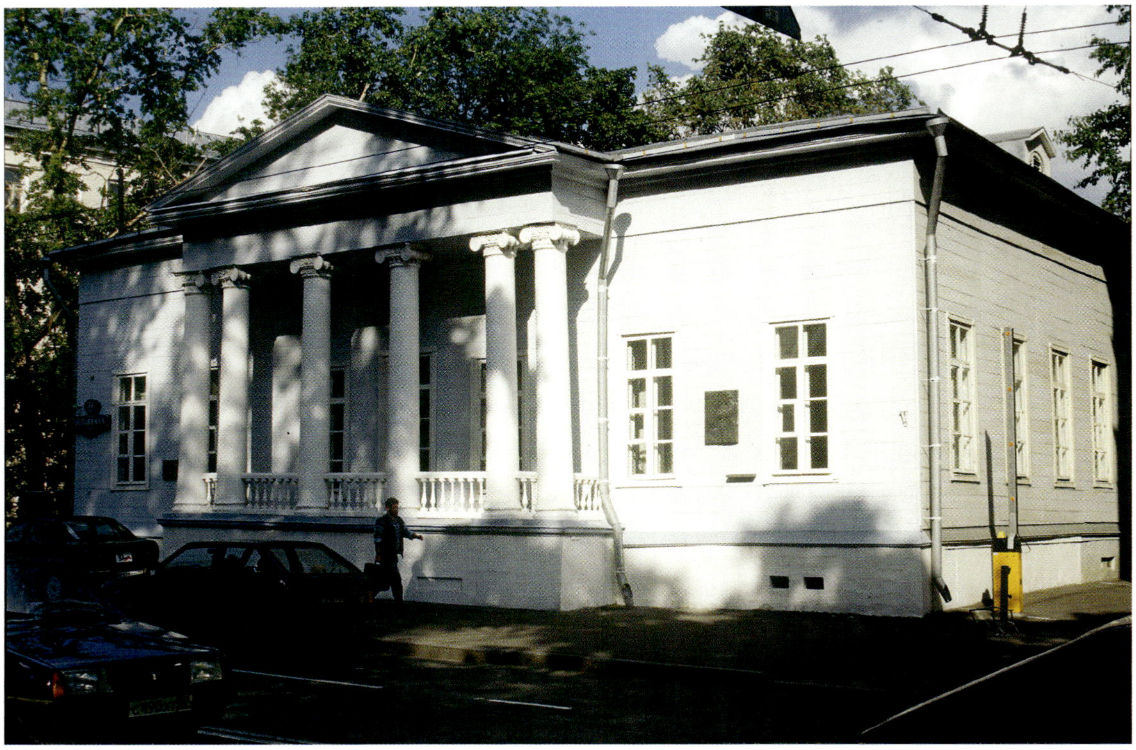

MOSCOW. Ivan Turgenev Museum, Ostozhenka Street 37. Originally built in 1819, the house was the residence of Ivan Turgenev's mother, Varvara Turgeneva, from 1840 until her death in 1850. May 25, 2000.

of Ivan Turgenev (1818–83), who frequently stayed at the house during a formative part of his development as a writer. Indeed, the house serves as the backdrop in one of Turgenev's most famous—and most sentimental—works, the story "Mumu," written in 1852 and first published in 1854. The tragic story, whose title character is a little dog rescued by the mute yard keeper serf Gerasim, was widely interpreted as an indictment of the abuses of serfdom. Ostozhenka 37 is popularly known as "Mumu's House," and the building is now a museum to Ivan Turgenev. Originally clad in plank siding, the structure shown in my first photograph from the summer of 1970 (when it still served as a communal apartment) shows an exterior of stucco over lathing. The plank siding was restored in the late 1970s.

Nearby, at Ostozhenka 49, is another graceful wooden house built in the decade following the Moscow fire. Called the "Vsevolozhsky house" after one of its early owners, the house was also associated with the Loshakovsky family, acquaintances of Vavara Turgeneva. Although smaller than its neighbor, the Vsevolozhsky house is closer to the street and more richly decorated, with a hexastyle portico supporting a pediment with the Vsevolozhsky family crest. The facade has stucco medallions with images of Apollo and the muses.

A simpler, but more typical, example of the urban estate house both before and soon after the 1812 fire is the house built in the early 1820s

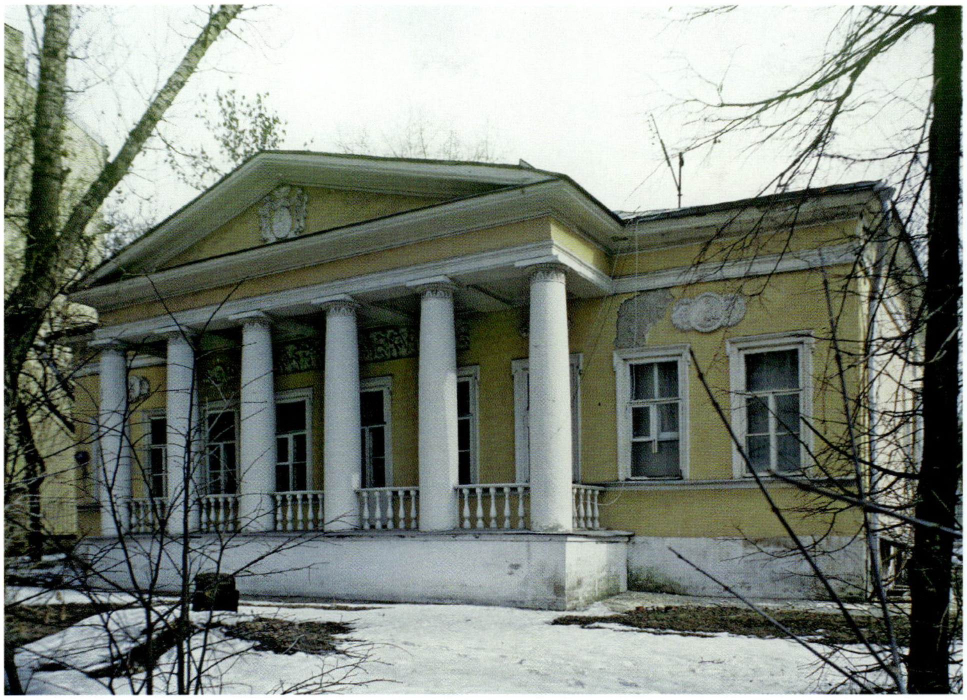

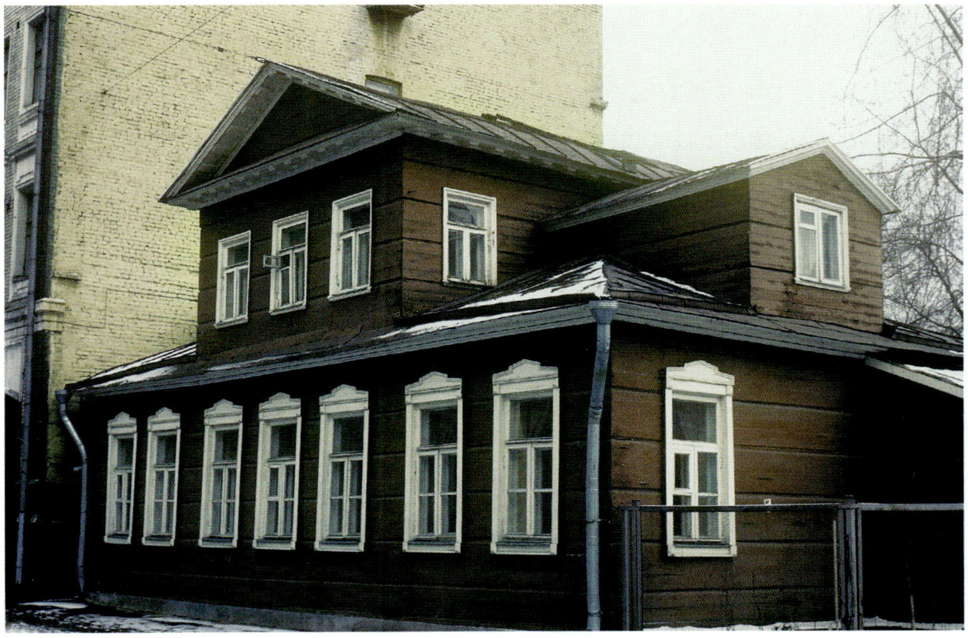

MOSCOW. Alexander Vsevolozhsky house, Ostozhenka Street 49. March 25, 2001

MOSCOW. Konstantin Krittsky house, Golikov Lane 9. Although the structure was recently rescued, its "restoration" involved painting the wooden siding a garish red with white trim. March 11, 1984.

at Golikov Lane 9 for the nobleman Konstantin Krittsky. Built close to the street, the house lacks a portico but is adorned with a *mezonin* and has plank siding with imitation rustication. All the ancillary structures in the back courtyard have been demolished, but the house itself has been preserved, albeit with questionable details from a 2013 restoration. Fortunately, I was able to photograph the structure before the current garish painting of the exterior.

Fyodor Dostoevsky's Childhood: The Darovoe Estate

Fyodor Dostoevsky (1821–81) is usually associated with the urban behemoth of Saint Petersburg, but there are relics of quieter spaces associated with the great writer, spaces built not of brick, but in the wooden traditions of the country estate. Dostoevsky spent several childhood summers in the 1830s at the modest family estate located at the village of Darovoe, 150 kilometers southeast of Moscow near the town of Zaraisk. The earliest reference to the village of Darovoe (likely derived from the word "dar," or gift) dates to the early sixteenth century. During that period the region formed Muscovy's first line of defense against Tatar raids from the south, and particularly from Crimea. Darovoe and the neighboring village of Monagarovo were among a cluster of outposts that belonged to the prominent Khotyainstev family in Kolomna. In 1830 the property came to the attention of Michael Andreevich Dostoevsky (1788–1839), a medic in state service who was engaged in quarantine enforcement during the cholera epidemic that swept through Moscow (and kept Pushkin at the Boldino estate). Already married for ten years, he and his wife Maria Fyodorovna (born Nechaeva) wished to acquire a place in the country for their family. The purchase was completed in 1831, and the family spent its first summer in Darovoe that year, when Fyodor was nine years old. The Dostoevsky family continued to live in an apartment at the Moscow Marinsky Pauper's Hospital, where their father served on the medical staff, but each summer the mother and children resided at Darovoe. The Darovoe property consisted of more than three hundred hectares, and Maria Dostoevsky proved an adept manager of the limited resources available to the family. In 1833 Michael Dostoevsky acquired the neighboring village of Cheremoshnya, with its one hundred peasants.

Years later Fyodor Dostoevsky would fondly remember the summers at Darovoe as a time of games with his brothers among the large linden trees and hollows on the estate. This imaginative play was stimulated by a reading of works such as Daniel Defoe's *Robinson Crusoe* and the novels of Walter Scott. On warm summer days the children swam in Mama's Pond, which Maria Dostoevsky had created from a nearby spring. The surrounding fields also left many memories. During his Siberian exile Dostoevsky remembered how the peasant Marei gently comforted him from fright at an imagined wolf near Darovoe. This memory of the goodness of the simple Russian people consoled Dostoevsky at a desperate time in his life, following his arrest in April 1849 for participating in a radical discussion group. Although his death sentence in December of that year was commuted at the last moment, he endured Siberian prison until the beginning of 1854 and served as an army private in Siberia for another three years until his rights were restored in April 1857.

Yet despite the loving memories, Darovoe had tragic associations for Dostoevsky. In February 1837 his mother Maria died in Moscow from tuberculosis. Her death at the age of thirty-seven was a devastating blow to his father, who retired from service and sent his sons Michael and Fyodor to school in Saint Petersburg. The rest of the family, including two younger sons and three daughters, moved to Darovoe. Life on the Darovoe estate soon became ridden with crises. Grieving for his wife and beset with financial problems, the elder Dostoevsky seems to have had increasingly antagonistic relations with the serfs who lived on the estate. Under circumstances that were never clearly ascertained, his lifeless body was found on June 6 (18), 1839, along the road to Cheremoshnya.

Following Mikhail Dostoevsky's death, the Darovoe estate was briefly kept in trust for his children and then passed to the younger son, Andrey. Fyodor Dostoevsky sold his share in 1844, and by 1852 his sister Vera (married name Ivanova) had purchased all shares of the estate. Under Vera Ivanova's guidance the estate gained new buildings for the Ivanov family and their guests. After many delayed plans, Fyodor Dostoevsky finally returned to Darovoe in 1877, four decades after his last childhood visit in the summer of 1836. Following the death of Vera Ivanova in 1896, the estate passed into the hands of her daughters, Dostoevsky's nieces. The only structure to have survived from the nineteenth century is the so-called wing (*fligel*). Opinion varies about whether it appeared following the 1832 fire, or whether it was built by the Ivanovs, perhaps as a guest house. After the Bolshevik Revolution one of the Ivanov daughters, Maria Alexandrovna Ivanova, became the dedicated curator of the small wing, which served as a village library. But with her death in 1929, all objects associated with the Dostoevsky family were moved to Moscow, and the wing became a nursery for the local collective farm. Only in 1990 did Darovoe achieve official status as part of the historic museum complex based in the town of Zaraisk. Today Darovoe and the adjacent linden grove are carefully maintained with a broad range of public support, including scholars and students from the regional center of Kolomna.

Dostoevsky at Mid-Life: Staraya Russa

The early 1870s were a time of intense pressure for Dostoevsky and his young family (by his second marriage), who were then living in the unhealthy physical environment of Saint Petersburg. His first daughter, Sophia (born in Geneva in 1868), had died before the age of one. His second daughter, Lyubov, was born in Dresden in 1869, while his son Fyodor was born in 1871 in Saint Petersburg. With the practical assistance of his young wife, Anna Grigorevna (nee Snitkina), Dostoevsky had begun to emerge

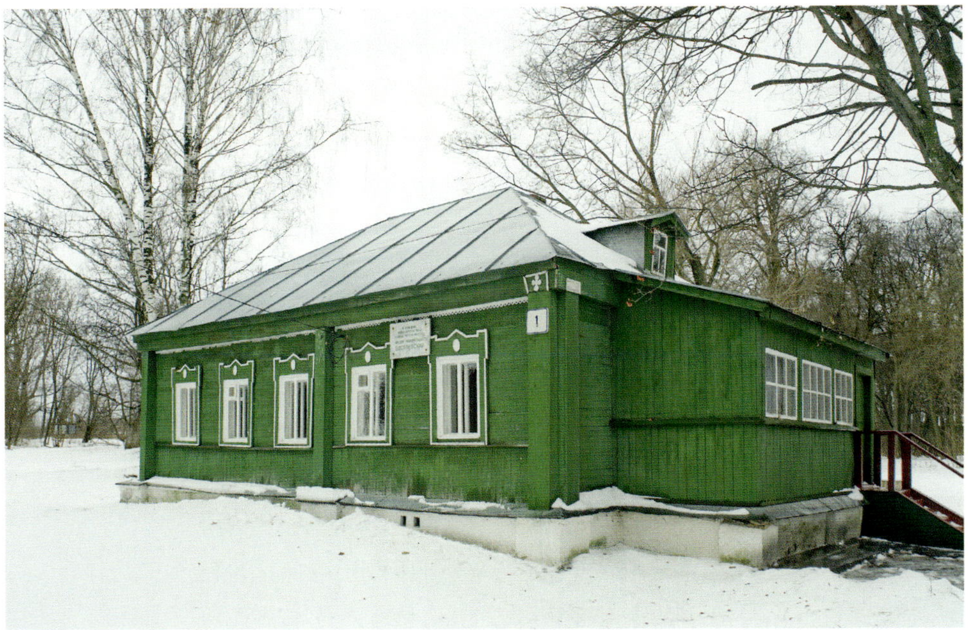

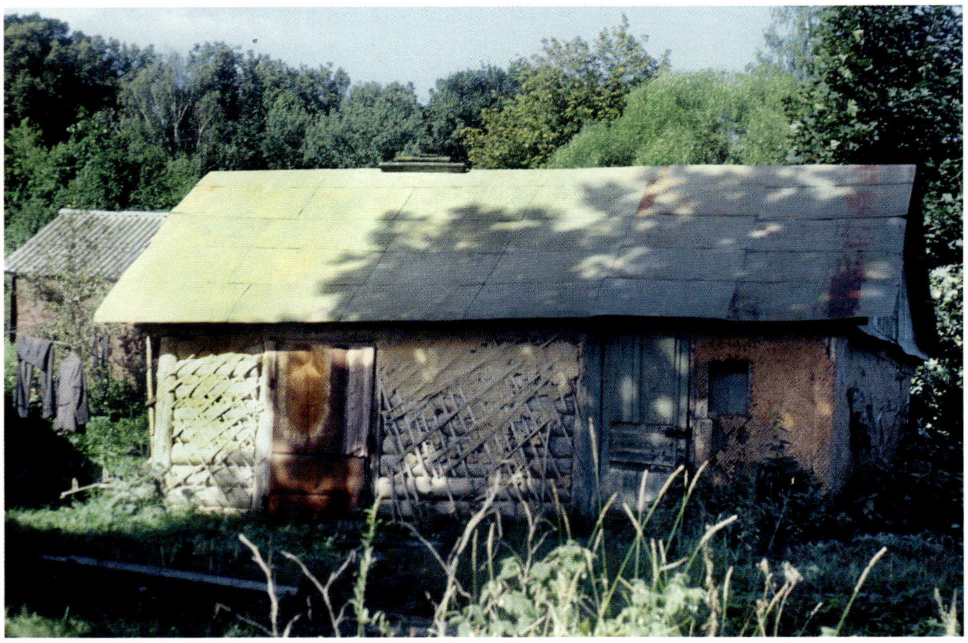

ZARAISK REGION. Darovoe estate, wing (*fligel*). Although the precise date of its construction is unknown, this is the only surviving nineteenth-century building on the estate that had belonged to Mikhail Dostoevsky, father of Fyodor Dostoevsky. January 3, 2015.

DAROVOE. Rare example of a simple log dwelling with clay daubed on a wattle lattice (for additional protection from the elements without the expense of plank siding). August 22, 2003.

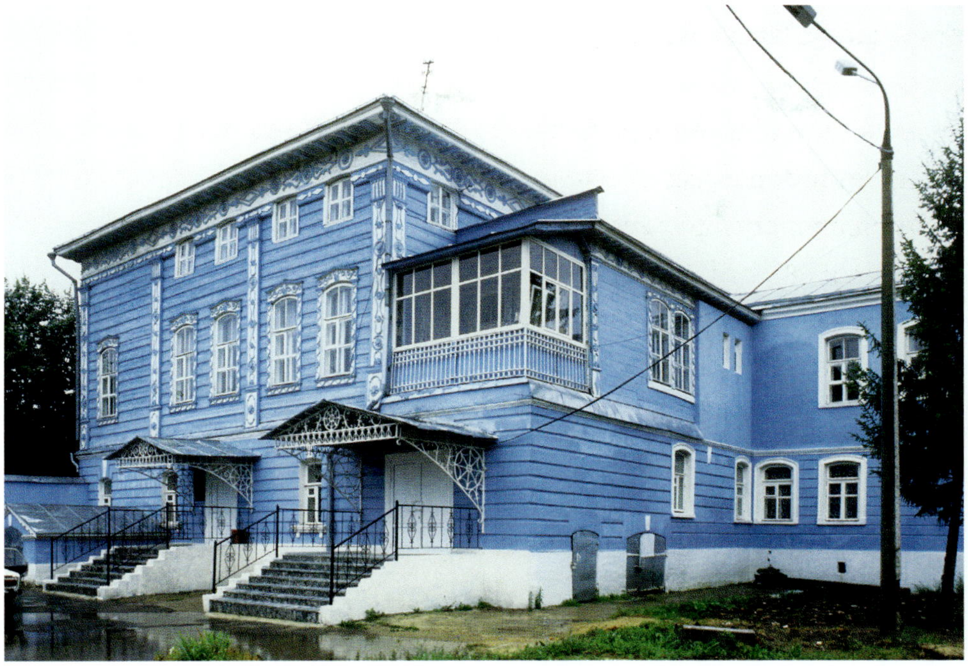

ZARAISK. Merchant house, Soviet Street 29. Built in the mid-nineteenth century, the house was converted into apartments. August 21, 2003.

from a mountain of debt and was able to consider moving with his family for at least the summer to a quieter, somewhat warmer environment. At the recommendation of friends, they decided to try the small provincial town of Staraya Russa, located 280 kilometers south of the capital in Novgorod Province. After a miserable, chilly first summer when they rented space from a local priest, his wife and children returned in the summer of 1873 and rented a two-story house belonging to a retired army officer, Alexander Gribbe. Dostoevsky's second son, Alexey, was born in this house in 1875 but died before his third birthday. Following Gribbe's death in 1876, Dostoevsky purchased the house (the first piece of property he owned). The literary works written here included his three late novels: *The Demons* (1872), *The Adolescent* (1875), and *Brothers Karamazov* (1880), whose setting (Skotoprigonevsk) draws features from Staraya Russa.

After Dostoevsky's death in early 1881, his widow and members of the family continued to return to the house on a regular basis until the outbreak of war in 1914. Enthusiasts established the house as a museum as early as 1909, and with the establishment of Soviet power, the building continued to be preserved as museum property. Even with this administrative support, the F. M. Dostoevsky House Museum—a wooden building, it must be remembered—might well have been destroyed during the war. Not only was Staraya Russa occupied by German forces from August 1941 to February 1944, but the town was also near the front line and subjected to

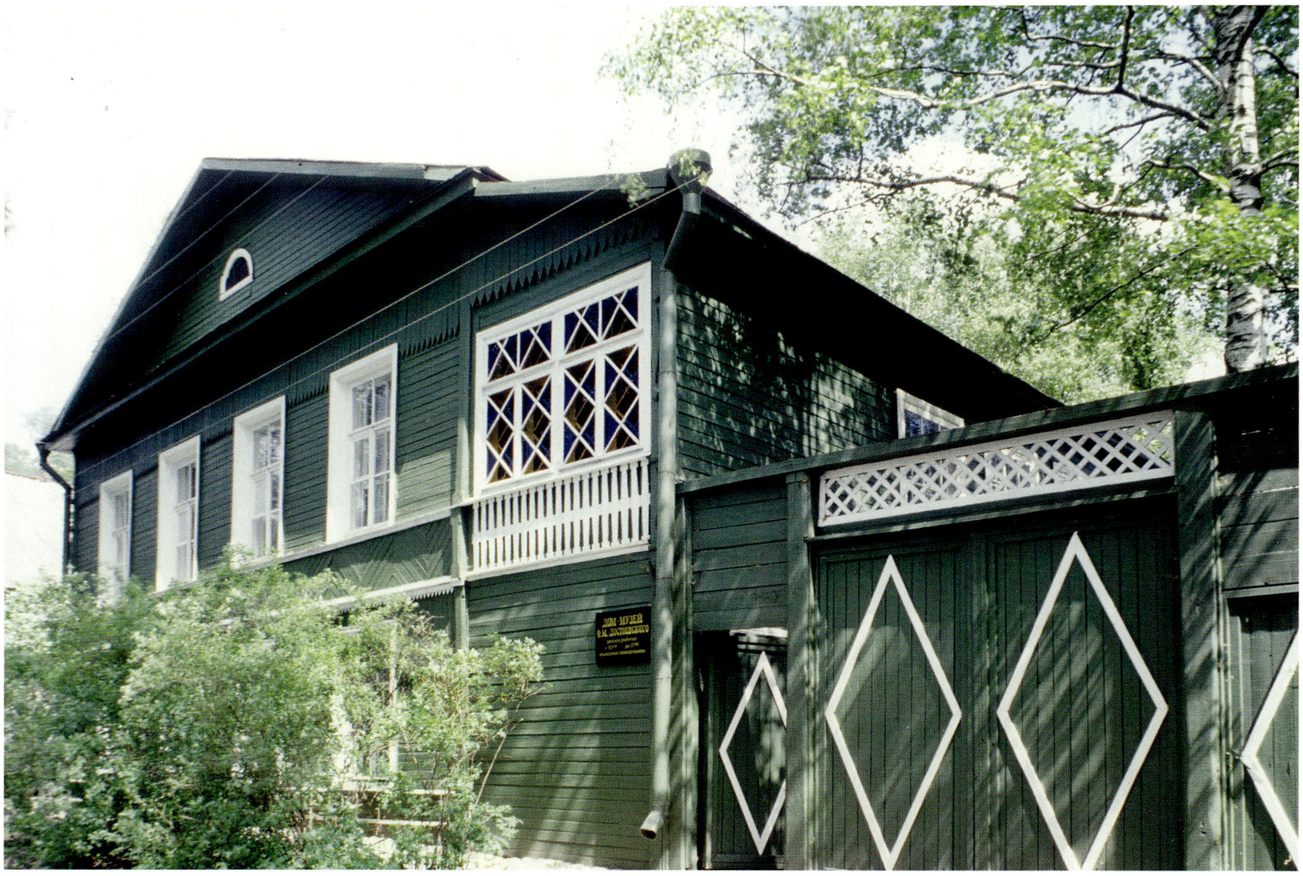

STARAYA RUSSA. Fyodor Dostoevsky House Museum. June 2, 1999.

frequent shelling. When Soviet forces finally retook the town, not only had it been depopulated, but almost every building was ruined. Astoundingly, the Dostoevsky House Museum remained unscathed, although in need of basic repairs. The first thorough restoration was completed in 1961, and in 1981 the house received the official name that it bears today.

On the exterior the structure is clad in plank siding painted dark green with simple white window frames and a few classicizing touches. The main facade is capped with a pediment, while an entrance area with a lower roof and doubled window extends to the right. The gathering of period furnishings and objects associated with Fyodor Dostoevsky continues to the present, and as a result the museum provides a presumably accurate interior view of mid-level nineteenth-century wooden housing. As usual, the interior walls are plastered and bear no traces of the log construction. The parlor and other rooms are amply illuminated by large windows, an increasingly common feature of nineteenth-century wooden dwellings in both urban and rural settings.

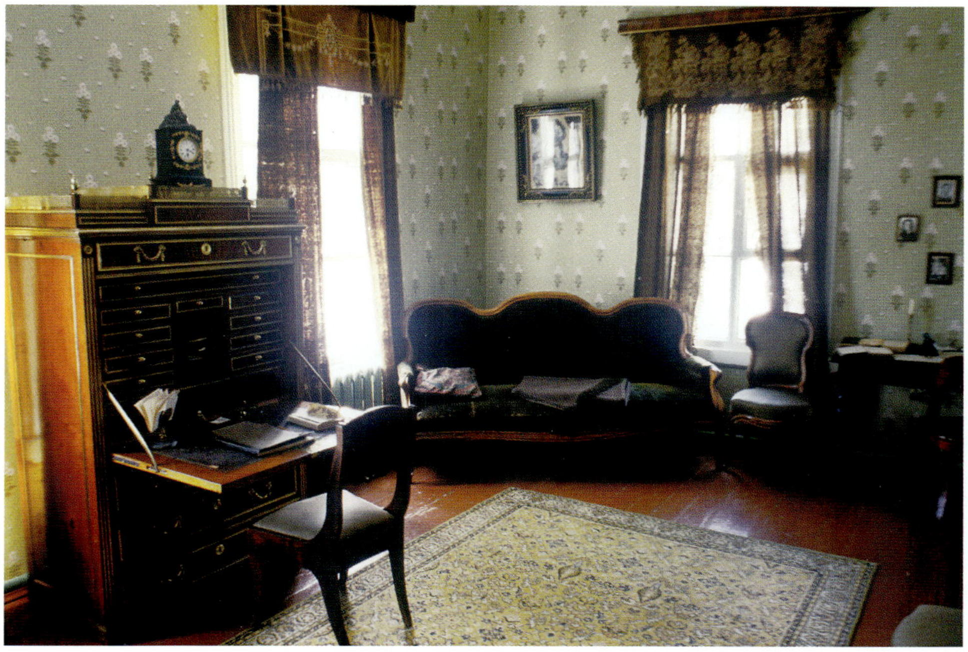

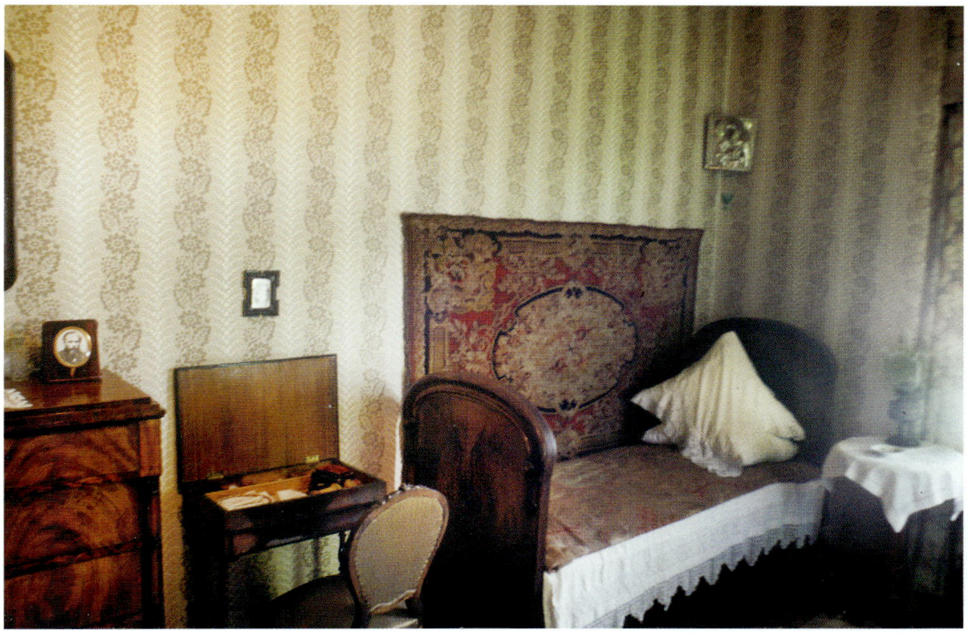

STARAYA RUSSA. Fyodor Dostoevsky House Museum. Dostoevsky's study. June 2, 1999.

STARAYA RUSSA. Fyodor Dostoevsky House Museum. Bedroom. June 2, 1999.

Leo Tolstoy and Yasnaya Polyana

The estate of Yasnaya Polyana ("bright glade") is universally linked to the life and work of Leo Tolstoy. He was born at the estate in 1828; it was here that he wrote two of the defining works of world literature; and it was from Yasnaya Polyana that he left in haste on the trip that would end his life. Yasnaya Polyana was the stage for Tolstoy's universal morality play. The estate, located just to the southwest of the city of Tula, became a pilgrimage site for Russians of all classes and for foreign visitors. Although the Yasnaya Polyana estate as received by Tolstoy's father had an imposing, largely wooden manor house, the main house that Tolstoy himself fashioned had a brick main house. Nonetheless, wooden structures were everywhere on the estate, including a few examples of the *izba*.

The earliest mention of the estate at Yasnaya Polyana dates to the middle of the seventeenth century. At that time the lands were held by the Kartsevs (or Karpovs), a nobility clan responsible for maintaining a regional line of defense against Crimean Tatar raids from the south. During the following century the estate territory was divided among several different owners. Tolstoy himself was interested in the history of Yasnaya Polyana and compiled notes on its early eighteenth-century owners—part of an unrealized project to write a historical novel set in the time of Peter the Great. In 1763 part of the estate was purchased by Major General Sergey Fyodorovich Volkonsky (1715–84), who continued to acquire adjacent holdings to expand the estate. His younger son, Nikolay Sergeevich Volkonsky (1753–1821), married Princess Ekaterina Dmitrievna Trubetskaya and moved to Yasnaya Polyana in 1799. Their daughter, Maria Nikolaevna Volkonskaya (1790–1830), married Nikolay Ilyich Tolstoy (1794–1837), a descendent of an ancient Russian clan elevated by Peter the Great. The Yasnaya Polyana estate served as Maria's dowry.

Leo (Lev) Nikolaevich was born on August 28, 1828, the fourth of five children (by today's calendar, his birthday fell on September 10; dates in this section are given in Old Style). He lost both of his parents at an early age (his mother when he was only two), but relatives saw to the well-being of the children, who moved between Yasnaya Polyana and Moscow. Further deaths in the family led to the children being adopted by an aunt in Kazan, where the younger children moved in 1843. In 1844 Leo entered the distinguished Kazan University but proved a desultory student. In 1847 he returned to Yasnaya Polyana, by now his inheritance, where he first encountered the intractable problems of serfdom. As his literary creativity began to flourish, Tolstoy made frequent trips to Moscow and Saint Petersburg, where he developed a love for classical music and considerable skill at the piano. He also fell prey to a gambling addiction that for the next few years threatened his financial security. In 1851 Tolstoy joined his beloved elder brother Nikolay in the army, which was then involved in a prolonged military campaign against Islamic insurgents in the Caucasus. With the

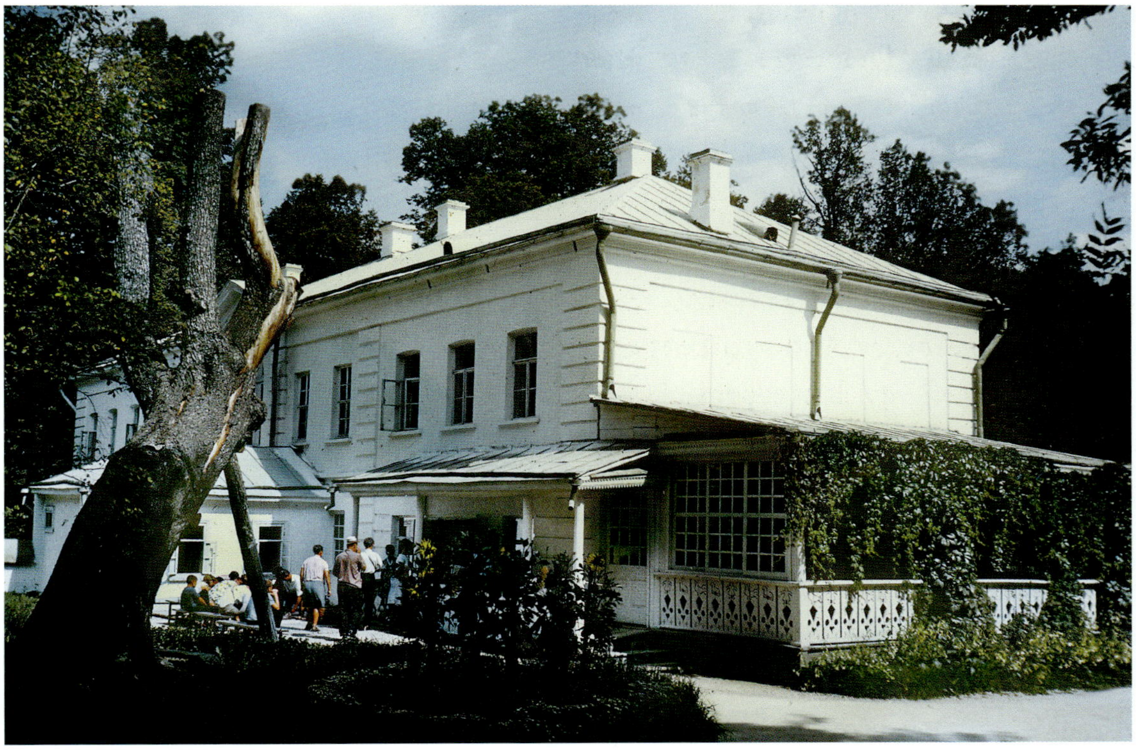

YASNAYA POLYANA ESTATE. Wing of original main house (not extant). Converted by Leo Tolstoy into the main residence for his family. Right: wooden porch with carved decoration. Left: trunk of ancient linden tree (later removed) under which Tolstoy rested and received visitors. July 28, 1970.

outbreak of the Crimean War in 1853, Tolstoy's military service moved to a new front, including the siege of Sevastopol that concluded with a bitter defeat in August 1855. (In 1854, he had sold the main estate house, a rambling, decrepit wooden structure he could not afford to maintain. By 1860 he had expanded one of the capacious two-story brick wings into the house where he and his family would live.)

In May 1861—shortly after the proclamation of the liberation of the serfs—Tolstoy returned to the estate after traveling in Europe and plunged into the role of social activist as an advocate for newly liberated peasants in legal disputes with the landowning nobility. In September the following year, Tolstoy married Sofya (Sonya) Andreevna Behrs, daughter of a prominent Moscow doctor descended from German nobility. She would bear him thirteen children, of whom eight lived to maturity. For a while, during the 1860s, life at Yasnaya Polyana seemed something of a gentry idyll. *War and Peace*, published serially between 1865 and 1869, was rapturously greeted by the reading public, enthralled by a mastery of detail drawn in large part from his knowledge of the family ancestry and its relation to Yasnaya Polyana.

War and Peace was followed in the 1870s by another masterpiece, *Anna Karenina*, first published in 1875–77. Although the heroine's fate unfolds primarily in Moscow and Saint Petersburg, the counterpoint narrative of

Levin and his wife Kitty takes place on an estate resembling Yasnaya Polyana. Yet despite this acclaim and the apparent devotion to a growing family, Tolstoy entered a period of depression and spiritual crisis that intensified in the 1880s, when his marriage to Sofya Andreevna was burdened with contention and dissatisfaction. The agony of Tolstoy's final decades is a separate topic, but through it all, Yasnaya Polyana provided a spiritual refuge as well as a place of pilgrimage for visitors throughout the world who wished to partake of the writer's wisdom. The Yasnaya Polyana estate became an assiduously maintained artifice, despite Tolstoy's attempts to escape the structures of exploitation. Tolstoy's family was not financially supported by the estate; rather, the estate was supported by Tolstoy's writerly income, managed by Sofya Andreevna. Tolstoy remained the *barin* (lord of the manor), morally sustained by the estate and dependent on the lives of "his" people whom he idealized but whose prospects were less than promising.

For all the love of the country estate from a literary and cultural perspective, widespread hostility to the gentry estate was evident from the burnings and destruction of estate buildings—including manor houses—that occurred between 1904 and 1906 and particularly after 1917. Even without this immediate violence, masses of peasants were ready to leave the estate system. Tolstoy's characters discuss this seemingly irresolvable problem at length in *Anna Karenina*. However, to Tolstoy and his admirers, the estate was an essential part of the persona and the life-system that he had created. Those humble huts were a stage set for a myth of the authentic life.

Tragically, Tolstoy himself ultimately proved incapable of sustaining the myth. On October 28, 1910, Tolstoy left the house in the middle of the night to escape an existence that he no longer considered bearable. Following his death at the Astapovo Station on November 7, his body was returned to Yasnaya Polyana, where it was buried on November 10 in a simple unmarked grave, a mound covered with grass. Other structures from Tolstoy's time—the stables, a few log houses, and the Kuzminsky Wing, where his school was briefly located—still stand at Yasnaya Polyana, along with much of the park originally laid out by his grandfather in the early nineteenth century. In 1921 Yasnaya Polyana was given official status as a national museum, and the interior of his house has been preserved much as he left it in 1910, a living link to one of humanity's greatest spirits, dedicated to a quest for justice and peace.

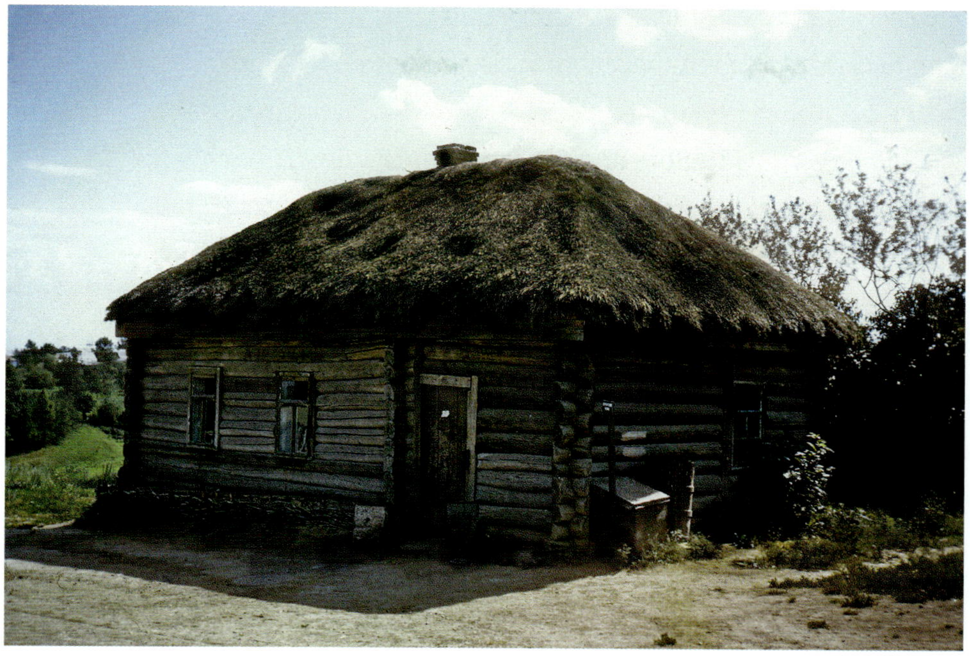

YASNAYA POLYANA ESTATE. Coachman's hut. Original nineteenth-century two-room *izba* with thatched roof. July 28, 1970.

Tolstoy's Final Journey: Astapovo Station

Fleeing what he considered to be an intolerable domestic situation in the fall of 1910, Tolstoy met death not at his estate of Yasnaya Polyana, but at a distant railway station known as Astapovo, some four hundred kilometers southeast of Moscow in what is now Lipetsk Province. Much has been written about these final days of the writer's life, but little attention has been given to the physical setting in which this momentous event occurred. The station's name came from the nearby village of Astapovo, known to have existed since the mid-seventeenth century. The toponym derived from Lake Ostapovo, in turn was related to the personal name "Ostap," pronounced "Astap" in standard Russian.

This rural backwater was transformed in 1889–90 with the building of Astapovo Station as part of the new Ryazan-Kozelsk Railway. By the late 1890s traffic through the station increased significantly with the development of what had become the Ryazan-Urals Railroad system. The Astapovo complex consisted of several buildings, including a substantial two-story brick station constructed in 1903 next to the original wooden station (1890; still in use). Behind the station buildings and slightly to the right are two one-story wooden structures: a house for the stationmaster and a first-aid station. Tolstoy arrived at Astapovo Station, already seriously ill, on October 31.

In his later years Tolstoy had become increasingly distraught by what he felt was a lack of sympathy for his social and moral views on the part of Sofya, who deeply loved him and had dedicated her life to his work and well-being. In the early hours of October 28, Tolstoy arose after a sleepless night, bade farewell to this daughter Alexandra (Sasha), and departed Yasnaya Polyana with his personal physician, Dushan Makovitsky. Fearing discovery, they covered a difficult path to the small station of Shchekino, where they boarded a train to Kozelsk Station (Kaluga Province). They journeyed that same day to the nearby Optina Pustyn Presentation Monastery, a renowned spiritual center that also played an important role in Fyodor Dostoevsky's life. Indeed, Tolstoy had met three times between 1877 and 1890 with Father (*starets*) Amvrosy, considered the prototype for Father Zosima in *The Brothers Karamazov*.

On October 28, Tolstoy twice approached the John the Baptist skete, or retreat, within the Optina Pustyn monastery where elderly monks venerated for their wisdom (*startsy*) resided. Each time he turned back, beset by doubt. Many have speculated on his motives for this unexpected visit, but there is little firm evidence about his possible intentions to reconcile with the Orthodox Church. Having spent the night at the hotel adjacent to Optina Pustyn, Tolstoy and Makovitsky made their way on October 29 to the Shamardino Convent, twelve kilometers north of Optina Pustyn. There Tolstoy visited his sister, Maria (1830–1912), who had entered the convent in 1891. The next day Sasha arrived with news that Sofya had learned of his whereabouts. That evening Tolstoy wrote a letter asking her not to follow him.

Early on the morning of October 31, Tolstoy left Shamardino with Sasha and Makovitsky for a jolting trip back to the Kozelsk Station. There they boarded a third-class car in the direction of Rostov-on-Don. Already in fragile health at the age of eight-two, exhausted by constant travel, and suffering in the smoke-filled, crowded primitive car, Tolstoy became ill with pneumonia. Toward evening Makovitsky and Sasha, alarmed by his obvious distress and rising temperature, decided to take him from the train at the nearest station, Astapovo. The efficient station master, Ivan Ozolin, recognized Tolstoy and promptly dealt with the emergency by providing him with a large room in the wooden house where Ozolin, his wife, and their three children lived.

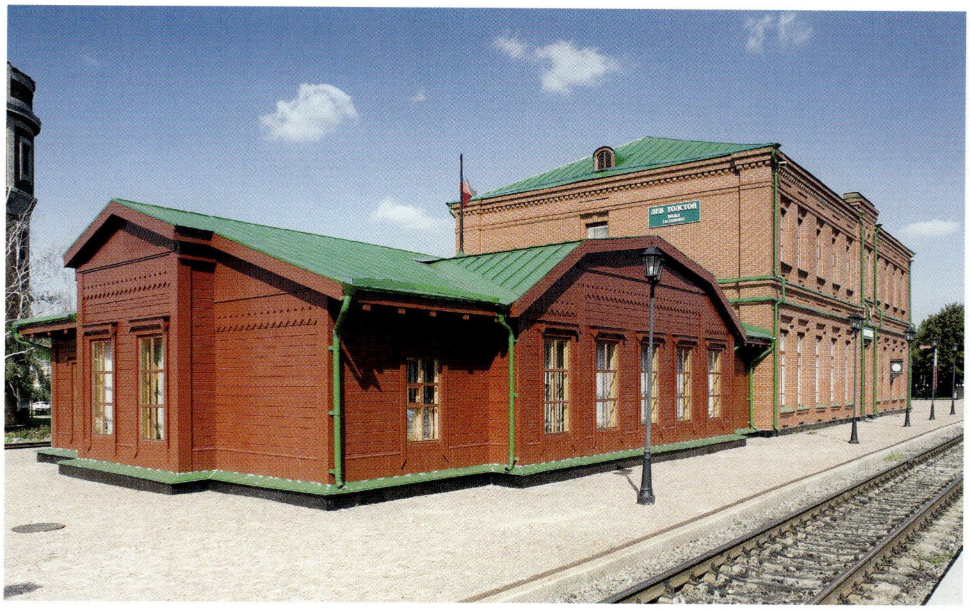

ASTAPOVO STATION (town of Lev Tolstoy). Original wooden station building (1890). Right: two-story brick station built in 1903. August 10, 2013.

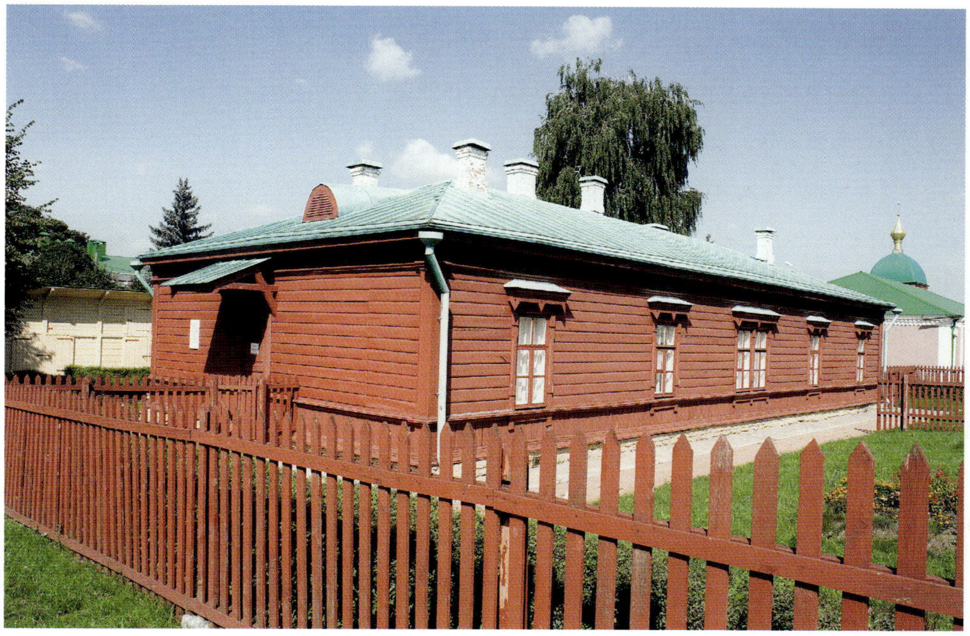

ASTAPOVO STATION (town of Lev Tolstoy). House of stationmaster, Ivan Ozolin, where the deathly ill Tolstoy was provided with the main room. August 10, 2013.

Over the next week Astapovo became an international sensation. Telegraph bulletins went out ceaselessly, reporters flocked to the station, and a film crew from the French Pathé News Company arrived toward the end. On November 2 Tolstoy's editor Vladimir Chertkov arrived (at Tolstoy's request), and that evening Tolstoy's son Sergey arrived. Sofya Andreevna, accompanied by other children, arrived by the end of the day in a first-class car that remained at the station and housed them for the duration. Those closest to Tolstoy prevented her from entering the stationmaster's

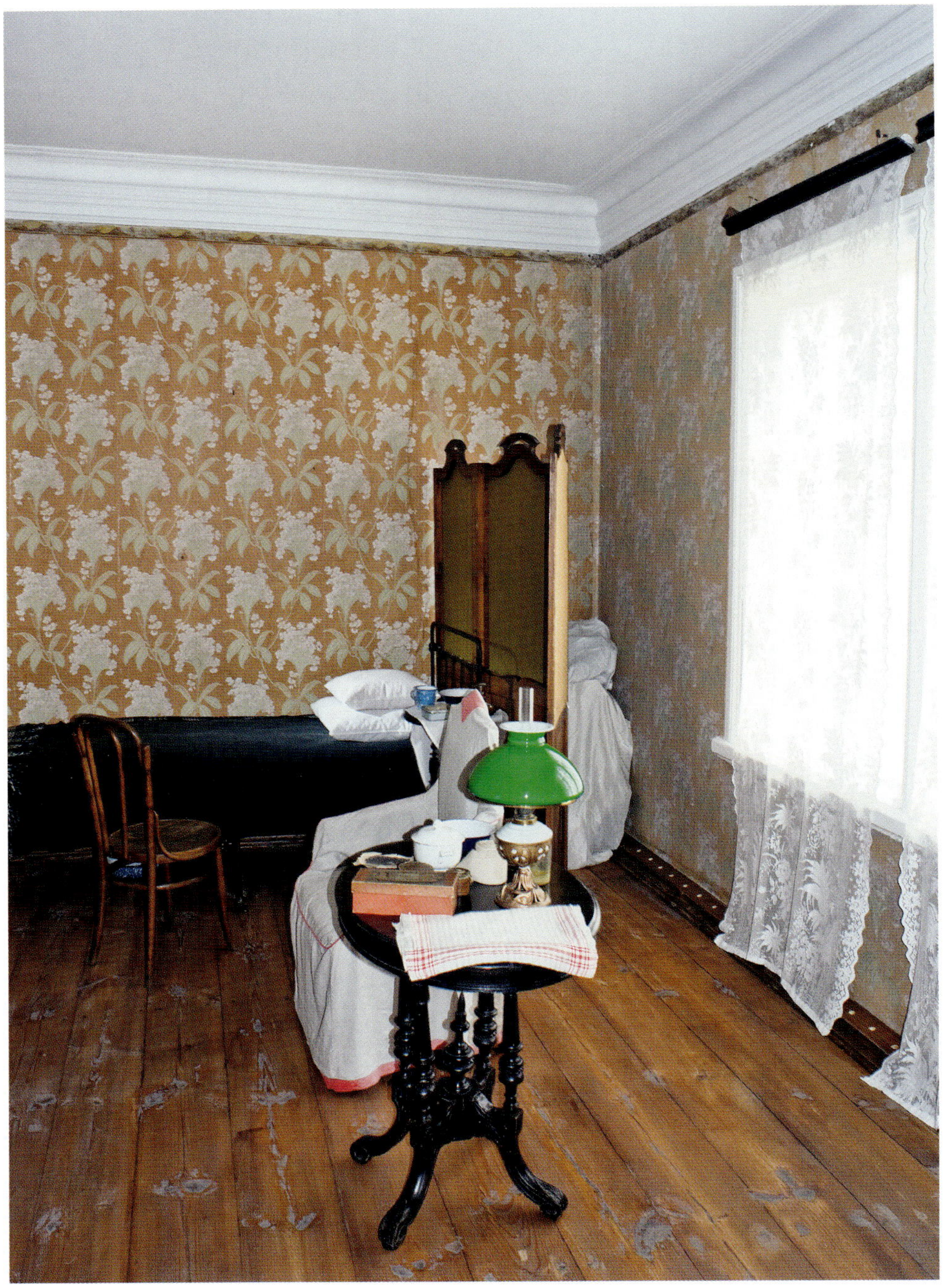

ASTAPOVO STATION (town of Lev Tolstoy). House of stationmaster, main room with the bed on which Tolstoy lay for a week until his death on November 7, 1910. August 10, 2013.

house. A succession of doctors descended on the station, but no expertise could prevent the inevitable. His wife was allowed into the room only when he had slipped into a coma. On November 7, at 6:05 a.m., Tolstoy died without Last Rites. (As a Lutheran of Latvian origins, Ozolin kept no icons in the house.) Ozolin decided to keep the bedroom as it was at the time of the great writer's death. The shadow of Tolstoy's recumbent head and torso cast by the bedside lamp was outlined on the wallpaper and has been preserved. Within a day a memorial plaque appeared over one of the doors to the room. The station clock stopped at 6:05, never to be reset. On November 8 a funeral cortege set off from Astapovo to Yasnaya Polyana. The next day Tolstoy was buried on the estate in a simple grave without a cross. Hundreds attended the burial under the watchful eyes of government agents. In 1918 Astapovo Station town was renamed "Lev Tolstoy," although the name "Astapovo" remains for the museum complex as well as for the nearby village. The shrine established by the good stationmaster Ozolin was maintained after the revolution and is now a national landmark, administered by the Tolstoy Museum in Moscow. As for the town now called Lev Tolstoy, it has a current population of slightly more than eight thousand and is the administrative center of a rich agricultural region. As of 2014 there is no passenger service at the station. Freight trains, however, still rumble through, past the large clock set at 6:05.

Muranovo

The beautifully preserved estate ensemble of Muranovo is remarkable for many reasons. The main house was converted by its owner, Evgeny Baratynsky, into a memorial to the great poet Fyodor Tyutchev (a relative), even though there is no evidence that he ever visited the estate (more on that below). The design of the manor is also a fine example of Russian Anglomania, a Romantic exercise intended to summon associations with the novels of Walter Scott and fantasy imitations of the life of British gentry. But the most curious feature—and the one most relevant to wooden architecture—is the construction of the main house, which is a brick shell encasing an inner log structure. Baratynsky's idiosyncratic design for the house is an unfolding series of surprises. On the exterior, the main facade appears at first glance to be a high-walled red brick wall with a central bay and octagonal crown, yet closer inspection also reveals an attractive log extension between the primary structure and a brick tower meant to complete the sense of a castle. On the interior of the main structure, containing some twenty rooms, the plastered wall surfaces with classical detailing give no indication of the material beneath. In fact, this brick mansion encases a log structure with a slight air pocket between brick and log that serves to moderate temperature extremes in both winter and summer. The vertical

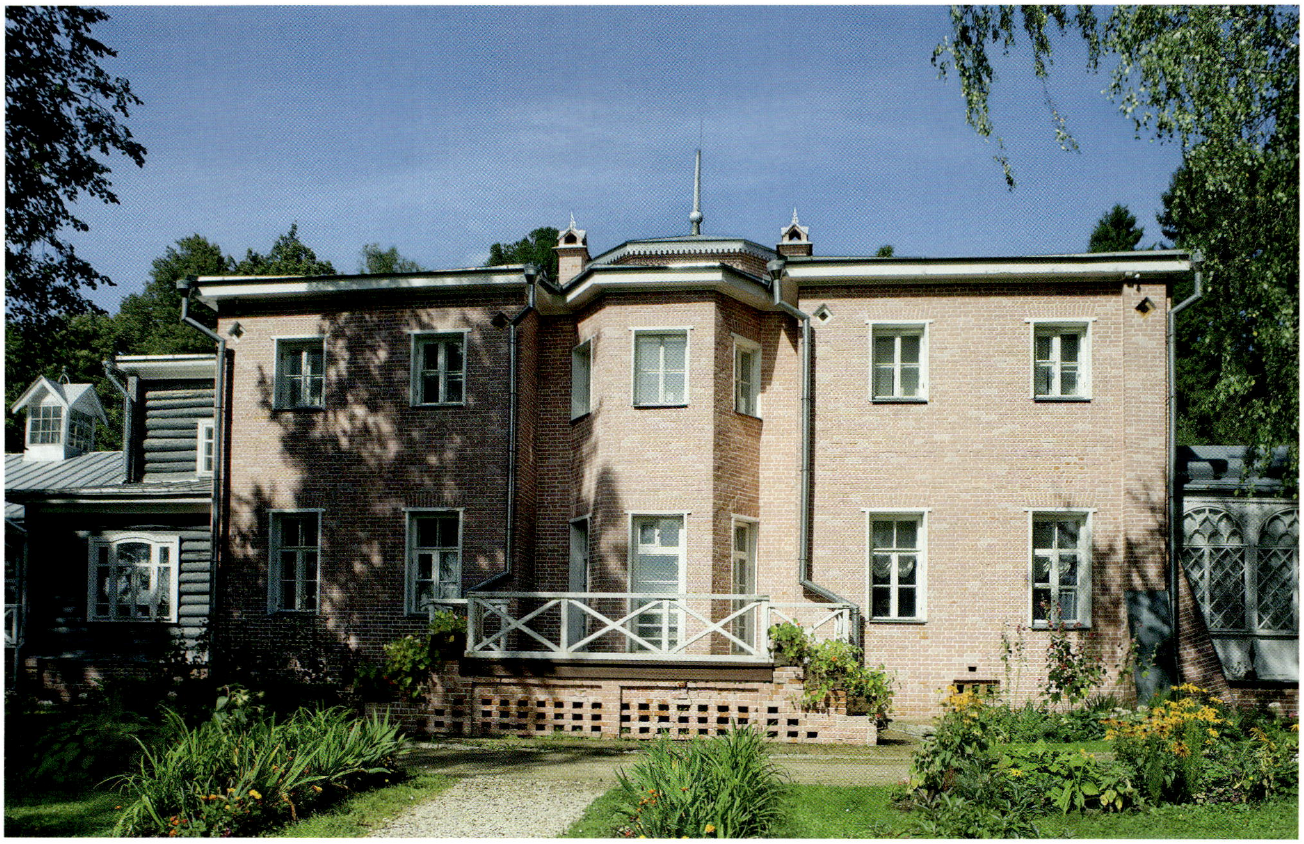

MURANOVO ESTATE. Main house, park facade. Brick facing over log structure. Partially visible on the left is a log annex extending from the primary structure. August 11, 2019.

logs of this construction are immediately visible in the entrance porch and hallway. Beyond this rustic introduction, however, the nearly twenty rooms richly exemplify Russia's nineteenth-century literary culture, suspended between the metropolis and the country estate.

The intricate literary history of the Muranovo estate began with its acquisition in 1816 by Elizaveta Engelgardt (1769–1821), wife of General Lev Engelgardt (1766–1836), who was connected at the highest levels of the Russian nobility and familiar with its early nineteenth-century cultural luster. In 1826 their daughter Anastasia (1804–60) married the poet Evgeny Baratynsky (1800–1844), a contemporary of Alexander Pushkin and one of the notable figures of the Golden Age of Russian poetry. Muranovo was considered Anastasia's dowry, and the couple, who also had a residence in Moscow, spent much time on the estate. Gifted in many practical areas and widely versed in European literature, Baratynsky undertook in 1842 to rebuild the estate house to his own design, with its Romantic literary echoes. After his sudden death in Naples in 1844, the estate was inherited by Anastasia's younger sister, Sophia (1807–84), who had married

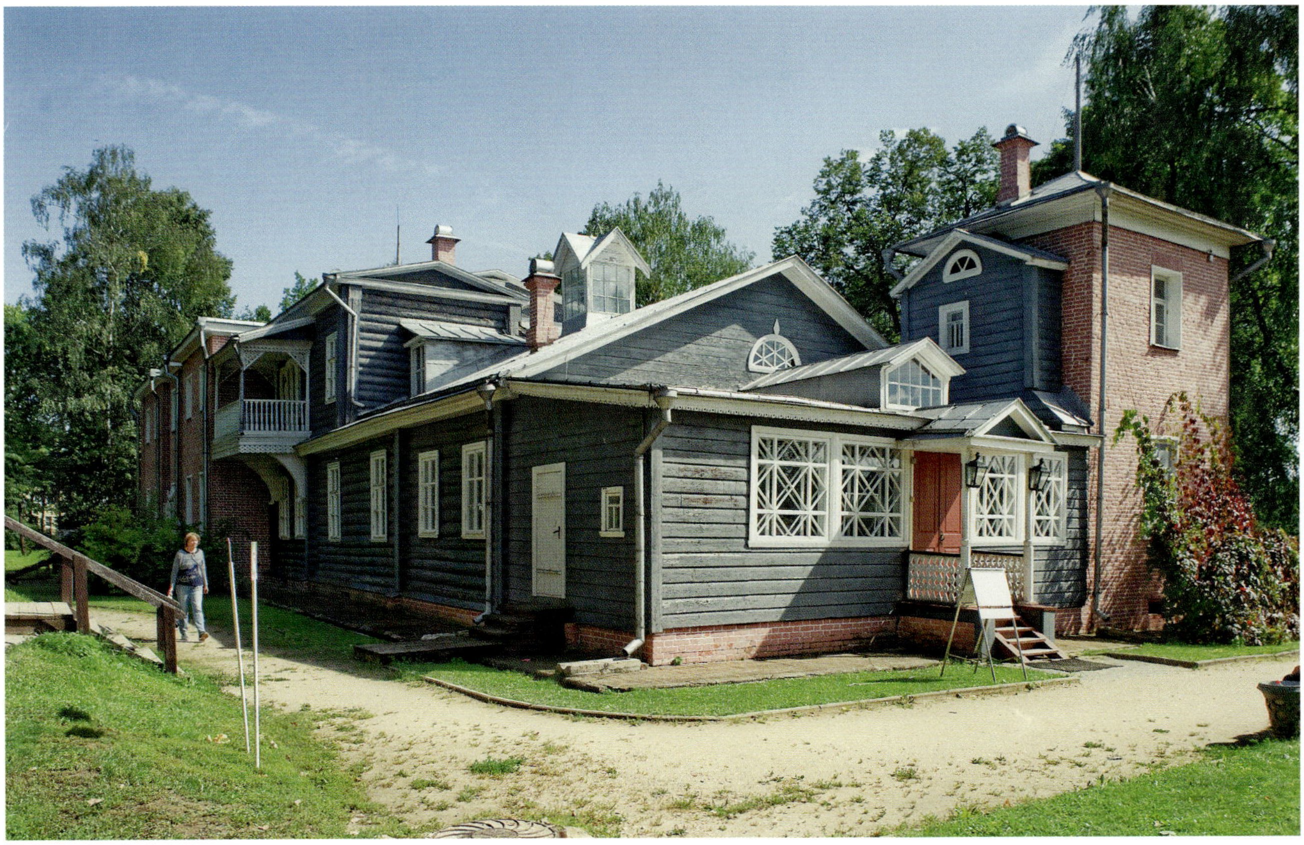

MURANOVO ESTATE. Main house, side view with log annex inserted into primary structure. August 11, 2019.

the writer Nikolay Putyata (1802–77) in 1837. In 1869, their daughter Olga Putyata (1840–1920) married Ivan Tyutchev (1848–1909), the younger son of Fyodor Tyutchev (1803–73), one of Russia's most renowned poets and a prominent conservative thinker. Having received the estate as Olga's dowry, the couple embarked on a life-long dedication to transform the house into a literary shrine, with its primary focus on the poet Fyodor Tyutchev.

Through this labyrinthine web of literary and family relations, Muranovo offers a broad insight into nineteenth-century Russian literary and ideological culture, with an orientation toward the conservative range of the political spectrum. For example, the writer Nikolay Gogol visited his friend Nikolay Putyata in August 1849 after staying with Sergey Aksakov at his estate of Abramtsevo, located only eight kilometers to the northeast. Although Gogol only spent one night, Putyata's literary passion designated that bedroom the "Gogol Room," with a strict instruction to leave everything intact and not to use the room any further. Such was the reverence accorded Russia's greatest writers. Muranovo was also closely connected

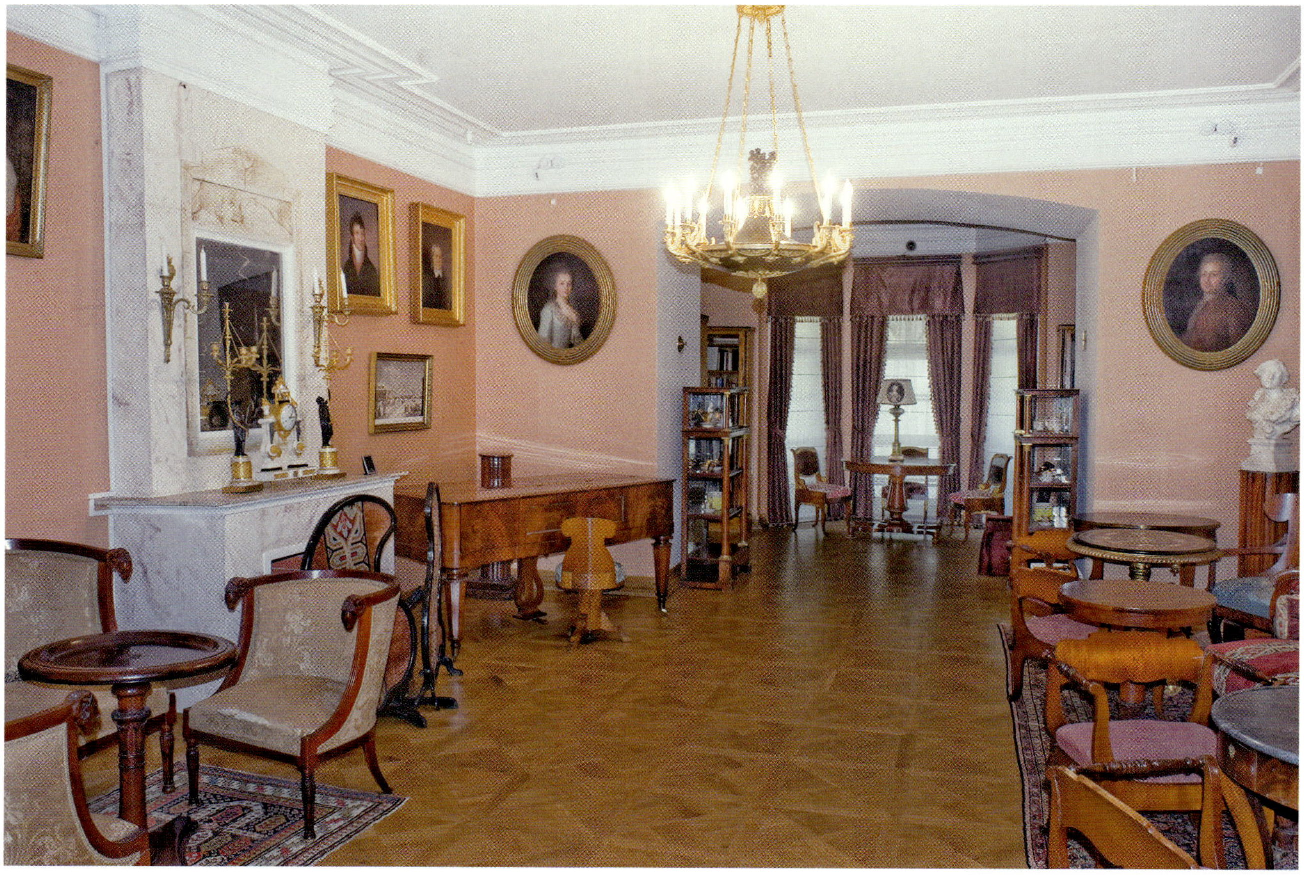

with the Aksakov family (related to the Tyutchevs by marriage), in particular Ivan Aksakov (son of Sergey Aksakov), an ardent Slavophile and proponent of independence of Slavs within the Ottoman Empire.

The primary focus on Fyodor Tyutchev arose from a combination of the poet's great renown and the fact that his son Ivan inherited many items belonging him. Indeed, the Muranovo house was able to accommodate authentic re-creations of the parlor, study, and bedroom from the poet's Saint Petersburg apartment. Following the Bolshevik Revolution, Ivan's son Nikolay Tyutchev (1876–1949) and his mother Olga (nee Putyata) decided to offer Muranovo to the state as a museum dedicated above all to Fyodor Tyutchev. Vladimir Lenin—a devotee of classic Russian literature—supported the proposal, the museum opened in 1920, and the Tyutchev family was permitted to remain on the estate in a curatorial capacity. Thus appeared one of the Soviet state's first literary museums. In 2006 a lightning strike started a fire in the house, and although response was prompt, much of the interior suffered from water damage. A two-year restoration concluded successfully in 2009, and the house museum was returned to full operation in 2015.

MURANOVO ESTATE. Main house, large living room, view toward alcove. August 11, 2019.

MURANOVO ESTATE. Children's house. August 11, 2019.

MURANOVO ESTATE. Wing (*fligel*). Early example of the Russian Revival style. Left background: kitchen building. August 11, 2019.

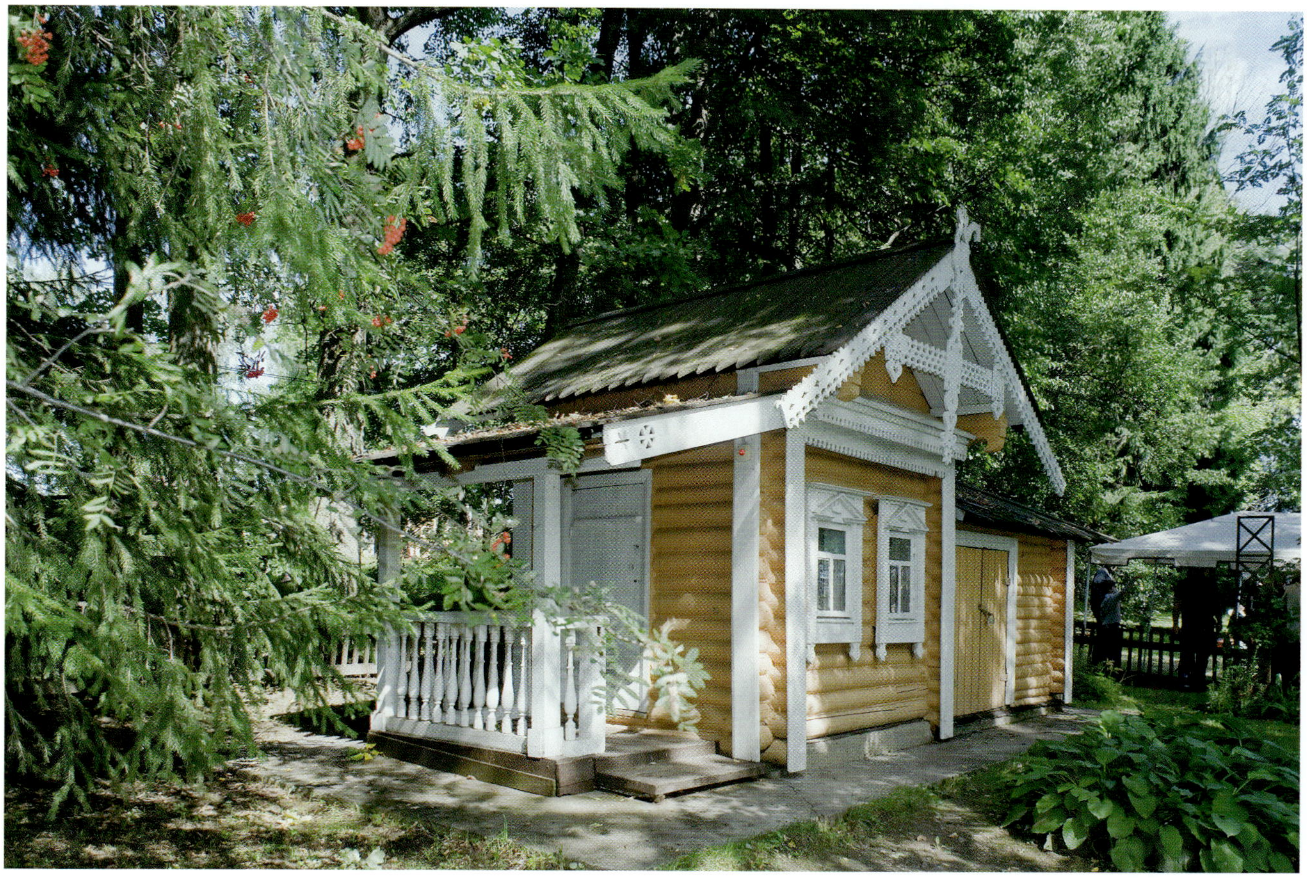

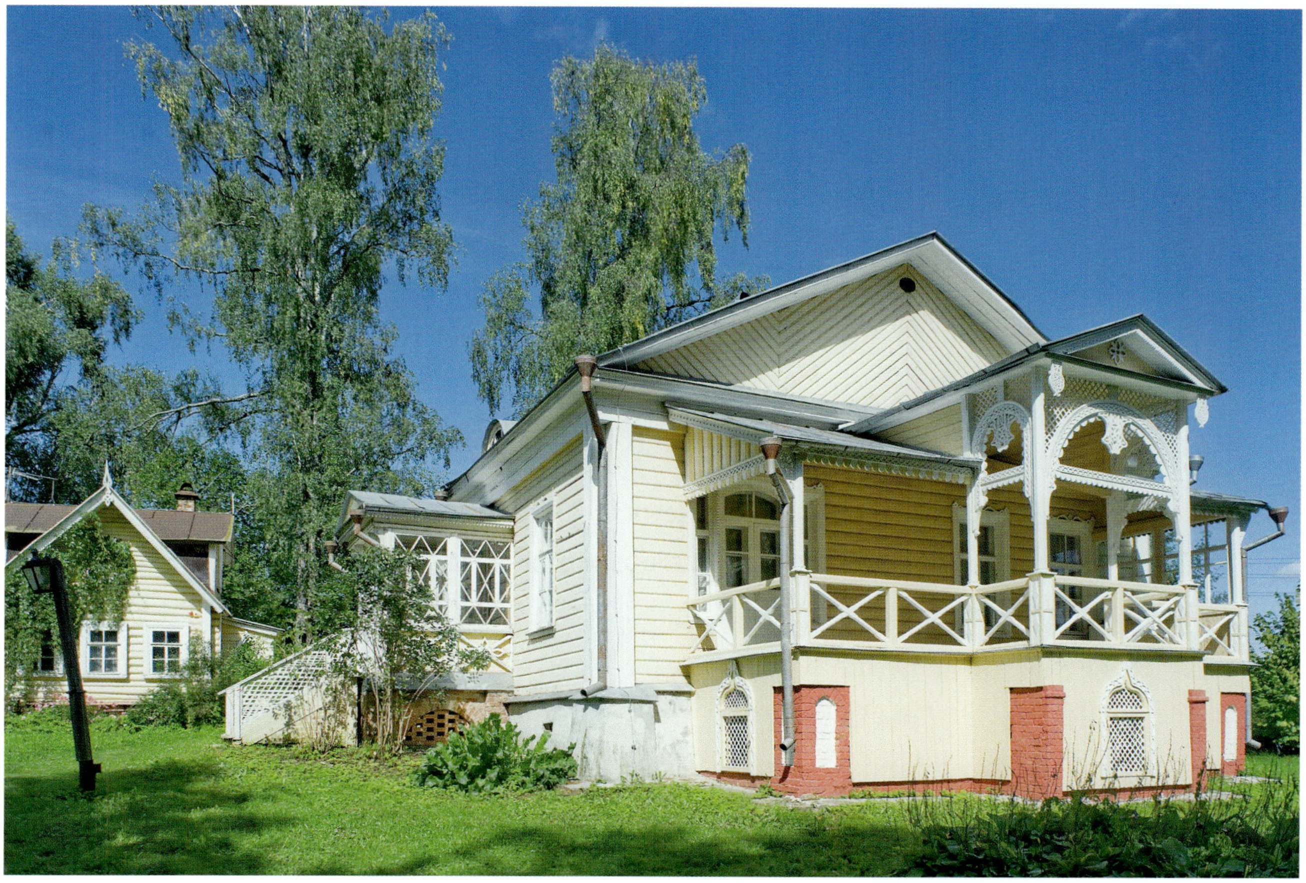

Additional structures include a delightful log cottage built in 1879 by Ivan Tyutchev for his mother Ernestine, widow of the poet Fyodor Tyutchev. Referred to variously as a dacha or "wing," the log structure was painted yellow and had plank siding over the pediments beneath the roof. Off to the left side was a separate kitchen wing built in a similar style. (For centuries, log structures could be, and often were, painted bright colors.) The estate grounds also had a log playhouse of fanciful design for the delight of extended family's children and grandchildren. Although the way of life that enabled estate culture vanished in the twentieth century, it is fitting that Muranovo, maintained by its owners as a monument to Russia's literary culture, should have survived in such comprehensive detail.

Anton Chekhov at Melikhovo

Anton Chekhov is associated with many places in Russia, from Taganrog—his birthplace and childhood home—to Moscow, where he attended medical school and matured as a writer, to Yalta where he purchased an estate in 1898 in an attempt to ameliorate the ravages of tuberculosis, from which he died in 1904. Within Chekhov's peripatetic existence, the village of Melikhovo, some seventy-five kilometers south of Moscow, became a refuge for some seven years, from 1892 to 1899. With its small wooden house and eighteenth-century log church, the Melikhovo estate not only offered Chekhov the peace to write some of his greatest works—including the plays *Seagull* and *Uncle Vanya*—but also provided an opportunity to continue his practice as a doctor for the local *zemstvo* (an organ of limited local government established in the 1860s to provide basic services such as education and health care in the provinces). This self-effacing, dedicated medical care provided Chekhov with a close view of the grinding poverty in which many local peasants lived, an experience that would enter some of his most profound stories.

The small estates around Melikhovo were owned by, among others, the Naumov family. In 1757 Andrey Naumov began a log church dedicated to the Nativity of Christ. (Most Nativity churches in Russia are dedicated to the Nativity of the Virgin Mary.) Consecrated in 1759, the church was a votive offering for the recovery of Naumov's daughter from a serious illness. Its form was a modest variant of ascending octagons over a square base. Subsequently, the population of the parish declined, resources were

MELIKHOVO ESTATE. Church of the Nativity of Christ. Originally built in 1757–59, the church burned in 1994. October 11, 1992.

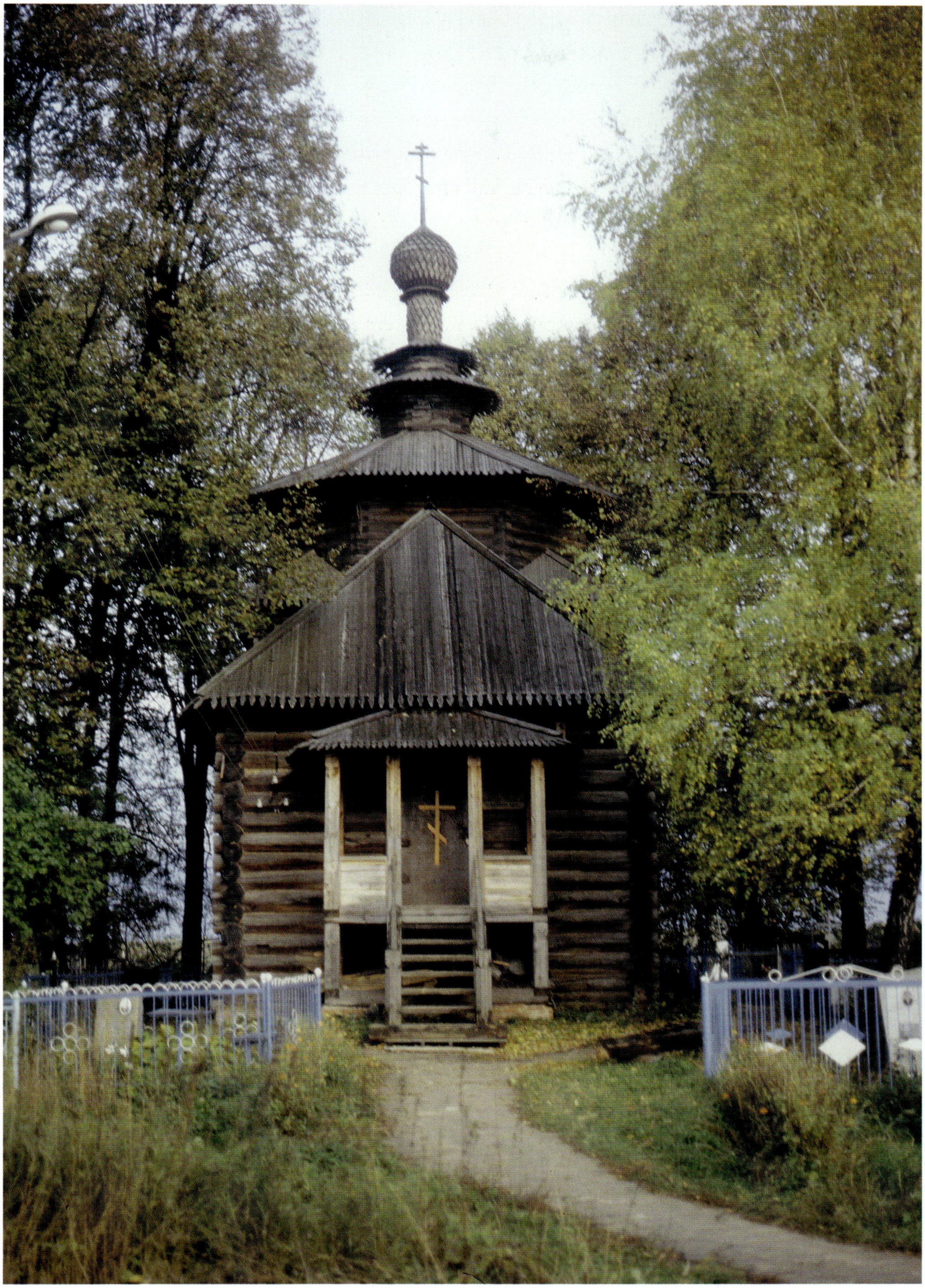

lacking to support a priest, and the church fell into disrepair. In 1834 the church and its bell tower were repaired by the Chufarovsky family, but resources were insufficient to maintain a parish. The church had again sagged, and the bell tower was dismantled when Anton Chekhov acquired the Melikhovo estate from the artist Nikolay Surokhtin in early 1892. In a letter of April 6, 1892, to his close friend and publisher Alexey Suvorin, Chekhov noted that despite the difficult conditions, funds were collected to observe Easter service, much to the satisfaction of the villagers.

Toward the end of his stay in Melikhovo, Chekhov, with the encouragement of local peasants, provided funds to repair the church and rebuild the bell tower in 1896. He was assisted in this by his father, Pavel, who had been a church choir director in Taganrog and continued to live in Melikhovo. In the 1930s, parts of the church were pilfered, but the basic structure remained intact for preservation when Melikhovo was declared a museum in 1939. Serious work on restoring the church began in the 1960s through the efforts of the artist Sergey Chekhov, the grandson of Anton Chekhov's brother Mikhail, who had frequently stayed at Melikhovo. Further efforts were undertaken in the 1980s by Yury Avdeev, who served as the director of the Chekhov Museum at Melikhovo from 1951 to 1987 and was

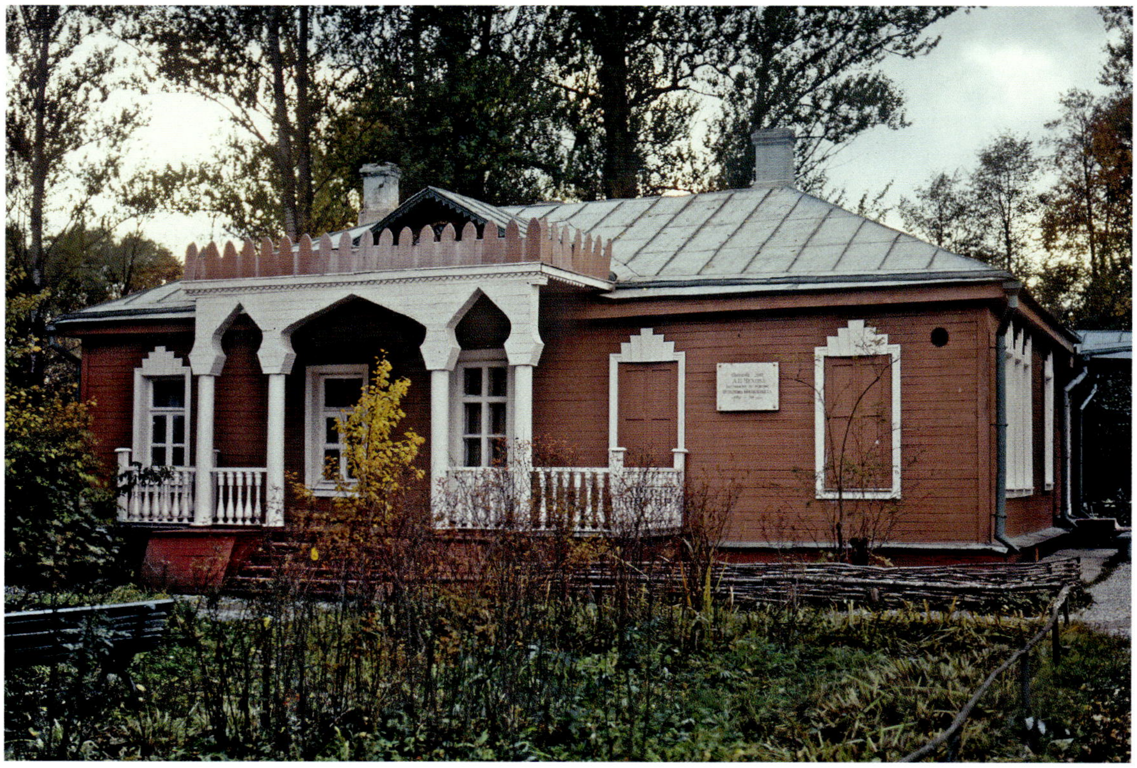

MELIKHOVO ESTATE. Main house, where Chekhov lived and received guests. October 11, 1992.

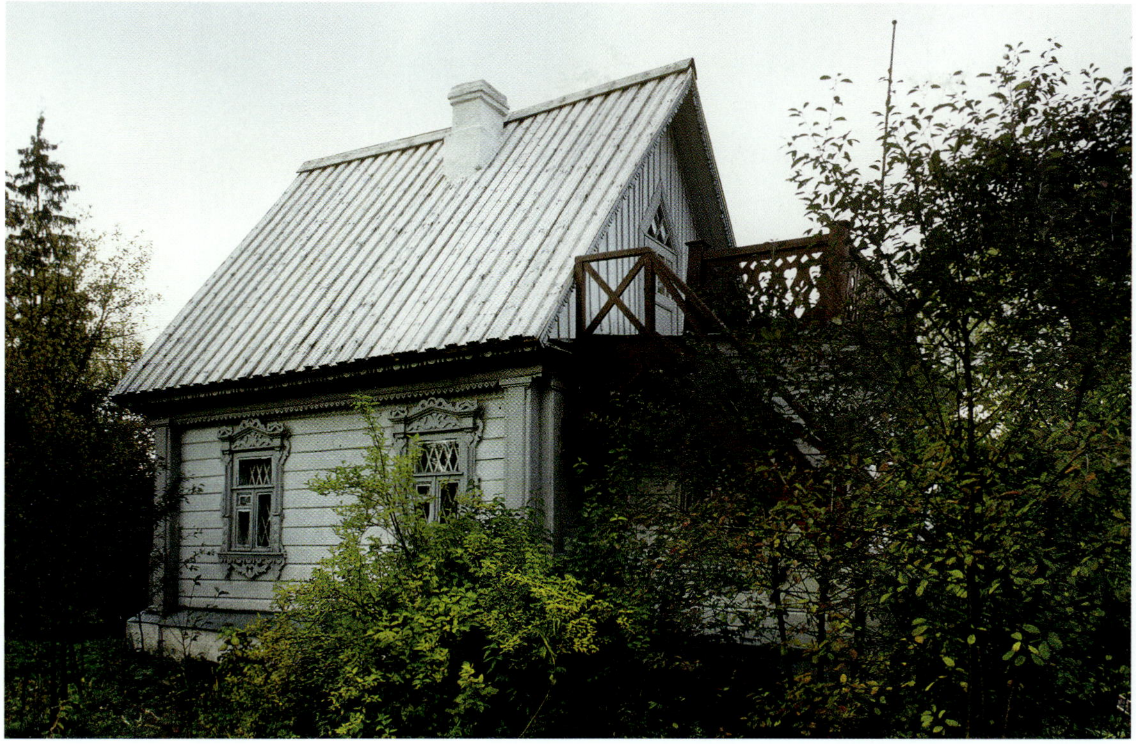

MELIKHOVO ESTATE. Summer house, where Chekhov did much of his writing. October 11, 1992.

buried at the church in June 1987. I was fortunate to be able to photograph the restored original church in October 1992. Just before Easter 1994, it was destroyed by fire, an all-too-frequent occurrence for Russia's wooden churches. Based on detailed measurements, a rebuilt Nativity of Christ Church was completed in 1999.

Other buildings associated with Anton Chekhov at the Melikhovo estate include the one-story house, dating from the 1840s with a playful pseudo-Gothic porch, and a kitchen wing built by Chekhov in 1893. Soon thereafter, a cottage, or summer house, was added originally for guests, but Chekhov himself grew enamored of the space and did much of his writing there. A marble plaque on the facade proclaims: "My house, where The Seagull was written." The design of this cottage has been attributed to Fyodor Shekhtel, Chekhov's close friend from student days and subsequently the leading architect of the *style moderne* (Russia's equivalent of art nouveau). Chekhov's letters, as well as memoirs of his brother Mikhail, show a deep affection for the Melikhovo estate, despite its occasional inconveniences. This love extended not only to the flowering garden and the surrounding nature—including the starlings in abundance—but also to the simple folk who came from surrounding villages to be treated gratis by the good doctor.

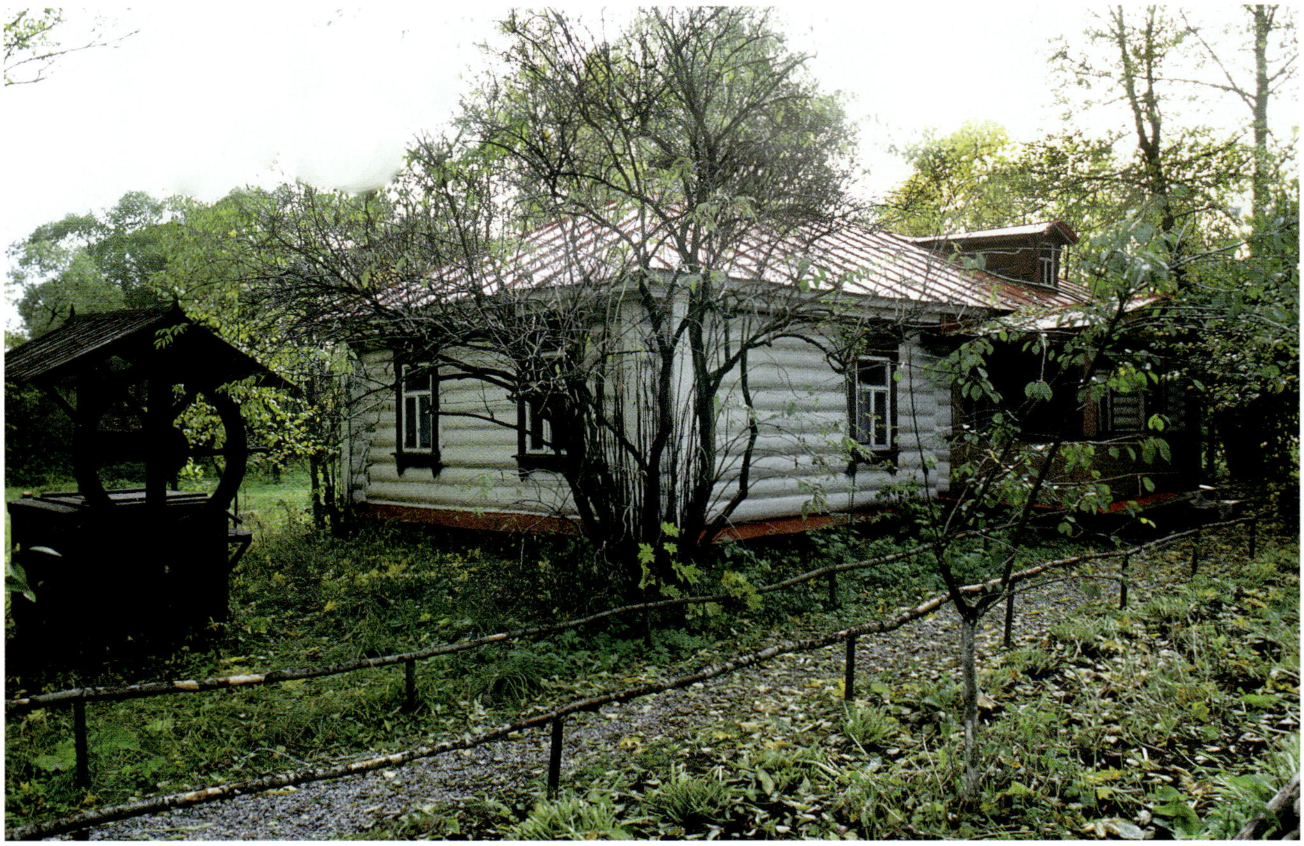

MELIKHOVO ESTATE. Kitchen wing. October 11, 1992.

Vladimir Nabokov at Rozhdestveno

In his memoirs and early stories, Vladimir Nabokov wrote with fond nostalgia of youthful summer days spent at a family estate at the village of Rozhdestveno, to the south of Saint Petersburg. The name of the village (and the estate) derived from the Church of the Nativity (*Rozhdestvo*) of the Virgin, which existed in one form or another since the early eighteenth century. In 1713 Tsar Peter I granted the village, together with a small palace and log church, to his son and heir Alexey. Five years later, Alexey would die from torture under interrogation at Peter's command. The village remained court property until 1797 when Emperor Paul I granted it to Nikolay Efremov, a highly placed official in the court administration who built the wooden neoclassical mansion that miraculously still stands. (The village was under German occupation from the early fall of 1941 until January 31, 1944.)

Rozhdestveno was always more a suburban residence than a functioning agricultural landholding. In the latter half of the nineteenth century the estate passed into the hands of various merchants until 1880, when

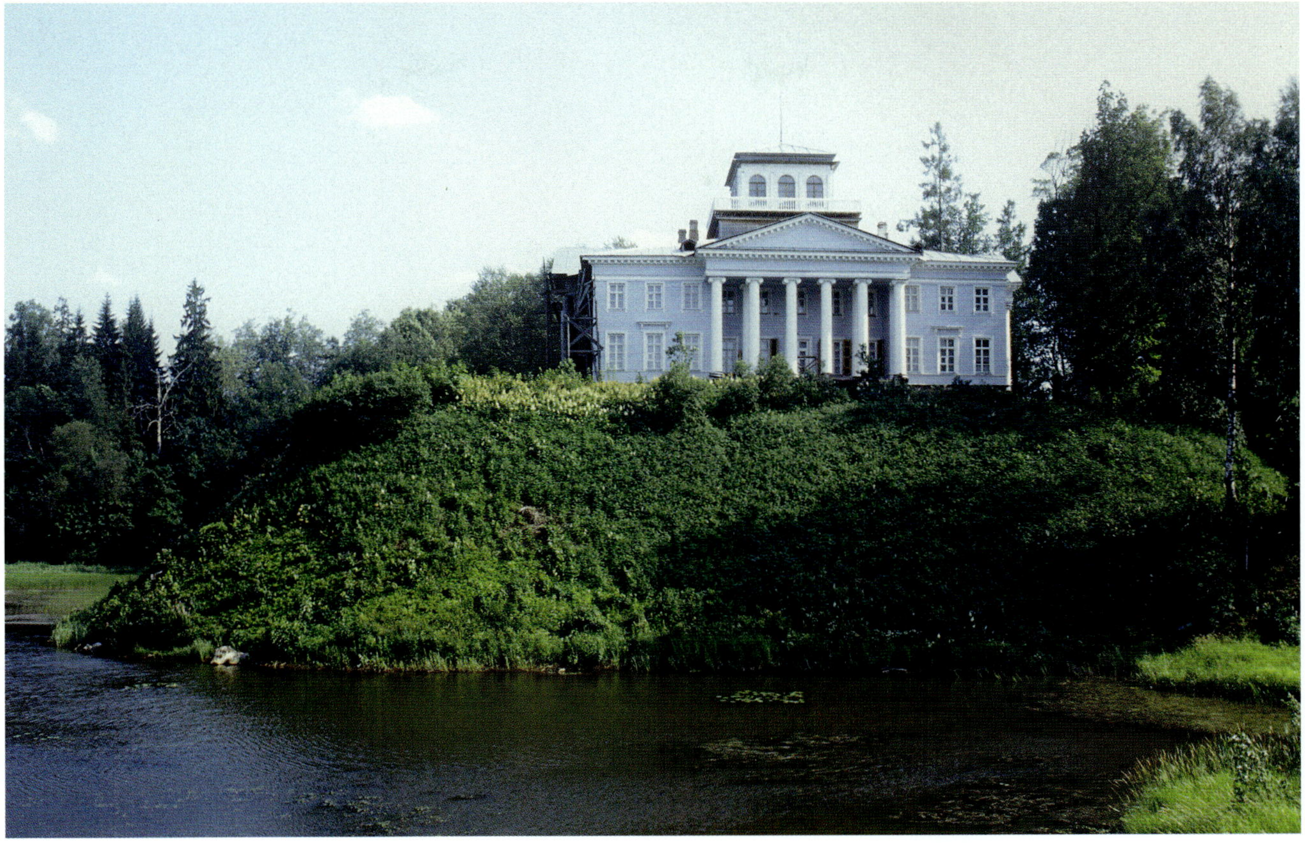

ROZHDESTVENO ESTATE. Main house. Owned by the Rukavishnikov family, the estate was inherited in 1916 by their relative and future literary titan Vladimir Nabokov. July 12, 2006.

it was acquired by Ivan Rukavishnikov (1843–1901), a wealthy mining engineer of Old Believer background who owned a substantial stake in the Lena Gold Fields. Rukavishnikov bought the estate for his son Vladimir, whose premature death at the age of sixteen in 1886 led to the founding of a local school in his memory. In 1897 his daughter, Elena (1876–1939), married the prominent lawyer Vladimir Nabokov (1869–1922), whose son Vladimir (1899–1977) would become one of the greatest writers of the twentieth century. With the elder Rukavishnikov's death in 1901, the estate was inherited by his younger son, Vasily, who never married and who planned to give his various properties to his sister Elena's three children—including the young Vladimir.

Upon Vasily Rukavishnikov's unexpected passing from angina in 1916 the Rozhdestveno estate became the property of his seventeen-year-old nephew—and the future writer—Vladimir Nabokov. A year later the estate was confiscated, and in April 1919 the Nabokov family departed Russia via Crimea as the vestiges of the old regime collapsed. In the early Soviet period, the Rozhdestveno mansion served as a dormitory for a veterinary school, and after the war it housed the village school. In 1973 the local

V. I. Lenin Kolkhoz acquired the mansion for its museum (founded in 1959), and the following year a few rooms were dedicated to an exhibit on Vladimir Nabokov's Russian years. In 1987, during perestroika, the mansion became the V. V. Nabokov Literary Memorial Museum, which it remains to this day.

One can understand the nostalgic ache that the great writer felt for Rozhdestveno, which was the source of so many pleasant, carefree memories. Emotionally and intellectually, Vasily Rukavishnikov was his closest relation on his mother's side and became something of a mentor to the young Vladimir. The estate house itself seems to have been calculated to summon reveries of an idyllic past, not only through its elegant neoclassical design but also in its picturesque location on a high bluff overlooking the small Gryazna River near its confluence with the Oredezh River. That shimmering image is "such stuff that dreams are made on."

Alexander Blok at Shakhmatovo

In a century filled with drama and tragedy for Russia's poets, the life of Alexander Blok was among the most turbulent. Born into a life of privilege, Blok embraced the Bolshevik Revolution with ecstatic fervor only to collapse in exhaustion, illness, and despair at the age of forty in August 1921. As will be seen below, 1921 would also prove a fateful year for the Moscow area estate of Shakhmatovo, where the Blok family spent their summers away from the heat and fetor of Saint Petersburg. The first reference to Shakhmatovo—whose name possibly derives from the name of a Tatar prince, Shah-Ahmad—occurs in mid-seventeenth-century administrative documents, which link the estate to the princely Obolensky family. Over the next two centuries, it passed through various hands until 1874, when it was acquired by Andrey Beketov, a distinguished botanist, rector of Saint Petersburg University, and the grandfather of Alexandre Blok. The estate had been recommended by a colleague and soon-to-be neighbor, the world-renowned chemist Dmitry Mendeleev, who lived at the nearby estate of Boblovo. The wooden manor house at Shakhmatovo dated from the early nineteenth century and represents a typical one-story dwelling crowned by a *mezonin* with an Italianate window.

In 1879, one of Andrey Beketov's three daughters, Alexandra (1860–1923), married Alexander Blok, a noted law professor at Warsaw University, and the following year their son Alexander (1880–1921) was born. Shortly thereafter, she broke off relations with her husband—purportedly because of his difficult, jealous character—but the Holy Synod (the main governing body of the Russian Orthodox Church) did not grant an annulment until 1889, at which point she remarried. Alexandra first brought the infant Alexander to Shakhmatovo in the late spring of 1881, when he was six months old. For decades, the extended Beketov-Blok family would come regularly to Shakhmatovo for stays between May and September. In contrast with Warsaw (associated with his father) and Saint Petersburg, Shakhmatovo represented for Blok all the wonder and freshness of Russian nature. Indeed, he and his friends carefully studied the natural surroundings, which have been preserved with special care for their relationship to Blok's youth and his literary work. Until the age of three, he, his mother, and nanny would stay in a small log annex (*fligel*) to the main house. In the summer of 1898, he met Lyubov Mendeleeva, daughter of Dmitry Mendeleev, and thus began a tempestuous relationship that led to their marriage in a nearby

SHAKHMATOVO ESTATE. Main house (reconstructed). July 8, 2010.

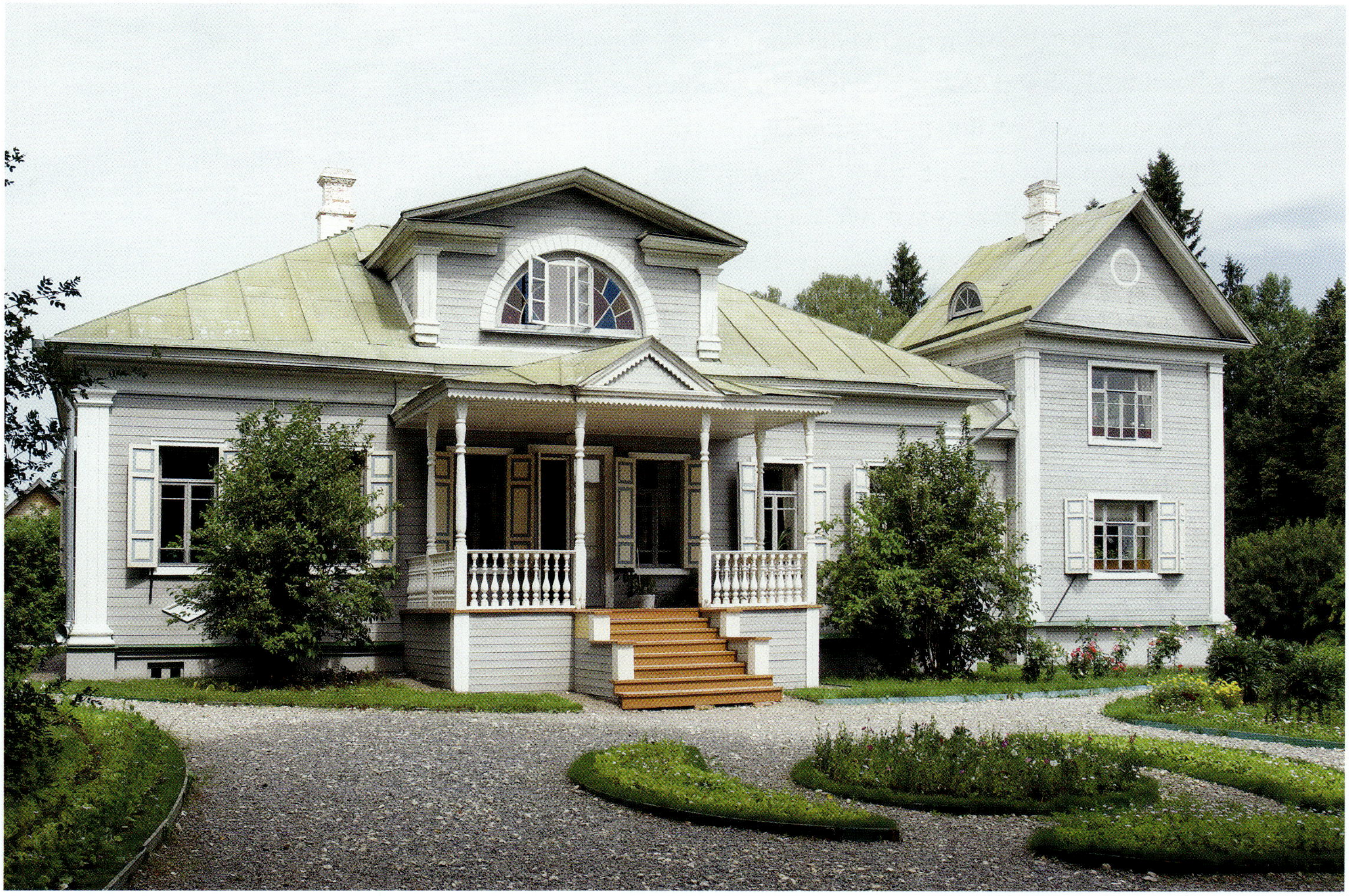

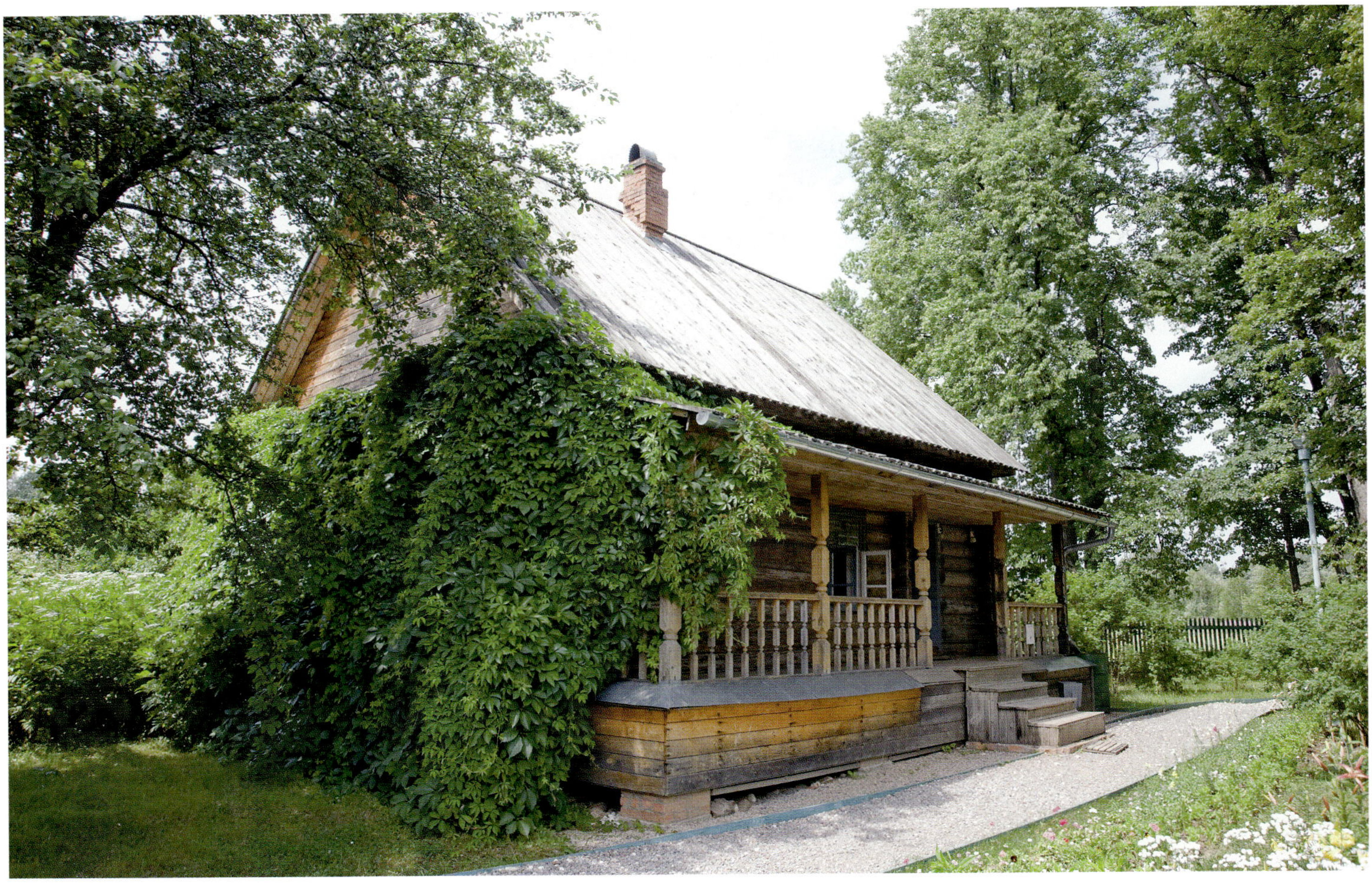

SHAKHMATOVO ESTATE. Wing (*fligel*) (reconstructed). July 8, 2010.

country church in the summer of 1903. The newlyweds spent the rest of the summer in the log house that was so familiar to Blok.

From 1898 to 1906 Blok was a student at Saint Petersburg University, and he continued to spend much of the summers at Shakhmatovo, but their duration decreased as Blok became more involved in a flourishing literary career and in travels abroad. His last, brief visit occurred in July 1916, when he saw his mother before enlisting in the army. The summer of 1918 was the final stay of Blok's mother at the estate. Thereafter, word filtered back that the house was being pilfered by peasants from surrounding villages, but Blok, who began as an ardent supporter of the revolution, seemed resigned to the destruction of the estate. His health steadily worsened from overwork, poor conditions, and an inability to go abroad for proper medical care. In a Russia wracked by chaos, famine, and violence, Blok died from endocarditis in August 1921. At approximately the same time, the estate house was destroyed by a fire whose origins remain undetermined.

Soon after the stabilization of the new Soviet regime, efforts began to recover the legacy of Shakhmatovo by devotees of the work of Alexander Blok, widely acknowledged as one of Russia's greatest poets. An invaluable source of information was his aunt, Maria Beketova, who in the 1920s and 1930s published several works based on her memories of the estate. To commemorate the centennial of this birth in November 1980, a memorial museum was established at the Saint Petersburg apartment where he lived from 1912 to 1921. During the same period, work began in 1976 on a thorough investigation of the Shakhmatovo grounds, and in 1984 the territory was declared a national preserve. In the 1990s, work continued on restoring the grounds along with the annex. Based on photographs, sketches, and archeological excavations, the main house was rebuilt of wood in 2001 to resemble the appearance of the house in 1910, with its attached two-story tower after Blok had made modifications. Several of the room reconstructions are related to family members and contain items that originally belonged to Blok and his relatives. Although the Shakhmatovo Museum is a reconstruction—like the rebuilding of the three estate houses associated with Alexander Pushkin in the Mikhailovskoe area—it demonstrates Russia's striving to re-create wooden structures of exceptional cultural significance.

PART II Where the Folk Live

FROM FOREST TO STEPPE

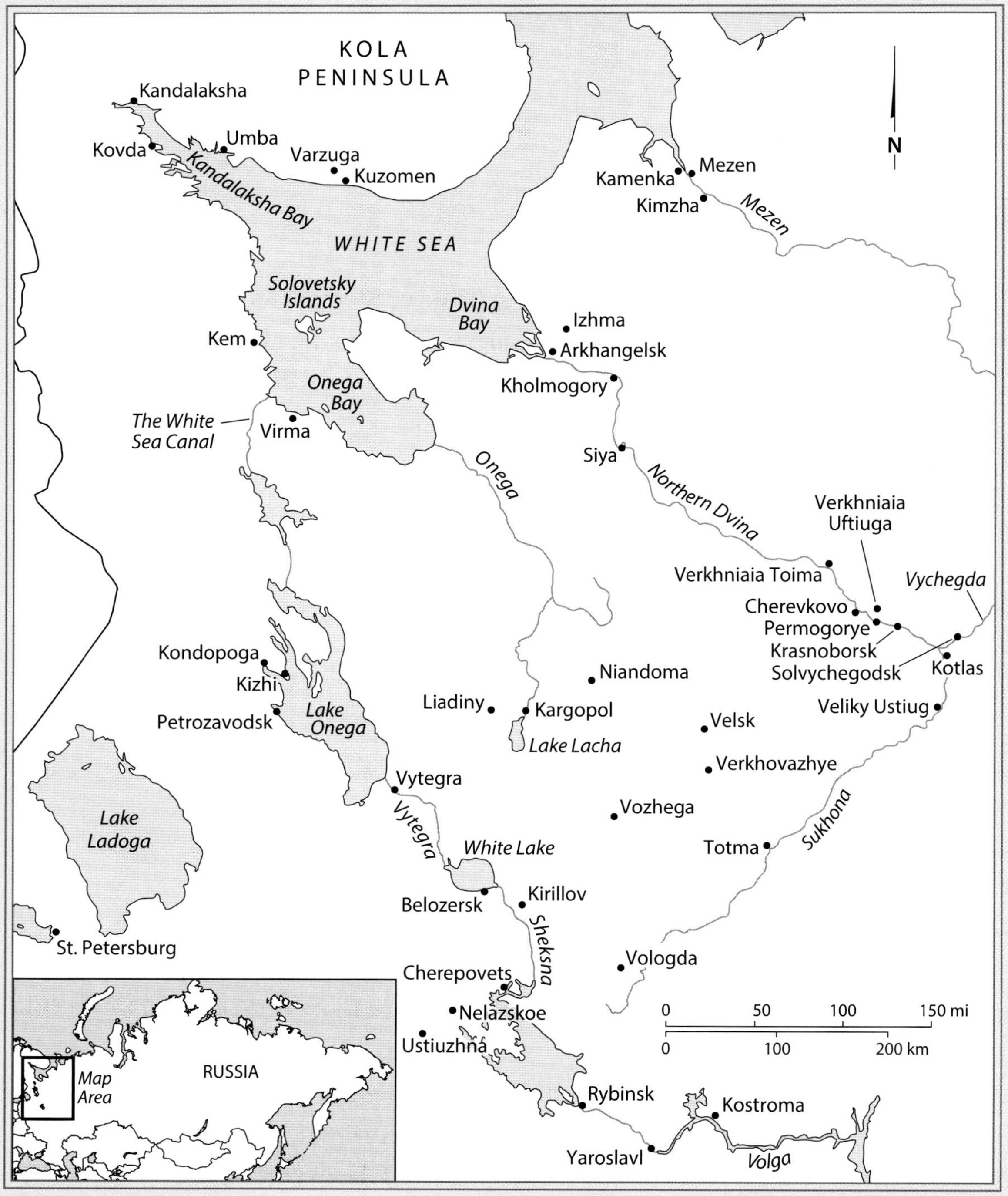

The Russian North.

CHAPTER THREE

The Russian North
Toward the White Sea

The variety and beauty of Russian log churches should not obscure the main purpose of wooden architecture, which was to provide housing. Although log houses were often humble affairs and even in the best cases would not have rivaled the distinctive form of the church, they, too, demonstrated artistry of design as well as economy of function. Although there are sporadic examples of eighteenth-century wooden structures still standing in cities such as Vologda, it is difficult to find wooden houses in Russia that can be verifiably dated before the mid-nineteenth century, particularly in Russian villages. It was accepted practice for log houses to be replaced frequently, not to mention the periodic purging of Russian towns and villages by catastrophic fires. Russian specialists have researched the possible forms of medieval Russian log dwellings, but I will not speculate on their appearance. The nineteenth- and early twentieth-century examples of log dwellings (including the *izba*) that I have photographed are entirely sufficient. Earlier characteristics, such as the absence of glazed windows or wooden floors, can be extrapolated, yet nineteenth-century developments visible in surviving examples of log houses (for example, the extensive use of milled lumber) offer a reflection of Russian habitat at a time of profound social and economic change.

Much will be shown of the variety and construction details of log buildings in the following chapters, but a few elementary principles suffice for the introduction. The range of structures is a remarkable demonstration of the properties of wood, from the simplest four-walled peasant *izba* to the massive log "fortress" houses of the far north (which sheltered extended families as well as livestock and forage), large urban multifamily dwellings, and even summer palaces. The main material for the basic structure was pine with its rich resin contents, but other conifers—particularly fir and larch (the hardest)—also played an important part in the building of log walls. Oak, long-lived and resistant to decay, could be used for support posts or foundation pilings but was less readily available than pine. Linden could be used for bathhouses (soft and pleasant smell) and barns (resistant to rodents) but was much less durable than pine. Birch was used for certain roof details that required a thinner, more flexible material. Aspen, a softer variety, was used for shingle roofs and other details requiring a smaller scale. Other varieties, such as maple, could be used for interior work (doors, furnishings in more elaborate houses).

Whatever the form, the methods of construction demanded a careful series of steps. The logs were cut in late fall or early winter after the final ring of the tree had hardened and when sap flow was minimal, thus reducing the possibility of moisture-induced cracking or decay. The felled timber was left to cure until the beginning of building season in the spring—typically after Lent. Logs were then trimmed, notched, and, if necessary, squared. The most common tools were the ax (of which there were various types adapted to specific functions) and the adze as well as wedged spikes for splitting logs and a primitive type of spokeshave, or drawing knife, for making concave incisions along a log. There was little use for saws, which would have opened the grain of the wood to moisture, as opposed to the proper stroke of the ax, which closed the grain. With long experience and deep traditions, Russians developed remarkable facility with the ax, which could be used to shape, as well as cut, timber. As a result, Russian log structures rarely used clay caulking but relied instead on the tight fit of one log above another. Round logs typically had a concave incision along the length of the log placed downward for a tighter fit with the log beneath. Materials such as moss or hemp were traditionally placed between the logs for insulation. Structures of squared logs were commonly joined with a dovetail notch that allowed greater precision. Churches frequently combined rounded logs for the main structure and squared logs for the apse containing the altar.

Nails were also traditionally dispensed with, not so much because they opened the wood to moisture and decay, but because iron was simply too valuable to spend on nails. The primary, indispensable use of iron was for the ax head, which was put to many uses in shaping the log. No iron was ever discarded. If an implement was irreparably deformed, the iron could always be salvaged and recast.

Nails were unnecessary even in the roof, whose planks—often double-layered—were laid next to each other with a groove fit and wedged at the top into a ridge beam. The logs just beneath the roof were extended in length to support an overhang for protection against moisture runoff. This flare (*poval*) is one of the most graceful details of Russian wooden architecture and is completely functional. The tips of the roof planks could be articulated with carved tips, which in sunlight cast a bold pattern of shadows against the texture of the log walls.

Despite a relatively small number of basic configurations, the variety of these dwellings offers a reflection of landscape, environment, and climate. The log house made survival possible in the most unforgiving of natural circumstances, and their decoration, illustrated in the photographs, not only satisfied a desire for beauty and status but also was intended to summon positive energy (the sun) while repelling hostile spirits.

The center of the peasant log house—whatever its size—was the large masonry stove used both for cooking and for heating the main living space during the long winters. The stove could be ventilated in two ways that define the basic types of peasant house: the "white" and the "black." In the former the smoke was released through a brick chimney, while in the latter the smoke drifted up toward the ceiling and along a wooden duct that collected the smoke and expelled it. This black variant was common even for large houses; and due to the ingenuity of the design, the smoke did not foul the entire living space, but only an area under the roof that could be scraped down.

The house typically formed the main component of an enclosed yard (*dvor*). In the more severe climate of the far north, these units were combined into a single, self-sufficient structure with three basic configurations: a long rectangular structure (known in Russian as *brus*) with the living quarters on one side and barn space for storage and livestock extended on the longer side; a rectangular structure with the barn attached to the side and extending back at a right angle (*glagol*); and, the most complex, a two story structure with the living quarters in front and the barn in back under a greatly extended roof (*koshel*).

Whether large or small, log houses were traditionally decorated with window surrounds and end boards that were carved or sawn in intricate designs. In the eighteenth and nineteenth centuries, patterns derived from folk motifs became particularly elaborate. During the same period, carpenters began to adapt urban architectural motifs, such as baroque window surrounds, that they observed during seasonal work in the cities or at the country dachas of city residents. These window surrounds, with their fretwork ornamentation often painted, have become a most visible expression of the Russian spirit in towns and villages. The object of various folk symbolic interpretations (icon frames, expressions of the "soul of the house"), the window decorations are usually painted in bright colors that contrast with the darkened, aged walls of the logs or the faded plank siding. Indeed, brightly painted surrounds are one of the most reliable indicators that the house is still inhabited and in reasonably energetic hands.

For large northern towns such as Vologda, wooden houses were the majority into the twentieth century. With the spread of sawmills, the log walls of these houses were frequently covered in plank siding, which provided opportunities for still more elaborate designs. Vernacular architecture thus served as a showcase for artisanal skills that reflected the owner's prosperity and link with Russian peasant traditions. The log house, as noted earlier, became a symbol of national identity in the nineteenth century.

The Sacred Ascent

The oldest surviving examples of Russian wooden architecture are churches, which could last three to four centuries, assuming that decayed logs were promptly replaced (a common procedure) and the roof maintained. Fire and the inevitable process of decay have, nonetheless, long since destroyed the work of early medieval Russian carpenters. Little has been preserved from before the eighteenth century, and attributions of log churches to the fifteenth and sixteenth centuries are rare. Nonetheless, much commentary on the characteristics of early Russian wooden architecture has proceeded on the assumption that such traditional forms were inherently conservative and can be inferred from surviving log buildings of a later period.

The simplest type of wooden church resembles the basic unit of the peasant house, with its pitched roof and rectangular "cell." The plan is linear, along an east-west axis, with one unit for the service and another, the *trapeza*, as a form of vestibule. Such churches often have two additional units: an apse containing the altar on the east and a bell tower attached to the vestibule on the west. The more elaborate churches of this type, like the larger peasant houses, were decorated with carved end boards (*prichelina*) protecting the roof beams and with carved galleries on raised porches. The variations on this form are many. Some examples display multiple gables with extensive carving and high-pitched roofs.

The vertical line is much more emphatic in a type of wooden church known as the "tent" (from the Russian word *shatior*), so named for the shape of its central tower. This type has a centralized plan consisting of a cuboid core that supports an ascending eight-sided tower. More complex variants display a cruciform plan with flanking domes. Often the core projected a gallery on three sides, raised above the highest snow drifts on a system of extended logs (*pomochi*). Details such as the gallery remind how closely aesthetics and function were combined in log churches.

The disfavor directed toward the tent tower by the church hierarchy in the late seventeenth century resulted in a waning of that design. Yet the Russian love of verticality in church design found expression in a third type of log church, the tiered (*yarusnyi*) structure, in which a pyramidal silhouette ascends in a series of diminishing octahedrons over the main part of the building. The vertical design of this church is accented by decorative barrel-shaped gables over the arms of the cruciform plan and repeated in smaller forms above the octahedrons. In the tiered form, as in most of the other types surveyed above, there were two basic methods of joining the pine logs: the notch (*oblo s ostatkom*) for round logs, and the mortised dovetail (*v lapu*) for both round and squared logs. As noted above, the dovetail joint was used when greater precision of detail and stability were required.

If the church culminated in a tent tower, the base of the tower would be surrounded by an overhang at a much lower angle (*politsa*). Such towers were usually planked, but in some instances they were covered with carved shingles, as were the cupolas. These shingles (*lemekhi* or *cheshui*, "fish scales"), among the most ingenious features of Russian wooden architecture, were curved and wedged to follow the contours of the wooden frame underneath. Typically, the shingles were carved from moist aspen, which ages from a golden hue to silver and forms a brilliant contrast to the dark walls of aged pine logs. The soaring vertical superstructure provided a system of ventilation to preserve the structure from rot. Yet the superstructure of tall wooden churches was not usually visible from the interior, which was capped at a low level by a painted ceiling, or "sky" (*nebo*), that prevented heat loss over the central part of the church.

It was not uncommon in Russian settlements to have paired churches at a venerated site called a *pogost*. In early medieval Russia, the term "pogost" referred to territorial centers surrounded by numerous hamlets that could be used to receive dignitaries, or guests, making official rounds in a largely rural country. This practice was applied particularly in the vast regions controlled by the major commercial center of Novgorod the Great. Through a natural social logic, these sites were soon graced with a church ensemble and cemetery. With the spread of serfdom in Russia, the country estate and its villages became a basic administrative unit. In the Russian North, however, serfdom and landed estates were largely absent, and the *pogost* retained its territorial status until 1775, with a limited role thereafter until the Soviet period. Ultimately, the term *pogost* came to be understood as the church ensemble and cemetery that arose at such centers. The *pogost* often had a large church for summer worship and a smaller one (more easily heated) for the winter. The churches were not built simultaneously; the ensemble evolved as parish means permitted, but the concept was always present. The final element of the *pogost* ensemble was a freestanding bell tower between and in front of the two churches. The *pogost* could be enclosed by a low wall of horizontal logs on a base of fieldstone, with square towers at the corners. The supreme example of the *pogost*—and of the genius of Russian wooden architecture—is on Kizhi Island in the northwest part of Lake Onega.

The achievements of Russian master carpenters can be seen both as a highly developed, specific response to a demanding physical and geographical environment and as an expression of values that can also be traced in Russian masonry architecture: the striving for verticality in church architecture, with its symbolic relation to God; the fondness for elaborate ornamentation; and a plasticity of structural form. The rigors of the far northern climate produced a shelter environment that excluded or reduced light—even in the precious and limited time when the sun was visible. The windows were small, and interior lamps—where they existed—were dim. Even more necessary and comprehensible was the urge to create vivid, towering forms of churches that would catch and reflect the light, whether from the blinding sun of a short winter day or a long summer evening. Such forms reaffirmed the survival of the community and sustained the spirit of those who sought refuge in the northern forests.

The Kola Peninsula

From a strictly geographical perspective, all of Russia seems north. Even the country's Black Sea coast at Sochi is on approximately the same latitude as Toronto. Yet when the Russians speak of the "North," they are usually referring to a historically rich territory of diverse ecology centered on the White Sea. The sea is the ultimate defining element in the culture and geography of this area, and the maritime focus is particularly evident on the Kola Peninsula (contemporary Murmansk Province), whose severe climate is modulated by sea currents that flow past the Arctic North Cape. The peninsula's northern shore is washed by the Barents Sea of the Arctic Ocean, while the south shore forms the upper (northwestern) boundary of the White Sea, a place of desolate beauty and the location of one of the most stunning log structures in Russia—the late seventeenth-century Dormition Church at Varzuga.

The way to Varzuga begins at the nondescript rail station at Kandalaksha, an important stop on the rail line to Murmansk. The asphalt road east leads 109 kilometers to the small town of Umba (population 5,500), which serves as the administrative center of the Tersky region and is located on the rapid Umba River, emptying into Kandalaksha Bay. The earliest written mention of Umba dates to 1466, and for centuries the settlement formed part of a network of villages belonging to the great Transfiguration Monastery on the Solovetsky Archipelago in the southwestern part of the White Sea. Contemporary Umba is a Soviet creation, yet the town still has a district with wooden houses and a small museum with the recreated interior of a local *izba*. Attempts to restore the wooden Church of the Resurrection on the left bank of the Umba River were halted when the parish preferred to meet in a modest structure more centrally located on the right bank.

Beyond Umba, the small, paved road becomes a dirt road all the way to Varzuga, some 135 kilometers to the east. Because there was no scheduled daily transportation, a colleague from Arkhangelsk and I stopped by the mayor's office, had a good chat, and he told us where to stand on the road to flag down a car going to Varzuga. The local police car accompanied us to add some authority to our request, but nobody came by. We asked the official car to take us to both parts of the village on either side of the Umba and then tried again in the late afternoon. After an hour or so, a car with a small open trailer finally appeared, stopped, and to our great

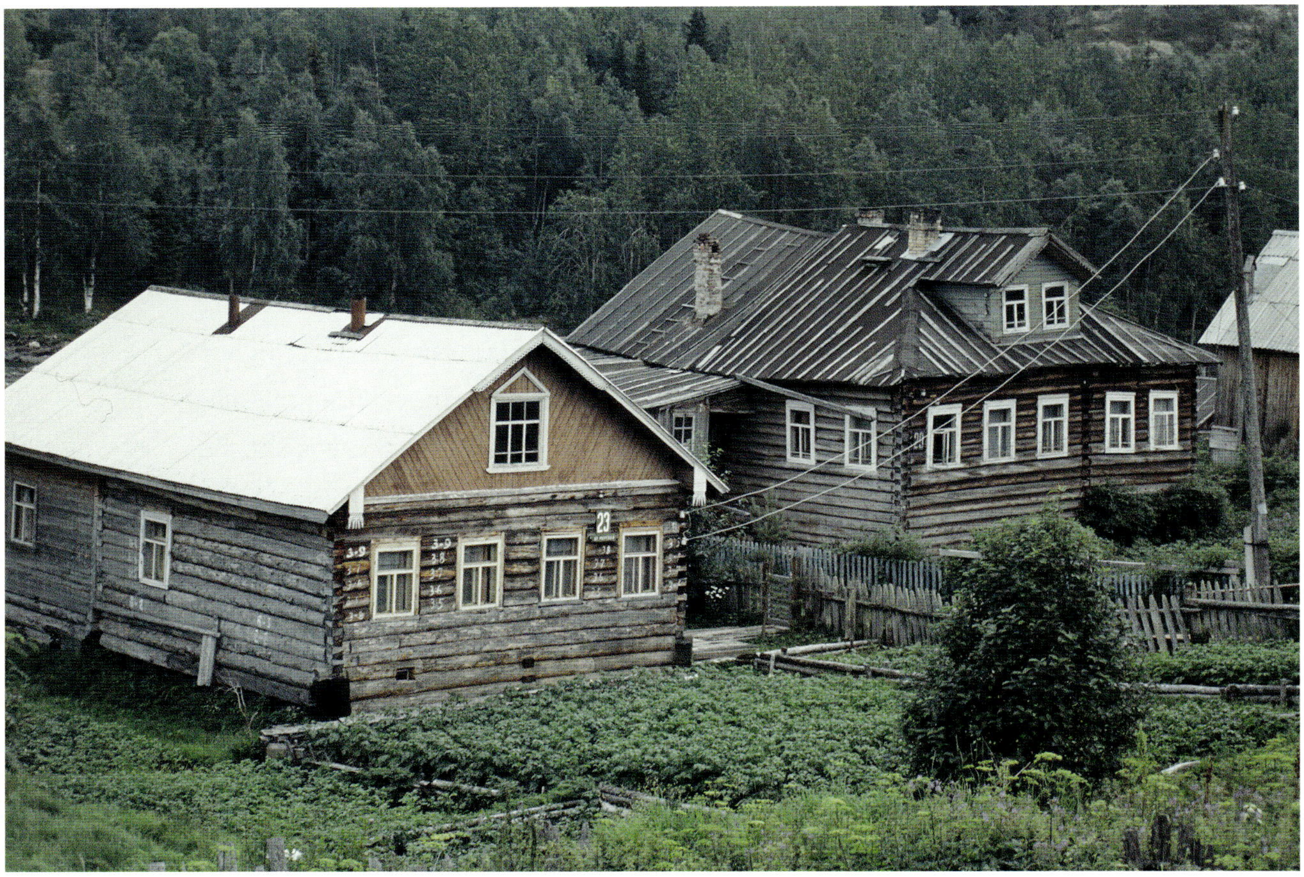

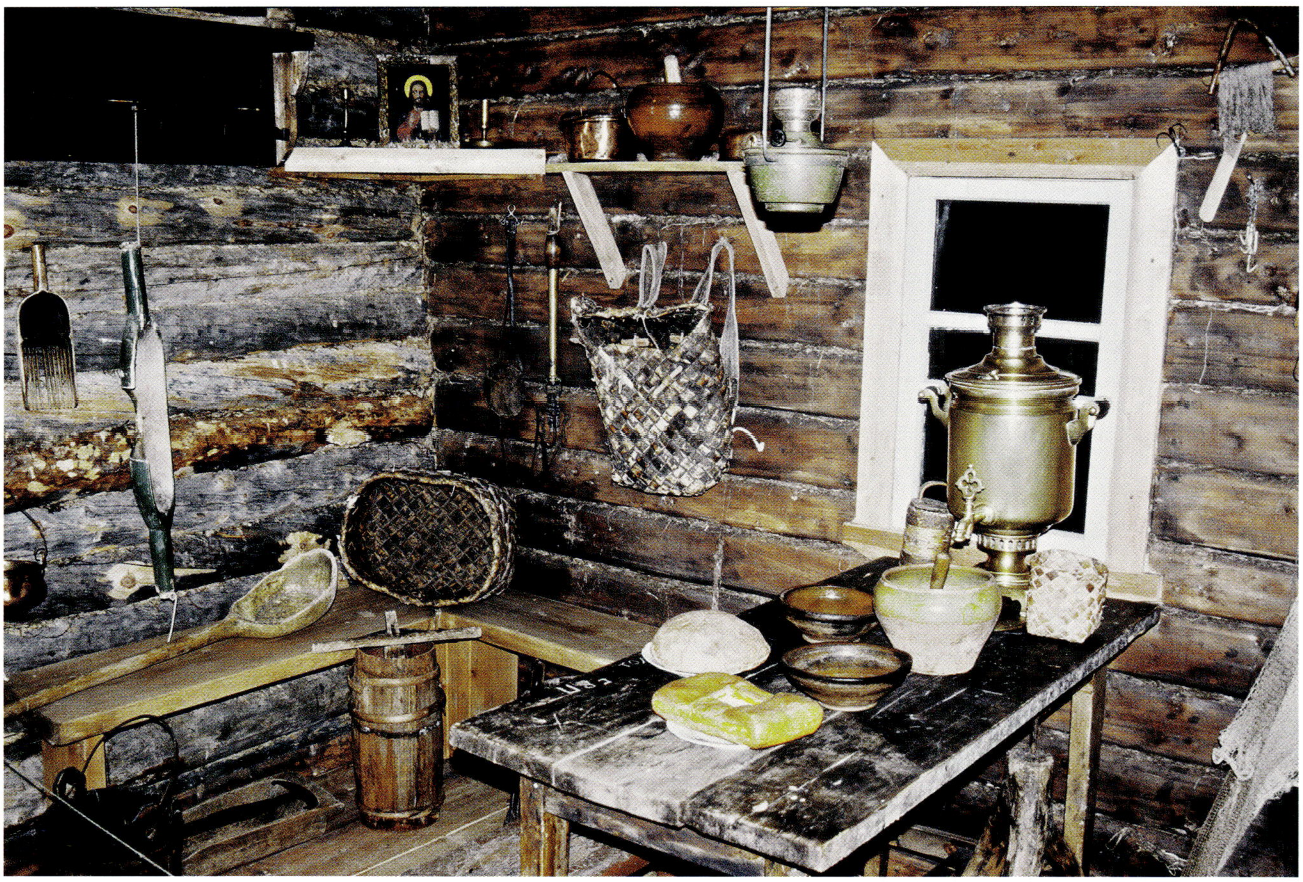

relief said that they were going to Varzuga. The driver and his wife were returning from a shopping trip over the nearby border with Finland, and among their purchases were crates of fresh vegetables, including large cucumbers. How odd, I thought, for them to import that quintessential Russian staple until I understood that the prosperity of the fishing center at Varzuga pushed vegetable gardens to the side for those who were too busy and had ample money to spend on the deluxe Finnish product. The car flew over the hard packed clay and sand road, and by late evening we arrived just at the richest light of the long northern sunset. The great log tower of the Dormition Church sprang into view, and my foot was out the door before the car had stopped. Unbounded, delirious joy!

UMBA. Standard Soviet-era log houses, Morskaya Street 23, 29. House on left has numbered logs, indicating that it was disassembled and moved from another location, a typical practice for centuries in Russia. July 20, 2001.

UMBA. Museum of Tersky Pomor People. Re-created interior of log *izba*, with items of everyday use including a samovar and containers of plaited birchbark. July 24, 2001.

Varzuga is commandingly placed along high banks on both sides of the Varzuga River twenty kilometers north of its mouth on the White Sea. The river is considered the beginning point of the Tersky Shore, the eastern edge of the Kola Peninsula. Some sources state that the current population of Varzuga is around nine hundred, but this figure includes other villages in the area. The 2010 census counts 363 residents in Varzuga itself. By contrast the population in 1910 was approximately one thousand. Varzuga is first mentioned in written sources in 1466, when the area was nominally under the control of the medieval trading city of Novgorod. By the end of the fifteenth century the area had entered the domain of Muscovy. From the latter part of the fifteenth century until the latter part of the eighteenth century, Varzuga was economically linked to various monastic institutions, above all the Solovetsky Transfiguration Monastery. The prosperity of Varzuga was, however, devastated in 1568 when the entire region, including Kandalaksha, was raided as part of a campaign by Ivan the Terrible's *oprichniki* to extort further revenues in support of his costly military campaigns. Like so much else in Russia during the latter part of the sixteenth century, the village would take decades to recover.

As in centuries past, the basic economic asset of Varzuga is its fishery, which continues to exist under skillful local management in the post-Soviet era. This enterprise provides jobs and a measure of stability for those who have lived in the area for generations. In recent years Varzuga has gained another source of income as a prime location for salmon fishing. Sports tourism has become a boon to many residents of Varzuga and is closely related to the fishery. The village has also recently been connected to the regional power grid, which ensures a dependable power supply. Although dwindling in number, wooden houses in these fishing villages show urban

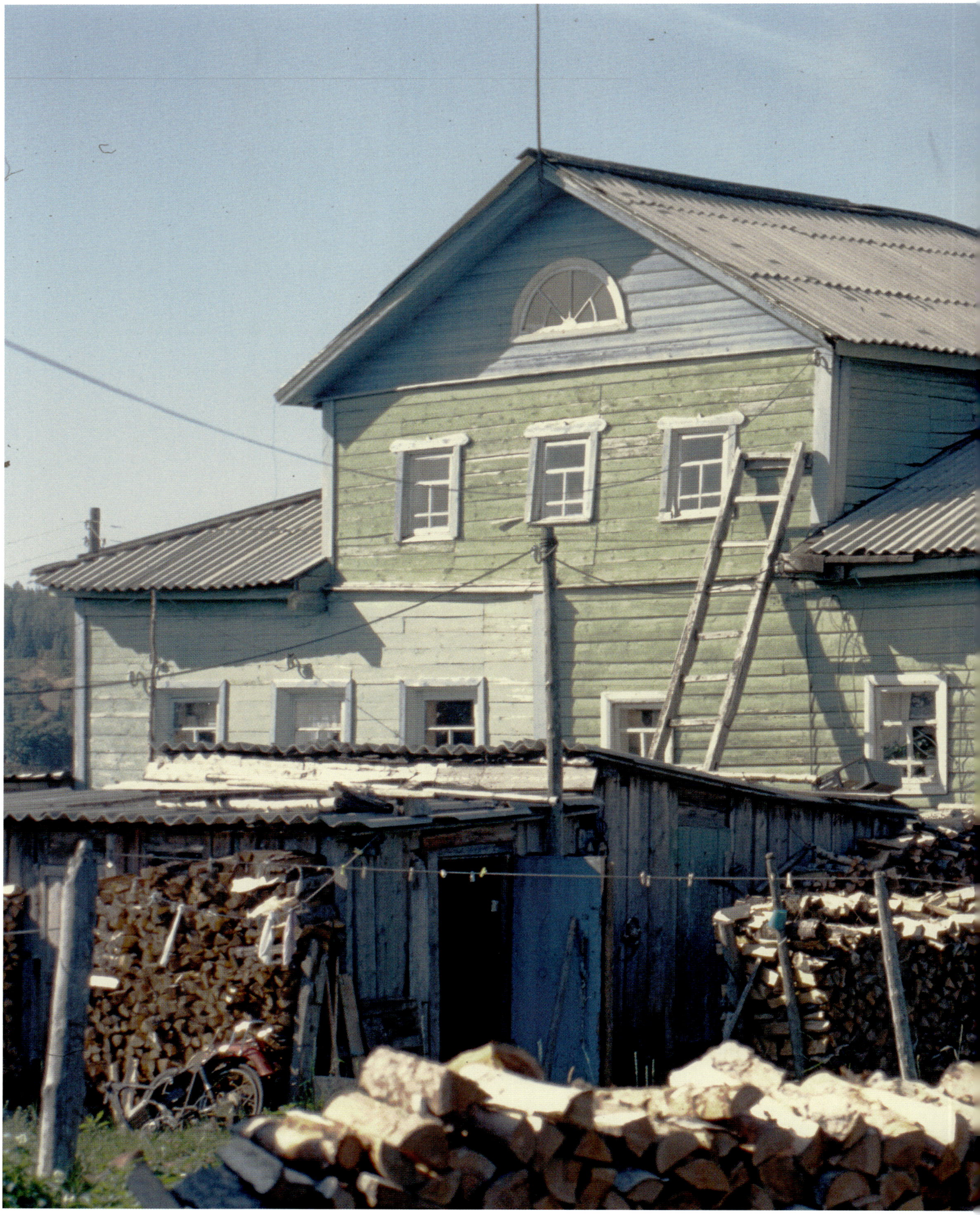

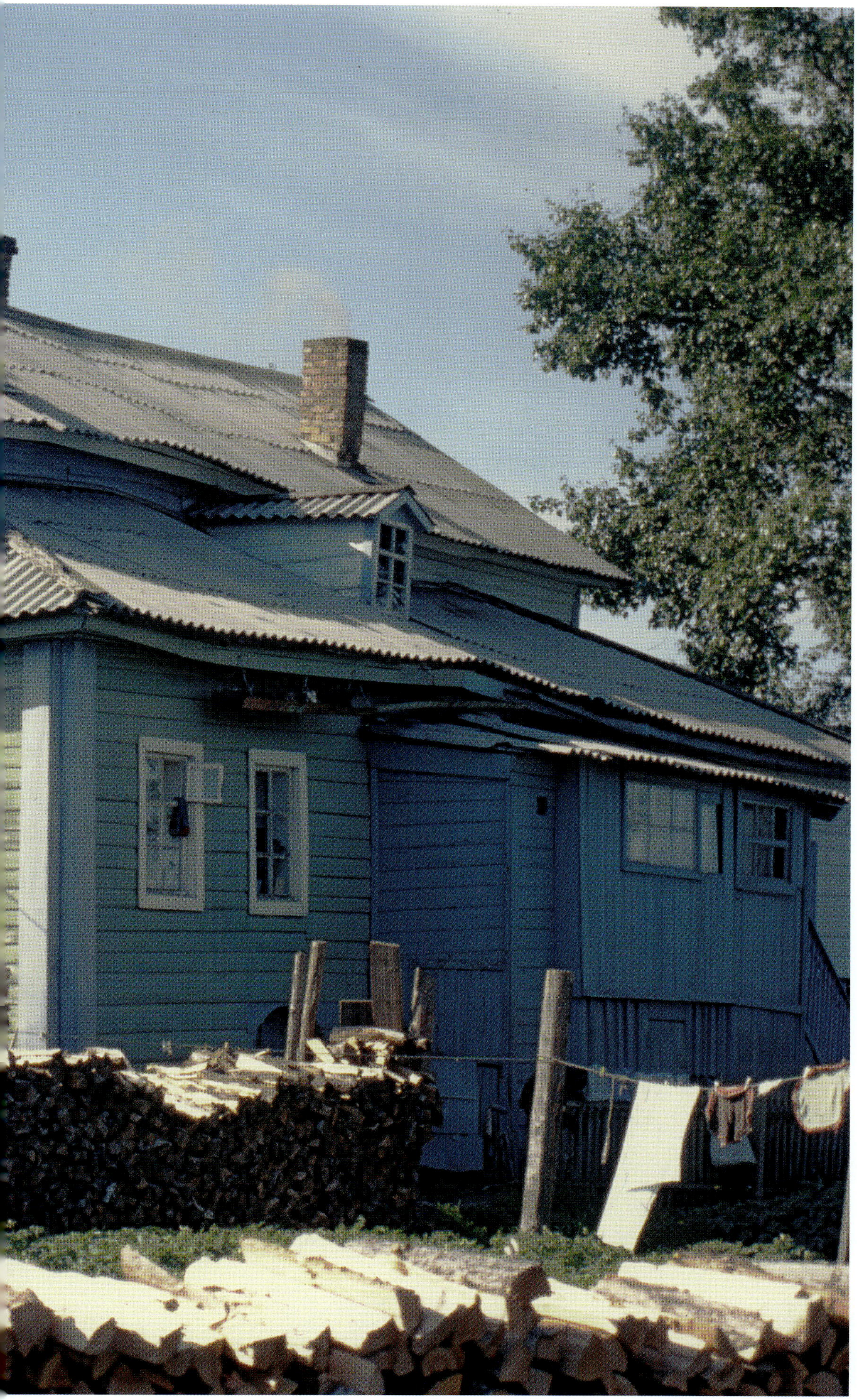

VARZUGA. Log house with half upper story (*mezonin*) built for wealthy merchant in 1867 and sheathed in plank siding. July 21, 2001.

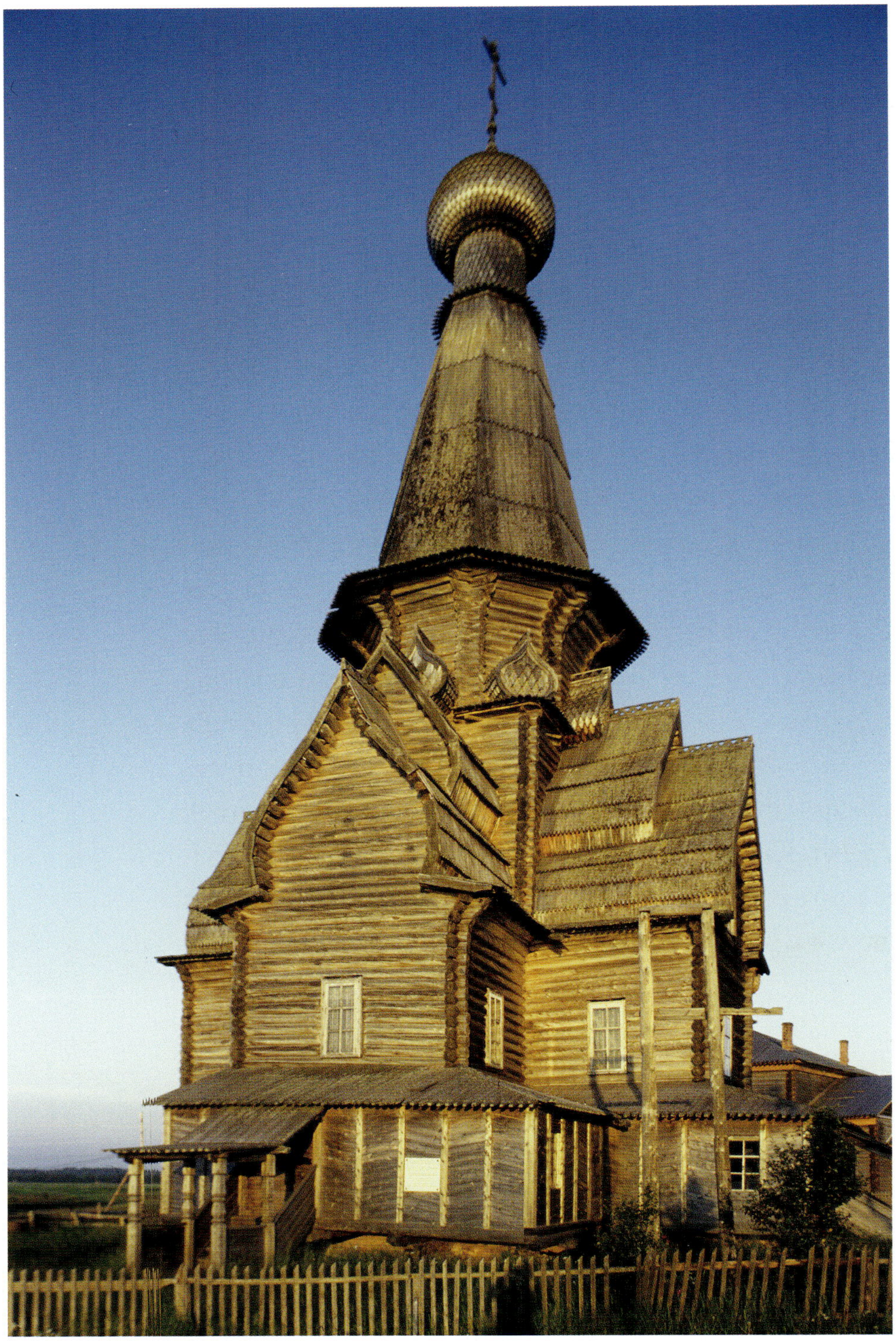

VARZUGA. Church of the Dormition, northwest view. Located just south of the Arctic Circle. Photograph taken close to midnight, July 20, 2001.

traits that distinguish them from the *izba*. Most of them have plank siding with modest classicizing details, as opposed to the decorative flourishes of the *izba* in northern agricultural regions.

The dramatic, soaring wooden Church of the Dormition of the Mother of God rises thirty-four meters above the high right bank of the Varzuga River. Remarkable for its construction logic, the basic structure from 1674 has withstood the elements in its exposed location. Modifications were made in the nineteenth century, when both exterior and interior were clad in plank siding painted white. A restoration completed in 1973 returned the upper part of the church to its original appearance with the remarkable artistry of its log construction clearly visible. Fortunately, I was able to photograph it in that state, for the church was recently again clad in painted plank siding that conceals important details of the log structure. Inside, the icon screen was dismantled for a halting restoration of the interior. Behind the village on both sides of the Varzuga River are high dunes covered with juniper bushes. Farther inland are dense forests of small conifers with a deep mossy carpet. The landscape is especially beautiful in the summer, a time of almost constant light.

The Varzuga River empties into the White Sea at the small village of Kuzomen. But its gritty endurance is evoked in weathered wooden houses and in a cemetery, whose crosses are nestled askance in dunes at the edge of the sea. Twice a week a converted truck provided transportation along the dunes back toward Umba and its blessed asphalt road. As the only scheduled conveyance, the lurching military green truck gathered riders from seaside villages rather than follow the straight arrow path that took us to Varzuga. Several hours later it reached the Kandalaksha Station, the point of departure for a return journey southward along the western shore of the White Sea.

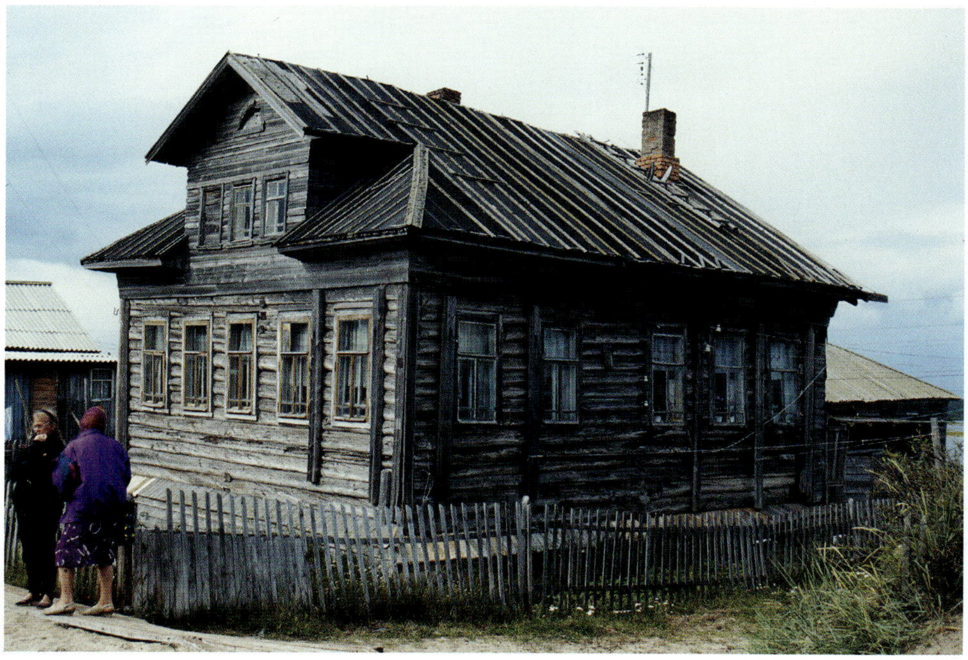

KUZOMEN. Built on sandy soil overlooking the White Sea, this late nineteenth-century house originally had plank siding (still visible on upper *mezonin*). July 23, 2001.

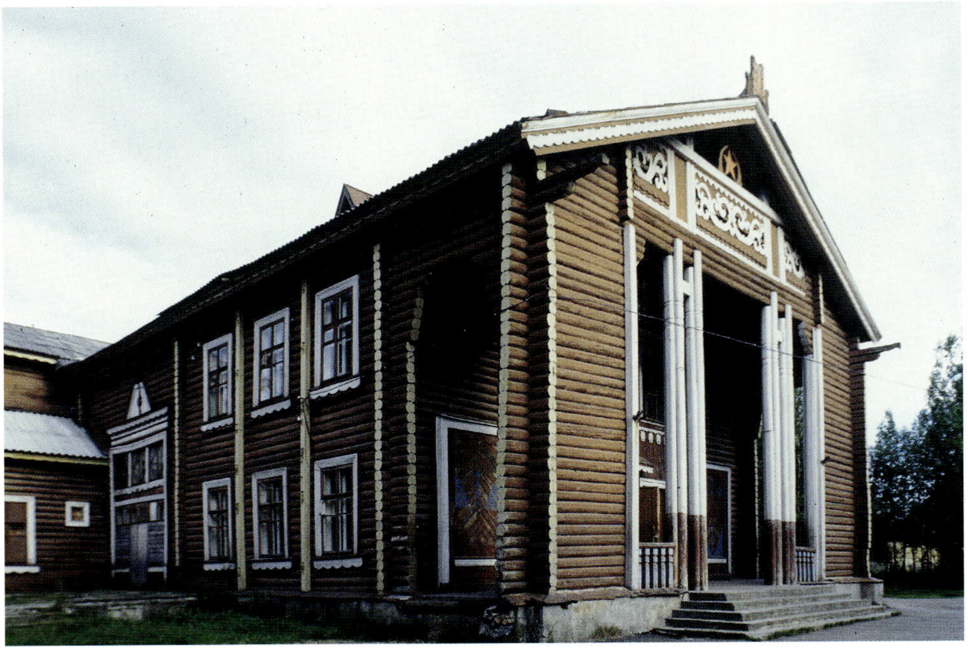

ZELENOBORSKY. House of Culture. Excellent example of log construction applied in Soviet-era community buildings. July 24, 2001.

For centuries the craggy western rim of the White Sea has supported ancient fishing villages that consolidated Moscow's hold on this challenging terrain. A number of these settlements, with soaring log churches, remained at the beginning of the twentieth century, but the modern age has dealt harshly with them. Most of the churches have vanished, and the few that remain are at risk. Among them is the Church of Saint Nicholas at Kovda, located on cliffs above an inlet of Kandalaksha Bay, an arm of the White Sea in southwest Murmansk Province.

Some three hundred kilometers down the coast is the regional center Kem in the Republic of Karelia. Known as a major port to the Solovetsky Archipelago and its great Transfiguration Monastery, the town has a dramatic history of its own, which, like that of the Solovetsky islands, combines elements of the spiritual with human tragedy. Kem is located primarily on an island known as Lepostrov ("Läppäsaari" in Karelian), which is flanked by the arms of the small Kem River near its confluence with the White Sea. During the medieval period these northern lands were tenuously held by the commercial power of Novgorod, whose authority was tested by Moscow's expansion. Because of its strategic location, Kem gained the unwanted attentions of hostile neighbors such as Sweden in the late sixteenth century. With Peter the Great's victory over King Charles XII at Poltava in July 1709 (a turning point in the Great Northern War), pressure on Russia's White Sea territory diminished.

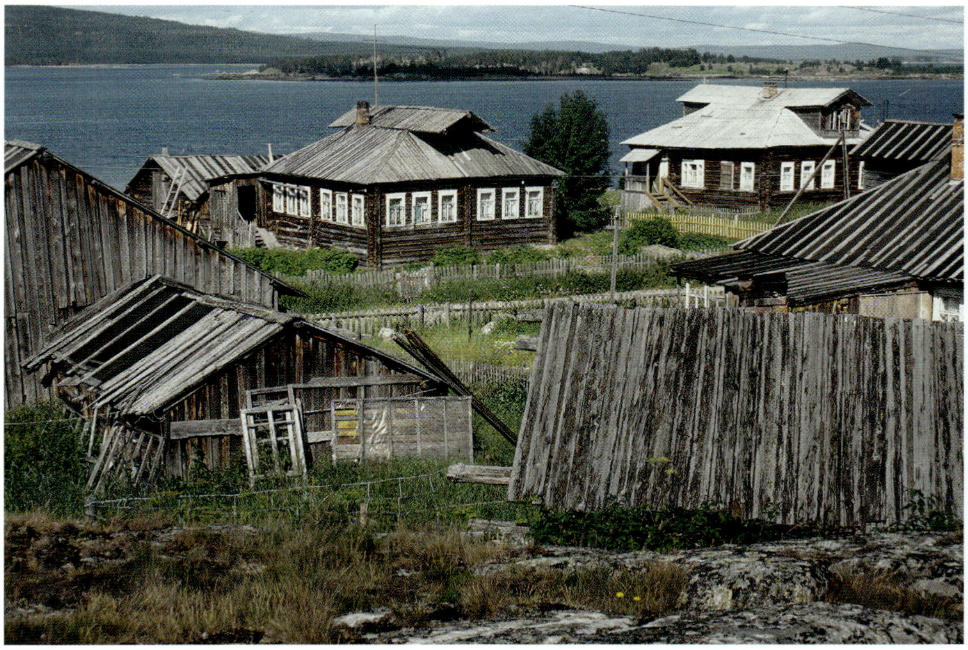

KOVDA. Log houses overlooking Kandalaksha Bay. Located in a dramatic but exposed location, these fortress-like square log houses have unusual lookout gables. House in center still has original plank roofing. July 24, 2001.

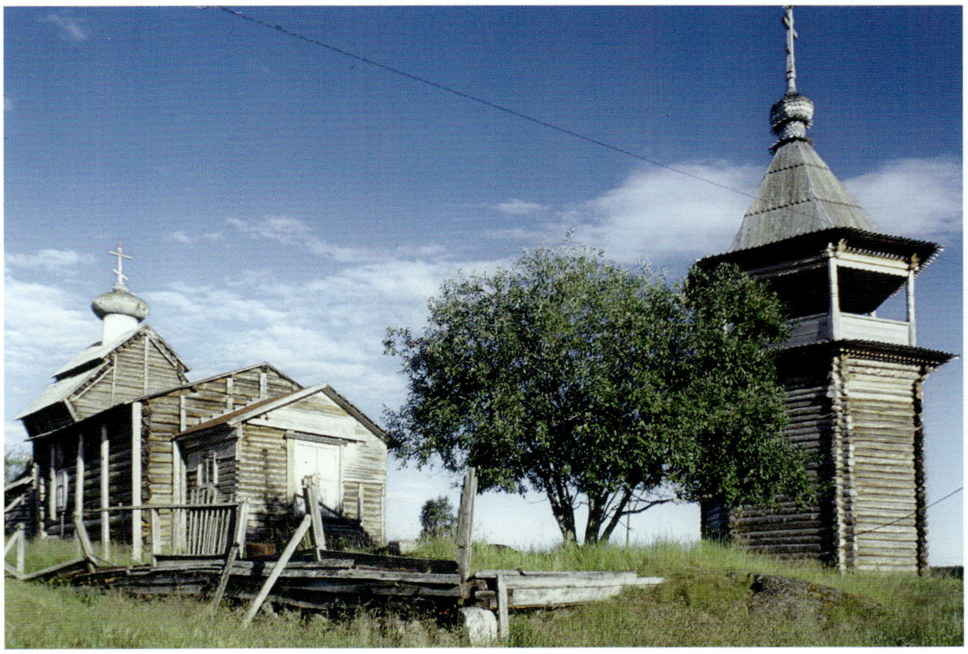

KOVDA. Bell tower and Church of Saint Nicholas, northwest view. During prolonged restoration, the nineteenth-century plank siding was removed. July 24, 2001.

To symbolize Russian power in the area, a cathedral dedicated to the Dormition of the Mother of God was erected in Kem in 1711–14. The building of the cathedral with logs is indicative of the distinctive culture of northern Russia, and the remarkable structure fully exploits the properties of wood. Its three tent towers, signifying the presence of three altars, soar above an elevated location on Lepostrov. Although partially obscured by trees, the Dormition Cathedral is still the town's dominant landmark. Despite wooden scaffolding from an ongoing restoration, the west (front)

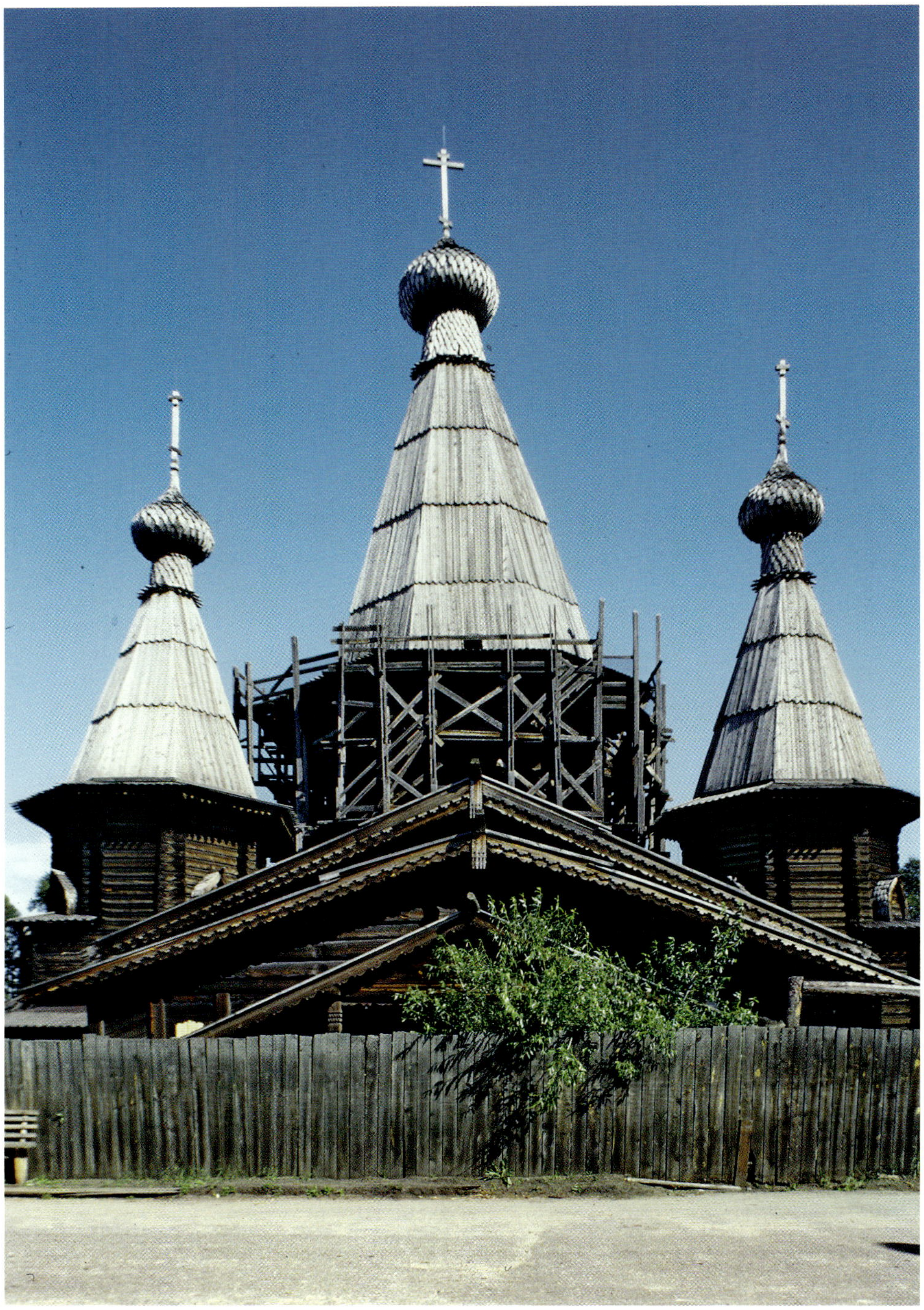

KEM. Cathedral of the Dormition of the Mother of God, west view. One of the few surviving cathedrals built of logs. July 25, 2001.

facade of the Dormition Cathedral was largely visible when I photographed it. A decorated porch leads to a wide one-story refectory with low pitched roofs. The ascending levels of three roofs provide a harmonious pedestal for the central tower, which rises from a square base to an octagon supporting an eight-sided tent tower. Some thirty-six meters high, the tower is crowned with a wooden cupola and cross. It is flanked by two smaller towers over chapels attached to the north and south of the main structure.

Farther south along the White Sea coast, the steep rocky outcroppings give way to salt marshes. In this setting, just over four hundred kilometers south of Kandalaksha, stands another coastal village, Virma, with its exquisite Church of Saints Peter and Paul, built perhaps as early as 1625 and rebuilt in 1759. The archaic structure rises like a living, organic form among the firs and other conifers that crowd the narrow coastline. Its crown of five cupolas, covered with silvery aspen shingles and surmounted with wooden crosses, rests on a distinctive flared roof, also clad in wooden shingles. As in the best examples of northern wooden architecture, function and beauty coexist in graceful harmony.

All of these coastal settlements have at one time or another had connections to the great Solovetsky Transfiguration Monastery, located on the Solovetsky Archipelago in the southwestern expanse of the White Sea. The islands form one of the most curious natural environments in Russia. Although buffeted by northern winds and sea currents, the same currents also moderate the northern climate and produce a rich ecological diversity. The archipelago's first known Russian settlement dates from 1429 when the monk Zosima joined forces with Herman, an illiterate hermit who had periodically visited Solovetsky Island. The elderly Zosima died in 1435, but the following year another monk, Savvaty, returned to the island and founded a monastery dedicated to the Transfiguration of the Savior. During this early period the monastery belonged to the domains of the Russian city-state of Novgorod, but after Novgorod's subjugation to Moscow in 1478 the Muscovite grand princes reaffirmed the strategic importance of this remote monastic outpost.

The great flourishing of the monastery occurred in the sixteenth century under the direction of Philip Kolychev, a Moscovite monk of noble origins who left his privileged existence in 1537, joined the Solovetsky monastic community, and in 1547 became its spiritual leader (*hegumen*). During the next eighteen years Philip guided an ambitious program of construction that transformed the monastery and created monumental buildings of stone and brick. Subsequently, wooden architecture played a secondary role in the Solovetsky architectural ensemble.

From a historical perspective, the archipelago's most notable wooden monument is the small Church of Saint Andrew, located on the outer Zayatsky Island and built in five days at Tsar Peter's command during his visit to the Solovetsky Monastery in August 1702. The dedication is deeply symbolic, for not only was Apostle Andrew supposed to have visited

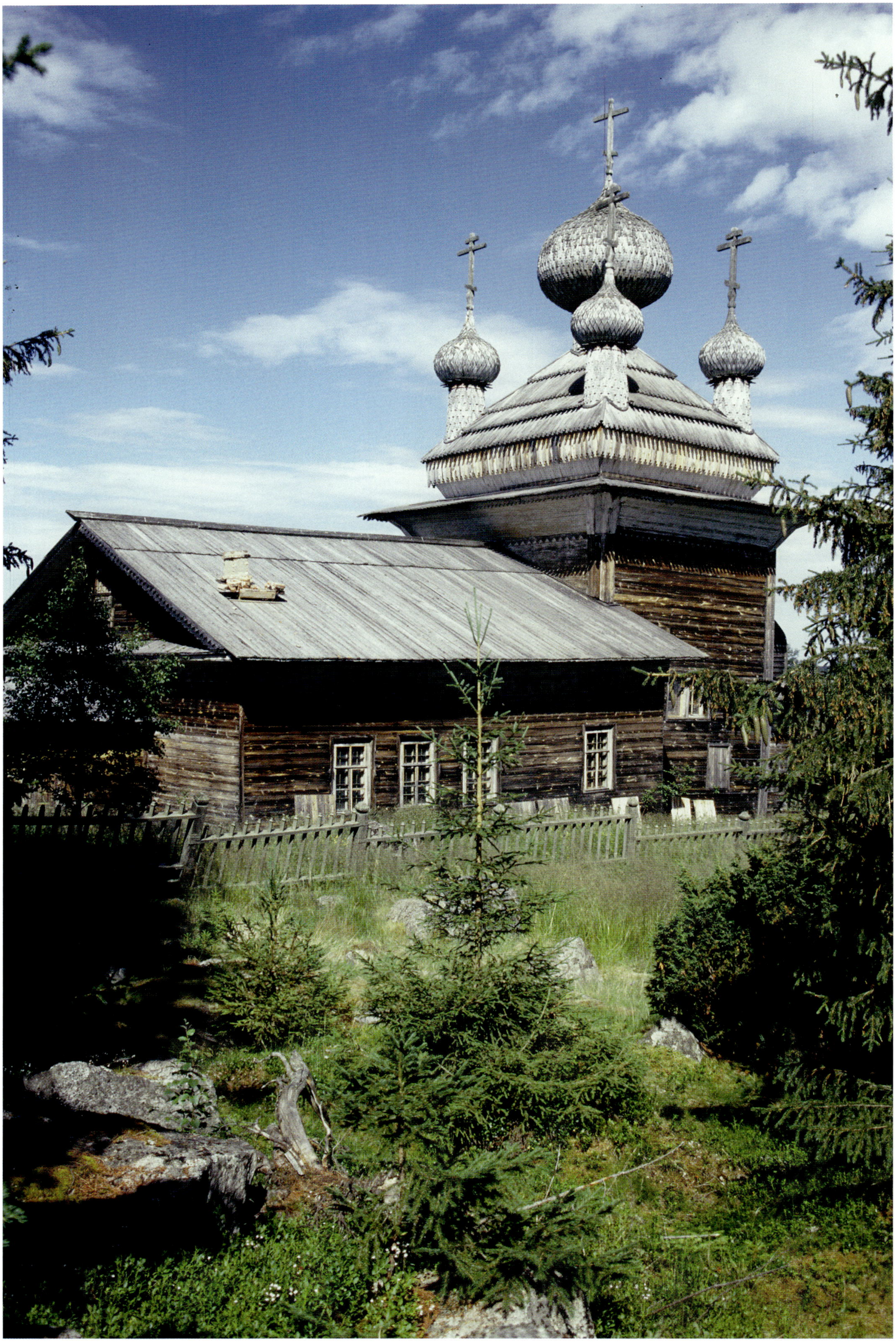

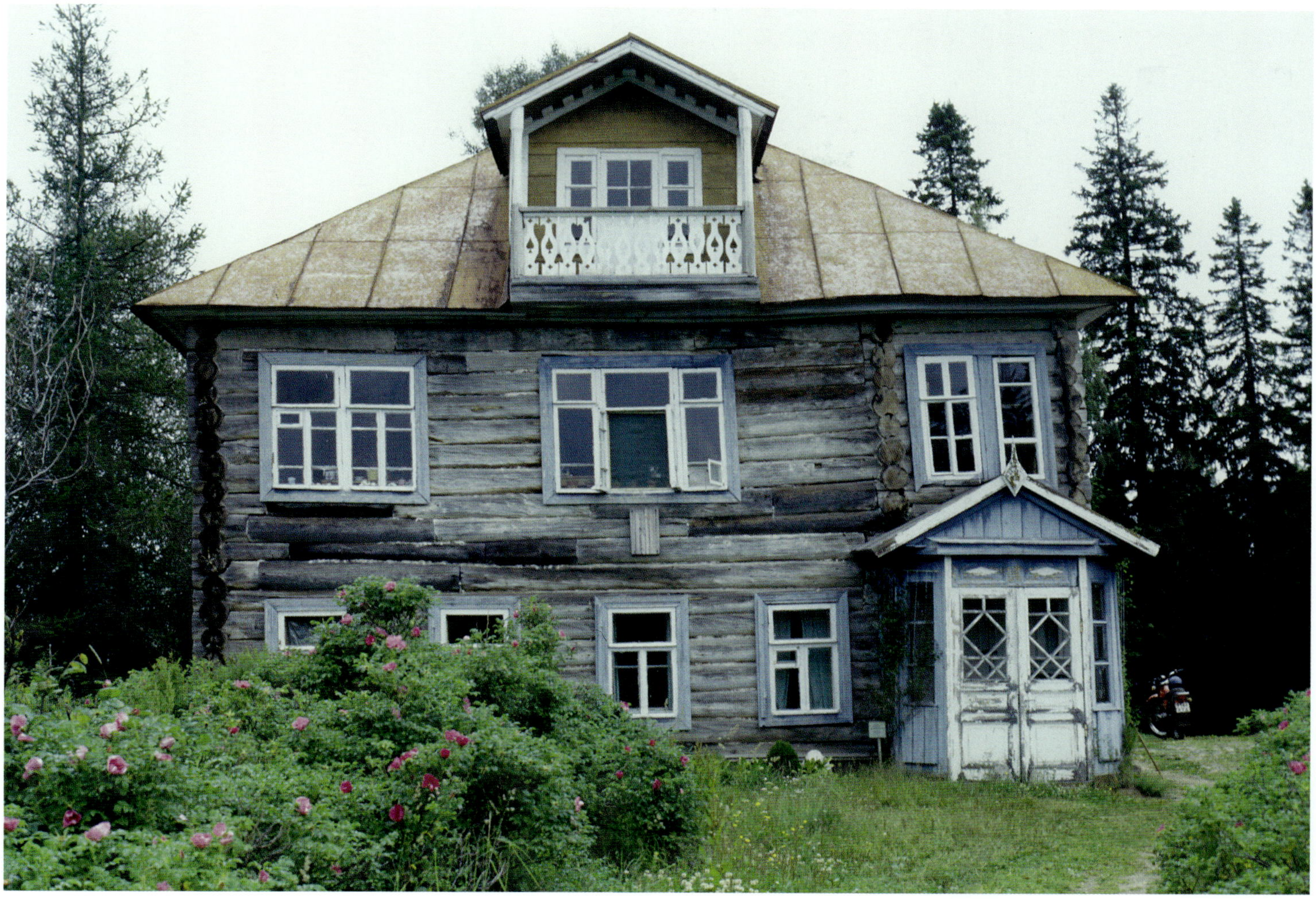

and blessed lands subsequently occupied by the Eastern Slavs, but he also acquired a reputation as patron of seafarers. Peter the Great personally designated Saint Andrew's cross—well known in England and Scotland—as the battle standard of the new Russian fleet. Upon completion of the church, Peter attended a prayer service as his squadron of thirteen ships stood at anchor off Zayatsky Island.

Peter the Great's dramatic success in the Great Northern War with Sweden (1700–21) changed the geopolitical balance of power in northern Europe and eliminated the age-old Swedish threat to Russia's North Sea domains. A unique surviving relic of the turbulent past is the log Mokhovaya Tower from Sumsky Ostrog, a fort originally established near the Suma River to protect the southwest holdings of the Solovetsky Monastery. Rebuilt in the late seventeenth century, the fort had six three-level towers, one of which survived into the twentieth century. In 1931 it was dismantled under the supervision of the renowned preservation specialist Peter Baranovsky and brought for conservation to the Kolomenskoe Museum. The logs were finally reassembled at Kolomenskoe in 2008.

VIRMA. Church of Saints Peter and Paul, southwest view. Nineteenth-century plank siding here intact but stripped of whitewash. July 7, 2000.

GREAT SOLOVETSKY ISLAND. Solovetsky Transfiguration Monastery, Saint Makary Hermitage at Khutor Gorka (hillock). Nineteenth-century dacha of archimandrite (abbot). July 26, 1998.

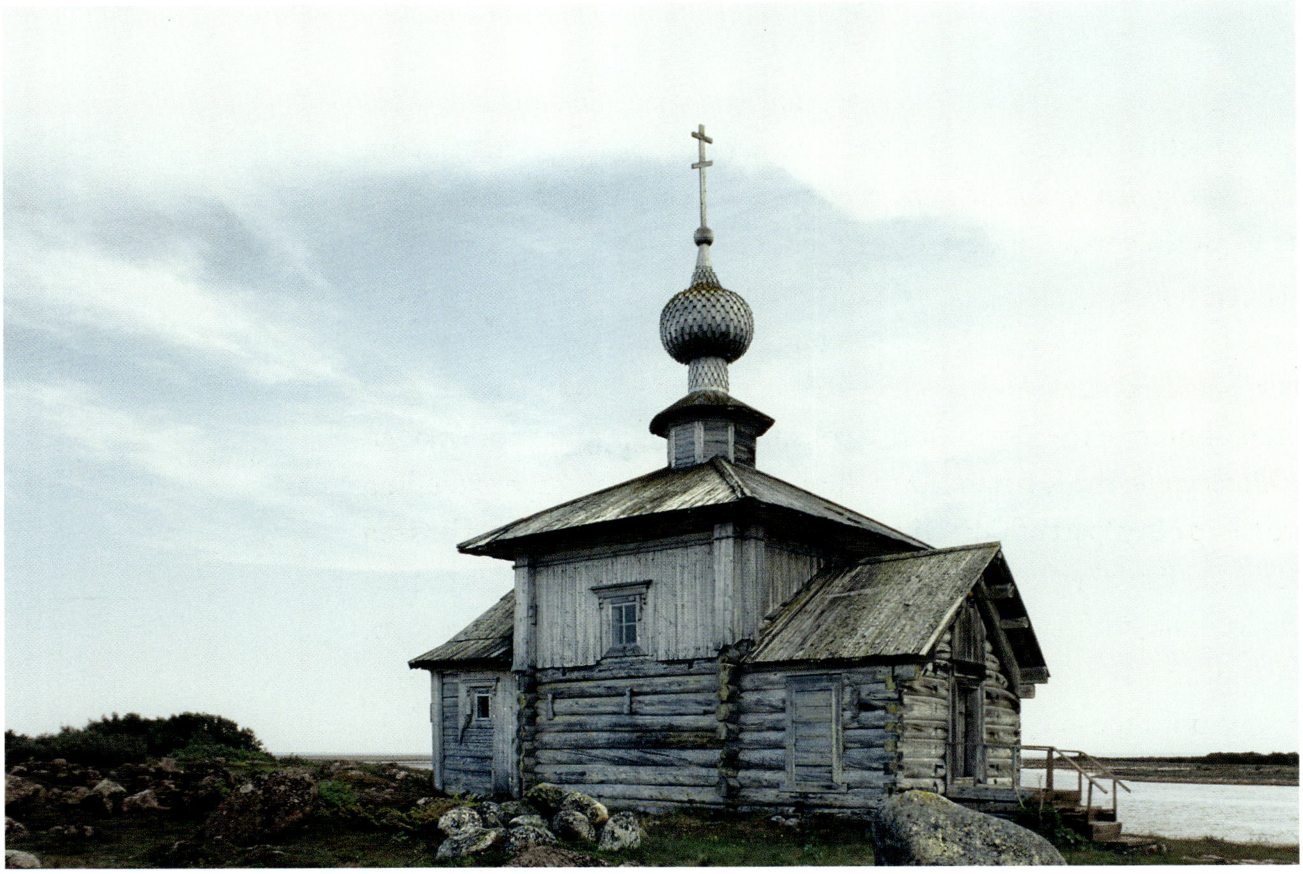

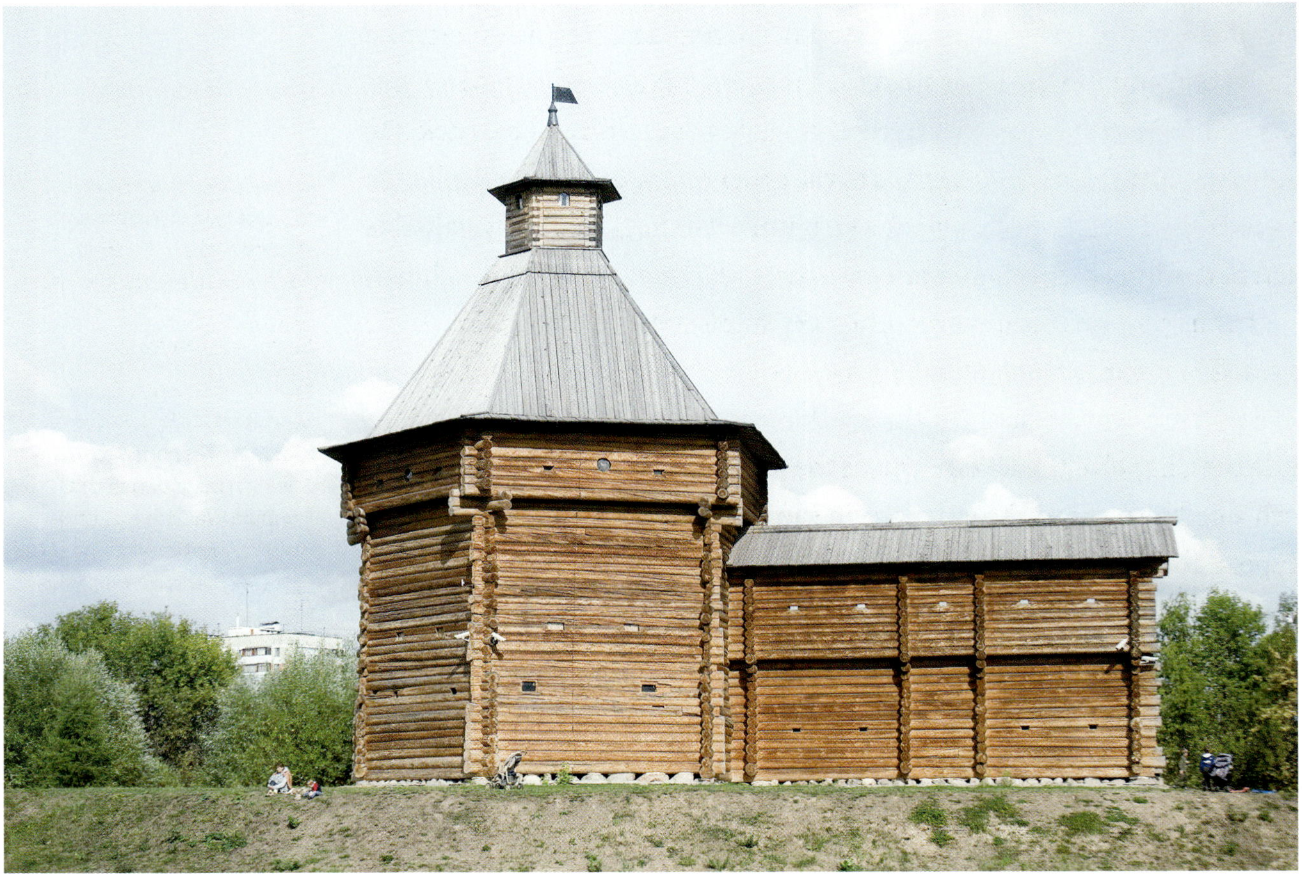

Lake Onega

Southward from Kem, the road leads to Kondopoga, located fifty kilometers north of the capital of Petrozavodsk on an arm of Lake Onega. With a decreasing population of some twenty-six thousand, it is now the third largest city in Karelia. The origins of a settlement on the site of Kondopoga date to the turn of the sixteenth century, when it was considered part of the territory of Kizhi Island. The growing importance of Kondopoga during the reign of Catherine the Great contributed to the construction in 1774 of the Church of the Dormition, a consummate monument of wooden architecture in the Russian North. Situated on a narrow cape extending into Chupa Bay (part of Lake Onega), the Dormition Church could be seen over water like a beacon from a great distance. To emphasize this prominent location, the master builders created a tower forty-two meters high.

During World War II Kondopoga was occupied from early November 1941 until the end of June 1944 by Finnish forces, at that time allied with Germany. Although the town's industry was ransacked, the Dormition Church—located on the outskirts—was untouched. A thorough study and conservation of the church was undertaken in the 1950s. In the 1990s the interior of the Dormition Church was again the object of careful restoration, even as the church was returned for active parish use. Despite structural issues that threatened a tall structure located near a body of water, the Dormition Church continued to receive visitors until disaster struck. On August 10, 2018, the church burned to the ground in a senseless act of arson by a local youth. In addition to the structure, all the historically valuable icons and ceiling paintings were lost in the fire. Plans to rebuild the church have been approved based on careful documentation before the fire, but a copy will never equal the artistic majesty of the original.

Surviving wooden architectural monuments in the Kondopoga area include the Chapel of the Kazan Icon of the Virgin at the village of Manselga. With a bell tower over the entrance in the west, the Kazan Chapel follows a typical form for wooden chapels in Karelia during the eighteenth and nineteenth centuries. A distinctive expression of this traditional form is the late eighteenth-century Chapel of the Three Prelates, originally at the village of Kavgora in the Kondopoga region but subsequently transferred to the museum on Kizhi Island. Like the Dormition Church, it has an elevated covered stairway to provide access over the high snows of the Karelian winter.

GREAT ZAYATSKY ISLAND (Solovetsky Archipelago). Church of Saint Andrew, northwest view. Built in 1702 by command of Peter the Great. June 29, 1999.

SUMA. Mokhovaya Tower, Suma Fort. Originally formed in 1582 in response to Swedish raids during the Livonian War, the fort underwent renovations during the following century when this tower was built. Disassembled in 1931 and brought to the Kolomenskoe outdoor museum in Moscow, where it was re-erected at the turn of this century. August 31, 2014.

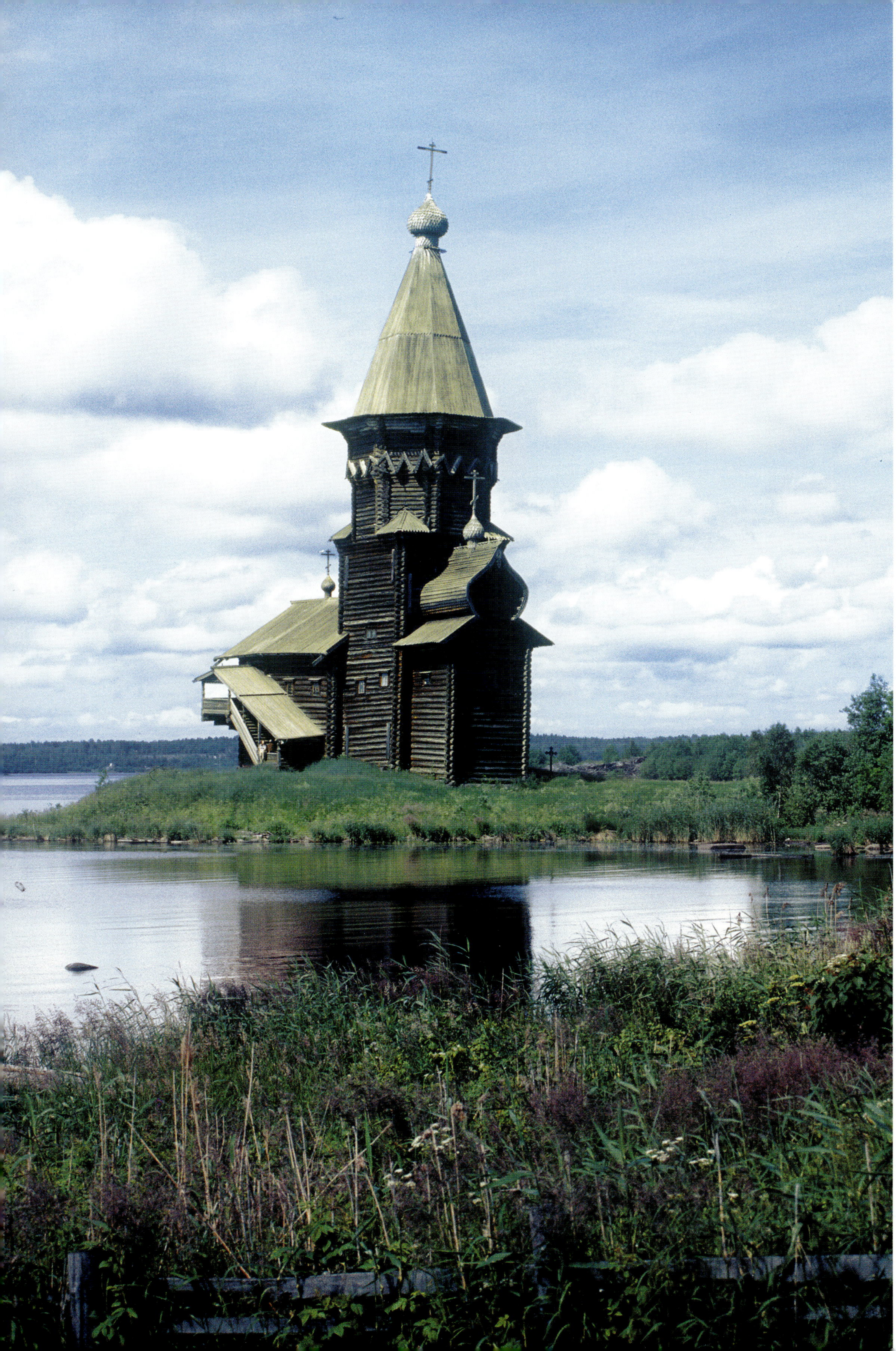

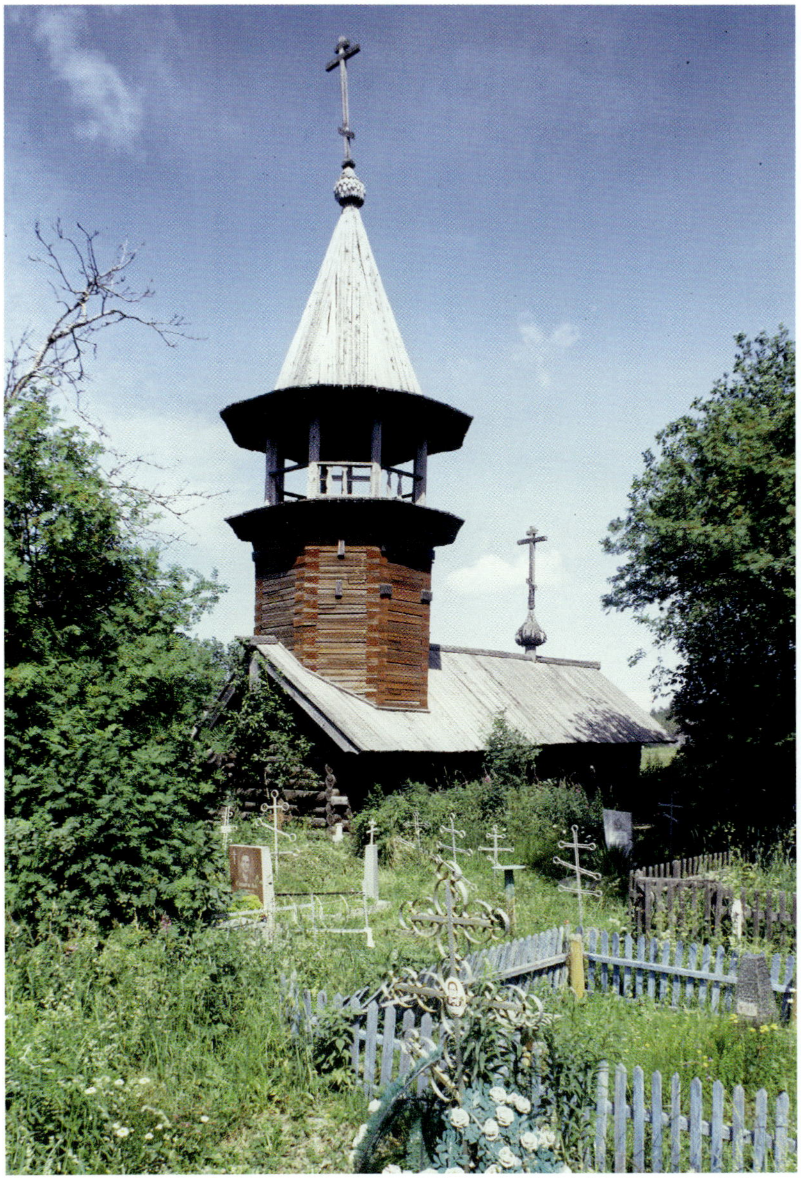

KONDOPOGA. Church of the Dormition, southeast view on the shore of Lake Onega. Destroyed by arson in 2018. July 4, 2000.

MANSELGA. Chapel of the Kazan Icon of the Virgin, southwest view. July 4, 2000.

A variation of the traditional wooden chapel in the Kondopoga region is the diminutive Church of Saint Peter at Martsialnye Vody (a word play on the Russian for "mineral waters" and the god Mars). Martsialnye Vody was founded by Peter the Great in 1719 at the site of mineral springs and is considered Russia's first spa. Peter visited Martsialnye Vody on four occasions between 1719 and 1724. Legend has it that the Church of Saint Peter was built to the tsar's own design, which combines traditional elements with a baroque dome over the main space. Although the spa fell into decline after Peter's death in 1725, it was revived in the late nineteenth century and again in 1964. The Martsialnye Vody spa functions to this day, with the Church of Saint Peter preserved as a link to the time of Peter the Great.

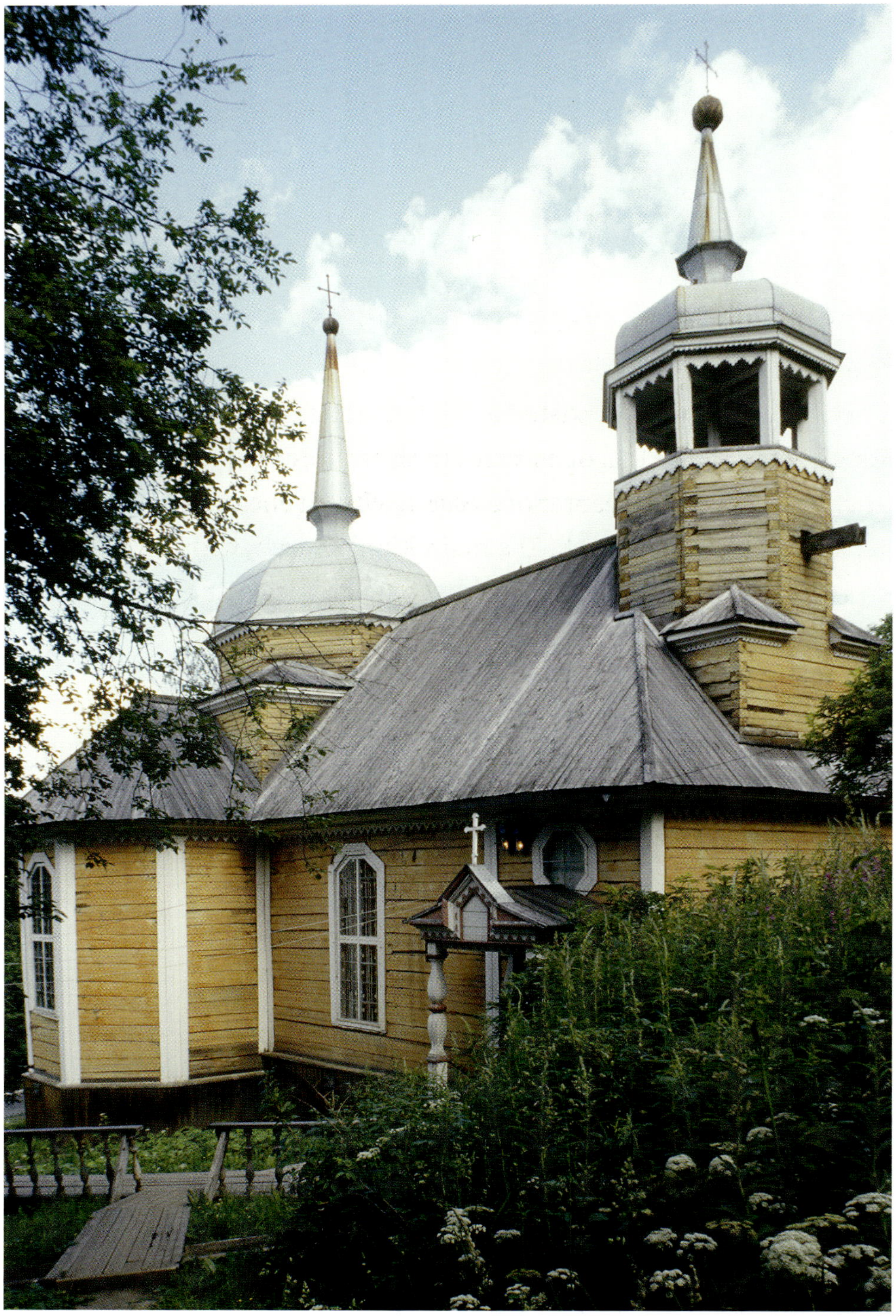

MARTSIALNYE VODY (Martial Waters). Church of Saint Peter, northwest view. July 4, 2000.

To the east of Kondopoga and on another northern bay of Lake Onega is the island of Kizhi, one of Russia's best-known heritage sites. Kizhi is unique in the range and distinction of its collection, centering on the original ensemble around the towering log Church of the Transfiguration of the Savior, with its twenty-two cupolas. In the late 1940s substantial restoration work began on the church, and in 1951 the first example of historic structures from other Karelian locations was brought to the island. With continued development Kizhi became a national architecture and historic museum in 1966 and was designated a UNESCO World Heritage Site in 1990. Kizhi Island now contains some of the oldest surviving examples of Russian log buildings, including one small church—the Resurrection of Lazarus—dated perhaps as early as the end of the fourteenth century.

The supreme example of the Russian wooden architecture is Kizhi's Church of the Transfiguration of the Savior, built in 1714 ostensibly in honor of Peter the Great's victories over the Swedes—although a church dedicated to the Transfiguration had existed at Kizhi since at least the early seventeenth century. Located on open space in the southwest part of the island, the church formed the center of a *pogost*, with an enclosed cemetery with a parish or district church. The main Kizhi church, with its many domes, produces an impression of overwhelming profusion and complexity; yet the design derives from rigorous structural and aesthetic logic. Its soaring pyramidal silhouette (thirty-seven meters high) signifies consecrated ground from a great distance, and the design of the structure reinforces that symbolic purpose at every point. The core of the Transfiguration Church is an octahedron, rising in three tiers and buttressed by extensions ("arms") at the four compass points. These extensions are also stepped, thus providing platforms for additional cupolas: twenty on the structure plus one at the top and another on the east side above the apse. This intricate pattern of cupolas and log structure is emphasized by the natural properties of the different woods: the dark walls of aged pine logs and the brilliant silver of the cupolas, covered with more than thirty thousand curved aspen shingles tightly fitted over the cupola frame. The design of this elaborate superstructure provided an efficient system of ventilation to preserve the structure from decay. Yet as was typical of tall wooden churches in the Russian North, the tower was not visible from the interior, which was capped at a low level by a ceiling (*nebo*) painted with saints and archangels over the central part of the church. This "sky" provided a culmination to the religious imagery of the icon screen in front of the altar. Unfortunately, this masterpiece was lost during World War II, and we know of its form through black-and-white photographs.

The Church of the Transfiguration was intended for use only during major church holidays in the summer. It was not uncommon in Russia to have paired churches for summer and winter. At the Kizhi *pogost*, the adjoining winter Church of the Intercession of the Virgin, built in 1764,

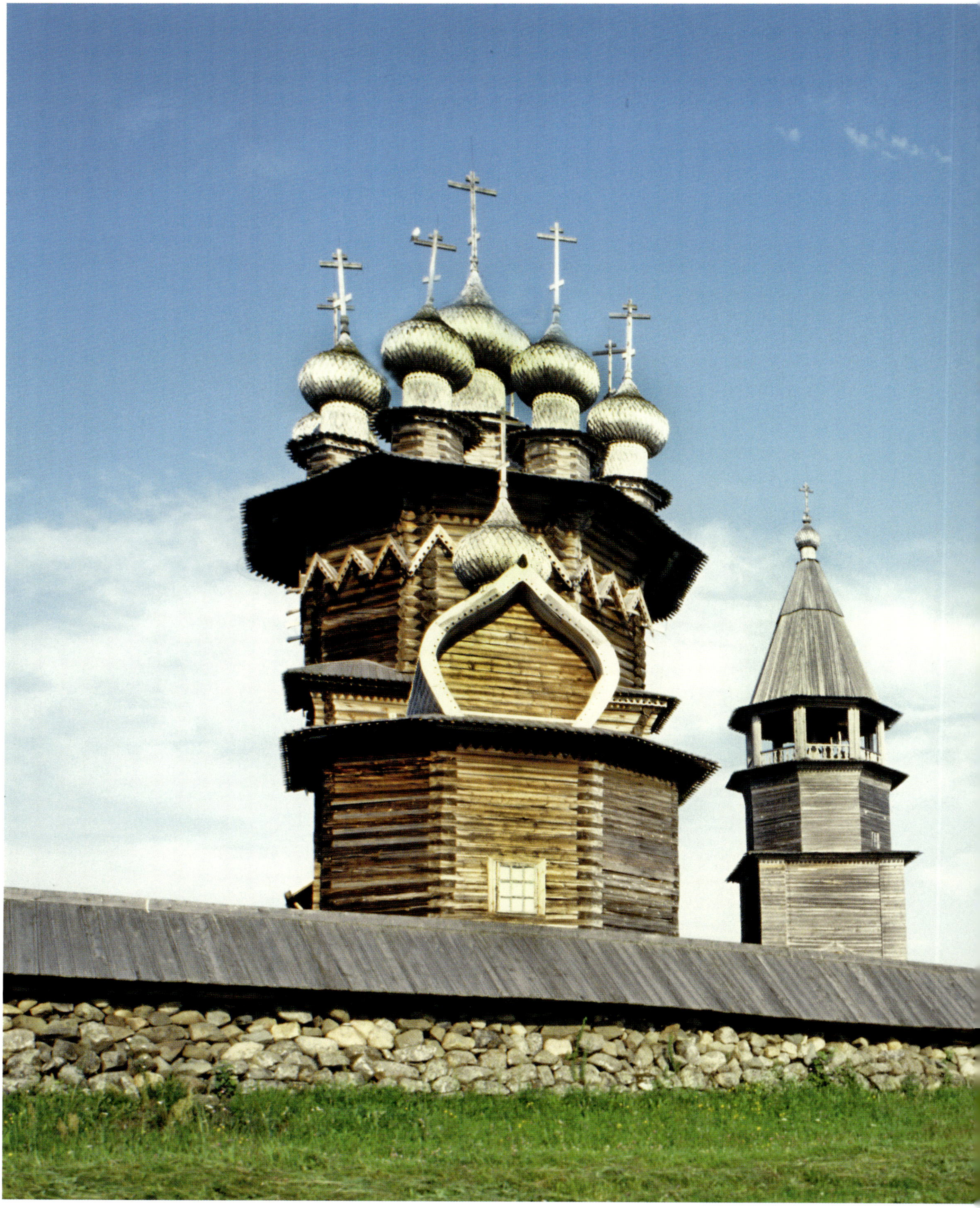

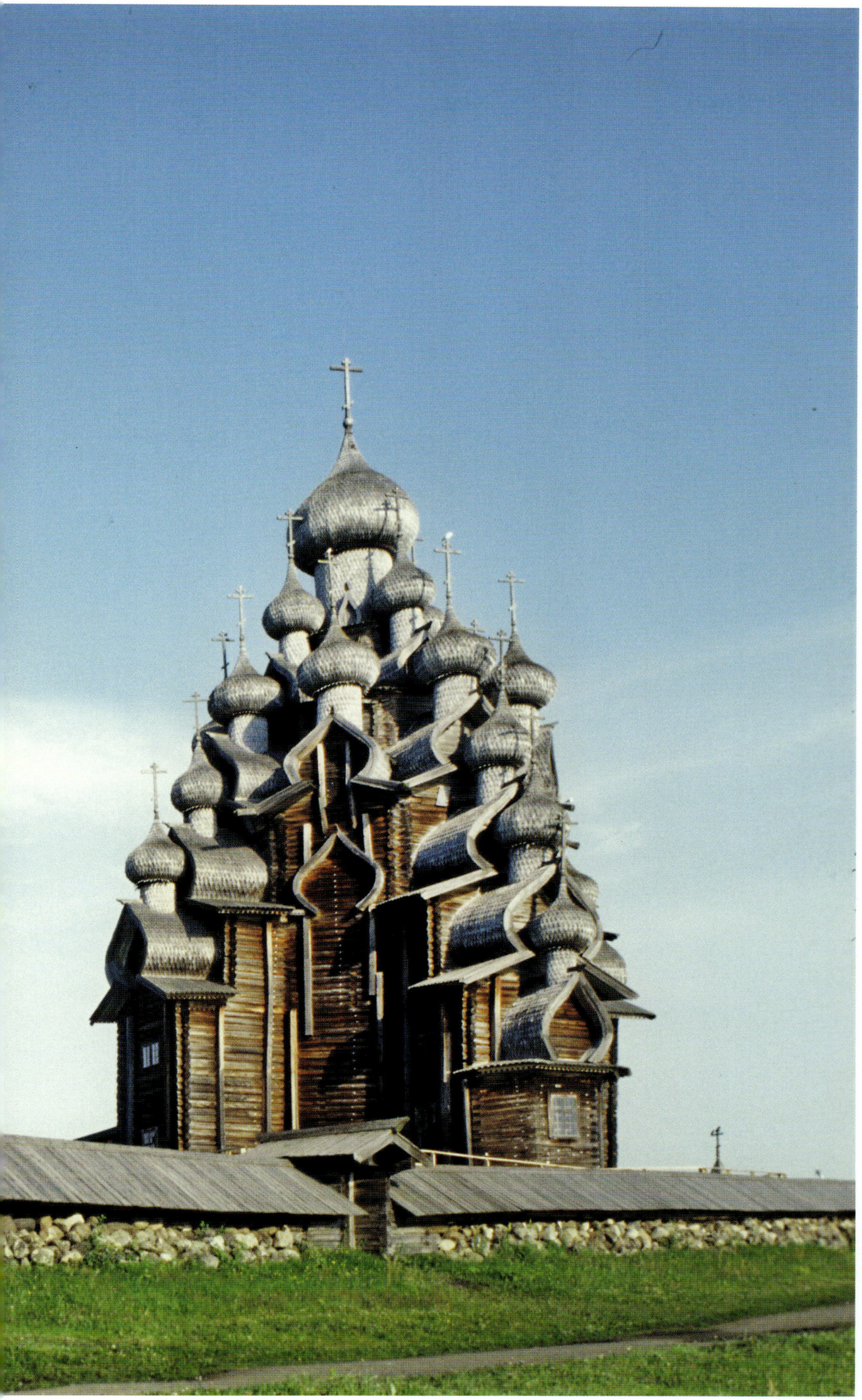

KIZHI ISLAND (Republic of Karelia, outdoor museum). Kizhi *pogost*. From left: Church of the Intercession, bell tower, Church of the Transfiguration of the Savior, east/southeast view July 13, 2007.

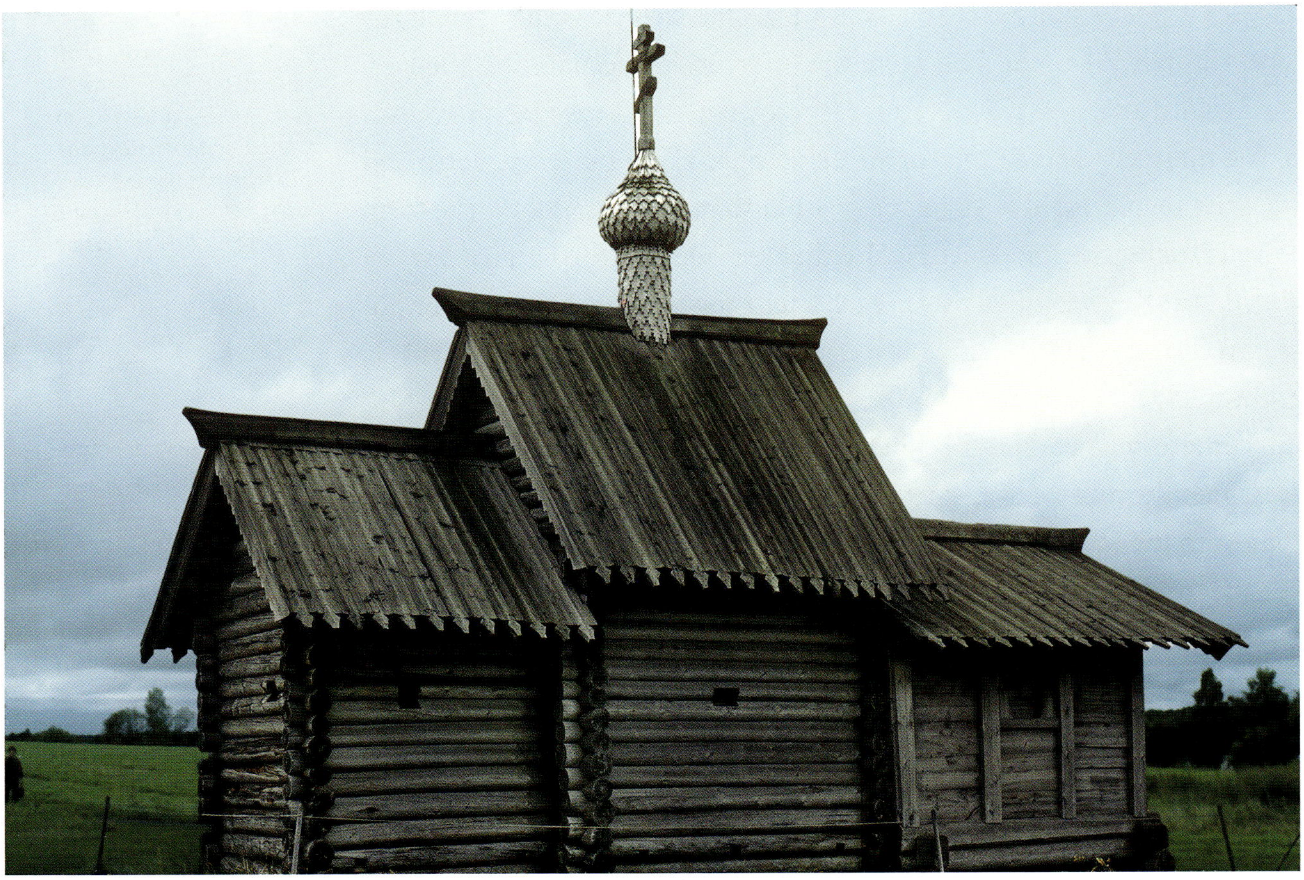

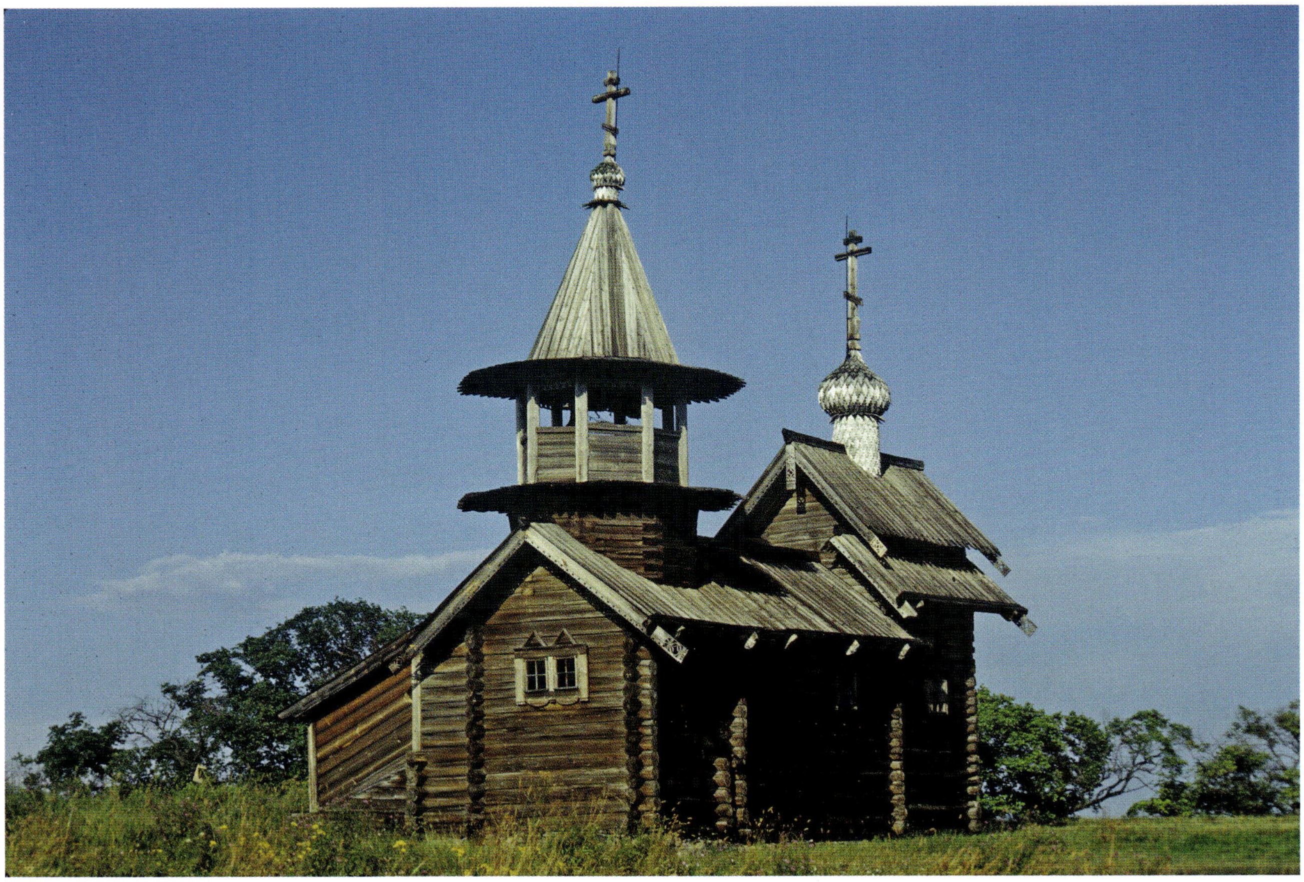

provides a visual complement to the ensemble. Whereas the Transfiguration Church soars, the Church of the Intercession accentuates the horizontal, with an extended refectory. Its crown of eight cupolas surrounding the main cupolas at the top of its octagonal core is a dramatic and satisfying resolution that enhances, rather than competes with, the form of the Transfiguration Church. The final element of the original *pogost* ensemble at Kizhi is a bell tower with a tent roof between and in front of the two churches. Originally built in the late eighteenth century, it was rebuilt in 1874 and renovated most recently in the early 1990s. The *pogost*, with cemetery, is enclosed by a low wall of horizontal logs on a base of fieldstone. The middle and northern parts of Kizhi also have their chapels, brought to the island from villages in the surrounding area. All of them have the modest charm and beauty characteristic of traditional Russian log architecture for places of worship, with decorative carved end boards and small wooden cupolas.

Examples of log houses, primarily from the late nineteenth century, are spread throughout Kizhi Island, from buildings grouped around the original church ensemble at the lower end of the island to other sites at the island's middle and northern parts. Taken together, these sites exhibit structures from various districts throughout the northwest region of Lake Onega, including villages inhabited by Karelians and Veps. The island also has two villages of its own—Vasilyevo and Yamka—with log houses whose traditional design complements those reassembled at the museum. In the severe climate of the far north, these houses provided living space as well as space for animals, supplies, and farm implements, all combined within a single, self-sufficient structure. As the examples at Kizhi show, such northern houses varied considerably in size and configuration. On display are three basic types, each with its own name. The simplest in plan is the *brus*, a long rectangular structure whose living quarters are at the front, while the larger space for storage and livestock extends along a single axis to the back. The front facade is framed by the two slopes of the roof, often with a balcony for a summer room under the peak of the roof. On the side are covered steps leading to the main floor. An impressive example in the south part of Kizhi is the Sergeev house. In the barns contained within these houses, livestock occupied the lower level, while hay and other supplies were kept on the second floor.

The most complex type of house design on display at Kizhi is the *koshel*, a two-story structure whose living quarters are underneath the long

KIZHI ISLAND. Church of the Resurrection of Lazarus, northeast view. Originally built in 1390 at the Murom-Dormition Monastery on the eastern shore of Lake Onega. Disassembled and brought to Kizhi by Alexander Opolovnikov in 1959. Considered the oldest surviving log structure in Russia. August 18, 1988.

KIZHI ISLAND. Chapel of Archangel Michael, southwest view. Originally built in the early eighteenth century at Lyolikozero village (northwest of Kizhi) and brought to the island in 1961 by Alexander Opolovnikov in 1961. August 6, 1991.

horizontal front of the main roof. Behind the living quarters was a barn under a greatly extended roof that originates from the same roof beam over the living quarters. When seen from the side, the barn looks like a large appendage extending from the house. (The basic meaning of *koshel* is "purse.") The Oshevnev house, near the Church of the Transfiguration, is a particularly good example. Houses with this design occasionally had a gabled half story with a balcony in the center of the front roof. An excellent example is the enormous Sergin house, now at the village of Vasilyevo on the western side of the island. The least frequent type of house plan on display at Kizhi is the *glagol*, whose name is derived from the archaic Russian name for the Greek letter gamma. This type consists of a rectangular structure with the barn attached to the side and extending back at a right angle (the top of the gamma).

The center of the peasant log house was the large brick stove, used not only for cooking but also for heating the main living space—the *zimnyaya izba* (winter house)—during the long winters. (In some parts of the north, the *zimnyaya izba* was a lower structure attached in parallel or perpendicularly to the main house.) Brick stoves usually had a ledge along the side on which a pallet could be placed for those who needed extra warmth, such as

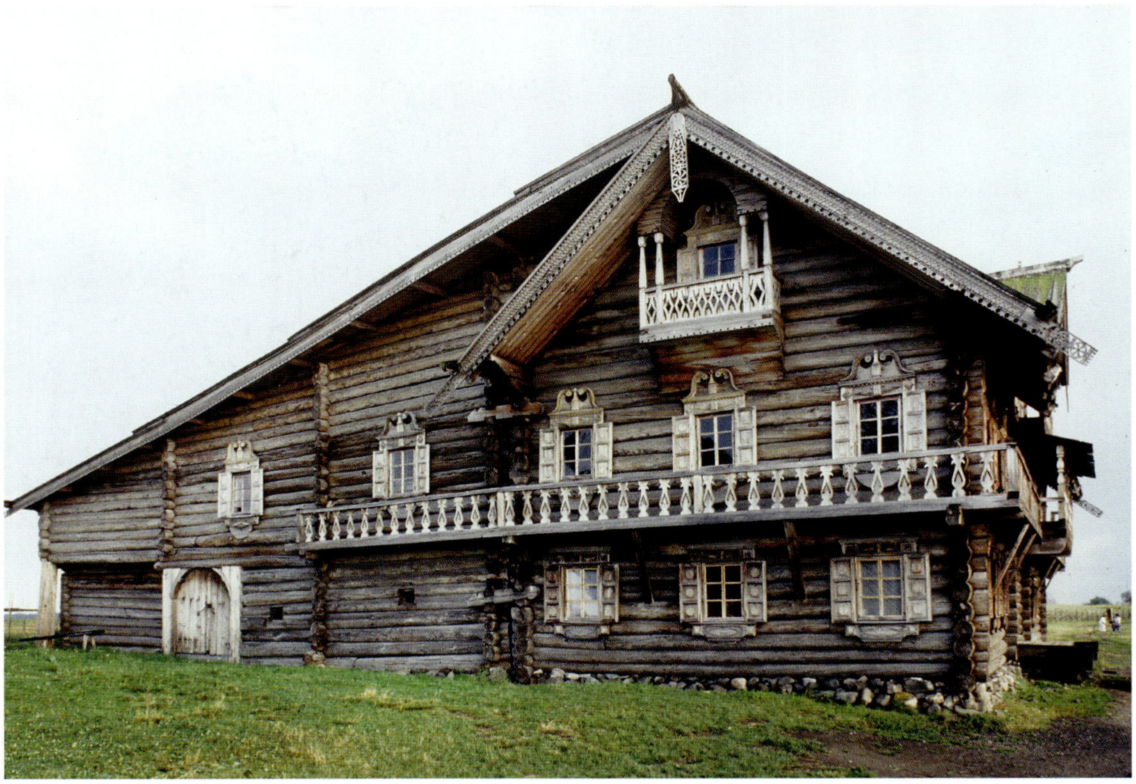

KIZHI ISLAND. Oshevnev house. Originally built in 1876 for a prosperous peasant family at the village of Oshevnevo, the structure displays every possible ingenuity for sustaining a large household in a severe climate, from the main living space in the front upper story to the capacious barn attached to the back with its own roof. Note at the back (far left) the stout logs supporting the upper part of the barn above the lower space for livestock, whose effluents caused the lower logs to decay more rapidly. The supports allowed weakened logs to be replaced without threat to the structure above. Restored in 1951 by Emile Ilyin. August 6, 1991.

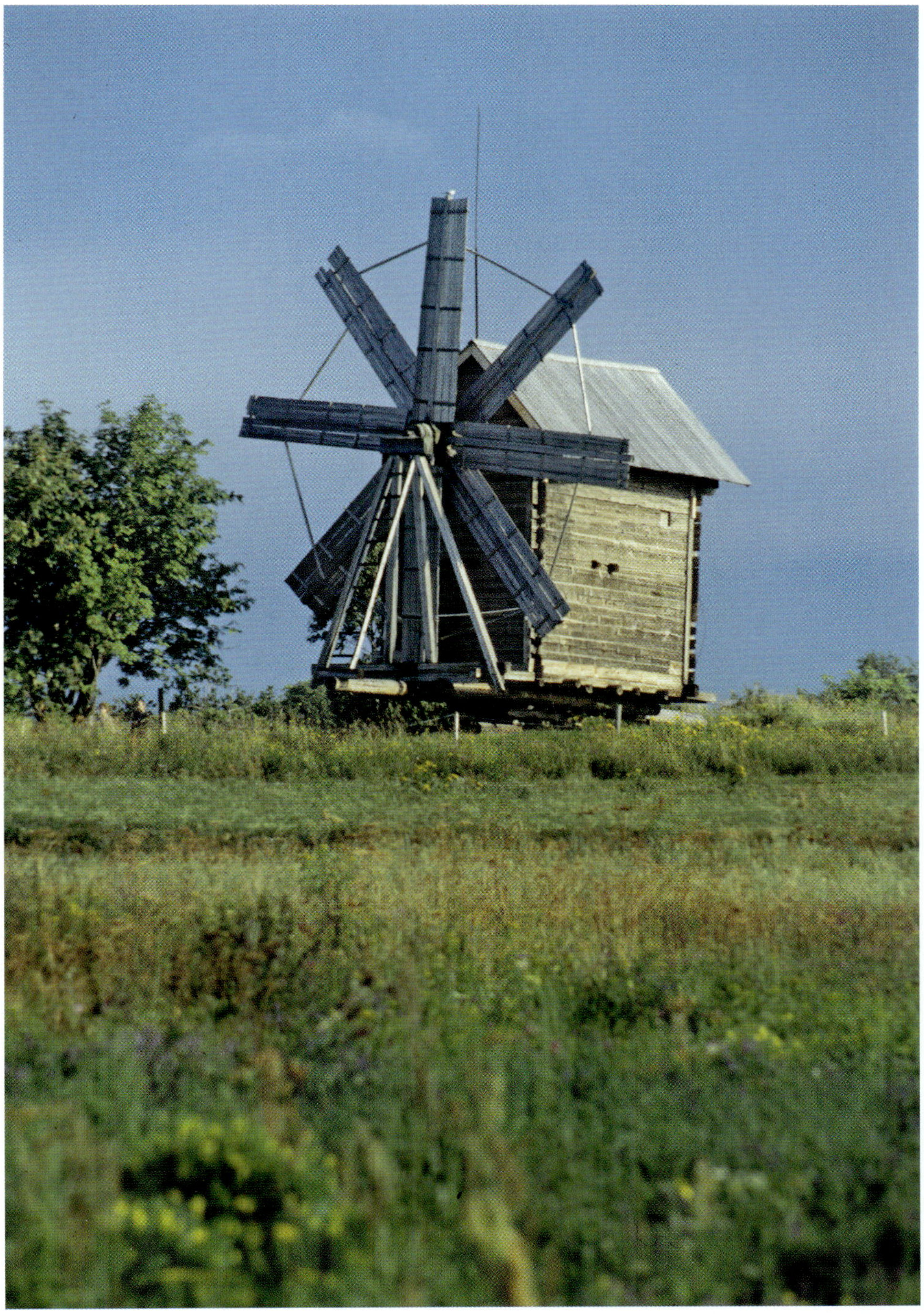

KIZHI ISLAND. Originally erected in the village of Volkostrov at the beginning of the twentieth century by the peasant Nikolay Bikanin, this windmill was restored in 1959 by Alexander Opolovnikov. Built around a central column, the square structure rests on a round base that permitted rotation to face prevailing winds. August 6, 1991.

the elderly or infirm. Space permitting, there was a separate bedroom for the head of the household. Children could be accommodated on wooden ledges beneath the ceiling in the main room, while a young married couple living with the family might have a separate space of their own. Large houses could also have an unheated room (*gornitsa*) with ample natural light and greater refinement for receiving guests in the warmer months. In some regions this space was known as a *letnyaya izba* (summer house).

Whether large or small, these log houses were decorated with elaborate window surrounds (*nalichniki*) and carved, or sawn, endboards for the roof. In the eighteenth and nineteenth centuries patterns derived from folk art became particularly elaborate. During the same period, carpenters began to adapt urban architectural motifs such as baroque window surrounds that they observed during seasonal work in cities such as Saint Petersburg. The larger houses displayed on Kizhi serve as a showcase for artisanal skills that reflected the owner's wealth and culture. The rigors of the northern climate produced a shelter environment that reduced natural light—even in the limited time when the sun was visible. In compensation, northern masters created vivid forms that would catch and reflect the light, whether the tower and cupolas of a church or the decorative wooden carvings on the facade of a log house. Such forms reaffirmed the survival of the community and the longings of the soul.

Lake Onega served as a conduit between the northwestern regions and the southern heartland, but it was also something of a barrier. By the eighteenth century, the challenge of linking Saint Petersburg—founded in 1703—with the interior of the country led to the development of a waterway between the new imperial capital and the Volga River basin. The first major component of the waterway was a canal that linked the Vytegra River, which flows into Lake Onega toward Saint Petersburg, and the Kovzha River, which flows south into White Lake. In 1799 this segment was named the Mariinsky Canal (in honor of Maria Feodorovna, wife of Emperor Paul I). Its administrative center was the settlement of Vytegra, located on the river of the same name. First referred to in written documents at the end of the fifteenth century, Vytegra had by the early eighteenth century become a crossroads for trade between the northern port of Arkhangelsk and Saint Petersburg. The canal continued to support Vytegra's prosperity throughout the nineteenth century. Most of its houses were built of wood, and a few have been preserved, as well as a picturesque Russian Revival chapel from the 1880s.

Just to the west of Vyetgra is the village of Paltoga, referred to as a *pogost*, which traditionally meant that it had at least one church and a cemetery. Paltoga had two churches: the wooden Church of the Epiphany, built on a rise in 1733; and Church of the Icon of the Virgin of the Sign (Znamenie), built of whitewashed brick in 1810. Both churches still stood in picturesque ruin at the time of my visit in 2006. The wooden Church of the Epiphany is especially interesting as an example of wooden architecture. Its basic

VYTEGRA. Chapel of Saint Isaac of Dalmatia, southeast view. August 28, 2006.

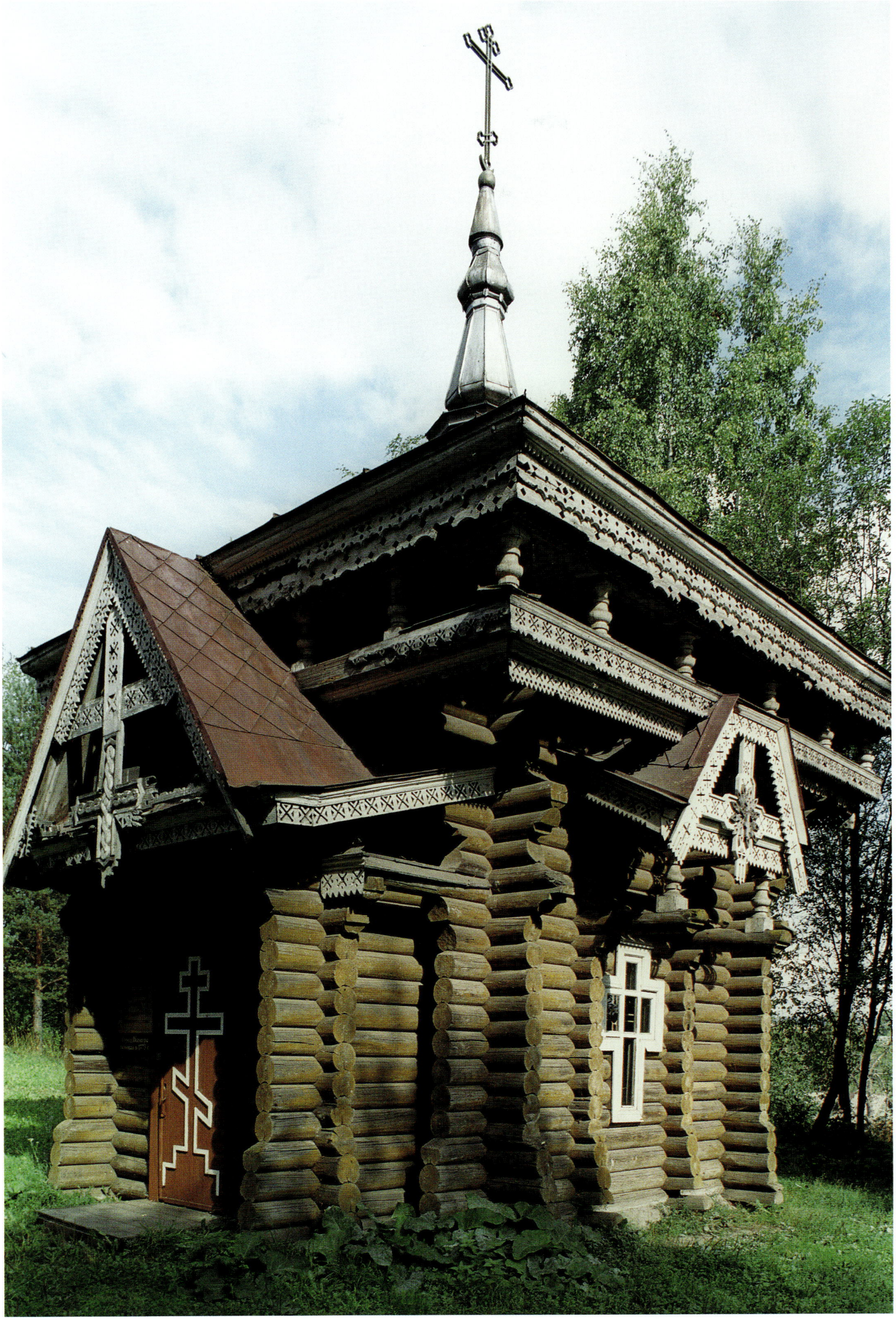

structure is a cube crowned with a much smaller cube that serves as a core for the church's five cupolas. The largest cupola rises at the center of the crown, while the other four cupolas rest on barrel gables that extend on the four points of the compass. This distinctive arrangement is found in a few other northern churches built at the turn of the eighteenth century. During the early Soviet period the church was closed and deprived of four of the five cupolas. An effort to restore the structure began in the 1990s, and the cupolas were rebuilt with the re-creation of shingle covering. As I have often observed, the restoration was abandoned mid-course. By 2006, when I was there, the church was already in a state of extreme disrepair with rotting scaffolding, and in 2009 the structure collapsed. Efforts were made to conserve what was left of the lower log courses, and by the summer of 2014 the rebuilding was well underway. By 2020 the reconstruction was complete, yet much of the original structure was lost in the collapse.

Forty-five kilometers due north of Vytegra is the remarkable log tower of the Church of Elijah the Prophet at the village of Saminsky Pogost, located on the Samina River. Saminsky Pogost was likely formed by the fifteenth century and became one of two parts of the larger Andomsky Pogost. (The Samina flows into the Andoma River, which empties into Lake Onega.) Its church ensemble, including a cemetery, arose on the right bank of the Samina River. The earliest documented church at Saminsky Pogost was built in 1652 and dedicated to Elijah the Prophet, but the church was destroyed by fire at the end of the seventeenth century. Wooden churches frequently fell victim to fires (including those caused by lightning strikes), but in this case, there is an added irony: Elijah was considered the patron saint of fire. Although work began on a replacement in 1692, the new Elijah Church was not consecrated until ten years later—an atypically long time for a wooden church. Superbly proportioned, the Elijah Church has a tall, square base culminating on each side with flared log courses (*poval*) that protect the walls beneath from excessive moisture. The top logs serve as a base for triangular gables. The gables transition to an octagonal structure that also culminates in flared log courses. They, in turn, support an apron of short boards at the base of a soaring tent tower capped with a cross over a cupola clad in carved shingles. Such tower churches formerly dotted the Russian North, but fires and neglect have severely depleted their number. Usually the tent tower consisted of vertical planks over a skeletal frame, but in the case of the Elijah Church, the massive tower had ascending, progressively smaller octagonal courses covered by plank

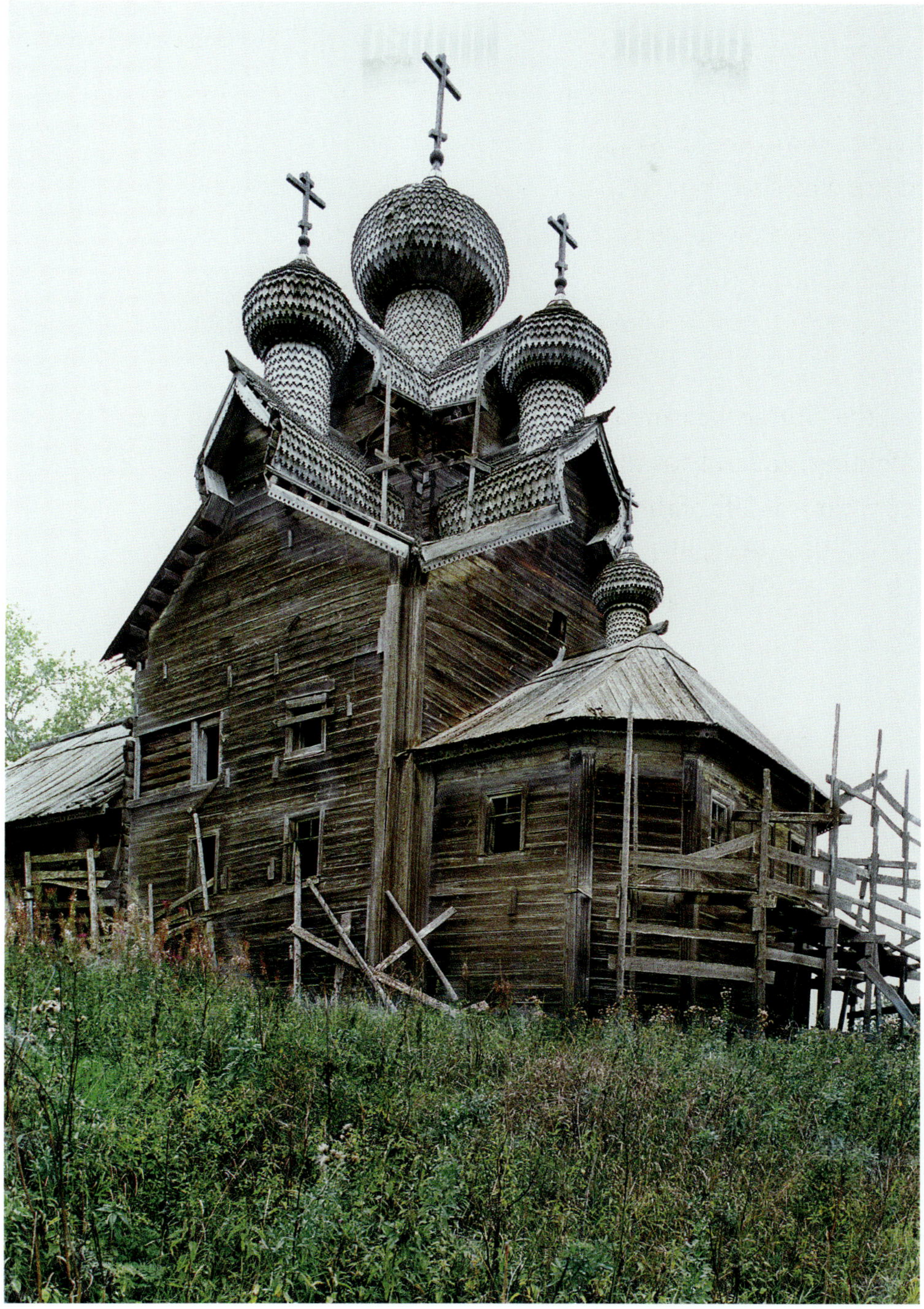

PALTOGA POGOST. Church of the Epiphany, southeast view. Collapsed in 2009. Rebuilt by 2020 with loss of much of the original structure. August 28, 2006.

cladding. An attached structure on the east end contained the main altar (as required by the Russian Orthodox Church). A larger extension on the west contained a vestibule that served the parish community. During the nineteenth century, the structure's exterior was covered with plank siding painted white, and a bell tower was built over the west end of the vestibule. On the interior the church had an icon screen, many icons of which were probably painted in the eighteenth century, with nineteenth-century additions. It also had a painted ceiling, or "sky."

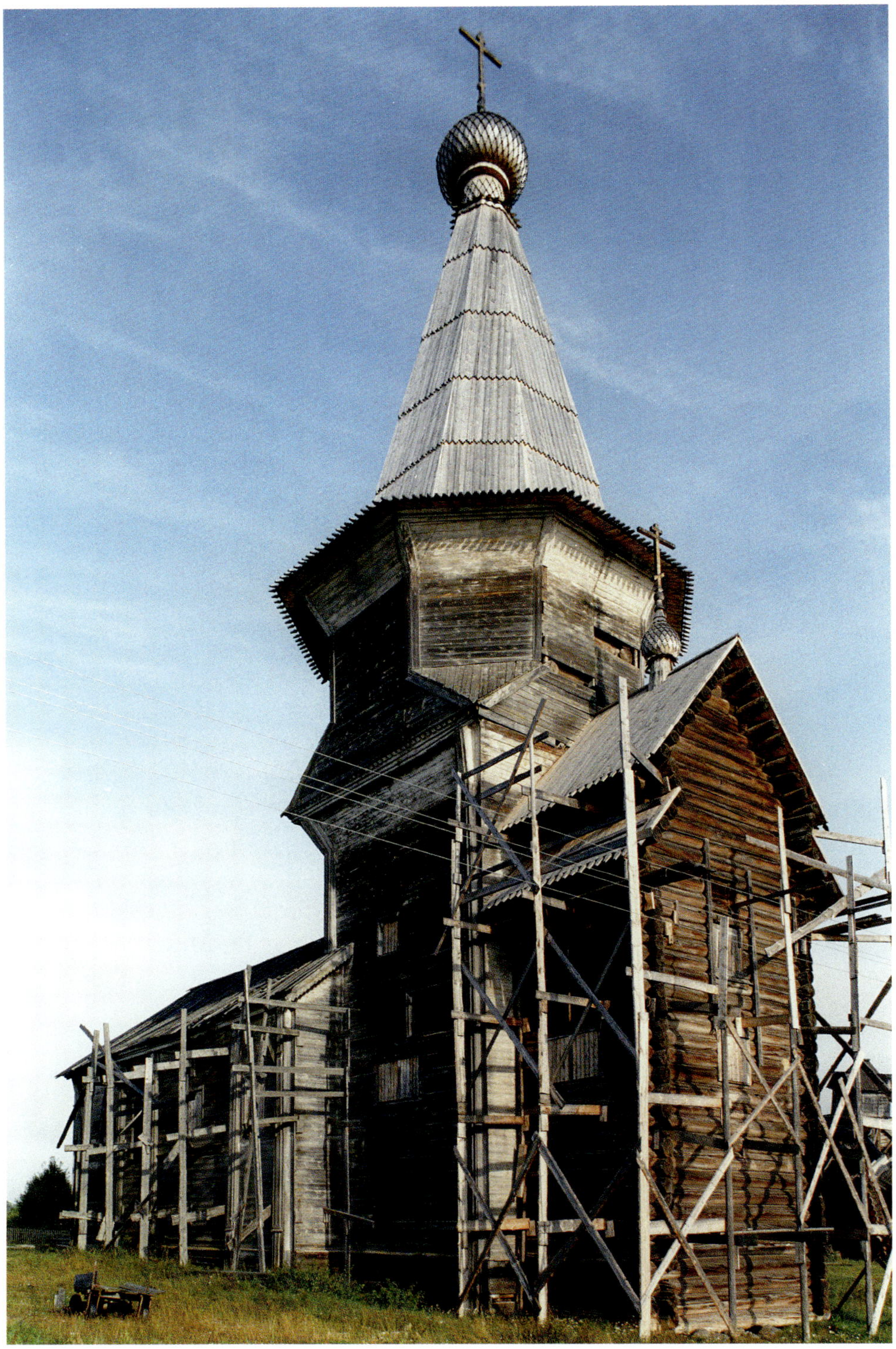

SAMINSKY POGOST. Church of Elijah the Prophet, southeast view. Under process of restoration with weathered plank siding partially removed. August 28, 2006.

In 1897 the Elijah Church was complemented by a wooden church dedicated to the Tikhvin Icon of the Virgin—a sacred image especially revered in the northwestern part of Russia. With the establishment of Soviet power, both churches were closed, and the cemetery overlooking the river was effaced. The Elijah Church was eventually converted into the village club. In 1954, the club director was ordered to remove the icons and the painted ceiling. Instead of destroying them, he had them covered with blue paint. This solution enabled some of the icons to be salvaged years later and placed in the Vytegra Museum. Around 1979, the Elijah Church bell tower was pulled down. (The bells had long since disappeared.) At the same time, the remarkable church was declared an architectural monument and limited conservation was undertaken to prevent further deterioration of the main structure. At the beginning of this century, these efforts were supervised by the preservation workshop of Alexander Popov, but no attempt was made to rebuild the nineteenth-century bell tower. Traces of these efforts were still visible at the time of my visit in August 2006. The plank siding was retained to reduce costs and as a means of protecting the log structure. As its population dwindled (twenty-one inhabitants as of 2010), Saminsky Pogost has lost most traces of organized village life. However, the Elijah Church has been reconsecrated, and each year on Elijah Day (August 2) a priest visits to conduct the liturgy.

And what of the neighboring Andoma Pogost? Only a shell remains of its early nineteenth-century brick church, yet a nearby village with the lush name of Troshchigino harbors an enchanted log Church of the Resurrection nestled within the fir trees of a cemetery. Begun in 1902 with funds from a merchant from the city of Pskov, the church was completed the following year and dedicated to the Ascension. Its bell tower was funded by a local entrepreneur of peasant origins. Closed and ransacked in the 1930s, the former church was used as a storehouse, but the cemetery remained. This at least saved the structure, which was restored by a local entrepreneur at the turn of this century and consecrated anew to the Resurrection in 2002. This delightful example of the early twentieth-century neo-Russian style beckons toward a wood-paneled interior (with a new icon screen) that seems especially appropriate to this shrine in the brooding northern forest.

Back to the Vytegra River, the most impressive landmark on the Mariinsky Waterway was the spectacular wooden Church of the Intercession of the Virgin at Ankhimovo. Built in 1708 on the site of a former sixteenth-century convent overlooking the Vytegra, the Intercession Church was tragically destroyed in 1963 by a careless fire apparently set by vagrants. This complex structure with its multitude of domes has now been rebuilt in a very different location. In the medieval period (fourteenth–fifteenth centuries) the village of Ankhimovo was the center of an area known as Vytegorsky Pogost, part of a network of large villages created beyond Lake

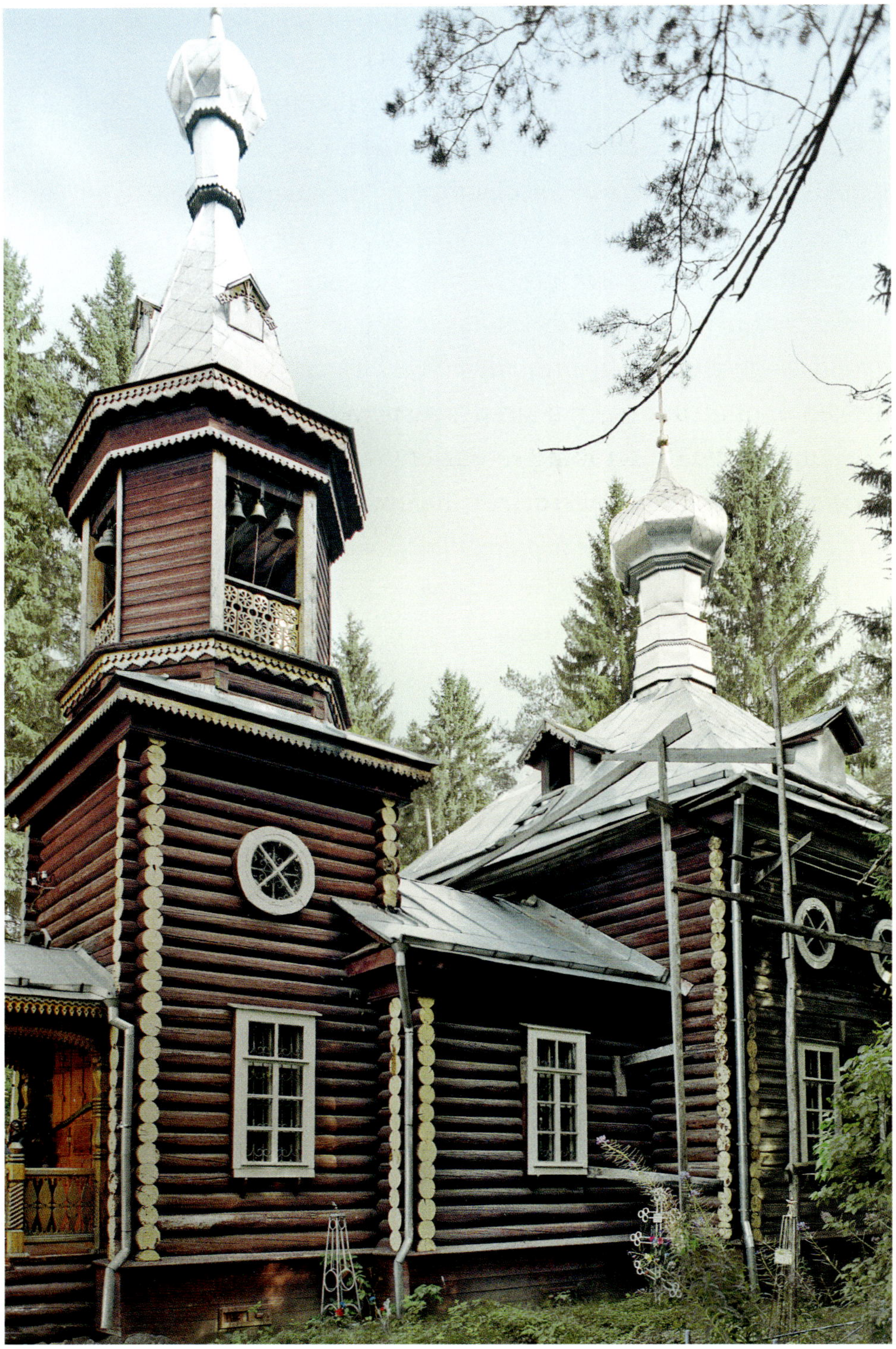

ANDOMSKY POGOST. Church of the Resurrection, southwest view. August 28, 2006.

Onega by settlers from Novgorod the Great. This region of the Russian North acquired special importance for Peter the Great's geopolitical strategy after the founding of Saint Petersburg in 1703. One can assume that this grandiose structure, as well as the similar, renowned Church of the Transfiguration at the Kizhi *pogost* (1714), served to proclaim Russian presence in the strategic territory around Lake Onega.

Toward the end of Catherine the Great's reign, the Intercession Church was taken apart, repaired with a replacement of decayed lower logs, and repositioned on a stone foundation in 1793. Subsequently, the massive log structure was entirely encased in plank siding painted white. Built of massive pine logs, the soaring form of the Church of the Intercession consisted of an octagonal core structure with four large extensions at the compass points. These extensions in turn ascended in two stages, with each level supporting cupolas over peaked barrel (*bochka*) gables. The four sides located between the compass extensions rose as unobstructed majestic facades. The center of these diagonal facades displayed an outline of the barrel gables that crown the flanking extensions. The structure's summit displayed a crown of eight domes, originally covered with aspen shingles. At the lower level on the west side, the church was encased by a gallery supported by extended projecting logs. This area, which contained the main entrance, served as an elevated vestibule particularly necessary during long, snow-laden winters. On the east side of the church the apse, which contained the main altar (dedicated to the Intercession), supported additional domes, as did flanking chapels dedicated to Saint John the Divine and to Saint George. Depending on the period, the total number of domes has been calculated as twenty-four or twenty-five.

After the disastrous fire of 1963, thoughts of re-creating the Intercession Church were based on detailed measurements done in the late 1950s by the leading specialist on wooden architecture, Alexander Opolovnikov (1911–94). Yet resources for such a large project were unlikely, particularly at such a remote location. Four decades after the fire, however, the vision of a reconstructed Intercession Church materialized on the territory of Nevsky Forest Park, located along the Neva River to the southeast of Saint Petersburg. This outdoor museum was conceived as a project to re-create lost monuments of wooden architecture and was given the name Bogoslovka after an estate that had existed in the area during the nineteenth century. The centerpiece of the project was the Intercession Church, its resurrection supported at the highest state and church levels. Built in 2004–7, the design of the reconstructed church followed measurements recorded by Opolovnikov and strove to re-create the earlier eighteenth-century appearance, although some details remain conjectural. There is no plank siding over the log structure, and aspen shingles cover the domes. Choosing and curing the timber for such a large structure assumed special importance. The pine logs, felled in Karelia's rocky terrain, were chosen

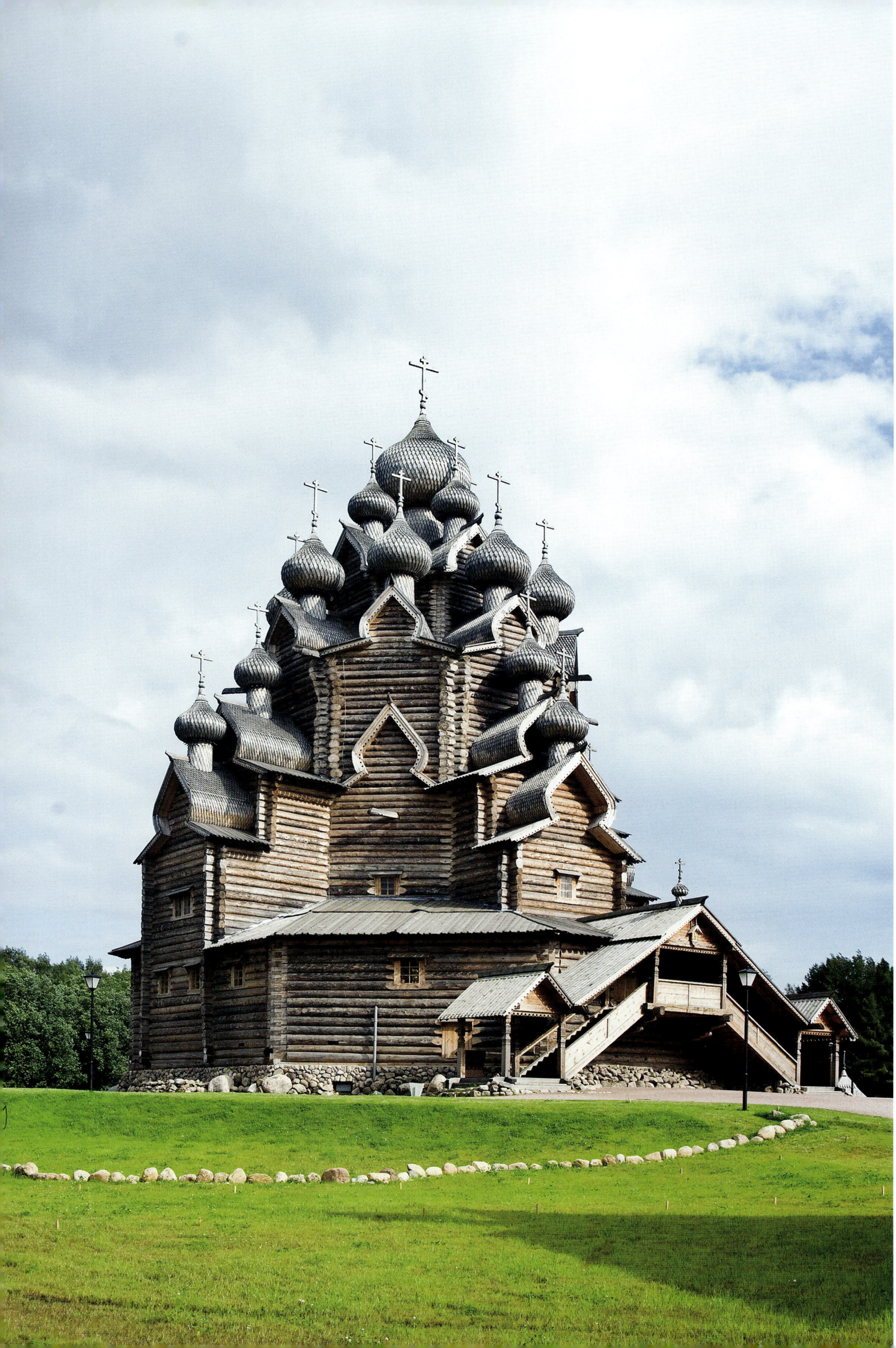

with a minimum of twelve rings per centimeter, indicating slow, solid growth.

The park territory surrounding the Intercession Church is enclosed by a wooden wall copied from an eighteenth-century original at Lyadiny Pogost near Kargopol, of which more later.

A major transit point in the journey down the Mariinsky Waterway was the town of Belozersk (current population around 10,000). The "Beloozero" mentioned in the *Primary Chronical* under the year 862 is now considered to have been at another location, but whatever the details of its origins and early location, the town was always connected with White Lake (Beloe Ozero). Although smaller than Lakes Ladoga and Onega, White Lake has been a pivotal link between those two lakes and the Russian heartland.

The architectural heritage of Belozersk consists primarily of brick structures, but it had one wooden landmark of national significance. Built in the 1690–96, the Church of Elijah the Prophet ascended in three tiers from a cuboid base to a large wooden cupola clearly visible from the southwest corner of the town citadel. This base was built of round notched pine logs, while the apse, which contained the altar on the east side, was constructed with the tighter dovetail joint. The west side had a vestibule and a covered porch. On the interior of the main structure, the logs were scraped flat to create an even surface that could be painted. The east wall displayed a large five-tiered icon screen that flared to the right and left on the upper levels. During the Soviet period the nearly 120 icons, painted at the end of the seventeenth century, were removed for preservation to the Belozersk Museum, but most were subsequently transferred to nearby Kirillov for better conditions at the museum of the Saint Kirill of Belozersk Monastery. At the top of the main structure was a painted ceiling (*nebo*) consisting of trapezoidal panels angled upward, with a square image of Christ in the center. I was fortunate to be able to photograph the interior of this masterpiece in 1999, including the main panel of the Crucifixion.

Over the decades of its closure, this historic structure was threatened by lack of repair. In the 1970s a restoration of the walls removed nineteenth-century plank siding and brought the structure into basic use as a museum. However, lack of maintenance led to further disrepair, including the threat of seeping ground water. Plans for a thorough restoration were proposed to meet celebrations of the 1150th anniversary of Belozersk in 2012. The structure was disassembled in 2010, but thereafter restoration plans have foundered among competing projects and priorities.

ANKHIMOVO (original location). Church of the Intercession of the Virgin, northwest view. Built in 1708, the church was destroyed by fire in 1963. In 2007 this replica was completed at a park on the Neva River to the southeast of Saint Petersburg. August 17, 2009.

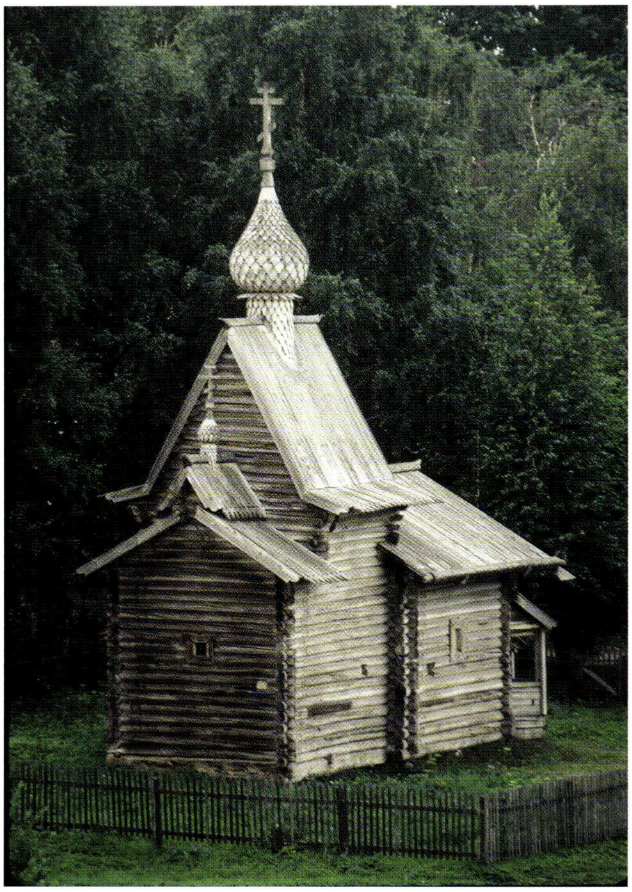

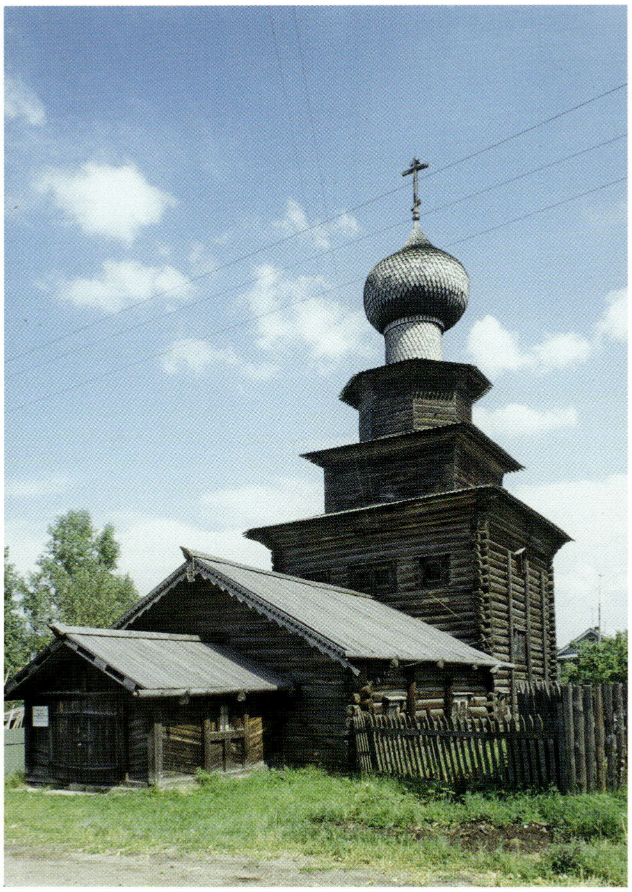

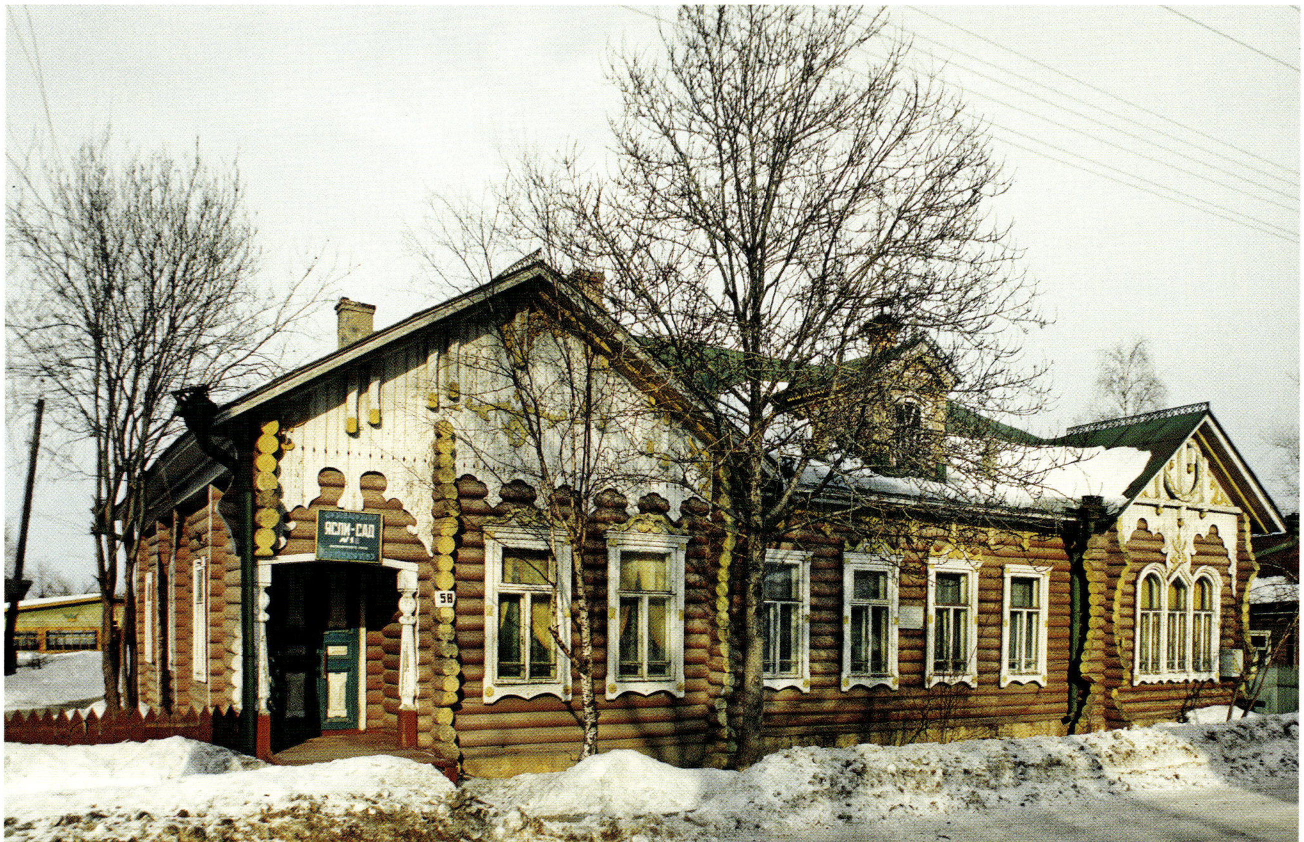
ЯСЛИ-САД

A happier story can be told of the graceful, tiered Church of Elijah the Prophet at Tsypino, located near one of Russia's most revered cultural and spiritual landmarks, the Ferapontov-Nativity Monastery, designated a UNESCO World Heritage Site for its early sixteenth-century frescoes. My encounter with the Tsypino church is a fortunate case of being present before and after a major restoration. I stumbled upon the site in July 1999, when the forest growth surrounding the log ruins was being cleared, and I returned fifteen years later, in June 2014, when the Elijah Church stood in its splendidly restored form.

The village of Tsypino is now tiny, but its origins date at least to the sixteenth century, and in the late nineteenth century it was the center of a thriving agricultural parish with over twenty villages. At that time, it was adjacent to a sacred space known as Tsypinsky Pogost, which consisted of the Elijah Church as well as a brick church built in 1800 with altars dedicated to Saint George and Saint Demetrius of Thessaloniki. The entire territory of the *pogost*—including parish houses and

KIRILLOV. Church of the Deposition of the Robe, northeast view. Built in 1485 at the nearby village of Borodava, this ancient, *izba*-like shrine exemplifies the most basic form of log church architecture. Brought in 1958 to the museum territory of the Saint Kirill of Belozersk Monastery. July 31, 1996.

BELOZERSK. Church of Elijah the Prophet, southwest view. Disassembled in 2010 for capital restoration, this major monument from the 1690s has lost much of the original material and has stood half-rebuilt for years without discernable progress. New promises have been made. July 23, 1999.

BELOZERSK. House built in the early twentieth century for the Pozdynin merchant family. An excellent example of *style moderne* decorative fantasy applied to a log structure. March 3, 1998

TSYPINO. Church of Elijah the Prophet at Tsypinsky Pogost, southeast view. Photograph taken July 15, 1999, when the territory around the abandoned structure was beginning to be cleared.

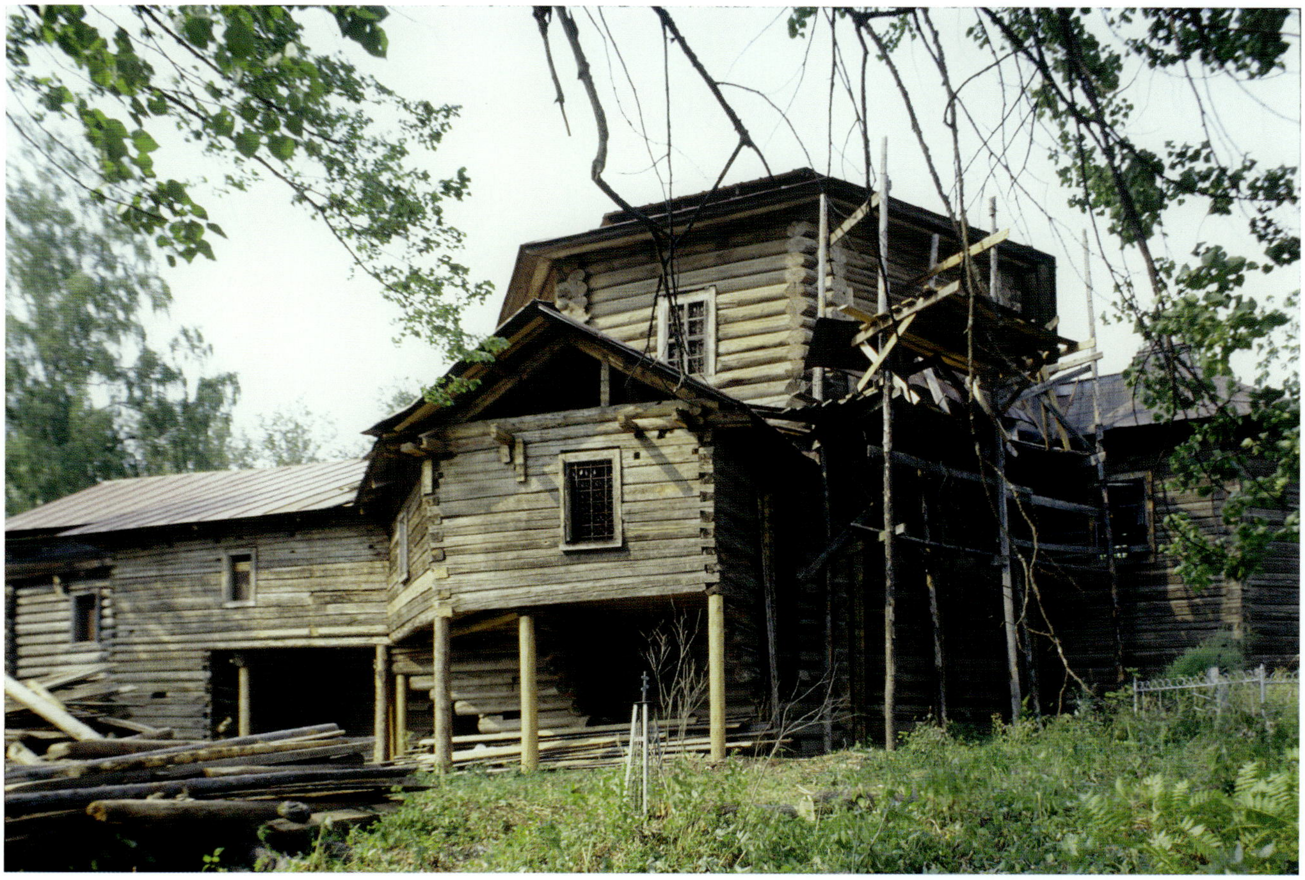

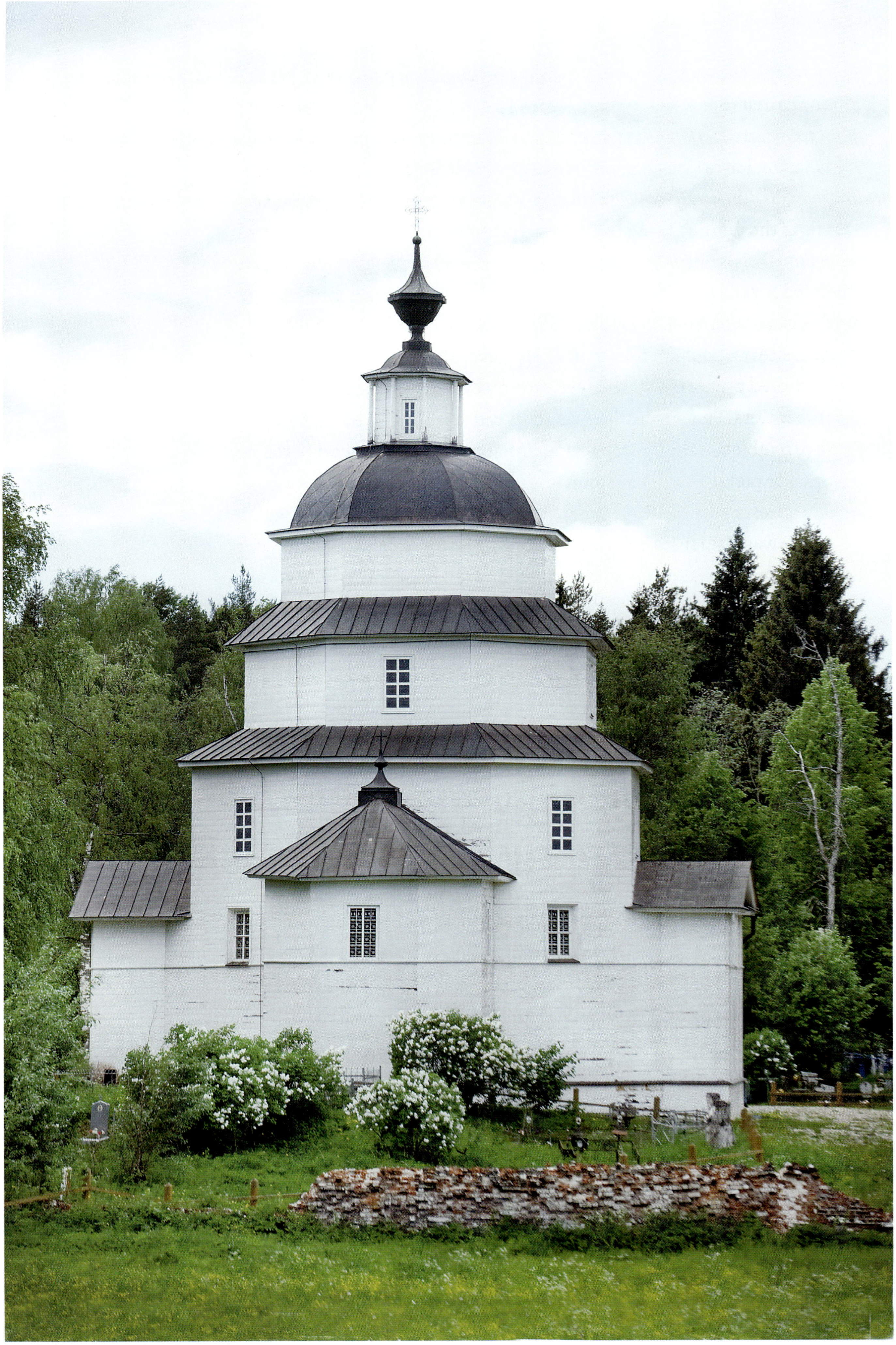

a cemetery—was surrounded by a solid wooden fence painted white. The Elijah Church that stood in the nineteenth century was built of pine logs and consecrated in 1756. Its tall, spacious form consisted of three ascending octagonal tiers over an octagonal base, from which extended four arms of the cross. The east arm contained the primary altar, and the west arm served as the main entrance. The base structure of the church is encompassed on the south, west, and north sides with a raised gallery resting on extended logs, still visible in my 1999 photographs. The structural design is a marvel of functional ingenuity and aesthetic harmony, enhanced by an ideal site overlooking the small Elijah Lake. The interior of the church was centered on a large icon screen that rose into the canopy formed by the upper tiers. Four majestic rows of sacred images looked down upon those assembled in the church's wide octagonal space, unencumbered by columns or piers.

The priest of the Elijah Church for much of the late nineteenth century (1862–95) was Father Ivan Brilliantov, two of whose sons, Alexander and Ivan, became specialists in Russian history. Ivan played a leading role in the study and preservation of the extraordinary artistic legacy surrounding the Ferapontov-Nativity Monastery. Tragically, both would succumb to the wave of Soviet repression directed against regional historians in the early 1930s. Closed in 1935, the Elijah Church fell into decay. The cupola collapsed in 1958, and the two upper tiers fell soon thereafter. The icons had already been gathered at the nearby local history museum in the former Saint Kirill of Belozersk Monastery in the small regional center of Kirillov. The adjacent Church of Saint Demetrius of Thessaloniki was razed for brick, and most of the *pogost* structures were destroyed. Fortunately, this major example of Russian wooden architecture had been documented in photographs and was not totally forgotten. In 1995 a presidential order included the Elijah Church in the list of architectural monuments of national significance. When I first photographed the structure, in the summer of 1996, work had just begun on clearing the overgrown site around the surviving log courses of the base structure.

The restoration proper was begun in 2003 under the direction of Alexander Popov, a leading practitioner of historic restoration methods with an emphasis on log structures. The first task was to completely disassemble and study the remaining structure. An examination of stroke marks on the original logs led to the creation of extended, narrow-bladed axes replicating those used in the construction of this eighteenth-century structure. The

TSYPINO. Church of Elijah the Prophet at Tsypinsky Pogost, east view after restoration. June 1, 2014.

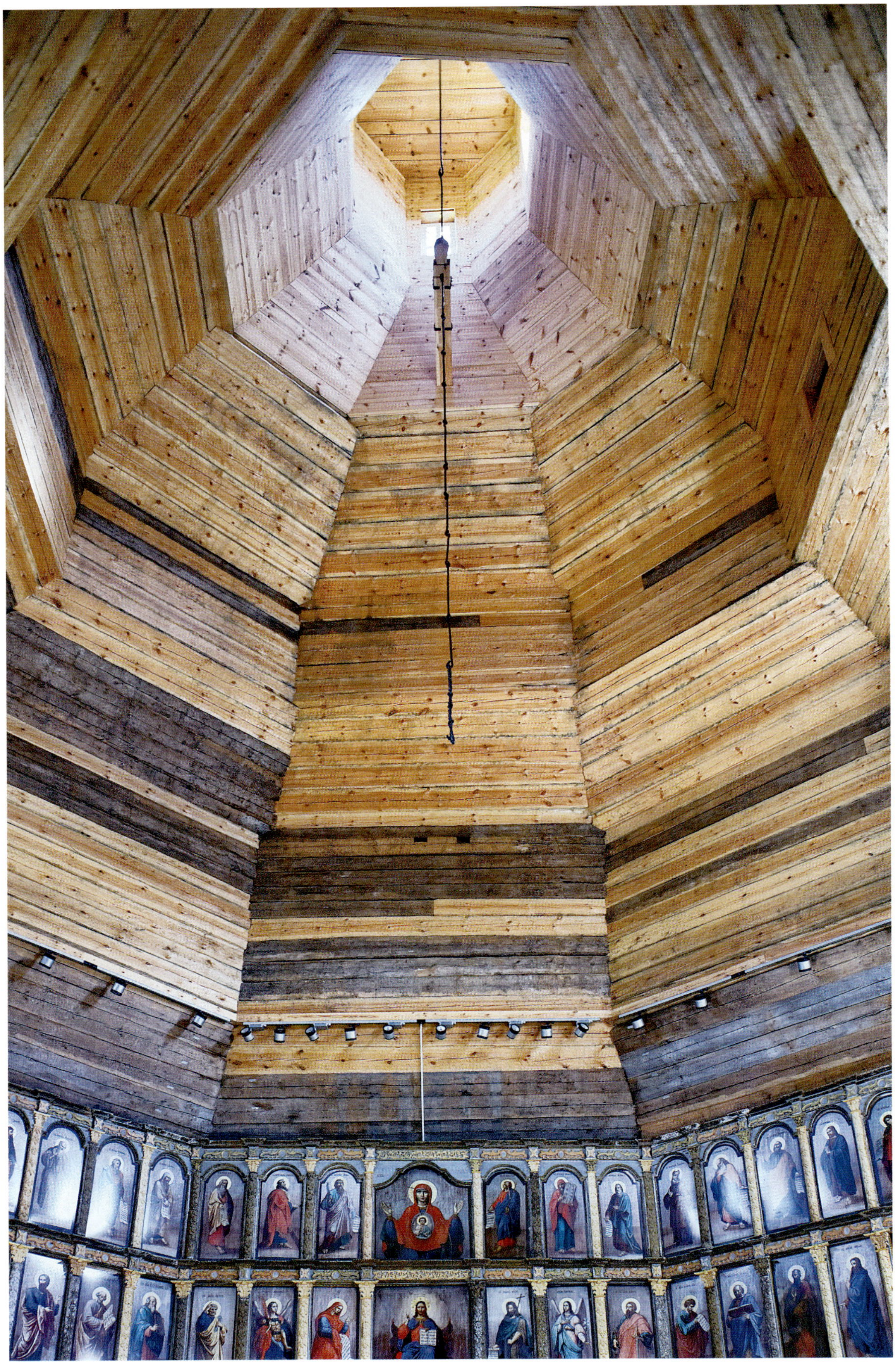

careful rebuilding of the church by master craftsmen extended through the summer of 2009, when the monument was reopened to visitors. As in the nineteenth century, the exterior has white plank siding. This cladding was typical practice in the nineteenth and early twentieth centuries, but postwar Soviet restorers of wooden architecture made a practice of removing the siding to gain the original appearance. A new approach restores the siding in cases where it is clearly documented. Some have argued that this helps preserve the log structure underneath, yet it also conceals structural elements and techniques such as those I photographed in 1999.

Work continues on the interior of the Elijah Church. In 2010 a reconstruction of the carved wooden icon screen was completed with photographic reproductions of the icons. A selection of the original icons is preserved in the museum at the Saint Kirill of Belozersk Monastery. Despite the continuing loss of monuments of Russian wooden architecture, the Church of Elijah the Prophet at Tsypino is a stunning testimony to what can be accomplished with the proper combination of historical documentation, technical expertise, and financial support.

A return to the Sheksna River eventually leads southwest to the city of Cherepovets (population around 318,000), known for the steel-producing center Severstal (NorthSteel), one of Russia's largest industrial enterprises. A major stimulus to Cherepovets occurred with the opening in 1810 of the Mariinsky Canal System, which linked Saint Petersburg with the Volga River basin at the town of Rybinsk. With few other settlements on the long Sheksna portion of the waterway, Cherepovets became a base for boat services and flourished under the energetic direction of Ivan Miliutin, a shipping magnate, industrialist, and civic leader. His wooden cottage has been carefully restored in a park overlooking the confluence of the Yagorba and Sheksna Rivers. Other restored historic houses include the magnificent Galskoy estate (see chapter 1) on the opposite bank of the Sheksna River. The villages surrounding Cherepovets, particularly to the south, have their share of wooden monuments, as my photographs show. How long they will survive is an open question.

The territory east and north of the Sheksna basin contains one of the richest treasures of the Russian North, the town of Kargopol, located in the southwestern part of Arkhangelsk Province. This small regional center (current population around 8,500) was founded perhaps as early as the eleventh century, and its remarkable masonry churches are a reminder of its former wealth from the sixteenth until the nineteenth centuries, when

TSYPINO. Church of Elijah the Prophet at Tsypinsky Pogost. Interior, view east after restoration with darker wood indicating original elements. June 1, 2014.

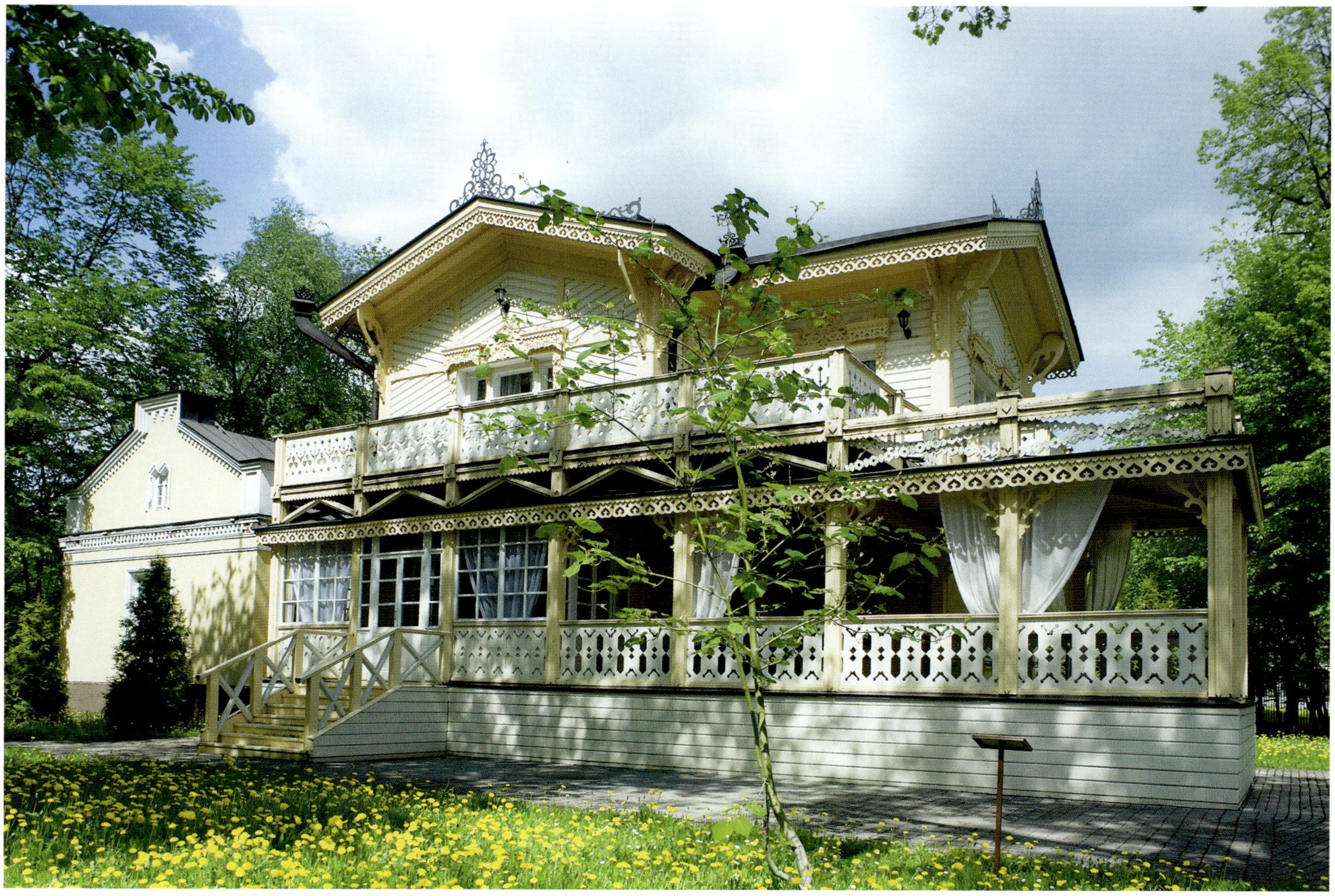

it was part of a strategic trading route from Lake Lacha northward along the Onega River to the White Sea.

Kargopol's historic core approximates its boundaries in the sixteenth century, and one of its charms is the concentration of museums and architectural landmarks within an easily accessible area. The town follows a regular grid plan from the time of Catherine the Great, and its dominant landmarks are churches of brick and locally quarried limestone, some dating back to the sixteenth century with blocks of one- and two-storied log houses, most of which are covered with plank siding. The windows display elaborately carved frames, and the eaves often have decorative cornices. In this town of merchants, craftsmen, clerics, and clerks, the carved decoration of wooden houses reflected a modest prosperity and way of life deeply rooted in tradition.

In the Kargopol region there are villages where the wooden architectural heritage has survived despite vulnerability to the elements and human carelessness. One of the most remarkable sites is the village of Lyadiny, almost forty kilometers from Kargopol. Although its population

CHEREPOVETS. Ivan Miliutin cottage (reconstruction). June 10, 2017.

NELAZSKOE (Cherepovets region). Church of the Dormition, northwest view. Built in 1694, this church is a beautifully complex, urbanized interpretation of a cruciform plan with a high central core culminating in three cupolas. The lower arms of the cross are crowned with large barrel gables. July 23, 1999.

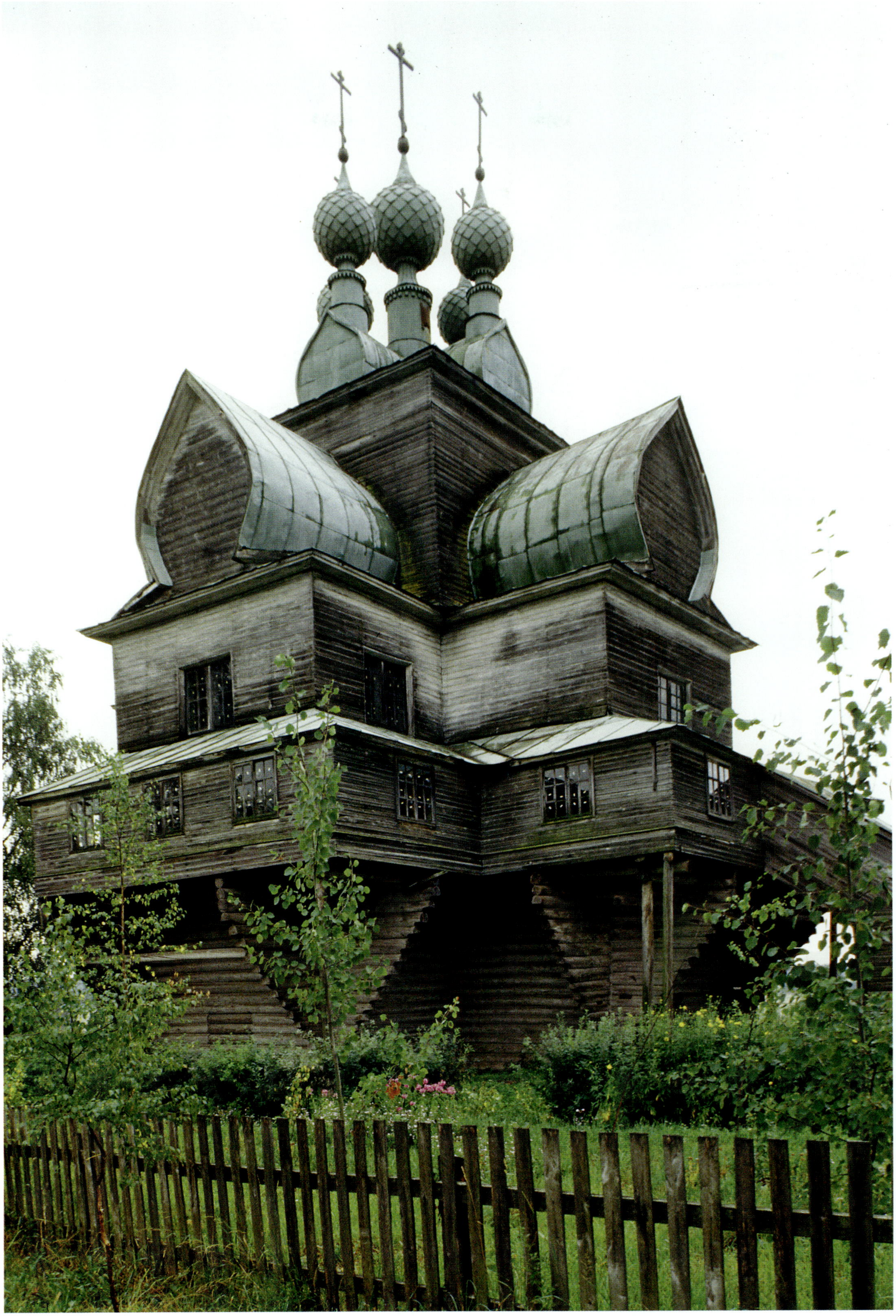

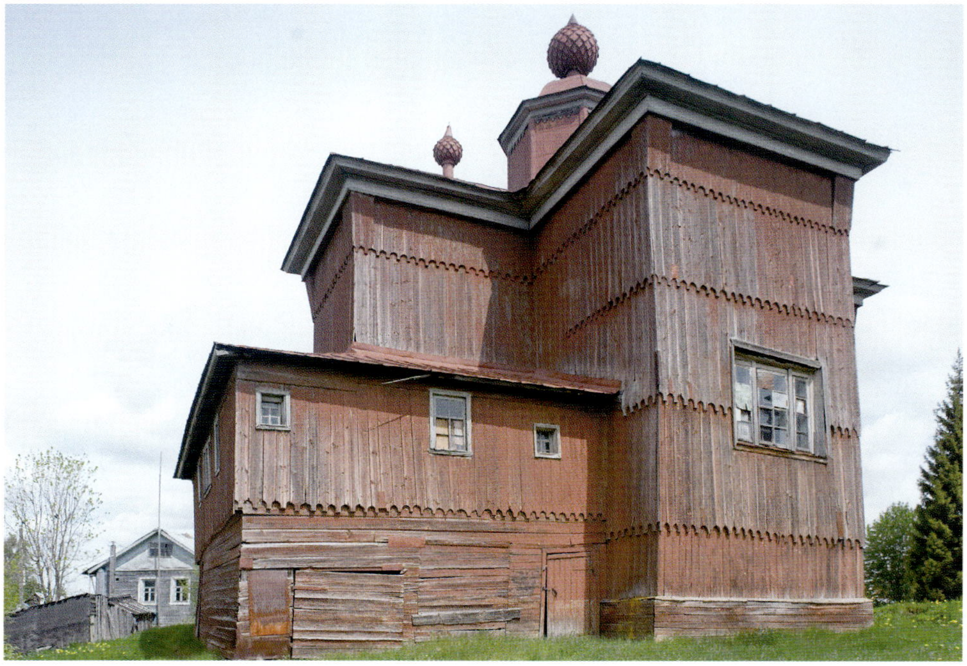

DMITRIEVO (Cherepovets region). Church of Saint Nicholas, southwest view. Built in 1673 at a center for producing bog iron, this intriguing cruciform church suggests similarities with the Nelazskoe masterpiece, but clumsy nineteenth-century modifications (including a truncated crown and shoddy siding) leave only a suggestion of what might have been. June 7, 2017.

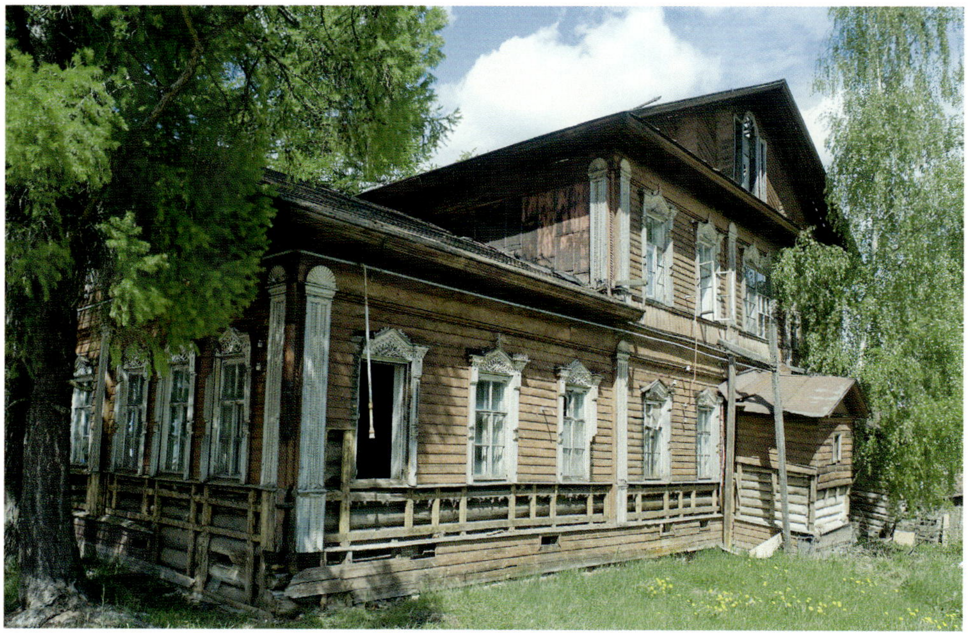

KOROTOVO (Cherepovets region). Peter Andriyanov estate house, park facade. Abandoned nineteenth-century house but structurally sound. Lower walls provide clear example of the attachment of plank cladding to vertical slats on log wall. June 7, 2017.

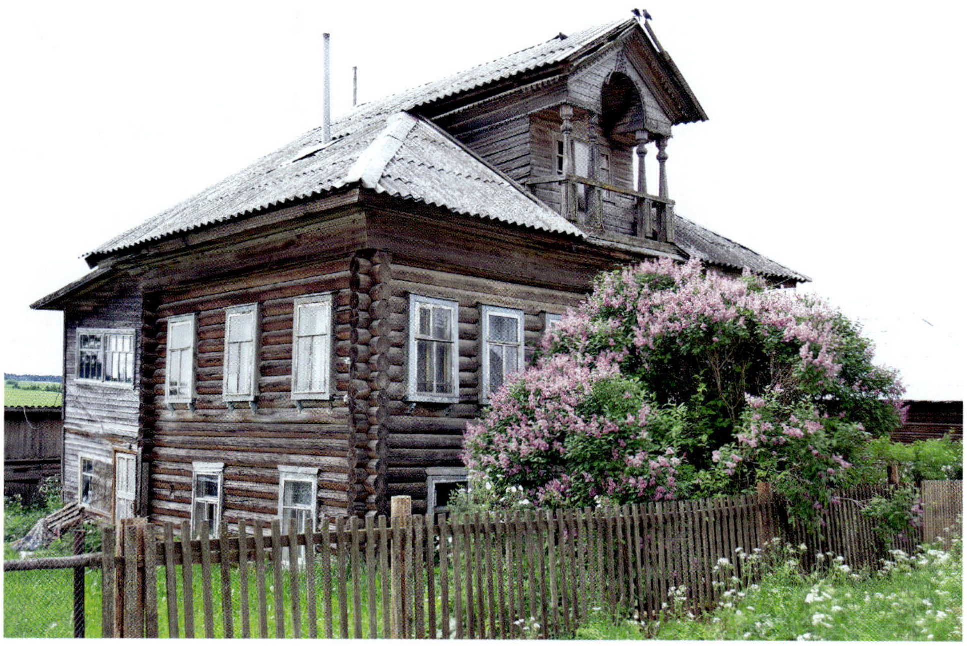

FOMINSKOE (Cherepovets region). Log house built at the turn of the twentieth century with upper gable containing summer balcony. Plank roof replaced with asbestos sheets. A fine example of transition of the *izba* to an urbanized form in small towns. June 10, 2010.

MYAKSA (Cherepovets region). Church of the Transfiguration of the Savior, northwest view. Consecrated in 2009, this log church, built with new construction methods, commemorates the renowned Leushino Convent, submerged with the creation of the Rybinsk Reservoir on the Sheksna River. August 9, 2015.

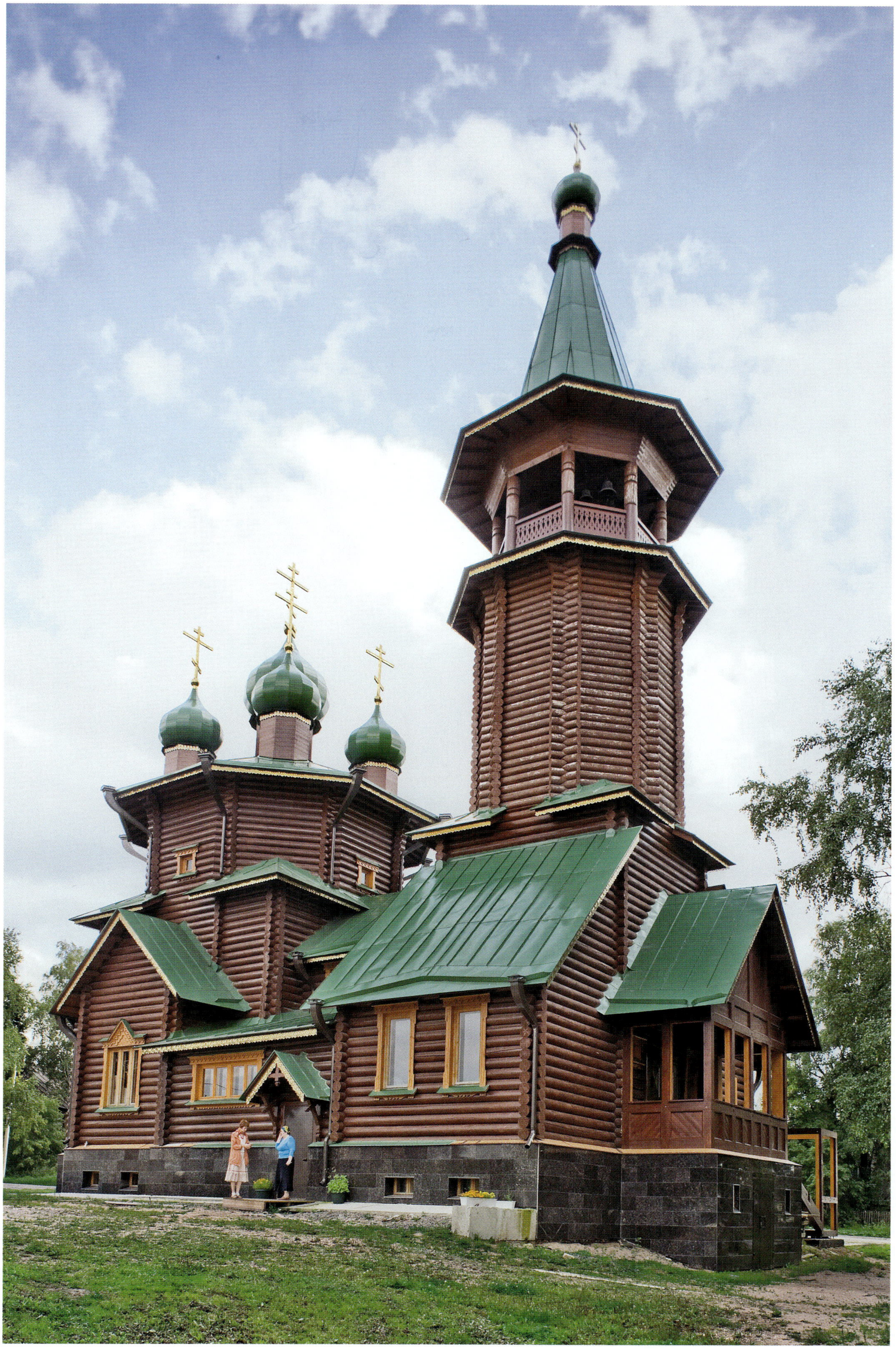

varies slightly between summer and winter, this hamlet of some seventy souls centered around an extraordinary architectural ensemble located on the territory of an ancient cemetery (*pogost*). The Lyadiny ensemble consisted of three parts: the Church of the Intercession with its soaring tent tower (completed by 1761); the nearby Church of the Epiphany (1793), crowned with a panoply of cupolas; and a large bell tower built in 1820. There was also a cemetery enclosed with a fence.

Within the Lyadiny cluster, the tall Intercession Church was used for summer worship, while the lower Epiphany Church, which could be more easily heated, served for worship in the winter. Before construction of the latter, the Church of the Intercession had an altar on the compact ground floor that could be used in the winter. In both summer and winter, illuminated by sun or wind-blown snow, the form of the Intercession Church produced an unforgettable visual impact. Sheathed in darkened plank siding, the structure of stout pine logs ascended to a cupola and cross at its high peak. On the interior, the ground-level chapel enclosed two massive log columns that supported the floor of the main worship space above. A narrow staircase ascended to this main space, and the first impression

KARGOPOL. Urbanized log house with painted plank siding, Zavodskaya Street 3. February 27, 1998.

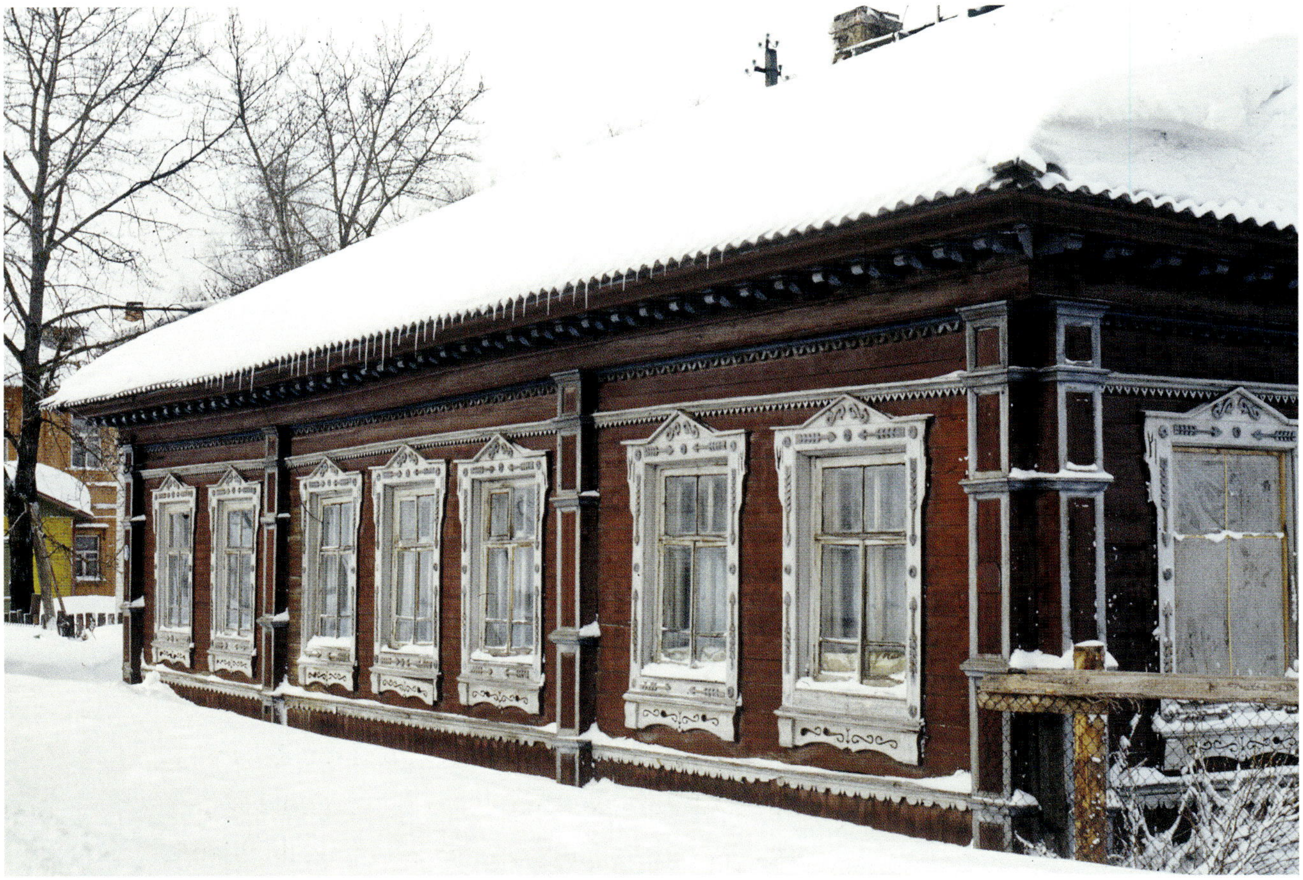

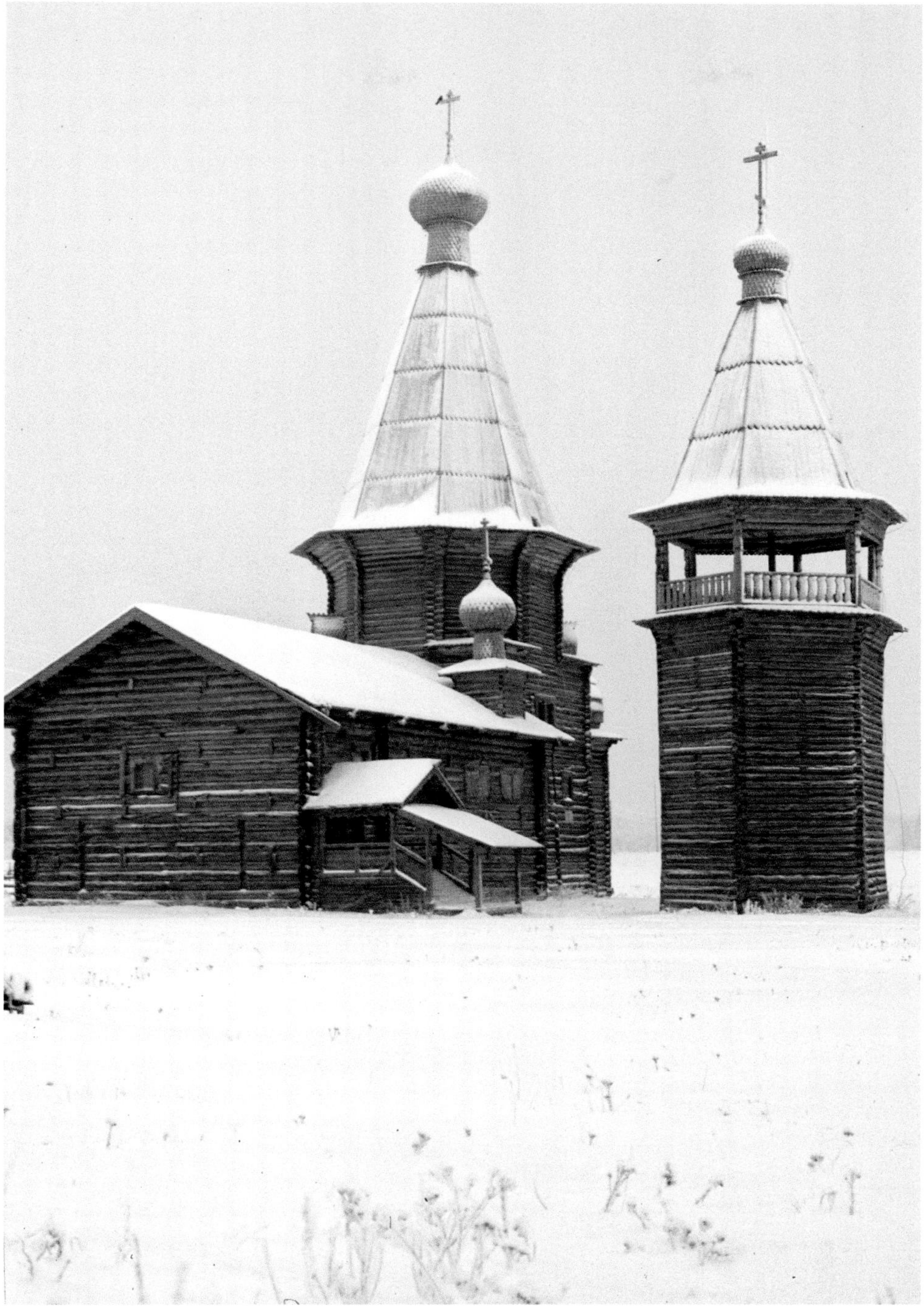

SAUNINO (Kargopol region). Bell tower and Church of Saint John Chrysostome, southwest view. Built in 1665, the structure is an excellent example of seventeenth-century log construction. Porch at southwest corner (probably late nineteenth century) leads to a vestibule with secondary altar. January 4, 1999.

was one of clean whitewashed walls in the vestibule. All the greater was the effect as one turned to the brightly colored icon screen and the painted ceiling, or "heaven," pitched over the worship space in an ingenious combination of art and traditional architecture.

These expansive heavens were a distinctive feature of northern Russian log church interiors, and some still survive. They create a polygonal canopy segmented by flat beams extending from the top of the walls to an

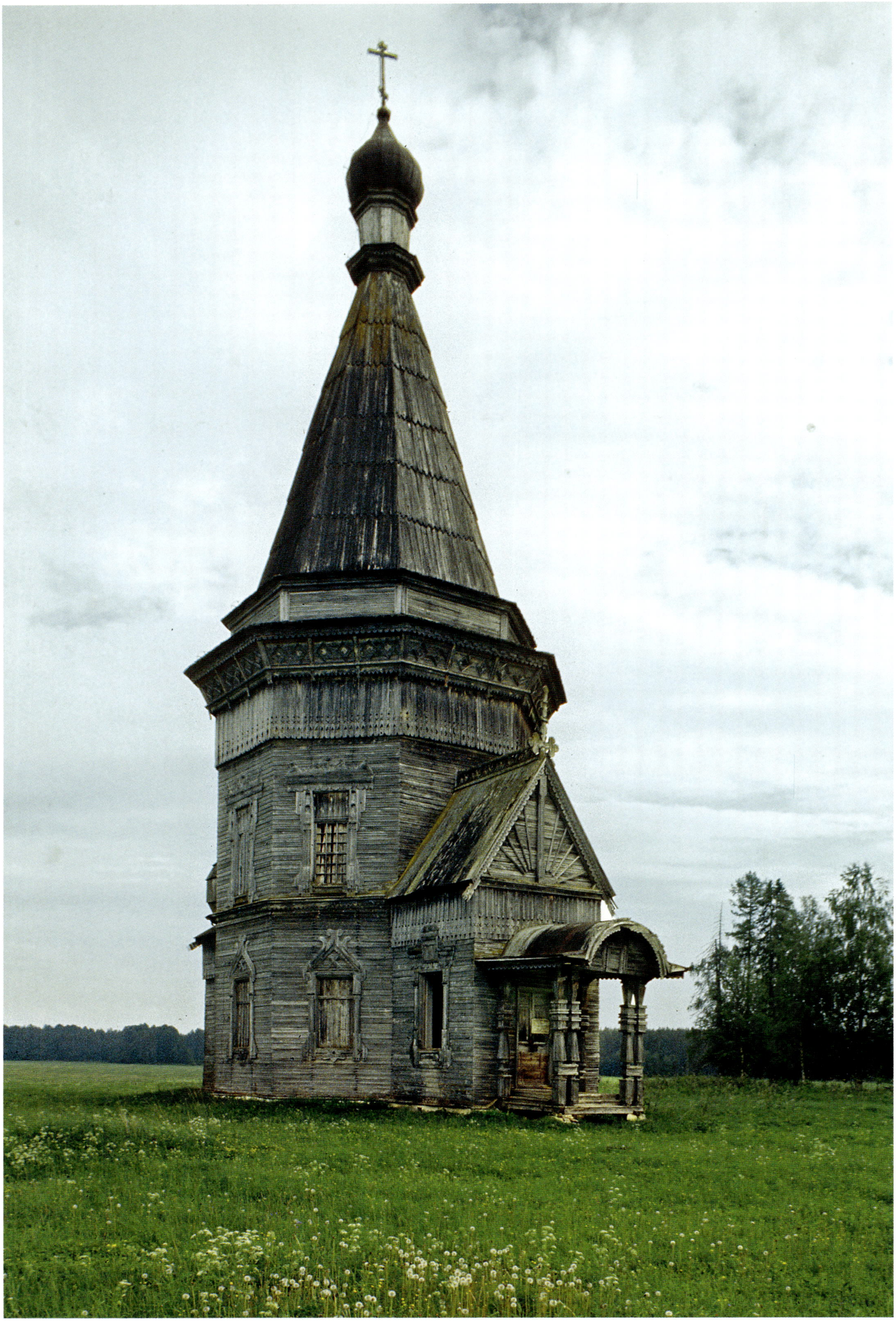

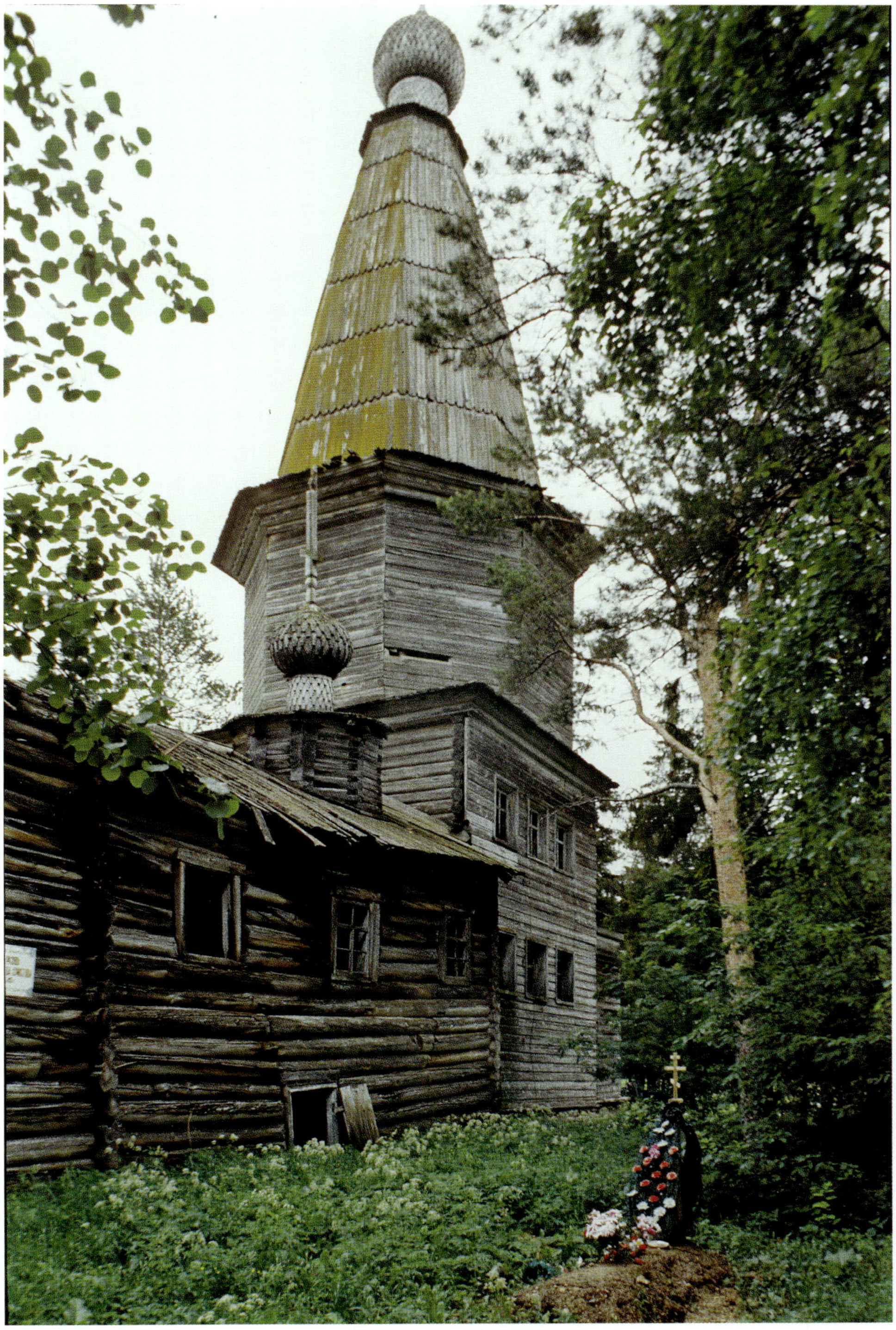

KRASNAYA LYAGA (Kargopol region). Church of the Purification, northwest view. Originally built in 1655, the structure has late nineteenth-century cladding in Carpenter Gothic style. Excellent example of tall tent tower. June 20, 1998.

BOLSHAYA SHALGA (Kargopol region). Church of Nativity of Christ, southwest view. Built in 1745, this superb, abandoned structure with surrounding cemetery is under threat. June 23, 1998.

elevated ring in the ceiling center with an image of the Savior. The beams incline upward and form a skeletal frame that is self-supporting between the walls and the ring at the center. The painted panels in the shape of narrow triangles are laid upon the frame without fasteners. Tension and gravity keep the panels in place. Its twelve long triangular panels depicted the Four Evangelists (Matthew, Mark, Luke, and John) and seven of the eight archangels: Michael, Gabriel, Raphael, Uriel, Yegudiel, Varakhiel, and Selafiel. The main panel above the center of the icon screen depicts the

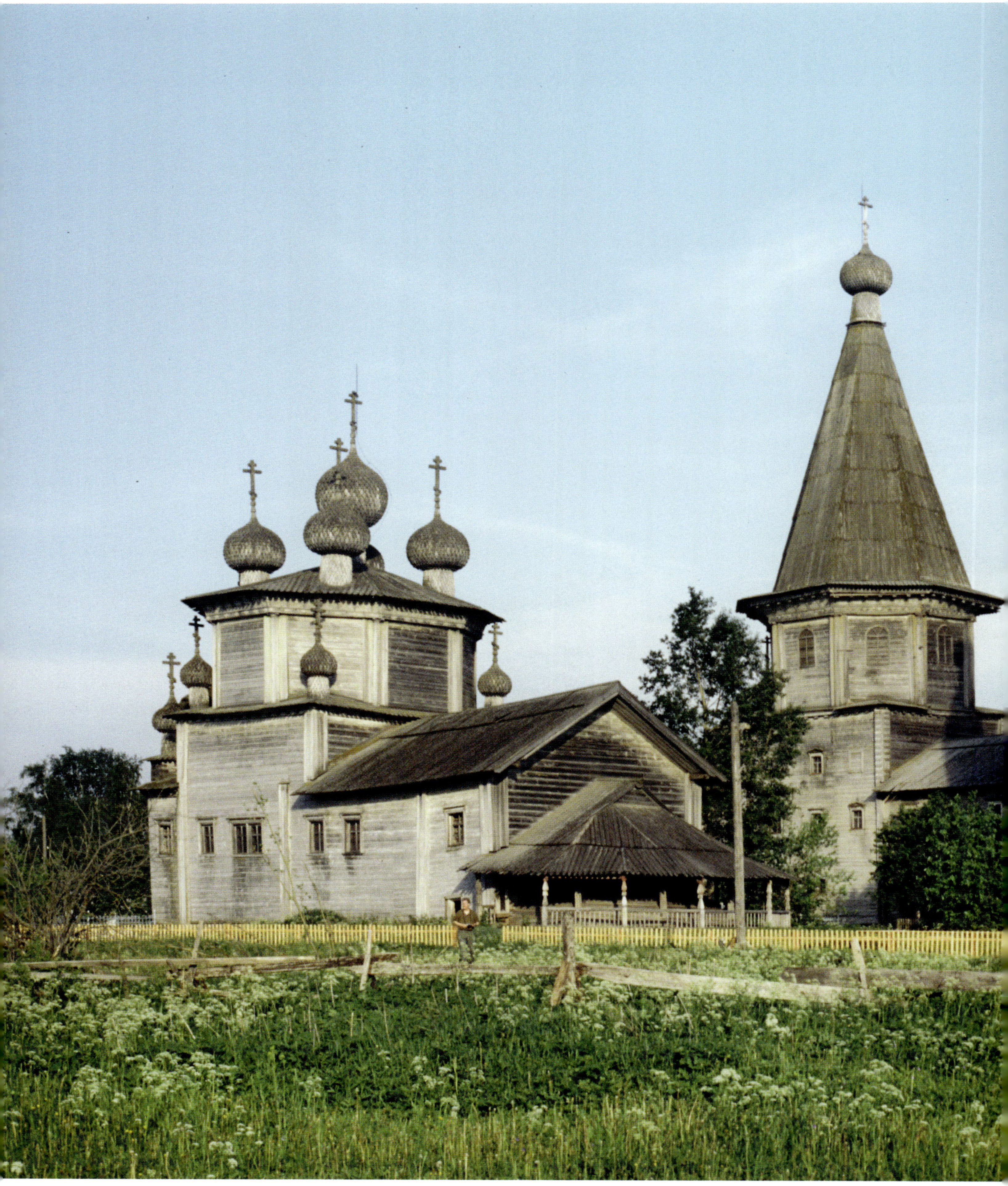

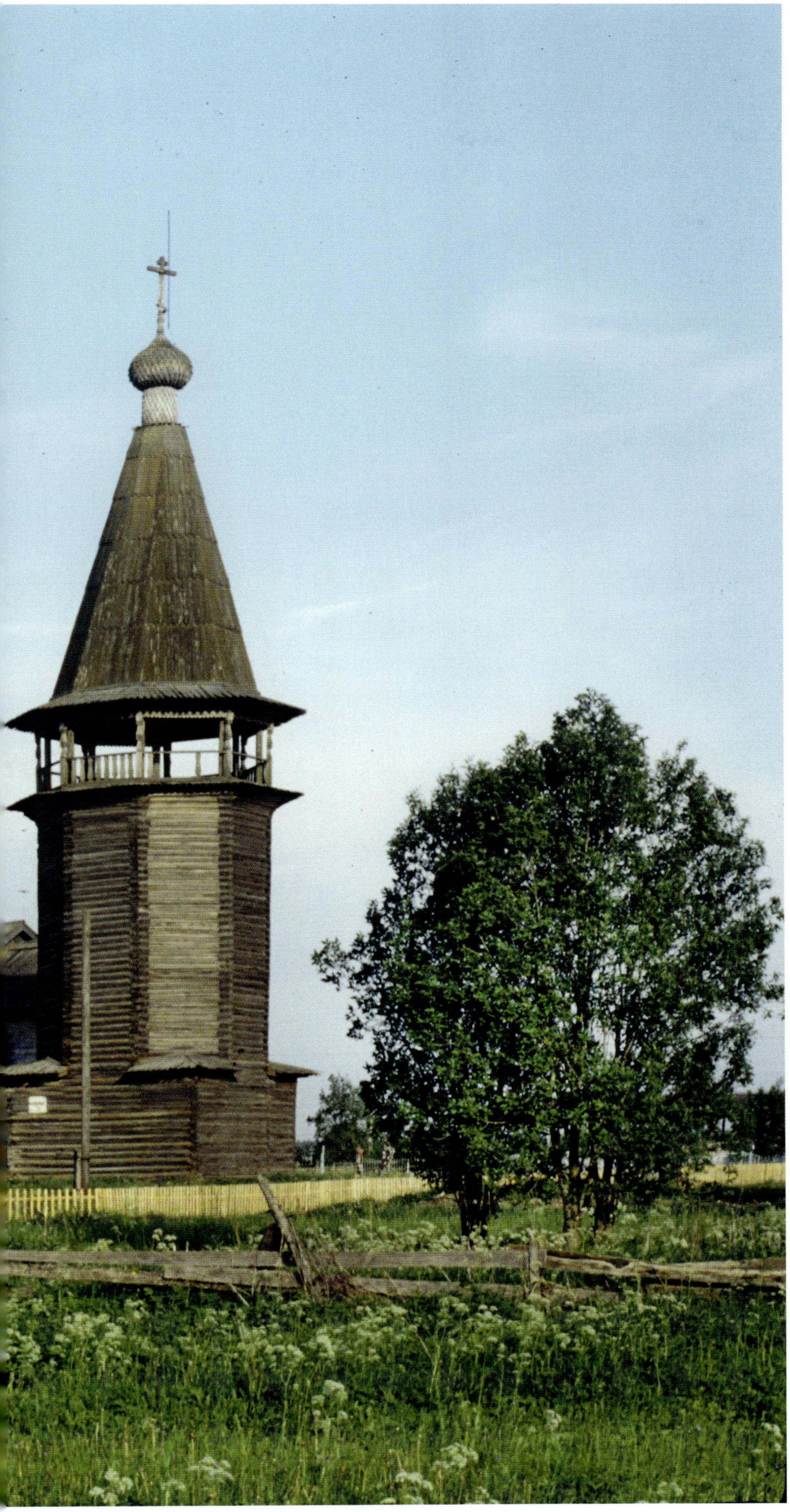

LYADINY (Kargopol region). From left: Church of the Epiphany, Church of Intercession, bell tower, northwest view. The latter two were destroyed by fire in May 2013. June 16, 1998.

Crucifixion, with Mary and other figures at the foot of the cross and Jerusalem in the background. The archangels Michael and Gabriel are painted with an especially rich aura of beauty. Archangel Raphael is accompanied with the boy Tobias holding his fish—a Jewish legend from the apocryphal Book of Tobit and known in Renaissance painting. Within the central ring is a depiction of the Trinity: Father, Son, and Holy Spirit. The twelve seraphim at the tips of the triangles are painted with appealing female masks. This festive and personal artistic expression has been attributed to an icon painter active in Kargopol in the 1760s.

On May 5, 2013—Easter morning—the Intercession Church was struck by lightning during a severe thunderstorm. The heat of the resulting fire was so intense that the nearby free-standing bell tower self-combusted. Firetrucks from Kargopol (some thirty-seven kilometers away) arrived in time to protect the Epiphany Church. Whatever the details of this national cultural catastrophe (failure of the lightning rod, and such), the dozens of photographs—interior and exterior—that I took with the cooperation of the Kargopol Regional History Museum have been archived and provide a comprehensive record of the masterpiece. They are complemented by photographs from a visit in the summer of 2014. As for the Church of the Epiphany, most of its interior art was lost or damaged during the Soviet period. The two churches at Lyadiny had complemented each other perfectly, with the lower silhouette of the winter Epiphany Church and its cupolas matched against the daring tower of the Intercession Church. The bell tower, with a pitched conical roof over the bell gallery, mediated between the two churches and the cemetery crosses.

For many decades when the church ensemble was closed, there was another shrine, a tiny log chapel (apparently dedicated to the Icon of the Miraculous Image of the Savior) in the hamlet of Kiselyovskaya, a part of Lyadiny. Access to the chapel was closely guarded by the local community, but I made a discreet request and was summoned one evening by an elderly woman in a kerchief who held the key. I understood the trust extended to me, and as she opened the heavy door, there was a sense of entering another dimension. The small interior was dimly lit in the evening summer light, but the burst of color was palpable. The warm colors came primarily from a wooden ceiling composed of painted boards radiating from a central ring with the image of Christ, while the surviving boards depict Christ on the cross flanked by Mary and John the Baptist, as well as archangels and the Four Evangelists. This chapel showed a simplified example of a type of

LYADINY (Kargopol region). Church of the Intercession, view east with icon screen and painted ceiling (*nebo*). Destroyed by fire in May 2013. June 29, 1998.

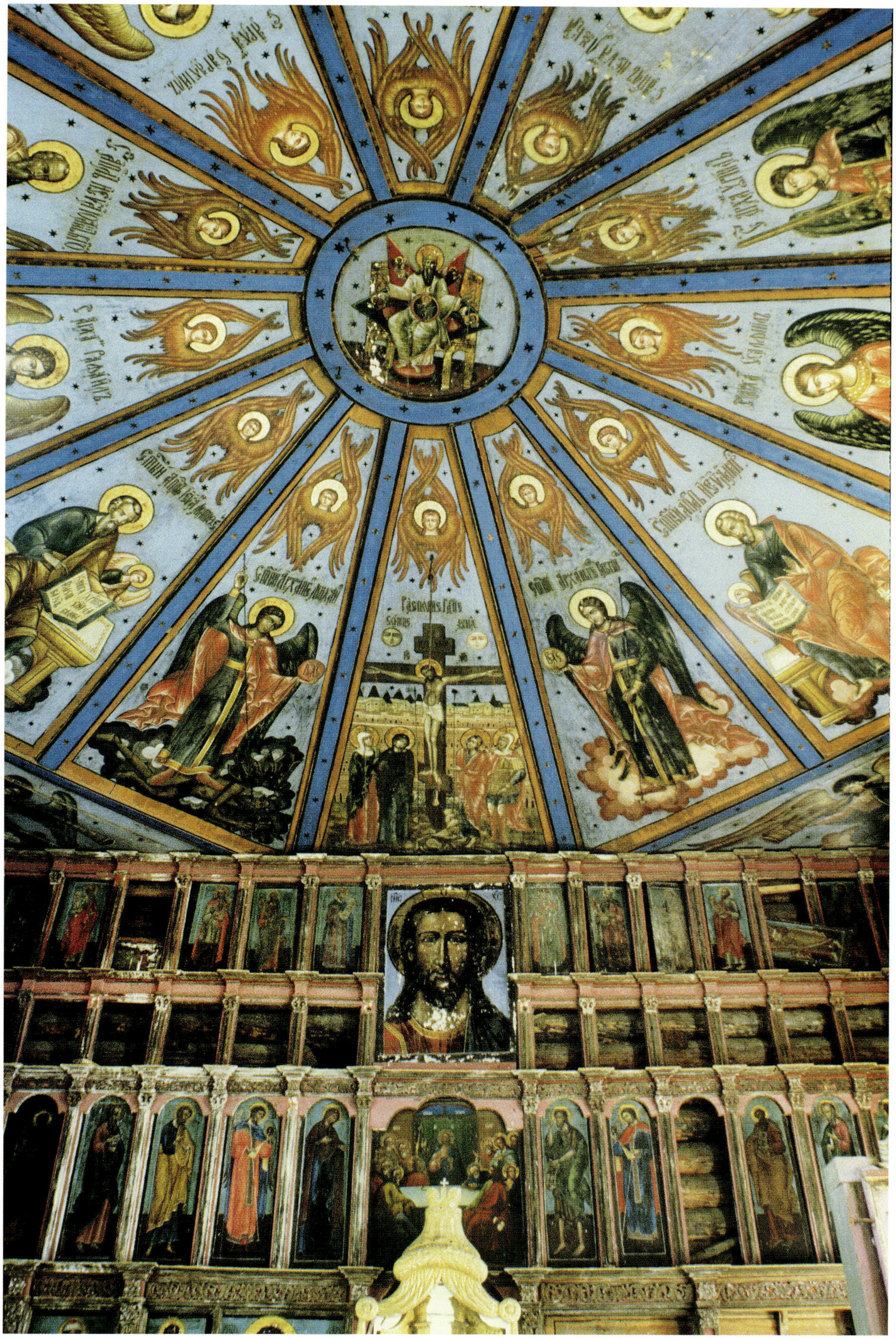

painted ceiling (*nebo*), yet the space was equally remarkable for the clothes and other textile items that draped the sides of the interior beneath the *nebo*. As part of a folk tradition, they served as votive offerings, petitions for divine succor against bodily ailments touched by the cloth. Indeed, the legend behind the Miraculous Image of the Savior refers to just such a healing miracle. Although documentation about the construction of the chapel is missing, it was likely built around the end of the nineteenth century. Even during the Soviet period, when public worship was highly restricted (if not banned outright), the chapel was protected and used by the dwindling community.

Many of the sturdy wooden houses in Lyadiny have been abandoned in a pattern of population loss long typical of the northern countryside. Dairy farming is still possible, but life in these rural areas is difficult. I will never forget my first visit, in early March 1998, just after a snowstorm. I was photographing the strange snow effects on the churches when a group of locals walked by. One of them said under his breath: "You photograph all this, but you have no idea how we live."

The tragic loss at Lyadiny further increases the significance of another towering log shrine with a painted *nebo* in the same region, the Church of the Epiphany at the village of Oshevensk. Oshevensk is, in fact, a cluster of settlements, including three hamlets picturesquely situated along the Churyega River. The Epiphany Church is in the first hamlet, Pogost. Built of pine logs in 1787, the Epiphany Church exemplifies the combination of structure and art in the Russian North. (The church is also referred to locally as the Baptism Church since the Epiphany and the Baptism of Christ are the same Orthodox holiday.) Octagonal in shape, the main structure of the church is crowned with a tall tent tower. The church bell tower stands separately to the northwest with its own vertical cap. The miracle of this church is the interior, which encompasses one of the largest such spaces among northern log churches. Its icon screen is enormous, yet few of the icons remain. The church was closed in the 1930s, opened during the war, and closed again in 1960 during Nikita Khrushchev's "final" campaign against religion. The church was reopened for prayer and occasional services in the late 1990s. During this long period, most of the icons in the main iconostasis were taken from the church. Only the uppermost row, dedicated to the Prophets, still had icons, which are visible in my earlier photographs. In October 2014 the church was broken into, and these remaining icons were stolen. Only the magnificent carved icon screen remained.

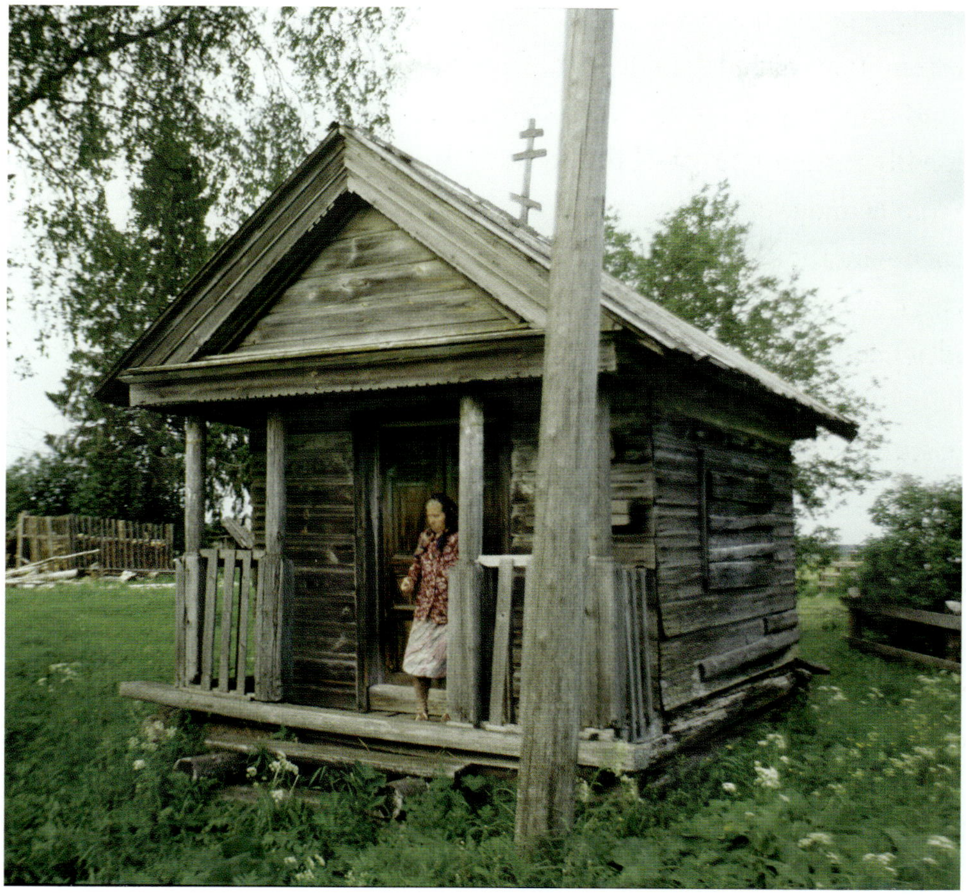

KISELYOVA (Lyadiny, Kargopol region). Chapel. June 16, 1998.

KISELYOVA (Lyadiny, Kargopol region). Chapel with painted ceiling (*nebo*) and votive offerings. June 16, 1998.

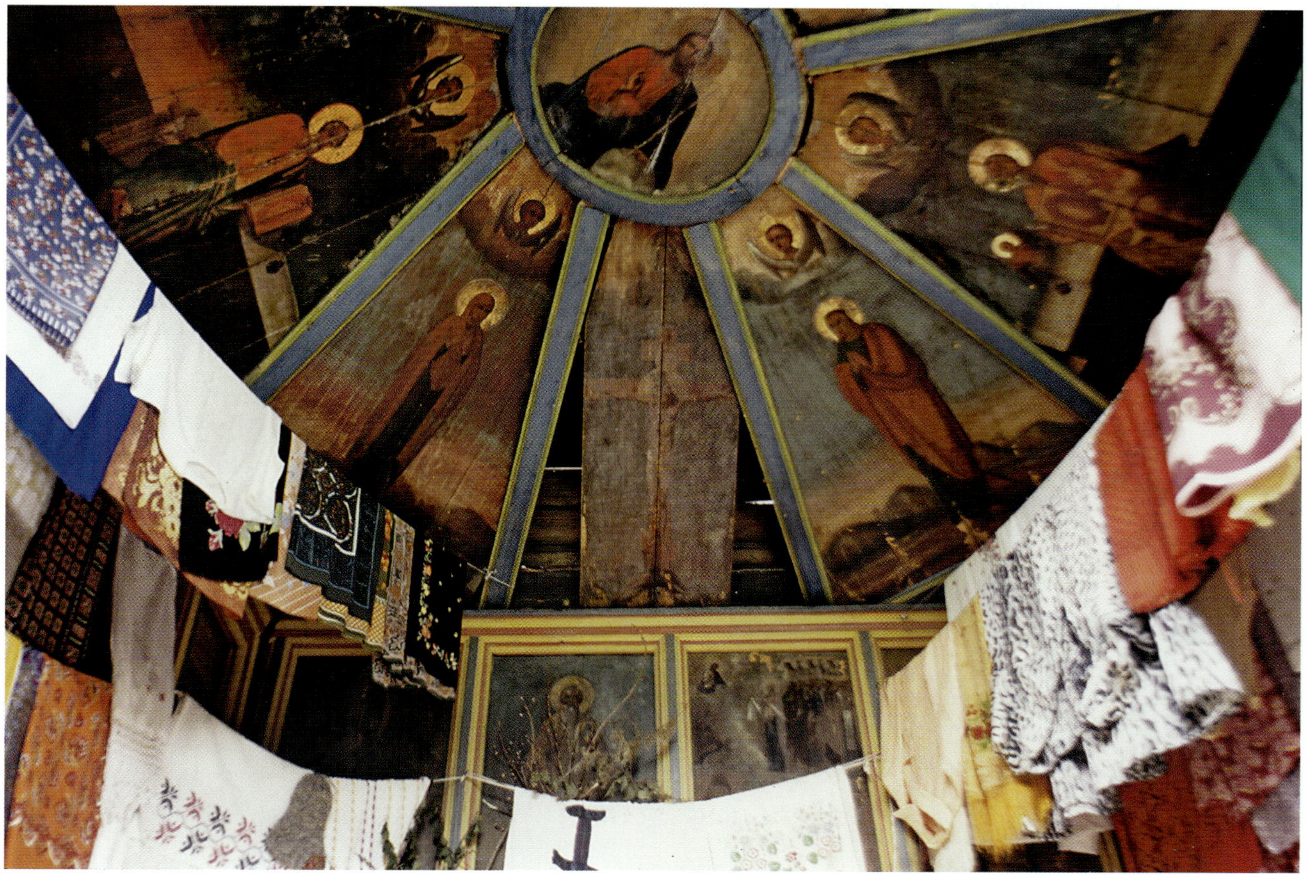

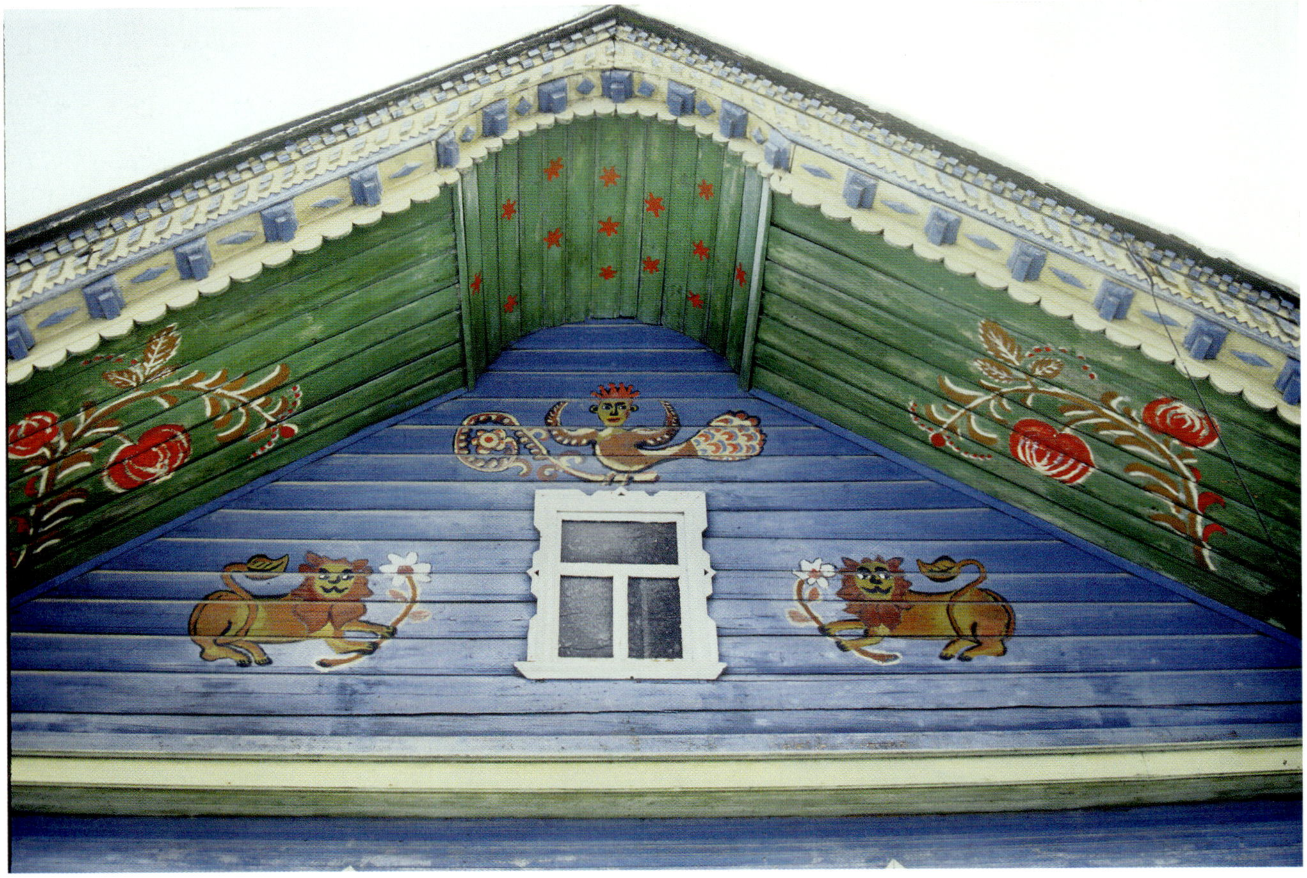

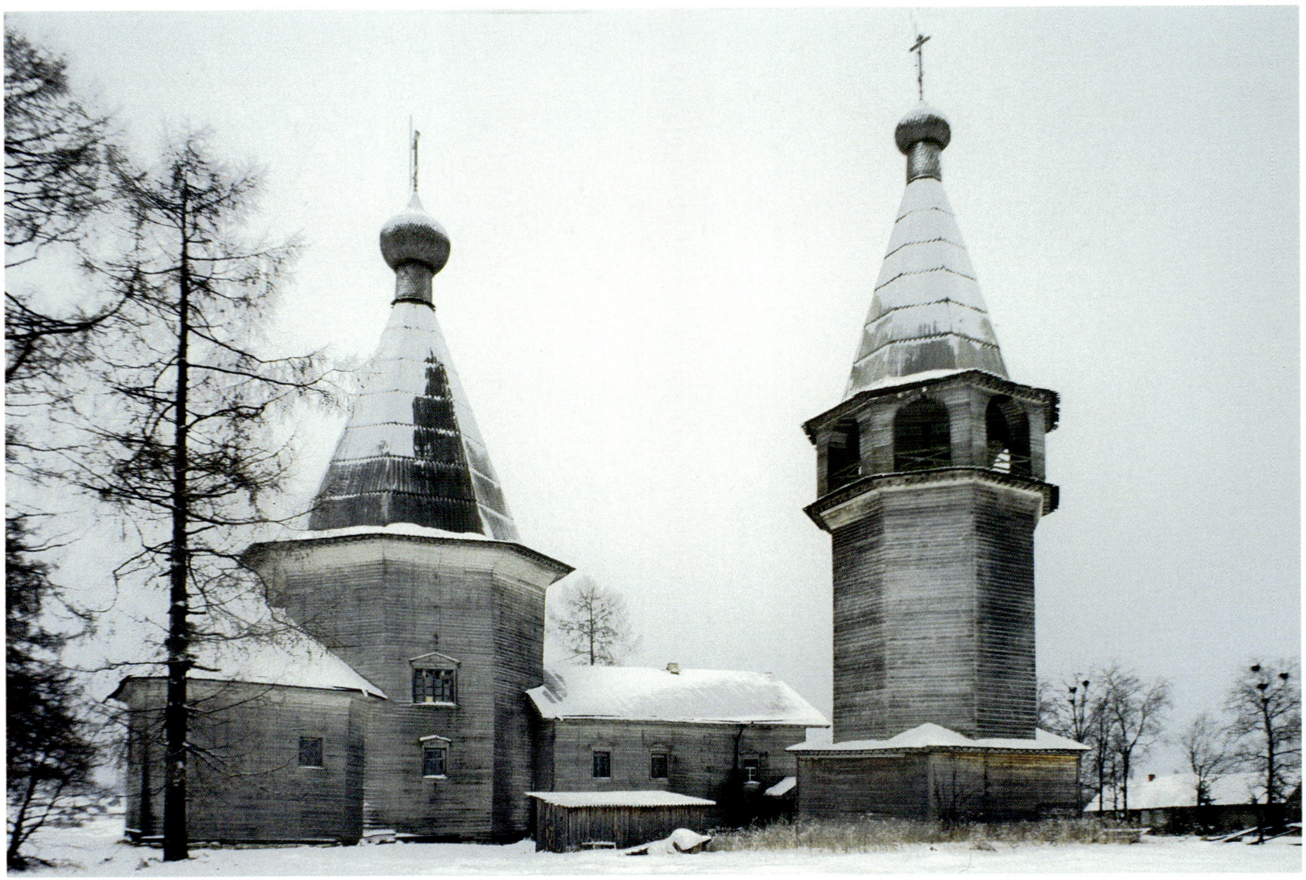

Although most of the icons have now been recovered, much work remains to restore them to their original place.

The most impressive display of art on the interior is the painted suspended ceiling (*nebo*), which still has its panels in place, although with sporadic damage to the painted surface. As at Lyadiny, the form of the *nebo* is a polygon segmented by beams framing triangular panels that extend from the top of the walls to a ring in the center. The paintings at the Epiphany Church have been attributed to the Bogdanov-Karbatovsky family, one of the dynasties of icon painters active in the Arkhangelsk territory in the latter half of the eighteenth century. Such artists brought new expressiveness to a traditional art in transition from tempera colors to oil paints.

The area north of the Kargopol region also has numerous wooden churches and chapels. Many of them are concentrated in an area around Kenozero Lake, part of the Onega River basin. The picturesque, unspoiled qualities of the Kenozero region led to the creation of a national park in December 1991. Since that time the painstaking work of preservation, conservation, and integration of local villages into the park structure has become a major enterprise. Of particular interest is the early eighteenth-century Pochozero ensemble of two wooden churches and a bell tower at the village of Fillipovskaya. Long under restoration, the ensemble has regained its former glory, at least on the exterior.

REKA (Kargopol region). Wooden house with painted eaves and pediment. Of special interest are the dancing lions, whose broad smiles and red roses bless the dwelling while warding off evil spirits. Above: magical bird Sirin. November 27, 1999.

OSHEVENSK (Kargopol region). Bell tower and Church of the Epiphany, north view. November 27, 1999.

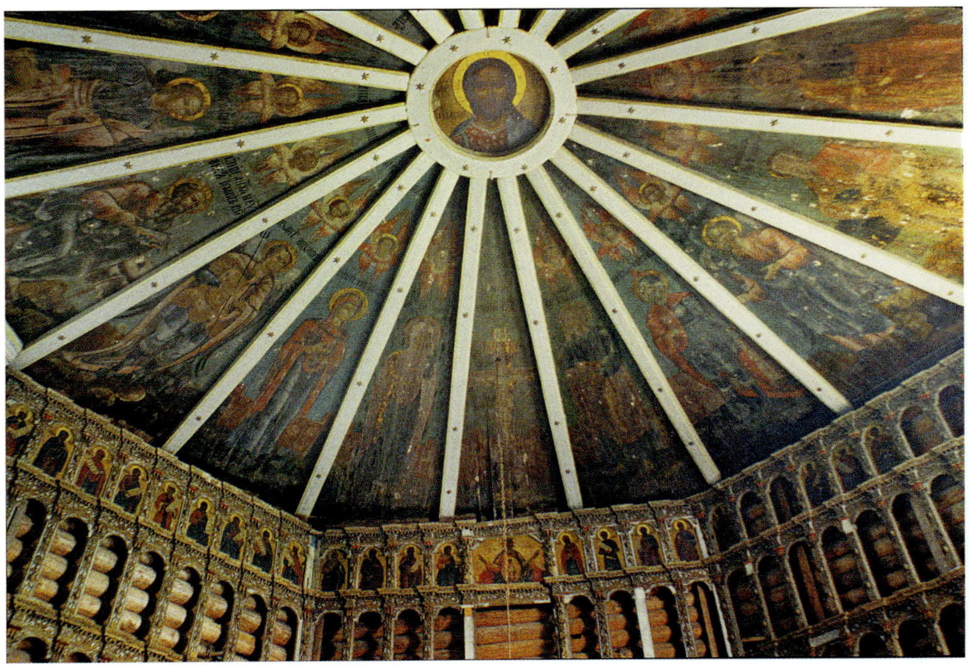

OSHEVENSK (Kargopol region). Church of the Epiphany. Segmented painted ceiling (*nebo*) and upper tier of icon screen. June 18, 1998.

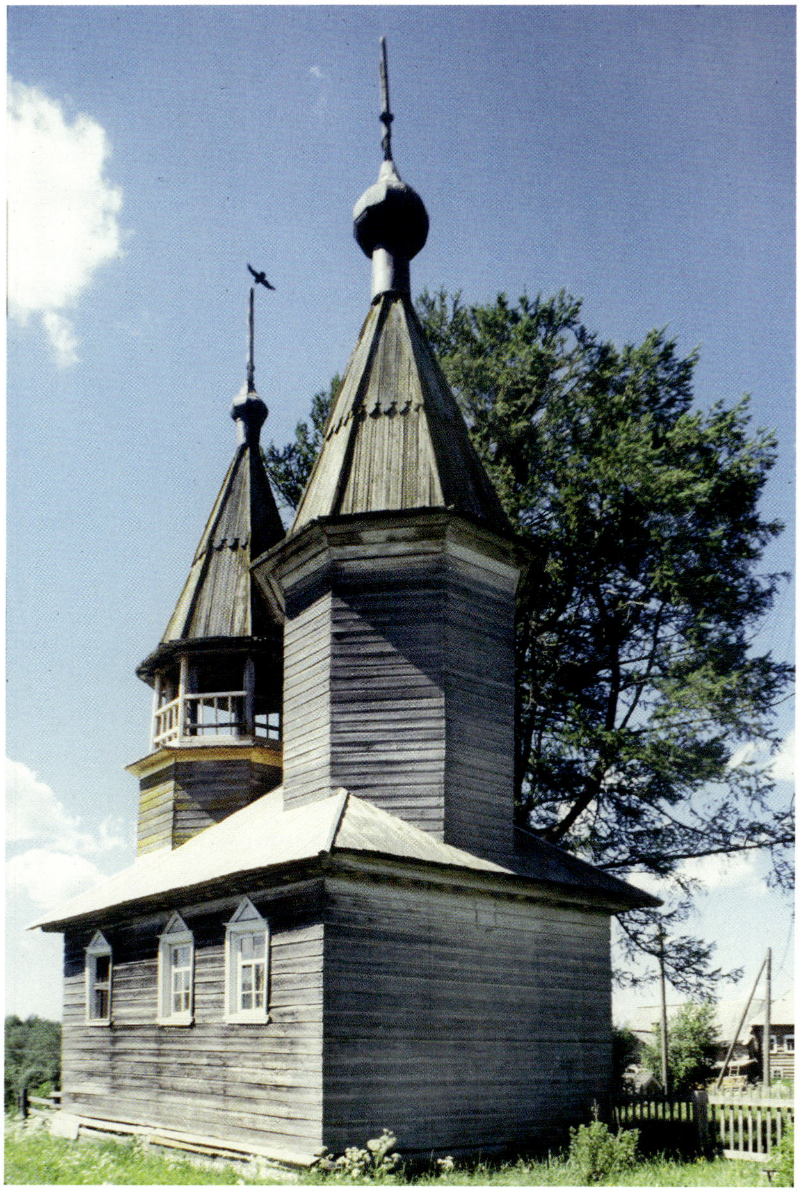

OSHEVENSK (Kargopol region). Chapel of Saint George, southeast view. This large chapel, built in the early nineteenth century in Niz (one of three hamlets constituting Oshevensk), is unusual in having a tent tower above the east part and a bell tower on the west end. June 18, 1998.

OSHEVENSK (Kargopol region). Extended log house with painted eaves. June 18, 1998.

OSHEVENSK VICINITY. This stunning work of natural art was created by a leaking cistern above a log water tower at a former collective farm. November 27, 1999.

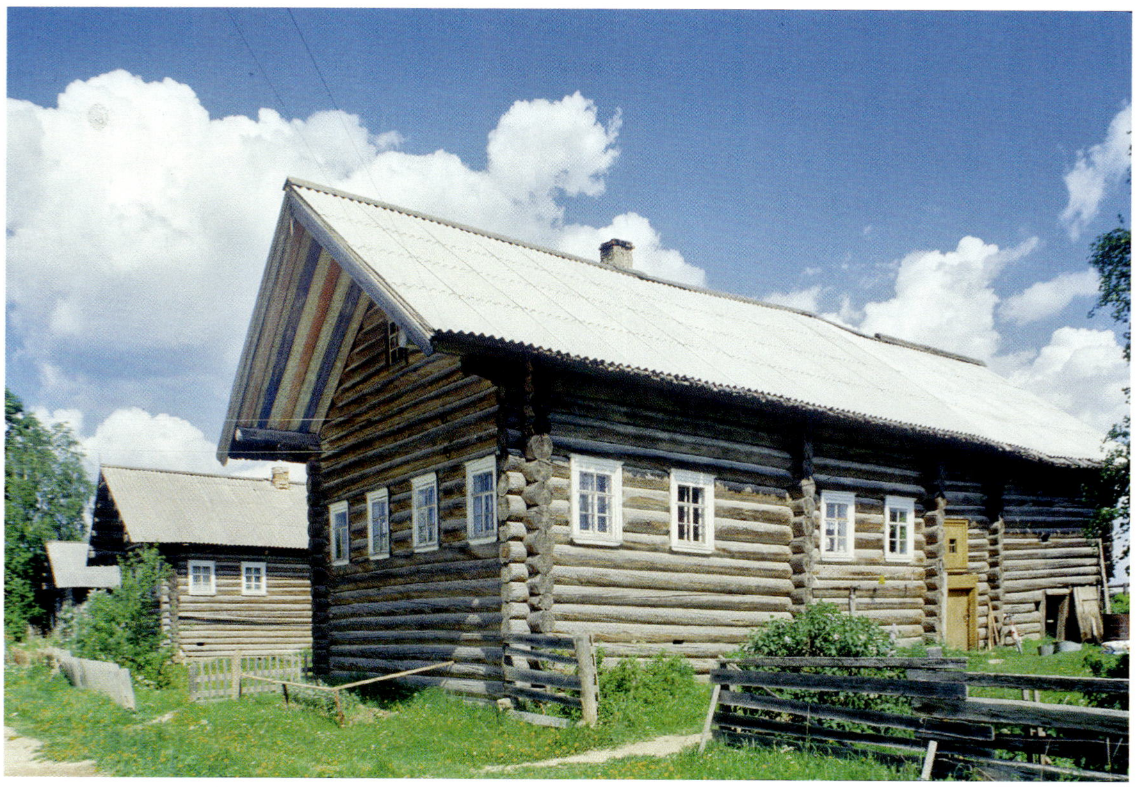

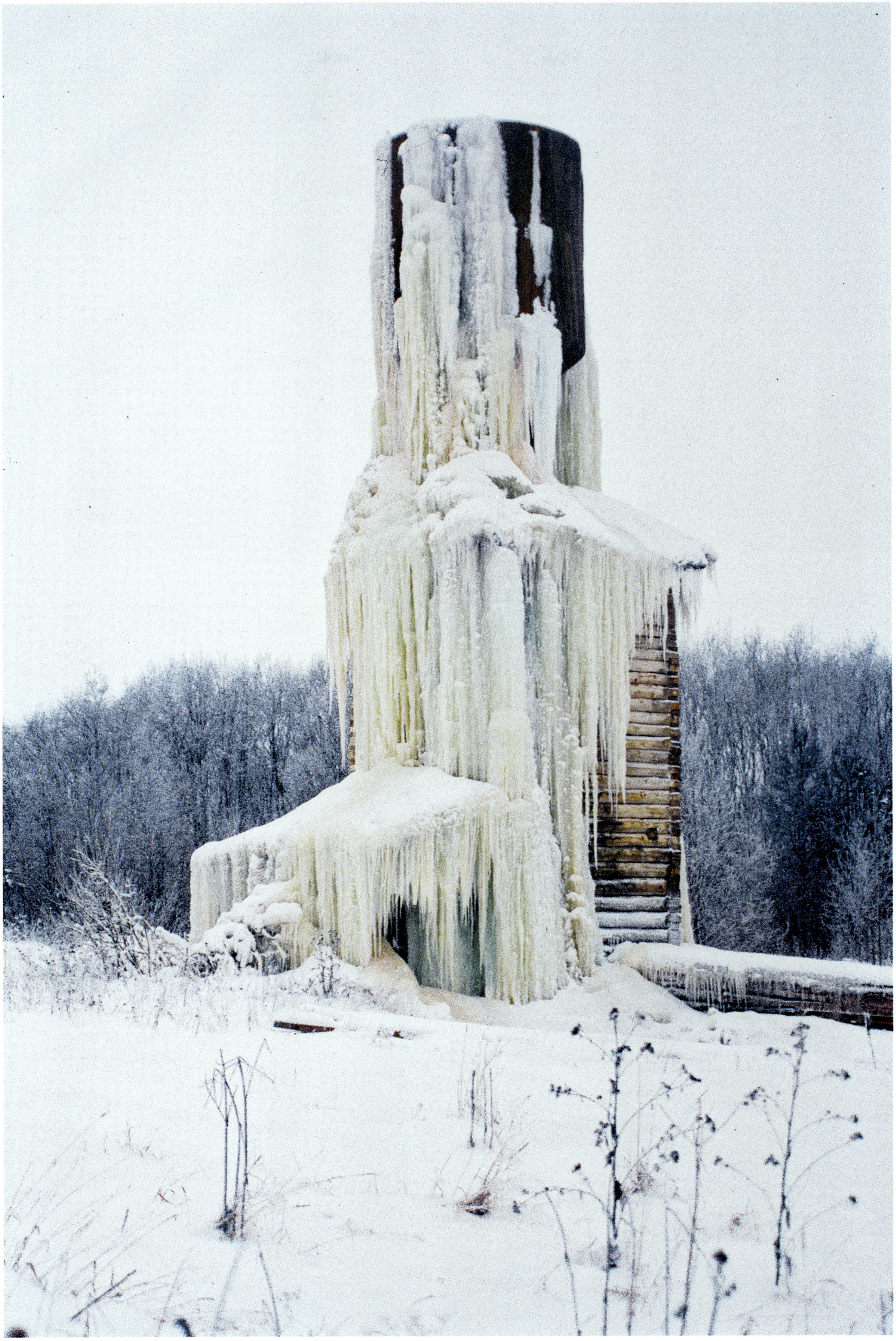

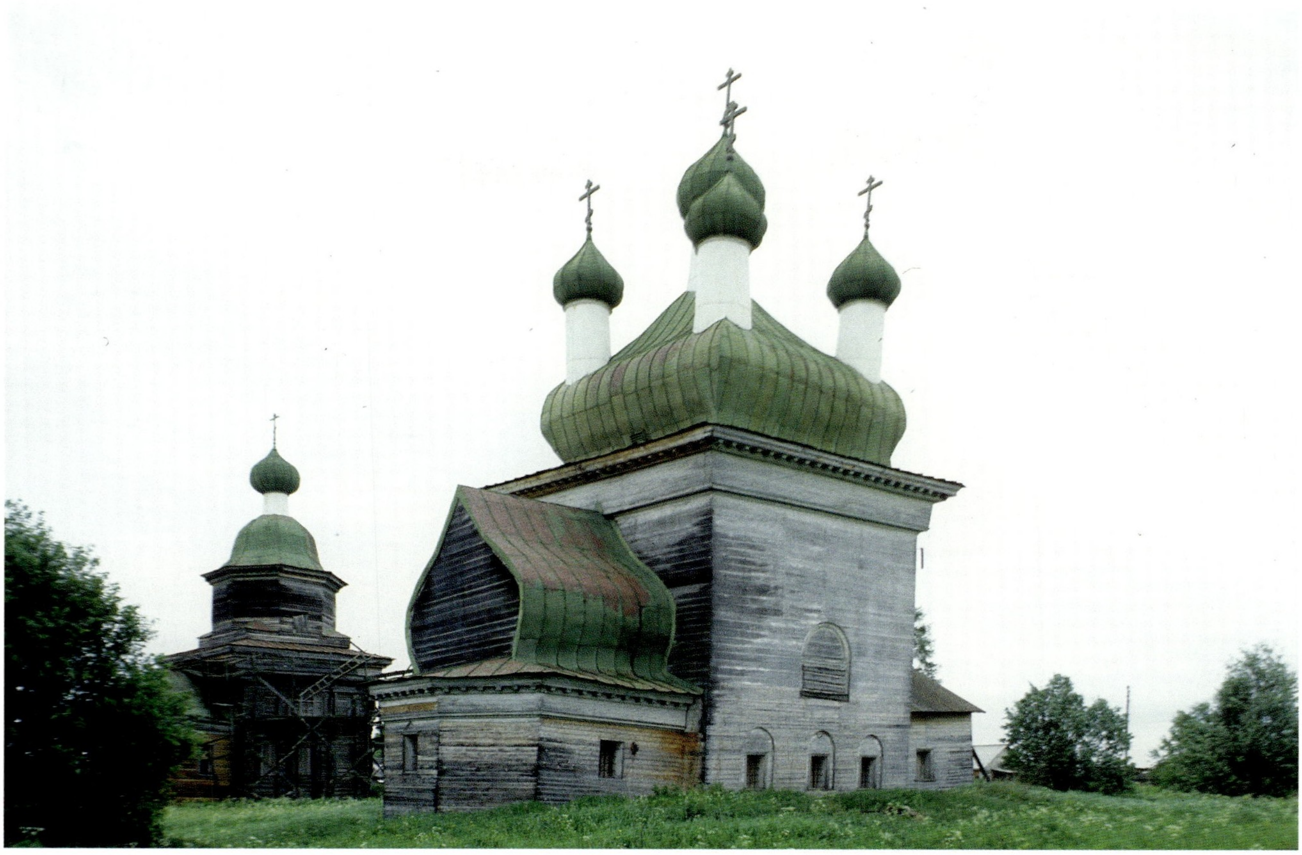

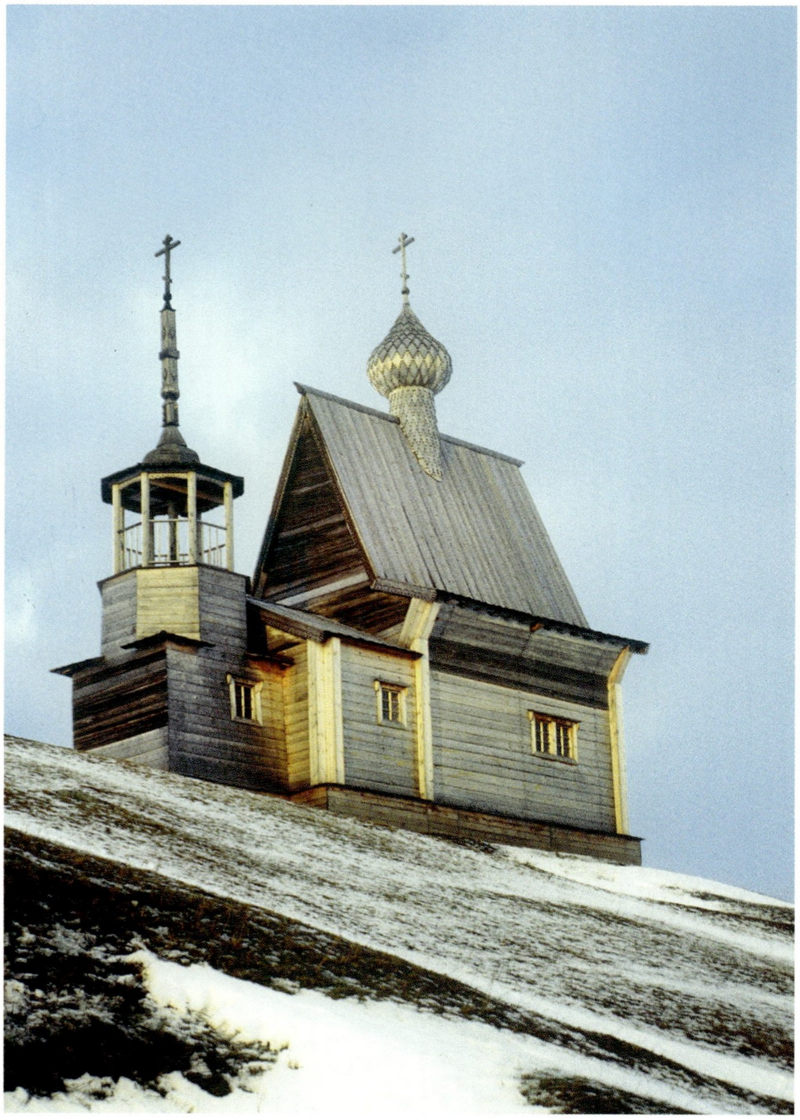

ARKHANGELO (Kargopol region). Church of Archangel Michael, northeast view. Built in 1715 with a flared roof supporting five cupolas. Left background: Church of the Purification (1803). June 26, 1998.

VERSHININO (Kenozero National Park). Chapel of Saint Nicholas, southwest view. Built in the nineteenth century with bell tower on west end. March 1, 2000.

VERSHININO. Chapel of Saint Nicholas with painted ceiling (*nebo*) and frame of icon screen. February 29, 2000.

ZEKHNOVO (Kenozero National Park). Chapel of Saint John the Divine, northeast view. Built in the eighteenth century with gallery on three sides under roof eaves. March 1, 2000.

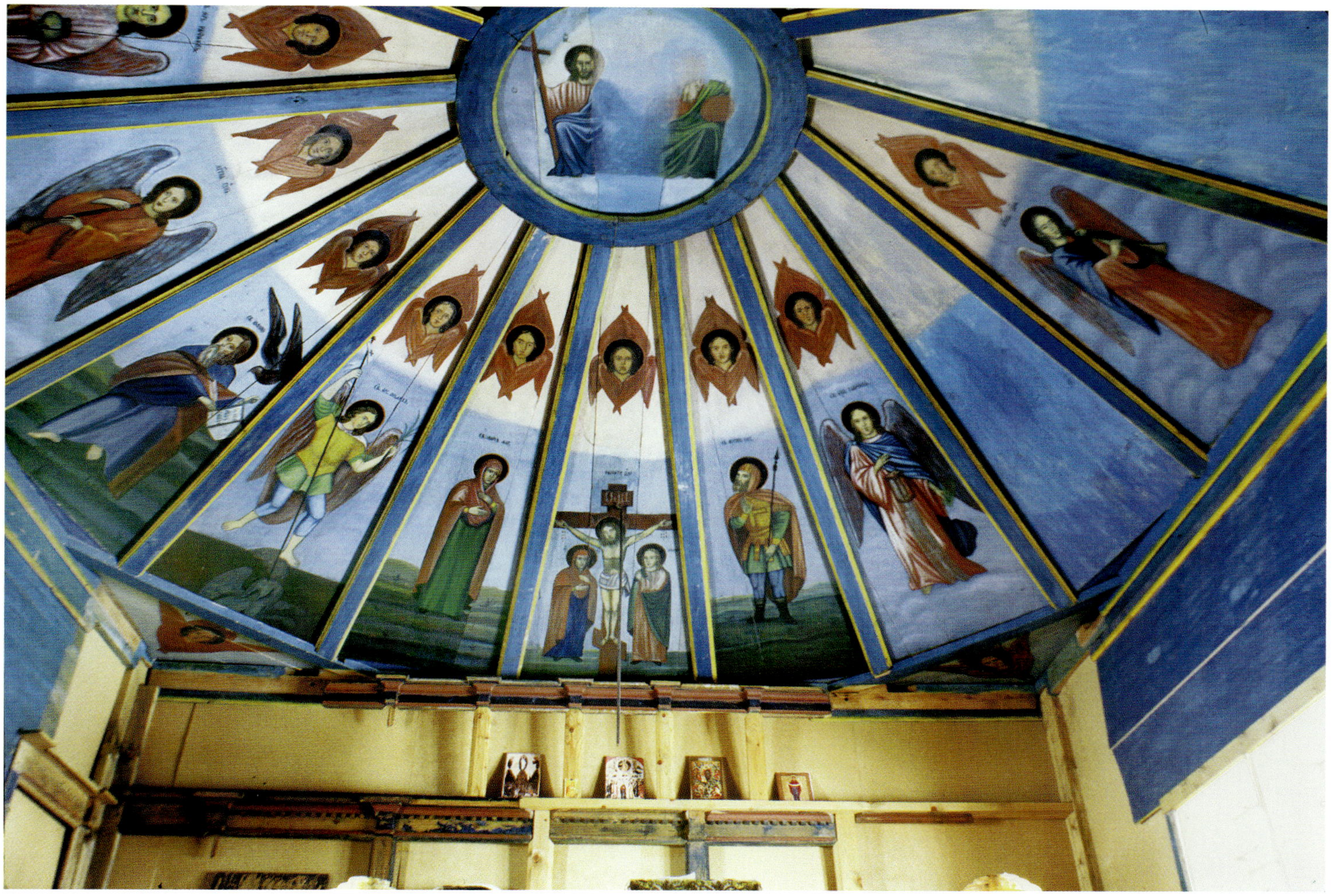

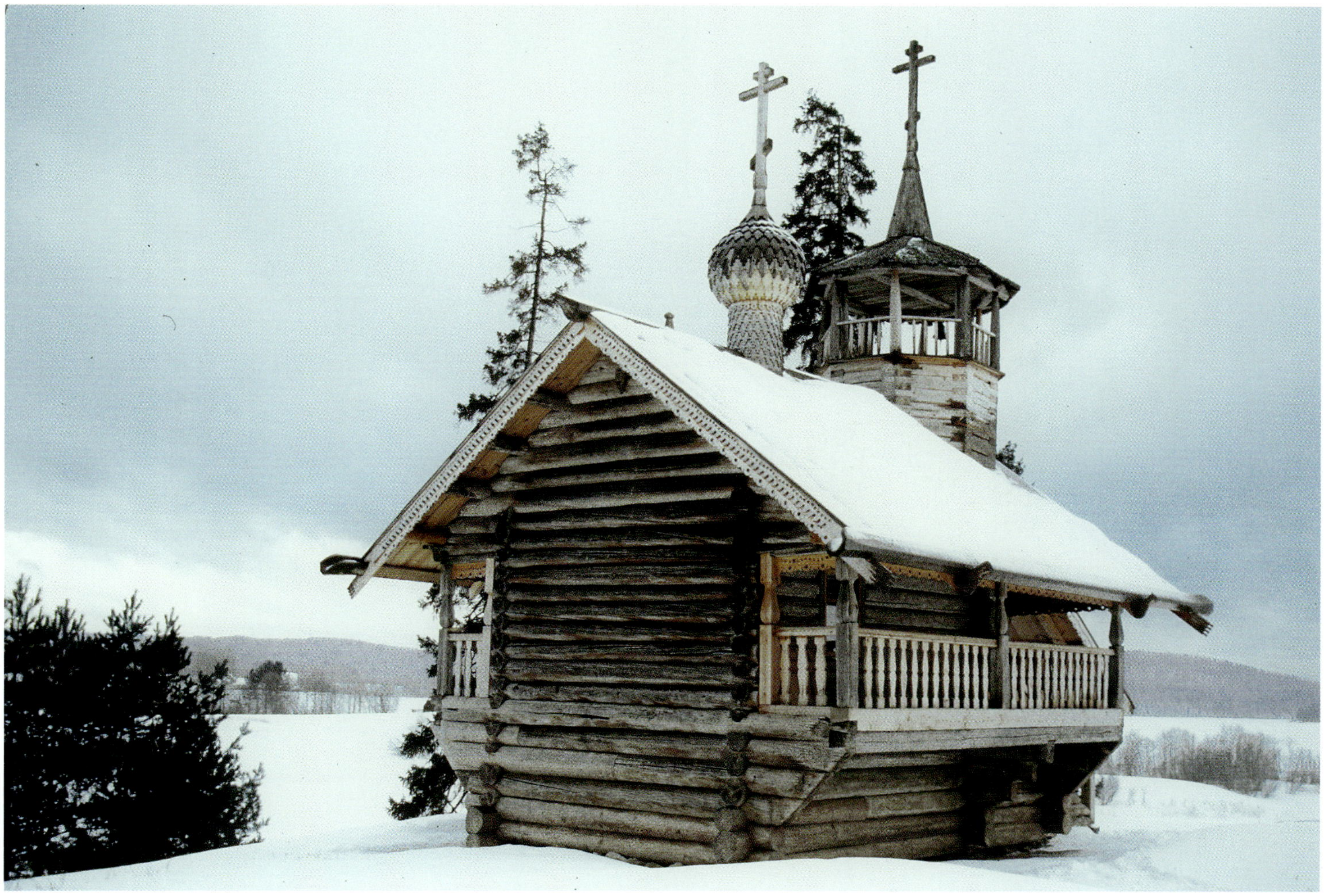

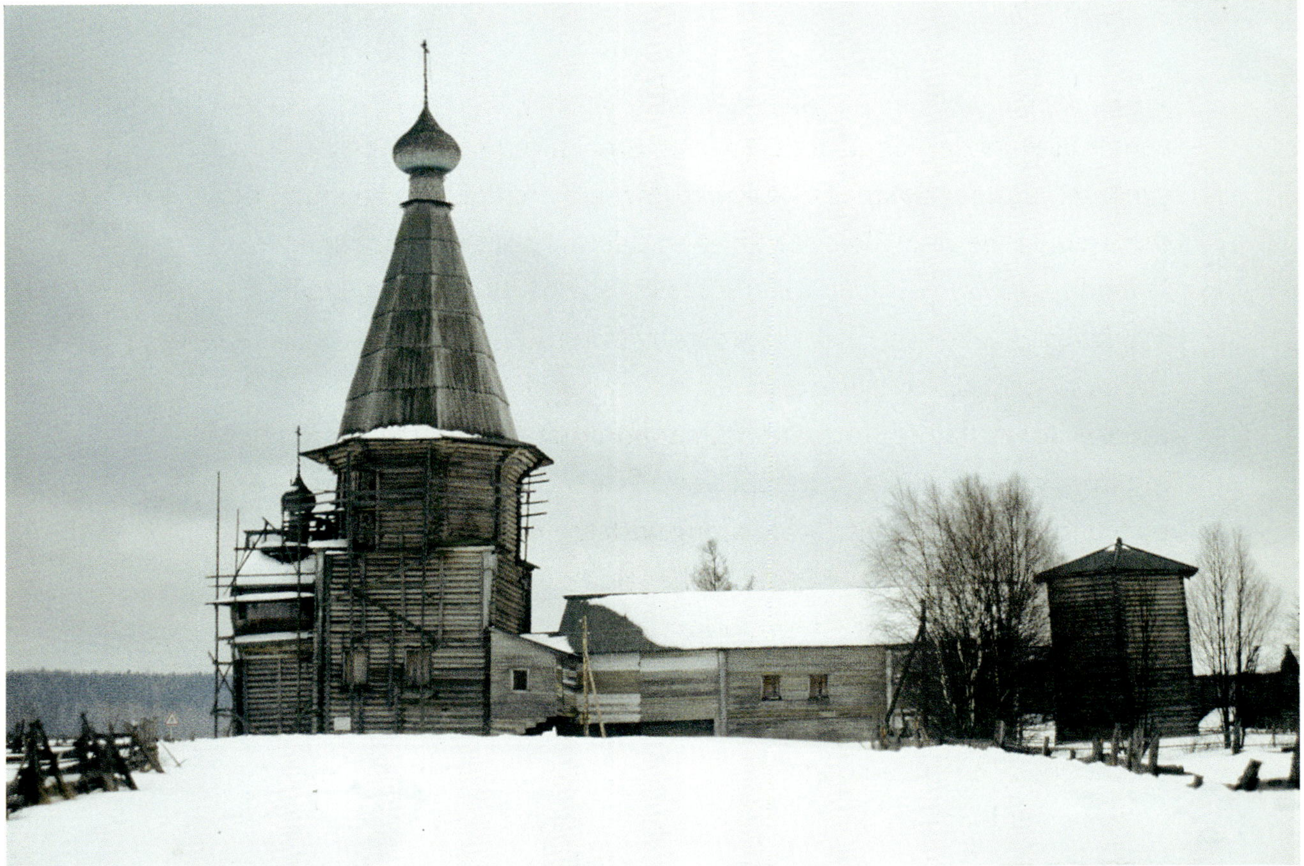

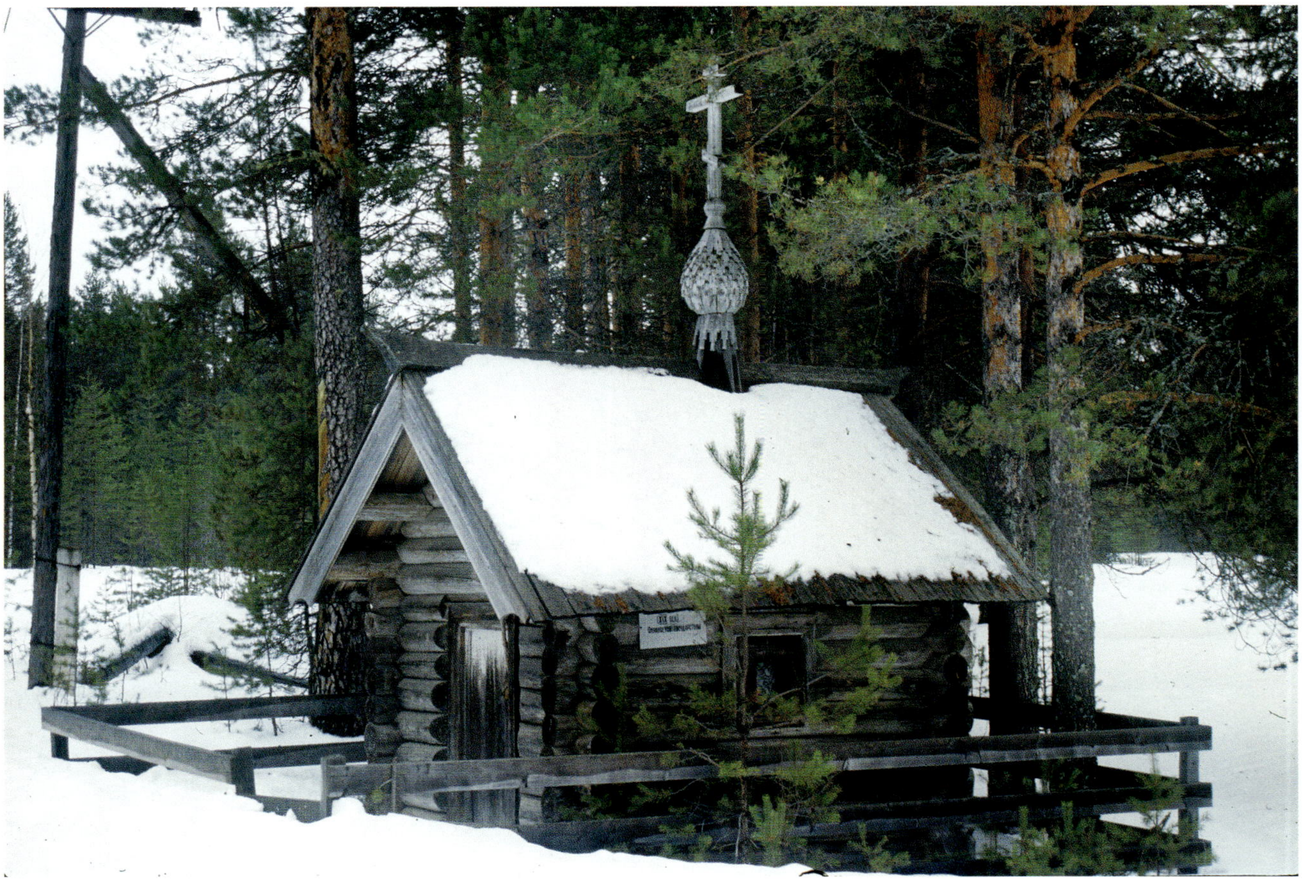

The Vologda Region

Two-hundred sixty kilometers due south from Kargopol is the regional center of Vologda (slightly over 310,000 inhabitants), whose rich cultural presence is due in no small measure to its many architectural monuments. Situated on the small Vologda River—a tributary of the Sukhona River—Vologda is sufficiently distant from Moscow (470 kilometers by road to the southwest) to allow its distinctive regional identity. The official date of the city's founding is given as 1147 (the same year as Moscow's "founding"), yet there is no verifiable information to support that date. With the growth of Moscow's power in the fourteenth and fifteenth centuries, Vologda was pulled into the Muscovite orbit, along with the rest of the Russian North on the path to the White Sea, and by the middle of the sixteenth century, it had become the major trading and administrative center of northern Russia. The Vologda River was linked to the Dvina River basin to the north and was close enough for portage to the Sheksna River, part of the Volga River basin. Vologda thus served as a distribution point for increasing trade with England, and subsequently Holland, by way of the Northern Dvina to the port of Arkhangelsk. The wealth of Vologda in the late eighteenth and nineteenth centuries is reflected in houses, brick and wood, that have survived throughout the town. Vologda was particularly known for the variety and extent of its wooden housing. Neglect, indifference, and lack of resources have taken their toll on these distinctive wooden residences.

FILLIPOVSKAYA (Kenozero National Park). Also known as Pochozero Pogost, this rare ensemble consists of two linked eighteenth-century structures: the Church of the Procession of the Life-Giving Cross (left) and the Church of the Finding of the Head of John the Baptist (under reconstruction). March 2, 2000.

FILLIPOVSKAYA (Kenozero National Park). Nineteenth-century Chapel of Saints Quiricus and Julietta, embraced by tall pines that provided the timber for northern shrines. March 2, 2000.

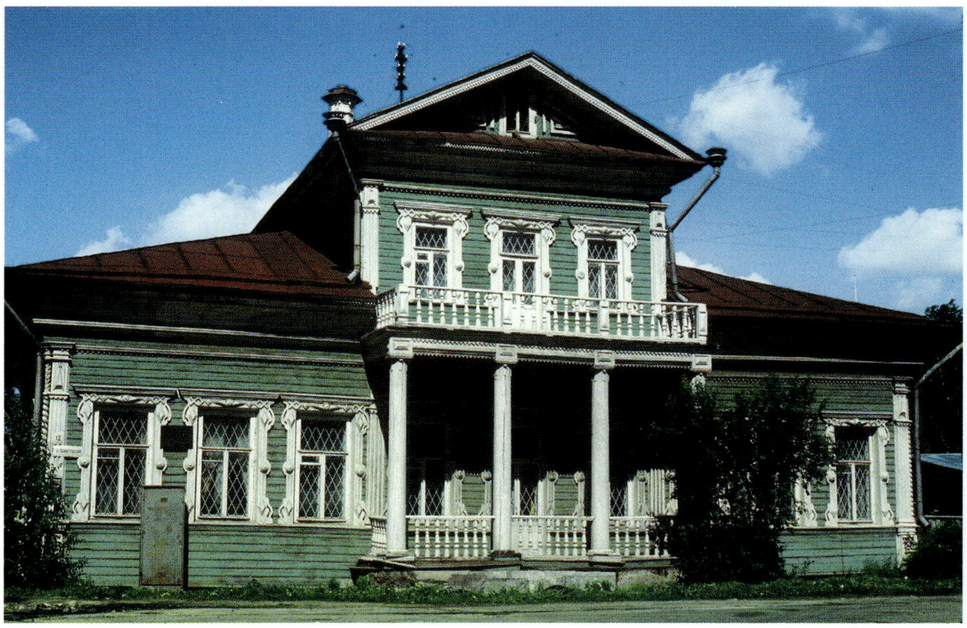

VOLOGDA. Zasetsky house. Built for a prominent family in the 1790s, this structure with portico and *mezonin* is a rare surviving example of an eighteenth-century house in an urban setting. Decorative window surrounds added in the late nineteenth century. June 6, 1998.

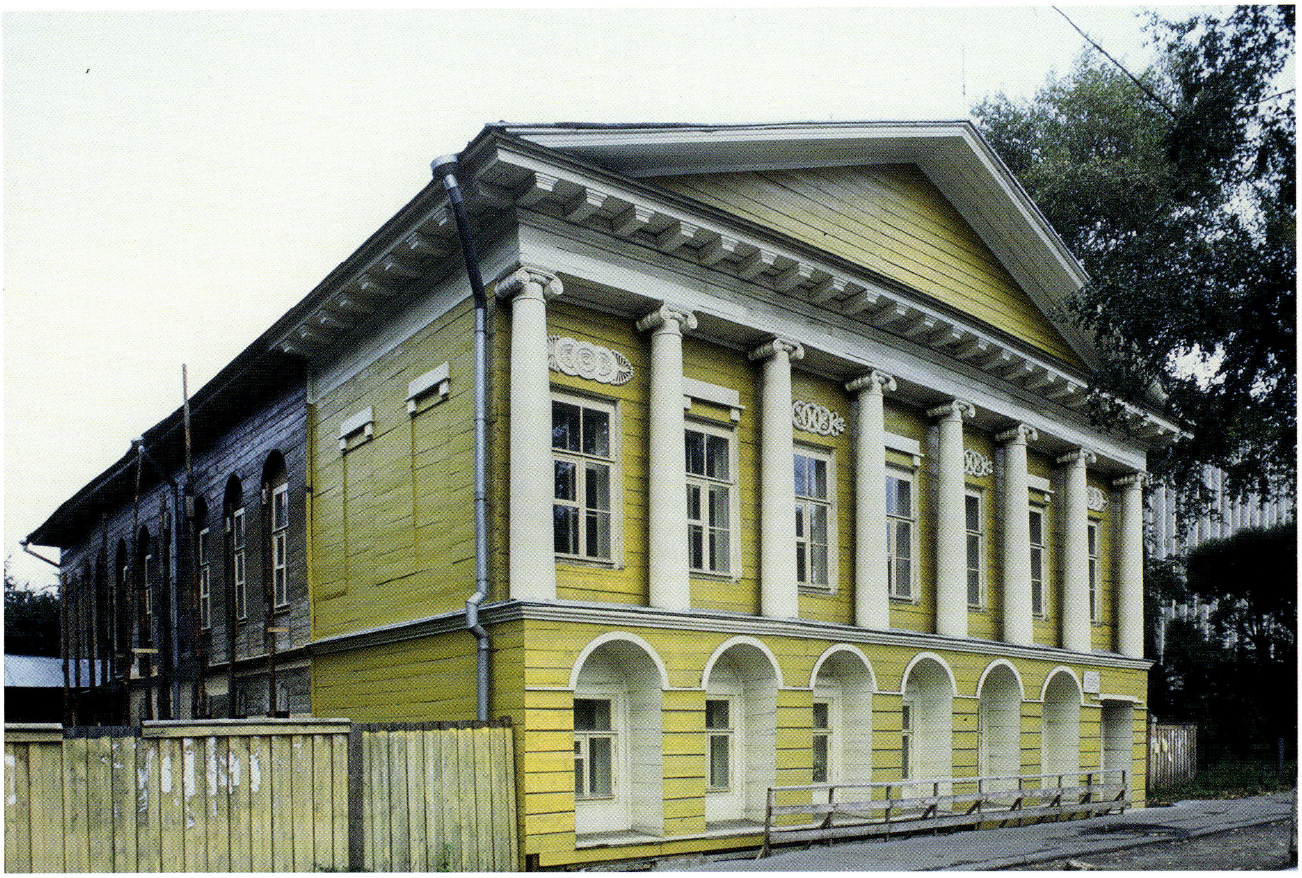

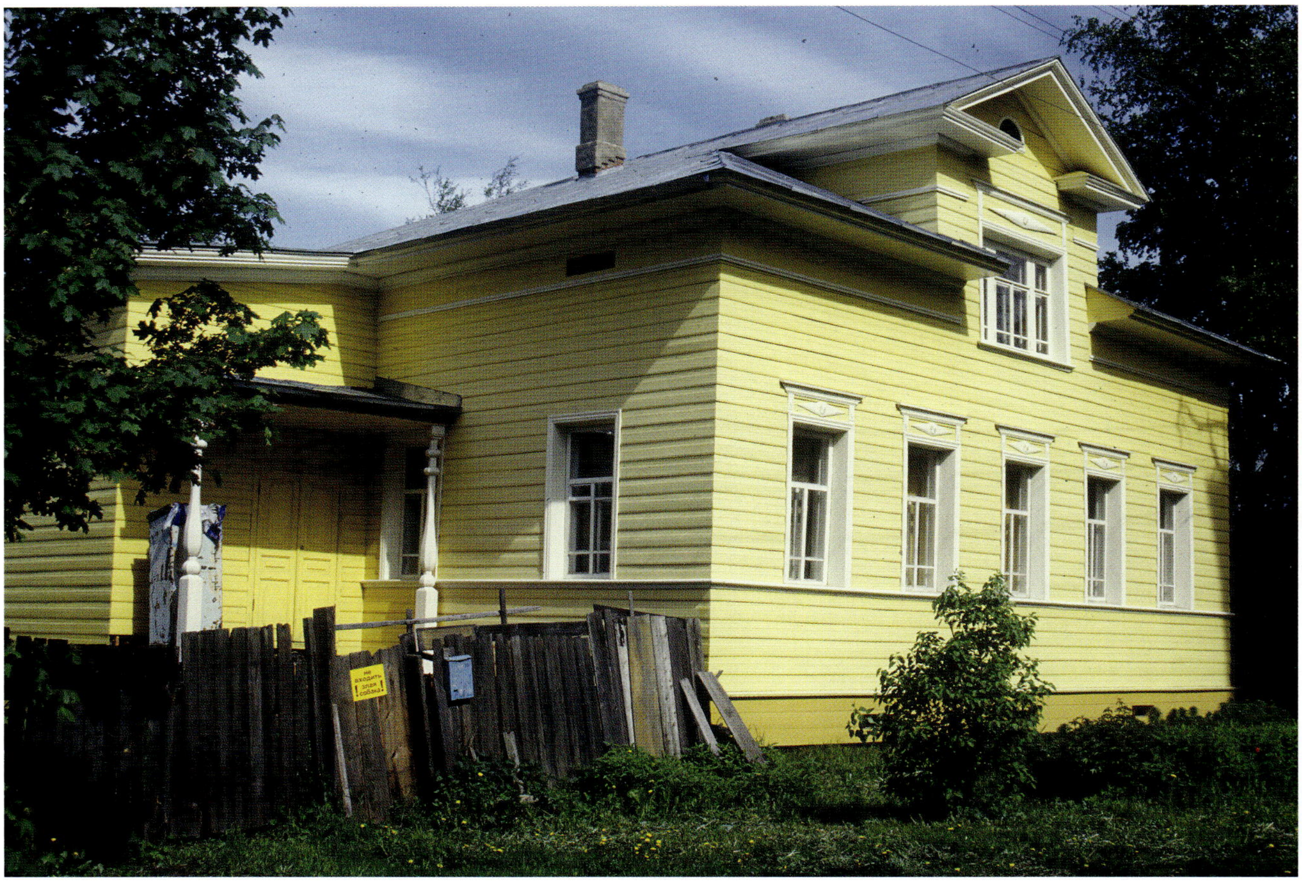

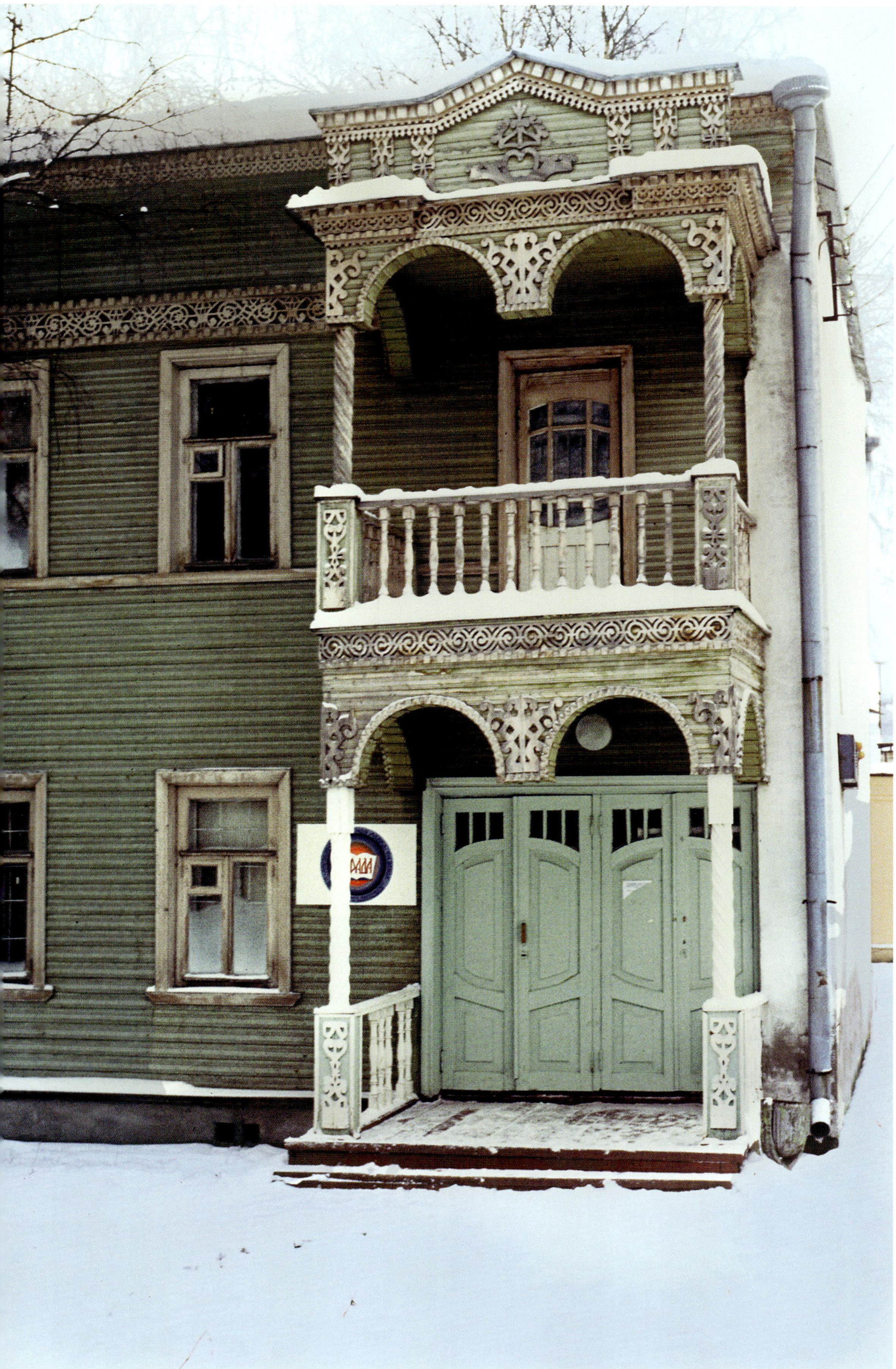

VOLOGDA. Levashov house. Built in 1829 for the nobleman Alexander Levashov, this large structure is one of the best classically inspired urban log houses in Russia. Encasing only the front part, the painted plank siding changes color (bright yellow, green) depending on the desire of the owner. Despite appearances, the portico columns extend to the ground. August 22, 2004.

VOLOGDA. Kulchitskaya house. Built in the 1820s, this typical example of an urban log dwelling has been painstakingly restored by the preservationist Mikhail Karachev. May 19, 2001.

VOLOGDA. House built in the early twentieth century by the merchant Alexander Samarin for his married daughter. Multifamily urban dwelling with decorative porch and paired doorways. January 3, 1997.

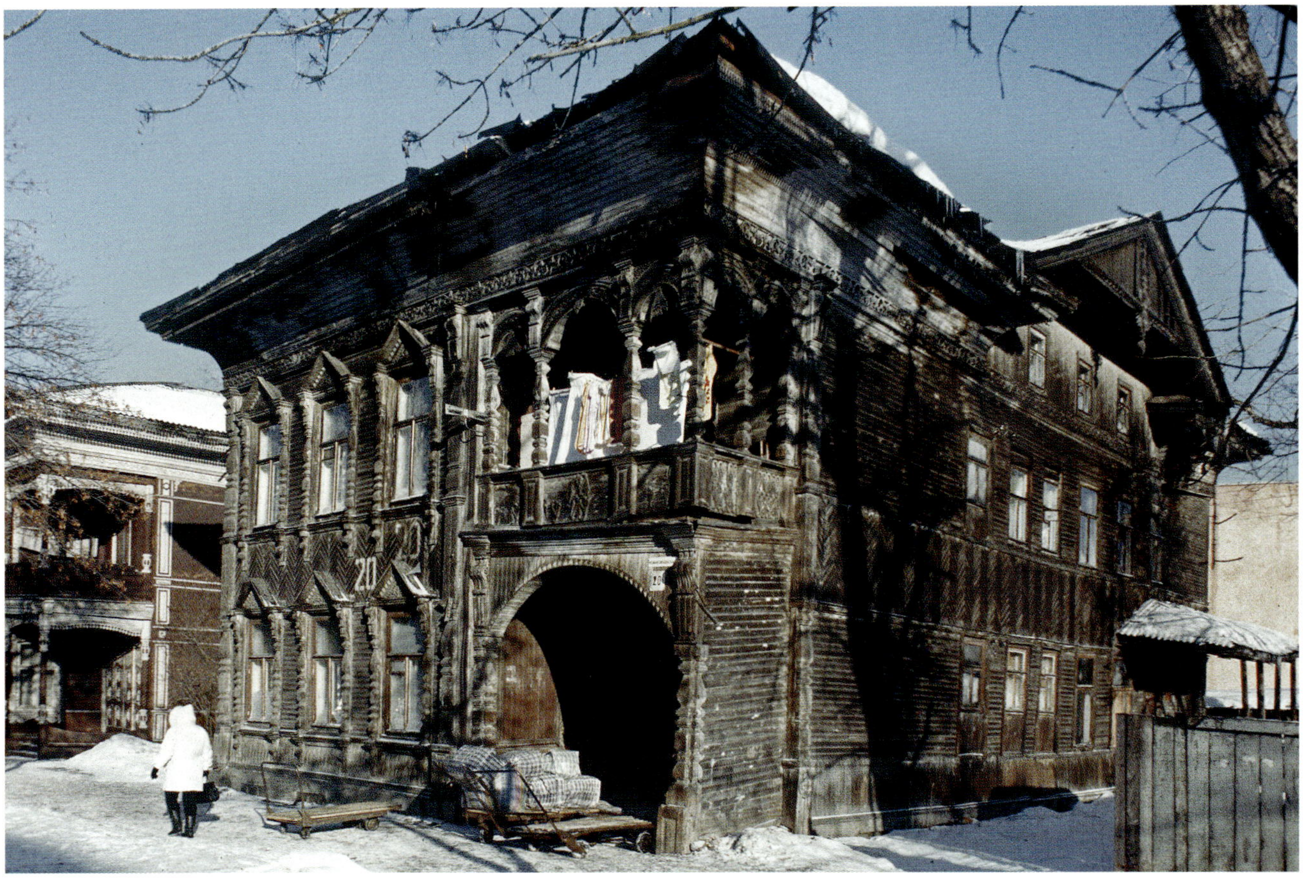
20

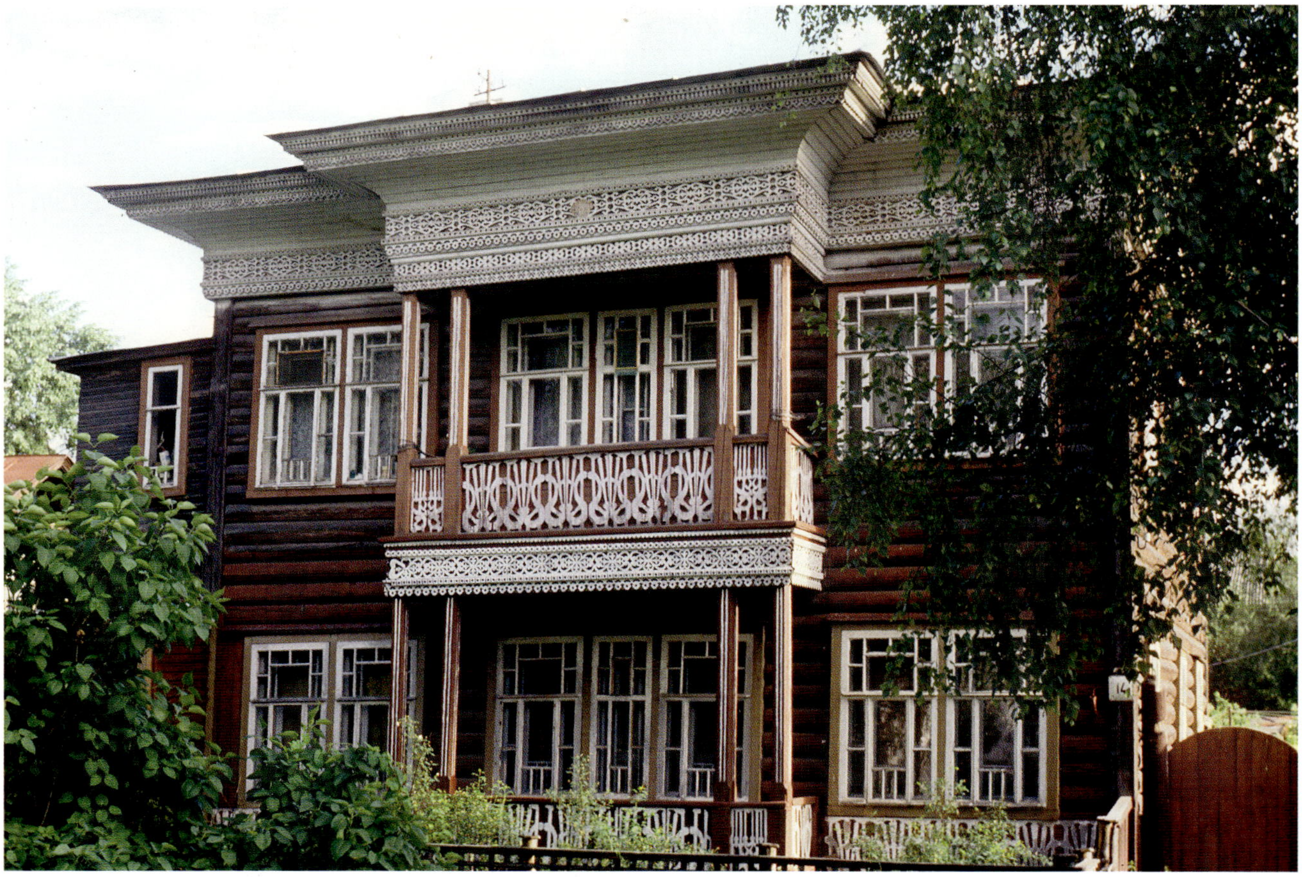

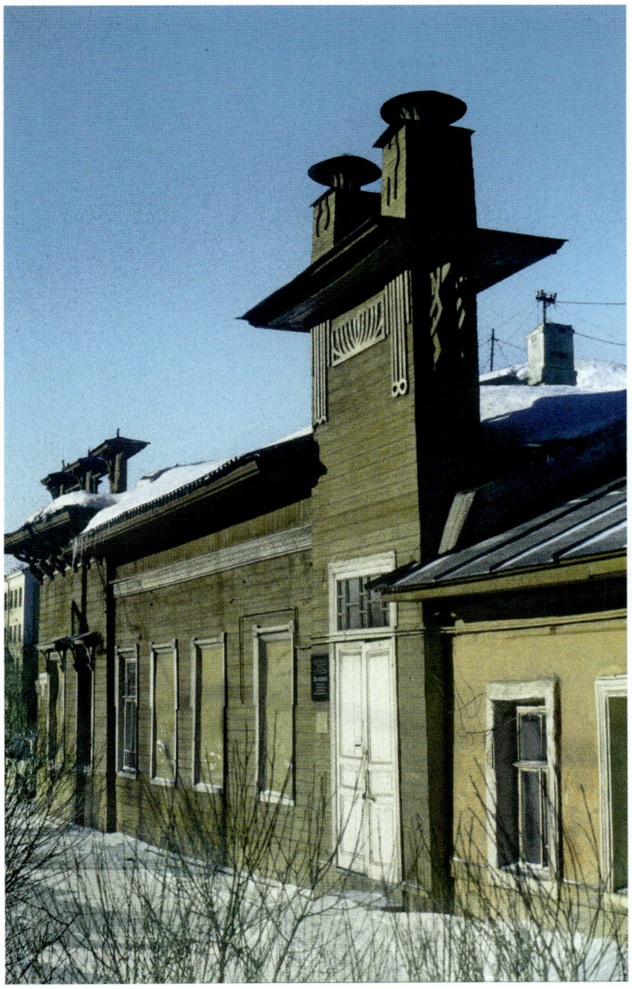

VOLOGDA. Kirkhoglanin house. Recent research indicates that the house belonged to Konstantin Naumov, a peasant who moved to town and became a seller of lacework—a renowned Vologda craft to this day. Definitive example of early twentieth-century merchant dwelling in Vologda, with porch beneath a loggia, paired doors (for upper and lower floors), flared cladding of eaves, and decorative carving. In the Soviet era, the house was converted to communal apartments with minimal maintenance. Recently restored as a cultural center. February 26, 1998.

VOLOGDA. Vorobyov house. Built in 1910 on a quiet lane near the Church of Saint Varlaam Khutinsky, this house is a riot of decorative fretwork in the *style moderne*. June 28, 1998.

VOLOGDA. Izvoshchikov house. Built in 1915 for a merchant family, the structure displays decorative details from the Vienna Secession movement. February 26, 1998.

Just to the northeast of town is the historic Savior-Prilutsky Monastery, founded in 1371 by Saint Dmitry of Priluki. Situated at a bend in the Vologda River, the monastic territory gained a stunning addition in 1962 with the reconstruction of the log tent tower Church of the Dormition from the long-abandoned Alexander Kushtsky Monastery, located near Kubenskoe Lake in Vologda Province. Although manuscript references lead some to state that the structure dates from 1519, other specialists assume that its existing form was frequently rebuilt and more probably dates from the seventeenth century.

To the northwest of Vologda is the Semyonkovo outdoor museum, initiated in 1979 to give a tangible sense of regional cultural traditions. The dominant feature of the Semyonkovo park is the Church of Saint George, originally erected at the turn of the eighteenth century at the village of Totsky in the Tarnoga region to the northeast of Vologda. Although plans for its preservation, together with careful measurements, were conducted

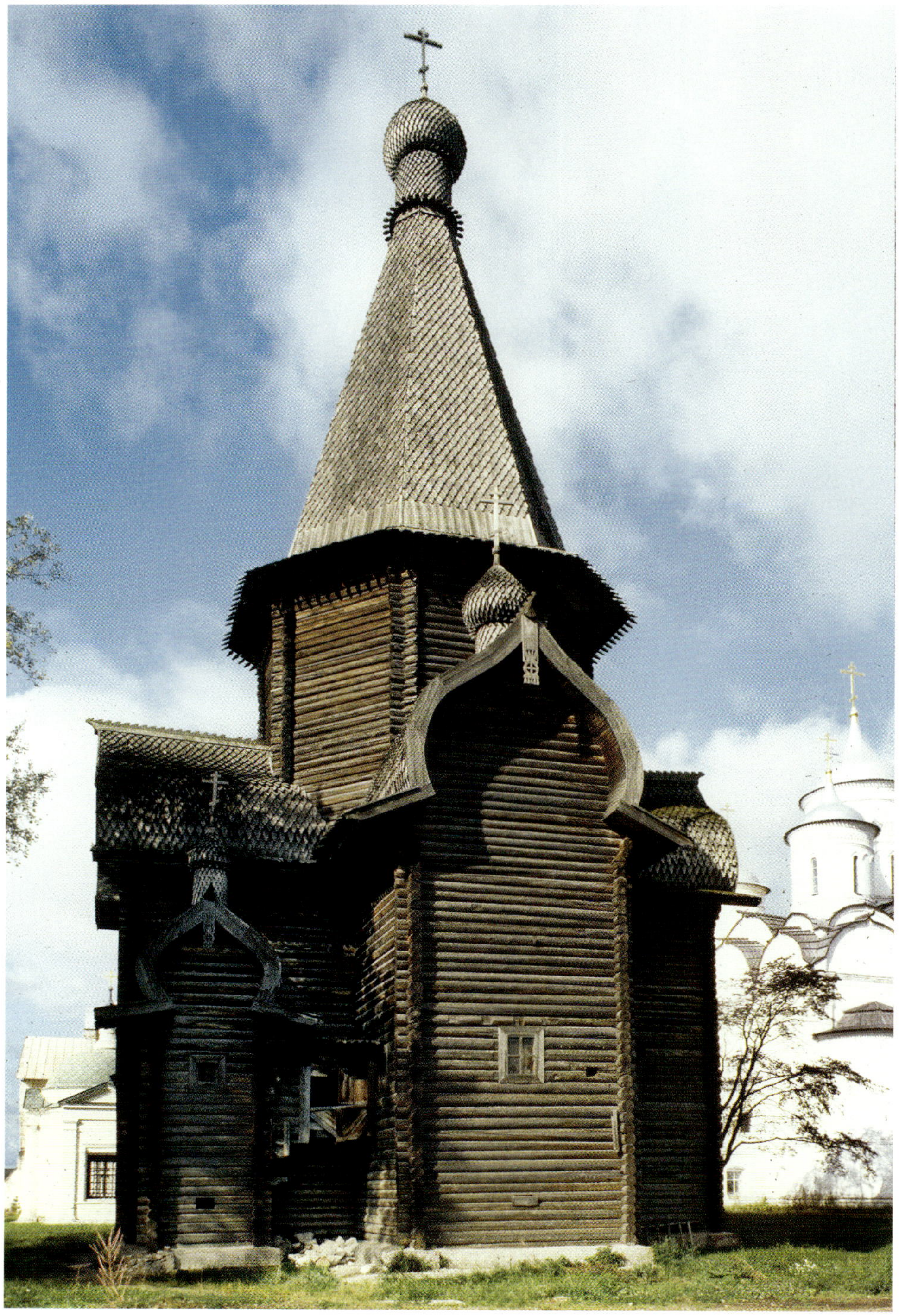

PRILUKI (Vologda region). Church of the Dormition, originally built at the Saint Alexander Kushtsky Monastery. Reconstructed in 1962 at the Savior-Prilutsky Monastery, whose Cathedral of the Procession of the Life-Giving Cross is in the right background. August 11, 1995.

in the early 1980s, delays led to a progressive degradation of the structure, so that the current version at Semyonkovo is an accurate reconstruction with a few original details. The form of the Saint George Church is a dramatic expression of the vertical often found in the Russian North. The base is a simple cuboid structure with an elevated porch and apse for the altar on the east side. In this case the apse is divided into two, with the north altar dedicated to Saint George and the south dedicated to Saints Boris and Gleb. The center of this sturdy base supports an octagonal

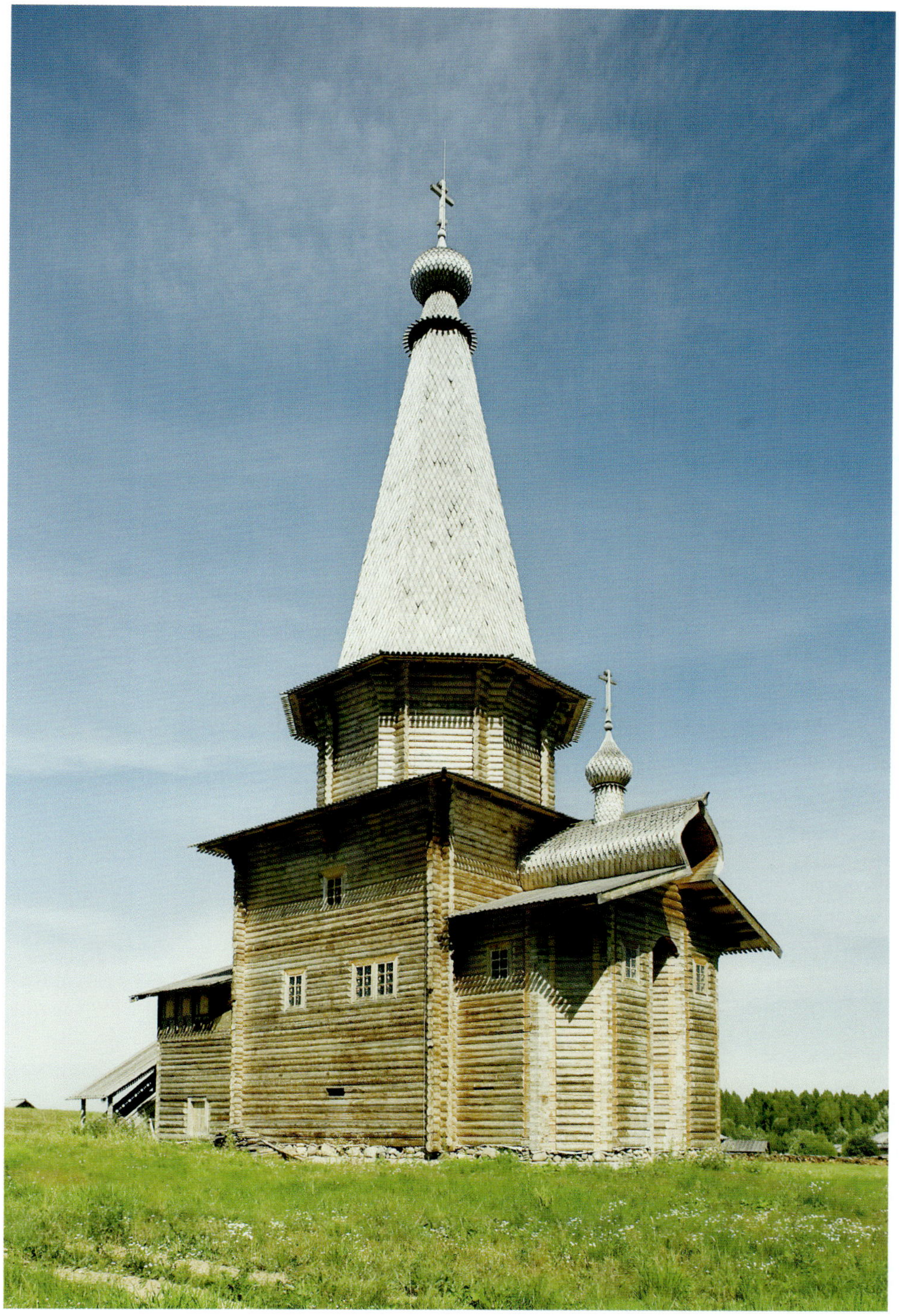

SEMYONKOVO (Vologda region). Church of Saint George (replica), southeast view. Originally built at the turn of the eighteenth century in the village of Totsky (Tarnoga region). July 23, 2011.

structure culminating in a flared roof to shed moisture. Above is a tent tower crowned with a cupola and cross. The total height is almost thirty-nine meters to the top of the cross.

The main part of the Semyonkovo museum is the collection of log houses reassembled on the park territory to illustrate the variety and artistry of regional folk architecture. One of the first examples to be brought to the museum (in 1985) is the A. E. Bolotova house, from the village of Korolevskaya in the Nyuksenitsa region to the northeast of Vologda. The basic part of the *izba* was originally built in the early nineteenth century in a simple rectangular plan of two floors. The ground floor had protected storage space in the front and animal pens in the back half. The upper floor had the main living quarters heated by a brick stove that was also used for cooking. The back half of the upper floor enclosed a large space for storing hay and farm implements. With increasing prosperity at the end of the nineteenth century, the entire *izba* was expanded by the construction on the right side of a parallel rectangular structure. The center of the enlarged house thus had two adjacent walls extending inward to provide increased structural support. This common practice created what is known as the "six-walled" *izba*, that is, four exterior walls and two extending inward from the middle of the front wall. The enlarged structure was graced with a balcony at the uppermost space under the large roof overhang, which protected against snow and rain. The main entrance was through an elevated stairway and porch on the side. Perpendicular to this large structure, there was also a one-story *zimnik*, or winter quarters, which could be more easily heated. Part of the family could live here in the winter, as well as young animals who would be vulnerable to the cold of the unheated animal pens under the main house.

Nearby is the house of A. I. Popova, brought to the museum in 1988 and originally built at the end of the nineteenth century in the village of Vnukovo, part of the Totma region northeast of Vologda. (The houses reassembled at the park have been arranged in a linear pattern typical of northern villages.) Like the Bolotova house, this *izba* has a rectangular

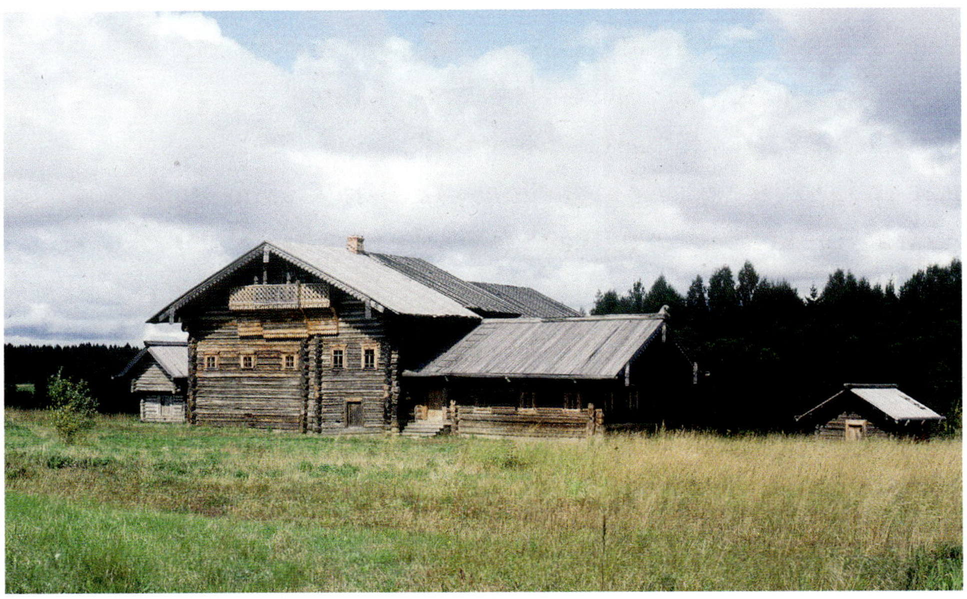

SEMYONKOVO. A. E. Bolotova house. Originally built in village of Korolevskaya (Nyuksenitsa region) in early nineteenth century with later additions. *Zimnik* (winter quarters) extending from right side. Log barn partly visible on left. August 11, 1995.

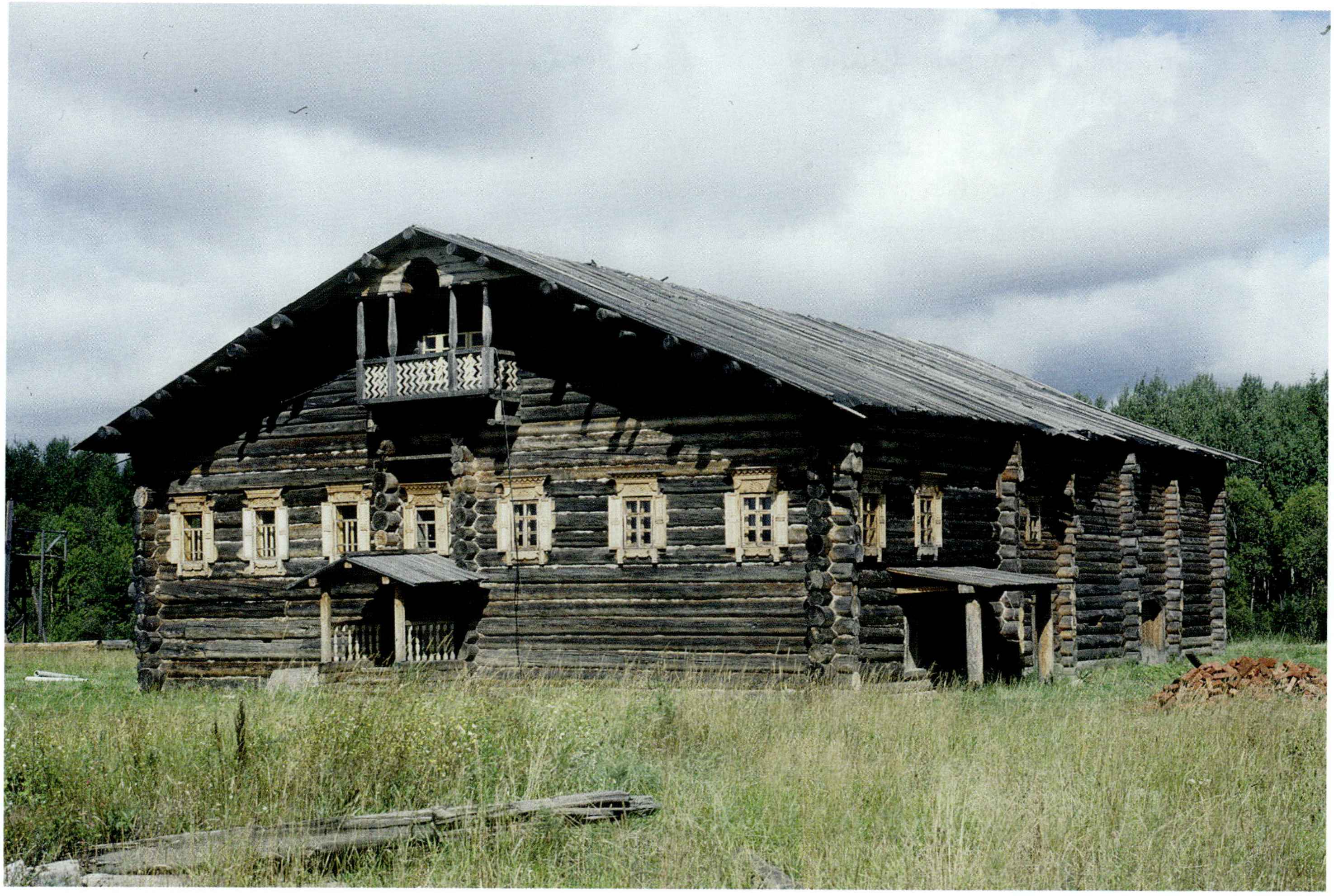

SEMYONKOVO. A. I. Popova house. Originally built in village of Vnukovo (Totma region) at end of nineteenth century. August 11, 1995.

shape of two stories with a balcony extending from the space under the roof, which provided an additional living area in the summer. The structure also has a six-walled plan, but since it was built all at the same time, the space between the two walls in the center is wider and designed to accommodate a stairway to the two halves of the upper story. Each half of the living space in the Popova house has a large brick stove. The main entrance is under a porch in the middle of the front wall. There is a smaller side entrance and a large ramp up to the hay barn in the back half of the upper level.

Simpler plans include the L. G. Zhukov house, built at the end of the nineteenth century in the village of Kalininskoye (Totma region) and brought to the museum in 1988. The Zhukov house is a five-walled *izba*, with the usual four walls of the rectangular two-level structure and a fifth supporting wall extending from the front into the interior of the house. The main entrance to the upper floor is through a porch on the right side that is also connected to an enclosed shed (known as a *staya*) for smaller livestock. The elongated barn at the back part of the house is narrower than the living space in front.

Another complex example of a five-walled *izba* is the E. A. Pudova house, built at the end of the nineteenth century in the village of Malchevskaya (Totma region) and brought to the museum in 1990. The exterior is graced with a fine bow-shaped balcony The layout of the upper floor is atypical: The summer living space at the front leads to the hayloft, but behind the hayloft is a winter *izba* with a separate entrance next to the

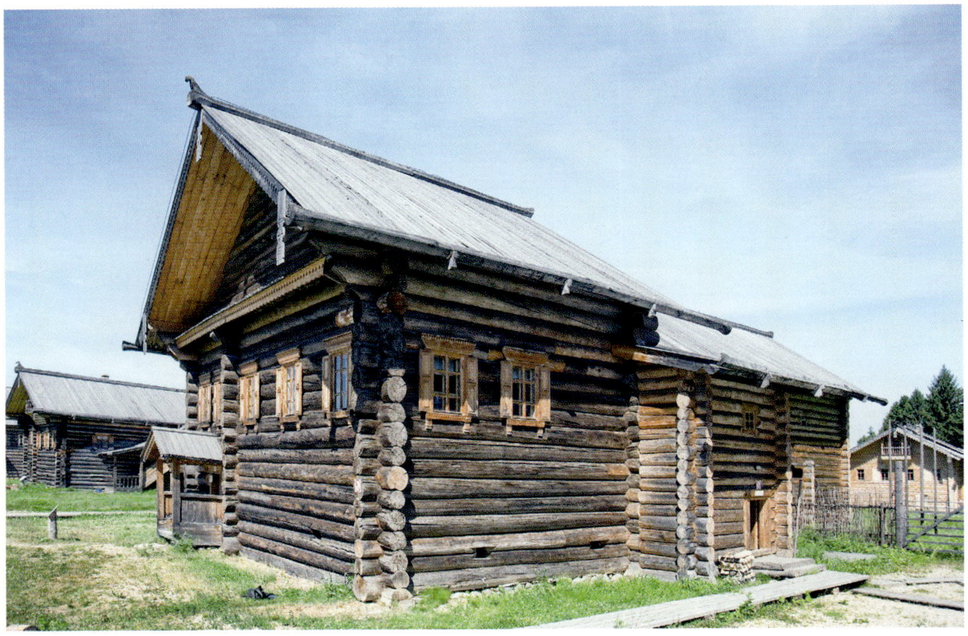

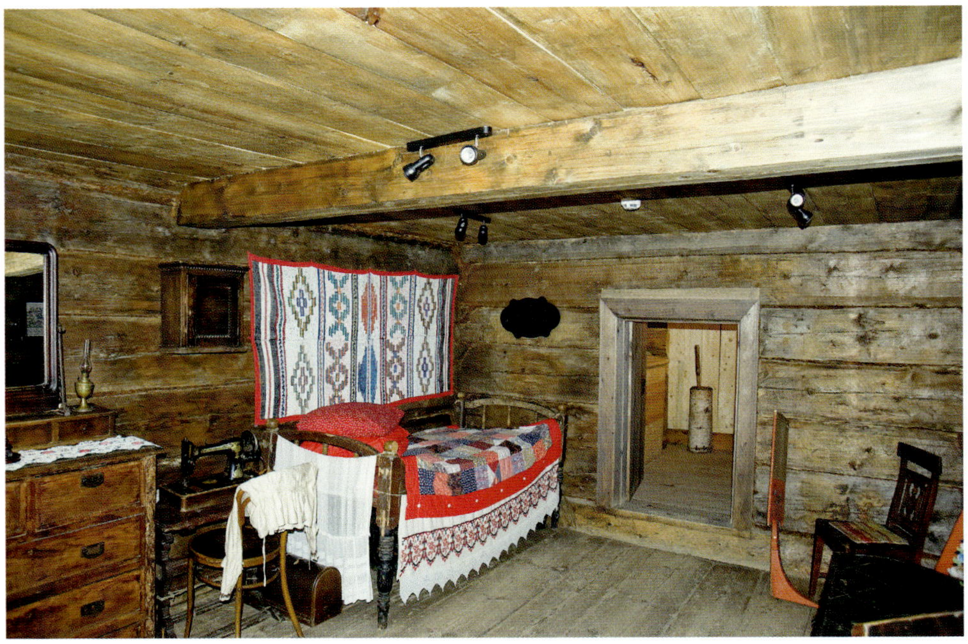

SEMYONKOVO. L. G. Zhukov house. Originally built at end of nineteenth century in village of Kalininskoye (Totma region). July 23, 2011.

SEMYONKOVO. L. G. Zhukov house. Main room. July 23, 2011.

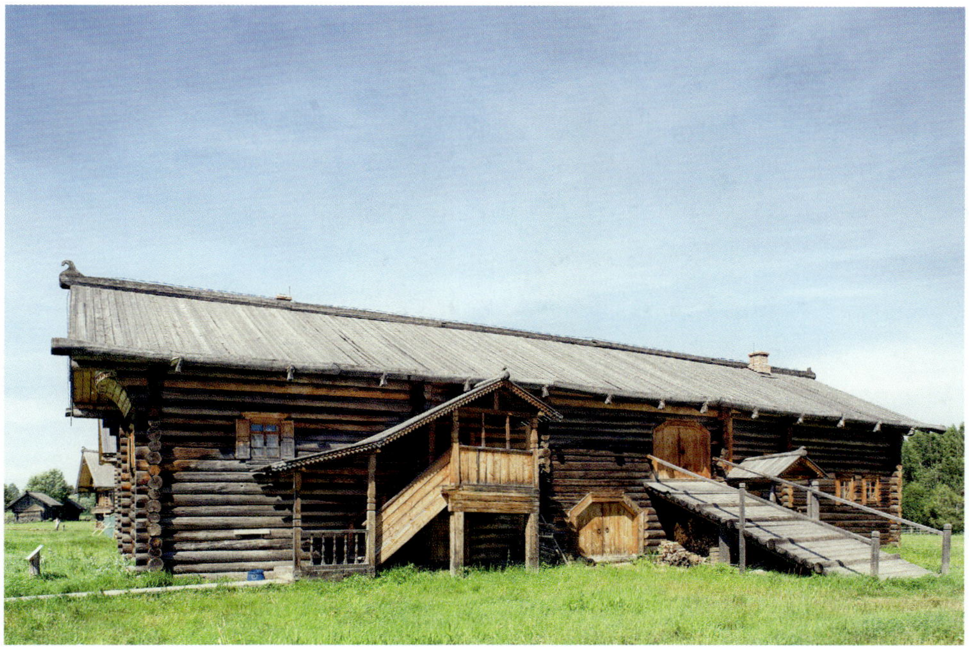

SEMYONKOVO. E. A. Pudova house, right side with elevated porch to main entrance and ramp to hayloft. Right: entrance to winter living space. Originally built at end of nineteenth century in village of Malchevskaya (Totma region). July 23, 2011.

hayloft ramp on the right side. On the left side is a long, enclosed shed for smaller livestock. As with other houses at Semyonkovo, the interior is attractively designed to give a sense of the living space of these dwellings, which sustained life in a severe environment.

The Semyonkovo museum park also displays various ancillary structures, such as separate barns, storehouses, icehouses, bathhouses, and, more recently, windmills. Among them is a reconstructed black bathhouse from the village of Shangino and now part of the Zhukov farmstead. In this type of bathhouse, the smoke rises from the stove through the heated stones and thoroughly disinfects the interior before accumulating under the roof and escaping through cracks in the structure. Having undergone this experience, I can say that it is quite bearable, and the odor of the smoke is washed away with a thorough dousing of water and soap.

Unfortunately, many landmark wooden structures in the Vologda territory have not survived. A notable example is the Church of the Nativity of the Virgin in the remote village of Popovka-Kalinkinskaya (Vozhegda District), which I photographed in April 2001. At that time the church already had a noticeable lean, but when the chairman of the village (current population: fourteen) let me into the interior, he could only speak of the need to attach "rubberoid" beneath the high ceiling to contain moisture leakage from the cupola. This, of course, had little to do with the main, structural problem, but he had no resources to prevent the looming catastrophe. The church collapsed on August 6, 2003.

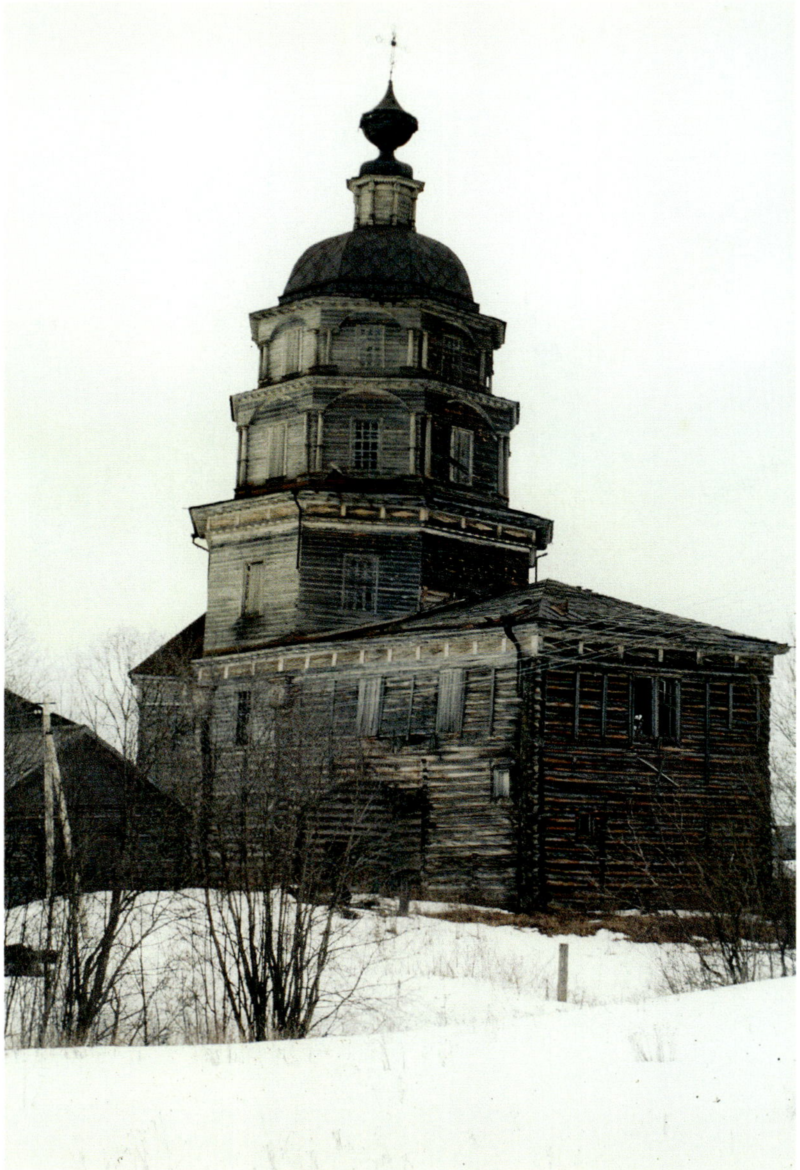

POPOVKA-KALIKINSKAYA (Vozhegda District). Church of the Nativity of the Virgin, southeast view. Built in 1783, this remarkable tiered church shows a visible lean that would lead to its collapse in 2003. April 1, 2001.

The Russian North is dotted with small towns whose architectural monuments reflect an earlier period of economic enterprise and strategic importance. Among the most distinctive is Totma, located on the Sukhona River midway between Vologda and Veliky Ustyug. Founded presumably in the early twelfth century, by the middle of the sixteenth century Totma had become a center of salt refining, developed by monasteries in the Vologda region. In return for their efforts in producing that essential commodity, the monasteries received tax exemptions. The other major force in the development of Totma's lucrative salt works was a Stroganov family branch headed by Afanasy and his son Grigory. Tsars Ivan the Terrible and Peter the Great visited Totma numerous times—a sign

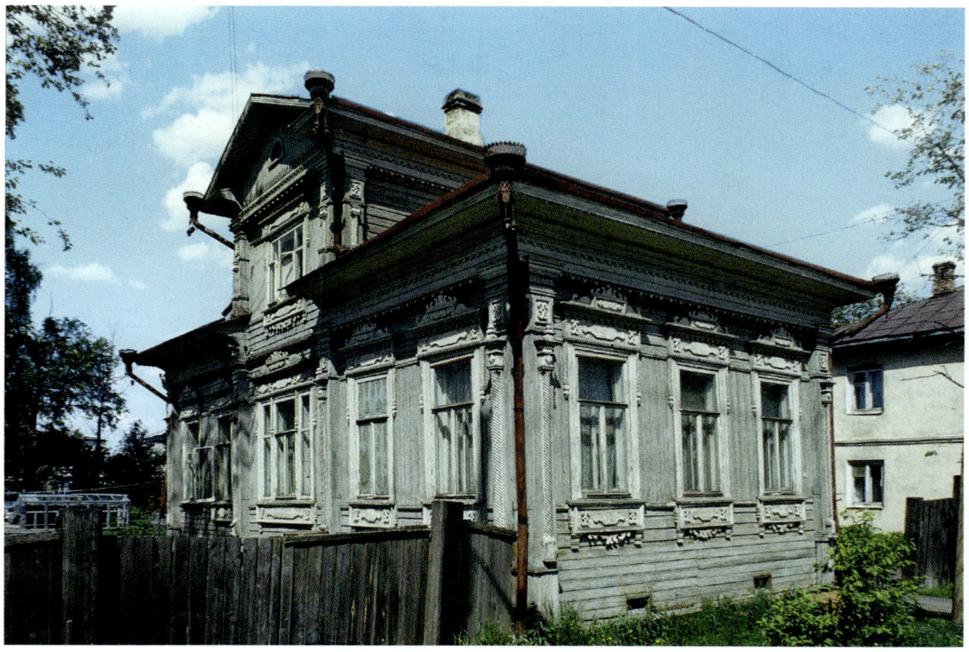

TOTMA. This small, richly detailed structure (Lenin Street 41) is an excellent example of a mid-nineteenth-century merchant house with *mezonin* in a town setting. June 21, 1998.

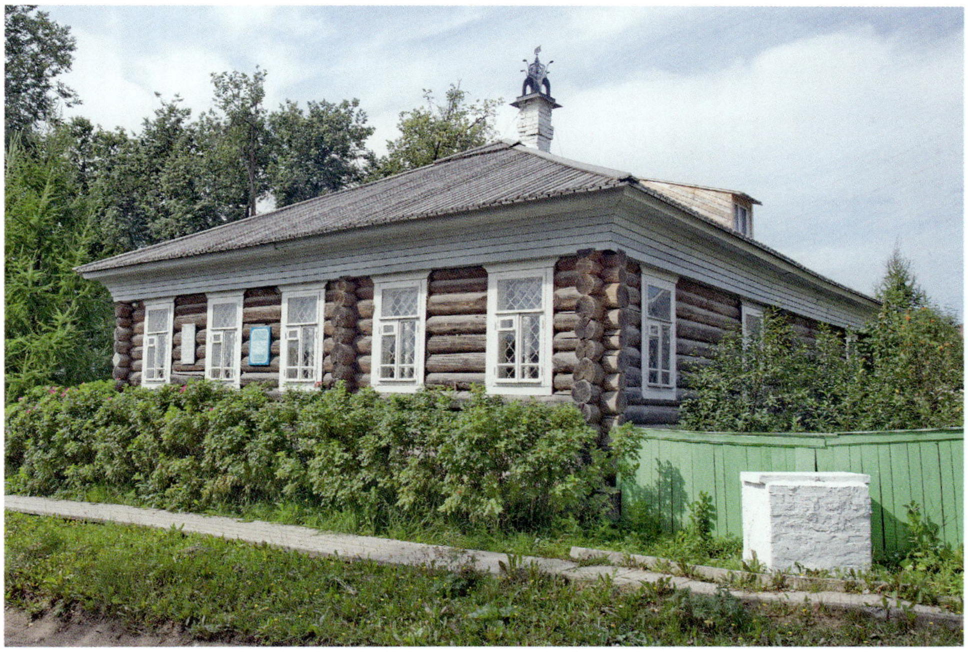

TOTMA. Ivan Kuskov house. Built in the late eighteenth century, this house belonged to the founder (in 1812) and first commandant of Fort Ross in California. August 8, 2014.

of its strategic significance in the northern territories. Salt was not the only source of wealth for the Totma region. Fur-producing animals also played a significant role. As in other northern Russian towns, the preservation of log houses in Totma has often yielded to the construction of monotonous brick apartments. Fires have also taken their toll. Yet Totma has retained a harmonious relation to the surrounding landscape, partly because of nineteenth-century economic stagnation compounded by the lack of a rail link.

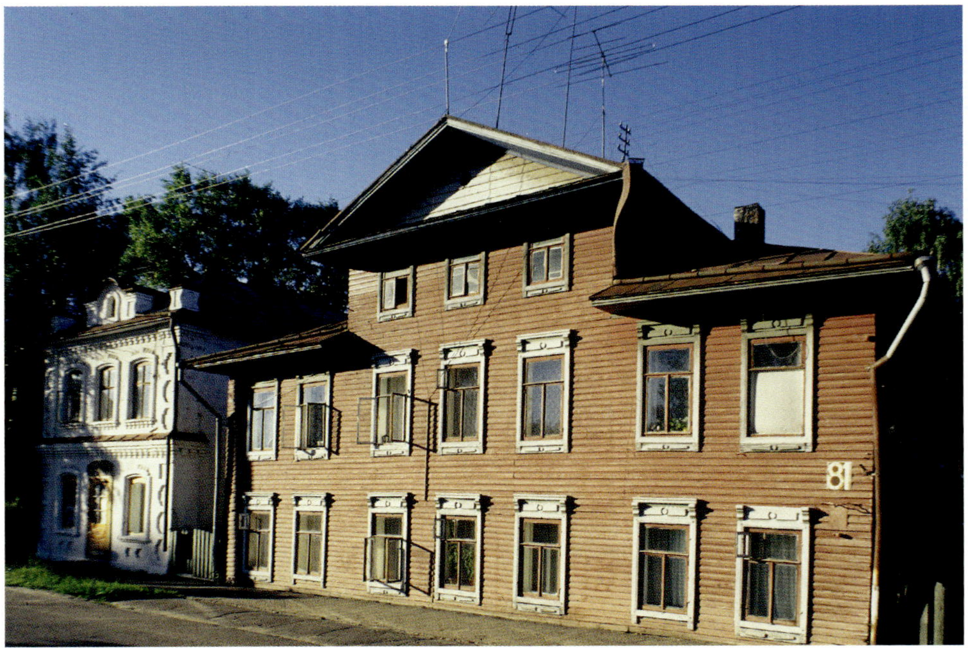

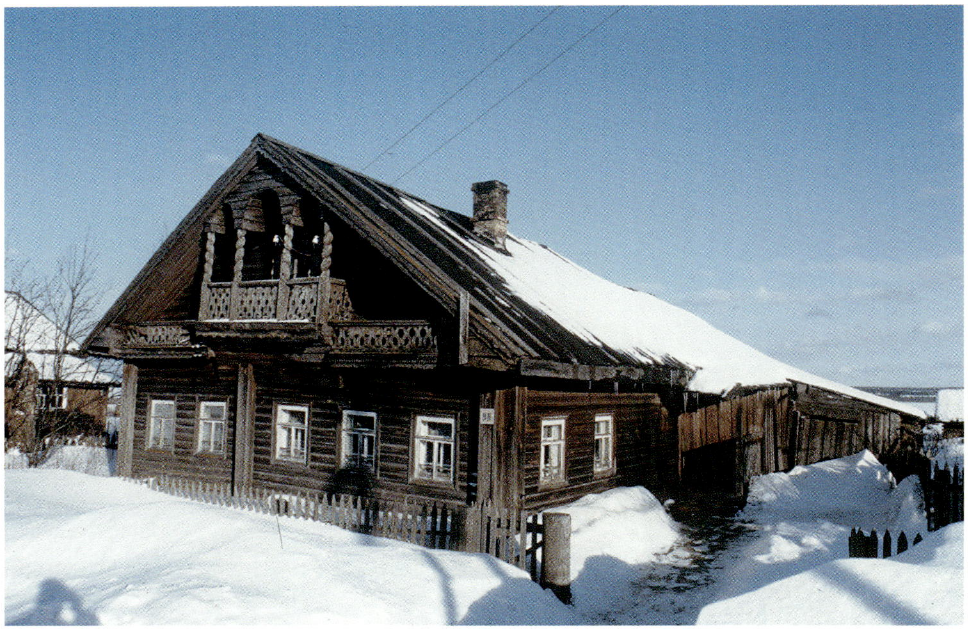

VELIKY USTYUG. Late nineteenth-century log house (Uspenskaya Street 81) with painted siding. July 18, 1999.

MOROZOVITSA (Veliky Ustyug region). Late nineteenth-century *izba* with decorative summer balcony and attached barn. I met the ninety-year-old owner of this jewel of a traditional house. After her death it was demolished. March 7, 1998.

The Sukhona River meanders northeast and ends at the town of Veliky Ustyug. Located on the left bank of the Sukhona, the town combines an appealing ensemble of historic architecture with a hauntingly beautiful natural setting. Although the development of Saint Petersburg in the eighteenth century lessened Ustyug's significance in transportation and trade through the Northern Dvina conduit, the town continued to prosper as a regional mercantile center. Ustyug was highly regarded for crafts such as leather and metal working, as well as the production of fine enamel objects. Its silversmiths developed specialized skills in the *niello* technique, and their work was in demand not only in the north but also in Saint Petersburg, including the imperial court. These commercial ties to cities such as Saint Petersburg led to a familiarity with the lavish decorative forms of eighteenth-century religious art. Although the town's surviving wooden houses are less elaborately decorated than those in Vologda, the surrounding villages still contain wooden houses that combine the traditional with the baroque.

In the vast expanses of the Russian North, rivers were historically the essential arteries of communication between communities set within dense forests and surrounded by marshlands. Today these rivers are no longer actively used for transportation, and the population along them is

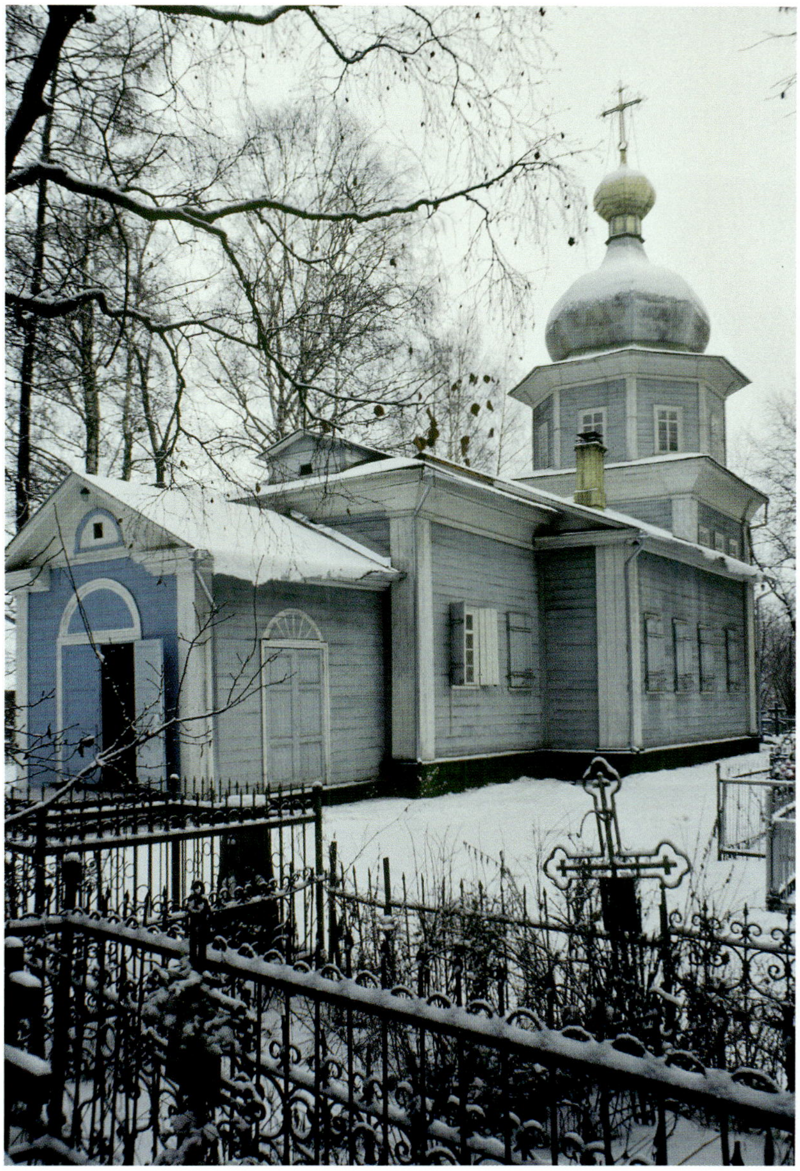

VELSK. Cemetery Church of the Dormition, southwest view. Built in 1793–95 with a baroque cupola elevated on an octagonal base. December 7, 1999.

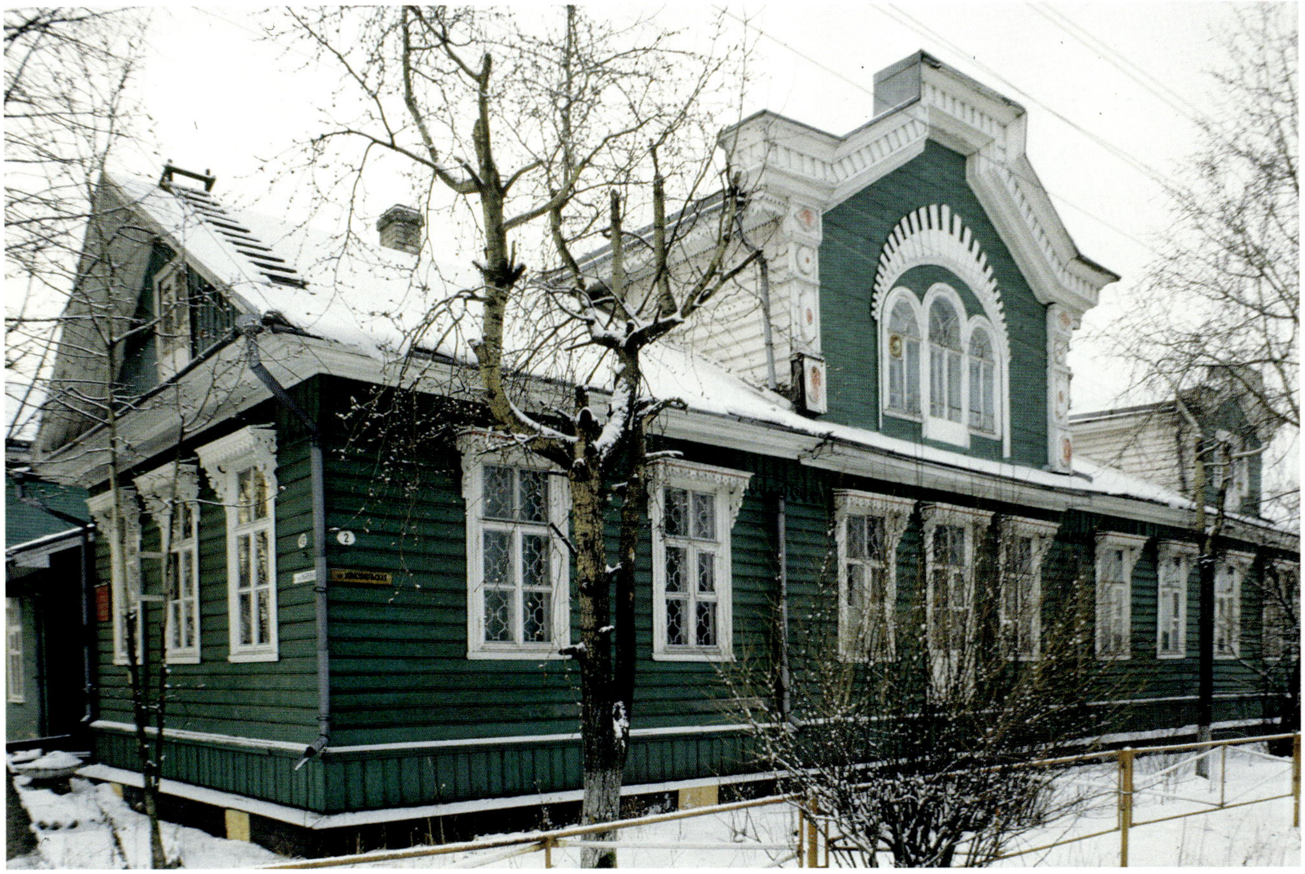

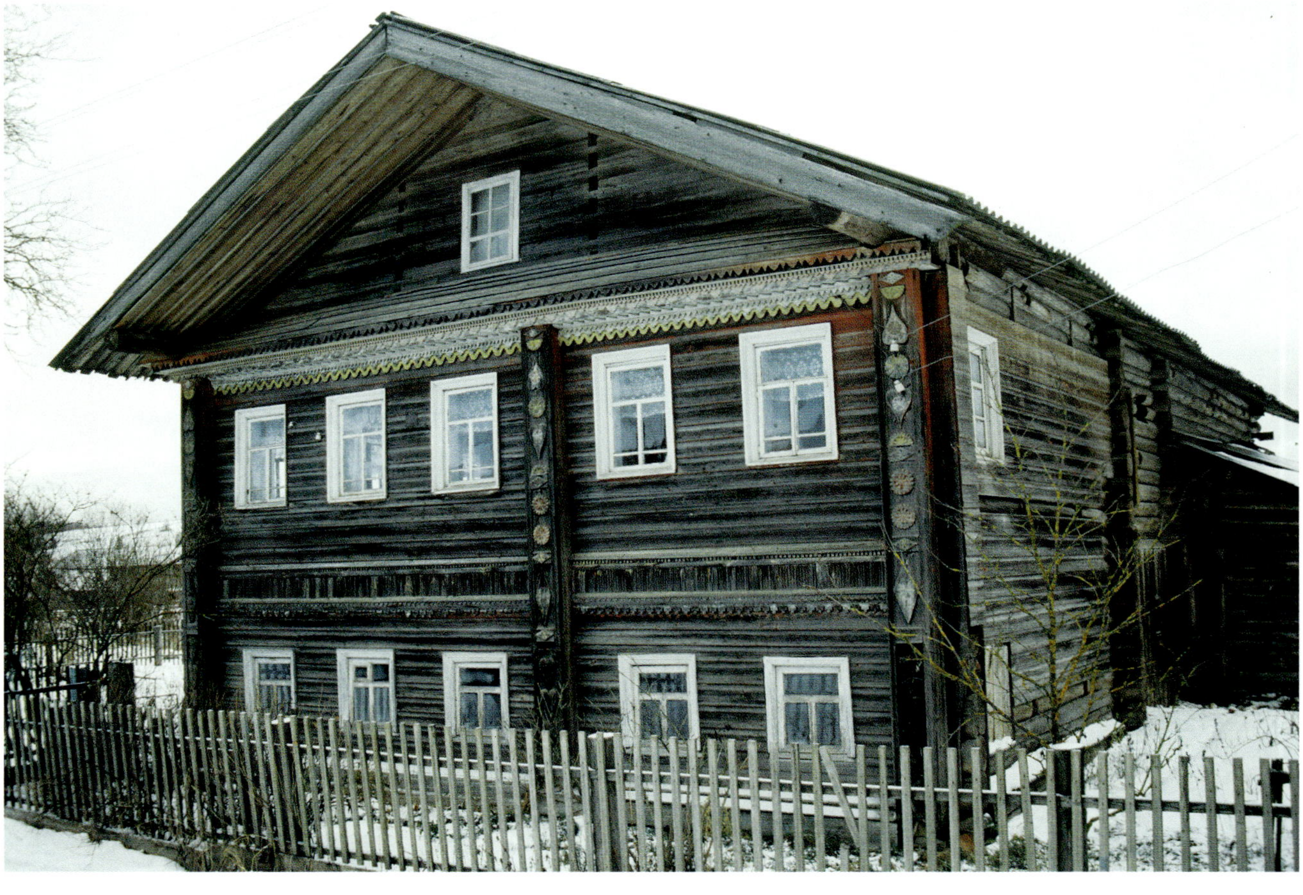

declining. But the rivers still lead to once viable settlements where remnants of traditional design and crafts have survived. One such river is the Vaga, the main left tributary of the Northern Dvina. Five-hundred-seventy-five kilometers long, the Vaga flows northward from Vologda Province to Arkhangelsk Province and enters the Dvina at the small town of Shenkursk. Its upper reaches are fed by a web of streams and small rivers, such as the Kuloi, Vel, Ustye, Pezhma, Shadrenga and Kokshenga. This aquatic network is nestled among gentle, rolling hills that form some of the most picturesque landscapes in the north. The area's many small rivers and lakes also provide an ample source of fish and wildlife.

The main regional town is Velsk (population about 22,000), located near the point where the small Vel River flows into the Vaga. Like most settlements in the north, the Velsk region was absorbed during the fifteenth century into the rapidly expanding territory of Muscovy during the reign of Ivan III (the Great). Velsk and its forests soon proved a reliable source of income for Moscow's princes. During the nineteenth century the Velsk region was included in the Crown Estates, managed especially for the imperial family. This gave a relatively favorable status to the peasants who lived and worked on the land. Velsk also benefited as an important way station on the Moscow-Arkhangelsk Road. This modest prosperity was reflected in several sturdy wooden houses for merchants and officials, as well as the wooden Church of the Dormition, built in the 1790s at the town cemetery.

Nearby villages continue to feel the impact of demographic shifts that have led in some cases to depopulation. Nonetheless, memories of old traditions remain, along with a few parish churches—most in an abandoned state. One historic village, Bereznik, is picturesquely located on the Vel River and is partially maintained by the Velsk Regional History Museum. In addition to a wooden firehouse and tower built in the early twentieth century, Bereznik has a large two-story nineteenth-century dwelling built for the peasant D. I. Kubennikov and known as a *kurnaya izba*, or "smoked" log house. The smoke from the brick stove on the first floor (*zimnyaya izba*, or winter quarters) did not exit through a chimney, but drifted upward through specially designed openings under the ceiling. As noted in the introduction, this form of heating had certain advantages (including economic use of firewood and fewer insects), although it became rarer over the nineteenth century.

VELSK. Astafev house. Built in 1910 for the nobleman Rafail Astafev, manager of the Crown Estates, the house has painted plank siding. Its imposing central *mezonin* encloses a tripartite window with a radiant crown and massive cornice. December 6, 1999.

PRILUK (Velsk region). Nineteenth-century *izba* of the five-walled variety with painted eaves and carved decoration. Structure includes extended barn. December 3, 1999.

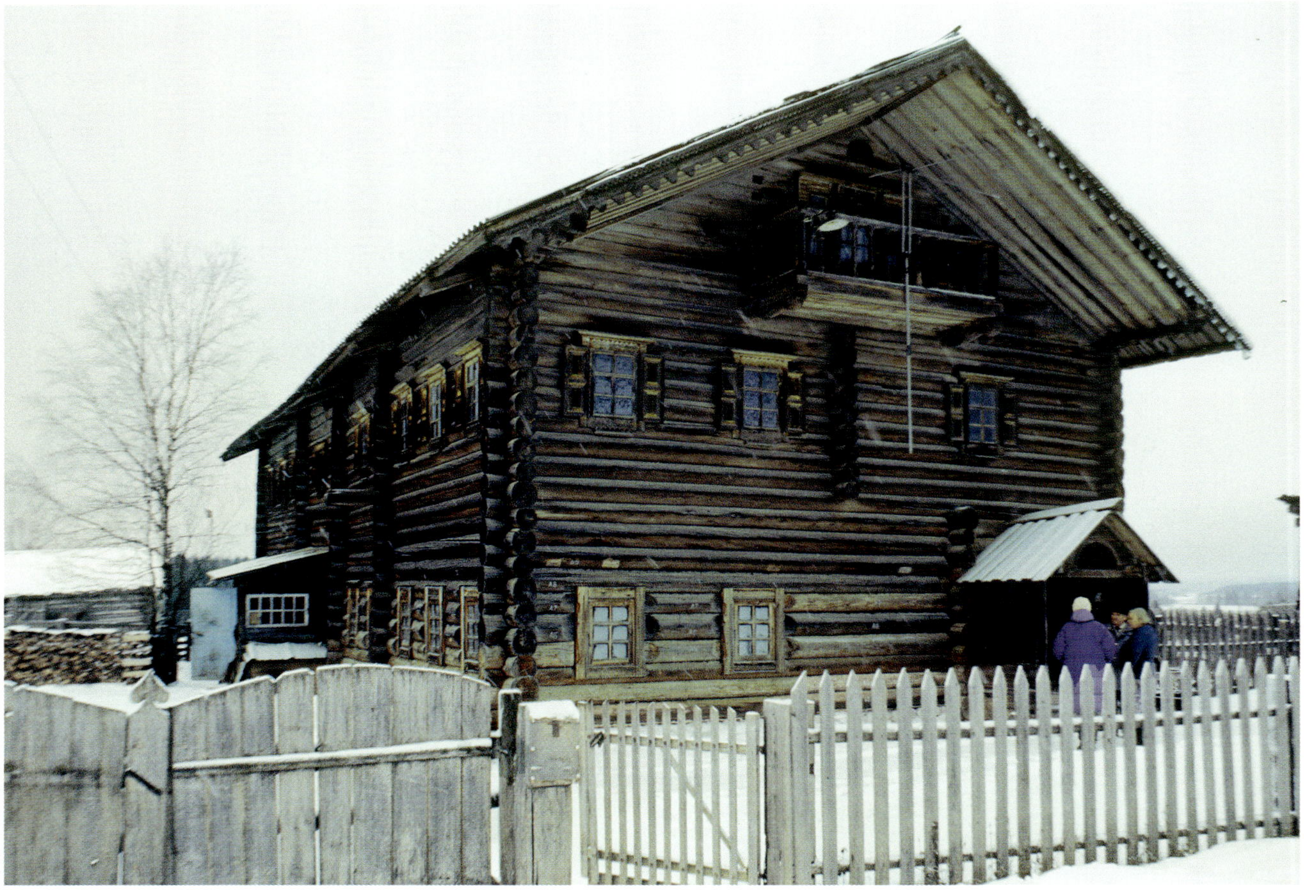

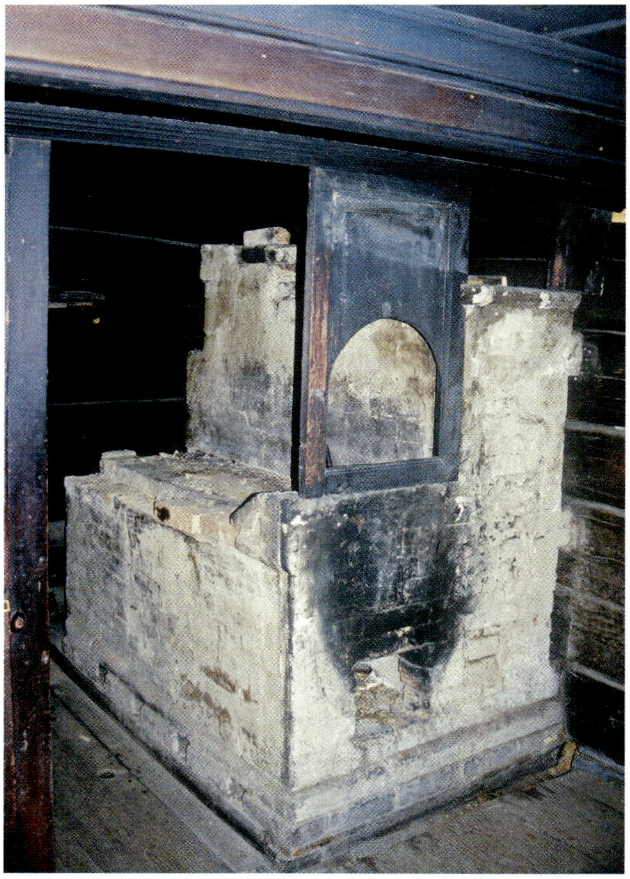

BEREZNIK. (Velsk region). D. I. Kubennikov house. Two-story *kurnaya izba* ("smoked" house) with a barn on part of the ground floor. Like many large houses in this region, it is adorned with a summer balcony and painted eaves. December 4, 1999.

BEREZNIK. D. I. Kubennikov house. Brick stove in winter quarters with soot-encrusted ceiling. December 4, 1999.

The center of the upper Vaga region is the town of Verkhovazhye (population 5,000), first mentioned in the early seventeenth century, when it struggled for existence in its remote location. Later in the eighteenth century the position of Verkhovazhye improved with the development of the Vologda-Arkhangelsk Post Road, which skirted the settlement to the north. During the nineteenth century a few imposing brick buildings were erected in the neoclassical style, but the small town—formally a village—was built largely of wood. During the mid-nineteenth century, it was known for the annual Saint Aleksy Fair, which attracted hundreds of merchants and peasants. In the summer of 1858 Tsar Alexander II passed through Verkhovazhye as part of his tour of the Russian North. A conflagration in 1879 reduced much of Verkhovazhye to ruins, but gradual rebuilding produced several wooden houses that still stand, including the two-story Yurensky house with its chevron-pattern siding.

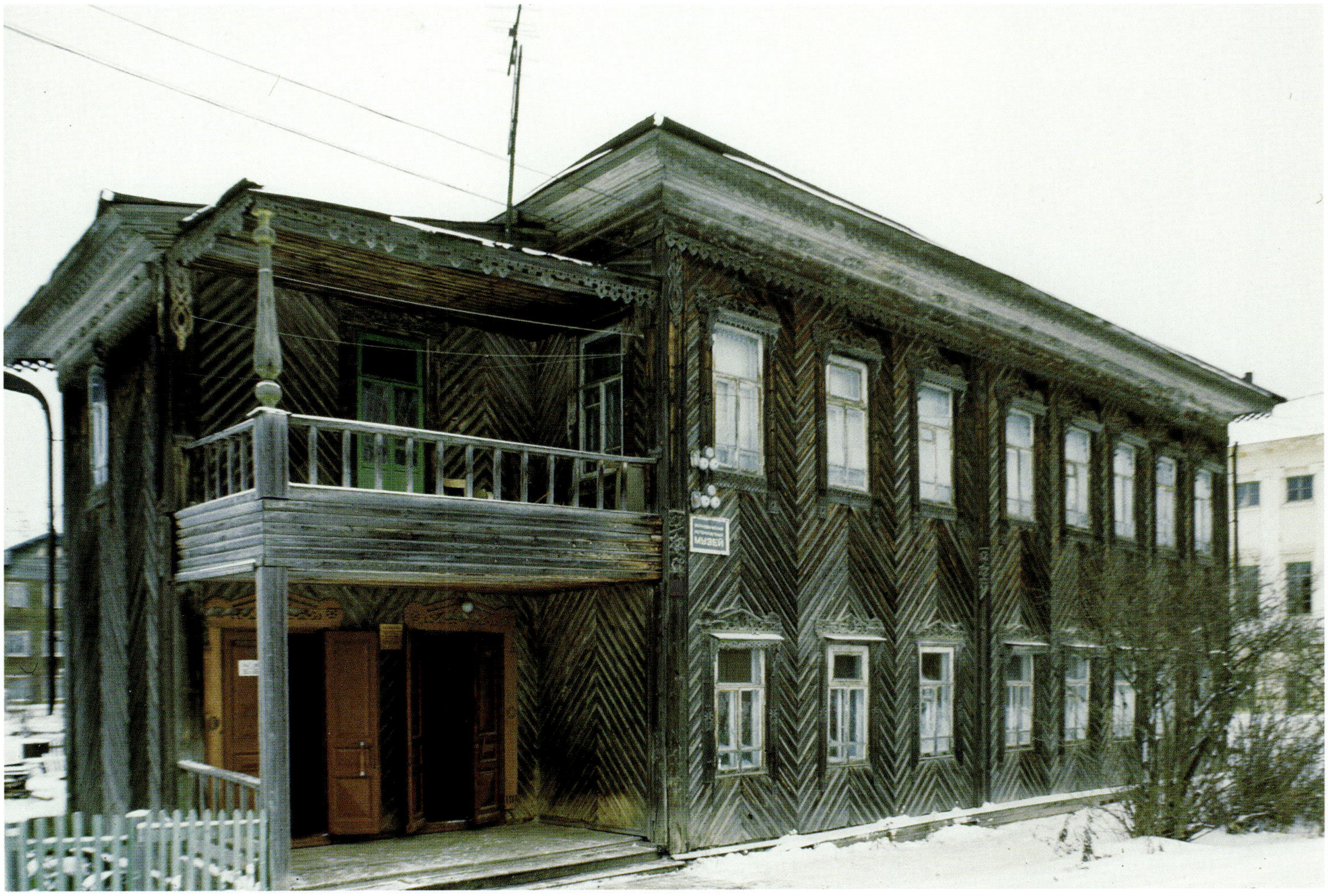

VERKHOVAZHYE. Yurensky house. A variant on the Vologda type of multifamily dwelling with a corner balcony and porch leading to paired doors. Walls clad in chevron-pattern siding. Now the Verkhovazhe Historical Museum. December 5, 1999.

Those interested in traditional Russian art will find obscure treasures in villages scattered throughout the Verkhovazhye region and the adjacent Velsk region, to the north in Arkhangelsk Province. The area has its brick churches, but the traditional culture of the upper Vaga region is most distinctively expressed in wooden houses and churches. Some of the houses, located in villages that have been nearly abandoned, are in a perilous state, yet there are surviving houses with unique decorative paintings on both exterior and interior, such as a rambling log dwelling in the hamlet of Ostrovskaya. Particularly notable here is the lion motif, symbolizing power and yet delightfully playful in this folk painting. In rare cases house interiors still displayed chromolithograph posters from the early twentieth century.

The aesthetic sensitivity is evident in the abandoned wooden chapels that dot the landscape near villages including Fedkovo, Nikiforovo, Selivanovo, and Semyonovskaya. Abandoned and weathered by the elements, these lyrical remnants of folk culture have fragments of paintings and

OSTROVSKAYA (Velsk region). House of Lions, so called because of the festive folk art on the main pediment. June 13, 2000.

OSTROVSKAYA. House of Lions, with the owner and sole remaining resident, Marfa Martynova, age seventy-two. June 13, 2000.

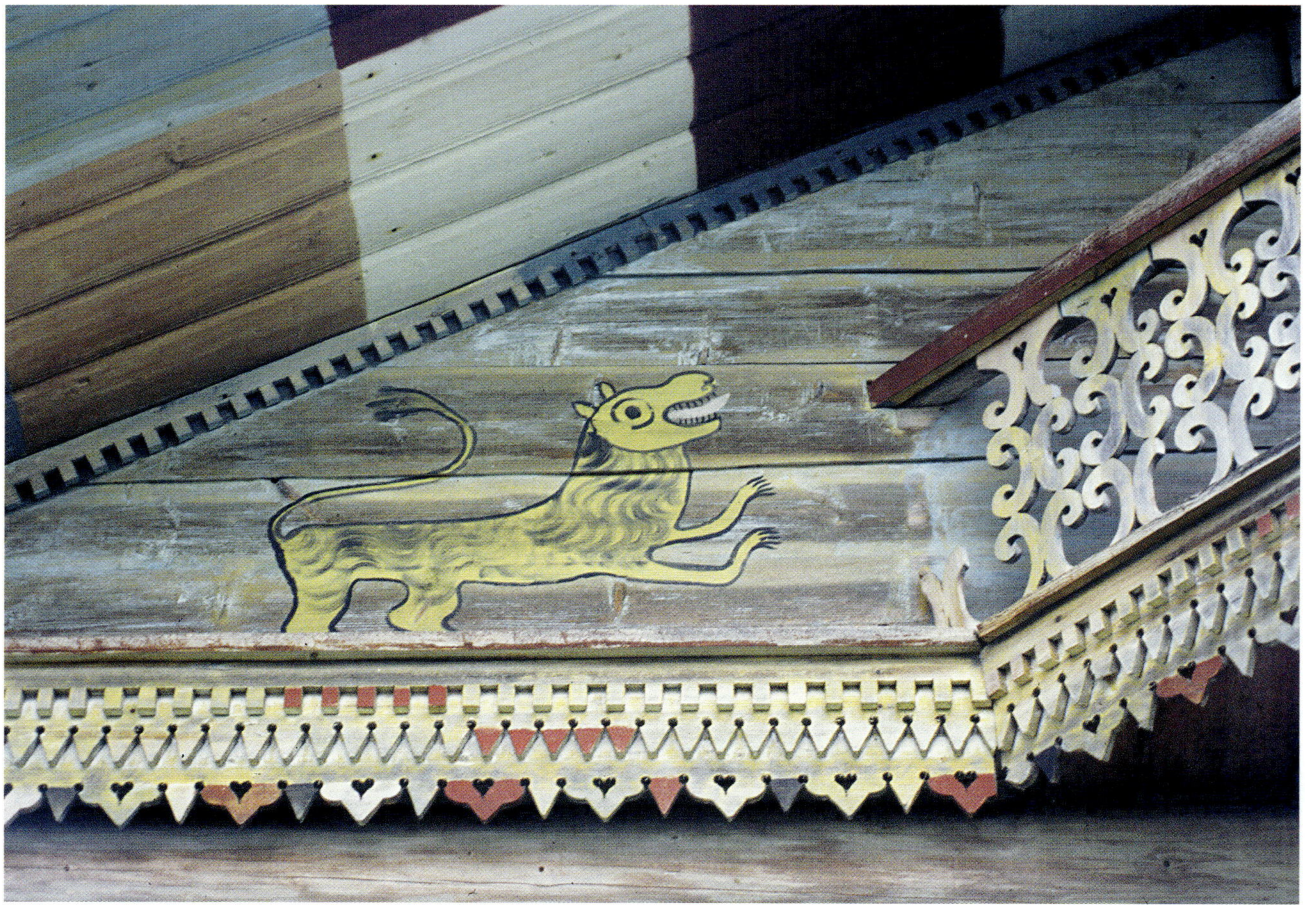

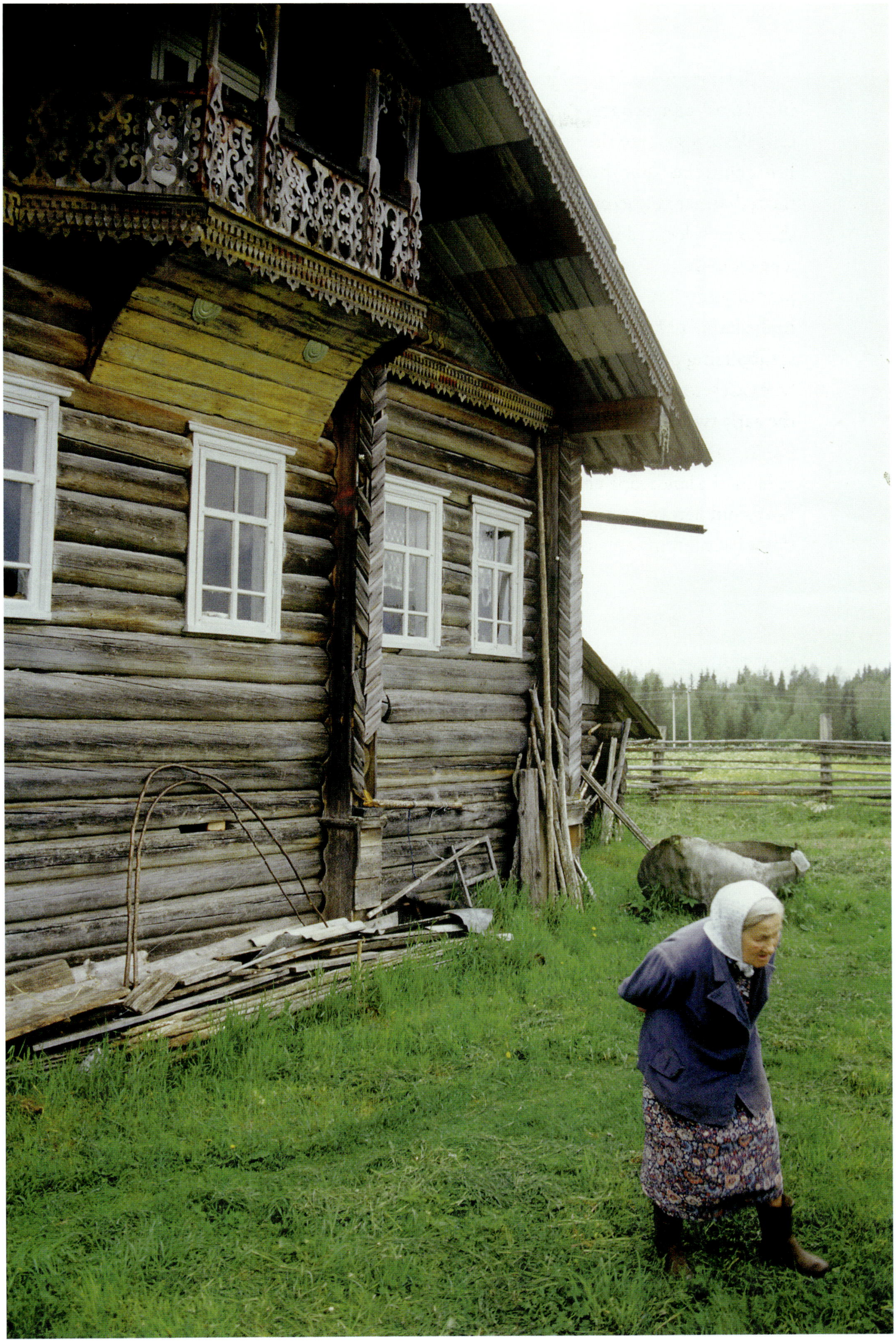

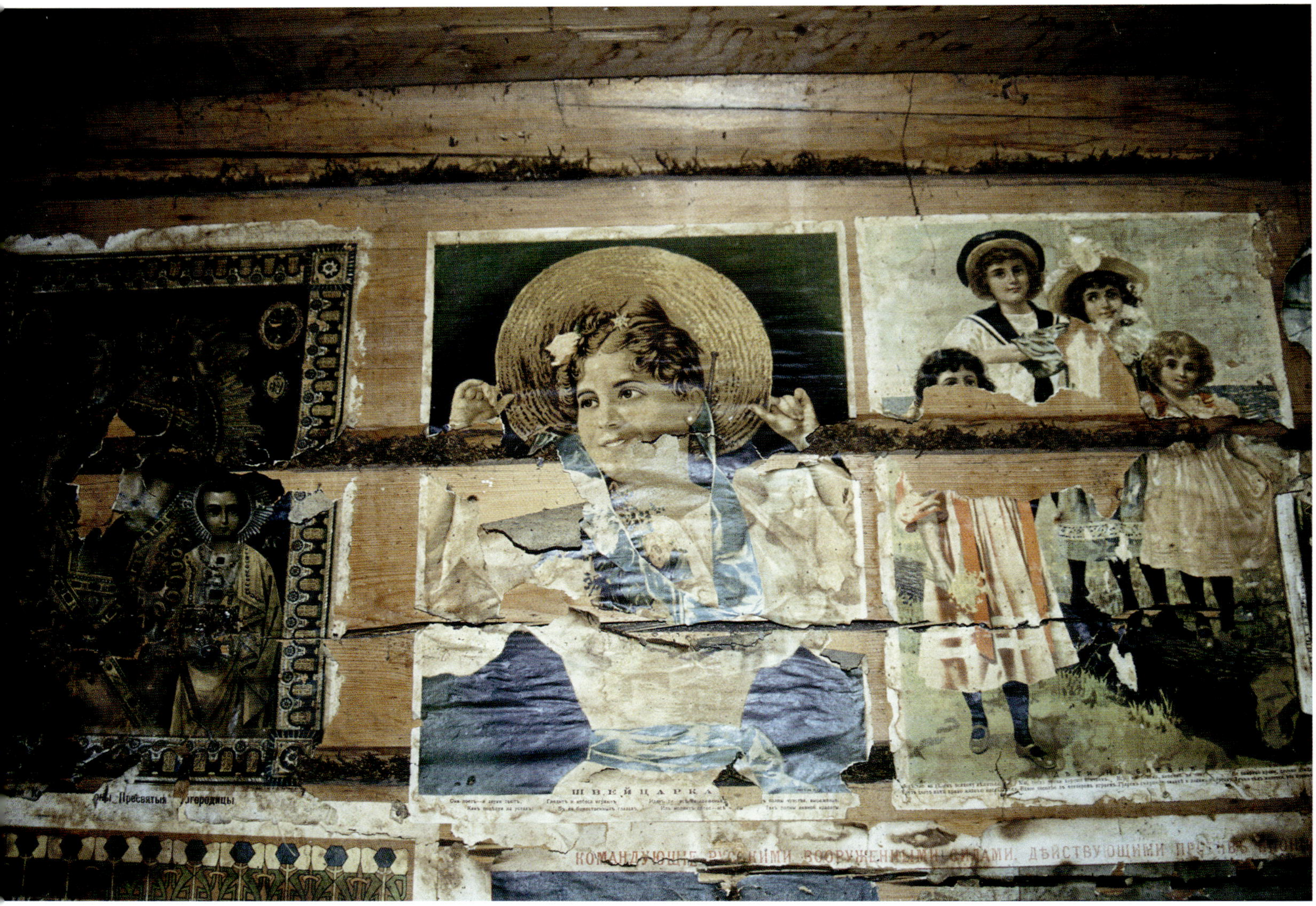

decorative art within. There are also large wooden churches, such as the Church of the Resurrection at Kozlovskoe, built in 1791 near the Kokshenga River just north of the border between Volodga and Arkhangelsk Provinces. In a recent restoration the plank siding of the church has regained its white color. These capacious houses of worship show a more expansive sense of space than the traditional log churches of an earlier period, with their dramatic tower forms. The increased size and simpler forms of churches such as the one at Kozlovskoe suggest a wide and active parish life in large northern villages.

OSTROVSKAYA. House of Lions. Main room, walls covered with tattered chromolithographs of the royal family and propaganda from the Russo-Japanese War. June 13, 2000.

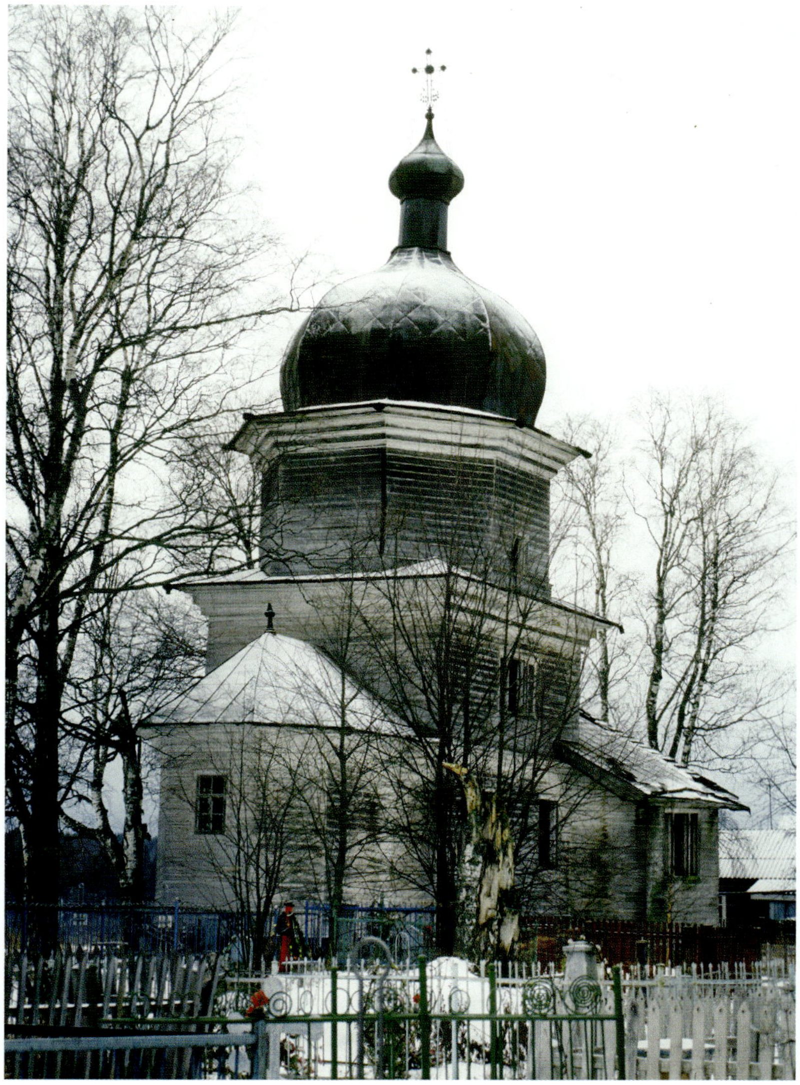

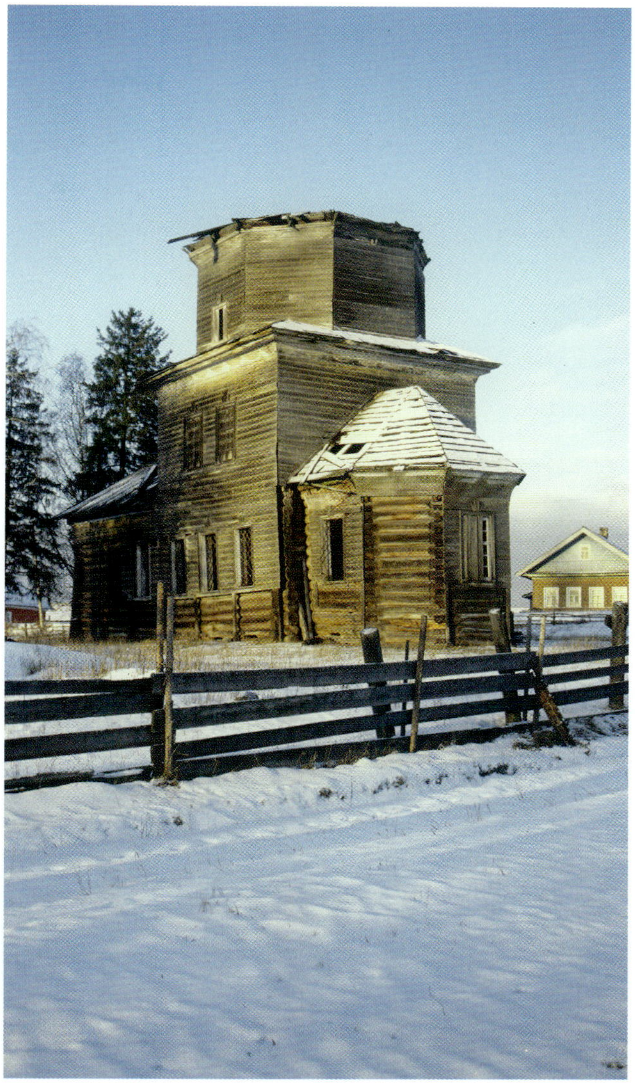

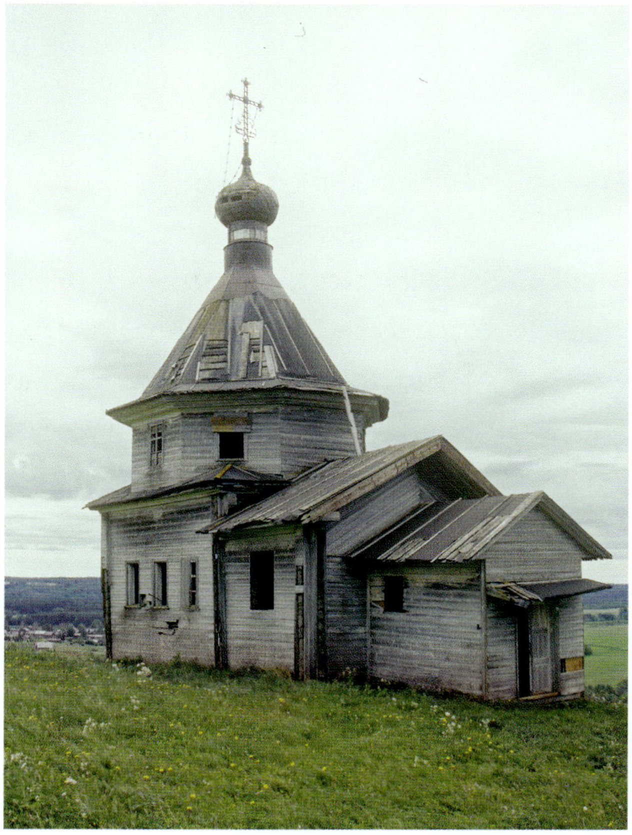

ROSTOVSKOE (Velsk region). Cemetery Church of Elijah the Prophet (1756), north-east view. December 4, 1999.

NIKIFOROVO (Velsk region). Built in late 1760s and originally dedicated to Nativity of the Virgin, this church was rededicated to Elijah the Prophet after a late nineteenth-century renovation. Southeast view. The long-abandoned structure burned on July 19, 2016. December 3, 1999.

SEMYONOVSKAYA (Velsk region). Chapel of Saints Zosima and Savvaty in Serednyaya, northwest view. Built presumably in the late eighteenth century. June 14, 2000.

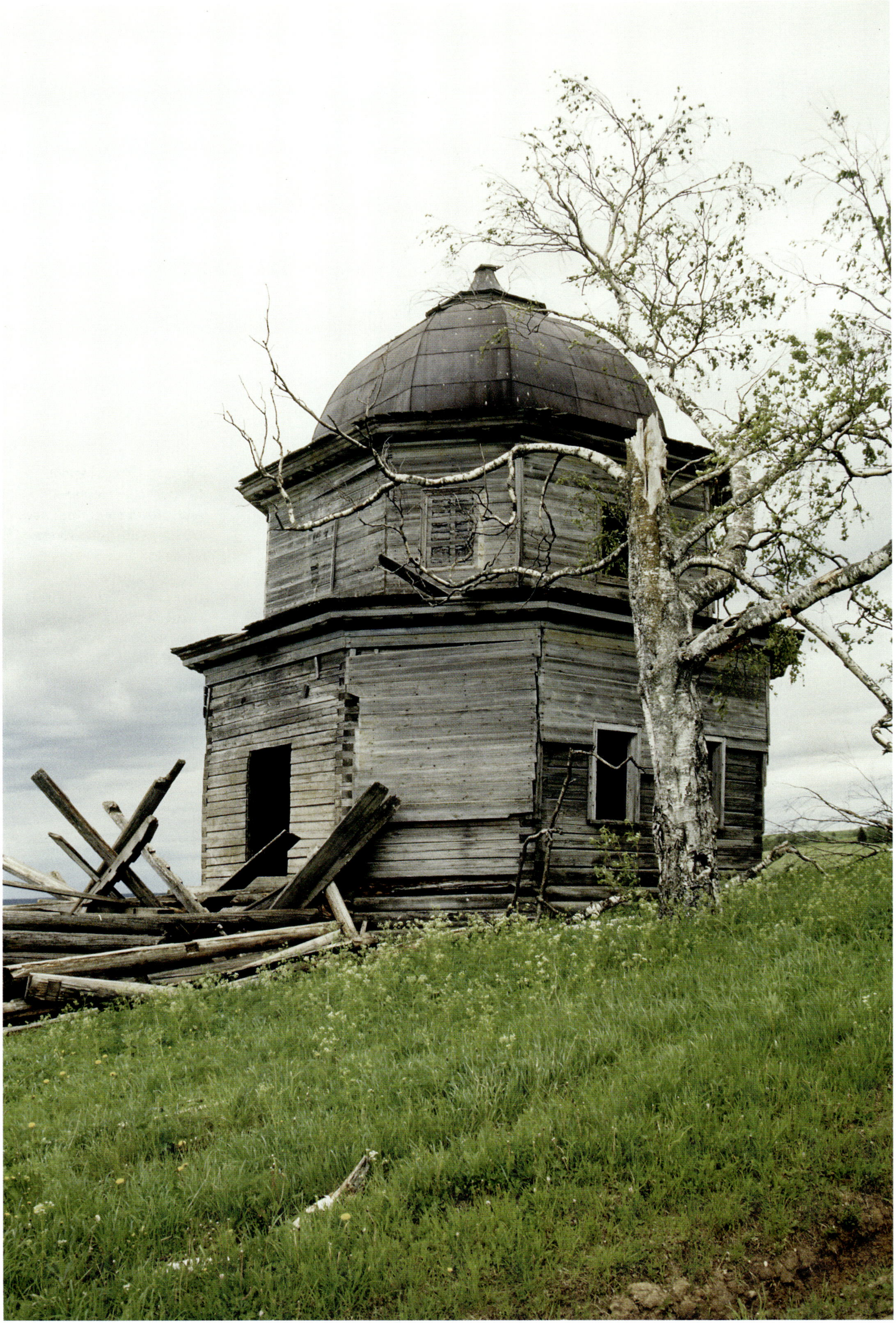

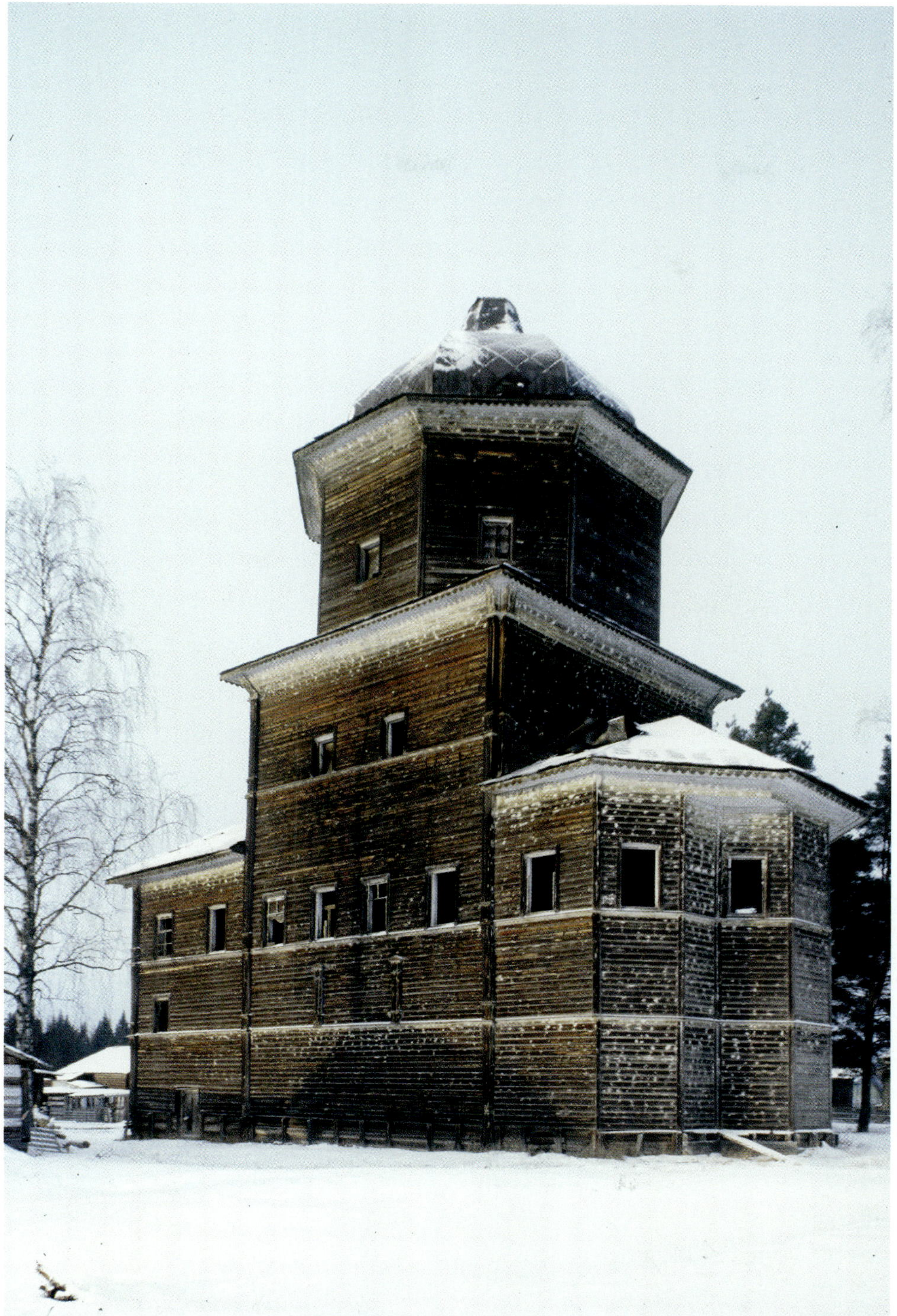

FEDKOVO (Velsk region). Chapel of Saints Quiricus and Julietta, southwest view. Built in 1848 overlooking a valley, the unusual rotunda-like structure has two octagons supporting a large dome. On the left are logs of a collapsed narthex. June 14, 2000.

KOZLOVSKOE (Velsk region). Church of the Resurrection, southeast view. Originally built in 1791, in the nineteenth century this large structure for a prosperous parish was covered with whitewashed plank siding, splotches from which are visible in this photograph. Exterior restored and repainted in 2012. December 5, 1999.

The Northern Dvina: Pathway to the White Sea

From its origins at the town of Veliky Ustyug to its mouth near the port of Arkhangelsk, the Northern Dvina is not one of the world's major rivers in terms of size, although at 744 kilometers long it is the longest river in the north of Europe. (Another Dvina River—the Western Dvina—is in Latvia, where it is known as the Daugava.) Yet, from the sixteenth to the beginning of the eighteenth centuries, the Dvina River basin, including the Sukhona and Vychegda Rivers, served as Russia's outlet to the West. Through the vast territory of the north—from Siberia to the Kola Peninsula—moved furs, forest products, fish, and that most essential of commodities, salt. Yet few are aware of the cultural heritage represented by the forgotten churches and houses along the river.

One particularly interesting area extends inland from the Dvina's right bank near its confluence with the Vychegda River, a tributary that stretches some 1,100 kilometers northeast toward the Ural Mountains and Siberia. This corner of the Dvina was known for its metal works and had abundant resources for salt—one of the most valuable commodities in the medieval period. Solvychegodsk means "salt of the Vychegda," and the area is replete with salt springs as well as a small brackish river, the Usol, and a brine lake, the Solonikha. The first Russian settlements in the area probably arose in the fourteenth century with the support of Novgorod, whose explorers would have recognized the value of a site near the crossing of two major river routes: north to the White Sea and east to the Urals. Wealthy entrepreneurs such as the Stroganovs, who arrived in the middle of the sixteenth century, received privileges from the Muscovite state to establish and maintain settlements for salt production. The Stroganovs created a salt monopoly in the sixteenth century that brought them enormous power, and Solvychegodsk became the center of a private empire based on salt refining, trading, and exploring Siberia. The patriarch of the dynasty, Anika (Ioanniky) Stroganov (1497–1570), whom Ivan the Terrible allowed to maintain an army of his own, exploited the wealth of vast areas of the Urals and Siberia, in return for which the domains of the tsar were greatly expanded at relatively small expense. It was he who began the lavish Stroganov patronage of the arts that produced splendid cathedrals in brick and stone, yet most of the dwellings in Solvychegodsk were built of wood.

As new trading routes led to a decline in its commercial role in the eighteenth and nineteenth centuries, the town became a small resort, known for its mineral waters and springs but also used by the tsarist government as a place of exile. Among the log structures was a one-story house with *mezonin* owned by a young widow Maria Kuzakova (1874–1941). Her husband, Stepan, had died in 1905, apparently in the disastrous Russo-Japanese War. She supported herself and five young children by renting to political exiles, among whom was Yosif Dzhugashvili—later known as Stalin—who lived there from January 10 to July 6, 1911. (Dzhugashvili had several northern exiles from which he seemed to escape at will, including

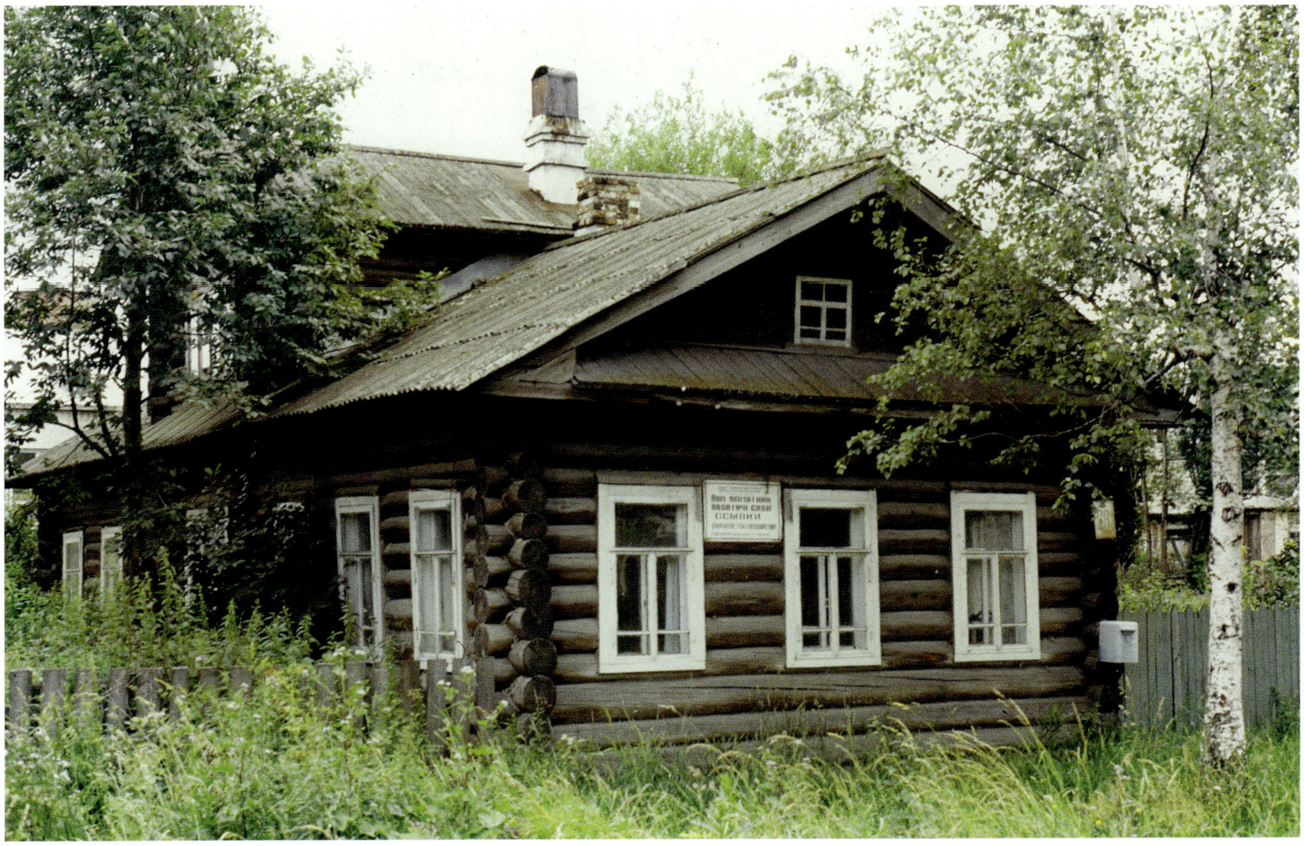

SOLVYCHEGODSK. Kuzakov house (now Political Exile Museum). House where Yosif Dzhugashvili—Stalin—lived as a political exile in 1911. July 28, 1996.

a previous stay in Solvychegodsk in 1909 lasting two months.) The young exile received a rental allowance from the tsarist government of seven rubles forty kopecks from which he rented a furnished room and purchased bread and milk. His main meals were with a group of exiles at another house, presumably with fewer children. On the dictator's fifty-fifth birthday in 1934, the room where he lived was preserved and proclaimed the I. V. Stalin House Museum. In 1937 Kuzakova transferred the house to the state in exchange for an apartment in Leningrad, where she died in December 1941 during the Siege of Leningrad. Such was the devastating fate of millions. Following Nikita Khrushchev's de-Stalinization campaign, the museum was maintained under a different guise. The Stalinist period inflicted much damage on the architectural heritage of Solvychegodsk, as elsewhere. Of the town's twelve brick churches at the beginning of the twentieth century, eight were destroyed and two others left in ruined state. None were built of wood.

To the north of Solvyghegodsk, however, traditional wooden architecture asserts itself stunningly in the village of Verkhnyaya (Upper) Uftyuga, located on dirt road along the small, winding Uftyuga River some

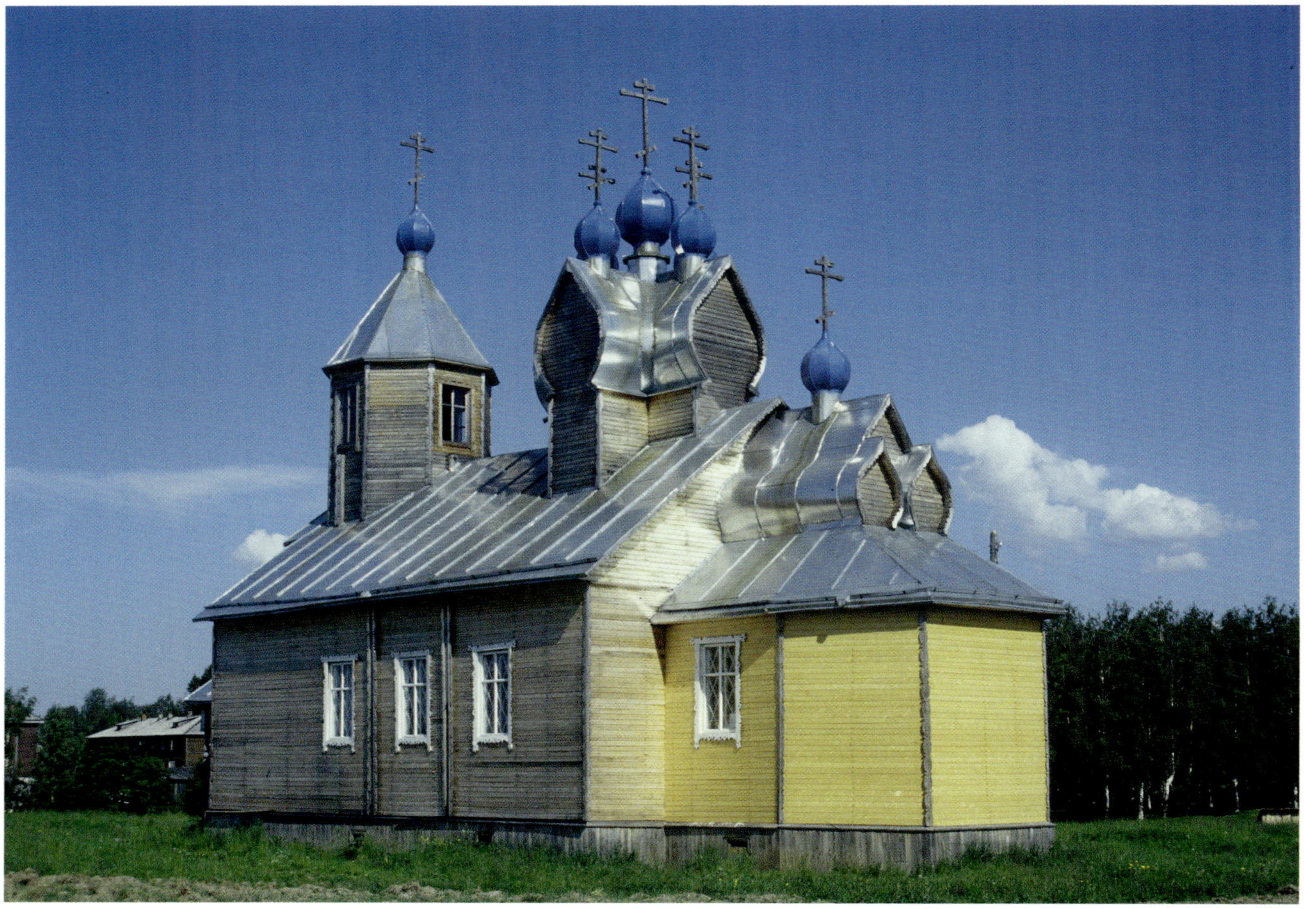

forty-five kilometers inland from the right bank of the Dvina. The village center is marked by the Church of Saint Dimitry (Demetrius of Thessaloniki), a magnificent tower shrine built in 1784 and carefully restored in the late 1980s. The most striking feature of the Church of Saint Dmitry is its tent tower, which comprises more than half the forty-meter height of the church. The eight-sided tower rises above a low octagonal log base, which in turn rests on the large cuboid structure. The tower culminates in a cupola covered in wooden shingles. On the east side is an extension for the apse (with the main altar) crowned with a small gable and cupola. The church is constructed of stout pine logs, tightly fitted, and notched at the ends. Just beneath the base of the tent tower, the logs are extended to support a flare (*poval*). This extension bolsters the tower and creates a roof overhang (*politsa*) that protects the lower walls from excessive moisture runoff. The flare design is both functional and one of the most graceful details of Russian wooden architecture. The vertical form of the Church of Saint Dmitry is fronted by a simple raised gallery to which a covered stairway ascended from the ground level, thus lifting the main entrance above the winter snow drifts.

VERKHNYAYA TOIMA. Church of Saint George, southeast view. Built in 1997, the church attempts to place traditional elements on a modern box structure. Destroyed by fire in January 2015. June 23, 2000.

VERKHNYAYA UFTYUGA (Krasnoborsk region). Church of Saint Demetrius of Thessaloniki, northwest view. June 25, 2000.

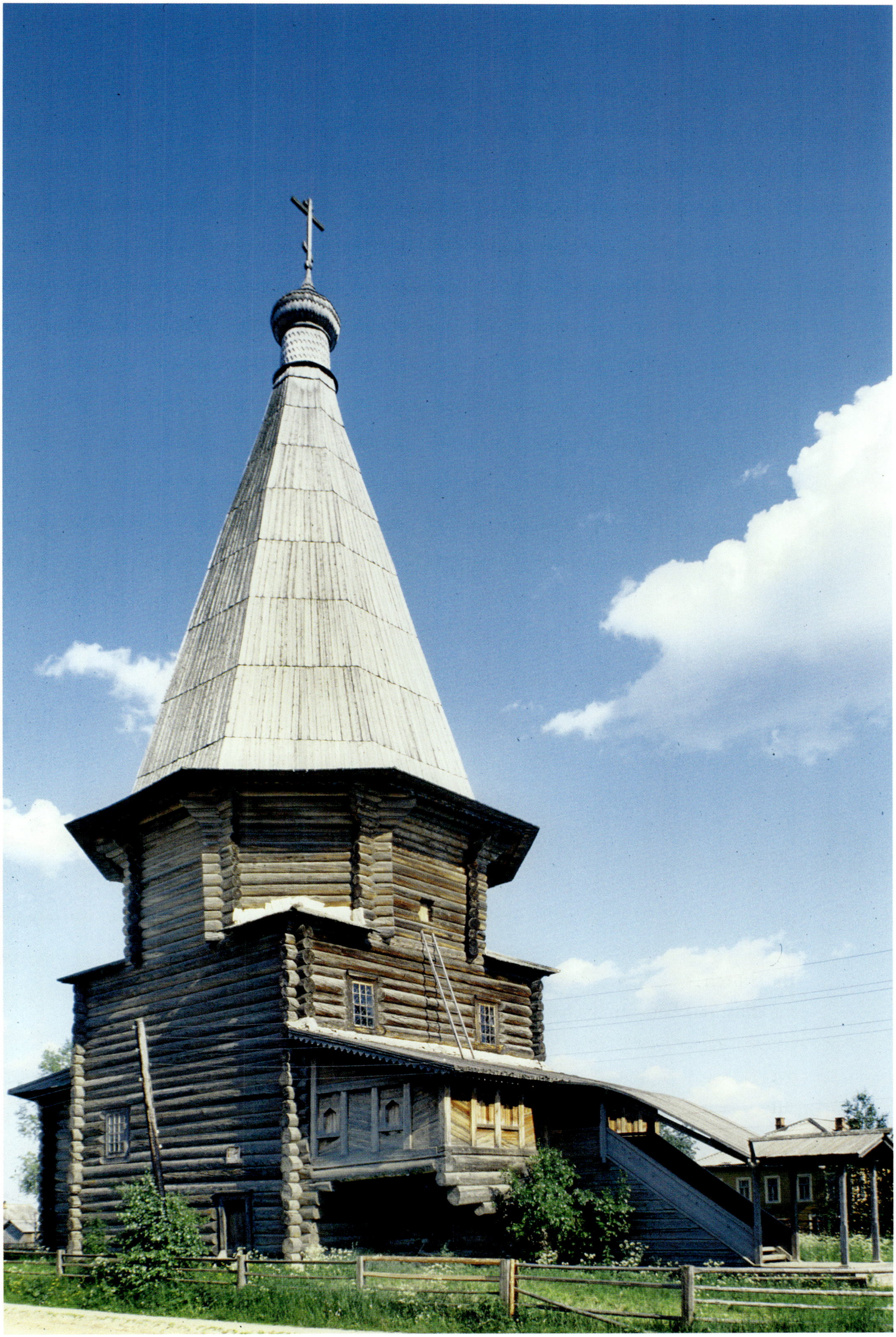

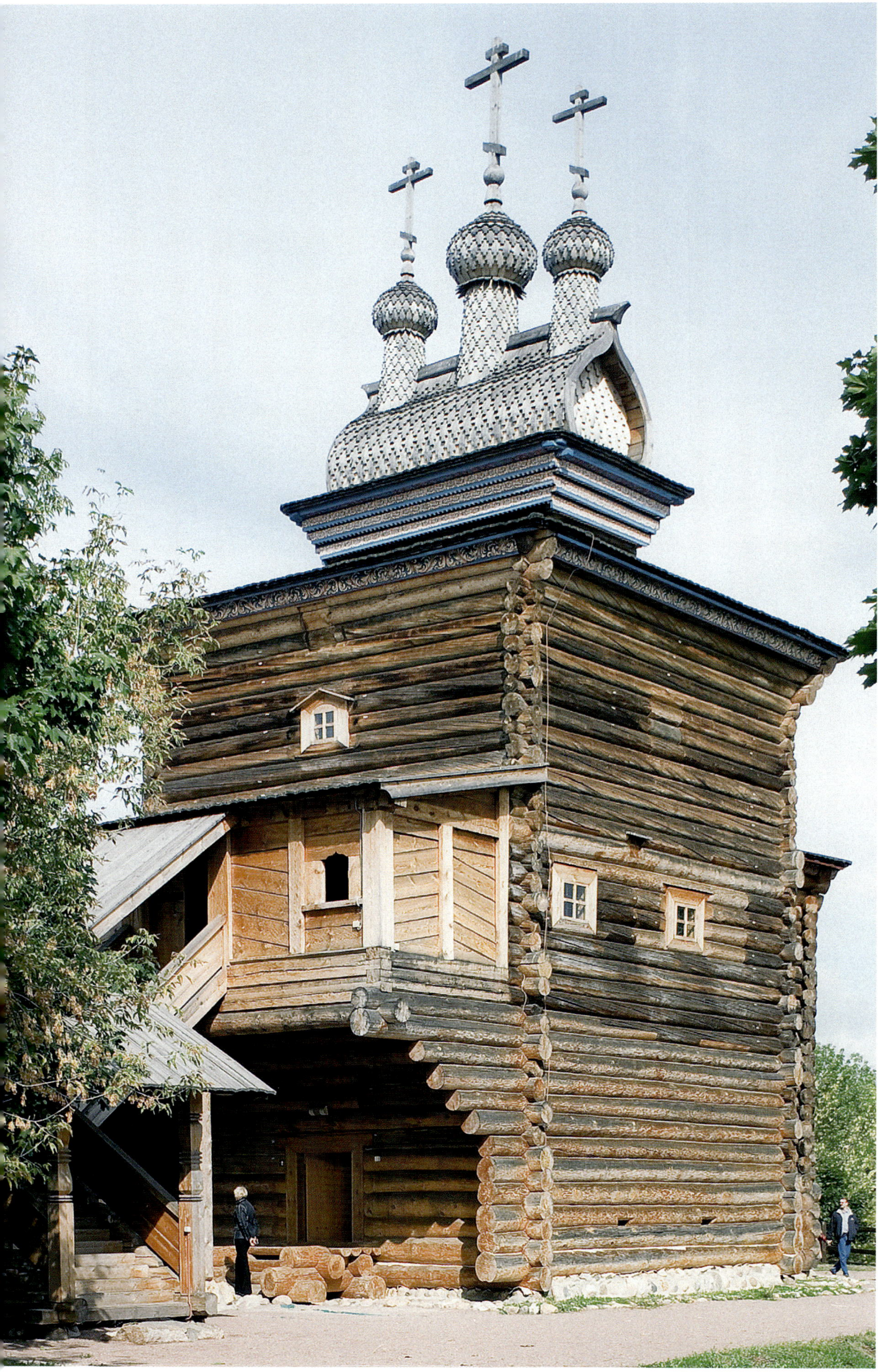

SEMYONOVSKAYA (Verkhnyaya Toima region). Church of Saint George, southwest view. Originally built in 1685 and modified over the centuries, this distinctive church shows similarities to the urbanized churches at Nelazskoe and Permogorye. Abandoned in the 1930s, the structure was disassembled and rebuilt in 2010 at the Kolomenskoe outdoor museum. August 31, 2014 .

BOLSHOI DVOR (Krasnoborsk region). Grain silo. An intriguing attempt to encase a round structure in wooden planks. June 21, 2000.

TSIVOZERO (Krasnoborsk region). Octagonal bell tower built in 1658. June 25, 2000.

To the south of the Uftyuga River, back country roads (often little more than sandy tracks) wind through the pine forests in the direction of Solvychegodsk. This region between the Uftyuga and Vychegda Rivers has remarkable wooden houses, which even when abandoned, give a sense of the folk traditions characteristic of the Russian North. These large domiciles usually have two levels that encompass living quarters in the front and a barn for storage and livestock in the back. All components are under an extended roof. Log houses traditionally have decorative window surrounds (*nalichniki*) as well as end boards along the front edges of the roof. A distinctive feature of many houses in this area is the curved form of their roof. This bowed form was considered to facilitate snow shedding, although roofs in most areas of the north have a simple slant or pitch. Whatever the origins, this unusual, bowed roof design provides an aesthetic grace note.

The path to Solvychegodsk goes through the once-flourishing village of Tsivozero, also known as Tsivozersky Pogost, site of a small, darkened form of a log bell tower. This archaic octagonal structure was built in 1658 to accompany a church dedicated to Saints Florus and Laurus. Although the church itself has long since disappeared, the intricate design of the bell tower provides a rare example of ancient traditions in log construction and decoration.

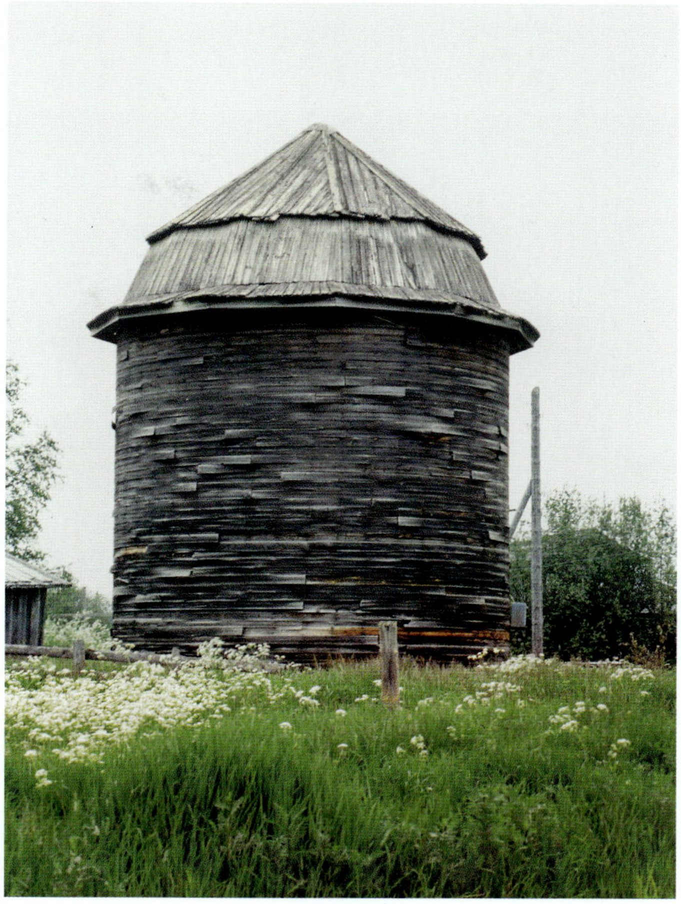

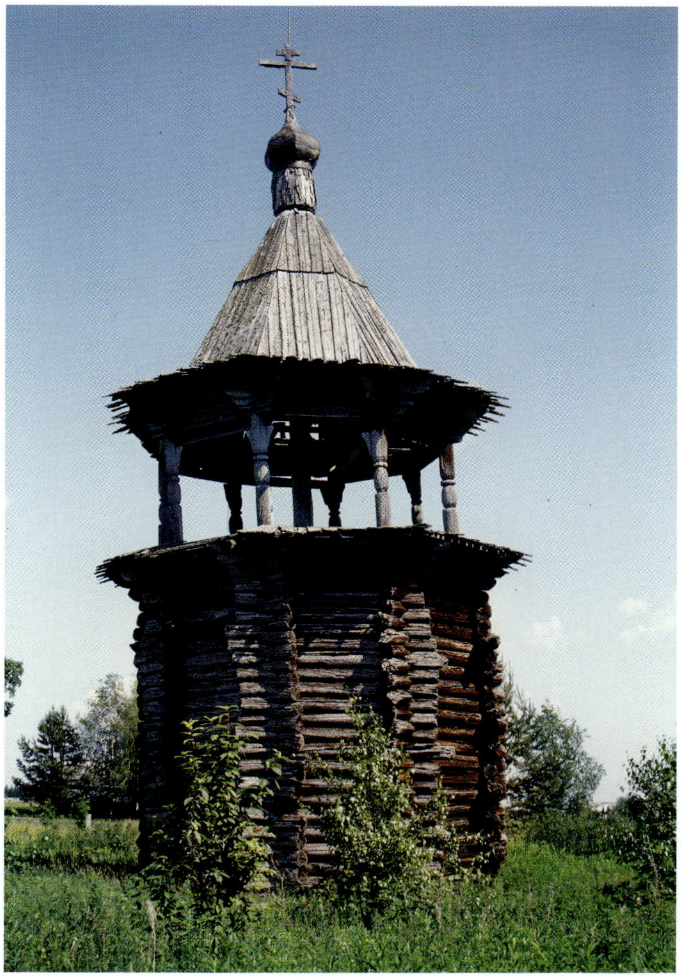

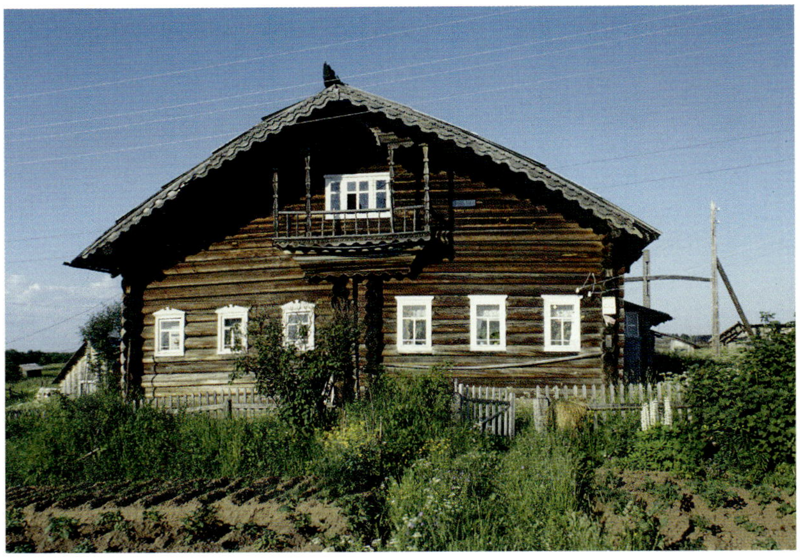

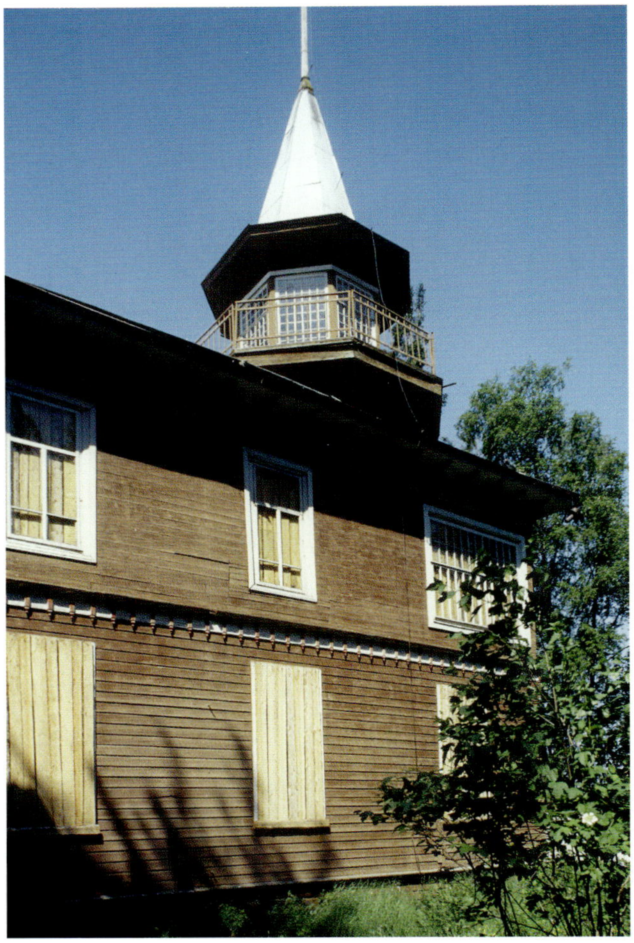

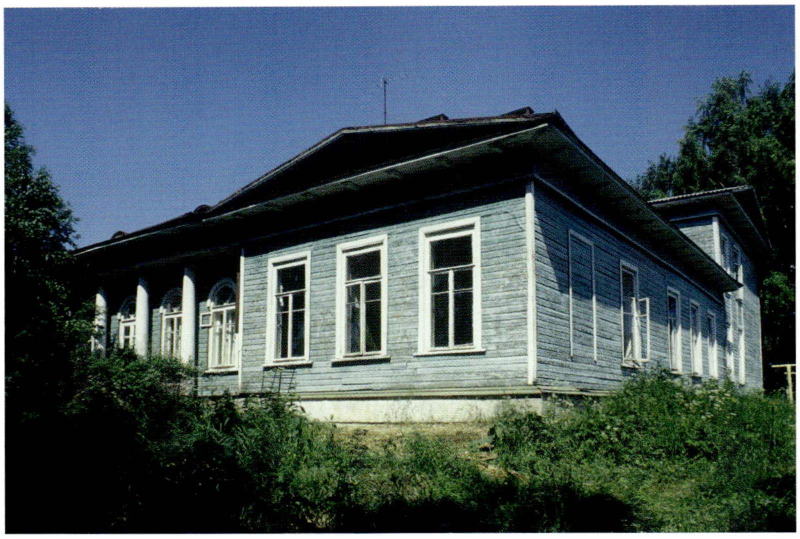

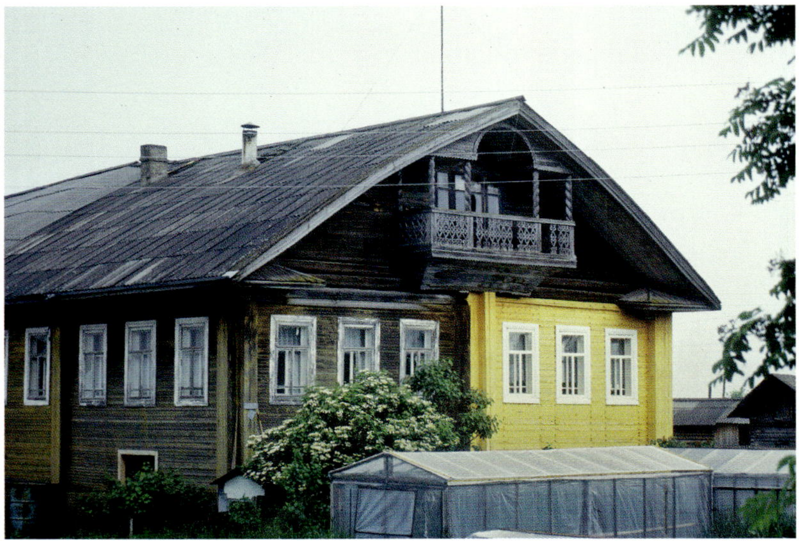

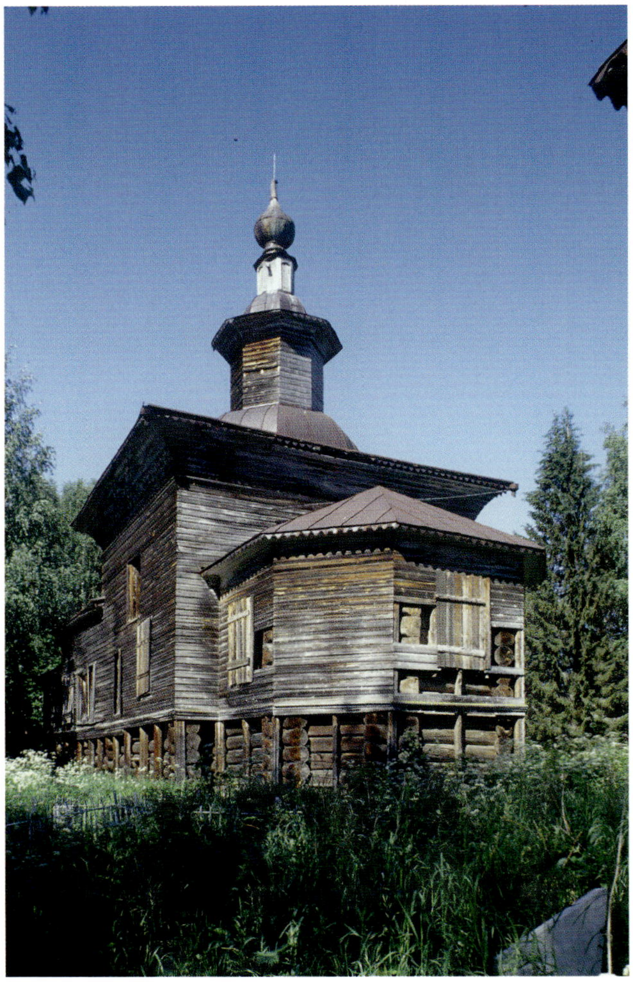

By the beginning of the twentieth century, a modicum of prosperity in the Dvina basin could be seen in imposing merchant houses built in river towns such as Cherevkova, on the left bank of the Dvina some five hundred kilometers south of Arkhangelsk. During the eighteenth century the village became a center of gold embroidery, which flourished in nearby Solvychegodsk, the center of Stroganov artistic culture. Contemporary Cherevkova (population around 1,000) still has examples of these merchant houses, built of wood and richly decorated with carved facades and summer balconies. Particularly notable are the capacious houses built in the late nineteenth century in the hamlet of Ovsyannikovskaya (part of Cherevkovo) by members of the extended Gusev merchant family. After the Bolshevik Revolution, the Gusevs, who came from peasant origins, were disenfranchised and deprived of their hard-earned property. The houses were converted to communal dwellings, the condition of which continues to decline for lack of proper maintenance; yet the extraordinary skill of their anonymous carpenters is still on view.

The most important heritage site to the south of Cherevkovo is the ensemble of two churches at Permogorye, a village mentioned in documents as early as 1379. Both churches—one of wood, one of brick—tower above the

KRIVTSOVSKAYA (Krasnoborsk region). Six-walled house with decorative summer balcony and bowed roof with carved end boards. June 25, 2000.

SOLONIKHA (Krasnoborsk region). Salt springs sanatorium building designed with neoclassical elements designed by artist Alexander Borisov in 1927. June 25, 1999.

FROLOVSKAYA (Krasnoborsk region). Six-walled log duplex with summer balcony and bowed roof. Foreground: lilacs in bloom and plastic sheet green house for tomatoes. June 22, 2000.

YERSHEVSKAYA (Krasnoborsk region). Estate house of artist Alexander Borisov. The artist's design included a lookout tower from which he could see the Northern Dvina River. June 25, 1999.

SHELOMYA (Krasnoborsk region). Church of Saint Nicholas, southeast view. Originally built in 1642 with subsequent modifications. June 25, 1999.

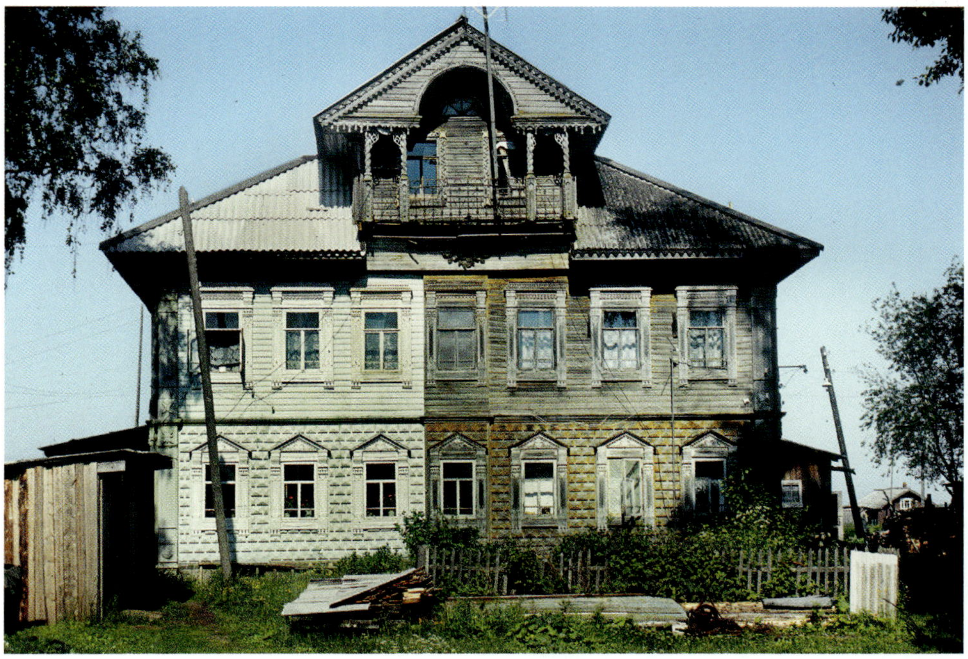

CHEREVKOVO (Krasnoborsk region). Ivan S. Gusev house. This six-walled dwelling was built in the late nineteenth century with fourteen large windows on the main facade and a summer balcony with wrought iron decoration. In an elegant neoclassical reference, the ground floor is rusticated. June 24, 2000.

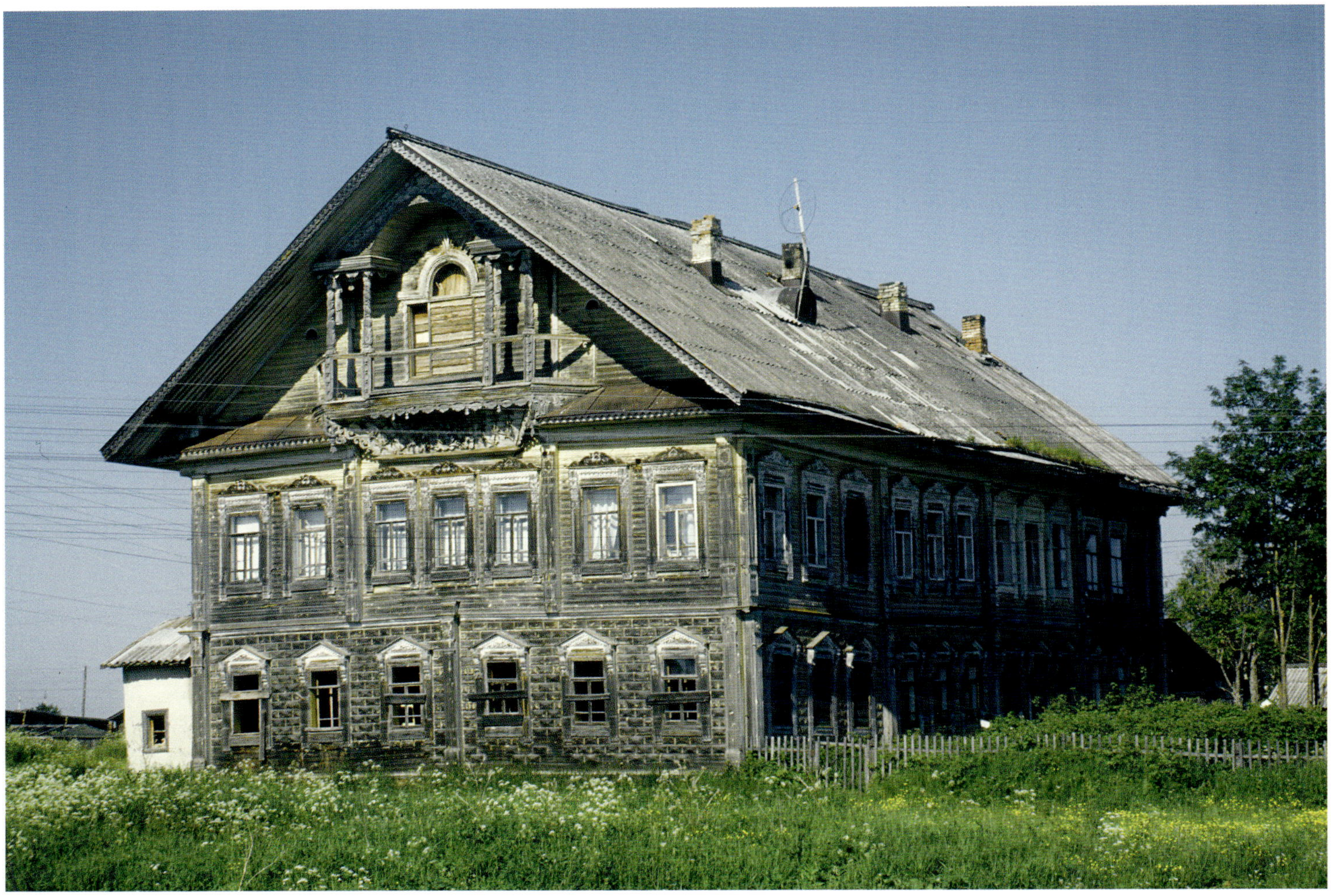

trees at the edge of the steep Dvina River bank. From the inland road, the distance between the two is more apparent. The extraordinary part of the Permogorye ensemble is the wooden Church of Saint George, built in 1665 and still standing with its three cupolas elevated on an elaborate cruciform platform. The platform is crowned with barrel gables, above which soar the cupolas. (This highly unusual design has a later counterpart—with five cupolas—at the village of Nelazskoe, near Ustyuzhna in Vologda Province.) In 1875 the structure was covered in plank siding, a controversial move that may at least have facilitated the preservation of this magnificent wooden temple. The Church of Saint George at Permogorye is a cultural beacon, a mark of the inexhaustible creativity of traditional architecture in the Russian North.

The Northern Dvina empties into the White Sea near the city of Arkhangelsk (current population around 414,000) and is one of Russia's most important, historic ports. The area was settled as early as the twelfth century by Novgorodians, who founded the Monastery of Archangel

CHEREVKOVO (Krasnoborsk region). Mikhail S. Gusev house. Built in 1886, this remarkable fourteen-room dwelling, with barn attached at the back, has thirteen windows on the main facade and twenty-four on the side. Like the neighboring house of his brother I. S. Gusev, the ground floor is rusticated while the upper story is crowned by a profusely carved balcony with a view toward the Dvina River. June 24, 2000.

PERMOGORYE (Krasnoborsk region). Church of Saint George, northwest view. Built in 1665, this structure with its distinctive crown shows similarities to its contemporary at Nelazskoe. Plank siding added in 1875. June 22, 2000.

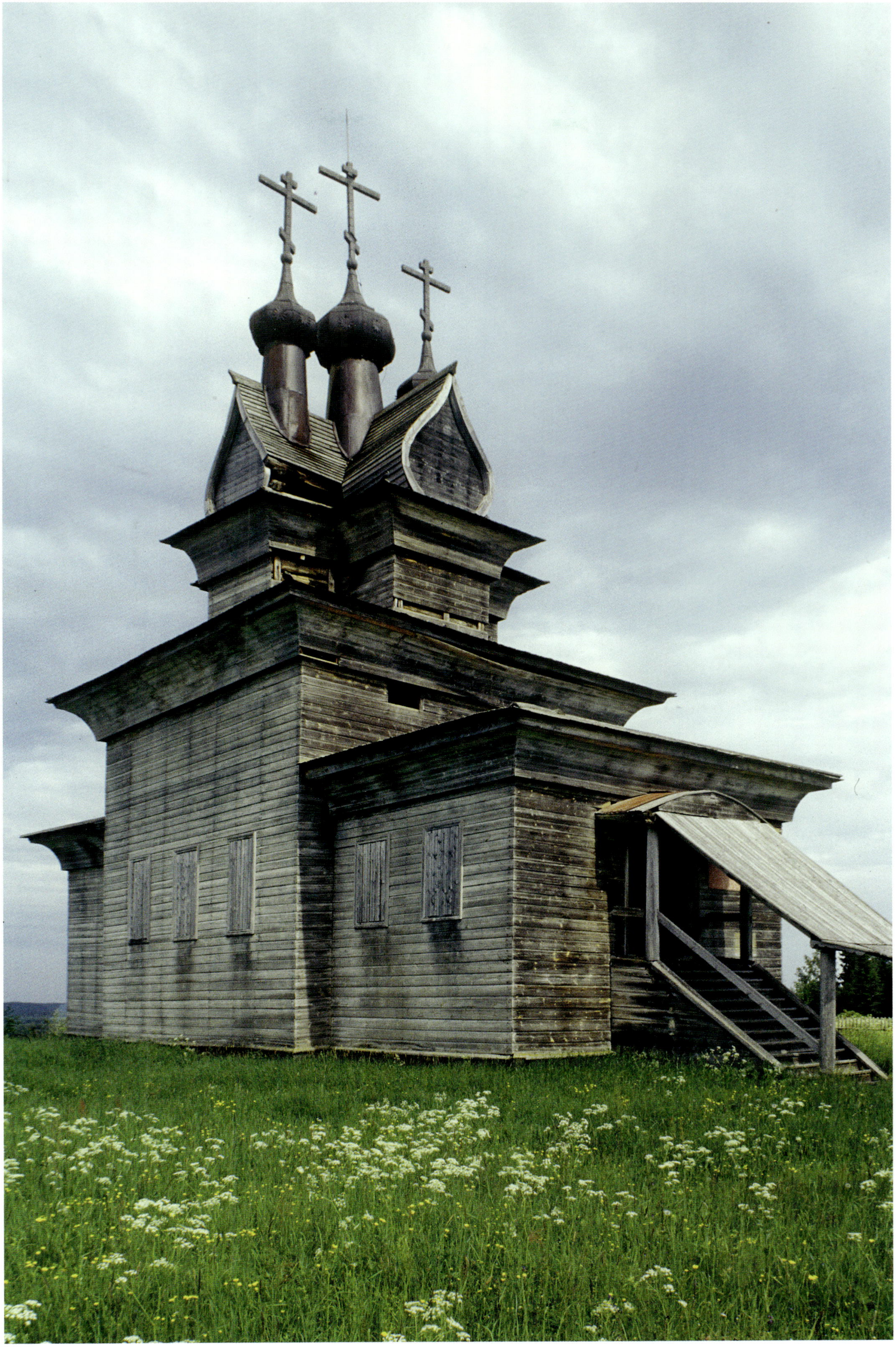

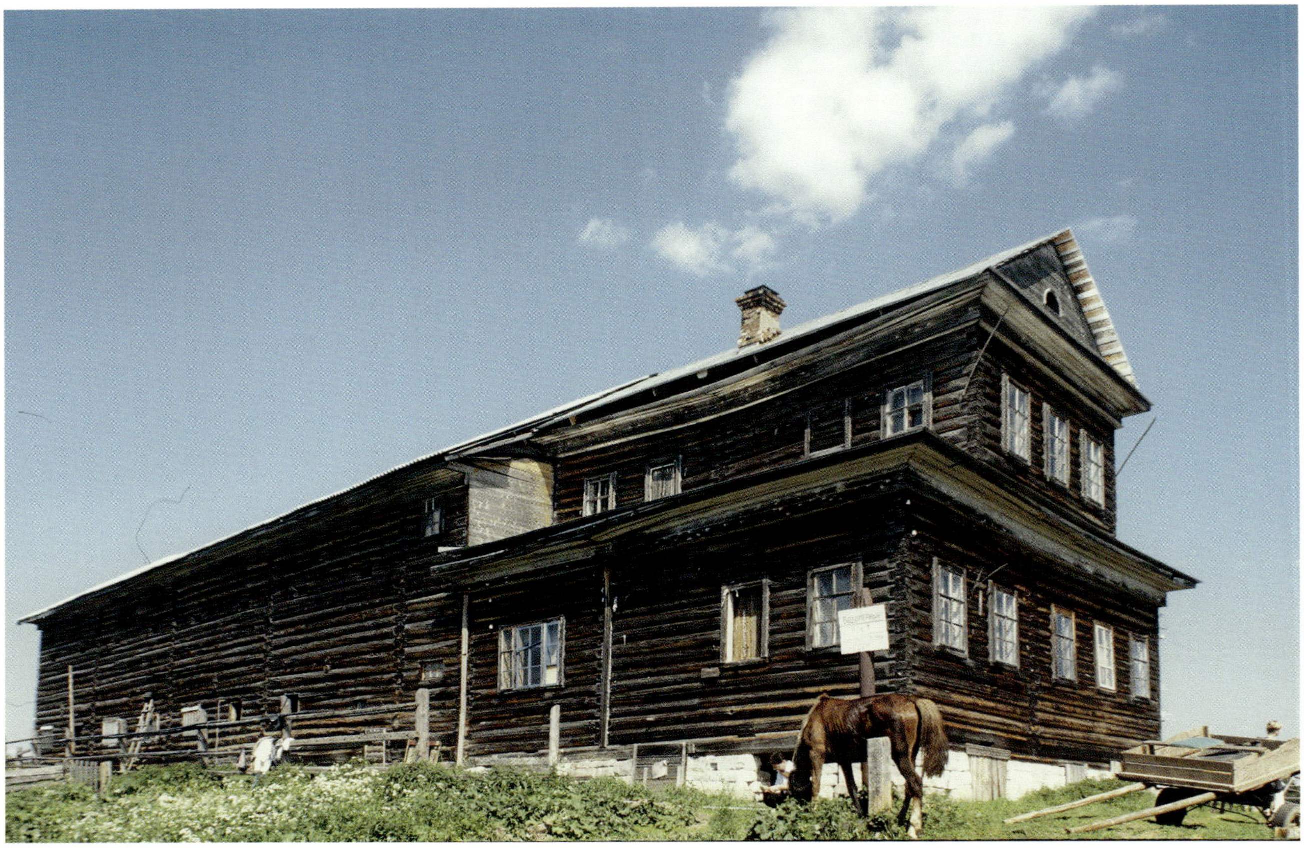

Michael. Until the late sixteenth century, the future site of the town contained little more than a wharf and the monastery, but growing trade with Western Europe led Ivan IV (the Terrible) to establish a settlement nearby. The name Arkhangelsk, derived from the monastery, did not appear until after 1613.

Although the development of Saint Petersburg in the early eighteenth century led to a decrease in the importance of Arkhangelsk as a port, the city remained an important center for shipping, shipbuilding, and industry (particularly forest products) during the nineteenth century. With the completion of a rail line from Vologda (and the central part of the country) in 1898, Arkhangelsk entered a period of accelerated development reflected in large mansions, many of which were built of wood. With intensified development of the central city after the 1950s, much of the wooden architectural heritage was demolished. In response to concerns from preservationists, city officials converted a central street with a few wooden landmarks into a pedestrian thoroughfare with additional wooden houses moved from other streets under redevelopment.

MONASTYR (Kholmogory region). Log house with attached barn near the Saint Antony of Siya Monastery. June 23, 1999.

ARKHANGELSK. Commerce Assembly (Club). Originally built in 1858 on Dvoryanskaya Street, the imposing Renaissance-style wooden building with its large ballroom served as a social center for the local merchant elite. In 1983 it was moved to Chumbarov-Luchinsky Street, thus establishing that area as a zone for preserving wooden monuments in the central city. June 24, 2000.

ARKHANGELSK. Andrey Chudinov house. Built in 1904 for a wealthy lumber magnate who came from a modest trading peasant background, beginning in his father's store at the village of Rakula. Before World War I, his firm was among the largest timber purveyors and exporters in the Russian Empire. In 1919 he emigrated to France, where he became a pillar of the Russian Orthodox community in Nice. November 22, 1999.

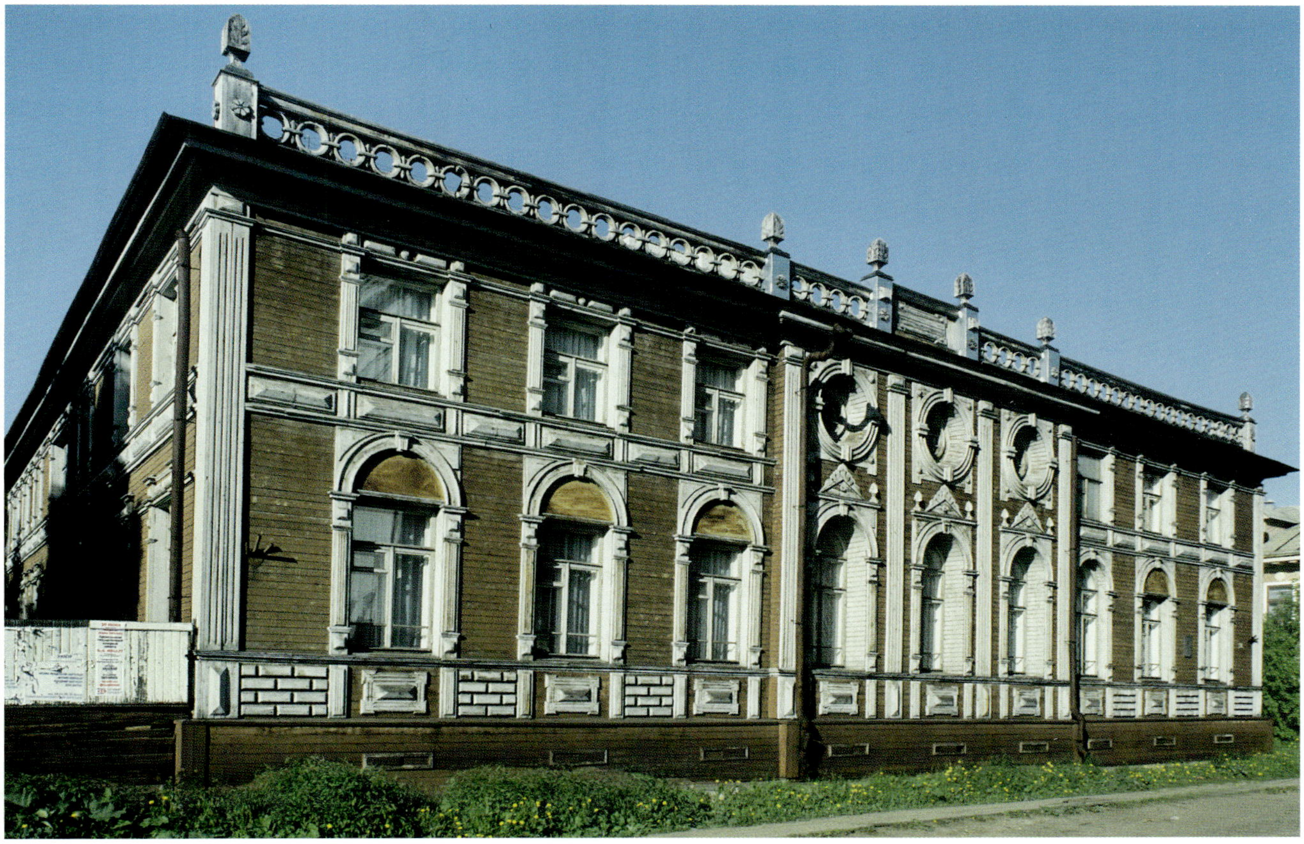

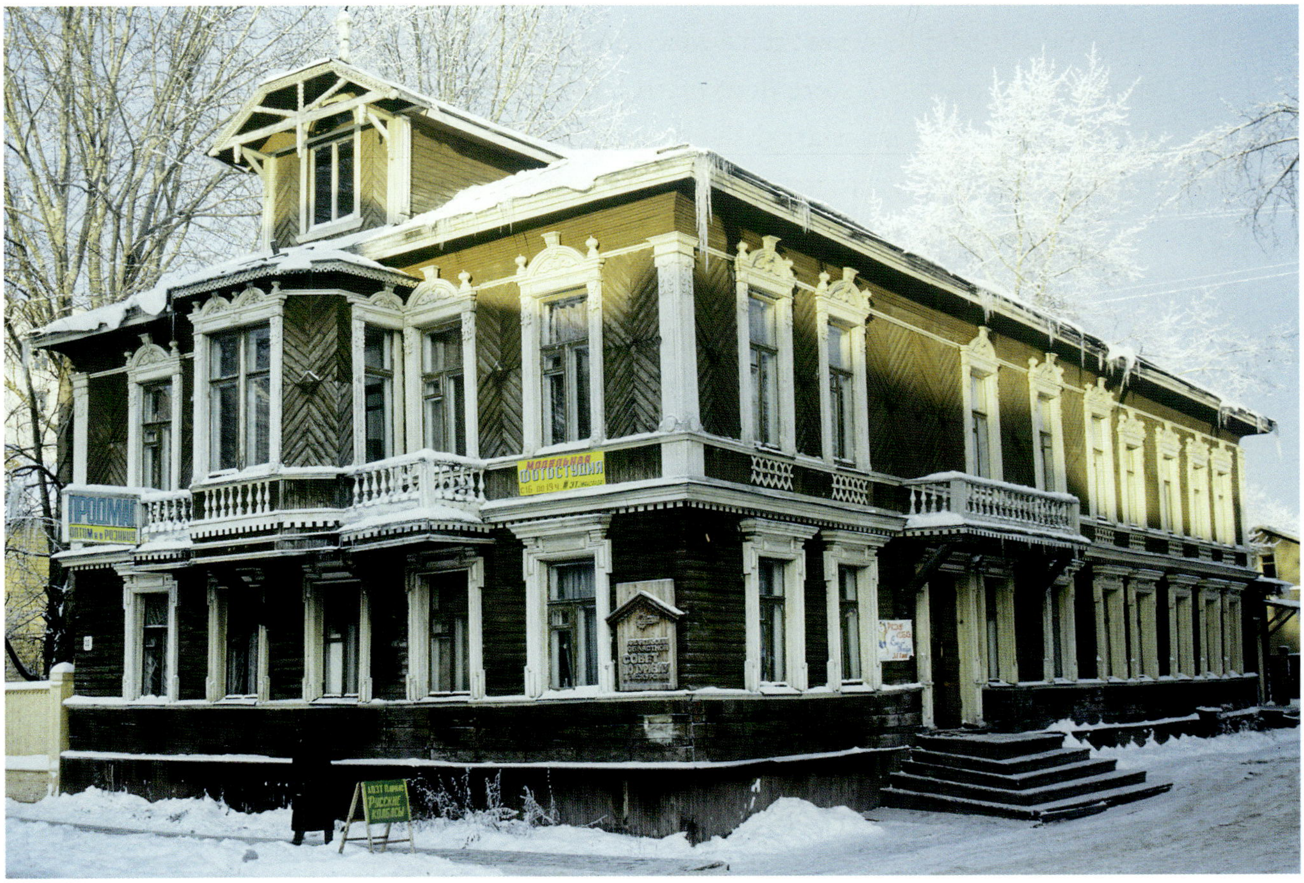
ПРОДМАГ
ОПТОМ и в РОЗНИЦУ
Модельная
ФОТОСТУДИЯ
СОВЕТ
Русские
колбасы

The environs of Arkhangelsk encompass villages with their own masterpieces in a marshy terrain marked with shifting delta channels of the Northern Dvina. One of the area's larger islands is Zaostrovye, bisected by the small Zaostrovka River. This land, nourished by frequent flooding, is the site of a paired log and a brick church near the village of Rikasovo. In 1683 the parish was permitted to build a new wooden church dedicated to the Purification, with secondary altars to Saints Peter and Paul and the second-century martyrs Saints Florus and Laurus. The design of the Zaostrovye church is idiosyncratic, with a central cupola resting on a sloping octagonal tower whose roof base was surrounded by eight wooden cupolas on high drums. The original roof had a flowing gable line that enlivened the square plan of the basic structure. In 1808 work began on a brick Church of the Purification to replace the wooden structure as the parish church. The wooden Purification Church, shuttered for decades, was repaired and reconsecrated in 1864 as the Church of the Intercession of the Virgin. Over the next half century, its highly unusual form was modified and disfigured. Closed during the Soviet period, the Church of the Purification/Intercession was the object of major work in the late 1960s that restored much of its earlier form. Even so, the work was never completed, and necessary maintenance has been neglected.

Thirty-five kilometers to the southeast of Arkhangelsk is the village Lyavlya (also known as Khorkovo) on the high right bank of the Northern Dvina. It contains a remarkable, albeit deformed, example of northern tower structures, a late sixteenth-century church formerly dedicated to the Dormition and now known as Saint Nicholas. With trading links to Novgorod, Lyavlya was already in the fourteenth century the site of a monastery dedicated to the Dormition of the Virgin. In 1339 Grand Prince Ivan Kalita, wishing to extend Moscow's influence in the area, commissioned for the monastery a manuscript of the Gospels that is one of the earliest Russian parchment works, the Siisky Gospels. In the sixteenth century the Lyavlya monastery contained two wooden churches, the Dormition and Saint Nicholas. A fire in 1580 led to the building of a new log Church of the Dormition, whose archaic form has survived as a rare display of a church built from the ground up as an octagonal tower. With a massive log tower rising to an elevated tent crown supporting a large cupola, the Lyavlya church served as a landmark along the river. The east and west sides of the structure have extensions for the apse and vestibule, crowned with barrel gables. The west end originally had an elevated, cantilevered porch that

ZAOSTROVYE (Arkhangelsk). Church of the Purification (Dormition). Built near Rikasovo village in 1683, this idiosyncratic structure underwent modifications through the centuries, but its distinctive crown remained. June 10, 1998.

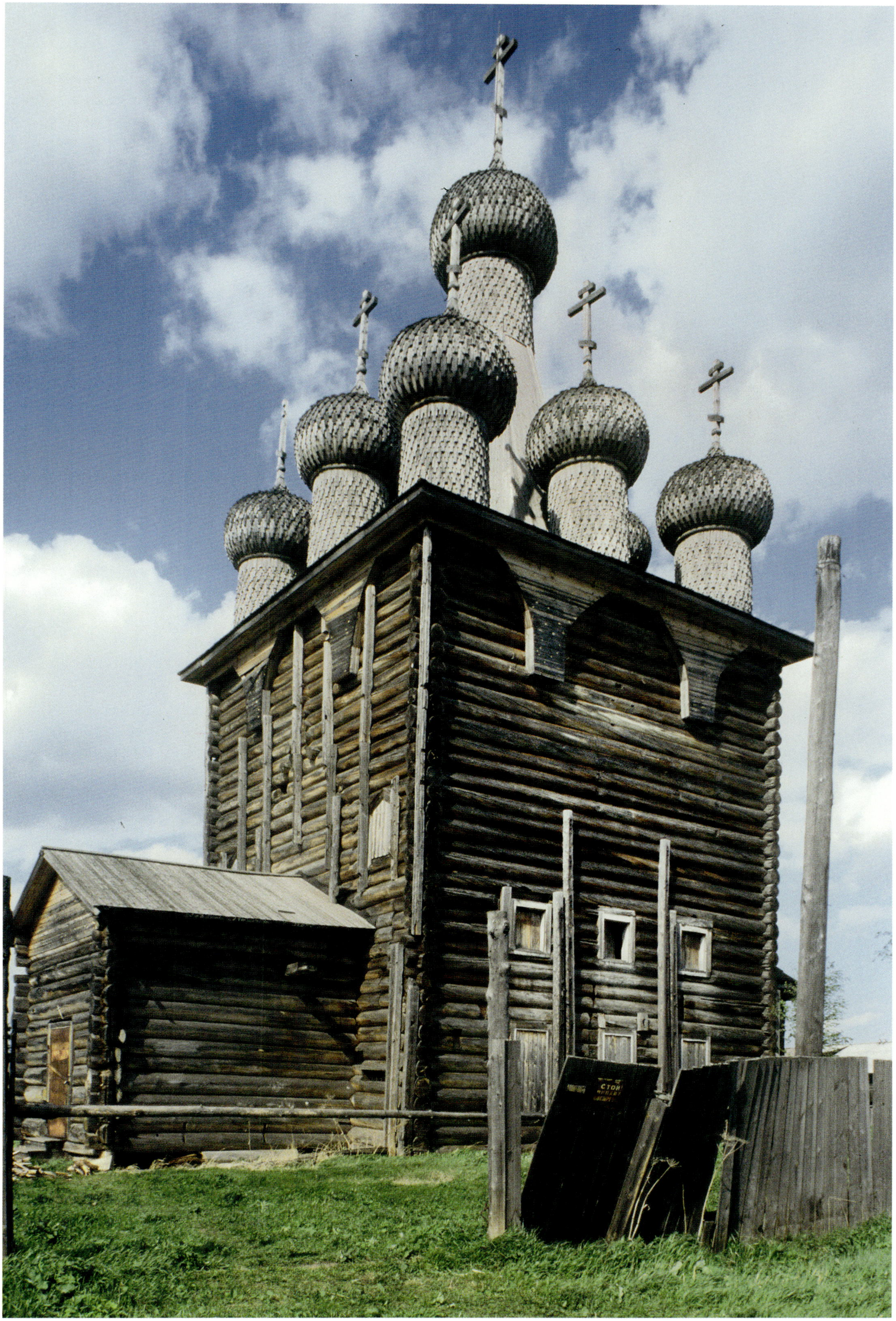
СТОЙ

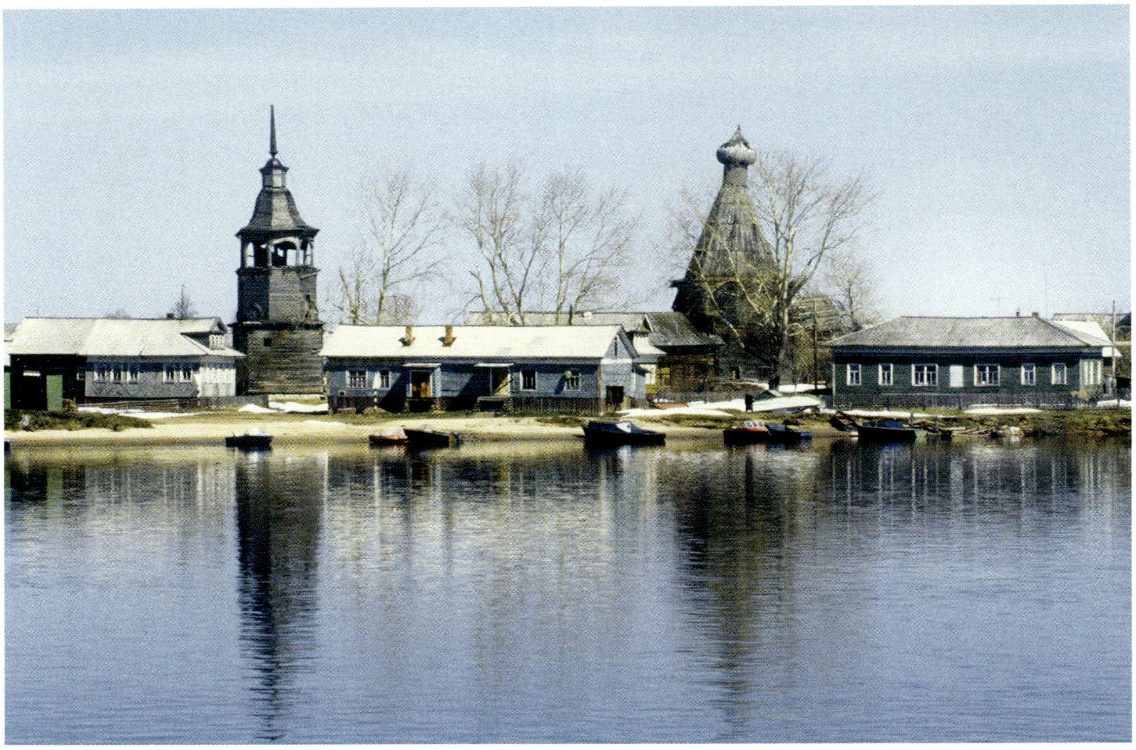

KONETSDVORYE (Arkhangelsk). This south view from the Dvina River delta includes Soviet-era wooden houses surrounding the Church of Saint Nicholas, bought and moved from a parish in Arkhangelsk in 1769. In 2004 the church was disassembled, measured, and reconstructed with entirely new logs. Only the separate bell tower retained its original structure. May 21, 2000.

LYAVLYA. Church of Saint Nicholas (formerly Dormition), south view. June 9, 1998.

enclosed the main entrance. Converted to a parish church in 1765 after the closure of the Lyavlya monastery, the Dormition Church was shuttered in 1805 because of structural decay. A brick Church of the Dormition had already been built nearby in 1804 to serve the parish. That might have meant the demise of the log Dormition Church, but in 1844 the governor-general of Arkhangelsk, Marquis Alexander de Traversay (1780–1850), visited the village and decided to restore the massive log structure. Although this was a remarkably noble gesture, the crude approach to "preservation" meant that two-and-a-half meters of decaying logs at the base were simply discarded and the remaining part of the octagonal church reassembled. Therefore, the imposing tower would originally have been eight feet higher. In 1845 the restored structure was reconsecrated as the Church

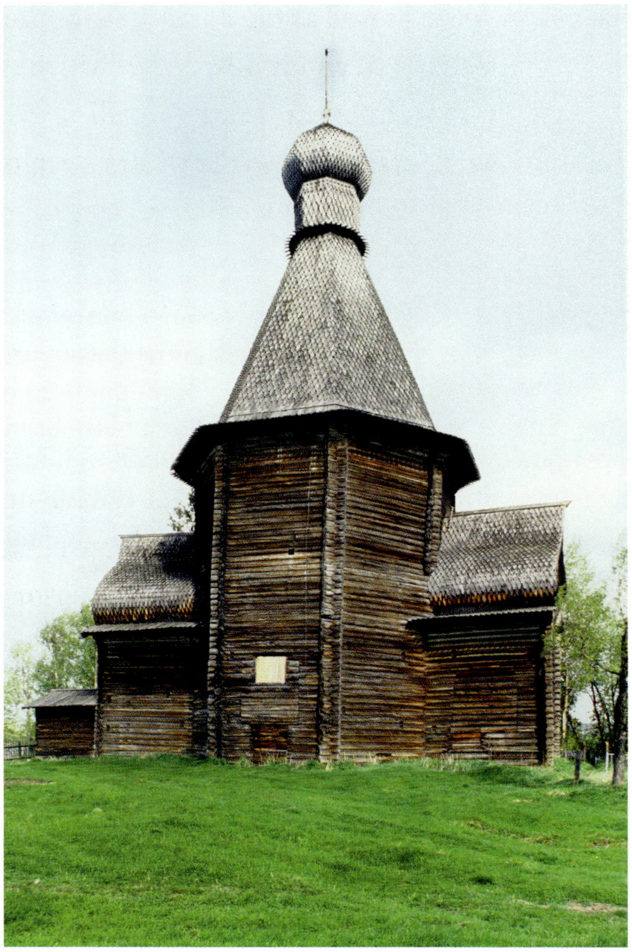

of Saint Nicholas, the name it bears to this day. During the Soviet period the durable structure withstood various uses, including a garrison club. In the late 1960s a restoration removed the planks and metal sheathing, rebuilt the cupola, and placed the original cupola frame—a rare example of traditional log design—within the church as a museum display. Practical considerations did not allow a reconstruction of the original height of the church. In the 1970s the Saint Nicholas Church was affiliated with the adjacent Malye Korely outdoor museum of wooden architecture.

One of the largest of Russia's outdoor museums, Malye Korely is located on high bluffs overlooking the Northern Dvina River some twenty-five kilometers to the south of the city of Arkhangelsk (population around 350,000). The southern boundary of the museum is the small Korelka River, which flows into the Dvina and gives the park its name. Opened to the public in the summer of 1973, Malye Korely is currently divided into six sectors spread over about 140 hectars of rolling forested landscape. These sectors represent distinct historic parts of the vast Arkhangelsk Province. On display are wooden churches and chapels, as well as log houses, barns, and a collection of windmills, one of which is visible from the entrance gates leading to the first sector, devoted to the western regions near the ancient town of Kargopol and scattered along the Onega River.

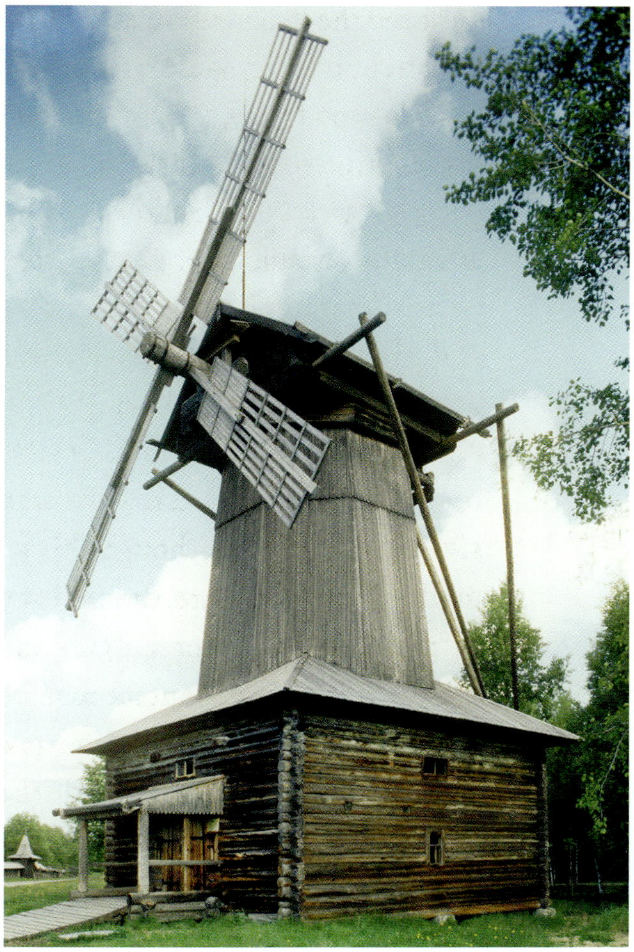

MALYE KORELY (Arkhangelsk region, outdoor museum). Windmill constructed in 1902 at village of Kozhposelok for Kozhozero-Epiphany Monastery. The complex structure, intended for large-scale production, has a rotating top braced to face prevailing winds. June 21, 2003.

In the woods near the entrance are two spacious log houses from the Kargopol region: the Pukhov house from the hamlet of Kiselyovskaya near Lyadiny and the Kirillov house, from the hamlet of Bolshoy Khalui near Oshevensk. Each house provides a sense of the arrangement of interior space in these northern fortress dwellings, which include an attached barn in the back to protect livestock and supplies from the long winters.

The centerpiece of the first sector is the Church of the Ascension (with a separate bell tower) erected in the village of Kushereka in 1669. Its five cupolas rise from a flared roof

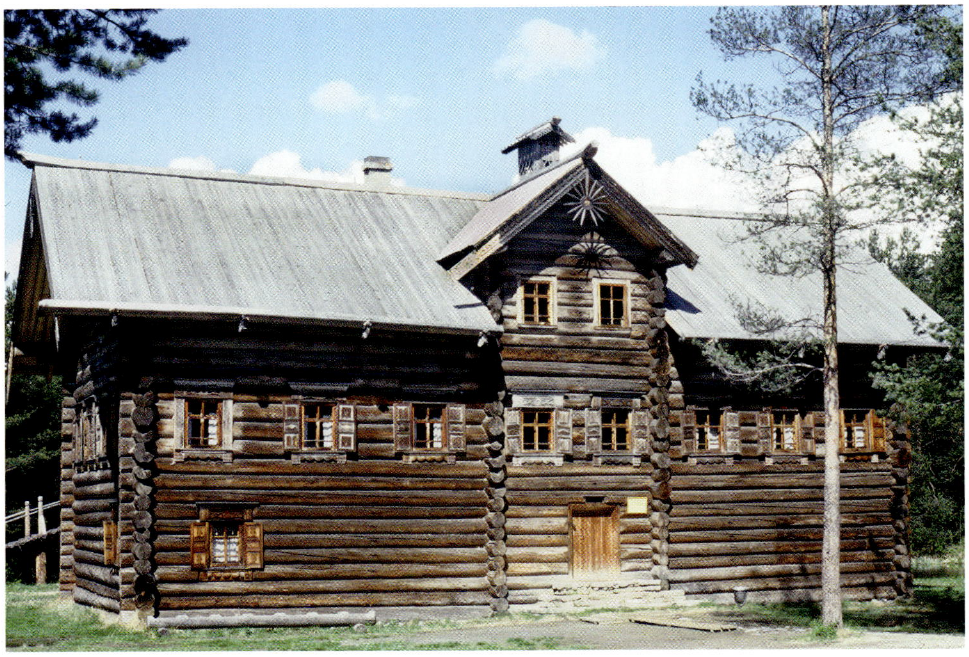

MALYE KORELY. This six-walled house was built in the early nineteenth century for the peasant A. F. Pukhov at the village of Bolshoy Khalui (Kargopol region). The first floor was used for storing goods and equipment, while the second was divided into living quarters for winter and summer. The barn was attached perpendicularly to the back. June 9, 1998.

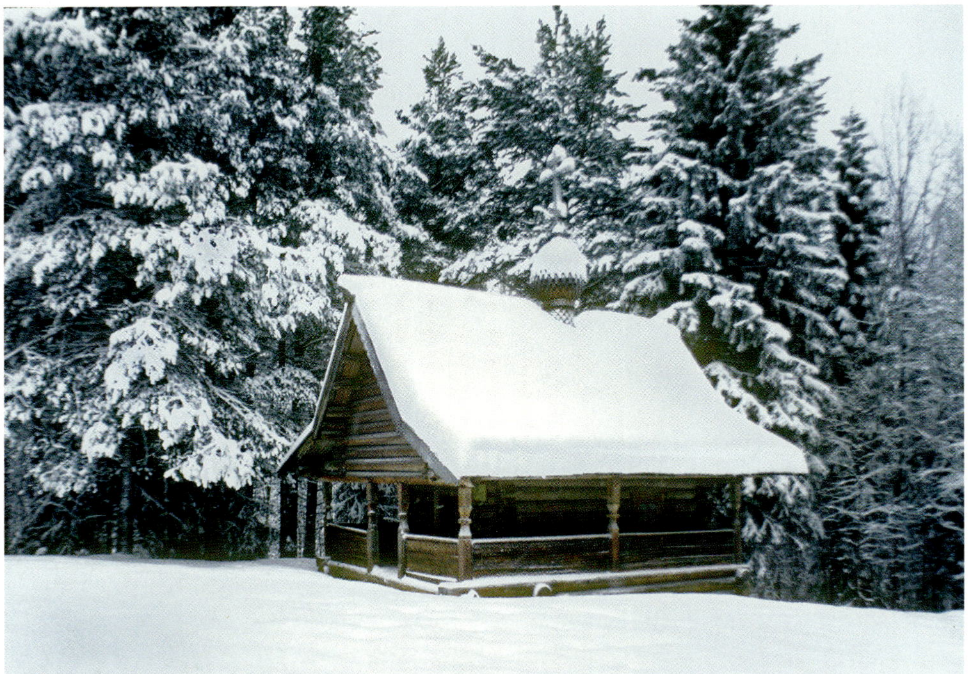

MALYE KORELY. Chapel of Elijah the Prophet, originally built in the eighteenth century at the village of Mamonov Ostrov (Plesetsk region). December 30, 1998.

with wooden shingles overlapping in a pattern known as fish scales. The interior had two altars. The one on the upper level was dedicated to Elijah the Prophet and to the martyr Saint Paraskeva, patroness of market day, while the lower level (heated for use throughout the year) was dedicated to the Ascension. No less impressive is a late sixteenth-century bell tower originally built in the village of Kuliga-Drakovanovo, part of the Krasnoborsk region at the southern reaches of the Dvina. Among the oldest surviving

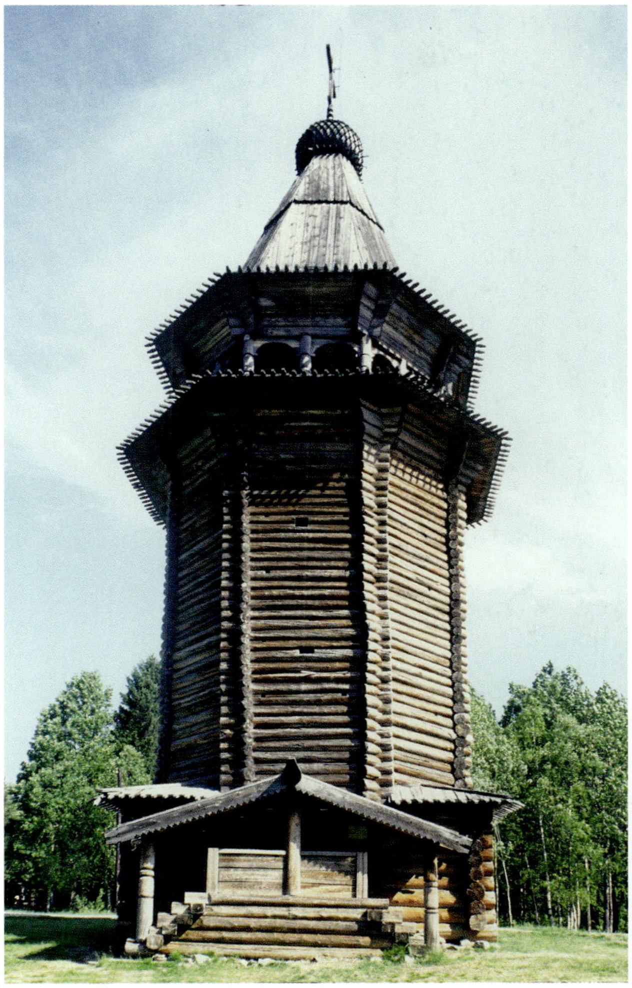 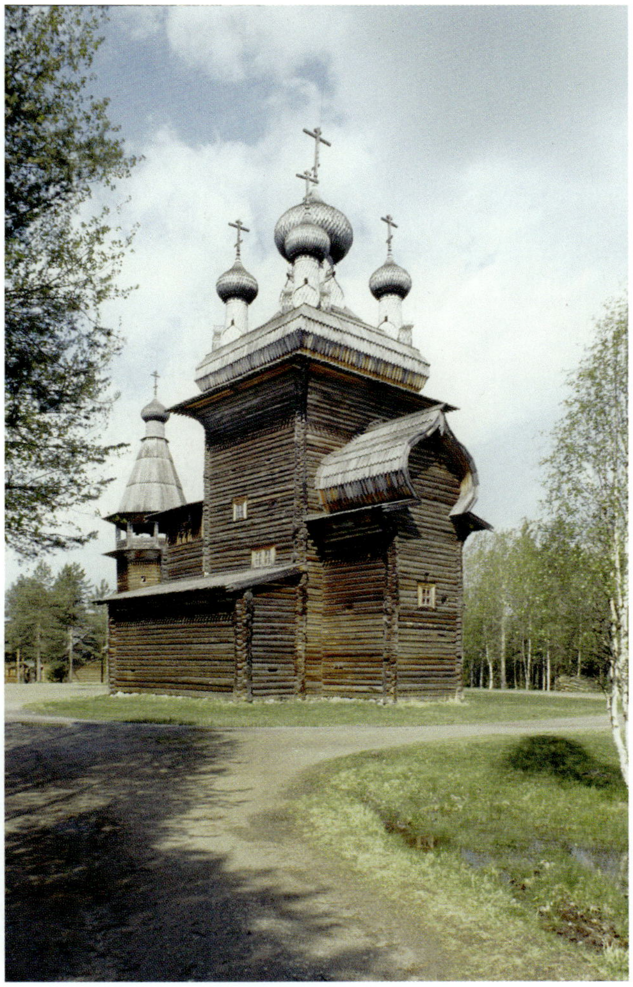

log structures in the Russian North, the bell tower rises some twenty-six meters on an octagonal shaft of horizontal log courses. The interior has three landings with flights of stairs leading to the open space for bells, which is sheltered by a tall tent roof.

A wooden pathway leads down a steep forested ravine to the second sector, devoted to villages along the Northern Dvina River. The dominant feature is the Church of Saint George from the hamlet of Vershina, near Upper Toima on the right bank of the Dvina. The church has a soaring tent roof typical of the Russian North. The interior has a partially preserved icon screen with baroque carving. Nearby are large houses combining intricate craftsmanship with strength of construction. Next to the Dvina sector to the south are the smaller Pinega and Mezen sectors, named after the Pinega and Mezen Rivers in the northeastern part of Arkhangelsk Province. Both sectors benefit from a picturesque setting on bluffs overlooking the

MALYE KORELY. Bell tower built in late sixteenth century at Kuliga-Drakovanovo (Krasnoborsk region). June 22, 1999.

MALYE KORELY. Church of the Ascension, southeast view. Built in 1669 at Kushereka village (Onega region). June 9, 1998.

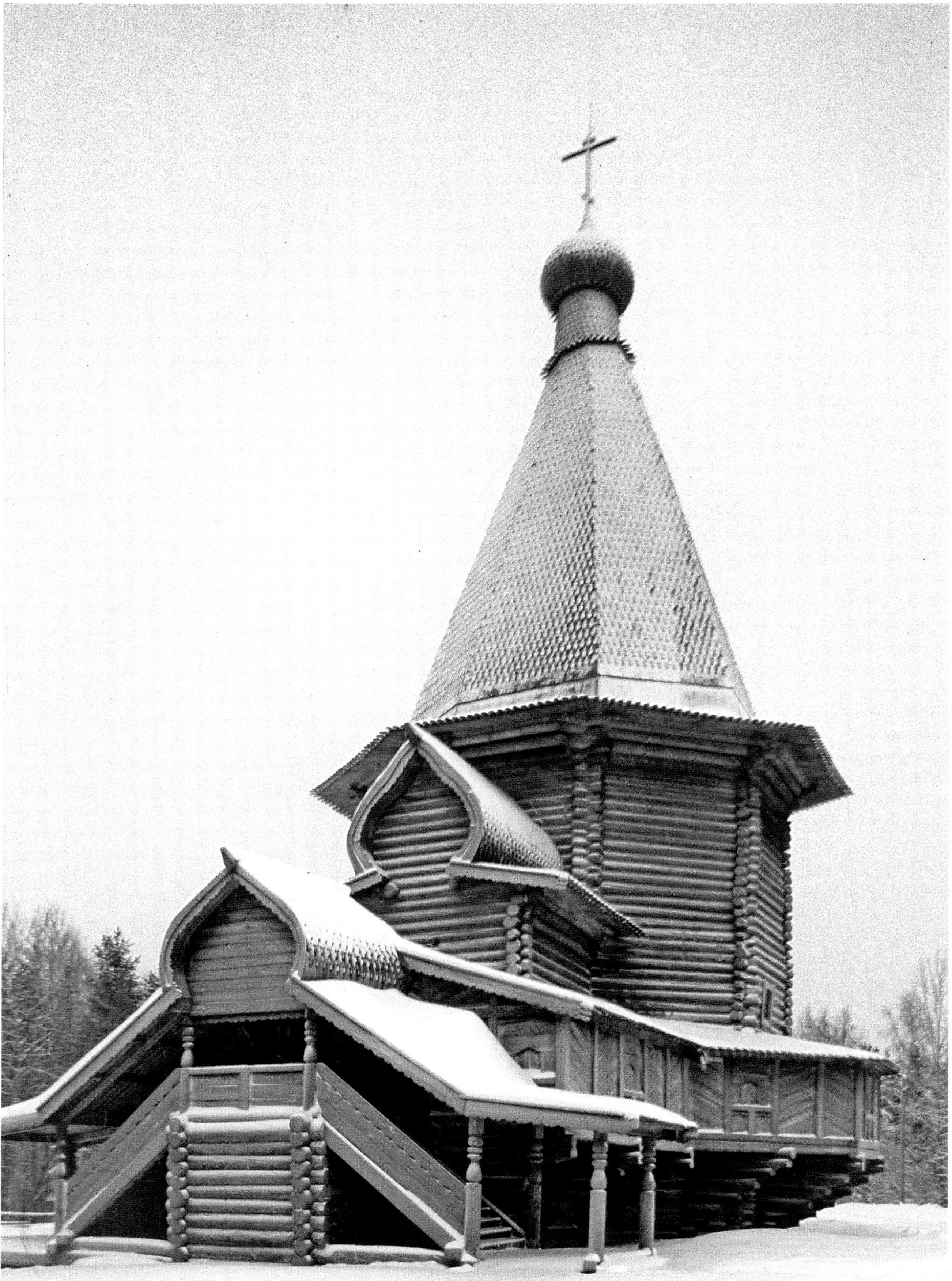

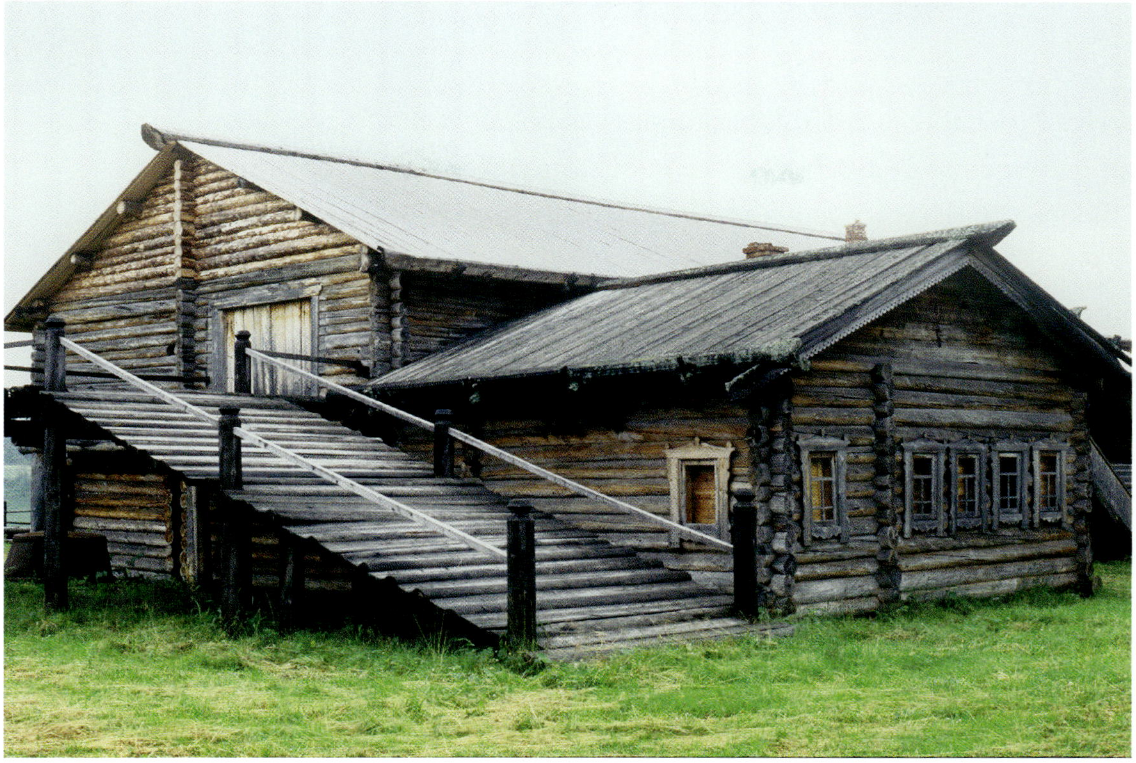

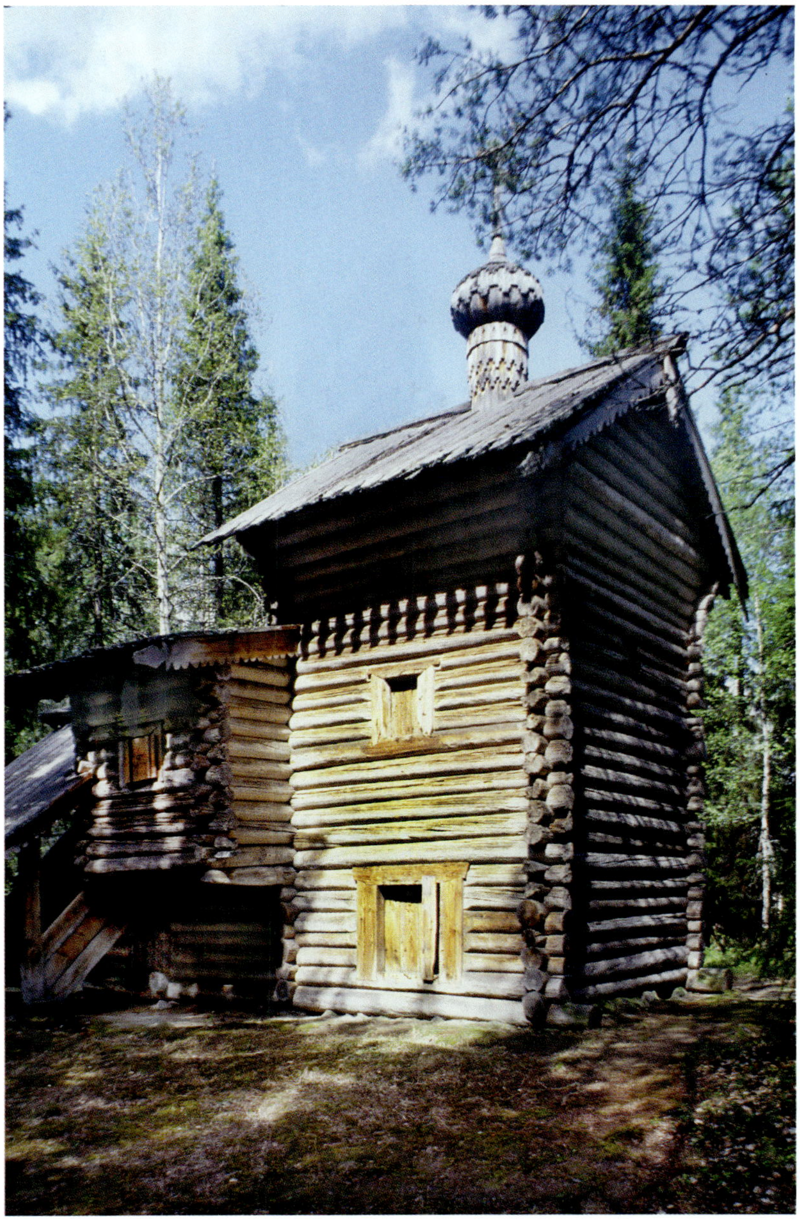

MALYE KORELY. Church of Saint George, southwest view. Built in 1672 at Vershina village (Verkhnyaya Toima region). December 30, 1998.

MALYE KORELY. M. Limonnikov house, built in 1920s at Yolkino village (Mezen region). View from back with ramp leading to attached barn and winter quarters extending on the right. July 27, 1998.

MALYE KORELY. Chapel of the Trinity, built in 1728 at Valtegorskaya village (Pinega region). June 9, 1998.

Korelka River, and both display examples of the *izba*, including dwellings that belonged to Old Believers, religious dissenters from the official Orthodox Church who were numerous in this part of the Russian North. The Pinega sector also contains the lovely Chapel of the Holy Trinity, built in the early eighteenth century in the village of Valtyevo with a compact grouping of entrance, vestibule, and main space elevated high above the winter snow level. The planks of the pitched roof have carved ends that cast a shadow design on the log walls.

Arkhangelsk Province—almost as large as Germany and Poland combined—still has old settlements that survive at their original location. A notable example is the village of Izhma (on the small Izhma River some twenty-five kilometers northeast of Arkhangelsk) with its archaic log Church of the Transfiguration. Crowned with a high four-sloped roof and five wooden cupolas, the structure dates to 1679, with modifications thereafter. Its stout proportions and diminutive windows suggest the blockhouse of a log fort, appropriate for a region in which survival was a perpetual struggle. The village houses are largely of the past century, one-story, usually with another half story containing a summer room at the top. The windows, with their painted frames, are double glazed and

IZHMA (Primorsky region). View across Izhma River toward west facades of the Church of the Transfiguration (1679) and the Church of the Resurrection (1887). The latter church was used as the village store. June 21, 1999.

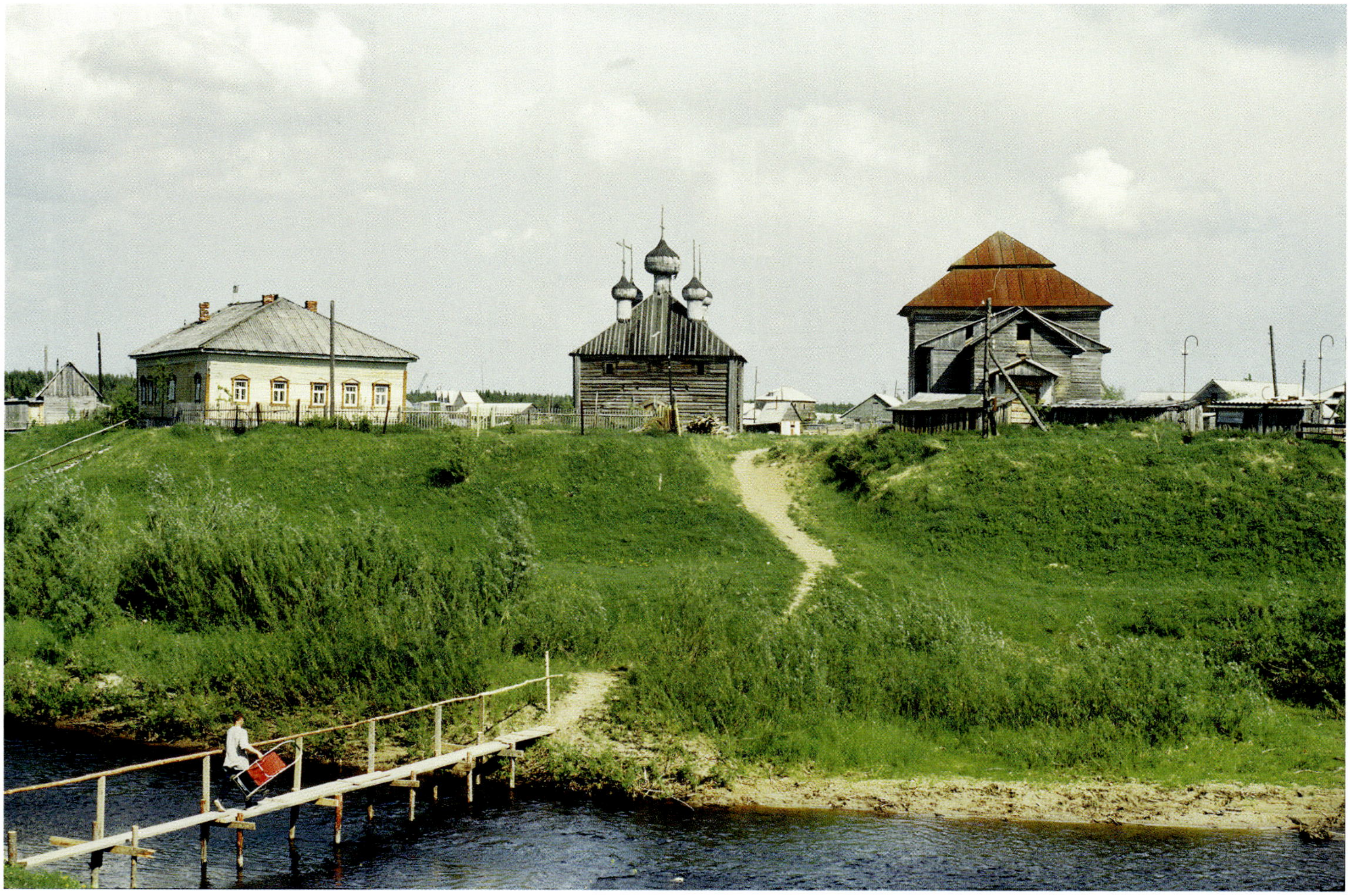

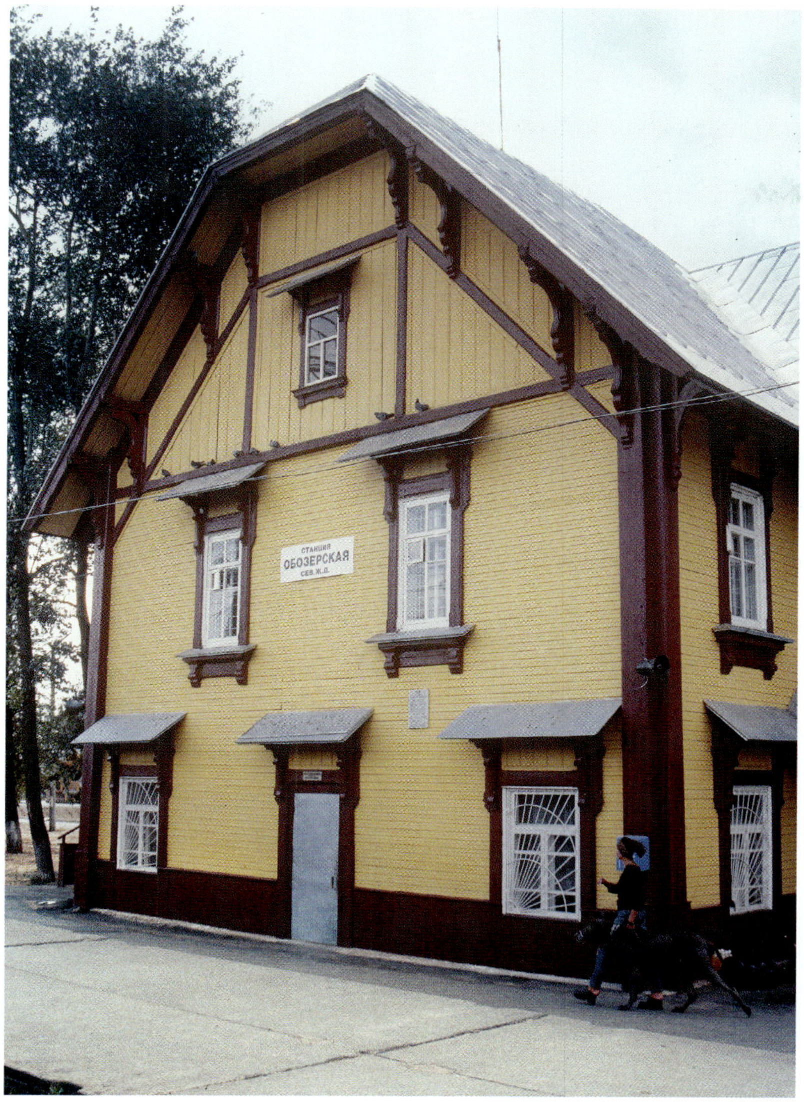

OBOZERSKY. Railroad station built in 1898 for northern extension of Savva Mamontov's Moscow-Yaroslavl Railway. Prominent Moscow architects Lev Kekushev and Ilarion Ivanov-Schitz created a uniform *style moderne* design that was economical (built of wood), durable, and functional. This is perhaps the best surviving example, located at a station that would become a major junction in 1940 and a critical point for Lend-Lease shipments from Murmansk during World War II. August 8, 2000.

SAINT NICHOLAS-KORELSKY MONASTERY (now in Severodvinsk). This East Gate was built in the late seventeenth century at the monastery located on the Nicholas arm of the Northern Dvina near its confluence with the White Sea. It was moved in 1933 to the Kolomenskoe outdoor museum in Moscow. August 31, 2014.

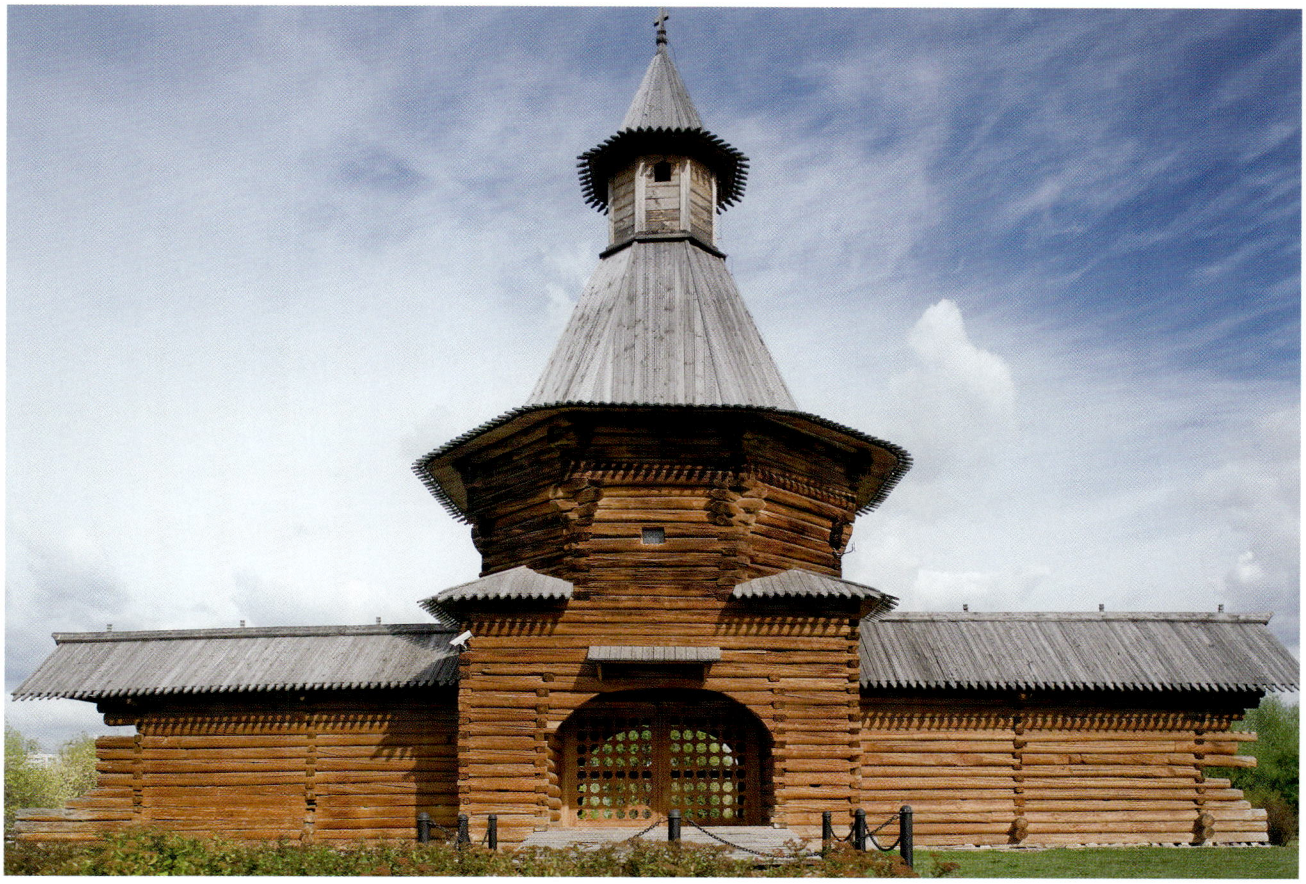

insulated to minimize heat loss during the long winters. Whether villages such as Izhma will continue to exist in their traditional form is open to questions, but for the present, Izhma represents a time when these settlements served an essential role in sustaining the Russian presence within a boundless northern territory.

Mezen River

The Mezen River—known for its major role in Russian expansion within the vast region east of the White Sea—empties into a bay of the same name near the merger of the White Sea with the Barents Sea in the Arctic Ocean. The mouth of the Mezen River is flanked by two towns, Kamenka and Mezen, both about five thousand in population. Mezen is the regional administrative center, while Kamenka has the region's largest employer, a lumber factory. I traveled to all three in both the winter and summer of 2000.

The cultural treasure, however, is the village of Kimzha, situated near the Arctic Circle at the point where the small Kimzha River flows into the

MEZEN. House built for merchant Ruzhnikov, Soviet Street 48. March 8, 2000.

KIMZHA. Three, six-walled houses with totemic horse's head at end of ridge log. Photograph in snowstorm, March 7, 2000.

KIMZHA. Five-walled house built around 1900 for Peter Ivanovich Deryagin. August 2, 2000.

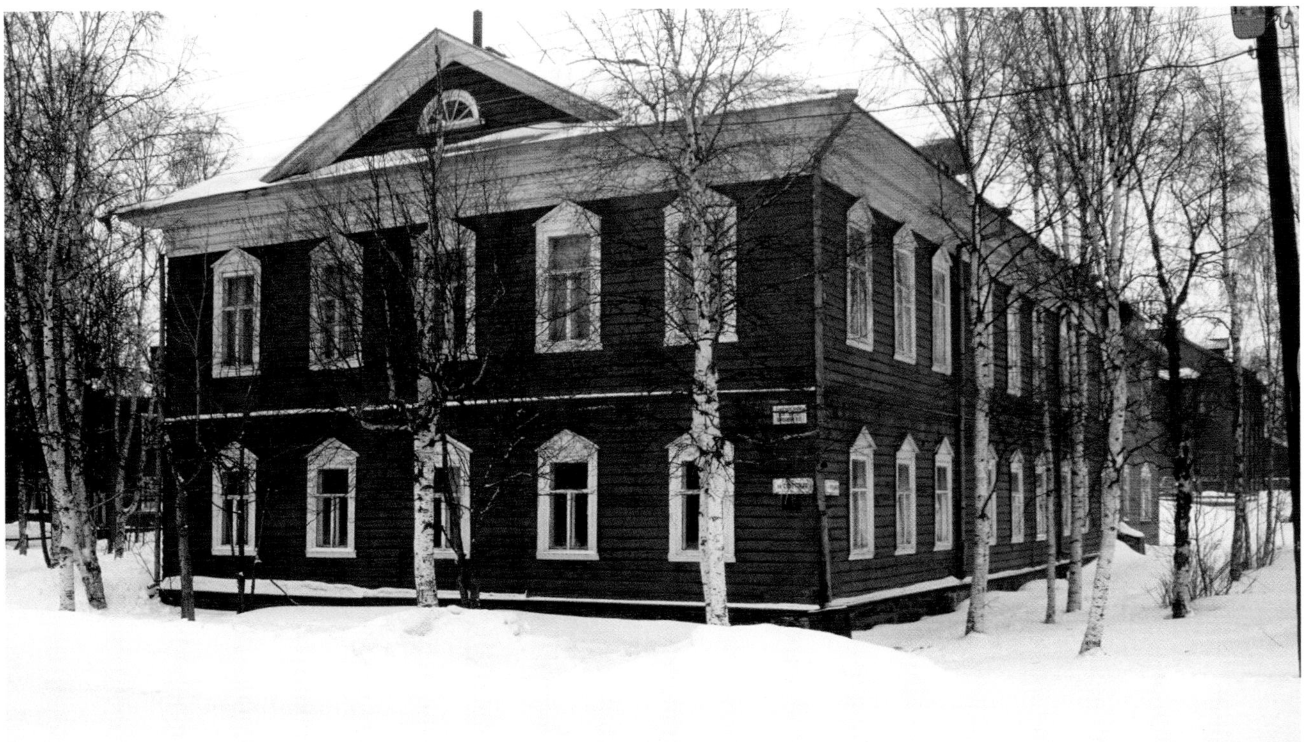

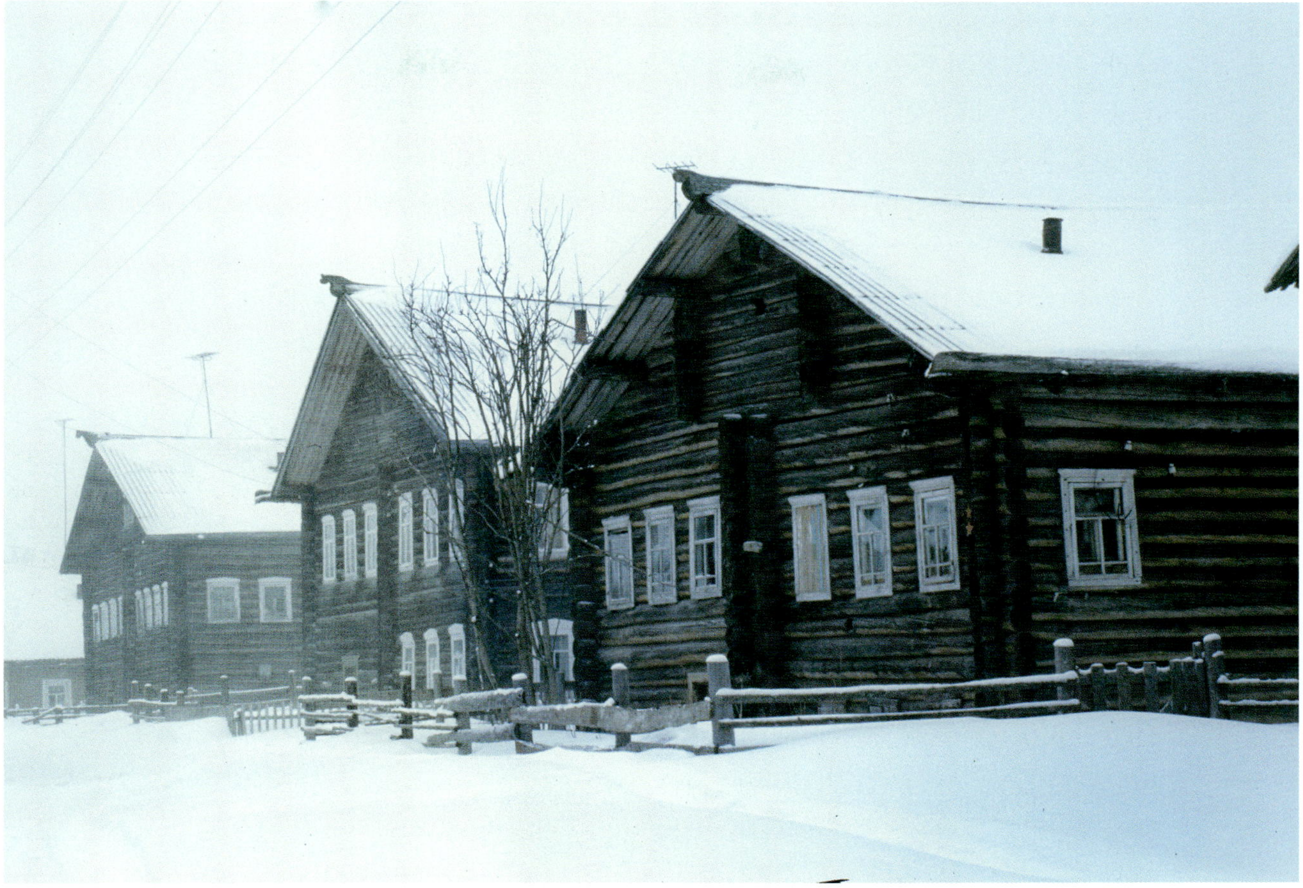

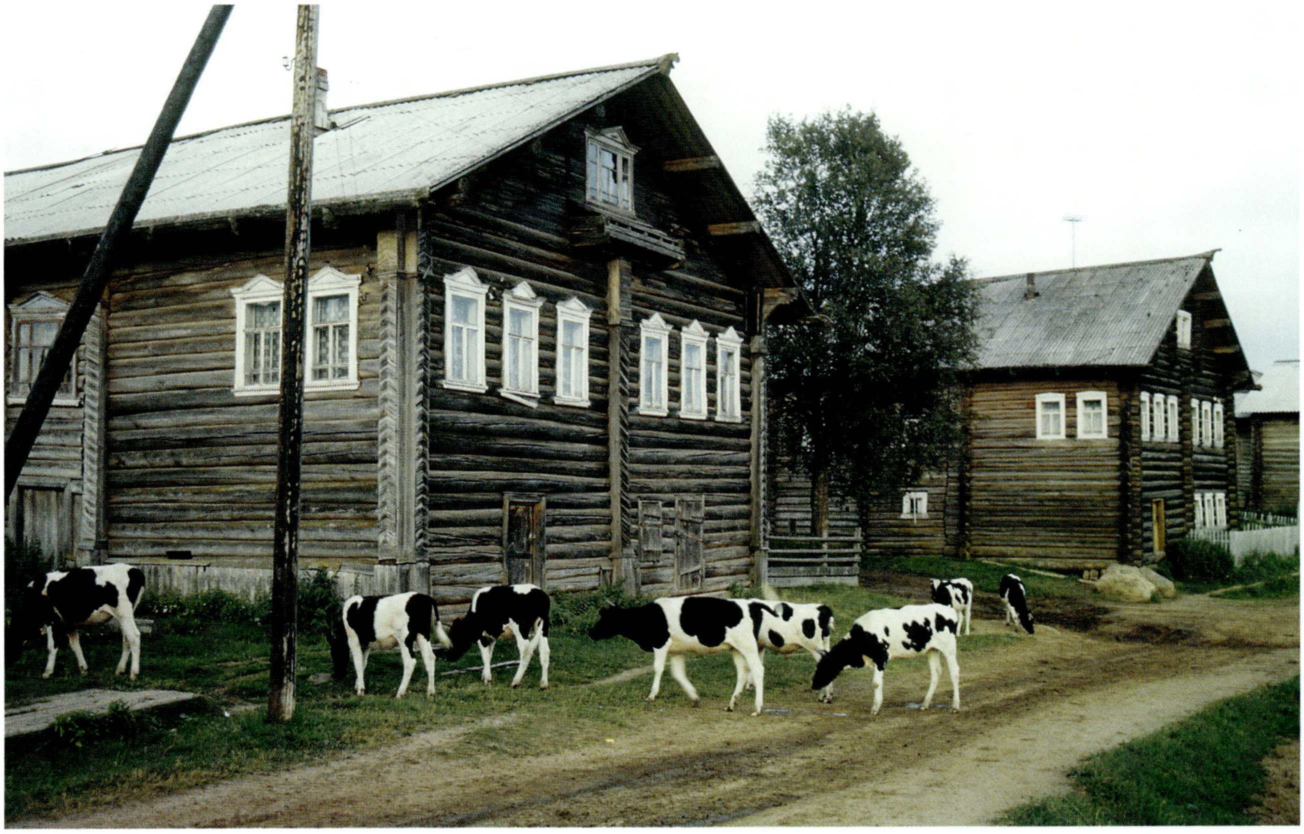

Mezen and founded at the beginning of the sixteenth century by settlers from the Pinega River area to the south. The current population of Kimzha varies between slightly more than one hundred in the winter, with a hundred or so more arriving during the summer, when relatives return to visit parents and grandparents. For much of the year, Kimzha lies in the grip of severe winter conditions, stiff wind and snow drifts produced by abundant moisture from the sea. Formerly, there was limited passenger transportation to the Mezen area from the major White Sea port of Arkhangelsk, but that route ceased decades ago. A year-round transportation option is by small plane from Arkhangelsk's Vaskovo Airport to Mezen, and from there by car (and boat) to Kimzha. During the winter there was an iced forest track, or *zimnik*, that wound northward from Pinega to Kimzha and Mezen. Yet that was a nerve-wracking, exhausting route, whose usefulness was curtailed by increasingly early spring thaws. Several years ago, a year-round gravel road (No. A11–004) was completed all the way to Mezen, with Kimzha as the road's main attraction.

From every perspective Kimzha is defined by the soaring vertical form of the Church of the Hodegetria Icon of the Virgin—more than twenty-seven meters high. A century ago, the Russian North was rich with examples of towering wooden churches, such as the Dormition at Varzuga. The Kimzha church, however, is the sole surviving example of a type with a high central tower and cupola flanked by four small cupolas on gables that buttress the tower. It is known that similar examples were created by carpenters active in the eighteenth century in the territory around the Pinega River. The daring form of the Kimzha church was enabled by a combination of superb carpentry and the use of larch logs, an exceptionally durable type of timber. In retrospect it seems remarkable that the Hodegetria Church was ever completed. Begun in 1700 to replace an early seventeenth-century church that had burned in 1699 from a lightning strike, the church was almost ten years in construction due to the limited resources of a small parish. After completion of the basic structure, another half century passed before its recorded consecration in 1763. (I was told that the delay was due to the local prevalence of Orthodox dissenters known as Old Believers, who had their own prayer houses.)

Miraculously, the Hodegetria Church has survived decades of alteration, neglect, and the constant threat of accidental fire. In the 1870s its tower and cupolas were sheathed in wooden fish scale shingles, while the

KIMZHA. Church of Hodegetria Icon of the Virgin, southwest view before midnight with log barn in foreground. July 31, 2000.

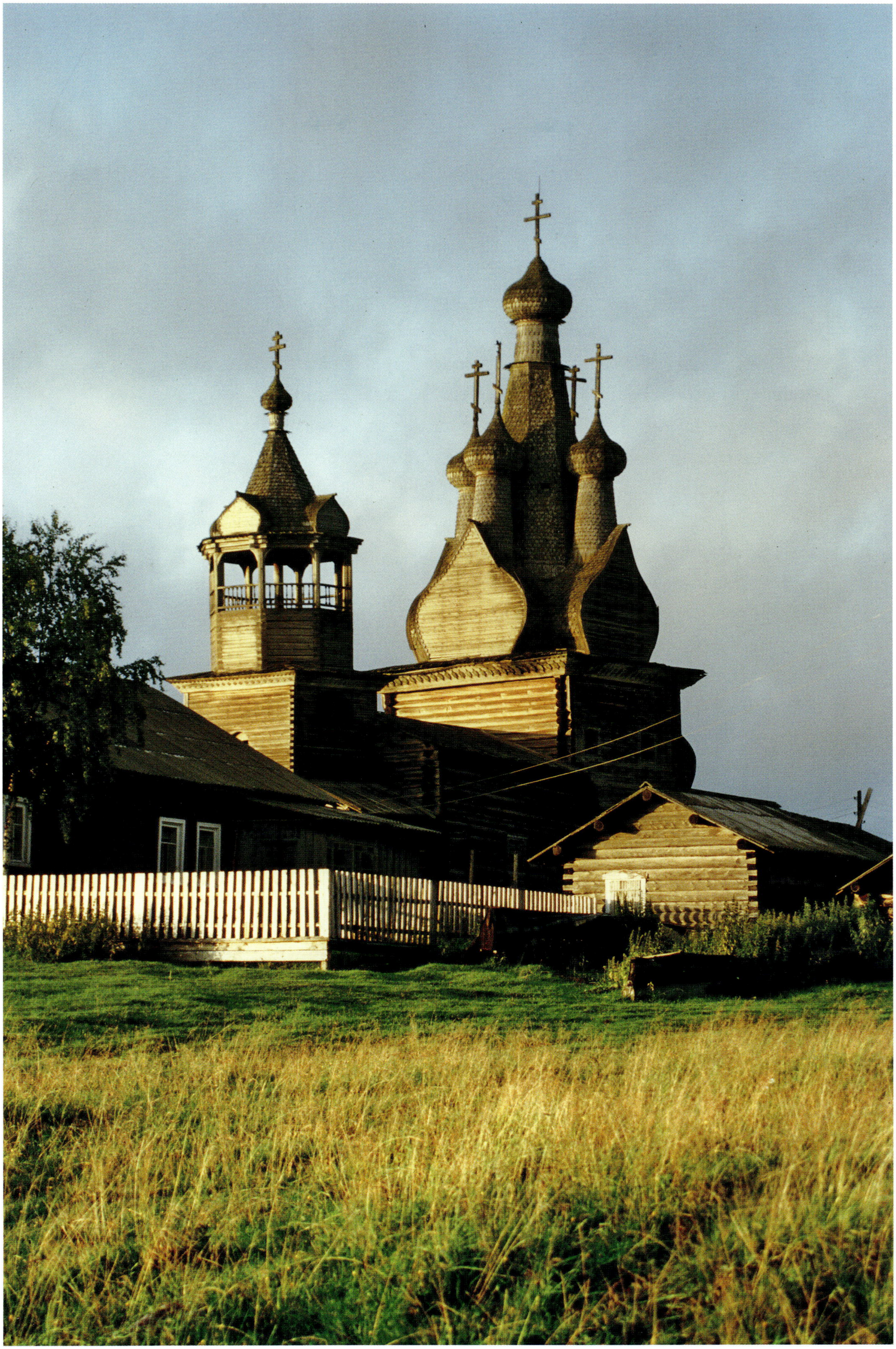

interior was surfaced with planks painted light blue. At the same time (1877–78), a bell tower was erected over the west porch. (An earlier bell frame stood apart from the church on the bank of the Kimzha River.) In the late 1890s the stout log exterior was covered with plank siding painted white with blue and green trim. Soviet restoration practice frowned on nineteenth-century white board cladding, and in the 1980s some of the planks were removed from the walls of the Kimzha church. A lack of funds halted this early restoration attempt, and in 2000 the church stood as an unintended display of restoration practice, half with siding and half without. A local committee succeeded in 1999 in having the padlock removed from the church, which had been closed for worship since the 1930s. Although the reconsecrated church was open for infrequent services led by a priest from Mezen, the building showed ominous signs of deformation.

In 2008 the entire structure was disassembled for restoration, but work was halted for prolonged periods because of contractual issues. The reconstruction was finally completed a decade later with new plank siding. As with other examples of wooden architecture in the Russian North, I consider myself fortunate to have photographed the Kimzha church when the original log structure still existed. The village of Kimzha has a certain magic perhaps best represented by the aquamarine shimmer of the aurora borealis that I saw on my first arrival in the winter of 2000. Together with the Hodegetria Church, the village makes an unforgettable impression with its massive log houses built in the late nineteenth and early twentieth centuries. Although some houses have been shuttered and others modified, Kimzha is a living environment preserved from another era.

Modern life requires amenities that are difficult to maintain in a remote rural environment. Despite these challenges, the preservation of Kimzha—the buildings and the community—seems remarkable. Many former residents of Kimzha have left for life elsewhere, yet this emigration has itself helped the village retain its age-old dimensions and appearance (in contrast to Varzuga). Some villagers are employed by the local administration, others have connections with the lumber plant in Kamenka, and others live on the remnants of agriculture. Although the former dairy kolkhoz, surrounded by rusting machinery, has dwindled, a large part of the dairy herd is now individually owned. Kimzha survived when dozens of other villages throughout the north vanished. There are several factors to explain this endurance, but the presence of the Hodegetria Church has played a central role in the village's cohesion. It remains the best-preserved, most significant traditional settlement in the Russian North.

KIMZHA. Windmill. Built at turn of twentieth century with upper structure rotating on elevated log base to catch prevailing winds. This striking design was widespread in the north and western Siberia. August 2, 2000.

MEZEN RIVER BANK (near Kimzha). Votive cross erected in 1887 by a merchant named Savvin to commemorate rescue from drowning. Figure of Christ draped in votive offerings (since removed to one side). Metal box at foot for votive candles and small offerings such as forest berries. August 3, 2000.

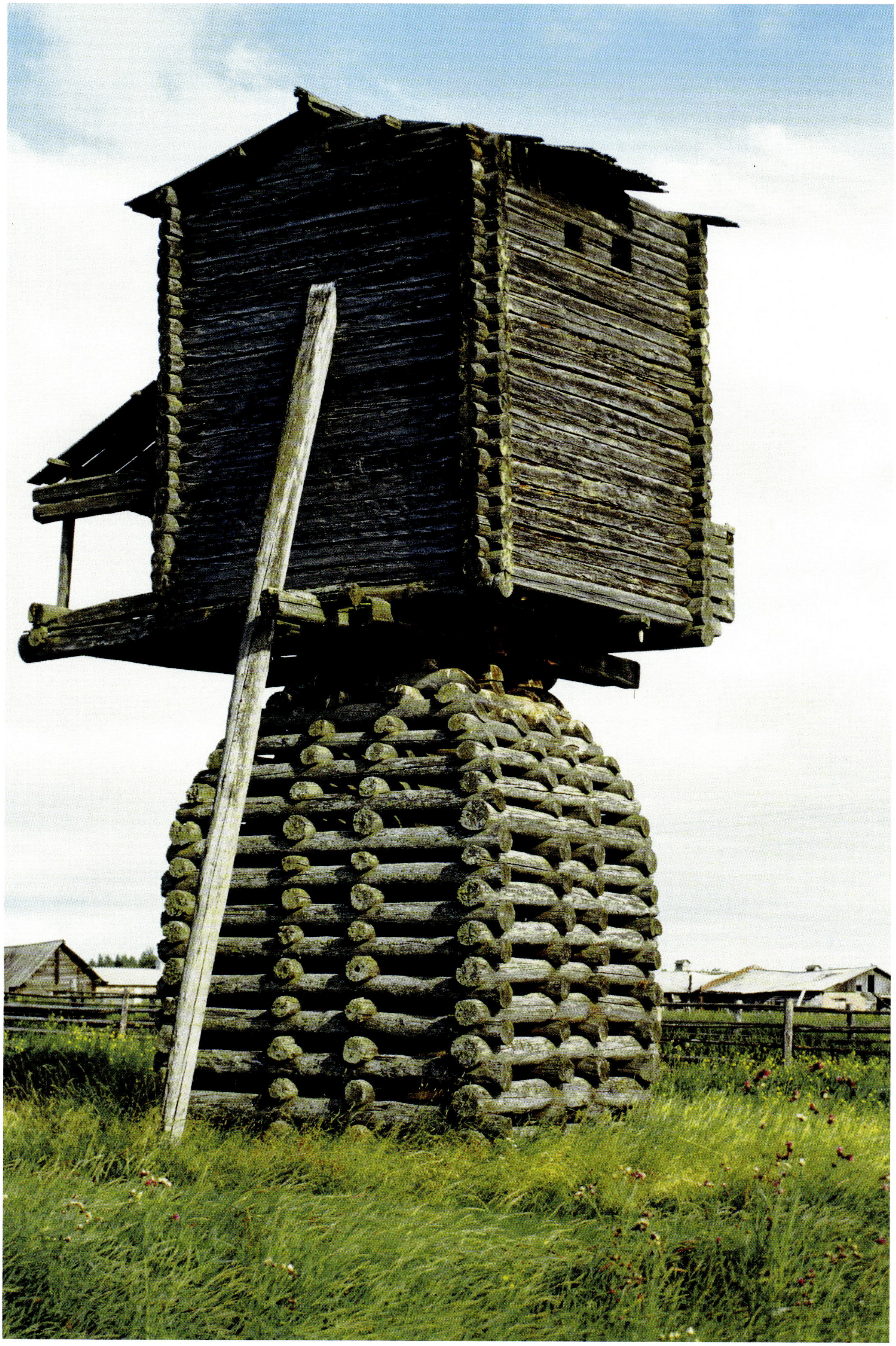

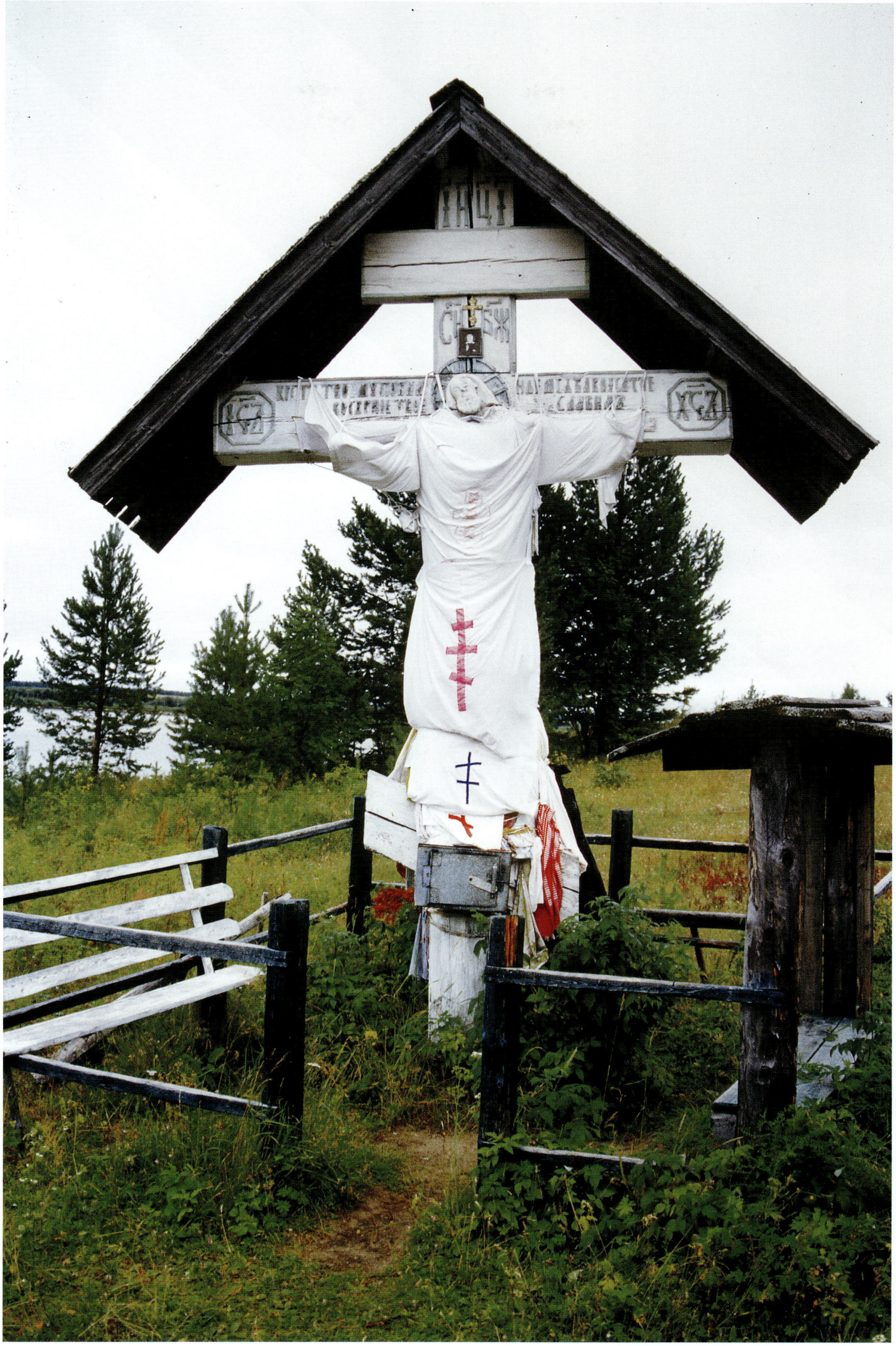

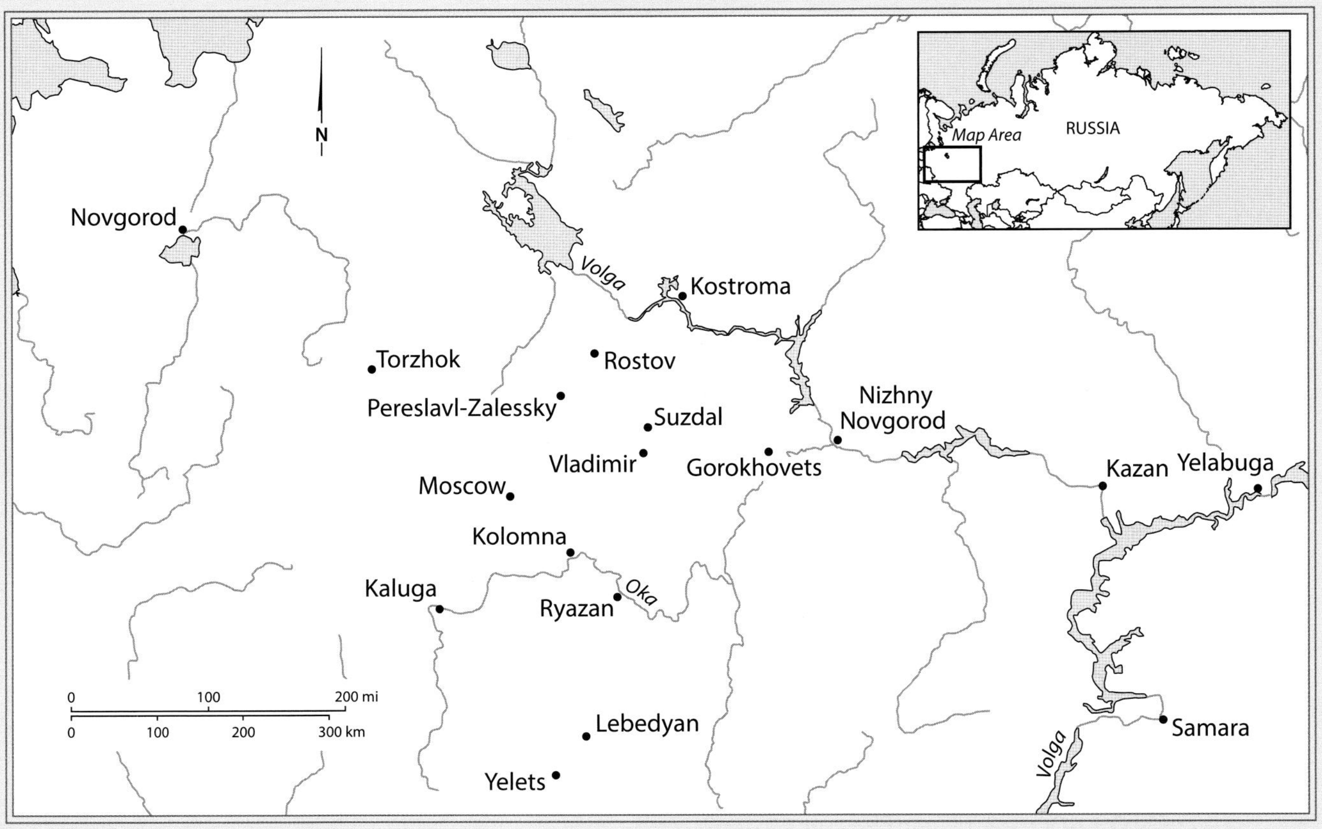

The Heartland.

CHAPTER FOUR

The Heartland

From Novgorod and Saint Petersburg in the northwest to the Don River basin in the southwest and the Volga basin to the east, the central part of European Russia defines that country's memory and identity. Each region within this geographic range shows specific features in the crafting of wooden buildings, yet there are general characteristics that span the entire area, such as the differences between the village *izba* (itself capable of many variations) and urban wooden dwellings. The following survey does not pretend to be exhaustive in describing this area, but the photographic evidence suggests the variety of expression and the ever-changing state of preservation.

Novgorod and Vitoslavlitsy Park

The city of Novgorod the Great, founded no later than the mid-ninth century, was one of the defining centers of medieval Russian culture and commerce, with a great Cathedral of Saint Sophia built in the mid-eleventh century. Although finally submitting to Moscow in the fifteenth century and sacked by Ivan the Terrible in 1570, Novgorod remained a repository of medieval Russian culture. Novgorod itself was built primarily of wood until the twentieth century, despite its renowned masonry churches and cathedrals from the eleventh to the eighteenth centuries. Medieval chronicles contain sparse references to large wooden churches in Novgorod, such as the town's earliest shrine dedicated to Saint Sophia (Divine Wisdom), apparently an oak structure of the late tenth century with thirteen "tops," or cupolas. From extensive archaeological and historical data, it is evident that wood was used for almost every type of structure.

Although little wooden architecture has been preserved within Novgorod, which suffered major war damage from late 1941 to early 1944, the area's wooden architectural heritage and traditional folk culture are on

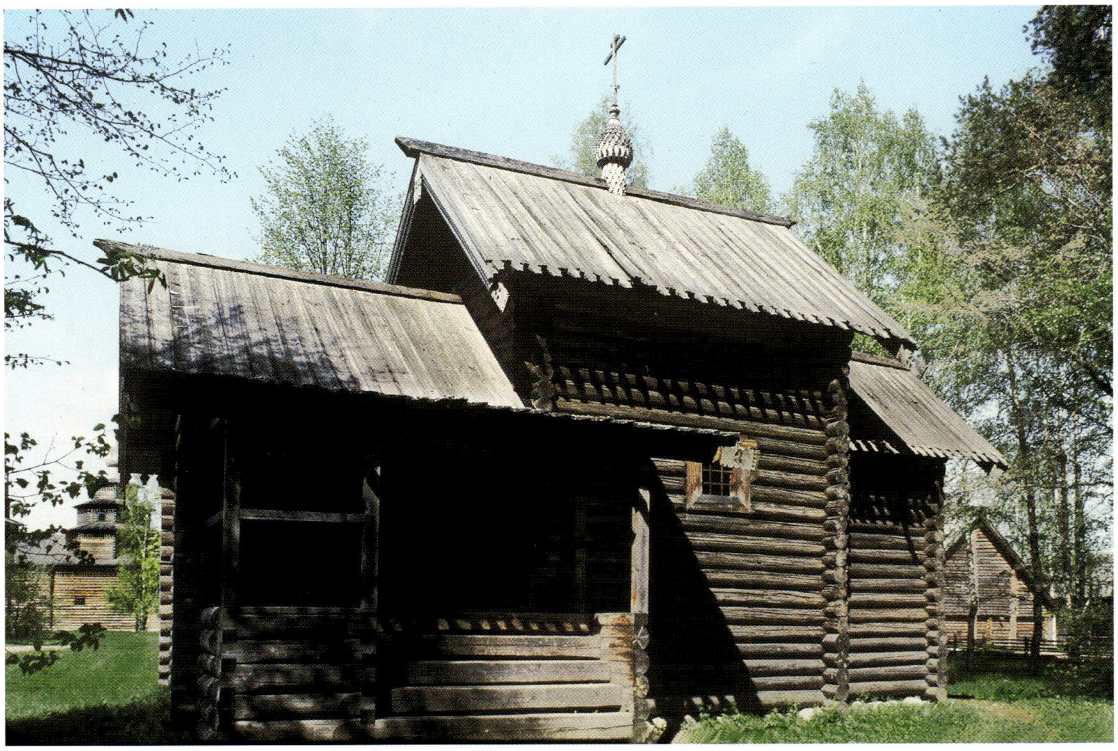

VITOSLAVLITSY (Novgorod region, outdoor museum). Church of the Trinity at the Rekon Hermitage, south view. Originally built in 1670s with modifications in the eighteenth century. May 19, 1995.

display at the Vitoslavlitsy outdoor museum, set within an ancient village estate surrounded by birch and pine groves. Established by state decree in 1964 and now one of Russia's most popular museum parks, Vitoslavlitsy has an array of structures ranging from small chapels to large churches, as well as houses with displays of period furniture and traditional crafts. My first photographs there were taken in October 1971.

The Vitoslavlitsy park serves as an encyclopedia of the variety of Russian wooden churches. Treated more carefully than houses, these structures could last for centuries if rotting logs were replaced and the roof maintained. Among the museum's array of log churches, the earliest examples date to the sixteenth century. The more elaborate churches had galleries on raised porches and were decorated with carved end boards that protected the roof beams. Similar decorative elements can be found on the larger peasant houses. The simplest type of wooden church (*pustyn*), illustrated at Vitoslavlitsy by the Church of the Trinity built in the 1670s at the Rekon Hermitage, resembles the peasant house, with its pitched roof and rectangular components. The plan is linear along an east-west axis, with the main part for worship and a smaller part in the west that served as a vestibule. An apse containing the altar projected on the east, as required in Russian Orthodox practice. Some examples had a bell tower attached at the west of the vestibule.

VITOSLAVLITSY. Church of Saint Nicholas at Myakishevo, north view. Restored at Vitoslavlitsy in 1976. A complex interplay of forms and volumes. June 5, 1993.

VITOSLAVLITSY. Church of Saint Nicholas at Tukholya, southwest view. Originally built around 1688 at the village of Ust-Volma, then moved to Tukholya. Restored at Vitoslavlitsy in 1967. May 19, 1995.

VITOSLAVLITSY. Church of Saint Nicholas at Vysoky Ostrov, southeast view. Excellent example of tiered tower construction integrated with linear design with bell tower at west end. May 30, 1992.

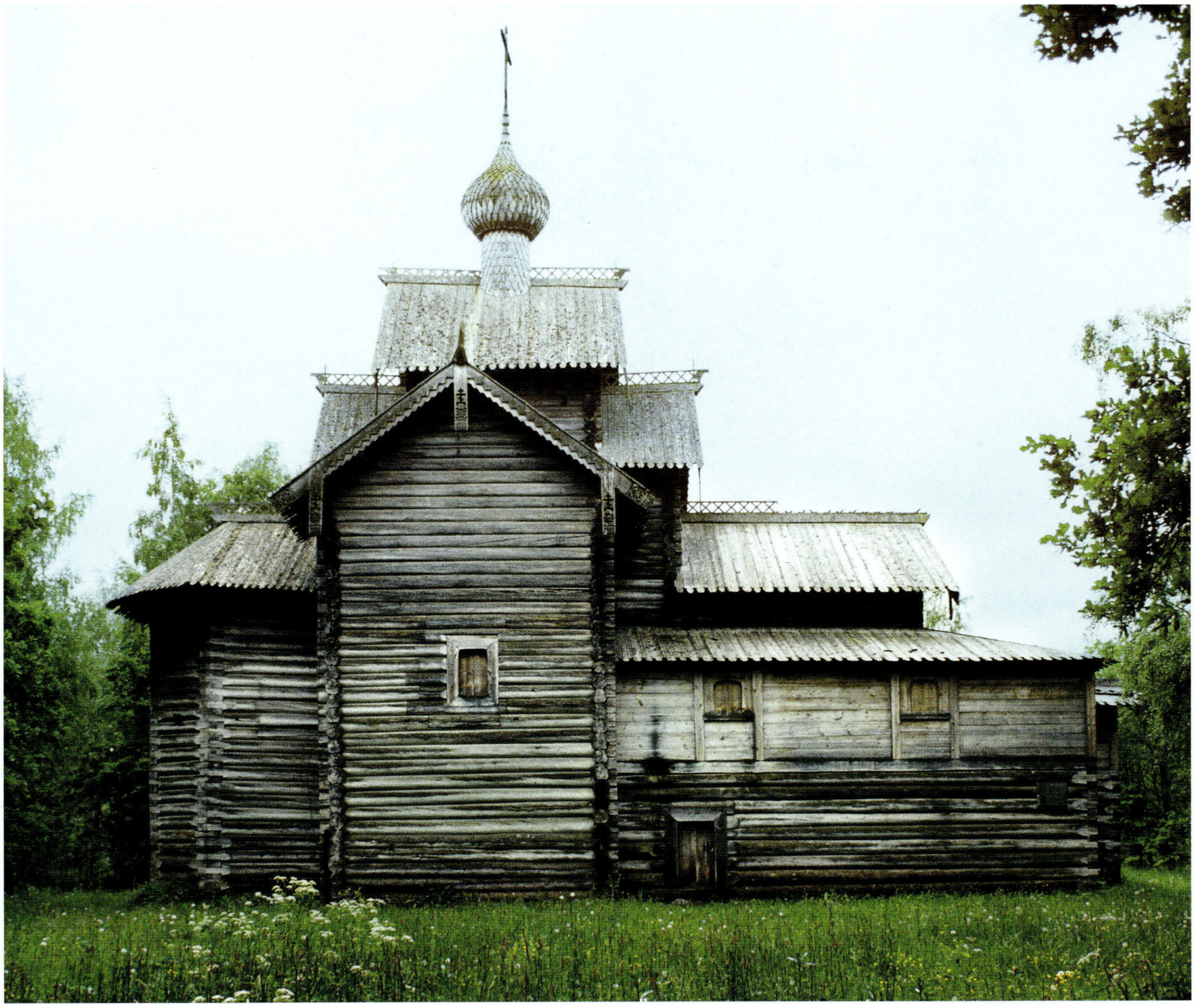

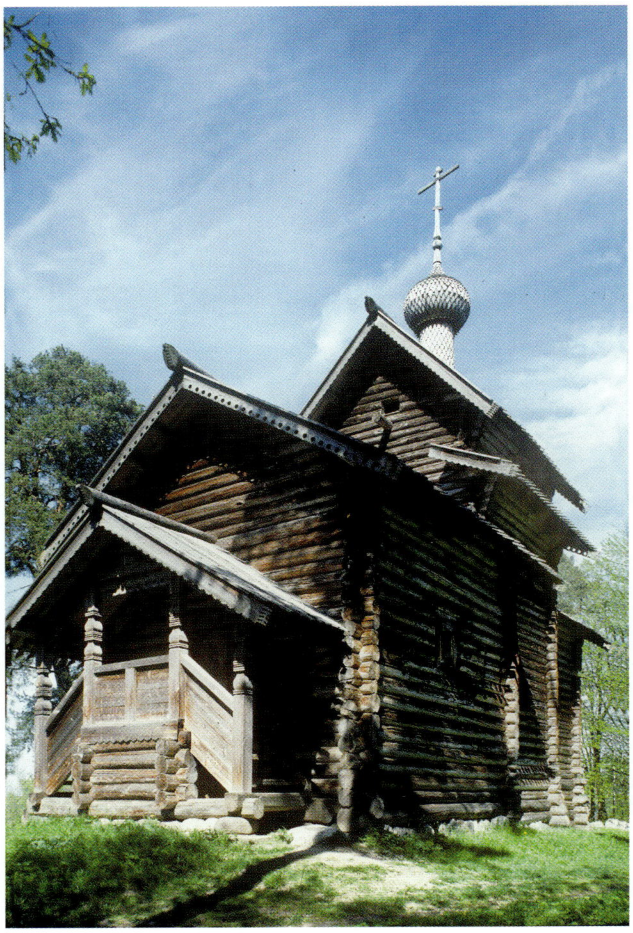

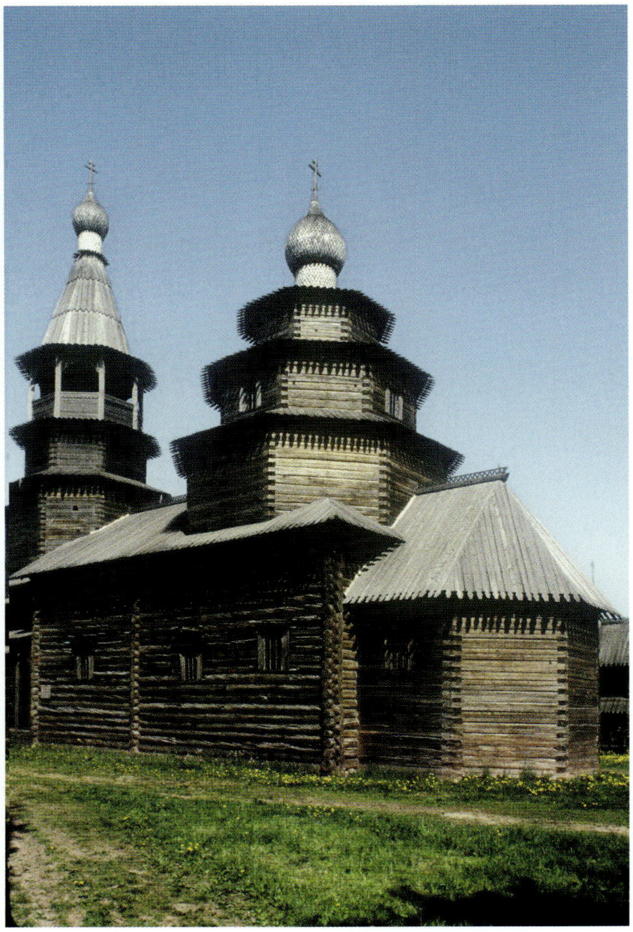

This linear plan could be elaborated by a roof with two planes above the main structure better to protect the walls from moisture, as in the Church of Saint Nicholas at Tukholya, built around 1688. Still more complex examples display multiple gables with decorative carving, such as the Church of Saint Nicholas at Myakishevo, built in the mid-seventeenth century. Designed to shed snow, their steeply pitched roofs are also a delight to the eye. The most daring structural approach was adopted in the design of tower churches. Their core structure ascends in a series of octagonal tiers over the main part of the building, an approach superbly illustrated by the Church of Saint Nicholas at Vysoky Ostrov (1757). In this linear plan, the tower above the Church of Saint Nicholas is set at the east end of a low vestibule. When seen from the east, the design suggests the form of a pagoda.

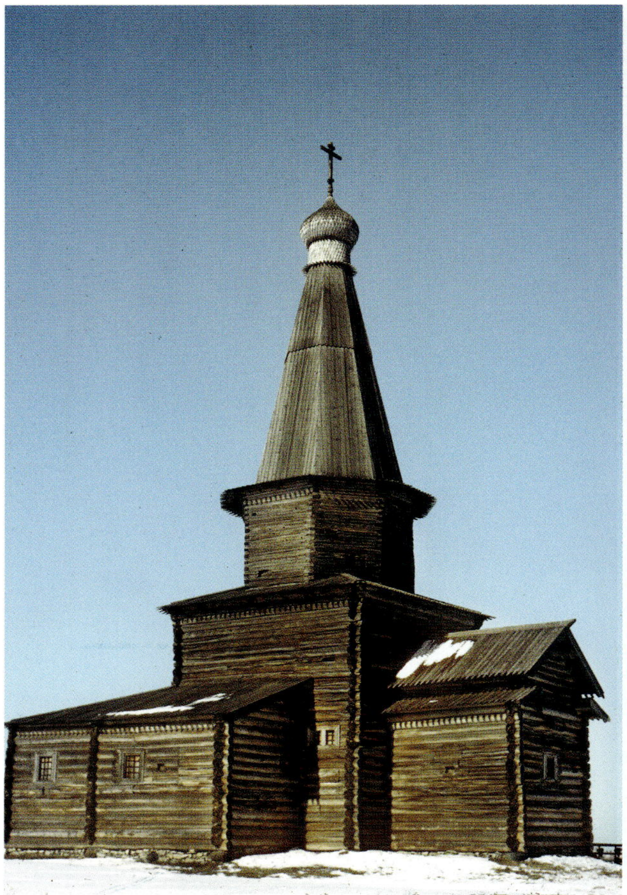

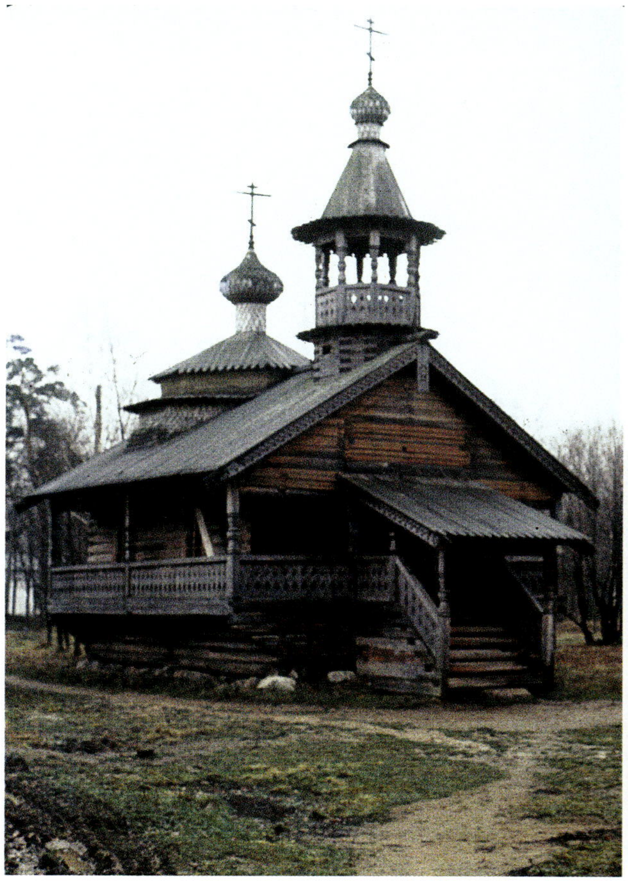

A variant approach to the vertical form is demonstrated in the tent type of wooden church, so named for the shape of its tall central tower (*shatyor*). Here the linear arrangement is replaced by a centralized plan, with a square base supporting an octahedron capped with a soaring eight-sided tent tower, illustrated in the Church of the Dormition at Kuritsko (1595). More complex variations of the tent tower show a cruciform plan with flanking domes, as illustrated in the Church of the Nativity of the Virgin at Peryodki, originally a monastic structure first mentioned in 1539. Side additions were made in 1699. The Peryodki church (approximately thirty meters high) has a gallery elevated above the highest snow drifts by a system of projecting logs.

The Vitoslavlitsy park also contains log houses (*izba*) and barns that combine the artistry

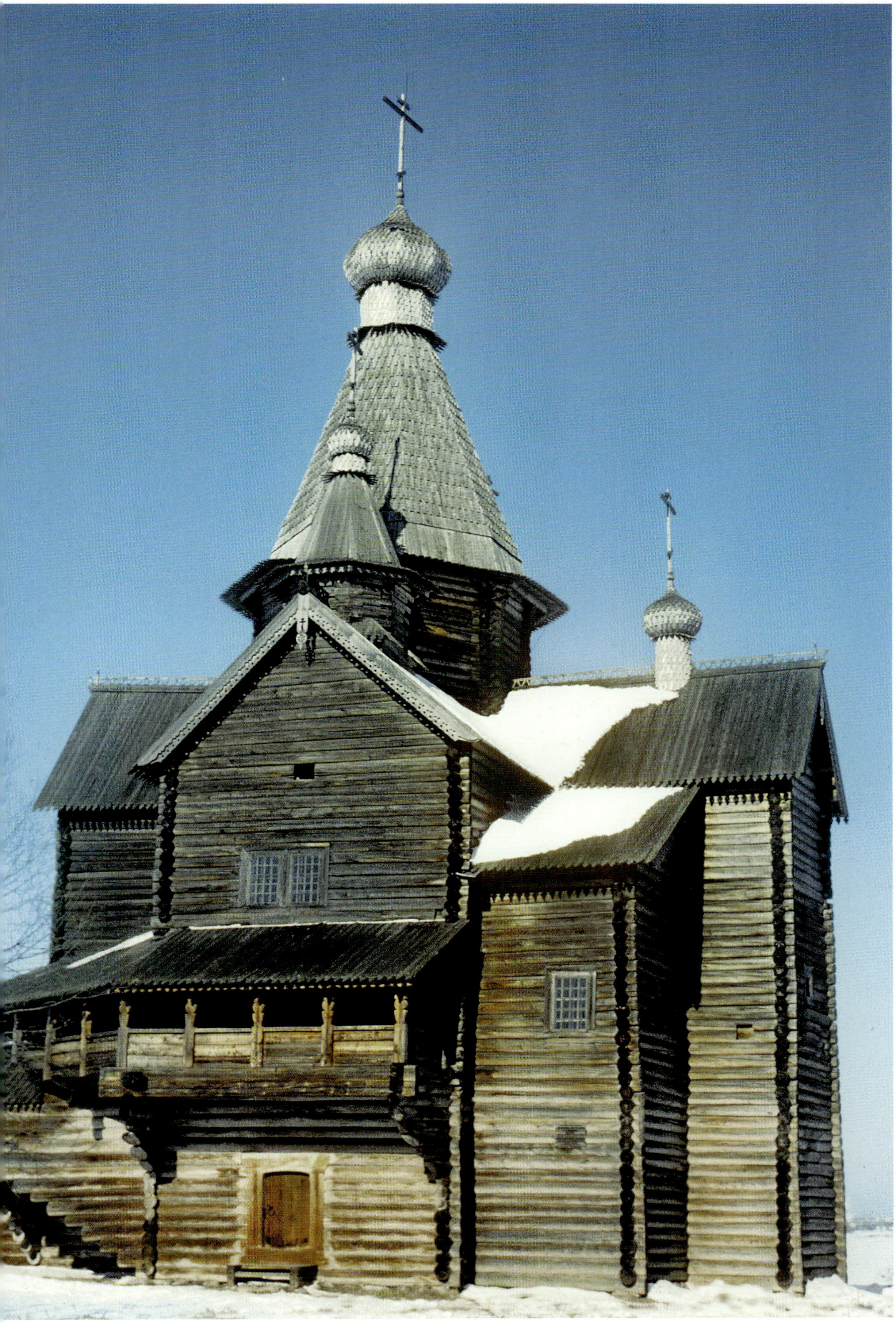

VITOSLAVLITSY. Church of Dormition at Kuritsko, south-east view. Austerely monumental, this tent tower construction became widespread in the Russian North. March 14, 1980.

VITOSLAVLITSY. Chapel of Mary Magdalene, south view. Built in the late eighteenth century at the village of Malyshevo. May 19, 1995.

VITOSLAVLITSY. Church of the Nativity of the Virgin at Peryodki, south view. Originally built in the 1530s, this is one of the earliest surviving examples of a tent tower over the main structure. The intricate cruciform plan gained secondary towers and domes at the end of the seventeenth century. The lighter color at the bottom indicates logs were replaced during restoration in 1968–71. March 14, 1980

of design with economy of function. The center of the peasant log house was the large masonry stove used not only for cooking but also for heating the main living space during the long winters. In the central part of Russia, the house typically formed the primary component of a yard enclosed by a solid fence and containing sheds for animals and farm implements. In the more severe climate of the far north, these units were combined into a single, self-sufficient structure.

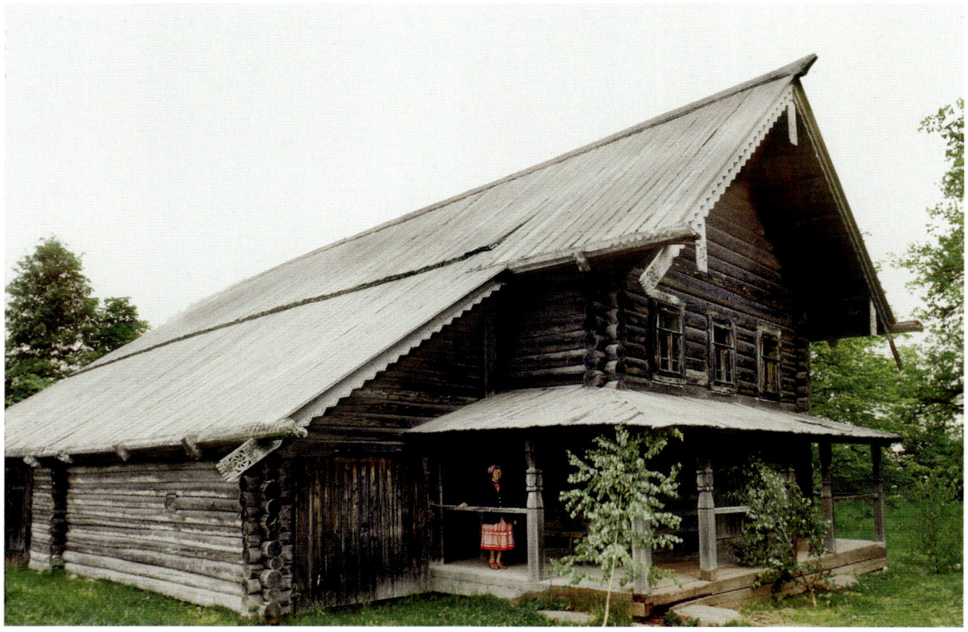

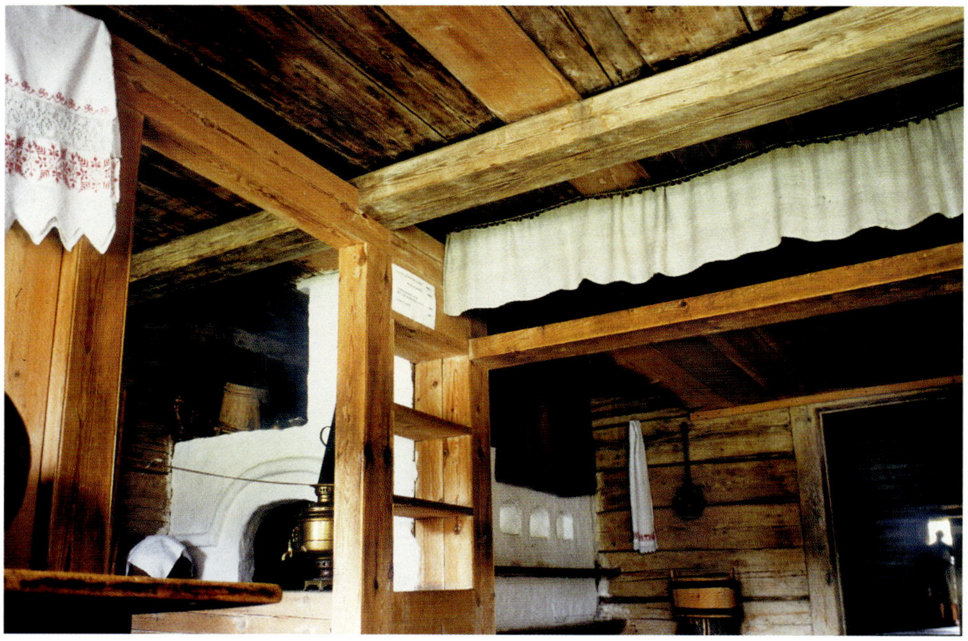

VITOSLAVLITSY. Vasily Tunitsky house. Built in the late nineteenth century at the village of Pyrishchi, this house with attached carriage shed was designed without a chimney (*kurnaia* or *chernaia izba*), thus allowing heated smoke to drift toward the ceiling and exit through openings in upper wall. June 5, 1993.

VITOSLAVLITSY. Vasily Tunitsky house. Main living space with brick stove and sleeping ledge for children. May 19, 1995.

VITOSLAVLITSY. M. D. Ekimova house, built in 1882 with four windows (considered a sign of status) and decorative carved elements. This unique photograph (October 21, 1971) shows both the house and the Peryodki church under restoration.

VITOSLAVLITSY. E. I. Tsareva house, built in the 1820s at the village of Pyrishchi. This view of attached barn at back shows stout logs supporting the upper part above the lower space for livestock, whose effluents caused the lower logs to decay more rapidly. These supports allowed weakened logs to be replaced without threat to the structure above. May 19, 1995.

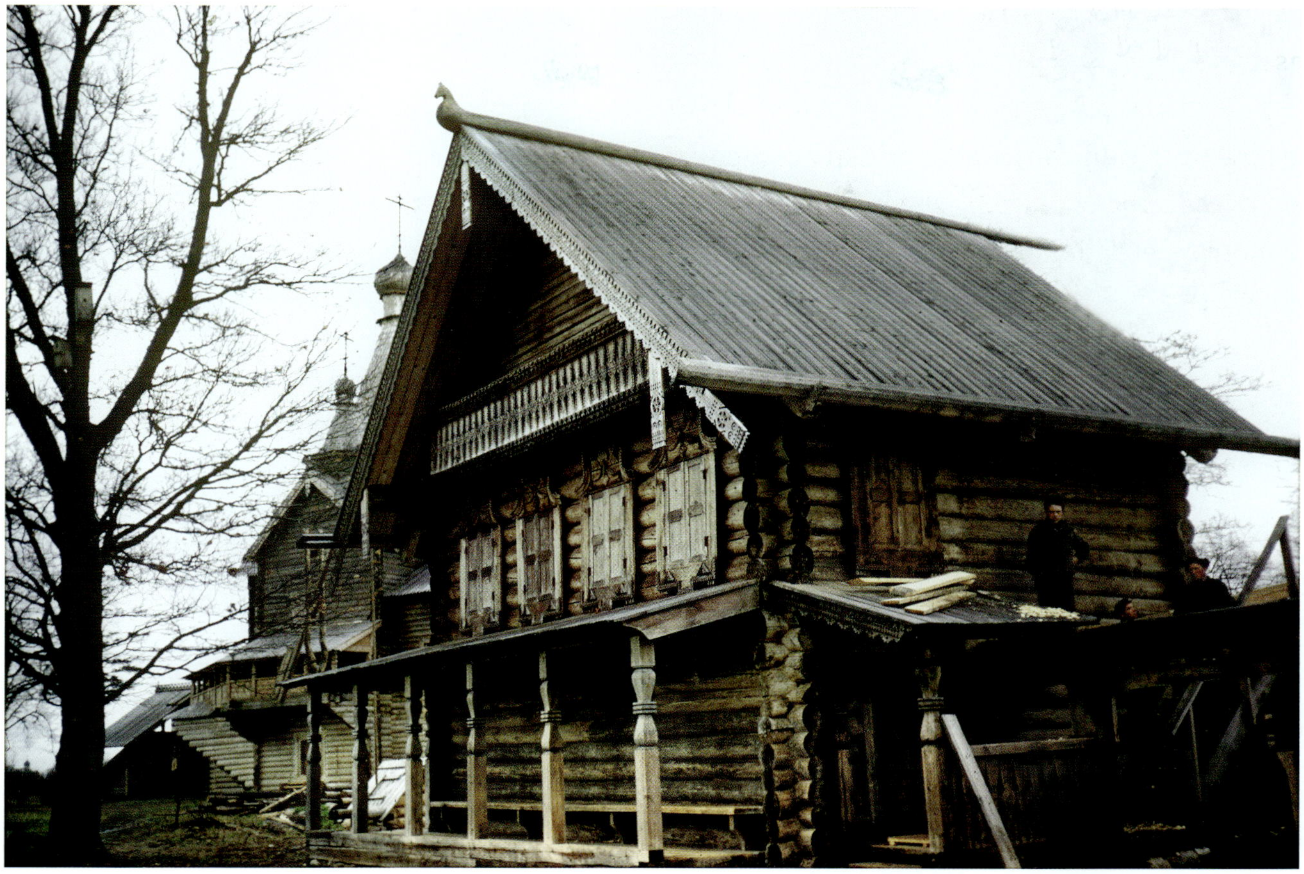

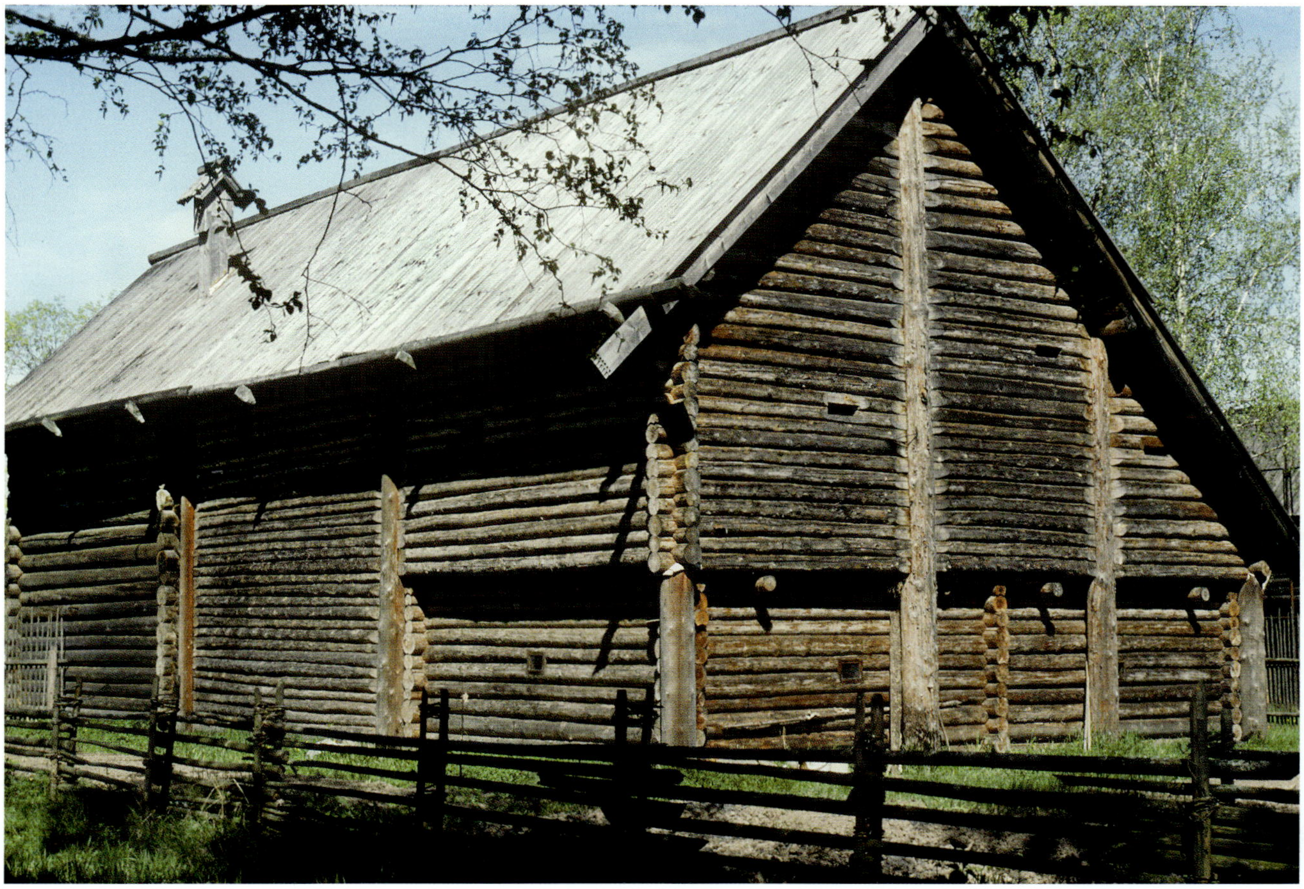

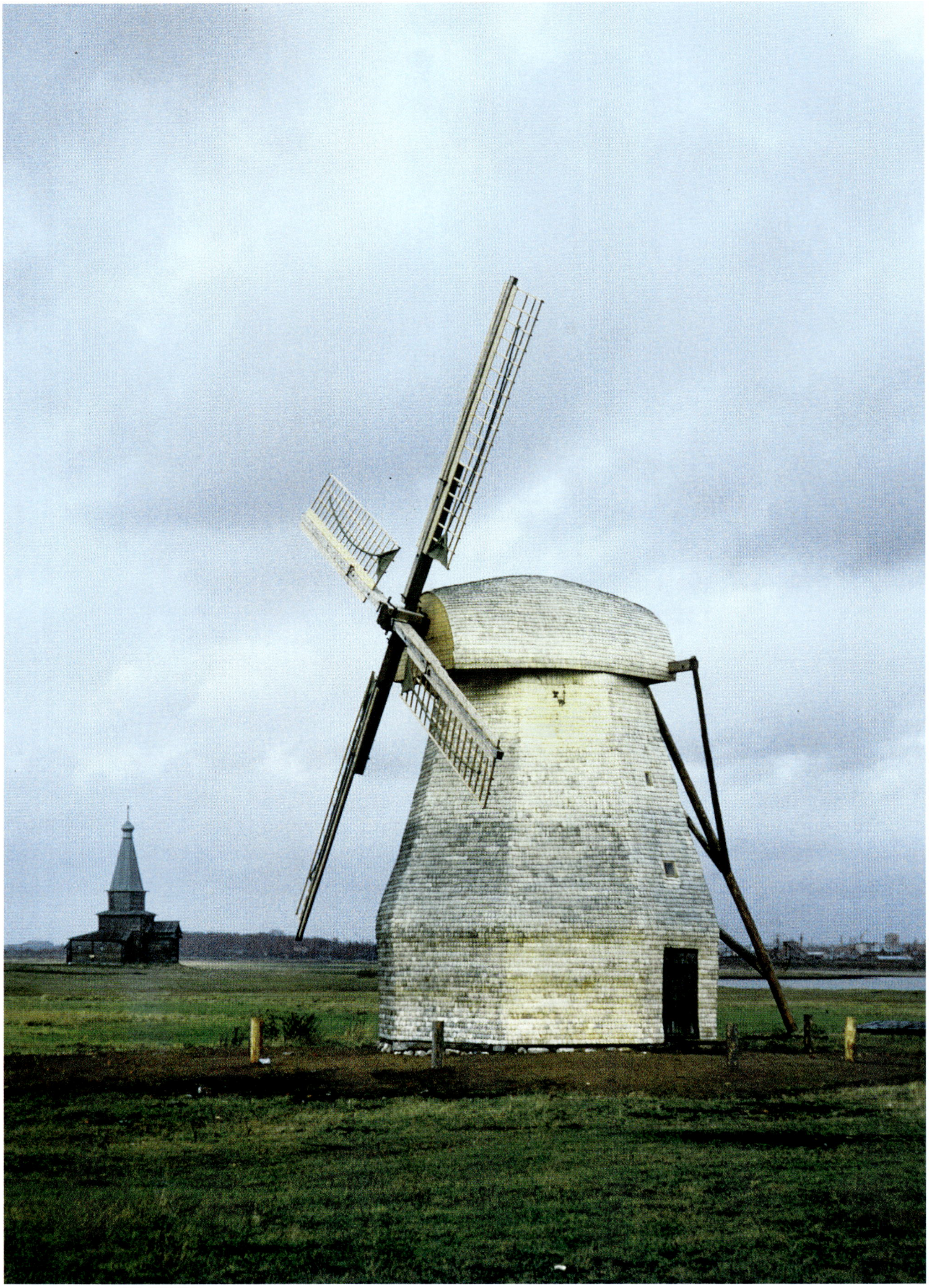

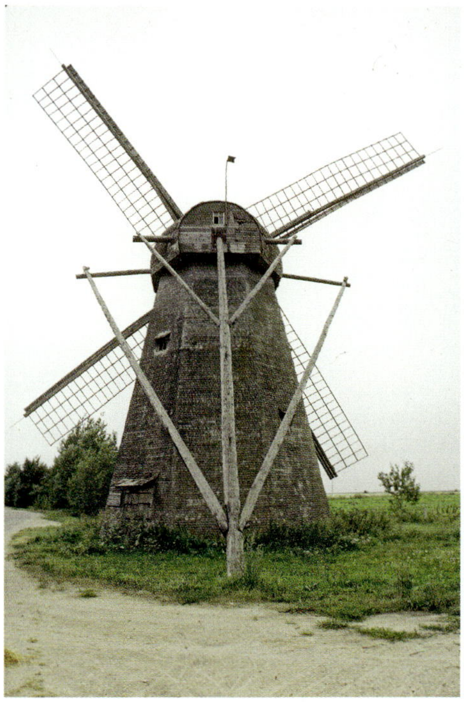

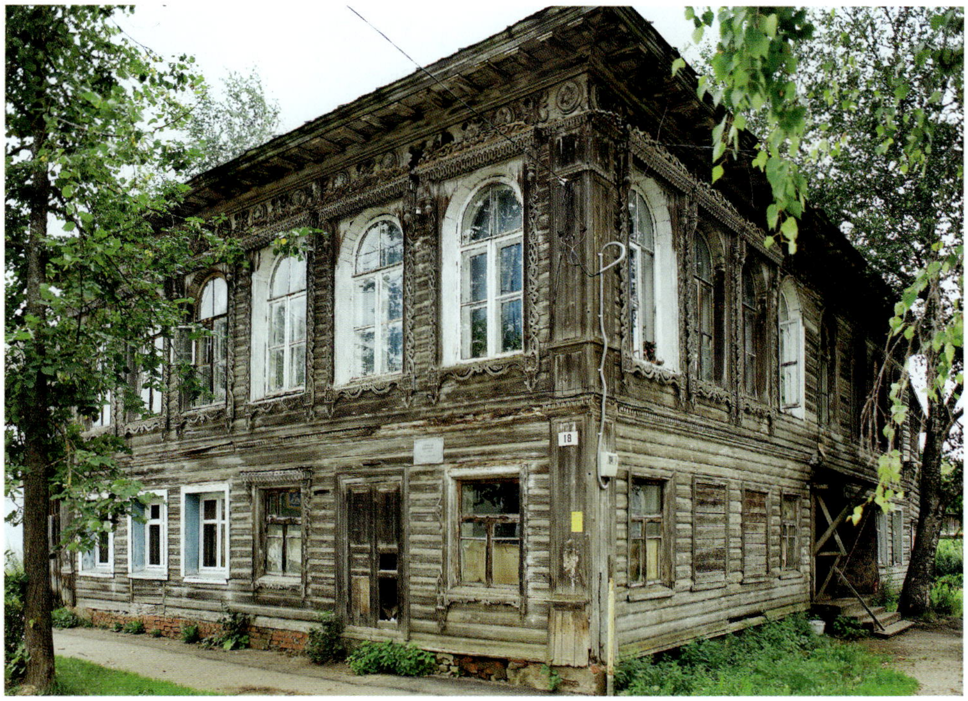

Another type of wooden structure traditional to the region was the windmill. Among these, the more advanced development is the tower mill (*shatrovka*) in which the movable cap (*shapka*), containing a horizontal shaft supporting the blades, rests above an enclosed tower. In Europe, there are numerous variations on this type, which can be used for pumping as well as milling. In Russia, I have photographed tower mills in which the main part—often octagonal—typically flares downward in a wood-frame structure covered with boards or shingles. Among my favorites are two tower mills in the vicinity of Novgorod. The first, clad in aspen shingles and fantastical in appearance, still stood with its blades on the original site near the Trinity–St. Mikhail Klopsky Monastery when I recorded it from all sides. The second mill, originally erected in the village of Ladoshchina in the 1920s, had just been restored at the Vitoslavlitsy park when I photographed it in October 1971. The lighter color of the replaced parts (such as aspen shingles) indicates the newness of the restoration. As of 2018, the mill is undergoing a capital restoration that includes the machinery. I remain fascinated by that windmill photograph taken fifty years ago with a small Konica camera. Having no idea of my vast photographic project that would unfold over the years, I was just there, in a muddy field, framing the object and catching the faint sunlight at the end of a stormy autumn day.

VITOSLAVLITSY. Windmill built around 1920 at Ladoshchina village. The octagonal tower supports a rotating cap. The light color of the shake shingles indicates recent restoration. October 21, 1971.

KHOTYAZH (near Novgorod). Windmill built in the early twentieth century near the Trinity–St. Mikhail Klopsky Monastery. The octagonal tower clad in shake shingles supports a rotating cap stabilized by poles fastened to the ground. Rare example of intact windmill on original site. August 11, 1994.

POSHEKHONYE (Yaroslavl region). Built for the merchant Vorontsov in the late nineteenth century, this house was one of the loveliest examples of a small-town dwelling, with large windows on the upper story, neoclassical cornice details, and fretwork decoration. Poorly maintained, abandoned, and ultimately burned (likely arson) in May 2019. August 9, 2015.

Moscow Region

Even into the twentieth century, Moscow had hundreds of urban wooden structures, although because of stucco over lathing, many of them were not recognizable as such. Now far fewer remain, including a few notable exceptions discussed in the first two chapters. The territory surrounding Moscow also has its monuments of wooden architecture, secular and sacred. Of particular note is the Church of the Purification at the village of Peski, formerly known as Vysotskoe, part of the land holdings of the powerful Resurrection Monastery on the Istra River (of which more below). A log Church of the Purification was originally built around 1705 through the support of local peasants, but that church was destroyed by a lightning strike in 1758. Another church arose on the site in 1759, but it too burned from a lightning strike in 1857. In 1858, the parish acquired a wooden church and bell tower built in 1774–76 for the neighboring village of Sereda, disassembled and erected it on the site of the destroyed church. (The disassembly of log structures—with the logs numbered in proper order—was a frequent practice.) Reconsecrated in 1860, the Purification Church, composed of ascending octagonal tiers, remained active throughout the Soviet period. The magnificent icon screen contains seventeenth-century icons.

In the town of Istra, fifty kilometers to the west of Moscow, there is a small museum of wooden architecture in the shadow of the great Resurrection Monastery (also known as "New Jerusalem") next to a sacred area called "The Garden of Gethsemane." Part of the New Jerusalem outdoor museum, which formerly included the Resurrection Monastery, the outdoor reserve began in 1970 with the reassembly of the log Church of the Epiphany, built in 1755–56 at the village of Semyonovskoe in Dmitrov District. At the museum the church was rebuilt in what was conjectured to be its eighteenth-century appearance, including an elevated gallery on the west side. Although modest in dimensions, the church was a textbook example of construction techniques. I was fortunate to photograph it in 1994, for in September 2000 it burned to the ground due to a short circuit and inadequate response by the park security. The most imposing structure remaining at the Istra park is a windmill presumably built in the late nineteenth century and brought from the village of Kochemlevo in the Kashin District of Tver Province west of Moscow. It has a rotating top, which is stabilized by construction of poles extending at the back of the

PESKI (Moscow region). Church of the Purification, east view. Originally built in 1774–76 at the village of Sereda, this monument is one of the most impressive surviving examples of a tiered church, its tower consisting of stacked octagonal tiers. June 30, 2019.

PESKI. Church of the Purification. Icon screen, created around 1900, contains several seventeenth-century icons. June 30, 2019.

ISTRA (Moscow region). Church of the Epiphany, southeast view. Originally built in 1756 at the village of Semyonovskoe (Dmitrov District), the church was moved in 1970 to an outdoor museum next to the New Jerusalem–Resurrection Monastery. Destroyed by fire in September 2000. June 11, 1994.

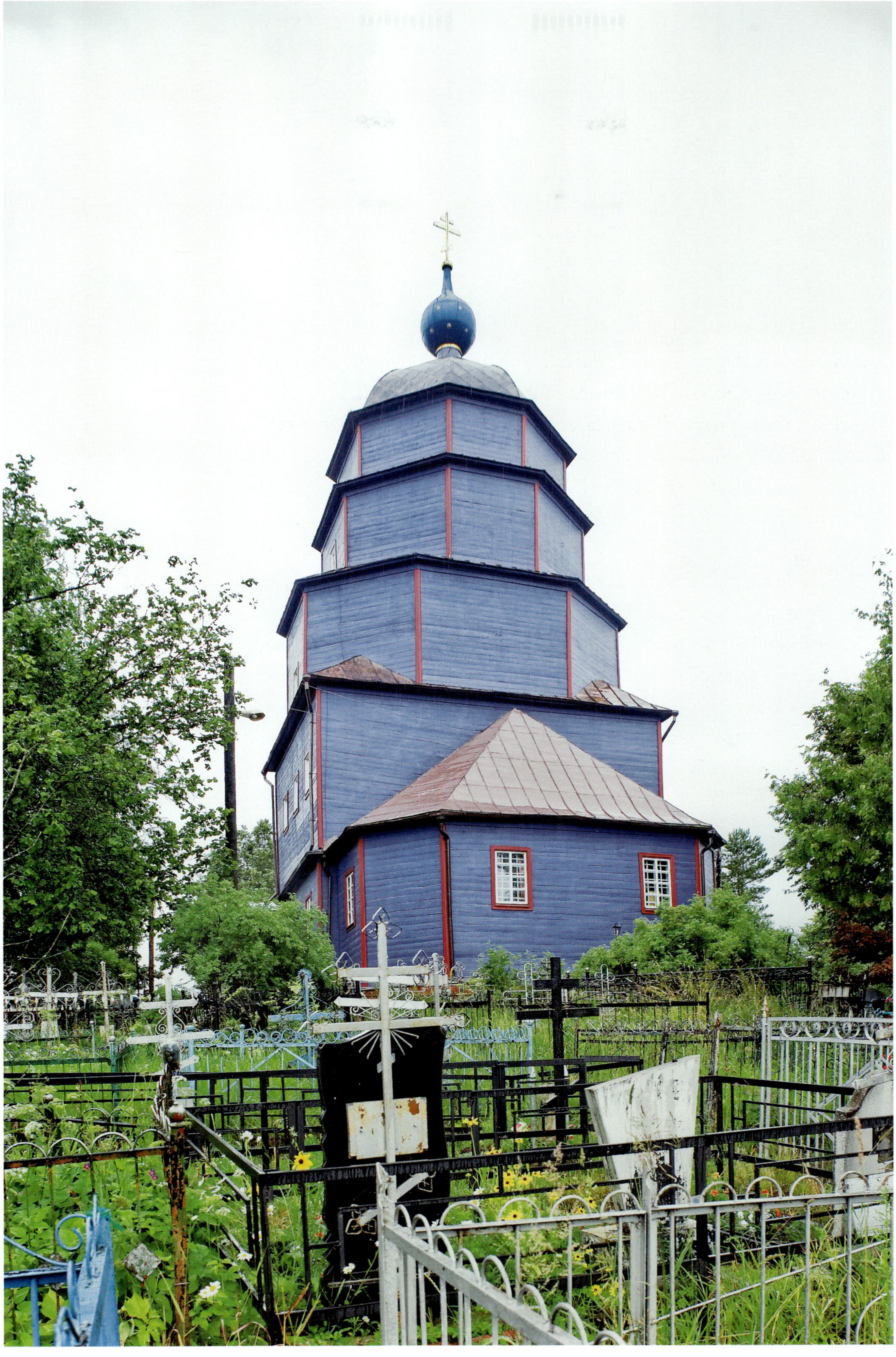

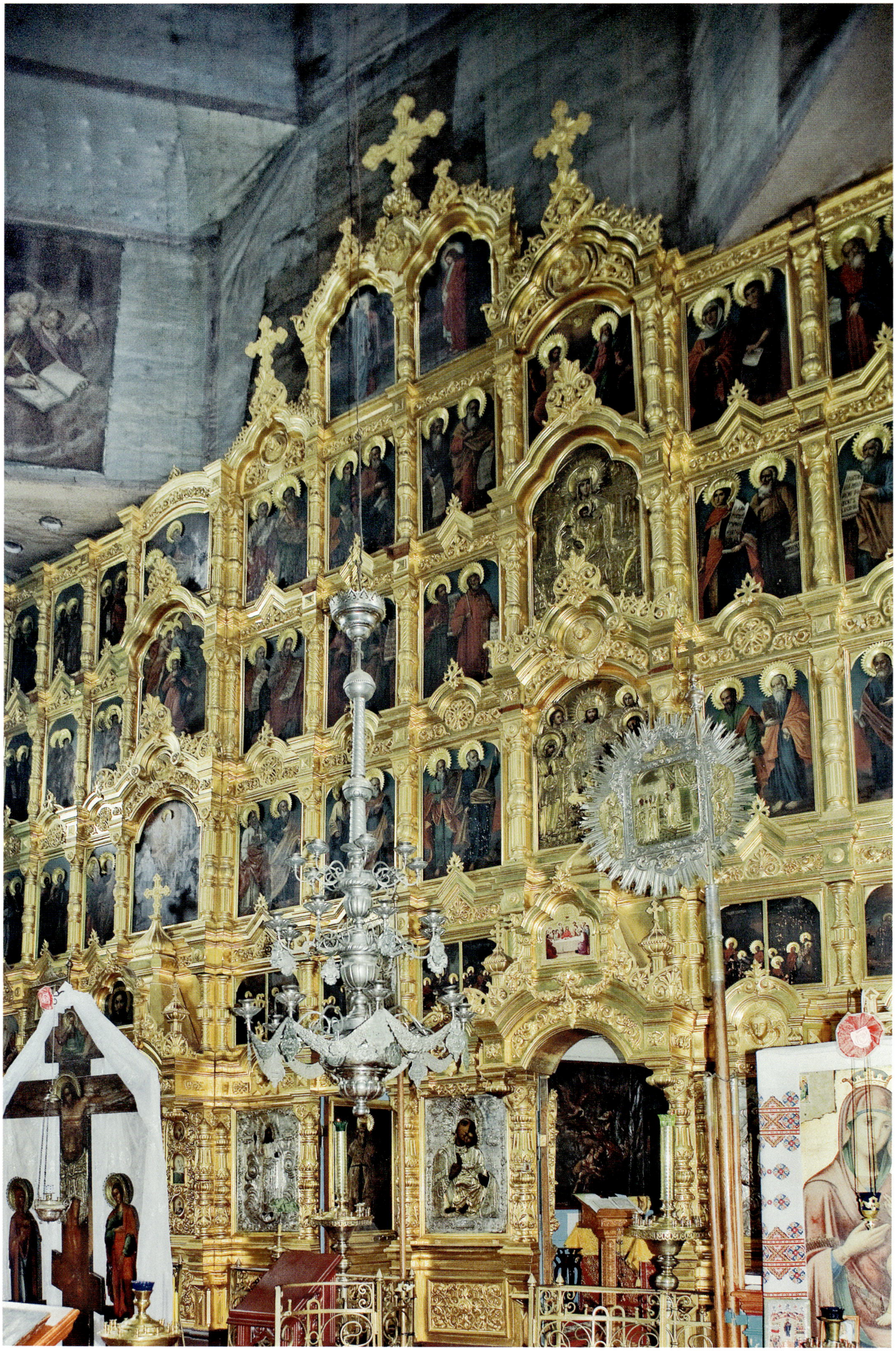

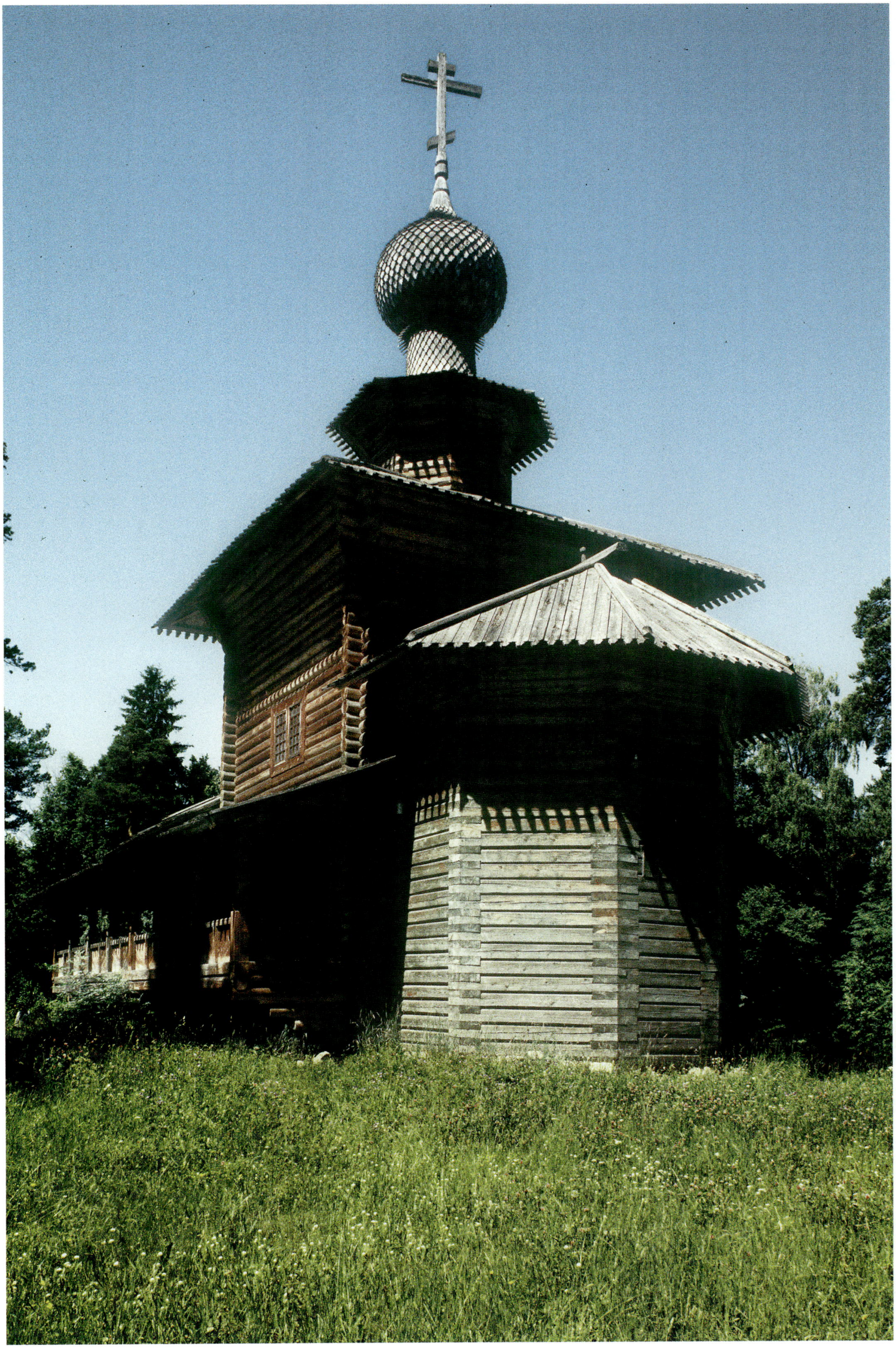

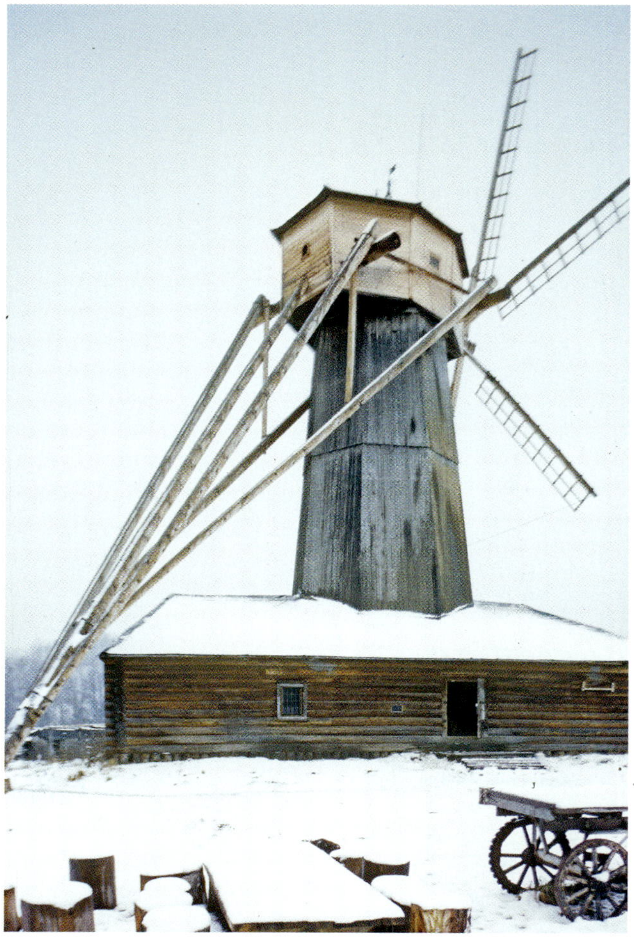

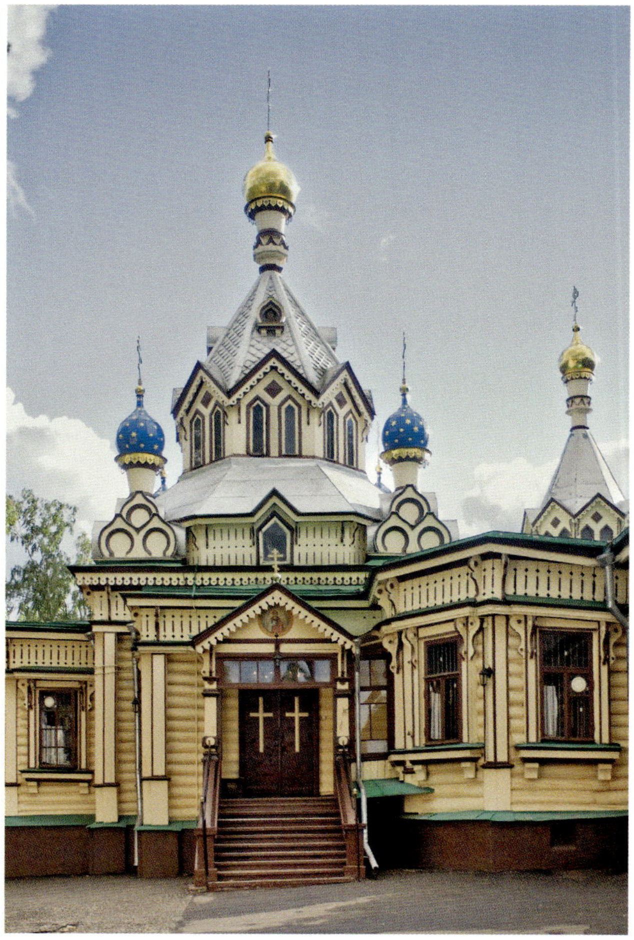

cap. Fully functioning as late as the 1950s, the windmill still has much of its original mechanism. I was fortunate to photograph this superb structure before its blades collapsed in August 2020.

One of the most appealing of Russia's provincial cities is Kolomna (population around 145,000), situated at the confluence of the Kolomenka and Moscow Rivers. Despite its proximity to Moscow, some one hundred kilometers to the north, Kolomna's rich cultural history has allowed it to maintain a distinctive identity. From the beginning of the fourteenth century Moscow's princes valued Kolomna as a strategic citadel guarding its southern border. Located near the point where the Moscow River flows into the Oka (the major western tributary of the Volga), Kolomna was traversed by trading routes from much of central Russia, thus creating the basis for an enduring merchant culture. In addition to its churches and bell towers, Kolomna has historic districts with houses from the nineteenth century, including wooden houses with ornate window surrounds. Some of the houses near the kremlin are associated with twentieth-century writers such as Boris Pilnyak and Anna Akhmatova.

ISTRA. Windmill built in late nineteenth century at village of Kochemlevo (Kashin District of Tver Province) and still functioning in 1950s. Superb example of a tower windmill with rotating cap. Brought to New Jerusalem outdoor museum in 1970s, periodically restored, but for lack of maintenance, its fate is uncertain. December 5, 2000.

UDELNAYA (Moscow region). Church of the Trinity, north view. Built in 1897 for a prosperous dacha community south of Moscow, the church shows fine detailing in the Russo-Byzantine style. Architect: Semyon Eibuschitz. August 30, 2014.

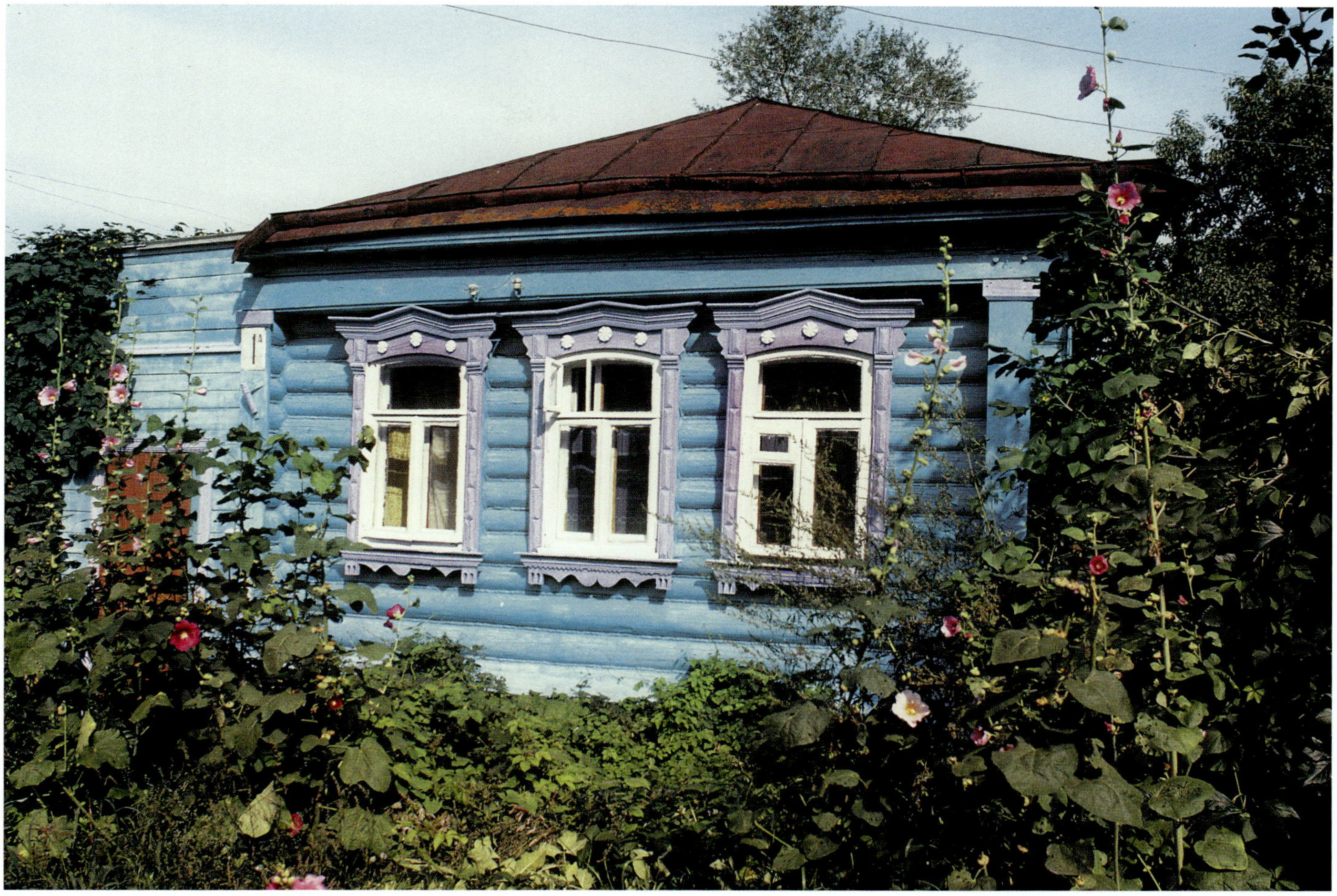

KOLOMNA. Log house, Moskvoretsky Lane 1A. Built in the late nineteenth century, this well-preserved urban house with original iron roof exemplifies the long-standing practice of painting log structures in bright colors with decorative window surrounds. August 20, 2003.

During the Soviet period new forms of wooden housing appeared, primarily for workers at the Kolomna Factory, founded in 1863 and subsequently a major producer of locomotives. Although the Kolomna Factory sponsored modern apartment blocks in the 1920s, many workers preferred to live in wooden houses with a small garden plot. Such houses continued to be built throughout the Soviet period. The most grievous blow to the wooden architecture of Kolomna occurred in 2005 with the overnight demolition of the large, festively decorated theater in Bobrovsky Park. Completed in 1899 with support of local industrial magnate Amand Struve (founder of the Kolomna Machine Factory) to provide entertainment for factory workers, this remarkable structure was demolished with the tacit acquiescence of the mayor's office, although public petitions had advocated for its preservation. In 2016 a loose replica was erected to house a kindergarten, an entirely different purpose.

To the northeast of Moscow, the main historical center is Vladimir. Whether the town was founded in 990 by Grand Prince Vladimir Svyatoslavich of Kiev or in 1108 by Vladimir Monomachus (also Grand Prince of

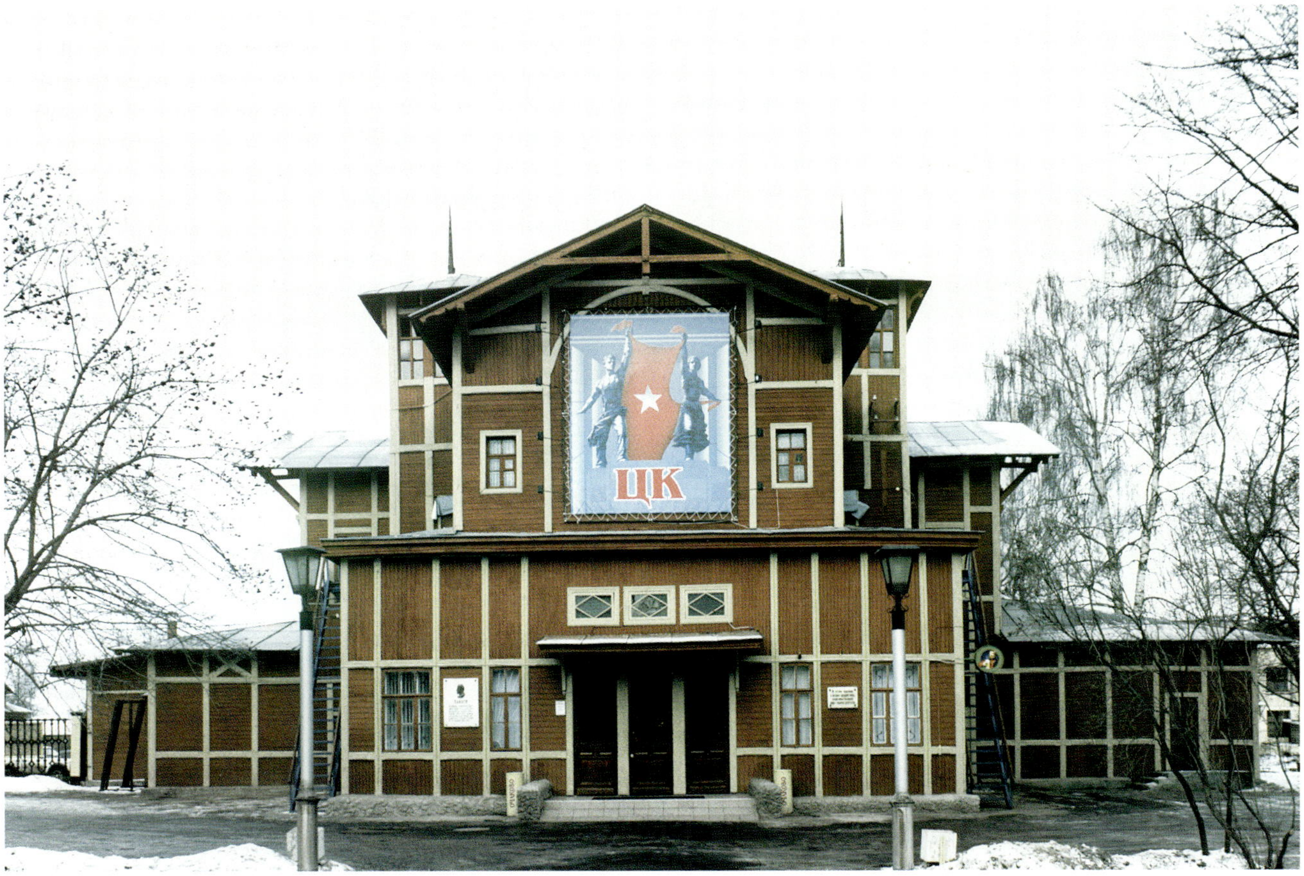
ЦК

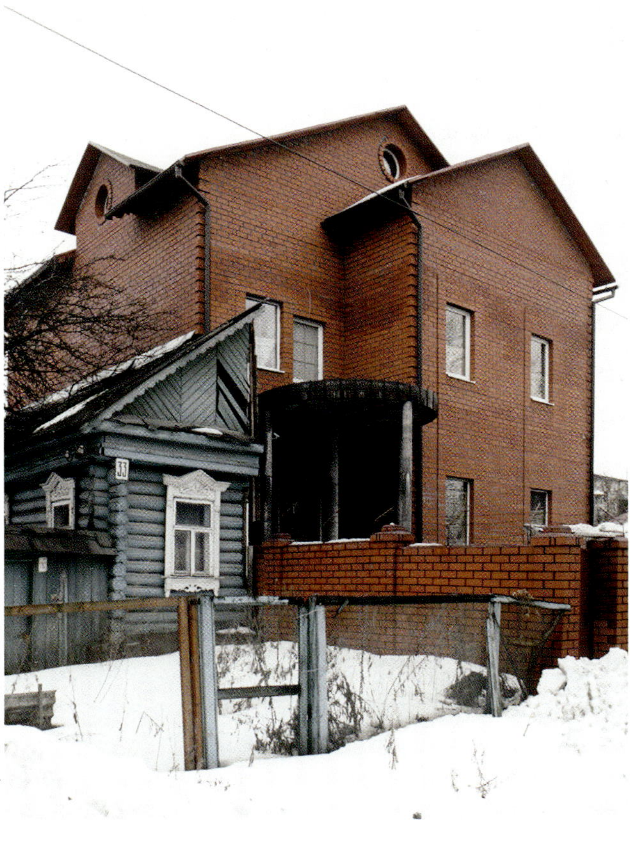
33

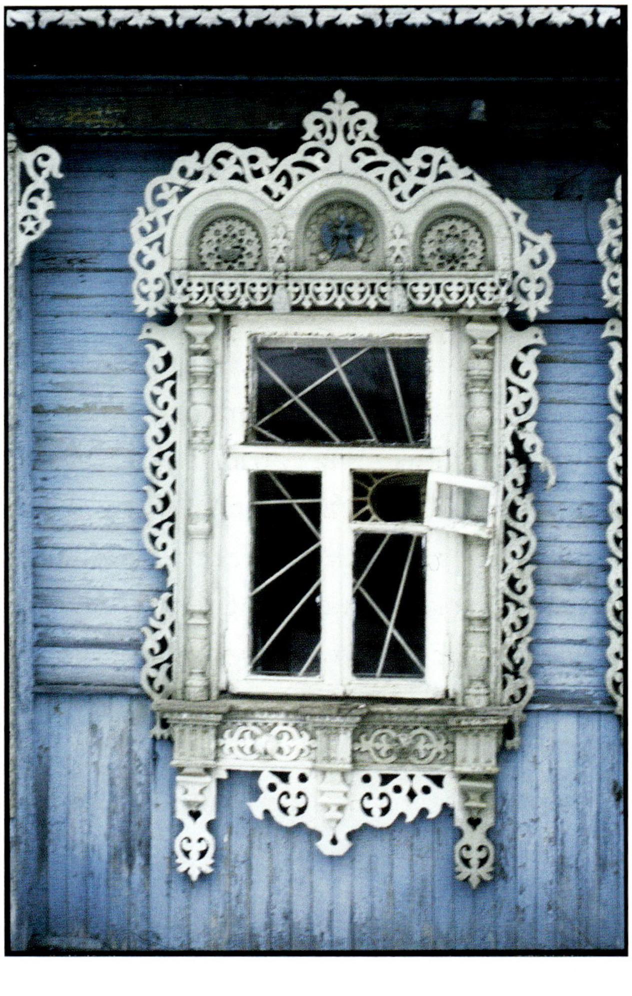

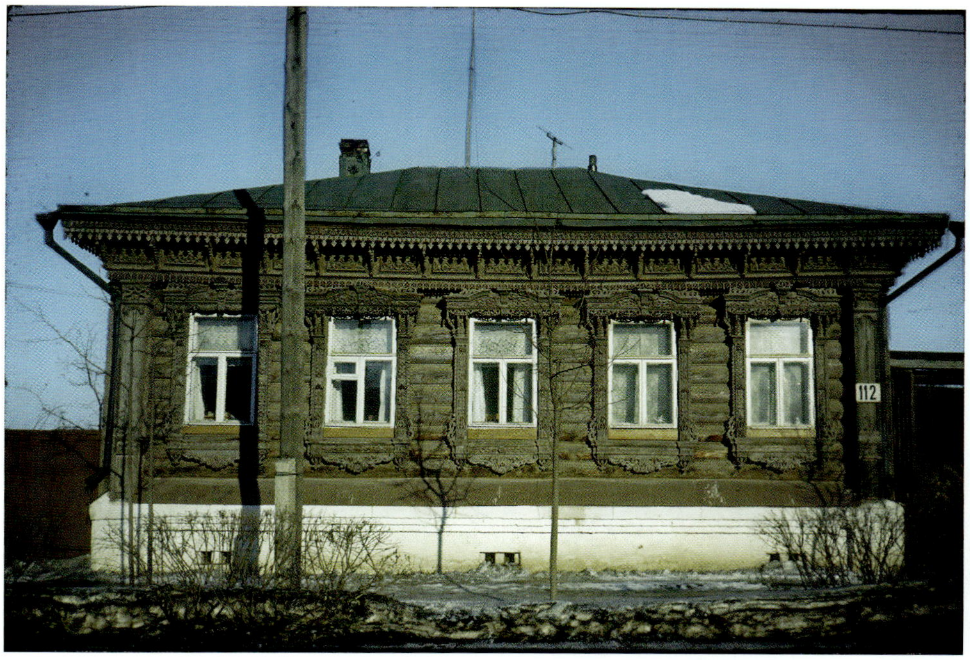

KOLOMNA. Theater in Bobrovsky Park. Completed in 1899, this festive structure was demolished by administrative fiat in 2005. December 28, 2003.

KOLOMNA. A house divided, Lenin Street 33. Half original wooden house and half new brick mansion. February 29, 2004.

KOLOMNA. House, Krasin Street 7. Built in first half of twentieth century, this log house has prefabricated siding and extravagant fretwork for the window surround. February 29, 2004.

VLADIMIR. House, Moskovskaya (?) Street 122. Exemplary urban log house, probably built at the turn of the twentieth century on a brick foundation with fretwork window surrounds and cornice, original iron roof. No trace remains. March 6, 1972.

Kiev) is a matter of historical debate, but by the twelfth century the town had become the political center of a fertile region of northeastern medieval Rus. Its turbulent history included devastation by the Mongol invasion in February 1238, but by the fourteenth century it entered the orbit of an expanding Muscovite state. By the end of the nineteenth century, Vladimir (current population 337,000) had become a rail and industrial center. As with other provincial towns, its habitat consisted largely of wooden houses, few of which have survived. The roads leading to Vladimir, however, are lined with wooden houses with festively painted window surrounds.

The wooden environment has been preserved to a much greater degree in the nearby small town of Suzdal (population around 9,200), which also claims one of the earliest and most frequently visited museums of wooden architecture in Russia. Situated on a rise across the small Kamenka River from the Nativity Cathedral compound and the Archbishop's Court, the museum park consists of two log churches, as well as log houses, barns, and windmills. This architectural heritage display rests on land formerly occupied by the Cave Monastery of Saint Demetrius of Thessaloniki, founded in the late eleventh century by monks from the Kiev Cave Monastery. The monastery was closed in 1764 as part of Catherine the Great's reorganization of the monastic system. Without a rail link and served by poor country roads, bucolic Suzdal and its ancient churches and monasteries existed as a neglected time capsule until the 1960s. During that

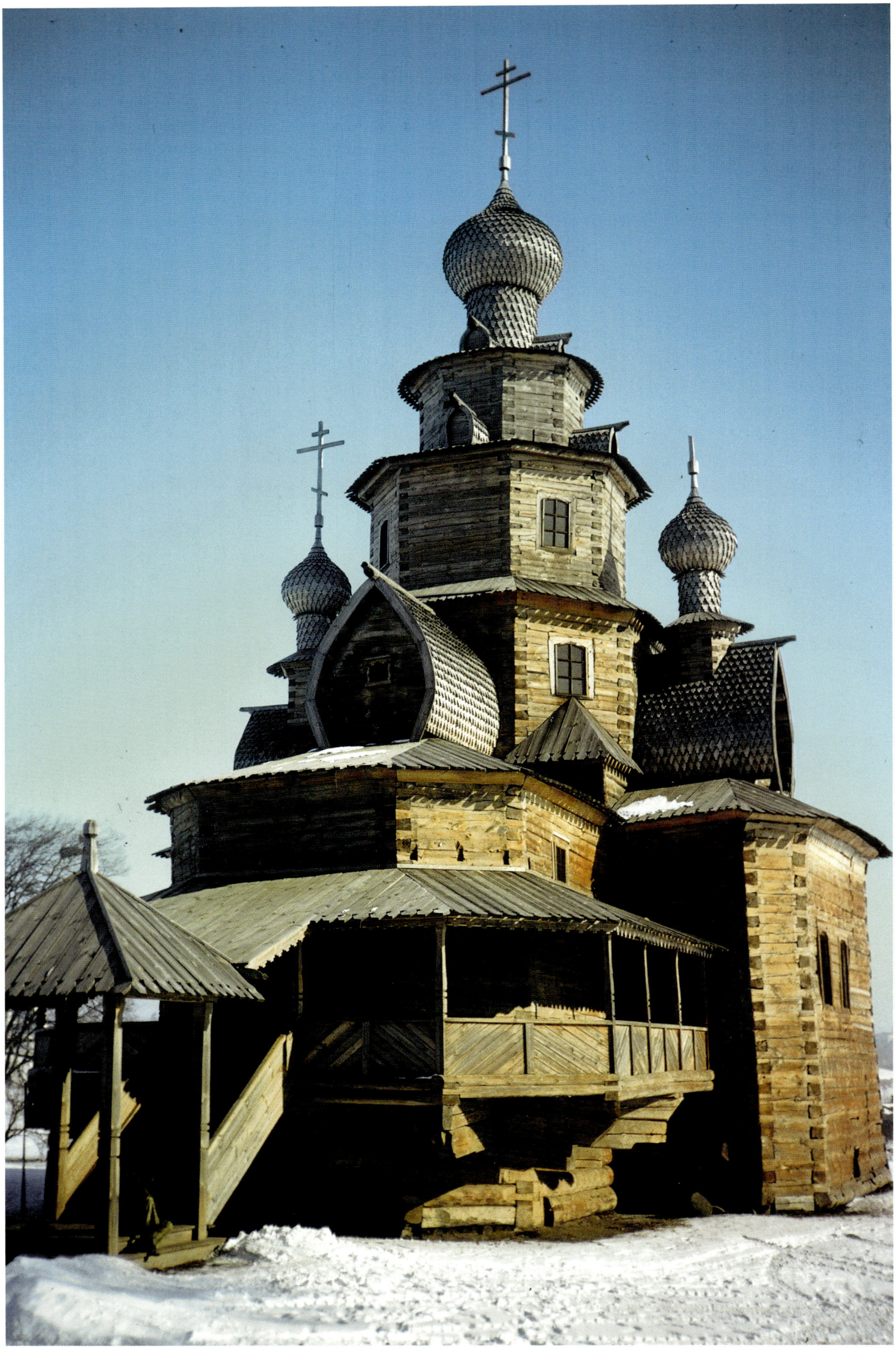

decade plans were formulated to convert this unique environment into a national preserve and a magnet for cultural tourism. In 1967 Suzdal was officially designated by the Soviet government as a historical heritage site.

An important component of this master plan, developed and supervised by Valery Anisimov, was the creation of a group of wooden structures brought from villages in the area surrounding Suzdal. The most imposing structure at the Suzdal museum of wooden architecture is the Church of the Transfiguration, built in 1756 at Kozlyatevo in what is now the Kolchugino District of Vladimir Province. The tower form of the Transfiguration Church consists of ascending octagonal tiers above a wide rectangular base structure. The roofs of the vestibule and the base structure are surmounted by barrel gables at the points of the compass, with an additional two over the apse on the east side for a total of six. The north and south barrel gables on the main roof support cupolas clad in aspen shingles. Each cupola is crowned with a wooden cross. The roofs of the upper tiers have their own diminutive gables, and the tower culminates in a wooden cupola with a tall cross.

The east side of the church is the most complex and contains not only the main altar, in the center, but also two side spaces for the sacraments and the clergy's vestments (known as the prothesis and the *diakonikon*). On the opposite side of the church a vestibule and raised entrance extend to the west of the base structure. The distinctive appearance of the Transfiguration Church derives from the form of its walls, which are built of squared logs tightly joined by a type of dovetail. (Usually, the logs are left in their round form joined with a simple notch.) It is possible that this form was required to support the bold vertical design of the tower. Every aspect of this tiered structure combines the functional with the aesthetic. On the interior the church has a white neoclassical icon screen with several surviving icons. The iconostasis ascends into the first octagonal tier of the tower and culminates with a gilded carving of Christ in Glory. In a highly unusual feature, the bare log surfaces of the octagonal tiers are adorned with large depictions of saints painted in oils in a naive style.

A short walk from the Transfiguration Church is the Church of the Resurrection from the village of Patakino (Kameshkovo District). This rustic structure was built in 1776 and served almost two centuries as a cemetery shrine. Although the design is simpler than the tower form of the Transfiguration Church, the Resurrection Church at Patakino has a visual richness of its own. The main structure of the Resurrection Church

SUZDAL. Church of the Transfiguration from the village of Kozlyatevo, southwest view. Built in 1756, the church was moved to the Suzdal outdoor museum in 1965. March 5, 1972.

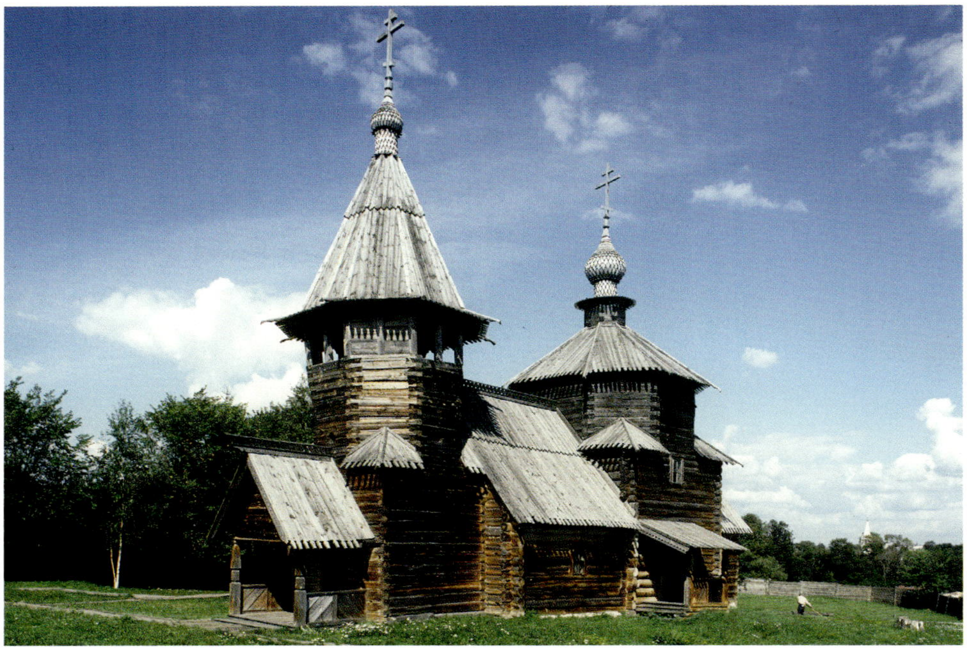

SUZDAL. Church of the Resurrection from the village of Patakino, southwest view. Built in 1776, the church was reconstructed at the Suzdal outdoor museum in 1970. August 4, 1995.

SUZDAL. Church of Saint Nicholas from the village of Glotovo, northwest view. May 23, 1996.

ascends from a cube to an octagonal top that culminates in a slanted roof with a small cupola and cross. On the east side is an elongated apse (containing the altar) with ornamental carving along the peak of the roof. The west side of the Resurrection Church has a vestibule that ends with a bell tower over the main entrance. This linear arrangement of components was typical of brick parish churches in the seventeenth and eighteenth centuries. Like the church from Kozlyatevo, the walls of this church were built of squared pine logs with dovetail joints. The interior has a preserved icon screen and is occasionally used for worship.

Around the two churches is a small collection of log houses reassembled at the museum. In typical Soviet practice, the houses were defined by the social strata of the peasants who inhabited them. They include a two-story house built by a "middle-status" peasant (*sredniak*) with an attic room and steep roof from the village of Log (Vyazniki District). Although the windows have simple shutters, the roof end boards are elaborately carved. On a rise at the top of the park are two tall windmills of pine logs from the village of Moshok (Sudogda District). The top of each mill rotates to catch the prevailing winds that power the grinding mechanism. Such village windmills would have belonged to prosperous peasants with the means to maintain the structure. The return path from the museum to the Suzdal kremlin crosses the Kamenka River near a row of small grain barns built at the turn of the nineteenth century at the village of Poltso (Murom

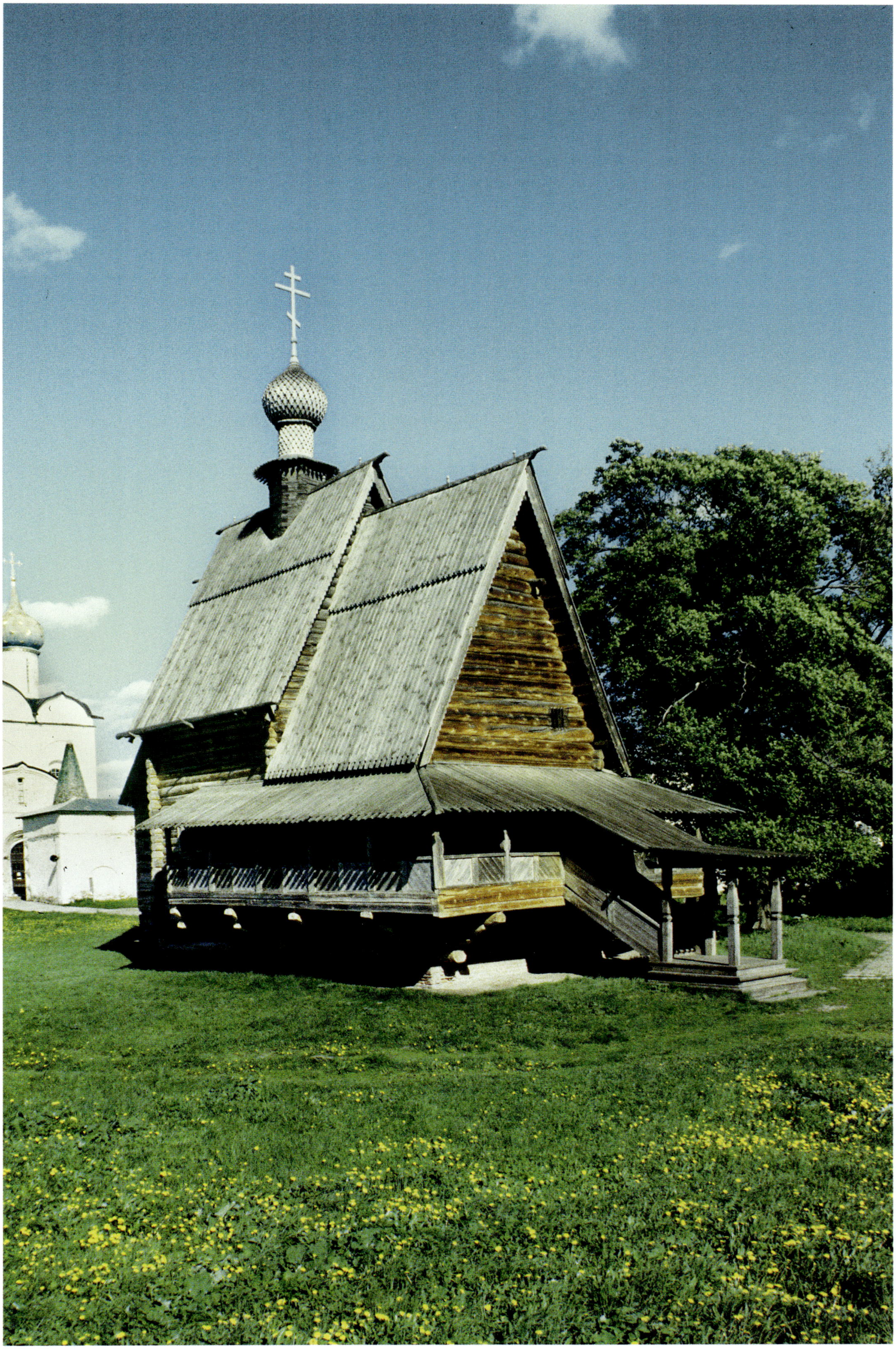

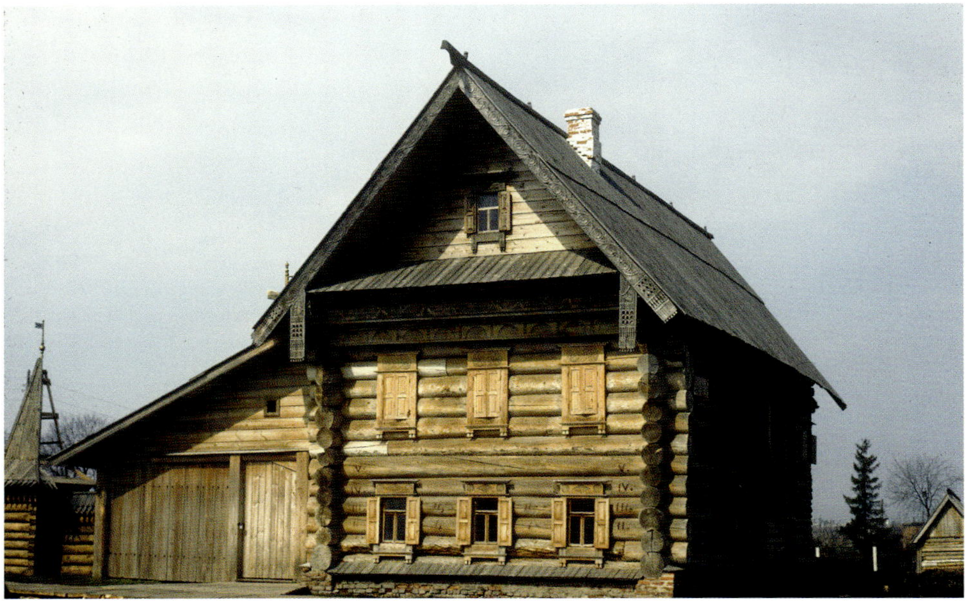

SUZDAL. House of "middle-status" peasant, built in nineteenth century in village of Log. April 27, 1980.

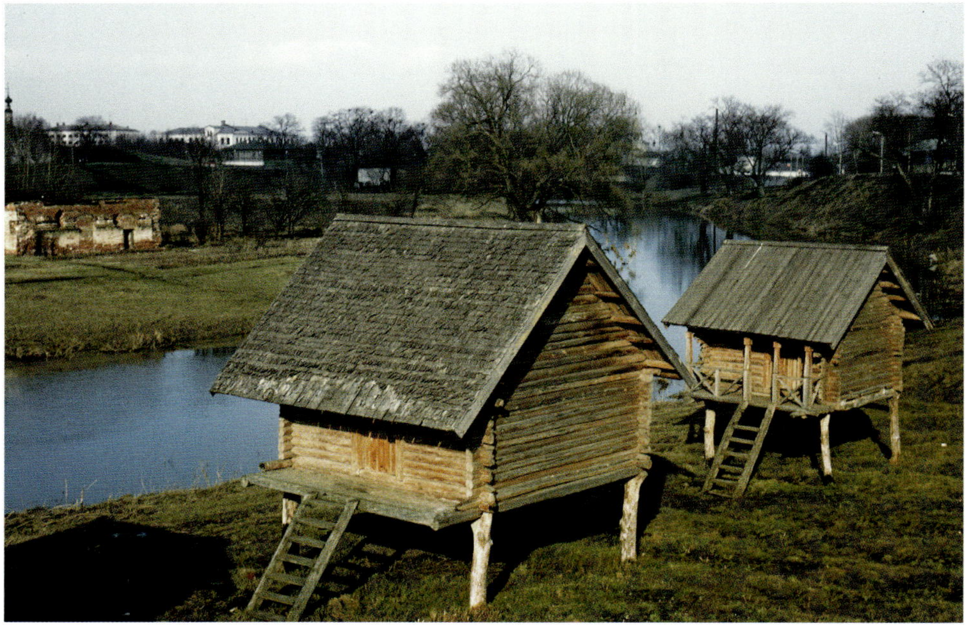

SUZDAL. Grain barns from Poltso village built on "hen's legs" to protect from spring floods. April 27, 1980.

region). Elevated on "hen's legs," such structures allowed easy access to the river and at the same time protected stored items from spring floods. This time-honored practice was attested by an archeological discovery of seventeenth-century piling remnants at the site.

The third wooden church on display at the Suzdal museum complex is located back across the Kamenka near the great Nativity Cathedral. Dedicated to Saint Nicholas, the small wooden church of simple design—a cuboid main structure with a pitched roof and single cupola—was built in 1766 at the village of Glotovo near Yurev-Polski. In 1960 the church was moved to Suzdal as the first example of traditional wooden architecture to be displayed at the future museum complex. The west side of the church is

SUZDAL. Windmill with rotating cap from Moshok village. Tentatively dated to the turn of the nineteenth century. June 18, 1994.

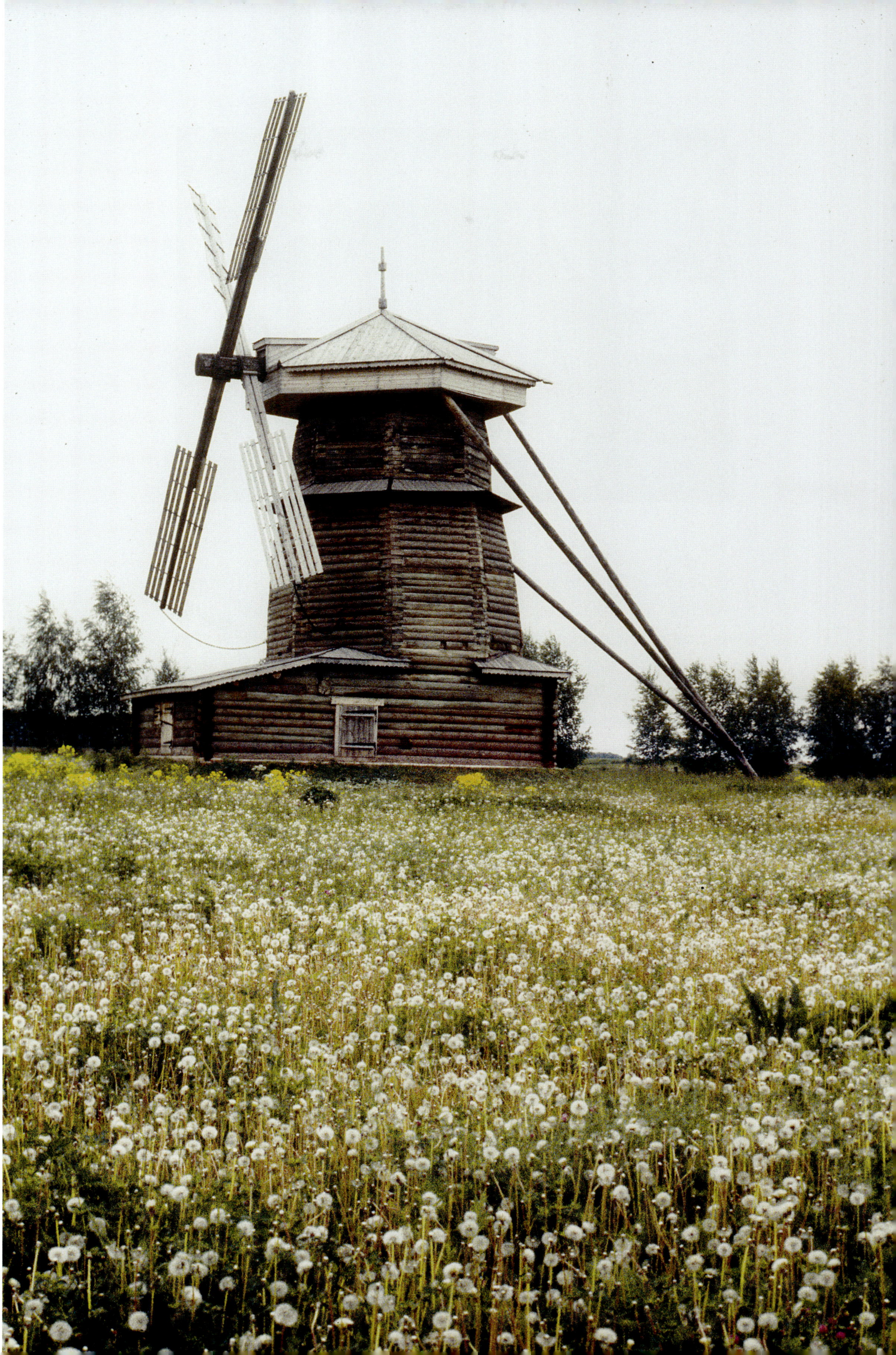

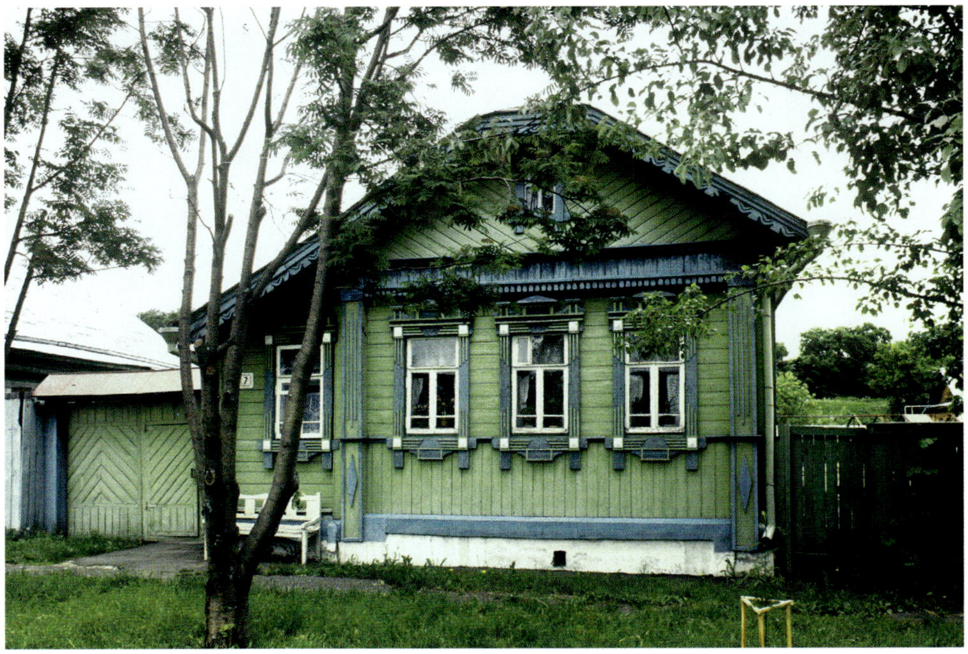

SUZDAL. Classic example of Soviet-era urban log house with painted siding, three windows, and courtyard gate. June 18, 1994.

clasped by an elevated enclosed gallery for protection against the winter elements. This gives the arresting impression of a structure floating in the landscape. Traditions of wooden architecture still exist in Suzdal, as seen from the many well-maintained wooden houses with decorative window surrounds. Most of the houses have plank siding typical for urbanized wooden houses, but others show log walls, and a few have revived an old practice of painting the logs in bright colors.

Near Suzdal is a smaller center of medieval culture, Yurev-Polski, founded in 1152 by Prince Yury Dolgoruky in an area of gently rolling fields and meadows that provide its name: Yury of the Fields. With the distribution of lands among Vsevolod III's sons in 1212, Yurev-Polski became the seat of a small principality under Sviatoslav (1196–1252). Within the settlement was the Monastery of the Archangel Michael, destroyed in 1238 during the Mongol invasion and revived in the mid-sixteenth century. Its territory was chosen in 1968 for a display of two small wooden churches: the Church of Saint George (early eighteenth century) from the village of Yegorye and the Church of the Intercession (1759) from Chernokulovo village. Both followed the simple, archaic form with a steeply pitched roof. Unfortunately, the latter church was destroyed by fire in 2001.

Beyond the Vladimir area and near the highway leading to Nizhny Novgorod is the small town of Gorokhovets (population slightly over 12,500), settled in the mid-twelfth century on the right bank of the Klyazma

River not far from its confluence with the Oka, which in turn flows into the Volga River at Nizhny Novgorod. This river network played a role in the prosperity of Gorokhovets, and the river basin also provided fertile land that produced an array of garden foods. The name of the town is derived from the word for pea (*gorokh*), and in 1781 the town was granted a coat of arms with a lower half consisting of five green pea vines supported by stakes on a yellow background. By the mid-seventeenth century, major

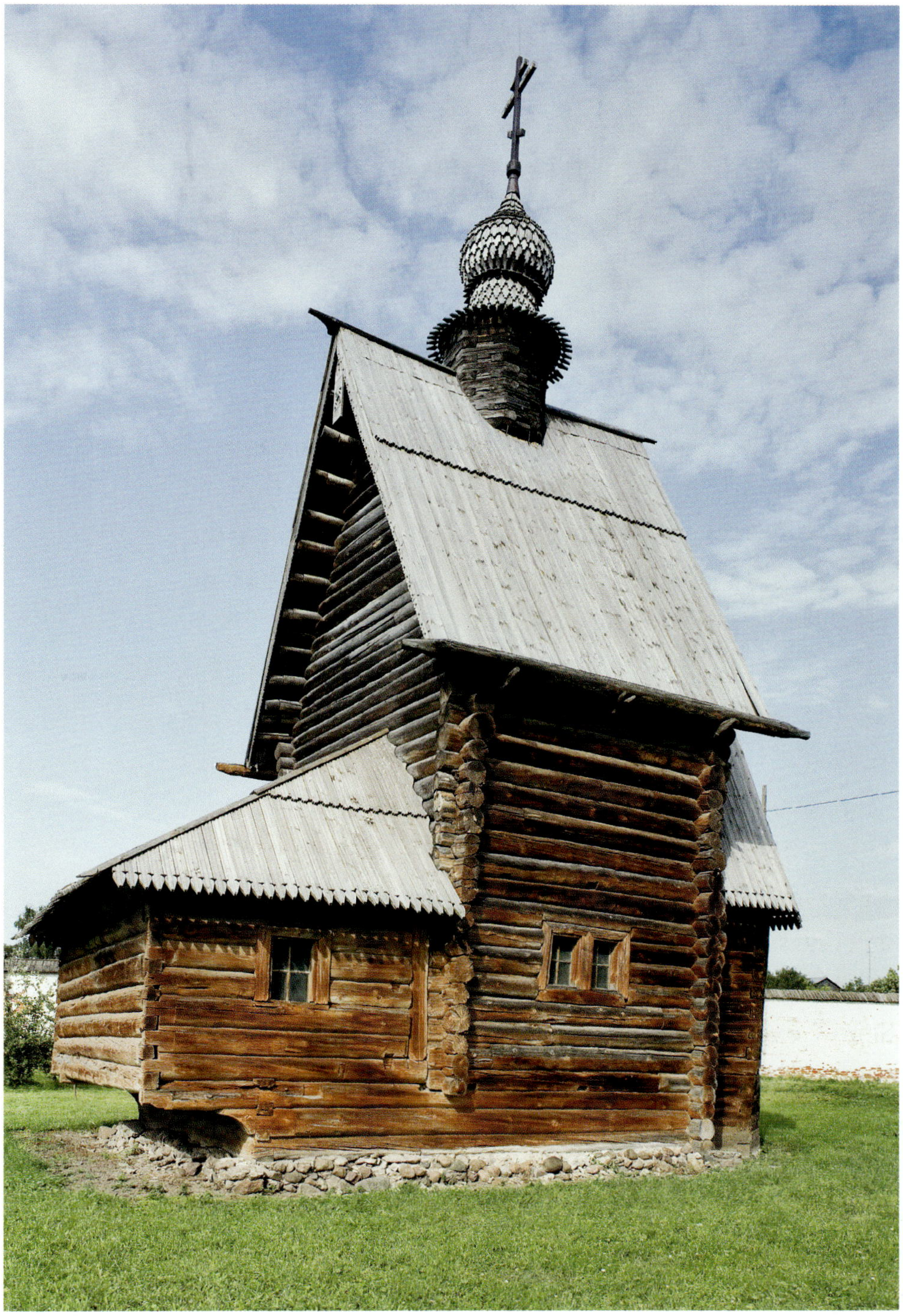

YUREV-POLSKI. Church of Saint George from Yegorye village, southwest view. Rebuilt at Monastery of Archangel Michael. August 21, 2013.

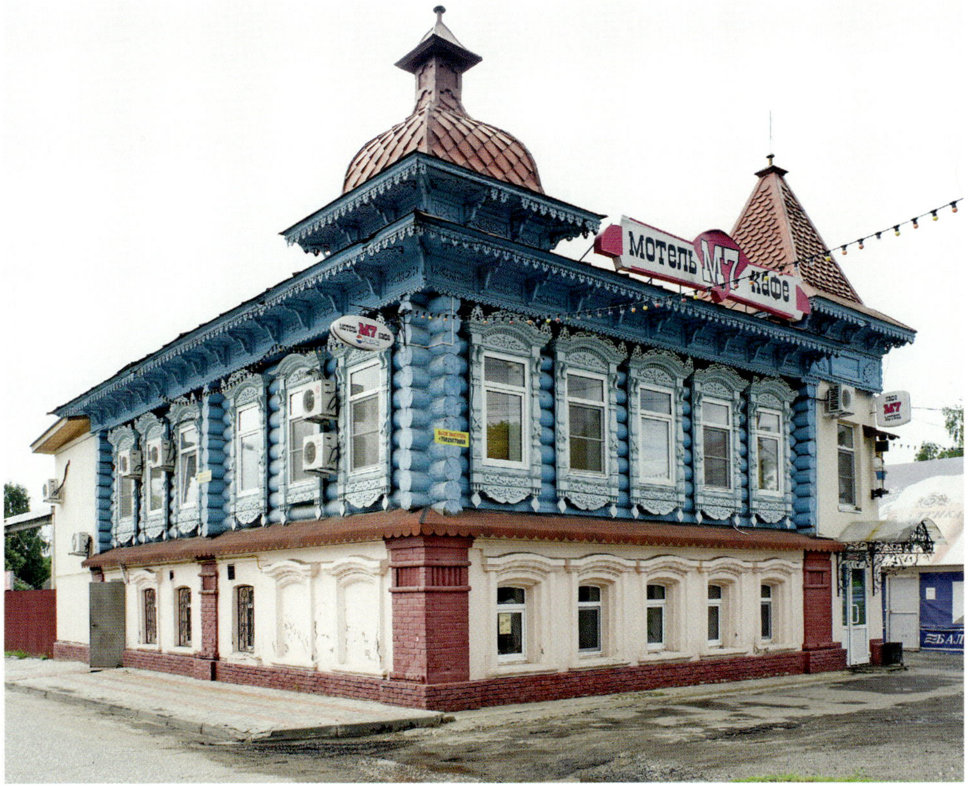

GOROKHOVETS. House in Russian Revival style built on a brick base for the merchant Kuchin at the end of the nineteenth century. July 10, 2011.

trade fairs along the Volga River near Nizhny Novgorod provided stimulus to local crafts—in particular leather working—and the bounty of the land provided produce to sell. During the late seventeenth and early eighteenth centuries, the trade of local merchants supported the building of white-washed churches, bell towers, and monasteries that still grace the town's verdant landscape. Although Gorokhovets began manufacturing cloth in the late eighteenth century, it never became a major textile producer. In 1875 the railroad from Moscow to Nizhny Novgorod passed the town by, but mercantile activity at the turn of the twentieth century was sufficient to support the construction of large wooden houses built for merchants, with flamboyant decorative details in a provincial art nouveau style.

The more northeasterly path from Moscow to Yaroslavl on the Volga River became an important pilgrimage and trade route passing through the town of Pereslavl-Zalessky (population slightly under 38,000). Nestled between bluffs overlooking Lake Pleshcheyevo, the settlement was founded in 1152 by Grand Prince Yury Dolgoruky and consisted of wooden structures surrounding a few notable masonry churches and monasteries. The approaches to town are still lined with small wooden houses that were built to urbanized designs in the Soviet era and decorated with painted, fretwork window surrounds.

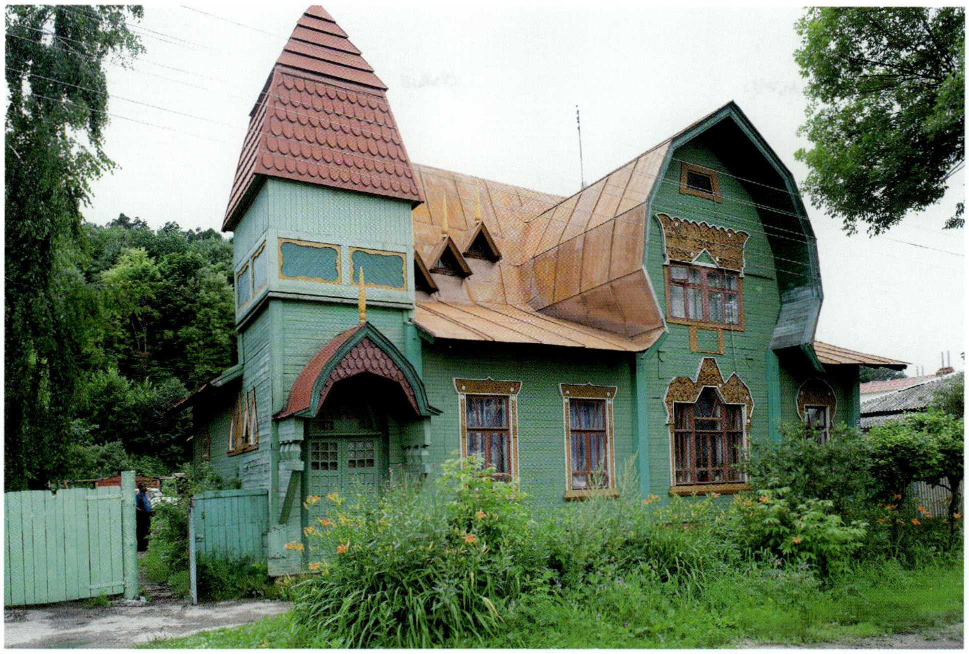

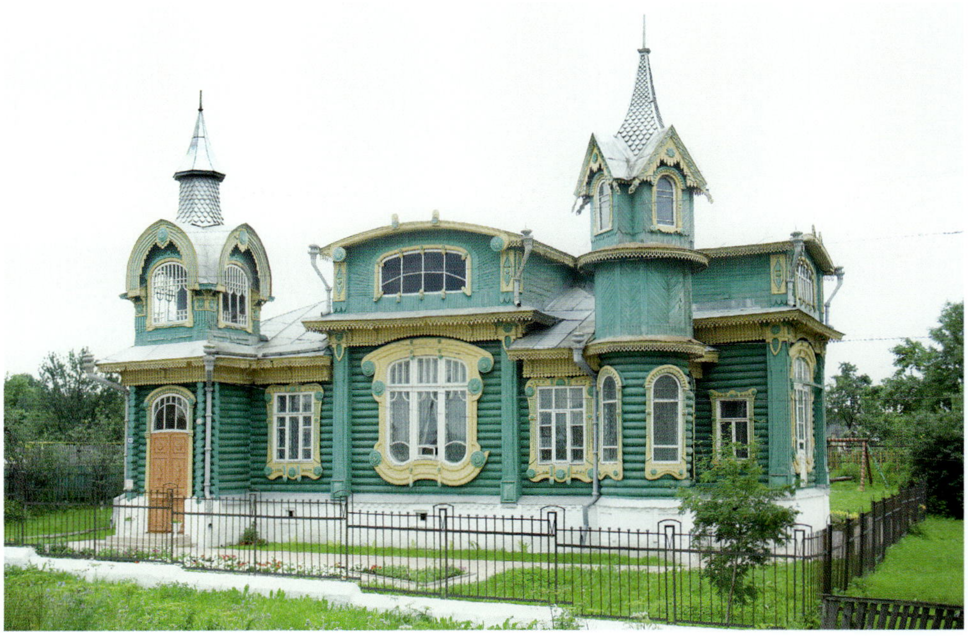

GOROKHOVETS. *Style moderne* house built in 1915 for Fyodor Prishletsov, president of the local government (*zemskaia uprava*). July 10, 2011.

GOROKHOVETS. *Style moderne* house built around 1911 for wealthy industrialist Ivan Shorin. July 10, 2011.

Similar wooden dwellings surround Rostov the Great (population 28,000; not to be confused with the southern city of Rostov-on-Don). Located beyond Pereslavl-Zalessky some 130 miles northeast of Moscow, Rostov is first referred to in twelfth-century chronicles under the year 862, thus making it one of the earliest historically attested settlements in Kievan Rus. The height of its architectural glory occurred in the late seventeenth century with the creation of the magnificent Metropolitan's Court, but thereafter the town's significance waned, and by the early twentieth

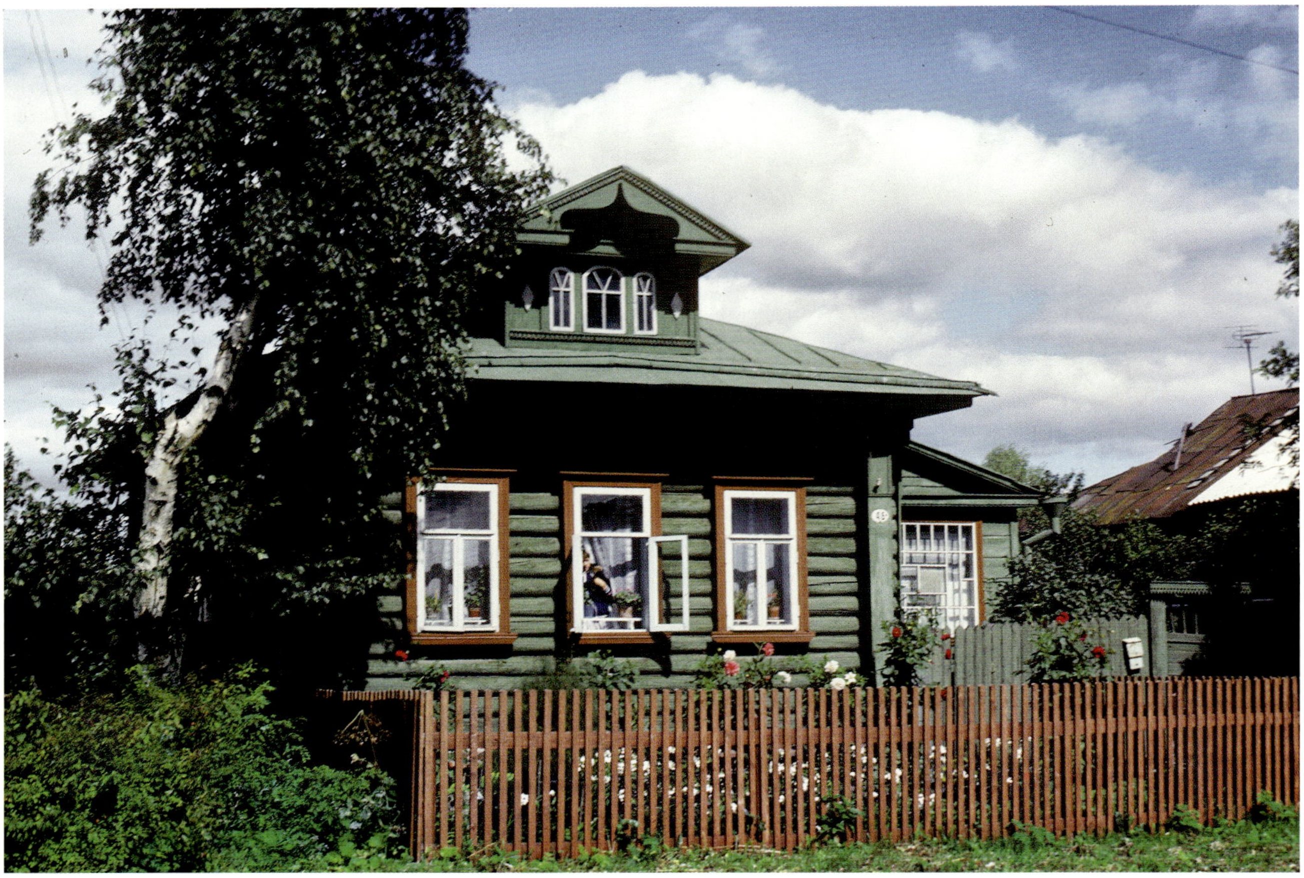

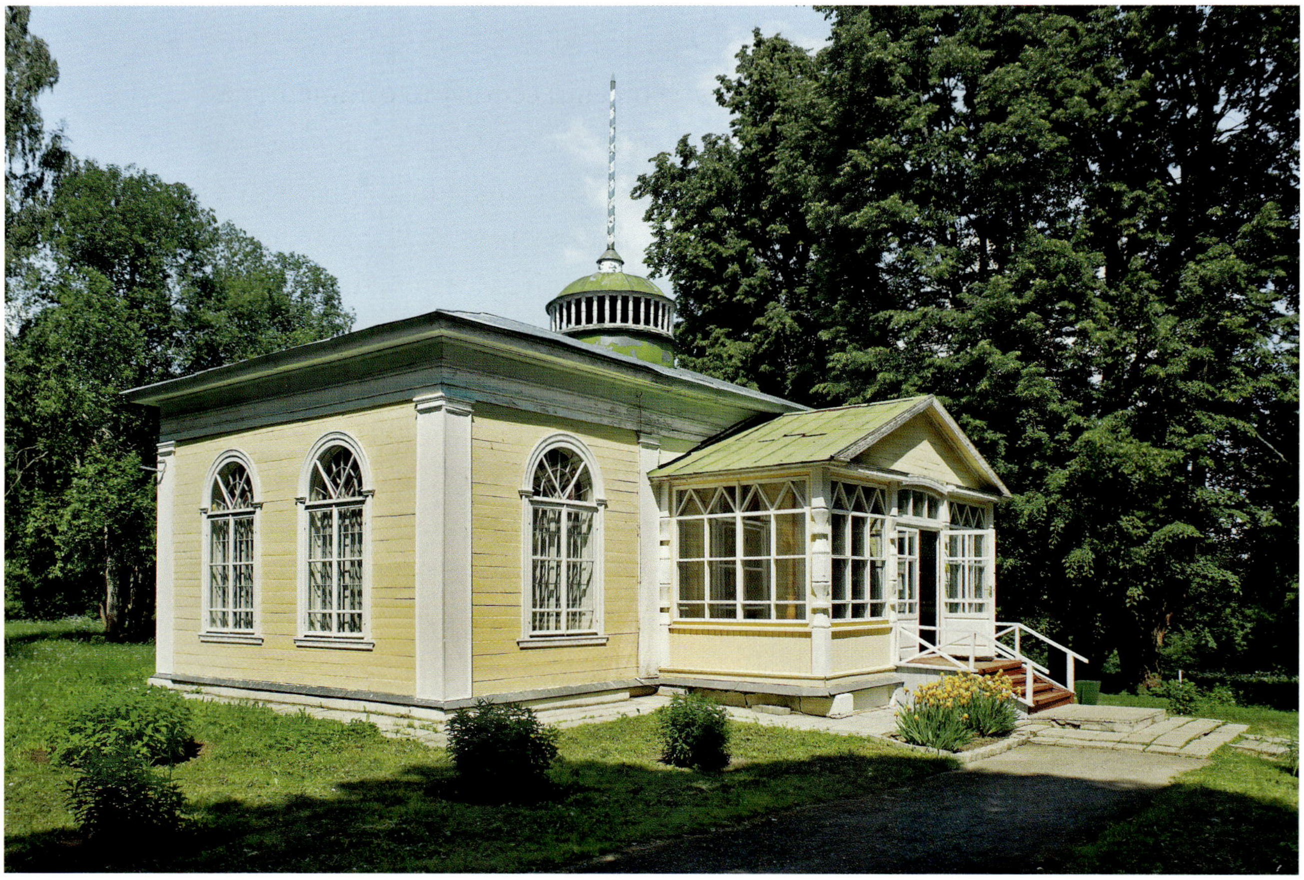

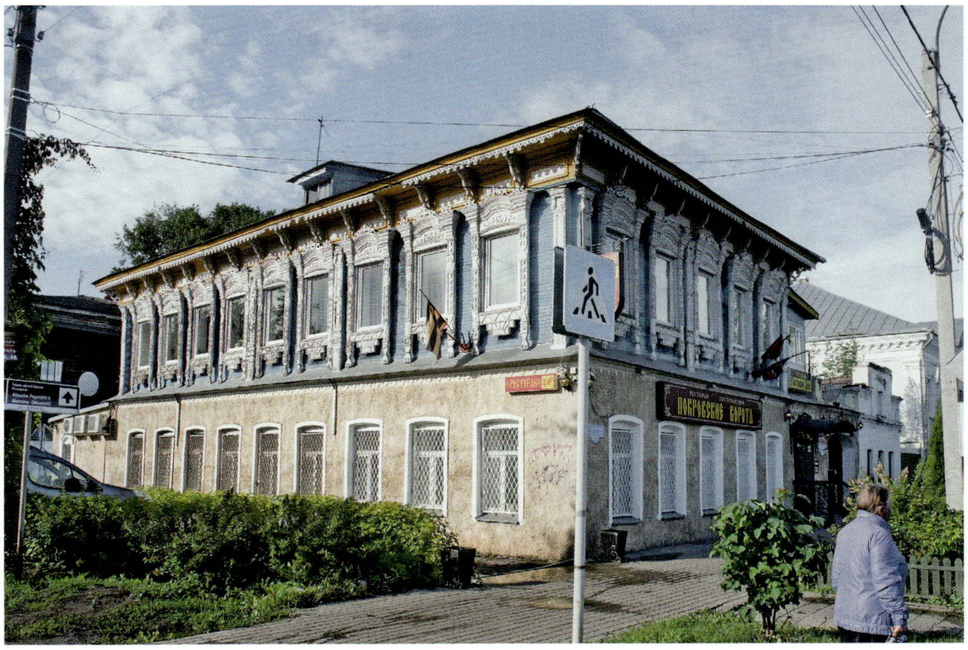

PERESLAVL-ZALESSKY. Standard Soviet-era painted log house with small *mezonin*. Such houses lined the approaches to provincial Russian towns. August 21, 1988.

VESKOVO (Pereslavl-Zalessky). Rotunda Pavilion, built overlooking Lake Pleshcheyevo in 1852 as a social center for the nobility on the occasion of the dedication of an obelisk to Peter I (the Great). The site is associated with Peter's early attempts to create a Russian fleet. June 7, 2019.

ROSTOV. Nineteenth-century commercial building, Lenin Street 28/18. Brick ground floor supports wooden upper floor with decorative window surrounds. July 6, 2019.

century, its modest economic role existed in the shadow of monuments created centuries earlier. Its wooden houses—few of which survive—reflect a provincial merchant style.

The area's main monument of wooden architecture is the Church of Saint John the Divine (in Russian "Bogoslov") at the village of Bogoslov, located at the western outskirts of Rostov near the small Ishnya River. The structure was built in the late seventeenth century to commemorate a vision of Saint John that had appeared to Saint Avraamy of Rostov centuries earlier. There is a divergence of opinion concerning the identity of Avraamy as well as the dates of his life. According to accounts of his life authorized by the church, his missionary activity occurred during the decades following the Christianization of Kievan Rus in 988. He eventually made his way to the settlement of Rostov and built a hut on the south shore of Lake Nero. At that time the local population consisted of a mixture of Finno-Ugric peoples who worshiped pagan gods. According to popular accounts, an awe-inspiring stone idol of the god Veles stood near Lake Nero and was widely venerated. Beset by the daunting task of countering the idol's power, Avraamy had a vision of Saint John, who gave him a miraculous staff crowned with a cross. With the staff Avraamy was empowered to overthrow the stone idol and convert its worshippers to the Christian faith.

The church that exists today was constructed in 1687–89 by Gerasim, archimandrite (abbot) of the Saint Avraamy-Epiphany Monastery. The

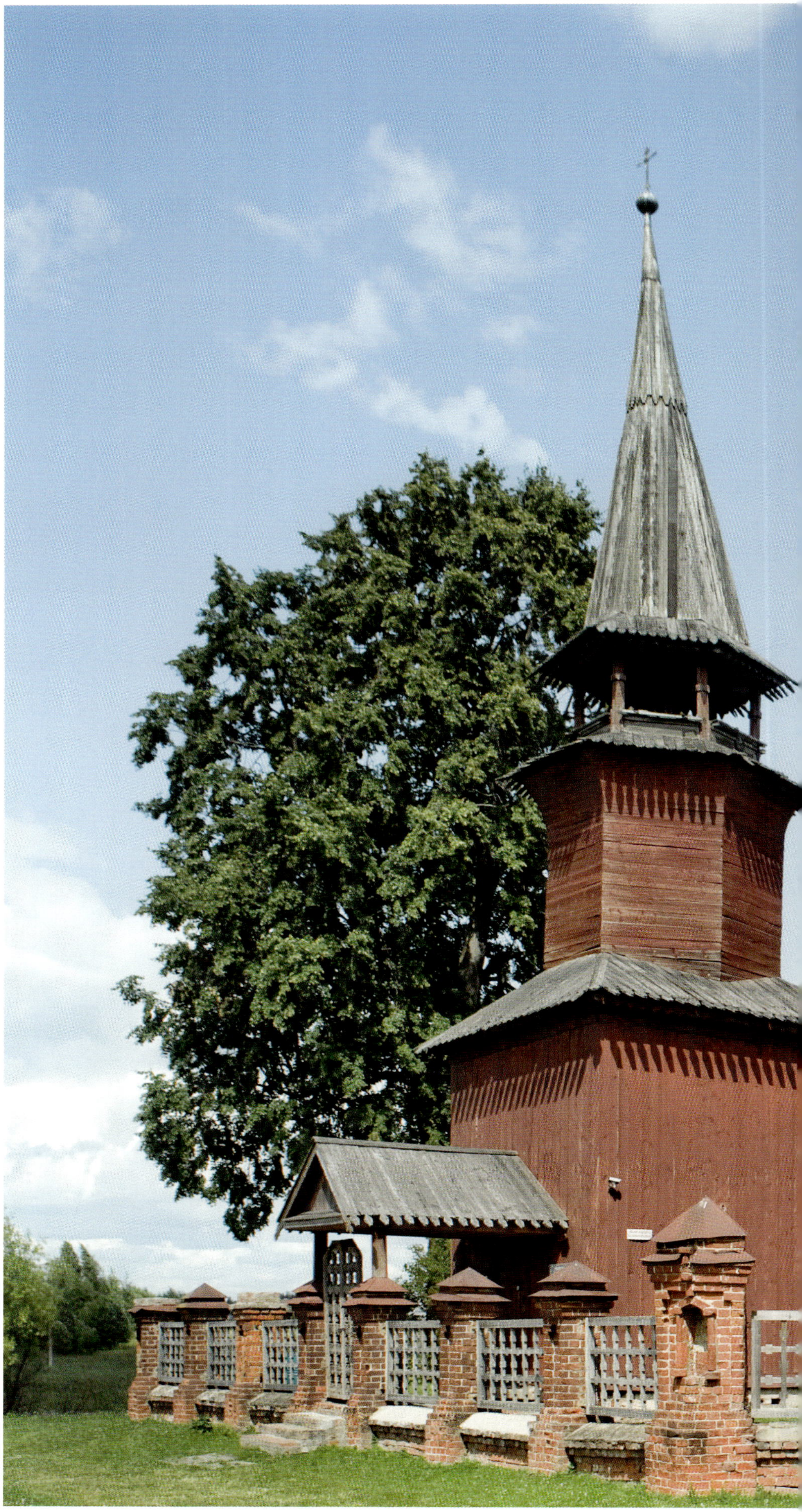

BOGOSLOV (near Rostov). Church of Saint John the Divine on the Ishnya, southwest view. July 8, 2019.

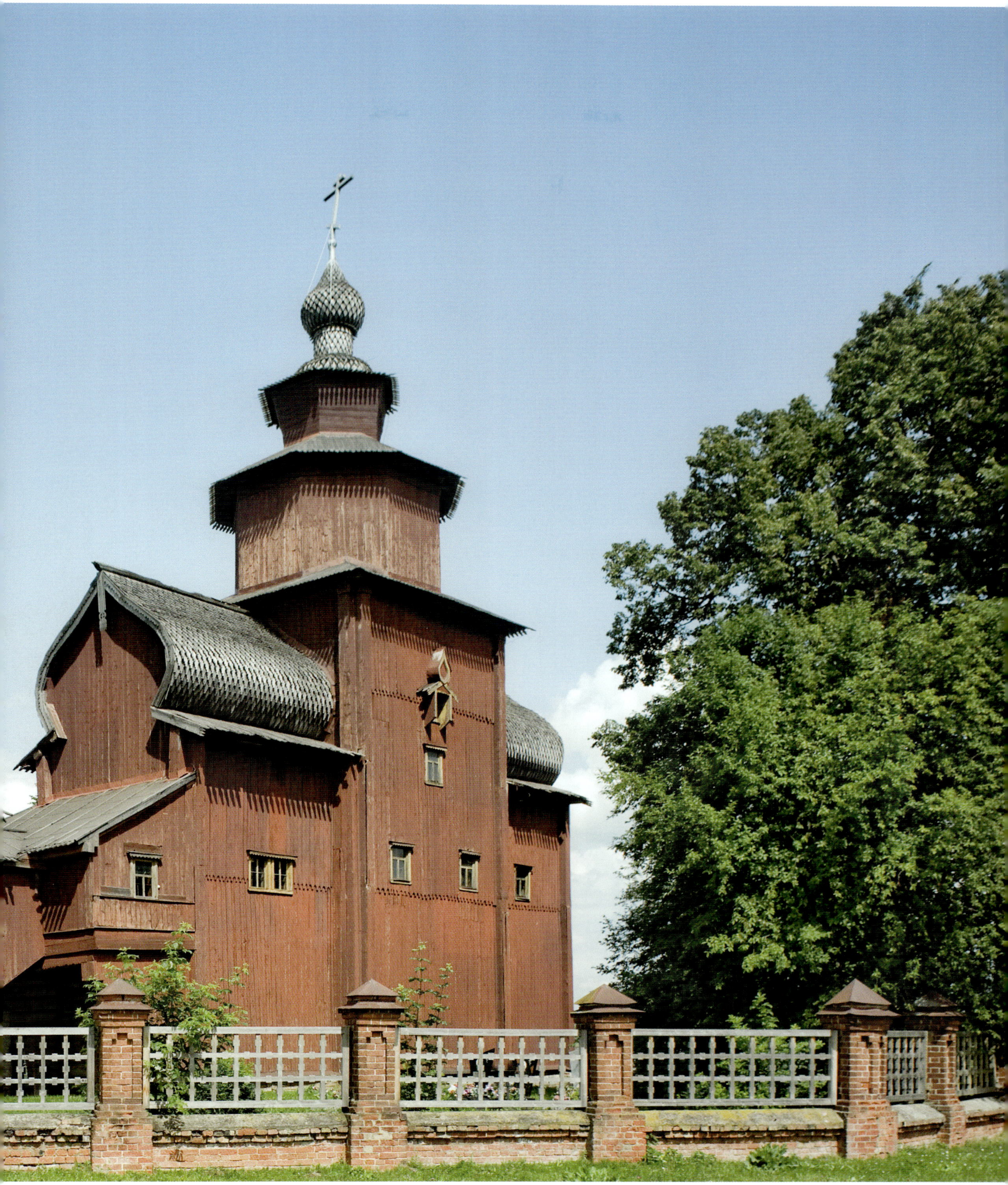

main structure ascends in an unusual sequence from a tall square base to an octagonal tier that supports a small hexagonal tier crowned with a cupola. The central core is buttressed by two extensions. The one on the east contains the apse with the altar, while the west extension serves as a vestibule. The extensions culminate in magnificent barrel (*bochka*) gables roofed with aspen shingles. Because of difficulties in maintaining the carved shingles, the upper part of the gable was protected with a plank roof. In a manner typical of such tiered churches, the main level was elevated some three meters from the ground, well above winter snow drifts. The west facade was marked by a covered stairway to the galleries and vestibule. The north and south sides were flanked by enclosed galleries supported on cantilevered log courses. Repairs in 1894 led to the removal of the south gallery because of its dilapidated state. The north gallery was preserved and braced by a brick pillar. The log walls were covered with plank siding and painted dark red during this period. The present hexagonal bell tower was added in the early nineteenth century.

On the interior the primary artifact was the Royal Gate, which served as the main entrance to the altar through the icon screen. This elaborately carved creation was originally made in 1562 by the monk Isaiah at the Saint Avraamy Epiphany Monastery. With the rebuilding of the Church of Saint John on the Ishnya, the splendid Royal Gate was offered by the monastery as the center of the church icon screen. In the late nineteenth century, the original was recognized for its superb craftsmanship and moved to the

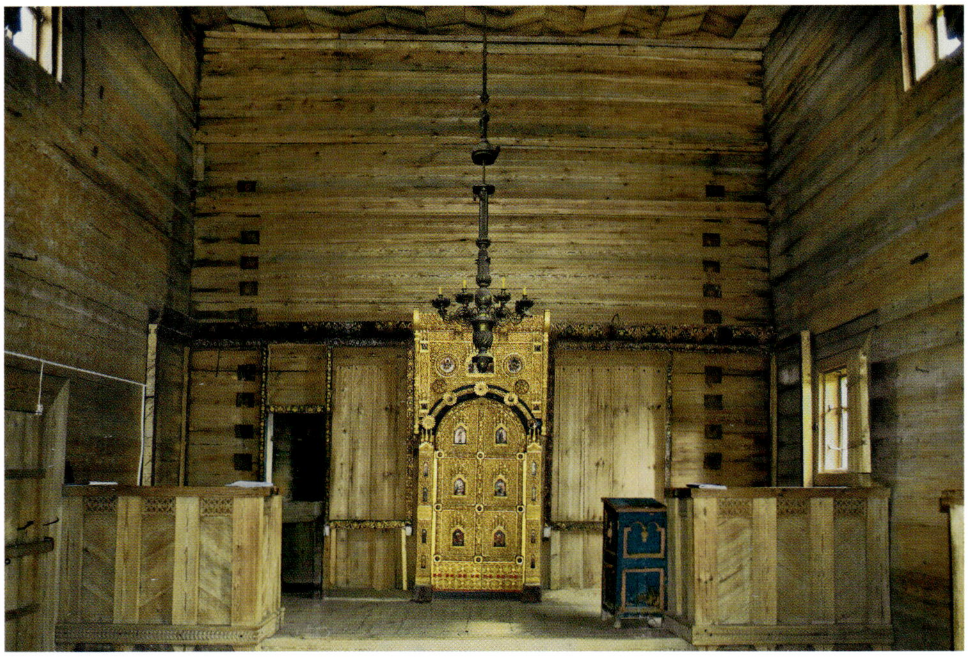

BOGOSLOV. Church of Saint John the Divine on the Ishnya, interior with late nineteenth-century reproduction of sixteenth-century Royal Gate of icon screen. July 8, 2019.

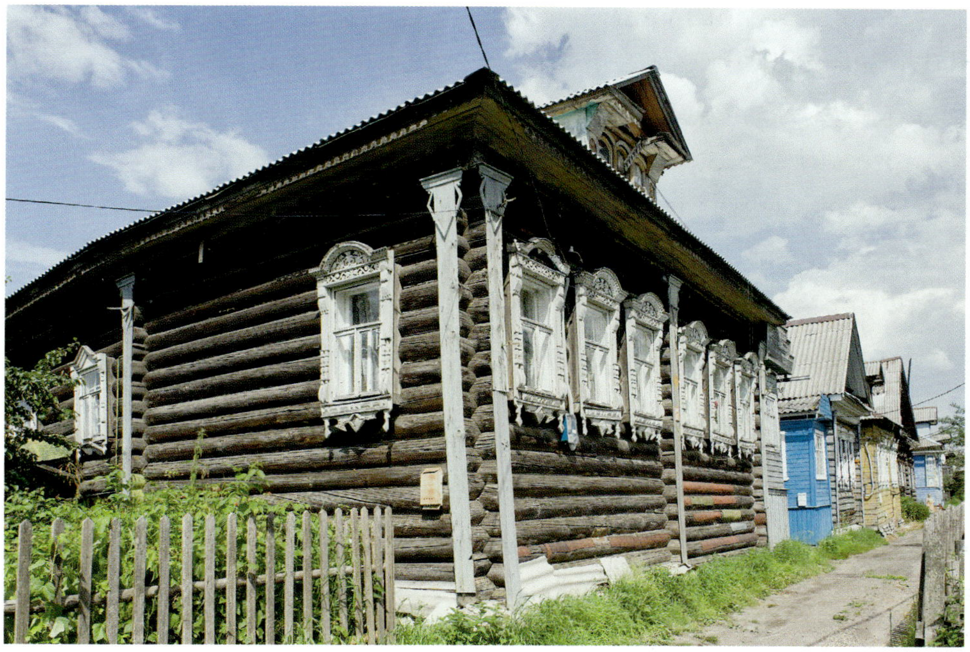

SULOST (Ivanovo Province). Well-maintained example of large village house built in early twentieth century. Freshly painted window surrounds form effective contrast to the dark log walls. July 12, 2012.

newly established Rostov Kremlin Museum, where it can be seen to this day. A reproduction of the carved artifact was placed in the church on the Ishnya before a visit by Emperor Nicholas II and his family during their brief stay in Rostov in late May 1913.

South toward the Don

The area south of Moscow was a route for invasion and raids from the thirteenth through the seventeenth centuries, and a line of defensive settlements, known as *zasechnaia cherta*, subsequently became provincial centers. To the southwest is Kaluga (current population around 330,000), whose beauty, enhanced by its location on tree-lined hills overlooking the Oka River, impressed nineteenth-century visitors. From the fourteenth century Kaluga served as fortress, and during the fifteenth and sixteenth centuries it became an important link in the *zasechnaia cherta*. During the latter part of the eighteenth century, Kaluga benefited from Catherine the Great's initiative to bring clarity and functional logic to the design of provincial Russian towns. The new plan for Kaluga was formulated in 1778 by Peter Nikitin, who also oversaw much of the construction. By the mid-nineteenth century, however, the town's commercial significance declined along with the decline of the Oka River as a transportation artery. The coming of the railway, in 1874, did little to reverse Kaluga's competitive

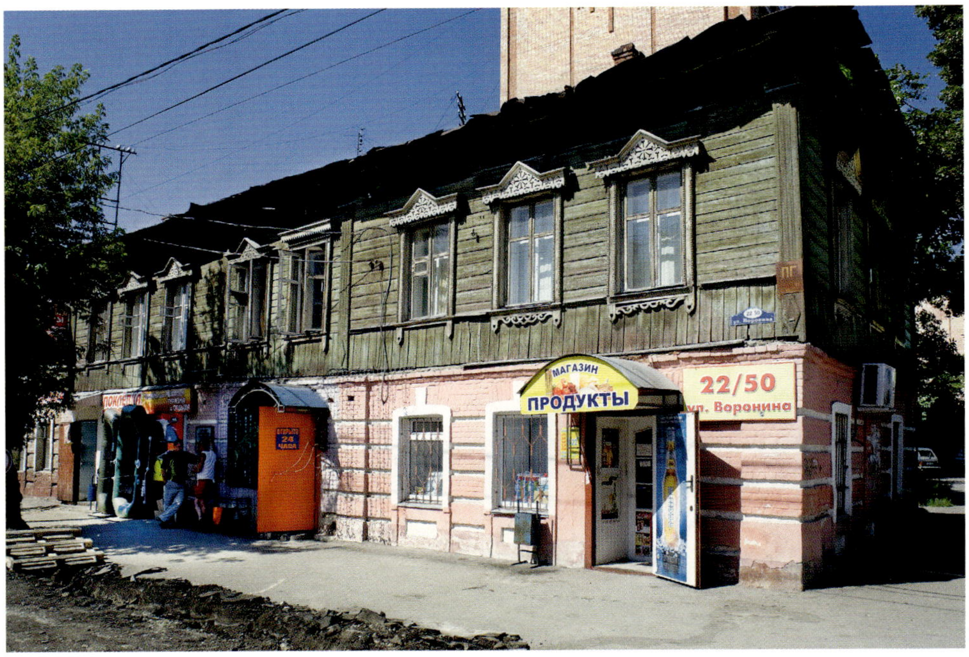

KALUGA. Nineteenth-century commercial building, Voronin Street 22/50. A mix of beauty parlors, barber shops, and auto parts. The windows have been replaced, but the iron roof is still there. July 17, 2010.

torpor. Most of its housing stock in the first half of the twentieth century still consisted of log structures, but with a few notable exceptions, the decline of these houses seems irreversible.

No Russian city is more defined by what it makes than Tula—samovars, gingerbread, and guns. Located about two hundred kilometers south of Moscow, Tula has some half a million inhabitants. Beginning in the seventeenth century, Tula became a center of metal working and armaments production, as small operations drawn from local iron deposits coalesced into larger units. For the public, however, Tula is associated with samovars, a type of enclosed urn—usually of copper or bronze—for heating water and brewing tea. The first documented production of samovars began in the 1770s at a family workshop belonging to Fyodor Lisitsyn, a worker at the Tula armory, and by the nineteenth century Tula samovars from several factories were sold throughout Russia. At the beginning of the twentieth century Tula had eight thousand wooden houses, and even in the middle of the twentieth century much of Tula's wooden housing stock was built before the First World War. A small fraction remains, particularly in a neighborhood known as Zarechye, an area of charming, diminutive, urbanized structures with modestly decorated shutters, built for factory workers. Often lacking conveniences, they sink into weed-clotted lots.

Among the ancient cities in the Russian heartland, few have endured a more turbulent history than Ryazan, located 180 kilometers southeast of Moscow, currently with a population of slightly over half a million. Already

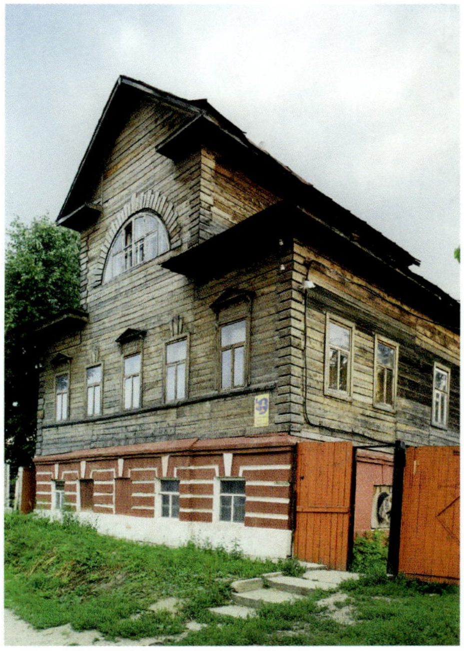

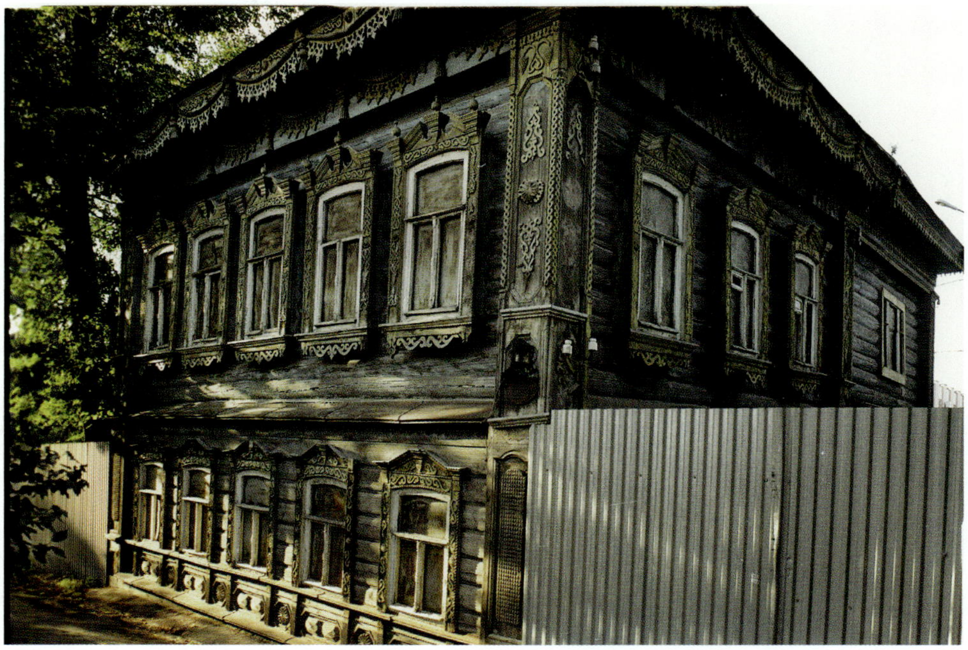

an important town in the eleventh century, Ryazan was completely devastated by the Mongols in 1237 and eventually revived at a different site nearby. In the 1890s Ryazan developed into a major railroad and commercial center, and some of the wooden houses built during that period still exist in styles ranging from neoclassicism to the Russian Revival. North of the city is the village of Konstantinovo, birthplace of Sergey Yesenin (1895–1925), Russia's beloved twentieth-century poet. Wooden structures, including the family house and a primary school, have been preserved as a monument to the poet.

TULA. Parish residence for Church of Nativity of Christ. A brick base supports a fine classically inspired wooden structure with corner rustication, window pediments, and an Italianate window in the large *mezonin*. July 20, 2006.

TULA. Senopalnikov house. Painted log structure with double glazed windows set within decorative fretwork. The draped cornice provides a festive culmination. July 20, 2006.

Nearly four hundred kilometers southeast of Moscow toward the upper reaches of the Don River is the provincial center Yelets (current population under 100,000), one of those Russian towns whose placid appearance belies a war-torn history. There are various dates proposed for the origins of Yelets (as early as 1146), but the first verifiable documentary evidence appears at the end of the fourteenth century. In 1395 Yelets was among the southern settlements razed by the great conqueror Tamerlane during his decisive defeat of Tokhtamysh, the Tatar ruler of the Golden Horde. In 1414 Yelets was sacked by a Tatar raid and abandoned. The settlement was revived in 1591 as one of the fortified points established on Muscovy's southern frontier during the reign of Feodor I (1584–98), son of Ivan the Terrible and the last tsar of the Rurikovich Dynasty. At the turn of the twentieth century, Yelets had a population of almost fifty thousand, with an active mercantile class and hundreds of wooden houses, a few of

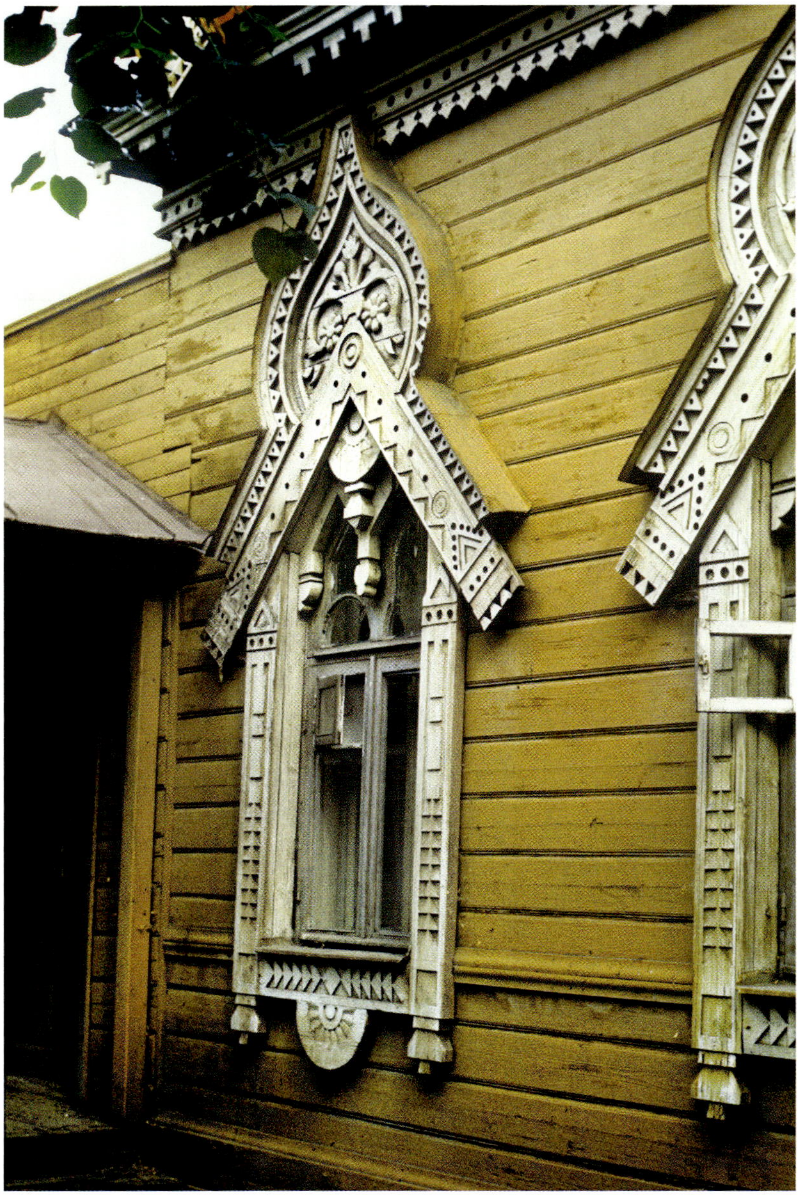

RYAZAN. House, Voznesensky Street 55. Distinctive window pediments in Russian Revival style similar to those displayed at Russia Pavilion designed by Ivan Ropet for the 1878 Paris Exposition. Pediment crowned with *kokoshnik* (traditional headdress). May 13, 1984.

KONSTANTINOVO (near Ryazan). Alexander Yesenin house, built in 1909, burned in 1922, rebuilt in 2001. Associated with the childhood of Russia's beloved poet Sergey Yesenin. June 6, 2008.

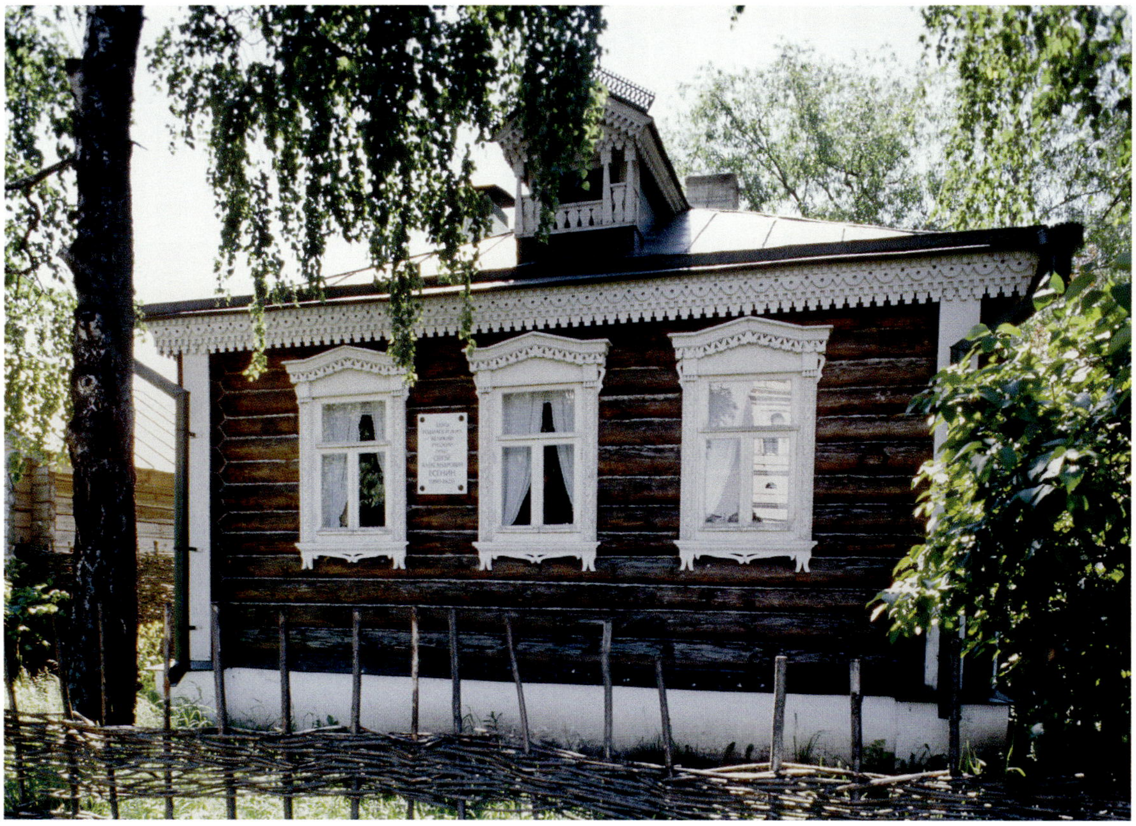

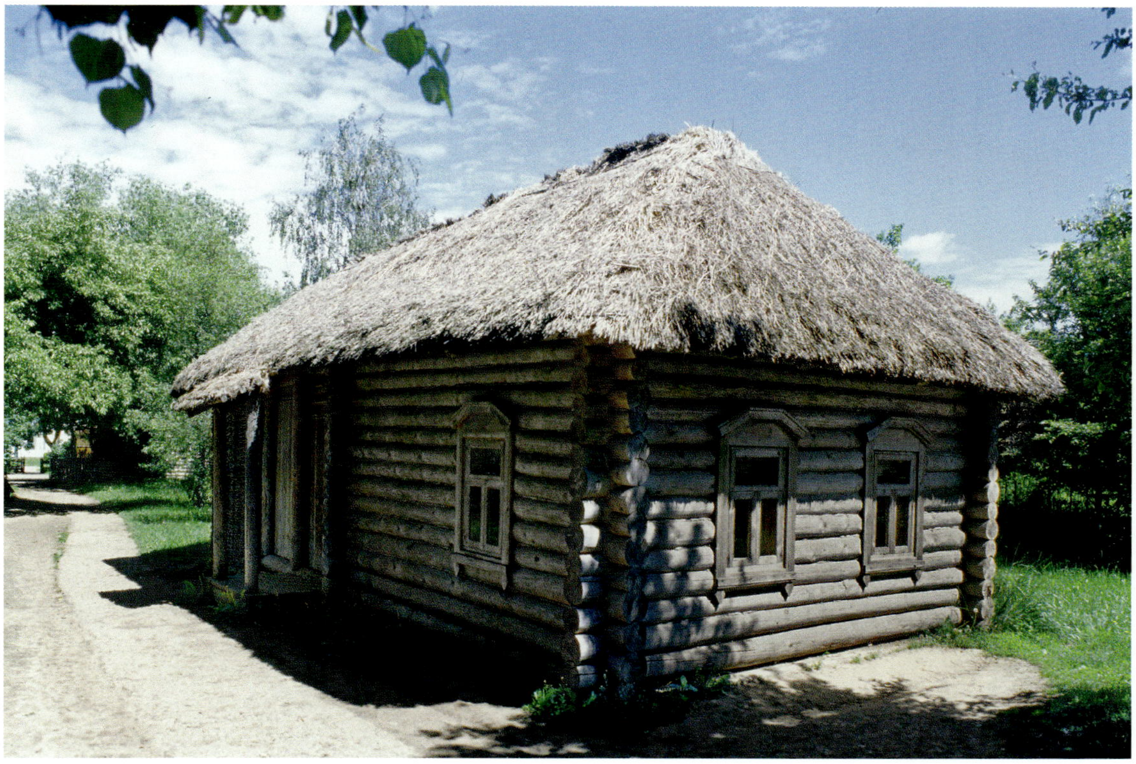

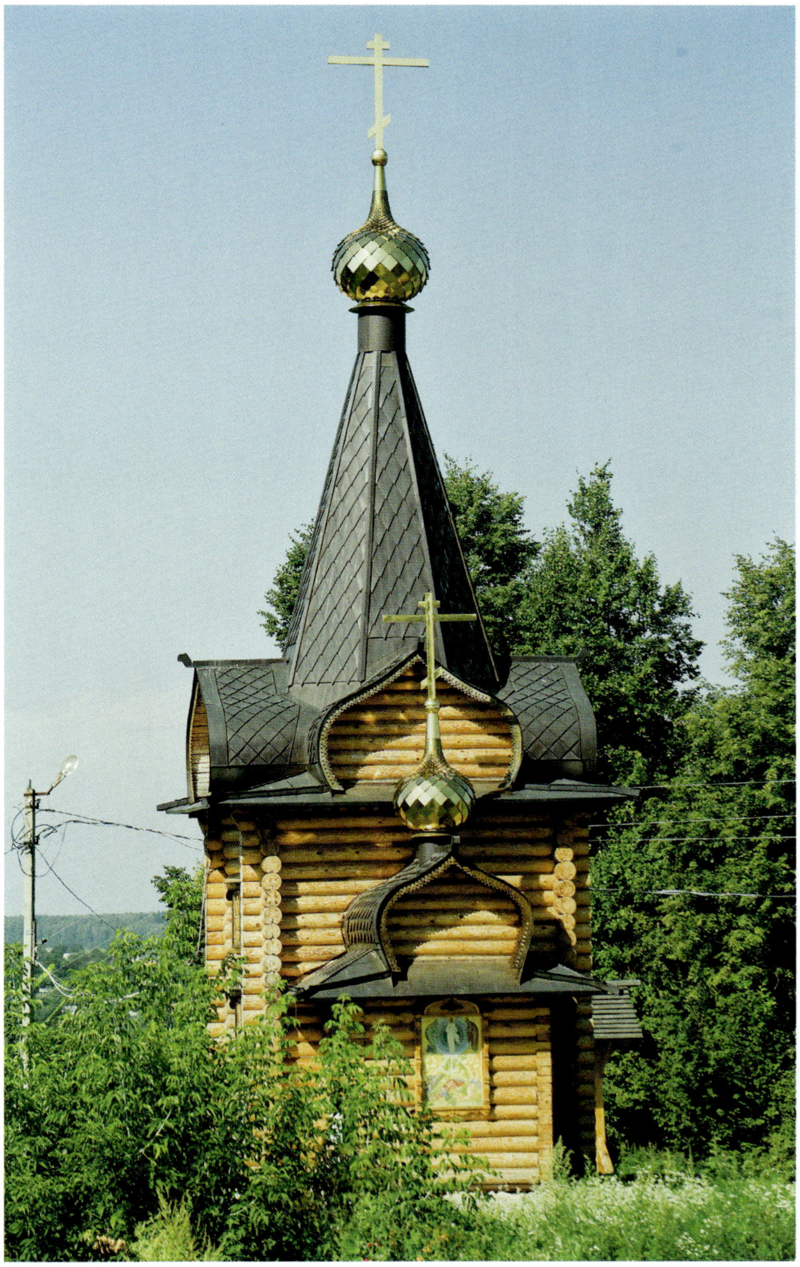

KONSTANTINOVO. *Izba vremyanka* ("temporary hut"), where Sergey Yesenin's parents lived after 1922 fire. Restoration. June 6, 2008.

MALOYAROSLAVETS. Church of the Transfiguration, east view. Built in 2008, this structure exemplifies the attempt to apply traditional elements in contemporary church architecture. August 7, 2016.

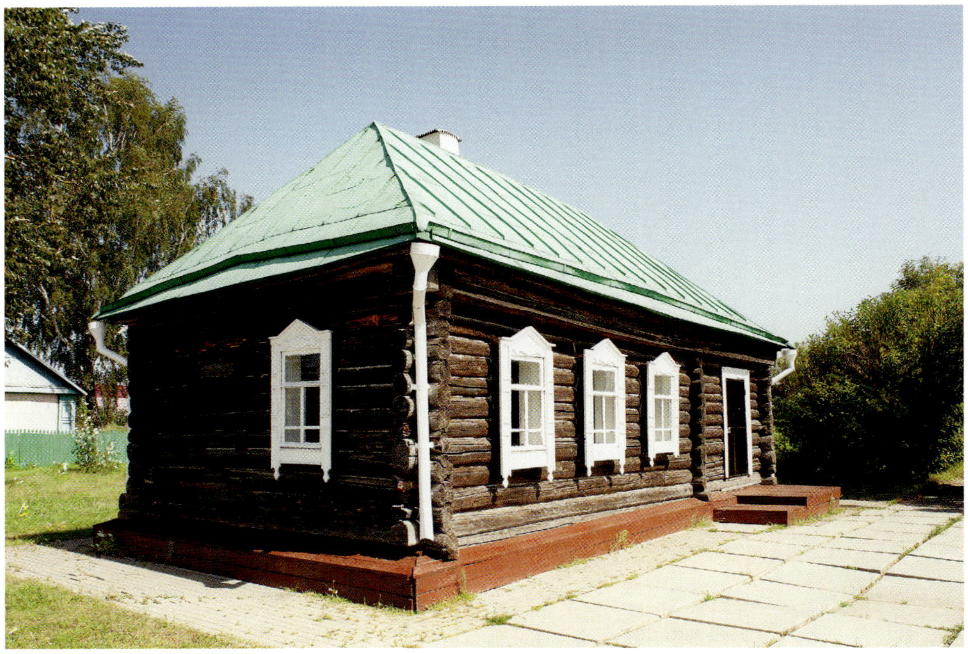

STRELKOVKA. Reconstruction of childhood *izba* of Marshal Georgy Zhukov. Already in disrepair during Zhukov's childhood, the *izba*, along with much of the village, was burned as a reprisal by German forces during their two-month occupation of the region in the fall of 1941. August 7, 2016.

which survive. Among them is the childhood home of Tikhon Khrennikov (1913–2007), a prolific Soviet composer, head of the Union of Soviet Composers from 1948 to 1991, and an unrepentant supporter of Stalin. The house is maintained as a museum, with Khrennikov's grave in an enclosed yard. The Yelets area is also closely connected with the childhood of the writer Ivan Bunin, whose family owned a modest country estate nearby. In 1920 Bunin and his wife emigrated to France, where in 1933 he received the Nobel Prize in literature. Nothing remains of the family estate.

In the same region is the smaller town of Lebedyan (population 20,000), located on the Don River some fifty kilometers south of the

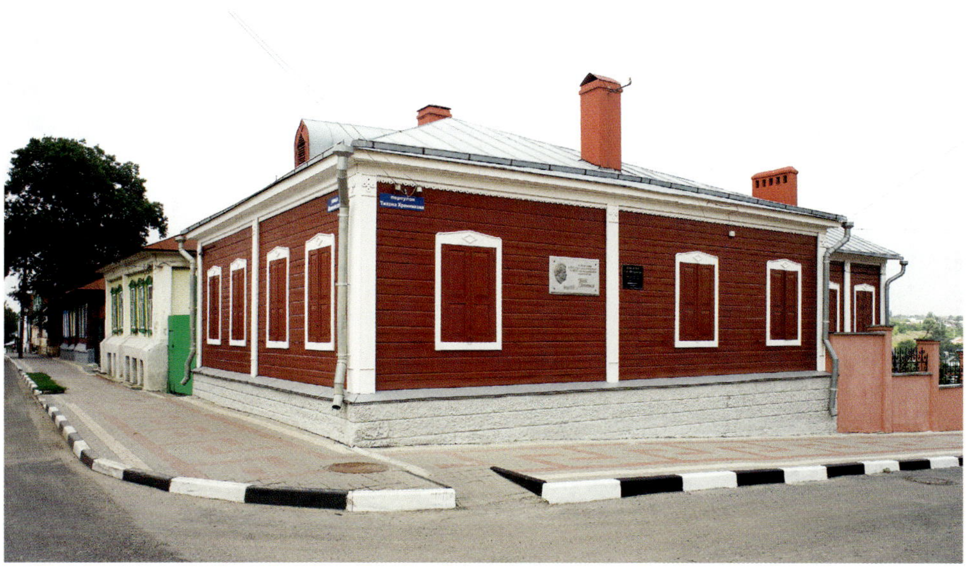

YELETS. Tikhon Khrennikov House-Museum. Childhood home of the composer. August 6, 2013.

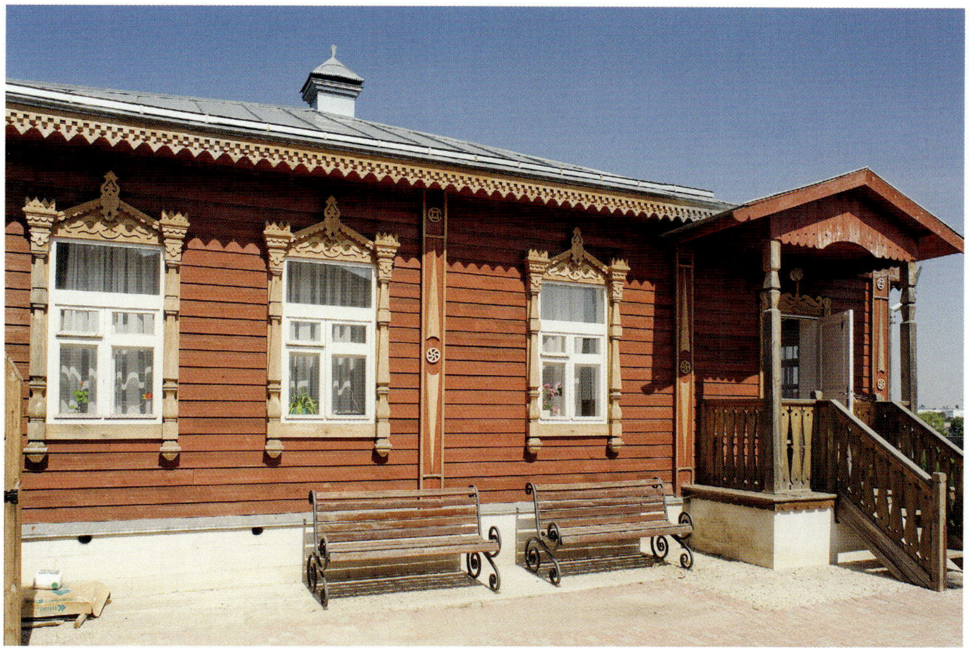

LEBEDYAN. Evgeny Zamyatin House-Museum. This late nineteenth-century house belonged to the writer's beloved maternal grandfather. August 10, 2013.

regional center of Lipetsk. The settlement dates from the late sixteenth century, when it served as a small fort in Russia's southern defense against steppe tribes. The town was advantageously situated on a high bluff above the Don, which is modest in size at this point. During the nineteenth century Lebedyan became an important horse-trading center, famed for its fairs and its racetrack, which attracted connoisseurs of horse flesh throughout Russia. Among the visitors was the writer Ivan Turgenev, who gave the town a leading role in one of the stories of his first renowned work, *A Sportsman's Sketches*. Lebedyan also appeared in the works of Leo Tolstoy and Ivan Bunin, who were raised nearby. The town's most famous native writer is Evgeny Zamyatin (1884–1937), whose father was a local Orthodox priest and his mother a gifted pianist. Zamyatin is best known for his dystopian fantasy *We*, a novel set in a futuristic police state. Completed in 1921, the novel was banned by Soviet censors, and Zamyatin lived under threat until his emigration to France in 1931. He is now honored by the town, which has made a museum of the wooden house where he spent his childhood.

The Middle Volga Basin

Referred to in written sources as early as 1138 but undoubtedly existing as a settlement much earlier, Torzhok thrived as a trading center located on the Tvertsa River just above its confluence with the Volga. (Its name derives from the word *torg*, or "trade.") As an outpost of the medieval commercial center of Novgorod the Great, the town was frequently contested. The rise of Muscovite power in the fifteenth century brought an end to Novgorod's independence in the 1480s, and in 1478 Torzhok entered the domains of Moscow's ruler Ivan III (the Great).

One of the most remarkable architectural monuments in Torzhok—indeed, in all Russia—is the log Church of the Tikhvin Icon of the Virgin, located a few hundred meters downriver from the majestic Saints Boris and Gleb Monastery. The church was originally dedicated to the Ascension—a dedication appropriately used for such astonishing tower churches as Moscow's Ascension Church at Kolomenskoe. Although the construction date is subject to debate, one version states that a wooden church was built on the site in the 1650s and then rebuilt in its present form in 1717. The tower seems to defy gravity as it rises thirty-four meters in three octagonal tiers over a square base structure that rests on a foundation of fieldstone. The west side of the first level is graced with a small vestibule, and the east side has a one-story apse containing the altar. For the most part the Tikhvin Church consists of closely fitted pine logs joined with notched ends. The logs of the apse, however, were squared and fitted in a tighter dovetail joint. In a daring play of balance and proportion, the tower is crowned by a single large cupola supported on a thin cylinder. Although other examples of tiered churches have survived in Russia, none rivals the height of this one.

Over the period of a century the church was frequently modified. In the early 1780s the foundation was reinforced with limestone blocks quarried in nearby Staritsa. (Log buildings could be braced for fundamental repairs.) Around the same period the plank roofing was replaced with metal sheathing, and in 1806 the west end of the vestibule was extended with the addition of a narthex. The shingles of the cupola and drum were also replaced with metal sheathing, apparently in 1828. In 1852–54 a new Ascension Church was built of brick nearby, and the wooden church fell into disrepair; but by virtue of its unusual, archaic form, local clergy were persuaded to repair the church. During this process the windows were enlarged, and the exterior was covered in plank siding. In 1883 it was reconsecrated to the Tikhvin Icon of the Virgin, although it continued to be known as the Old Ascension Church.

The church was closed by Soviet authorities in 1929, and the icon screen and other sacred objects were ransacked. Nonetheless, much interior wall

TORZHOK. Church of Tikhvin Icon of the Virgin, northwest view. August 13, 1995.

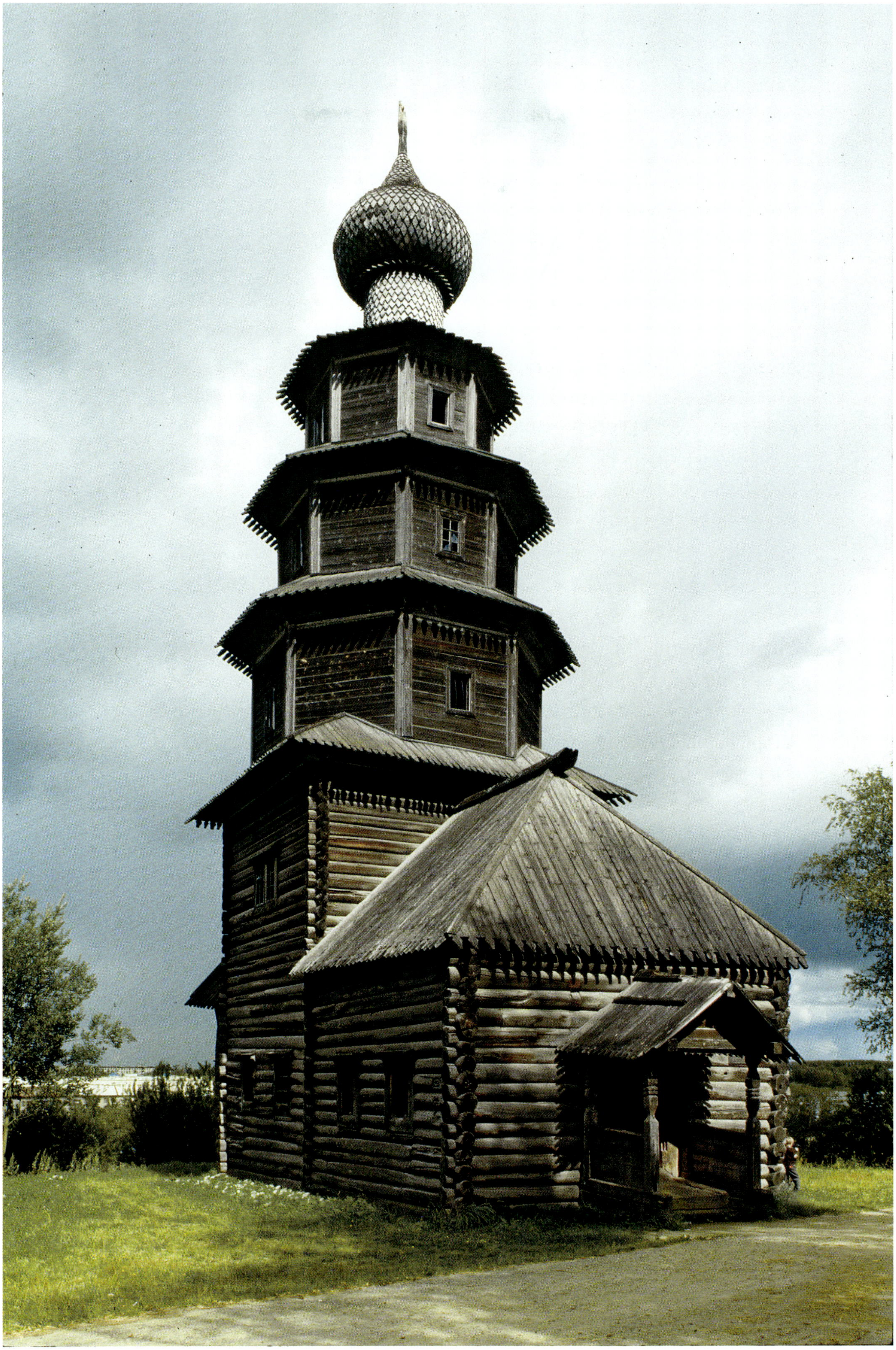

painting survived in the tower structure proper, including floral decorative flourishes in the bright colors of folk art. The upper tiers display eighteenth-century images of the Virgin Mary and church fathers done in a naive style with distemper paints. Additional wall paintings were created in the lower part at the end of the nineteenth century. The lower part of the east wall shows the ghostly outlines of the lost icon screen. Visible at the top are crossbeams that were earlier covered with a panel painted in tempera with an image of the Holy Trinity (now in the Torzhok Museum). Restoration efforts in the late 1970s and early 1980s removed much of the plank siding from the exterior and dismantled the late narthex, leaving the diminutive vestibule and a small porch. In 2006 the church was reopened for worship, yet its condition remained fragile for regular services. The resumption of restoration work in 2007 led to the seemingly interminable presence of scaffolding that obscured much of the structure. Although the scaffolding was recently dismantled and bracing beams were placed on the lower structure, the condition of the log walls continues to degrade.

To the north of Torzhok is a small outdoor museum established in 1976 at the former estate of Vasilyovo, which in the late eighteenth century belonged to the nobleman Dmitry Lvov. Dedicated primarily to traditional wooden architecture, the park contains both sacred and secular structures. In the former group are the Church of the Ascension built in 1737 at the nearby Spas-na-Sozi *pogost* and the Church of the Icon of the Virgin of the Sign, built in 1742 at the village of Pylyovo. Both churches conform to the simple cuboid form with a pitched roof and vestibule extension at the west side. In addition, there are two log chapels: Archangel Michael, built in the mid-eighteenth century at the village of Maksimovo, and the distinctive octagonal Dormition Chapel, built in the early nineteenth century at Findiriarevo village. Among the secular structures are a roadhouse and a fire station with a watch tower. The former estate park is a large part of the appeal of Vasilyovo.

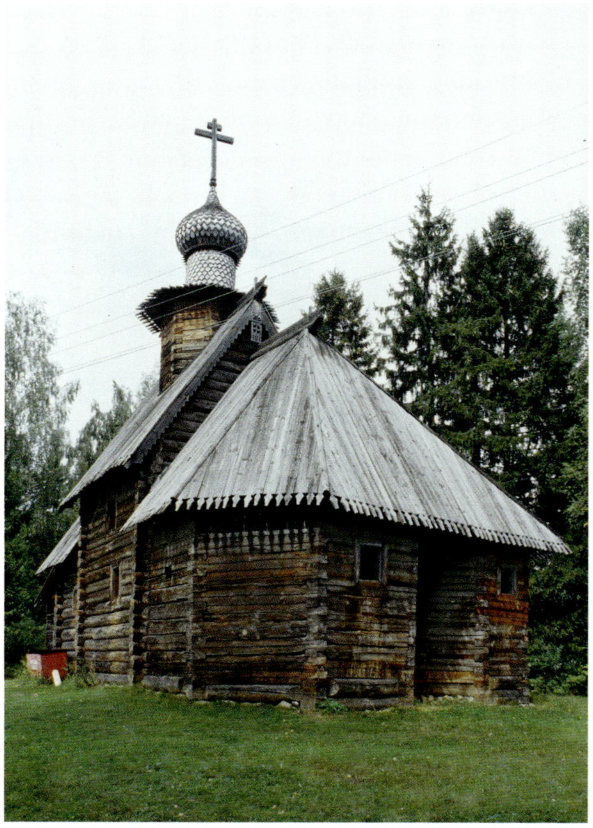

VASILYOVO. Church of the Icon of the Virgin of the Sign, southeast view. August 13, 1995.

On the Volga proper, the cities of Tver and Yaroslavl have little wooden architecture of significance. (Tver—then known as Kalinin—

suffered severely from German occupation and fighting during the final months of 1941.) Farther down the river, however, the city of Kostroma has devoted much attention to traditional wooden architecture. Although its origins are unclear, the earliest documented reference to Kostroma dates to 1213, when the settlement was burned by Prince Konstantin during a territorial feud with his brother Yury. By 1364 it had been absorbed into the expanding Muscovite state and became known for its monastic institutions, such as the Trinity-Ipatiev Monastery. Just beyond the monastery's south wall is one of Russia's earliest outdoor museums of wooden architecture, called Kostromskaya Sloboda ("Kostroma Old Quarter"). This park was founded in 1960 originally to rescue historic wooden structures in villages threatened by the rising waters of the Volga River with the creation of the Gorsky Reservoir and Hydroelectric Station. The park includes the spiritual aspect of wooden architecture, such as the graceful Church of the Icon of the Most Merciful Savior from the village of Fominskoe (Kostroma District), especially lyrical in its setting at the edge of a small pond that serves as a reflecting mirror from the east side. Dated to 1712 and brought to the park in 1968, the shrine has a tripartite design that proceeds from the apse (containing the altar) in the east leading to the main worship space, then a vestibule crowned with a bell tower. The west end is fronted by a raised decorative porch with carved end boards. The central space of the Savior Church supports a steeply pitched roof with a single cupola, yet the interior has a low ceiling to preserve warmth in the long winters. Fortunately, the icon screen at the east end has been preserved relatively intact.

A special example of the traditional tripartite design was the Church of the Transfiguration from the village of Spas-Vezhi (Kostroma District), originally built in 1628 and brought to the park in 1956. I was fortunate to have photographed it during my first trip to Kostroma in 1988, for it burned in 2002—the tragic fate of many Russians wooden churches. The Transfiguration Church was distinctive for its elevation on stout log posts (replaced with brick at the turn of the twentieth century), a means of protecting against deep snow drifts and flooding during spring thaws.

The oldest of the wooden shrines at the Kostroma park is the Church of the Convocation of the Virgin, built at the village of Kholm (Galich District) perhaps as early as 1552. If that date is accurate, this church is the most ancient surviving wooden church from central Russia. It is also one of the most complex, with an elevated enclosed gallery supported on cantilevered logs and encasing the structure on three sides. Additional support for the

KOSTROMSKAYA SLOBODA (Kostroma Old Quarter, outdoor museum). Church of the Icon of the Most Merciful Savior at Fominskoe, southeast view. August 13, 2017.

KOSTROMSKAYA SLOBODA. Church of the Transfiguration at Spas-Vezhi, southeast view. Destroyed by fire. August 22, 1988.

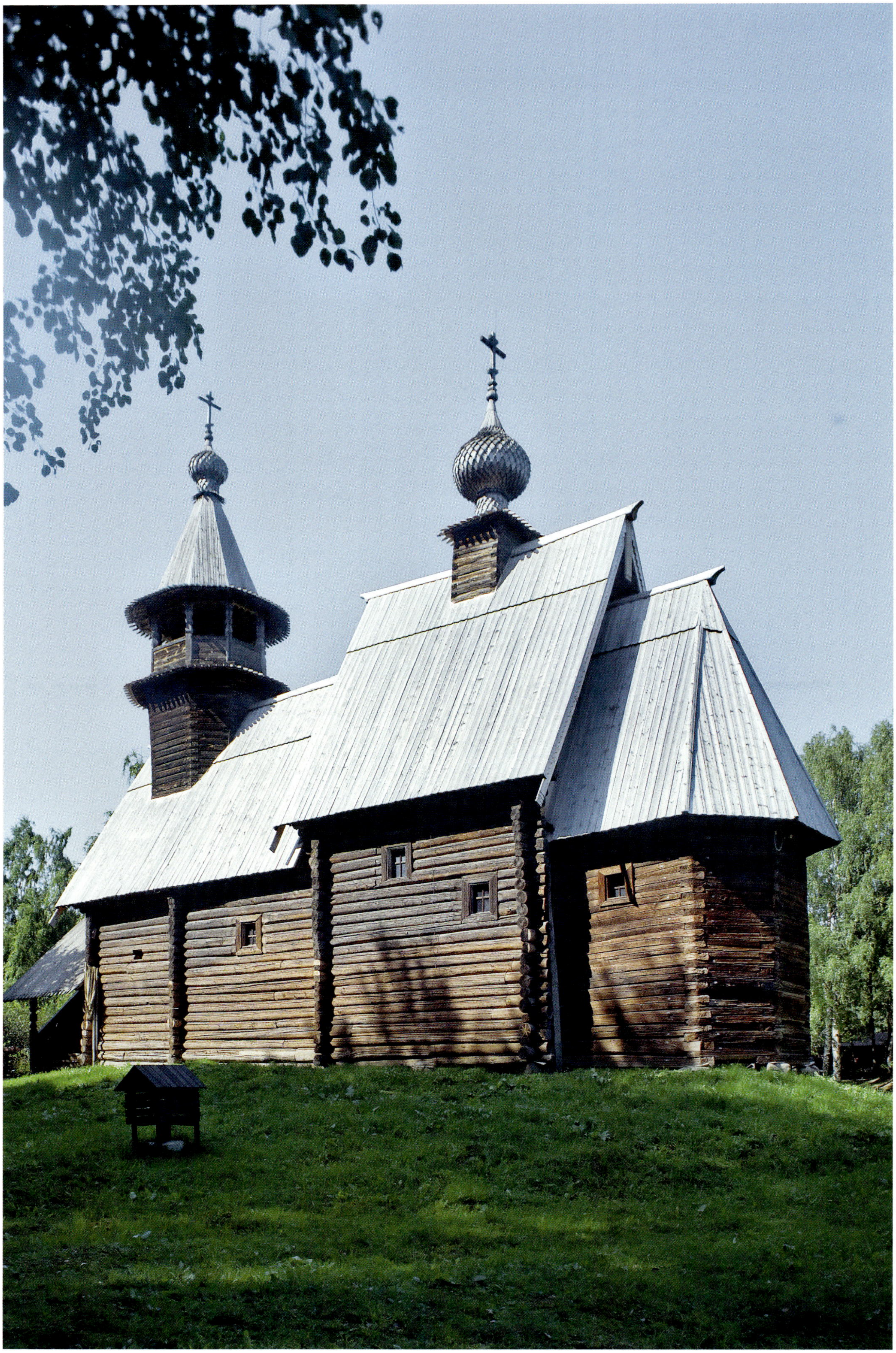

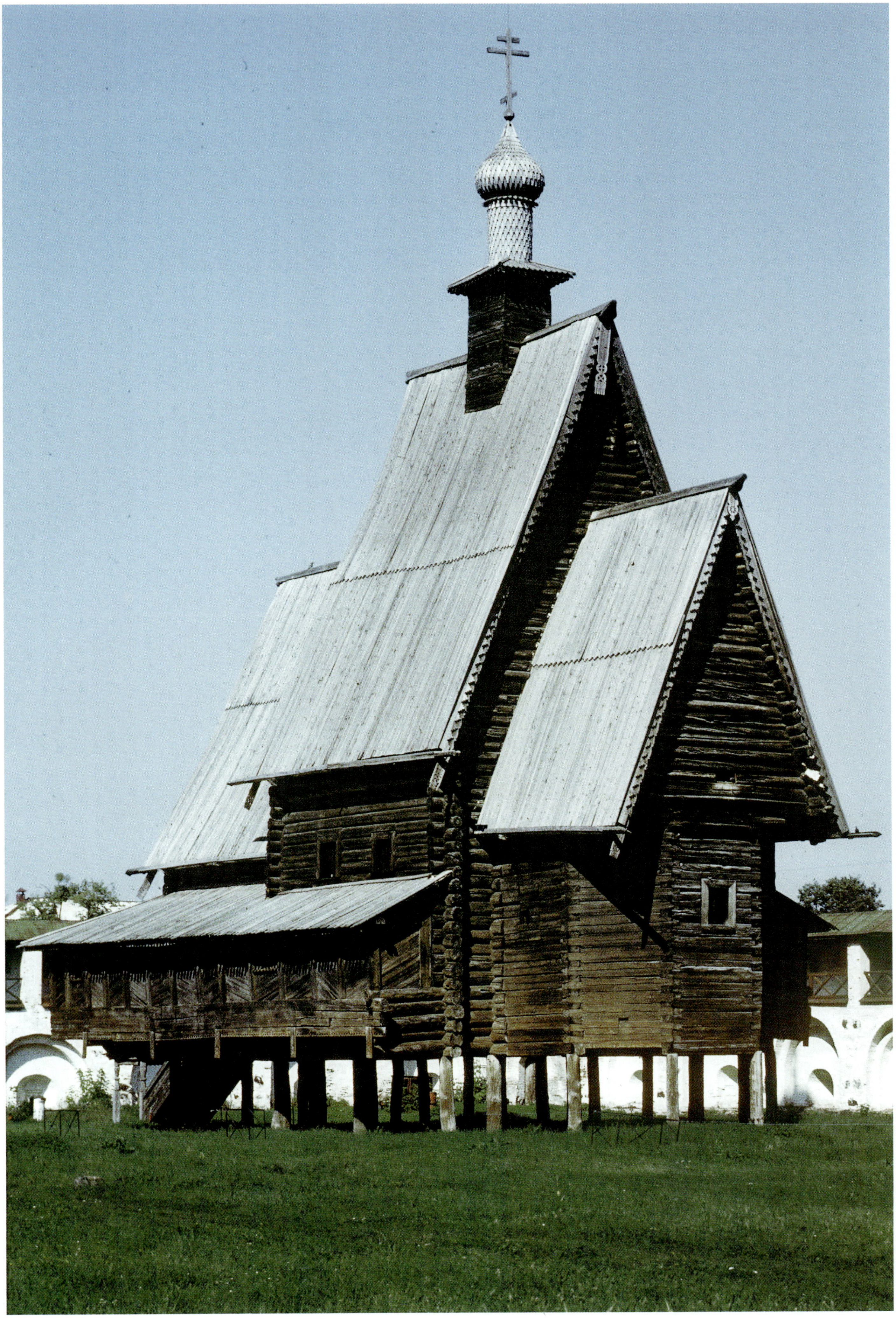

extended gallery is provided by brick piers (originally by log posts). The central part of this remarkable structure comprises two stacked octagons with irregular dimensions. The lower octagon is constructed of notched pine logs, while the smaller upper octagon consists of squared logs joined in a type of dovetail. This method provides greater strength at a critical point supporting the five cupolas that crown the church. The visual effect of these ascending levels creates a graceful silhouette, as if on a raised pedestal. As with many other log churches, the interior is capped with a low, flat plank ceiling to conserve heat. The objects that once graced the worship space of this church have long since disappeared.

The fourth log church at the Kostroma outdoor museum is simpler in design but impressive in its own way. The Church of the Prophet Elijah was originally built at the village of Verkhny (Upper) Berezovets in the Soligalich District. Because of its basic traditional design and the lack clear documentation, specialists have dated its construction widely over a range from the sixteenth to the nineteenth centuries. A plausible period for the building of the Elijah Church is the early 1700s, a century before the construction of a brick church dedicated to the Intercession. Renovations to the church occurred throughout the nineteenth century, when a porch on the west end was replaced with a two-story narthex, and the wooden roof was replaced with sheet metal. The distinctive features of the church come to the fore on the interior, which has been preserved to a rare degree. The carved icon screen is in a provincial baroque style originating in the eighteenth century with twisted columns and saturated decoration based on the grapevine motif. Of particular interest is the painted ceiling, or *nebo* ("sky"), with depictions of the Passion of Christ. The paintings—little more than sketches, probably copied from an illustrated Bible—were applied on triangular segments of stretched homespun canvas. The ring at the center contains a fully colored depiction of Christ Ruler of All.

The Kostroma display of wooden architecture also contains log houses ranging from the simplest *izba* to large structures for an extended family. Among the latter is the Mitry Lipatov house, a two story "house-fortress" originally built for a wealthy peasant in 1857 in the village of Kobylino (Makarievsky District). Located in the same district is the slightly smaller house of Andrian Serov, built at the village of Mytishchi in 1873. Both Lipatov and Serov achieved prosperity in the lumber business, and both commissioned the same master builder, Emelyan Stepanov-Zirinov, to

KOSTROMSKAYA SLOBODA. Church of the Convocation of the Virgin at Kholm, west view. August 13, 2017.

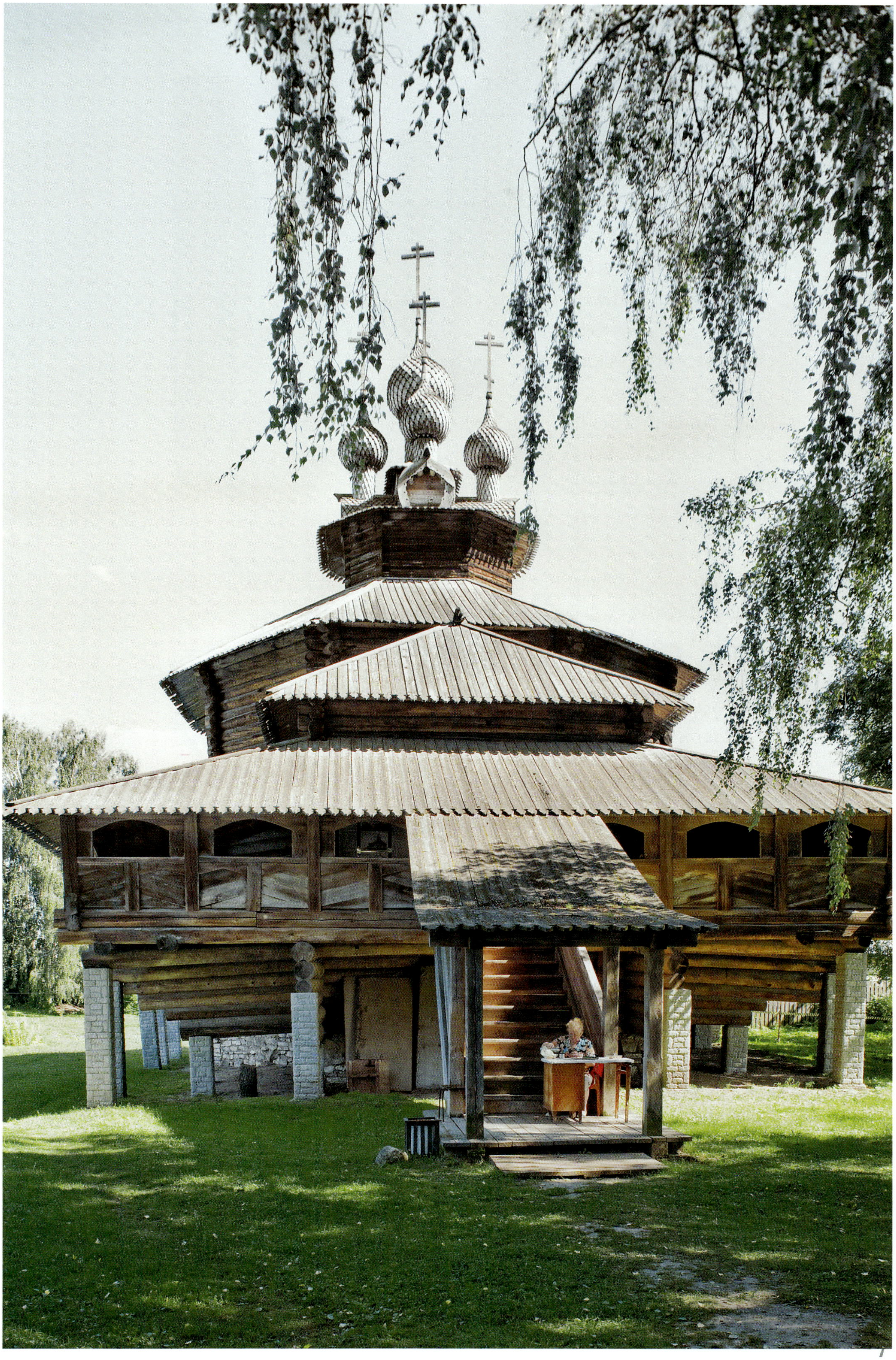

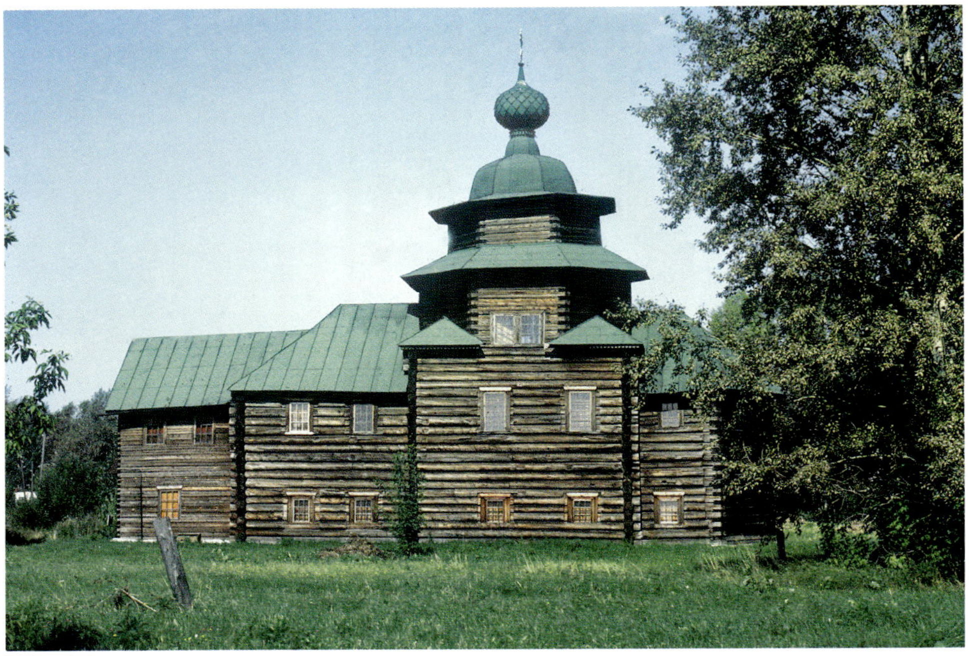

KOSTROMSKAYA SLOBODA. Church of Elijah the Prophet at Verkhny Berezovets, south view. August 22, 1988.

construct and ornament their massive dwellings. This attribution to the master builder is proclaimed on front of each house. At the Lipatov house, this unusual gesture occurs on the carved end boards of the roof and on the decorative cornice at the base of the roof. The upper facade of the Lipatov house is graced with a richly decorated central window including urban (baroque) ornamental elements. The Serov house also has carved end boards and a cornice with a brief inscription on it. Both houses proudly express the enterprising spirit of their peasant owners.

After Kostroma the Volga dips and bends before heading due east, past Kineshma to Yurevets, where it turns sharply to the south in the direction of Nizhny Novgorod. This bend, or pivot, on the high right bank of the Volga formed an ideal point to survey the river for a great distance. It also accounts for the remarkable beauty of the landscape within which the town is situated—high forested bluffs marked by ravines that descend to the main part of town along the river. Perhaps this beauty imprinted itself in some mysterious way on the imagination of the town's most famous son, the filmmaker Andrey Tarkovsky. The generally accepted date of the founding of the town is 1225, formally known as Yurevets Povolzhsky (on the Volga) to distinguish it from other towns with the same name. According to ancient accounts, it was founded by Prince Yury (a Slavic form of Georgy, or George), son of Prince Vsevolod the Great Nest, the last major ruler of Vladimir before the Mongol invasion of 1237. Legend has it that

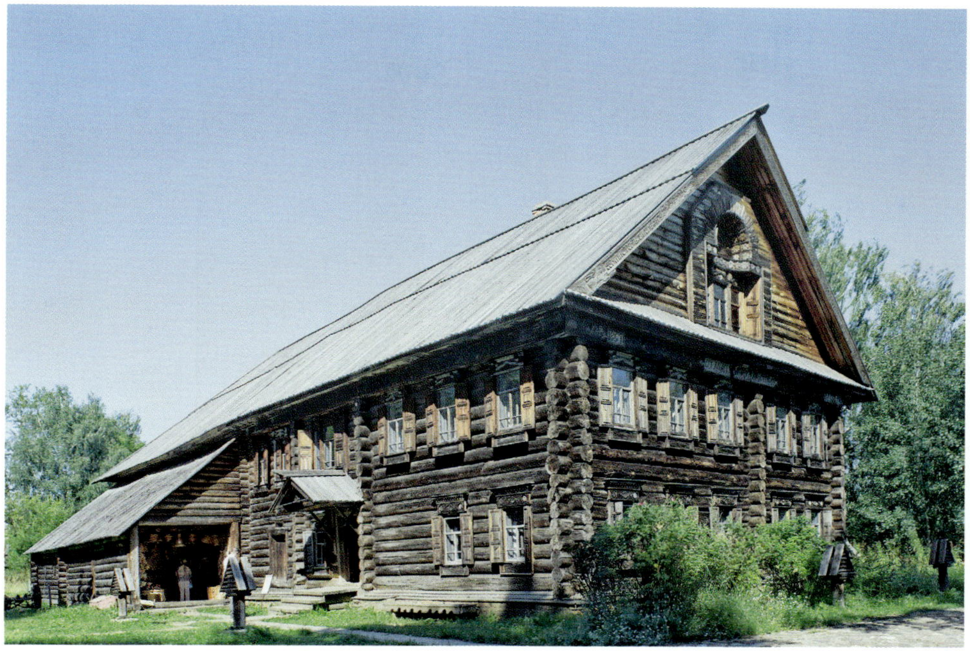

KOSTROMSKAYA SLOBODA. Mitry Lipatov house, built for the large family of a wealthy peasant. August 22, 1988.

during a river journey from Yaroslavl to Vladimir, Yury camped on the site and had a miraculous vision of an icon of Saint George. Responding to the heavenly sign, Yury built a log fort and a wooden church dedicated to Saint George. Such legends typically served to sanctify what was a pragmatic decision—in this case to guard and fortify a strategic river bend.

Just over a decade after Prince Yury's vision, the settlement suffered from the Mongol invasion in the winter of 1237–38—the same catastrophe that led to Yury's death during the Battle on the Seet River (March 4, 1238). The town revived under the authority of regional princes, and in 1452 it was absorbed into the holdings of Basil II (the Blind), grand prince of Moscow. During this period Yurevets was frequently attacked by Tatar raiders from the south, a threat eliminated in 1552 with Ivan the Terrible's conquest of Kazan. Despite its prominent geographical position, enhanced by a location opposite the mouth of the Unzha River, Yurevets was overshadowed by other towns along the Volga such as Nizhny Novgorod, some 190 kilometers to the south. Nonetheless, the Volga River provided the town with a transportation artery used effectively by local entrepreneurs in the nineteenth and early twentieth centuries. Their wooden houses are the most charming feature of Yurevets, but many are beyond repair.

The largest city on the right bank of the Volga is Nizhny Novgorod, considered to have been founded in 1221 as an eastern outpost defending the lands of Grand Prince Yury Vsevolodovich of Vladimir. Within two decades his principality would be devastated by the Mongol invasion, but Nizhny Novgorod (current population 1,214,000) maintained its strategic significance overlooking two major rivers, the Oka and the Volga. Drawn into the orbit of Moscow in the early fifteenth century, it would play an important role in the defense against and subsequent conquest of the Tatar Khanate of Kazan in 1552. The completion of the Moscow-Nizhny Novgorod Railroad in 1861 launched an industrial expansion that brought a population of nearly one hundred thousand by the turn of the twentieth century. At that time the city had thousands of wooden houses,

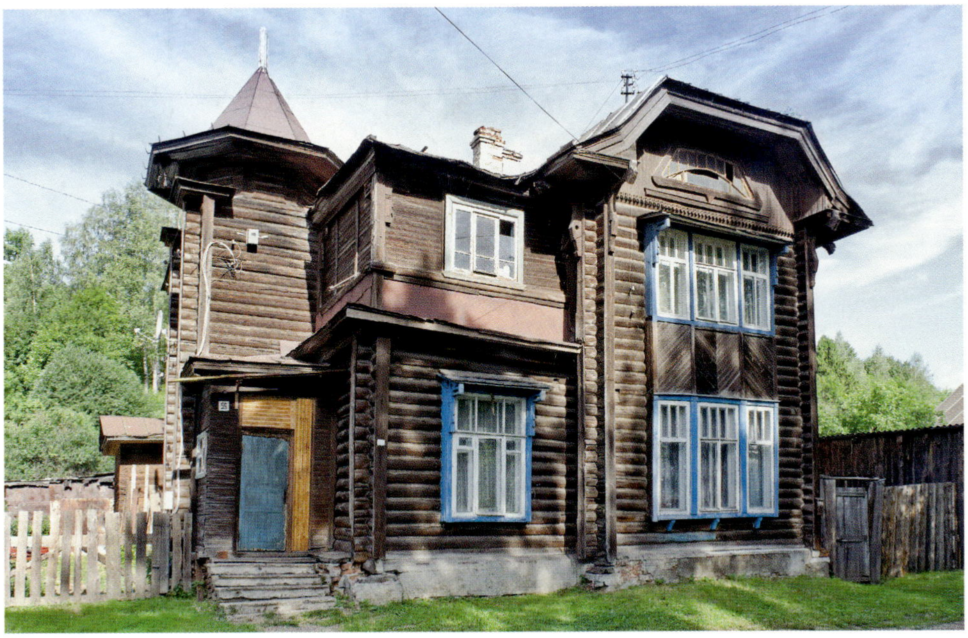

YUREVETS. House, Lenin Street 59. Fine example of early twentieth-century log dwelling in the rationalist version of *style moderne* with a minimum of decorative detail. July 15, 2012.

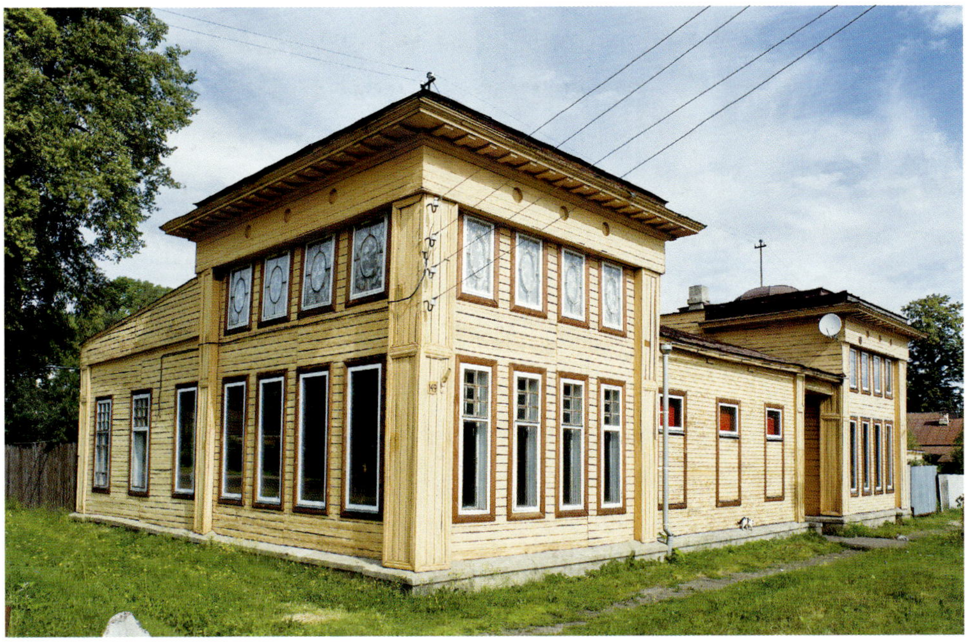

YUREVETS. Efimov house. Built in 1910s for a timber merchant, this wooden house is one of the most radical expressions of *style moderne* rational design. July 15, 2012.

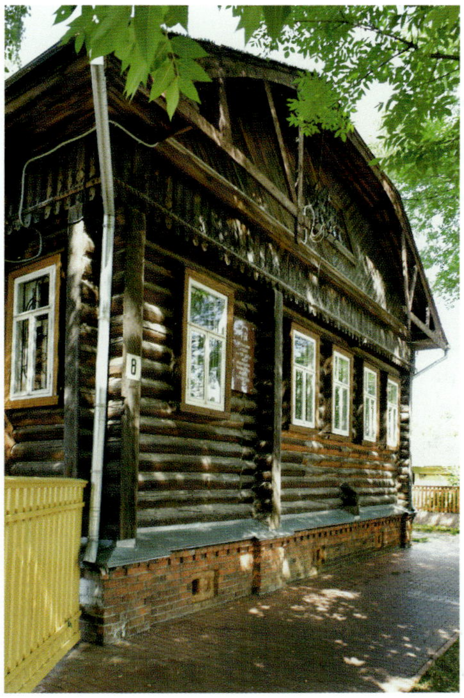

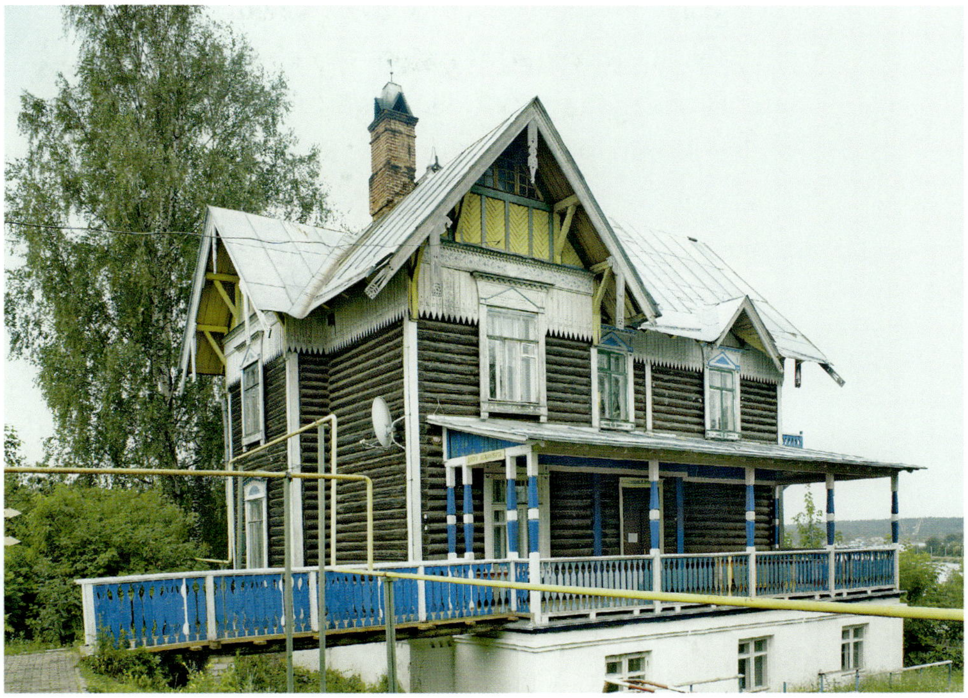

many built on brick ground floors and all with decorative detailing on the main facade. With urban redevelopment, their number has decreased exponentially.

There is, however, in the southeastern part of the city a modest outdoor museum devoted to traditional wooden architecture. Opened in 1973 on the territory of a former farmstead known as Shchyolkovsky Khutor (from which it takes its name), the park contains not only churches, chapels, and examples of the *izba*, but also large wooden houses built in villages but resembling urban housing design—a phenomenon reflecting significant social changes in nineteenth-century Russia. For example, the Pavlova house, from the village of Rakovo, was built by a peasant who had become a prosperous entrepreneur, thus setting him apart from the agricultural way of life. There is also a house moved from the center of Nizhny Novgorod to make way for an office building, an example of a limited attempt to preserve something from the urban wooden habitat. The churches at the park are both dedicated to the Intercession: a diminutive one built in 1672 at the village of Zelyonoe and an octagonal tiered structure built in 1731 at the village of Starye Klyuchishchi ("Old Wellsprings").

The destiny of Nizhny Novgorod has been closely connected with that of the next major city down the Volga River, Kazan, capital of the Republic of Tatarstan. A short distance upstream from Kazan is the small settlement

YUREVETS. Andrey Tarkovsky Museum. Early twentieth-century house where the stepfather of Tarkovsky's mother rented rooms in a communal apartment in 1933. The young Tarkovsky lived here in 1936 and again in 1941–43 (evacuation from Moscow). July 15, 2012.

KINESHMA. Parish House, Church of the Transfiguration. This early twentieth-century house exemplifies a picturesque merging of *style moderne* and Russian Revival decorative elements. July 16, 2012.

of Sviyazhsk, located on a prominent island hill now connected to the right bank of the Volga by a causeway. The crown of the hill is graced with churches and monasteries, one of which is now a UNESCO World Heritage Site. Yet despite this peaceful view, Sviyazhsk was from the moment of its founding at the center of one of the most dramatic, violent episodes in Russian history: the taking of the fortress city of Kazan by Ivan the Terrible in 1552. The Tatar Khanate of Kazan had been established in 1438 from the increasingly fragmented Golden Horde. Relations with Muscovy were

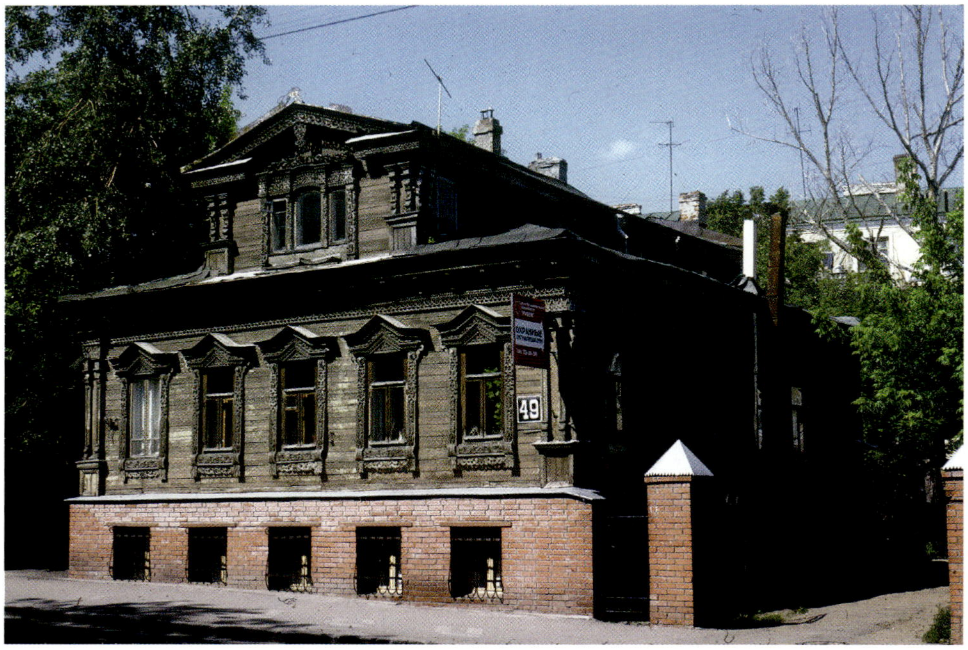

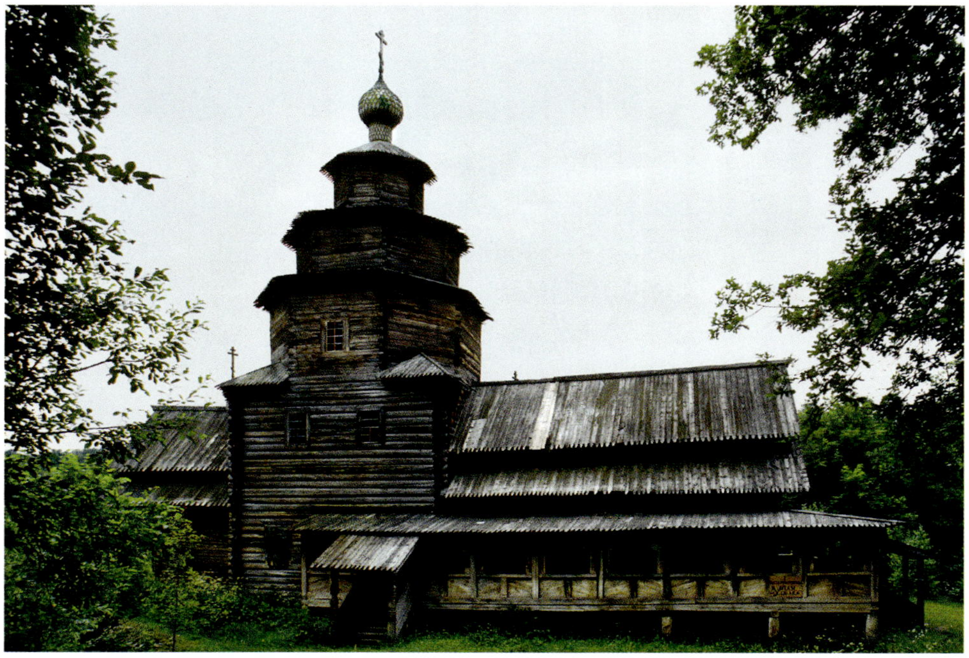

NIZHNY NOVGOROD. House, Belinsky Street 49. With its decorative fretwork, this is a typical example of the hundreds of wooden houses in the city before large-scale redevelopment. Demolished. June 22, 1996.

SHCHYOLKOVSKY KHUTOR (Nizhny Novgorod, outdoor museum). Church of the Intercession from the village of Starye Klyuchishchi, north view. June 23, 1996.

SHCHYOLKOVSKY KHUTOR. Church of the Intercession from the village of Zelyonoe, southwest view. Archaic in form, this small jewel has a rhythmical perspective of pitched roofs. June 23, 1996.

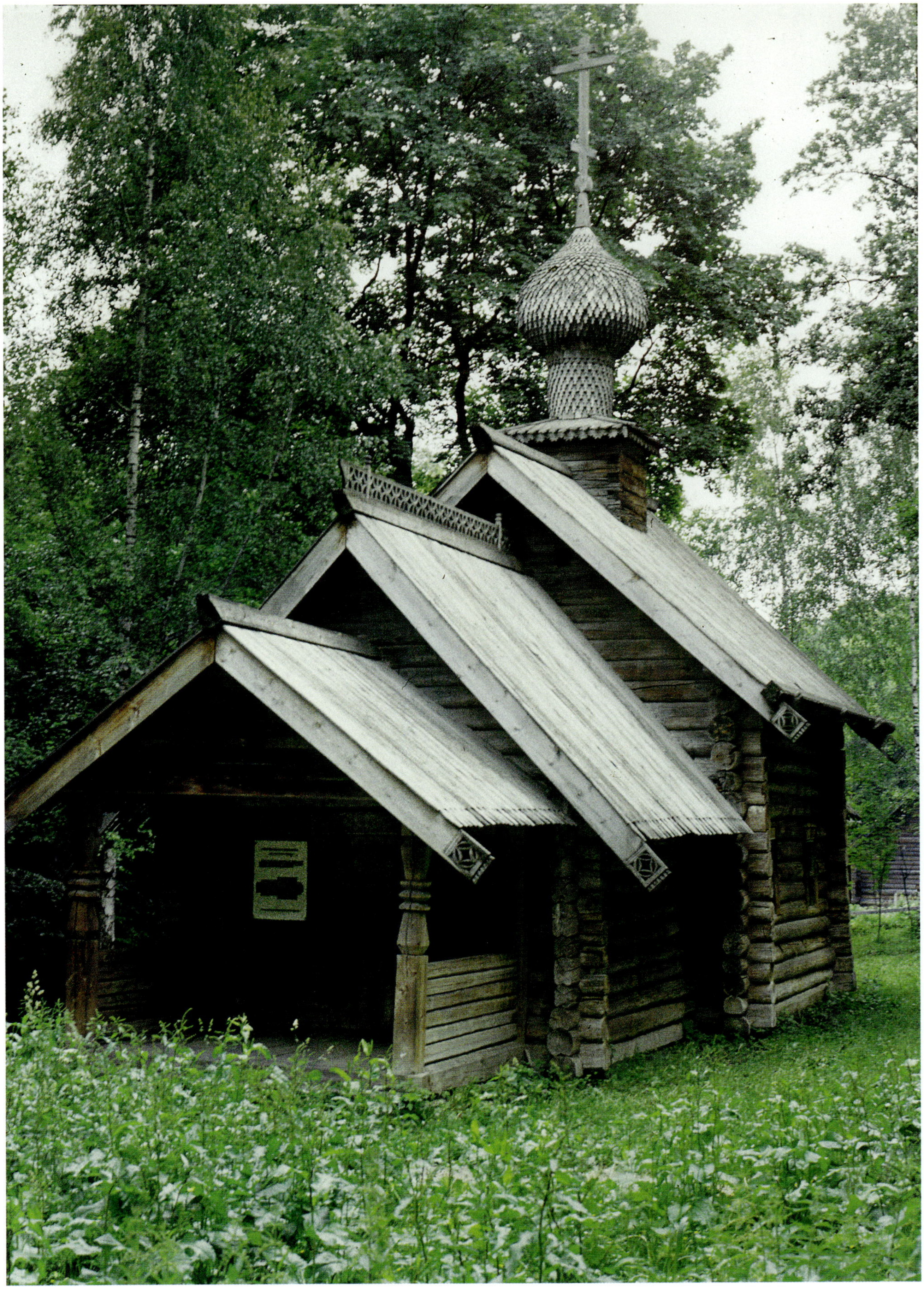

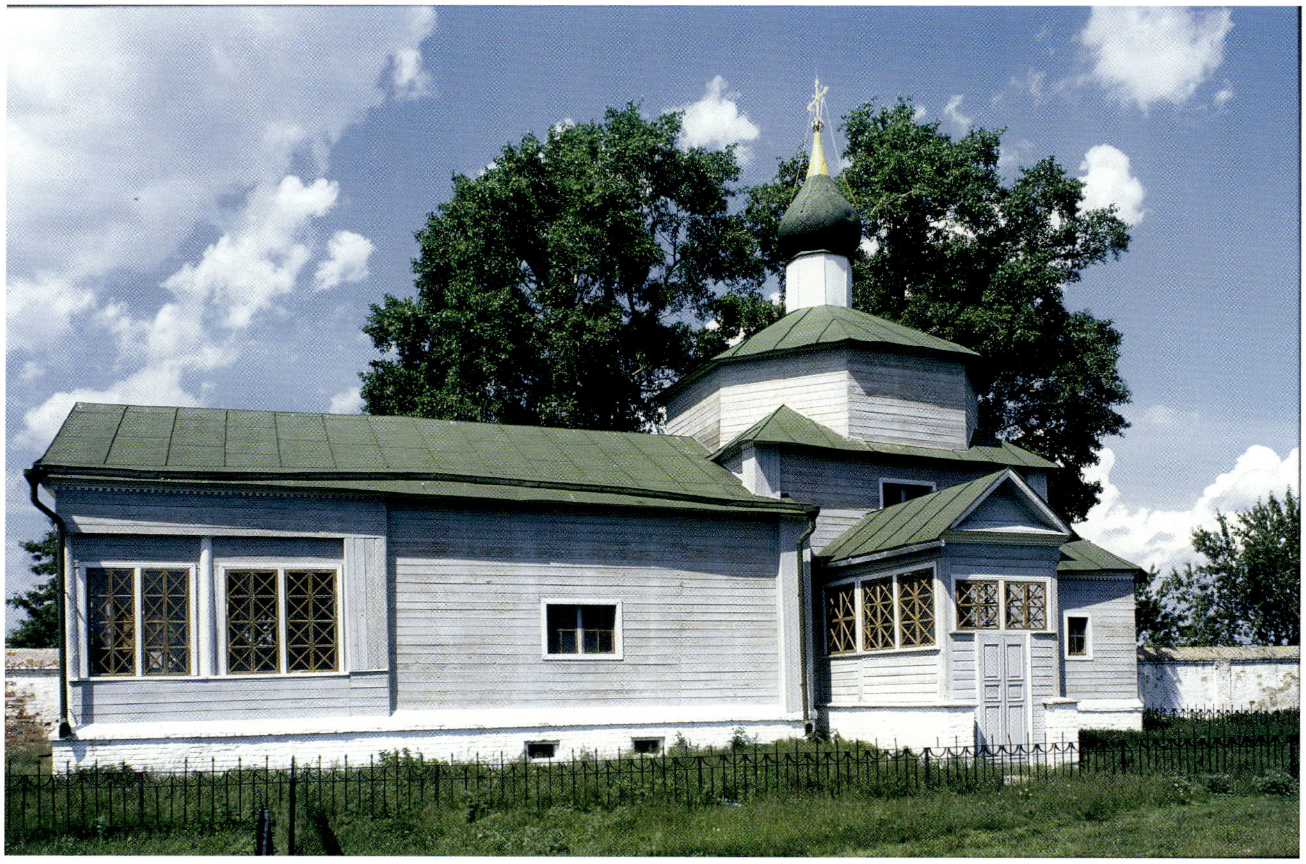

constantly changing as part of a complex pattern that involved not only Kazan but also the Crimean Khanate (established as an Ottoman vassal state in 1478), the Nogai Horde, and various smaller entities such as the Kasimov Tatars, who accepted Moscow's authority in the 1450s. Kazan, however, remained the primary challenge to Moscow in view of its strategic location on the Volga River near its confluence with the Kama, the major river draining the western Ural Mountains. As long as Kazan existed as a threat, Russian movement into and beyond the Urals into Siberia, as well as south toward the Caspian Sea, was blocked.

SVIYAZHSK. Church of the Trinity, south view. Although modified in the nineteenth century, it was originally built at the same time as the Sviyazhsk fortress and is considered the oldest Orthodox Church in Tatarstan. June 8, 2004.

Unsuccessful campaigns launched by Ivan in 1547 and 1549 from Nizhny Novgorod made it clear that a forward base, both accessible and defensible, was required to support such a complicated operation. The chosen site was a promontory that overlooked the Sviyaga River at its merger with the Volga some twenty-five kilometers north of Kazan. Ivan's massive offensive required the rapid construction of a fortress, and to that purpose thousands of logs were cut and shaped during the winter of 1550–51 near

Uglich, on the upper Volga. In late May 1551 Muscovite forces disembarked at the site of the future Sviyazhsk on land that traditionally belonged to the Chuvash people. The titular head of the force was the Kasimov Khan Shahgali, a calculated gesture that symbolized allegiance to Moscow among a significant group of Tatars. Trees on the hill were quickly felled in preparation for the fortress. With deft coordination rafts of logs were floated downriver, captured, and assembled within four weeks into a large fort whose territory exceeded that of the Moscow kremlin. Astounded by the rapidity of the fort's construction, large segments of the local population gave allegiance to Moscow. Inconclusive maneuvers and skirmishes over the next several months led to a renewed Muscovite assault, which began in early July 1552 and lasted until Kazan was taken by storm on October 2. Although critical to the support of Ivan's large army and its artillery, Sviyazhsk lost its strategic purpose after the conquest of Kazan and became a local religious center. Sviyazhsk has one historically important monument of wooden architecture—the small Church of the Trinity, built in 1551 during the construction of the Sviyazhsk fortress and considered the

KAZAN. Merchant houses in old Tatar Quarter, Kabannaya Street 13, 15. Built in the late nineteenth century, these richly decorated wooden dwellings were razed as part of large-scale redevelopments of central Kazan. July 9, 1985.

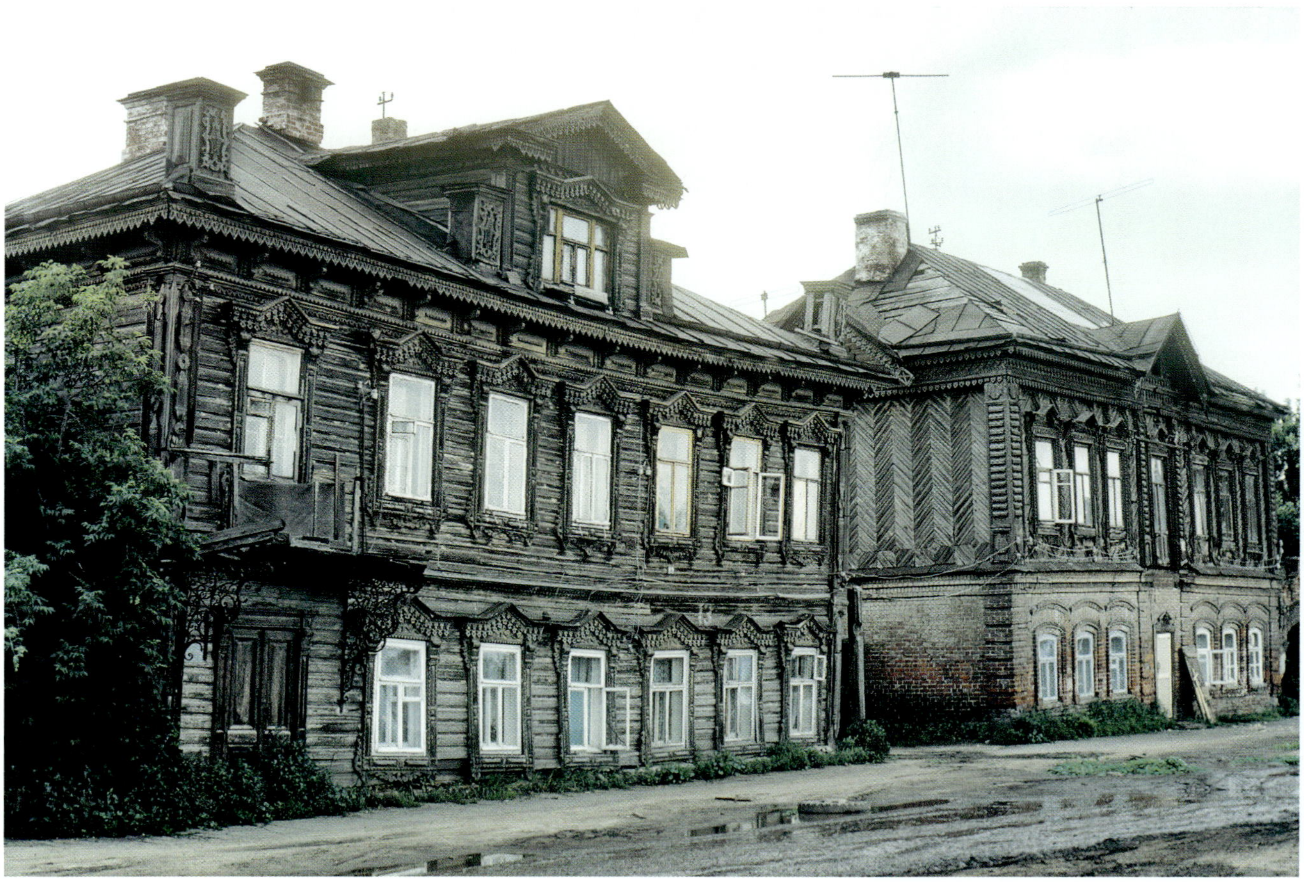

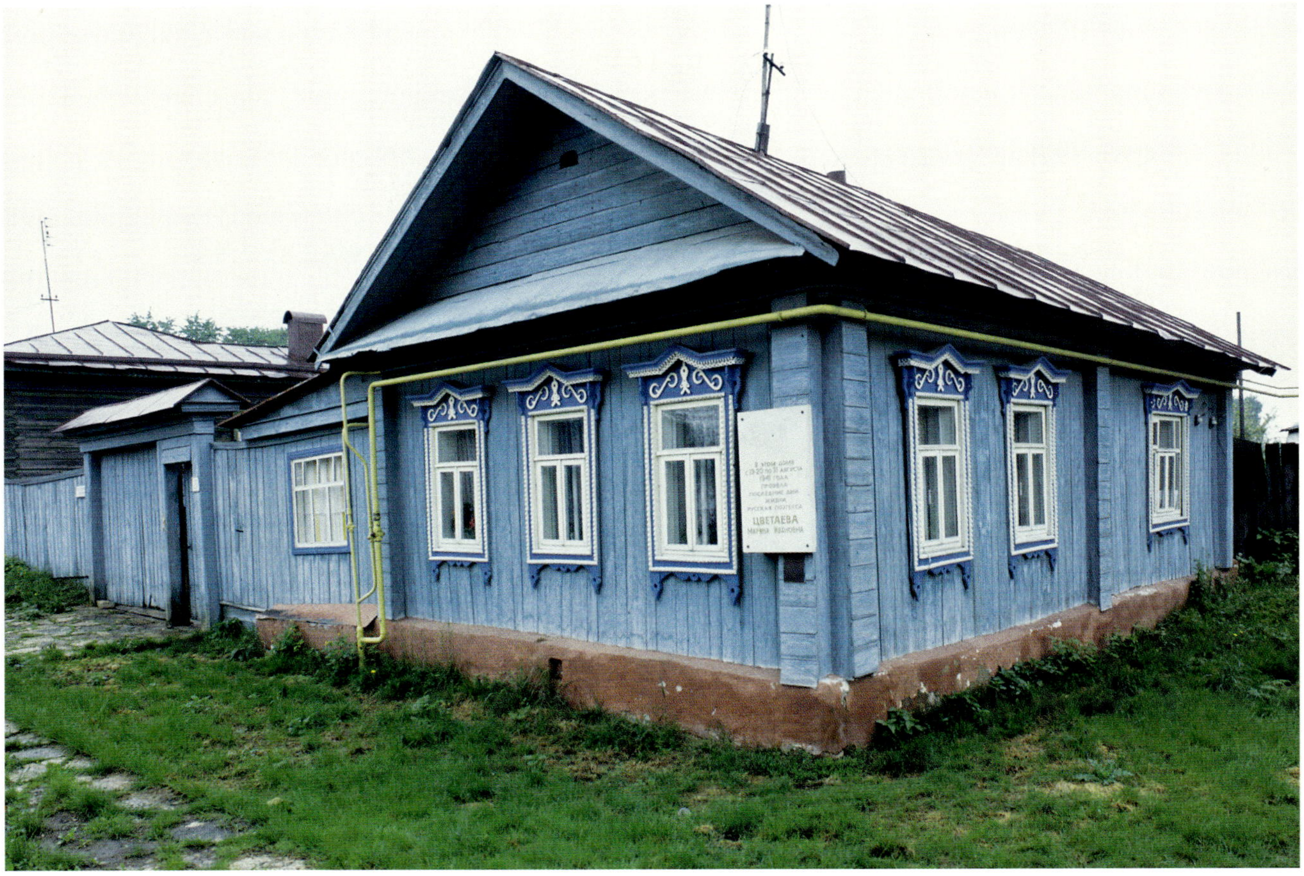

earliest surviving Orthodox Church in Tatarstan. Its stout larch logs have stood the test of time, although its crown was substantially modified in the nineteenth century.

Like Nizhny Novgorod, the city of Kazan (current population 1,315,000) experienced rapid commercial development in the late nineteenth century, accelerated by the completion of a railroad linking the city to Moscow in 1894. And like Nizhny Novgorod, Kazan had thousands of wooden houses, many of which had lavish facade decoration reflecting the prosperity of their Tatar and Russian merchant owners. Although I was able to photograph some remaining examples during my first visit in 1985, wide swaths of those wooden houses, poorly maintained and with uncertain ownership, had already been leveled. The pace of demolition increased during intensive redevelopment campaigns at the beginning of this century, when both the city administration and private investors were interested in clearing blocks of these houses for more profitable construction with modern amenities.

YELABUGA. House, Malaya Pokrovskaya Street 20. It was here that the great poet Marina Tsvetaeva spent her final days as an evacuee from Moscow before taking her life in the terrifying autumn of 1941. May 28, 2004.

CHIKINAS (Alich Tarkhan). Tatar village mosque with minaret, possibly dating from the nineteenth century. June 5, 2004.

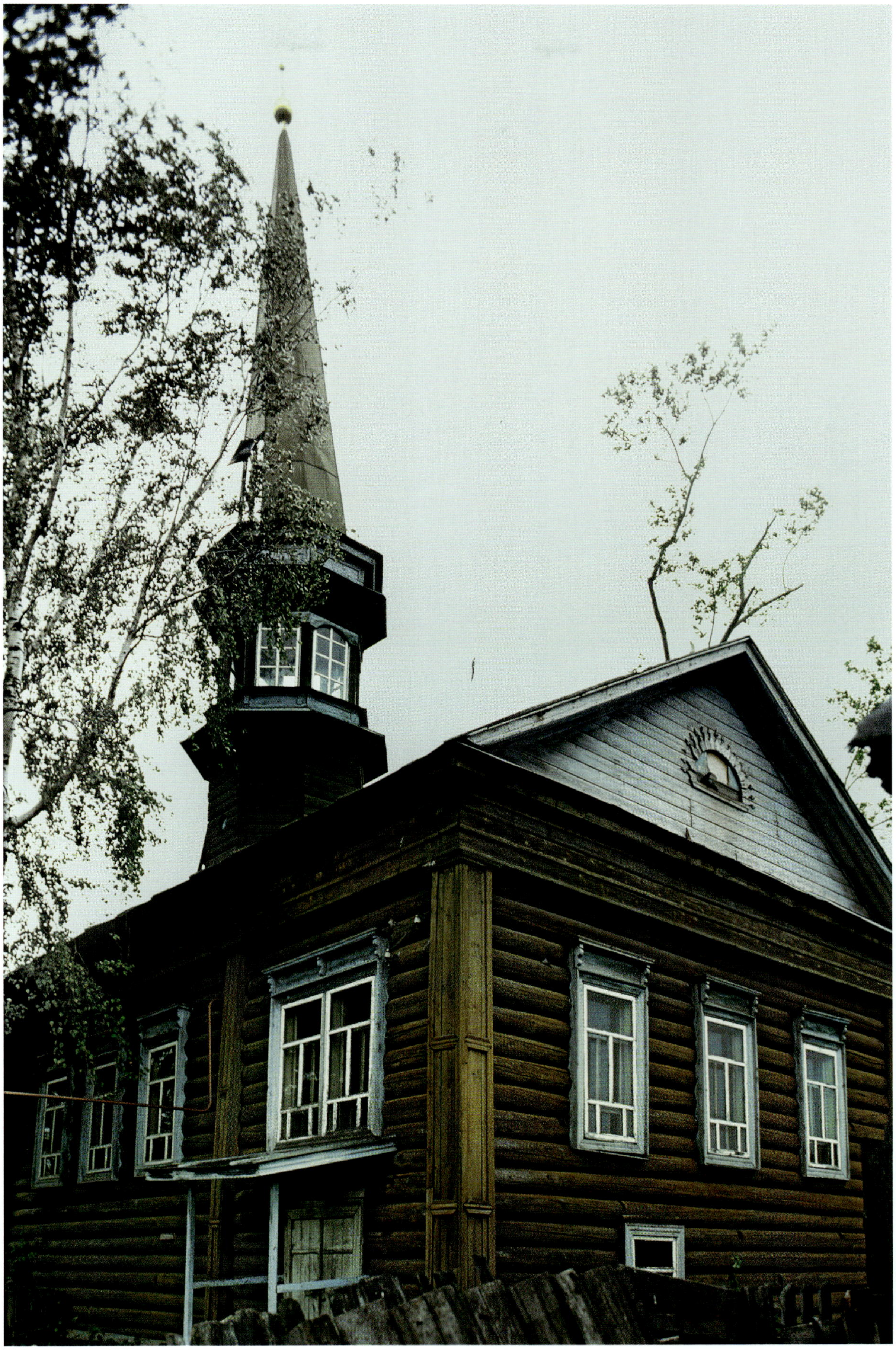

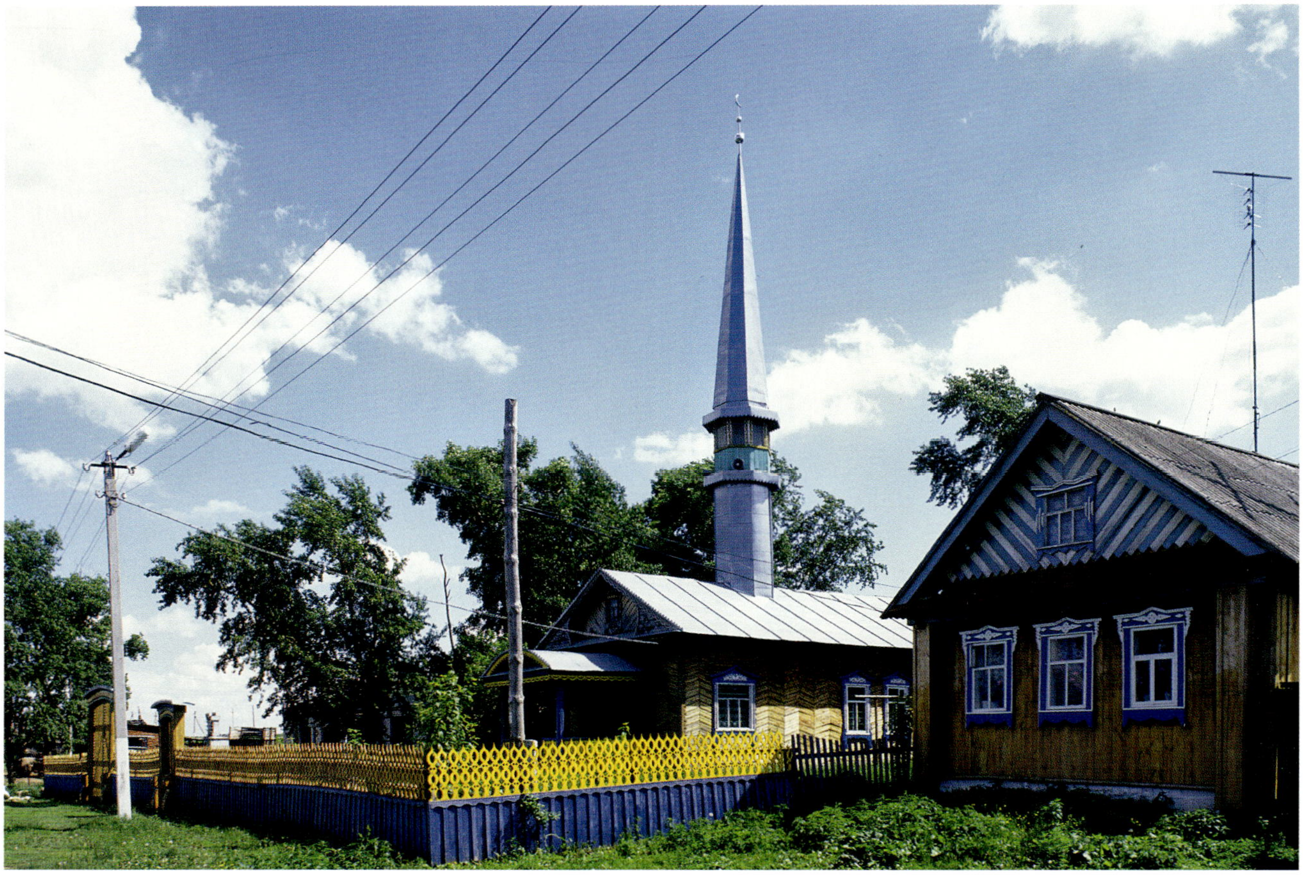

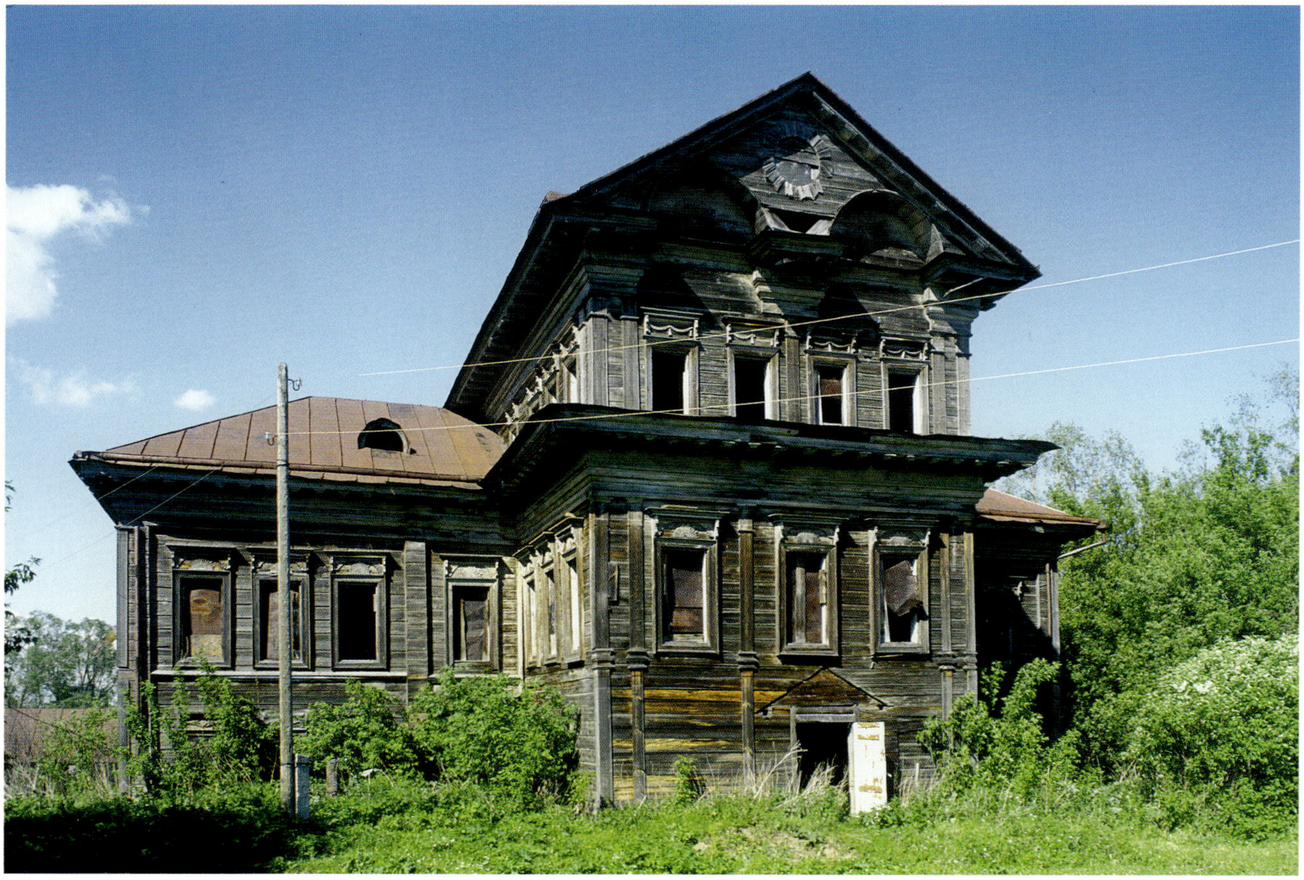

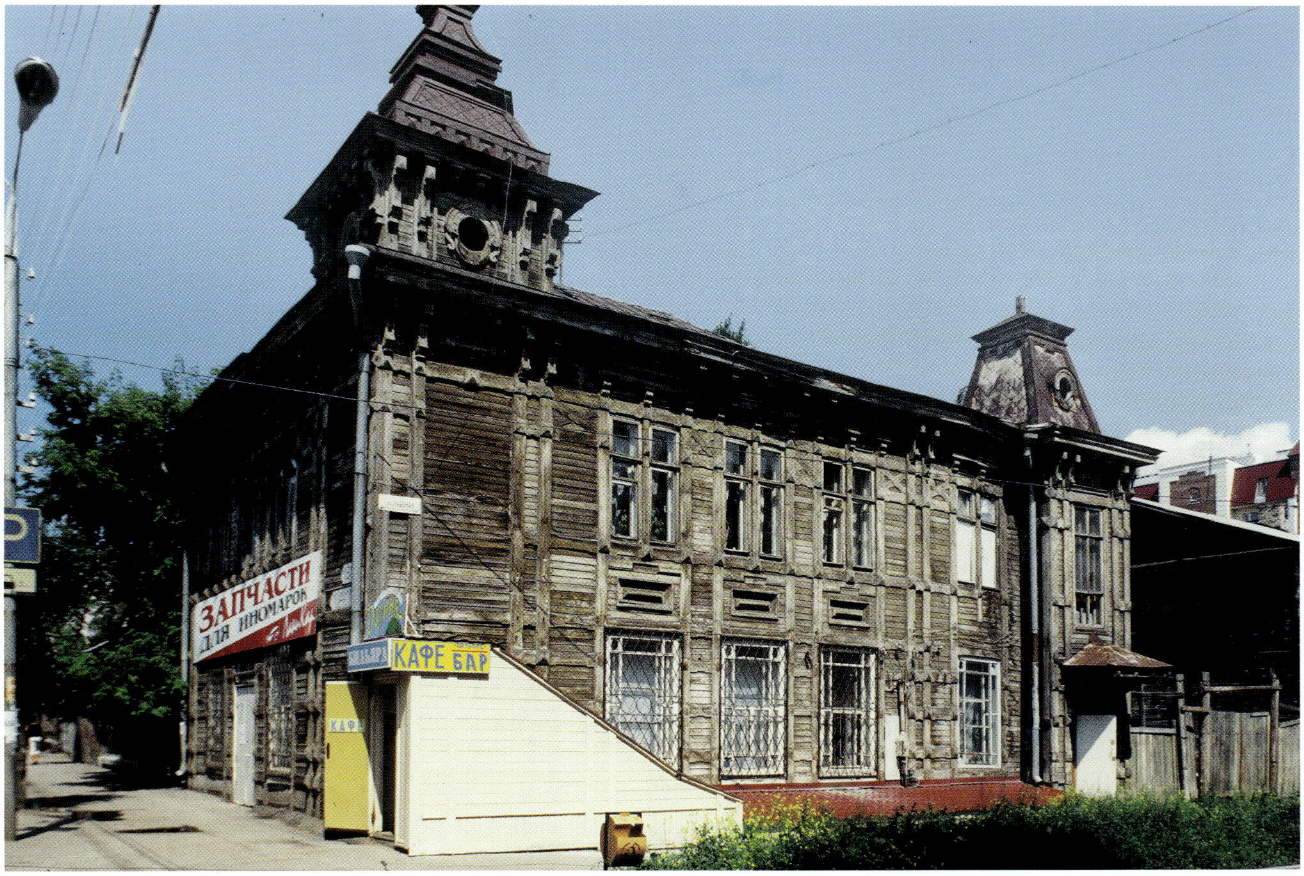

SAMARA. V. E. Prakhov building, Samara Street 151. This magnificent dwelling and store, designed with Beaux Arts elements in 1900 by the Jewish architect Zelman Kleinerman (who also designed the main Samara synagogue), is a rare success story of urban preservation. The neglected building that I photographed with a parts store for foreign cars has been repaired and freshly painted—although I consider myself fortunate to have recorded the texture of the unpainted walls. June 24, 2001.

The situation seems more favorable in smaller cities such as Yelabuga (current population 73,500), in the eastern part of Tatarstan. Situated on a high bluff looking over the broad plain of the Kama River, Yelabuga is especially favored by its physical setting. The artist Ivan Shishkin, renowned for his paintings of Russian nature, grew up in Yelabuga, and his family house, with its view of the sweeping vistas over the Kama, is now a museum. The surrounding pine forests seem to provide the air with a fragrance and freshness even within the town itself. Yelabuga was founded as a Russian settlement in the latter part of the sixteenth century, a time of expansion of such settlements on Russia's southern and eastern frontiers. By the end of the nineteenth century, the town had become a thriving trading center by virtue of its location on a major tributary of the Volga River. Yelabuga's entrepreneurial prosperity was reflected in the creation of a harmonious

KULLE-KIMI VILLAGE. Post-Soviet minaret and mosque with chevron plank siding. June 7, 2004.

BOLSHOI MENGER. Bakirov house, built for a Tatar merchant at the turn of the twentieth century with a distinctive double-arched pediment. June 7, 2004.

nineteenth-century architectural environment, in which wooden houses played an important role. At the time of my visit in the summer of 2004, many of these nineteenth-century houses still stood, and there were also districts with early Soviet-era wooden houses of standardized design. One of those houses, owned in the 1940s by the Brodelshchikov family, was the final dwelling of the great twentieth-century poet Marina Tsvetaeva, who found a room as a war evacuee from Moscow in the desperate fall of 1941. It was here that her tragic, immensely complicated odyssey ended with suicide on August 31, 1941. When I photographed it, the house where Tsvetaeva spent the final ten days of her life still served as a family residence, and a similar wooden house nearby had been converted into a memorial. The following year, the Brodelshchikov house, built in 1925, was purchased by the state and converted into the Marina Tsvetaeva memorial, with much of the 1940s furnishings intact. Curiously, the plank siding visible in my 2004 photograph, and which probably existed when Tsvetaeva was there, has been removed, revealing the log structure underneath.

In the countryside surrounding Kazan and Yelabuga, there are dozens of villages that are ethnically Tatar. With the return of religious observance, there has been a demand for village mosques, many of which are log structures. Examples built recently show the adaptability of wooden architecture to Islamic traditions in rural areas.

Beyond Kazan, the Volga River eventually passes through the high cliffs of the Samara Gorge, leading to the Samara Bend on which the city of the same name is located near the confluence of the Samara River with the Volga. The origins of the name are a matter of linguistic debate, but it first appears in a travel account by the traveler and writer Ahmad ibn Fadlan, who in 921 was attached to an embassy sent from al-Muqtadir bi-llāh, ruler of the Abbasid Caliphate in Bagdad to the king of the Volga Bulgars near present-day Kazan. As a Russian fortress, Samara (current population around 1,163,000) was founded in 1586 by decree of Tsar Feodor I, son of Ivan the Terrible, to protect Russia's interests and navigation along the lower Volga. The completion in 1877 of a railroad from Orenburg to Samara (and westward) led to accelerated growth for a city that was already one of Russia's largest river ports. The growing population, which doubled in the quarter century from 1875 to 1900, created a corresponding development of ornately decorated wooden houses. As elsewhere, urban development has destroyed most of these houses, decorated in the profuse "merchant style." A few surviving examples are delightful to behold, but barring the unlikely creation of a preservation zone, they will continue to decay at an alarming rate. Much the same could be said of the remaining two historic cities on the lower Volga—Saratov and Astrakhan—but this survey of traditional wooden architecture ends at Samara.

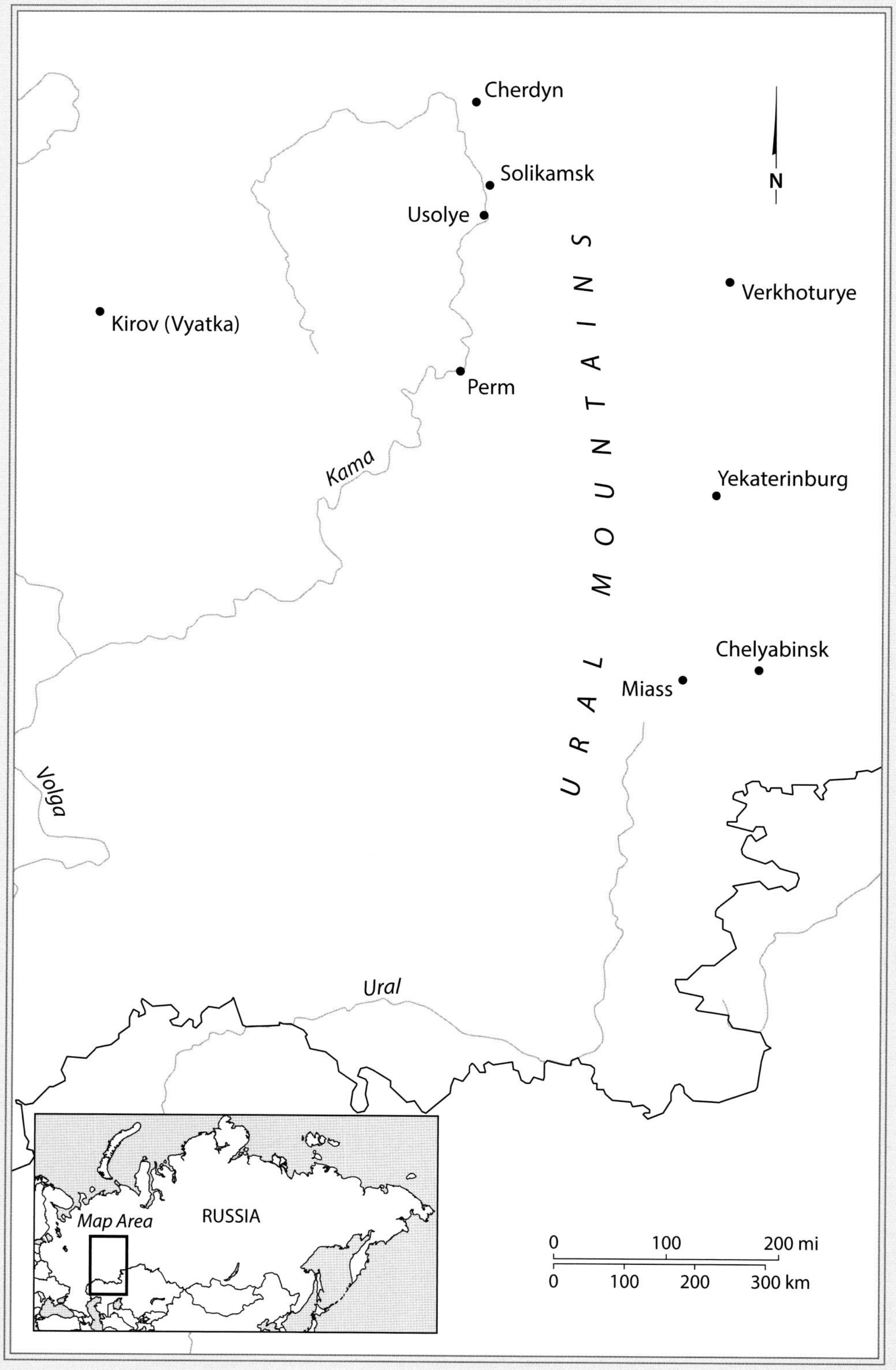

Cherdyn
Solikamsk
Usolye
N
URAL MOUNTAINS
Verkhoturye
Kirov (Vyatka)
Perm
Kama
Yekaterinburg
Chelyabinsk
Miass
Volga
Ural
Map Area
RUSSIA
0
100
200 mi
0
100
200
300 km

The Urals.

CHAPTER FIVE

Crossing the Urals

Toward the Northern Urals

As the dividing line between the European and Asian parts of Russia, the Ural Mountains are popularly considered the country's backbone. Extending from the Kara Sea in the north to Kazakhstan some 1,600 miles to the south, the Urals are not only a defining geographical feature but also the source of much of Russia's mineral wealth. This vast territory was assimilated by the Muscovite state in the fifteenth and sixteenth centuries as part of Russia's eastward expansion, which would reach the Pacific Ocean during the seventeenth century.

My overland route to the Urals in 1999 followed the old path from Moscow to Vladimir and Nizhny Novgorod, and from there to Vyatka (renamed "Kirov" after the assassination of the Leningrad party chief Sergey Kirov in 1934). There is a sense of boundary as the train crosses eastward over the majestic sweep of the Volga River and leaves behind the high, western river bluffs at Nizhny Novgorod. Here is the broad conduit along which merchants from the Orient and nomadic invaders from Asia's highlands moved toward the ancient territories of the Slavs. And in the opposite direction, Russia's merchants, troops, and settlers moved inexorably toward the east. Asia is still far, but Eurasia feels near at hand. Yet this is all still Europe. Kirov itself, located on picturesque hilly bluffs overlooking the Vyatka River is not even the beginning of the end of the European continent. This ancient town, first mentioned in Russian chronicles in 1374 under the name Khlynov, arose in an area along the Vyatka River that had been inhabited by Finno-Ugric tribes long before the first Slavs.

Unlike other historic Russian towns, Kirov (current population 472,000) did not revert to its pre-Soviet name after 1991. Preservationists and intellectuals attributed this stubborn indifference to the town's character as a sleepy, backward provincial hole (*dyra*), and I have always referred to it as Vyatka. Like every other Russian provincial center, Vyatka had its

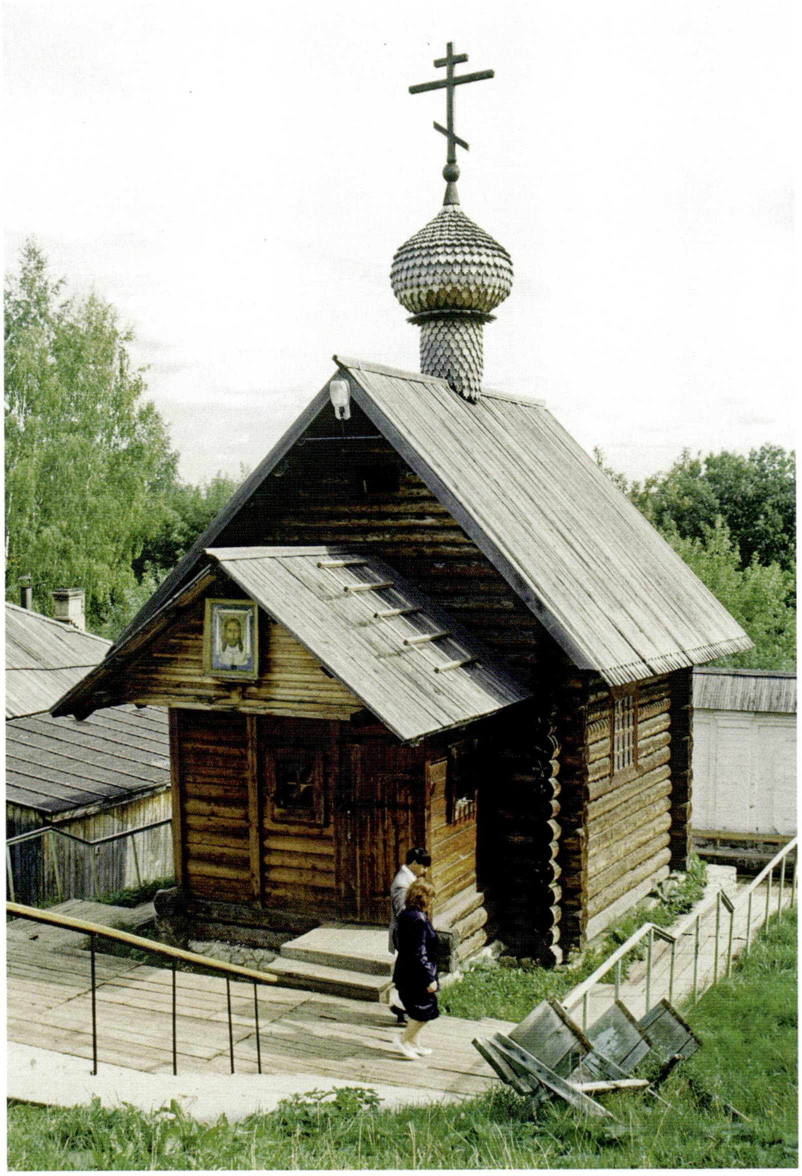

VYATKA (Kirov). Chapel of Saint Trifon of Vyatka, part of the Dormition-Saint Trifon Monastery, southwest view. Built in 1990 near a sacred spring, this is an early example of architectural traditions applied to contemporary church design. August 18, 1999.

share of festively decorated wooden houses, only a fraction of which are left, and as elsewhere, those committed to preserving traditional culture can only decry the loss.

Beyond Vyatka on the European side of the Ural Mountains, the metropolis of Perm is both an industrial powerhouse and a major cultural center, with slightly more than a million inhabitants. The main part of the city extends along the high east bank of the Kama River, with sweeping vistas across the river to the west. The toponym "Perm"—apparently derived from Finno-Ugric words *pera ma*, meaning "distant land"—is documented as early as the twelfth-century chronicle *Tale of Bygone Years*. At that time Perm was variously used to mean lands extending from the Vychegda

SLOBODSKOY. Church of Archangel Michael, originally built in 1610 at the Epiphany (later Elevation of the Cross) Monastery with the participation of Saint Trifon of Vyatka. Modified in the early nineteenth century; restored in 1957. August 19, 1999.

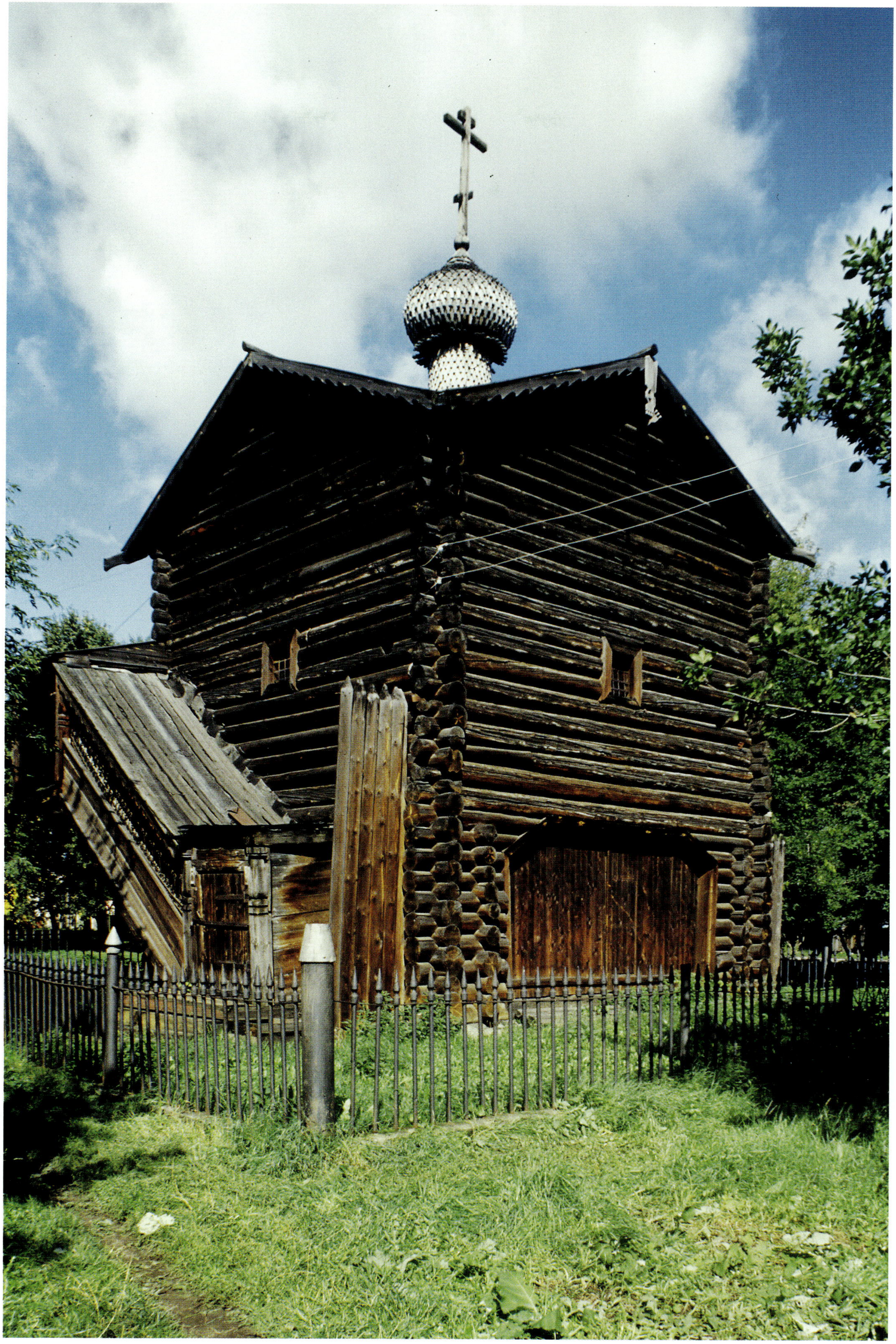

River basin to the Pechora and Izhma River networks in the north to the Vishera and Kama Rivers in the east and south. This territory was nominally controlled by the economic power of Novgorod the Great, whose hunters and traders were interested in its supply of valuable furs.

The city now known as Perm had its origins in the quest by Peter the Great (1672–1725) to exploit the rich ore deposits of the Urals and secure sources of high-quality industrial metals. As was the case for other Urals' towns (including Yekaterinburg), the guiding force in developing this area was Vasily Tatishchev (1686–1750), one of Russia's early professional historians. During the 1720s Tatishchev established settlements at mines, smelters, and metal-working plants throughout the Ural Mountains. In 1720 Tatishchev chose the seventeenth-century village of Egoshikha, located near the small Yegoshikha River, a tributary of the Kama. With nearby sources of copper ore, the site was considered ideal for a large smelter. Construction on the main Yegoshikha factory began on May 4, 1723, which is considered the city's founding date. The name Perm was officially adopted in 1781 after a command by Catherine the Great that transformed the large factory settlement into an administrative center for the Urals. Since its origins Perm has been associated with heavy industry, and by the 1860s it became one of the most important arms-producing areas in Russia. It would later serve as the model for Yuryatin in Boris Pasternak's novel *Doctor Zhivago*.

Typically, most of the wooden houses have vanished under the pressure of urban development, increasing land prices, and the difficulty of maintaining the material of wood in a heavily paved, urbanized environment. I have been able to document isolated examples of wooden houses in the central city, some of which are ornamented with festive decorative features such as carved window surrounds (*nalichniki*) typical of the late nineteenth and early twentieth centuries. One of the best-preserved examples is the house at Perm Street 67 consisting of a log structure on a brick basement. In 1883 the owner, Alexandra Tokareva, petitioned to expand the structure and rebuild the front part in a decorated manner derived from Russian interest in traditional vernacular folk styles (characterized as Russian Revival) in the latter part of the nineteenth century. With its elaborate carved and milled woodwork, the Tokareva house acquired the name *teremok* ("little tower chamber"), a term applied to similarly decorated structures in the Moscow area. In 1985 the Tokareva *teremok* was renovated for use as a small shop. It is now protected as a registered landmark. Most

PERM. Alexandra Tokareva house. Landmark example of decorative Russian Revival style. August 23, 1999.

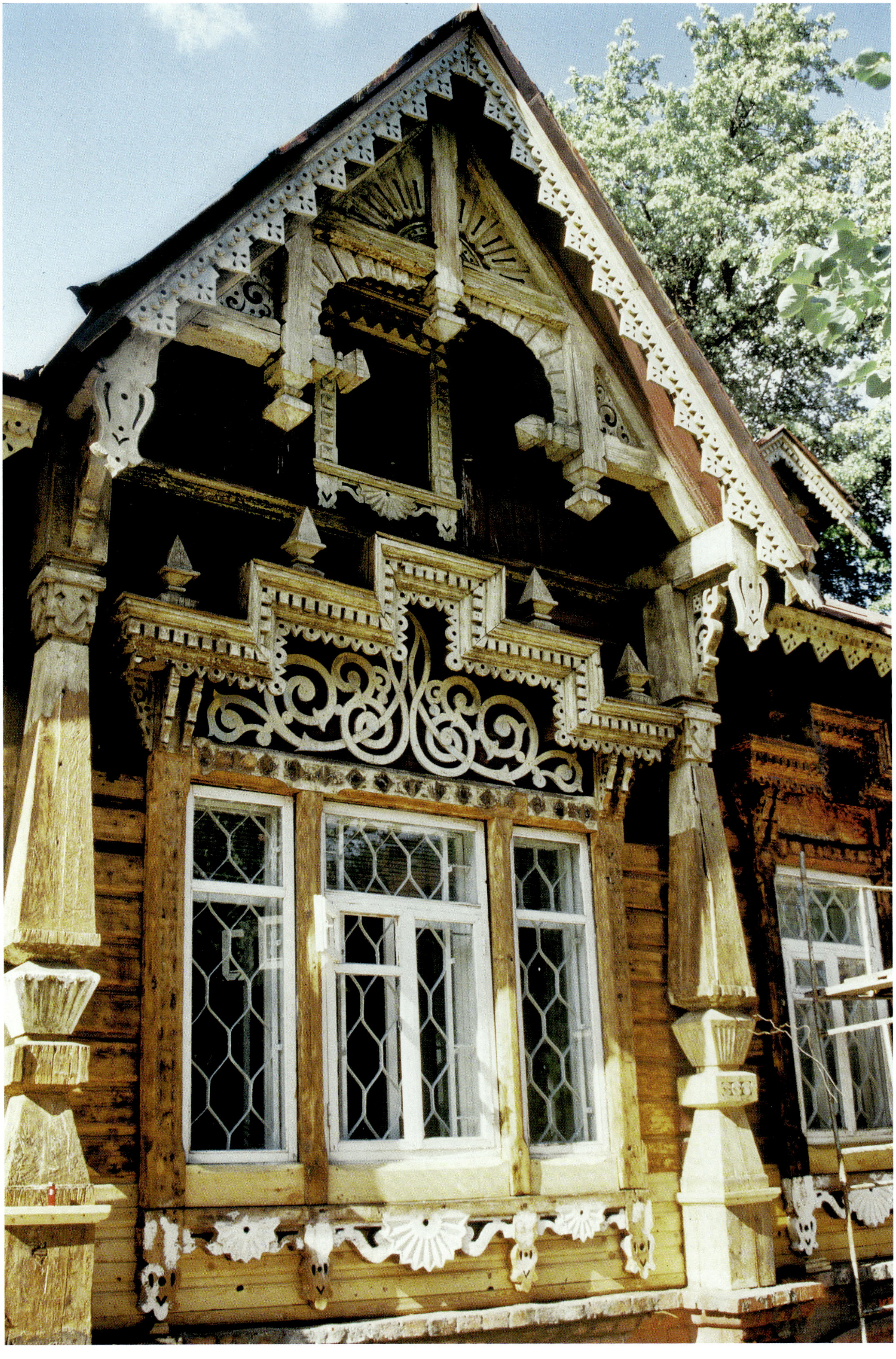

other wooden houses are likely to disappear. Yet Perm also pays a unique modernist homage to the properties of wood. Entitled "Perm Gate," this ingenious work was erected in 2011 by the artist Nikolay Polissky near the main Perm II Rail Station. Twelve meters in height, width and depth, the sculpture consists of 2,500 fir logs bound in chaotic fashion to create a thoroughly original triumphal arch.

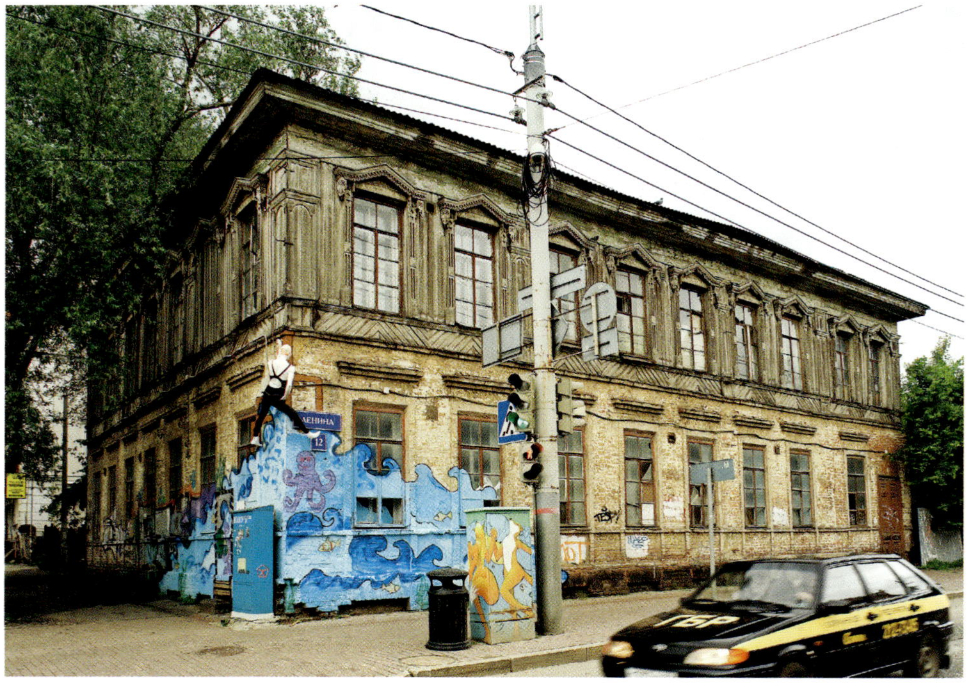

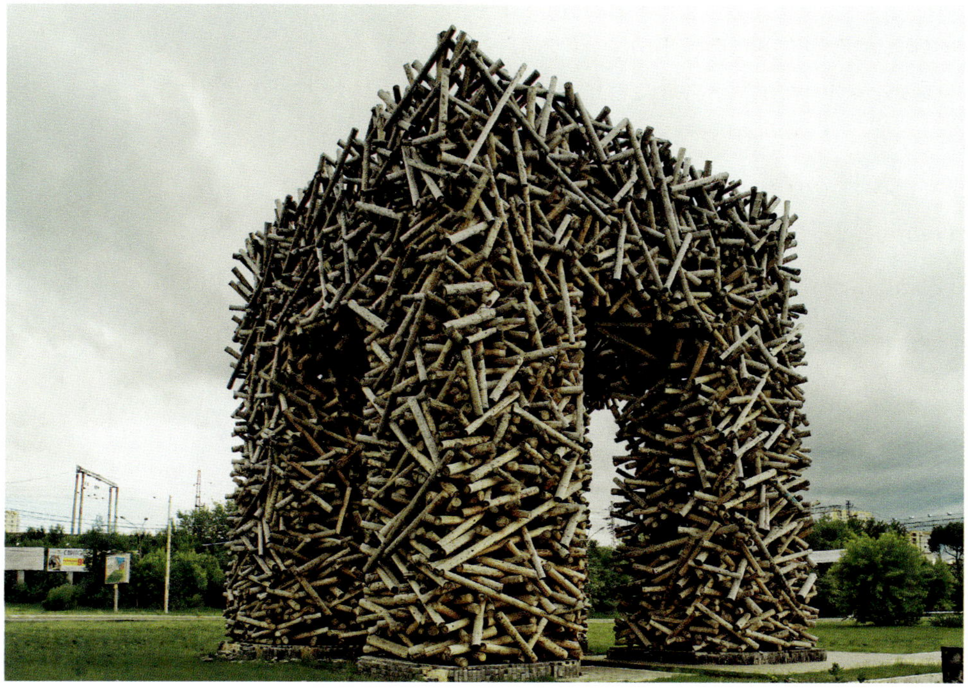

PERM. Residential building with wooden upper story, Lenin Street 12. Built in 1917 and abandoned in 2012, this fine classically detailed structure was reduced to a surface for street art with panache—already a harbinger of its demise. Demolished in 2022. June 15, 2014.

PERM. "Perm Gate." This ingenious tribute to the properties of the log was created in 2011 by the sculptor Nikolay Polissky near the main Perm II Rail Station as a portal to the city. June 15, 2014.

In the larger Perm area, the main architectural-ethnographic museum is known as Khokhlovka (pronounced HO-hlovka), named after a village nearby on the small Khokhlovka River. Located less than an hour's drive north of Perm, the Khokhlovka park is one of those special journeys back into the region's past. Architectural preservationists and scholars began plans for the park in 1969, and with the approval of the Ministry of Culture in 1971, regional authorities set aside a beautiful hilly site of some forty hectares leading down to the west bank of the Kama River Reservoir. The park opened to the public in 1980. The entrance is through a turreted log gateway typical of sacred precincts (*pogost*) found throughout the Russian North. The spacious natural landscape consists of clusters of log buildings transported from various parts of Perm Province. They include two churches and a bell tower, log houses (two of which have restored interiors), barns, a village fire station, and a windmill with its interior intact.

The two churches—the Church of the Nativity of the Virgin (1694) from the village of Tokhtarevo and the Church of the Transfiguration (1702–6) from the village of Yanidor—display some of the oldest forms in wooden church architecture. Both adhere to a traditional cuboid design built of pine logs, with a pitched roof of aspen shingles, an altar contained in an apse on the east end, and a refectory extending from the west side. The roof design of the Tokhtarevo church (from the Suksun region southeast of Perm) is particularly appealing, with a rhythm of different angles and shapes from west to east. The adjacent log bell tower, built in 1781 in an octagonal form, was brought from the village of Syra in the same area. In an unusual decorative flourish, the main cupola of the Transfiguration Church from Yanidor (Cherdyn region north of Perm) rests upon four intersecting barrel gables. As was often the case in severe northern climates, the Church of the Transfiguration was raised on a two-meter base (*podklet*) to place it above snow level. During a restoration undertaken in 1984–85 by Boris Gnedovsky and Gershen Kantorovich, an elevated porch and gallery were reconstructed on the west and north facades of the church, whose basic structure dates from 1694.

A unique part of the Khokhlovka display is an ensemble of factory structures brought from the town of Solikamsk, where they were used as recently as the 1950s as part of the Ust-Borovsk salt refinery. Following the path between these massive log buildings (constructed in the 1880s) from wellhead to brine pumping station, to refinery barn, to the shipping warehouse on the edge of the Kama River, the entire process is illustrated with

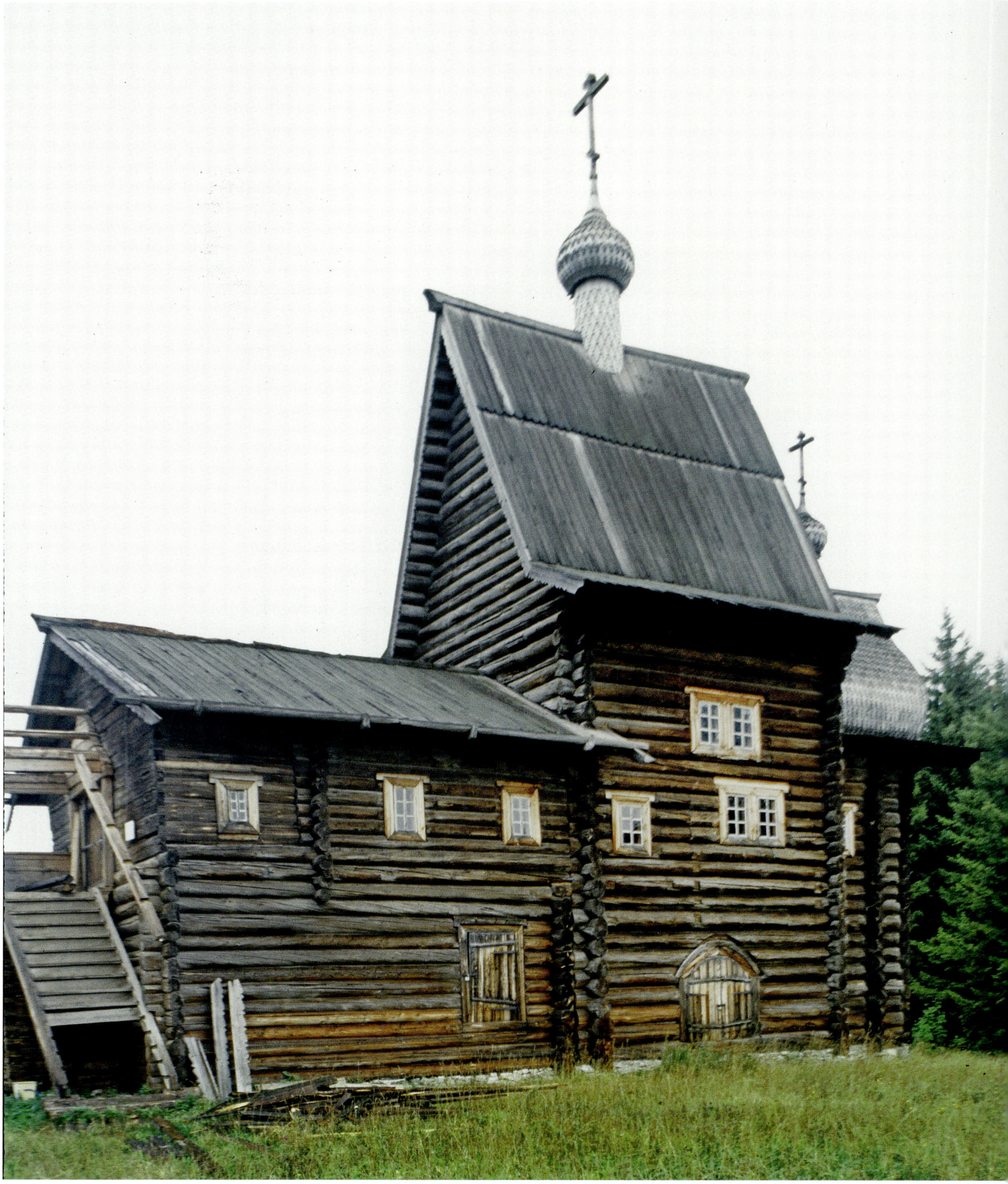

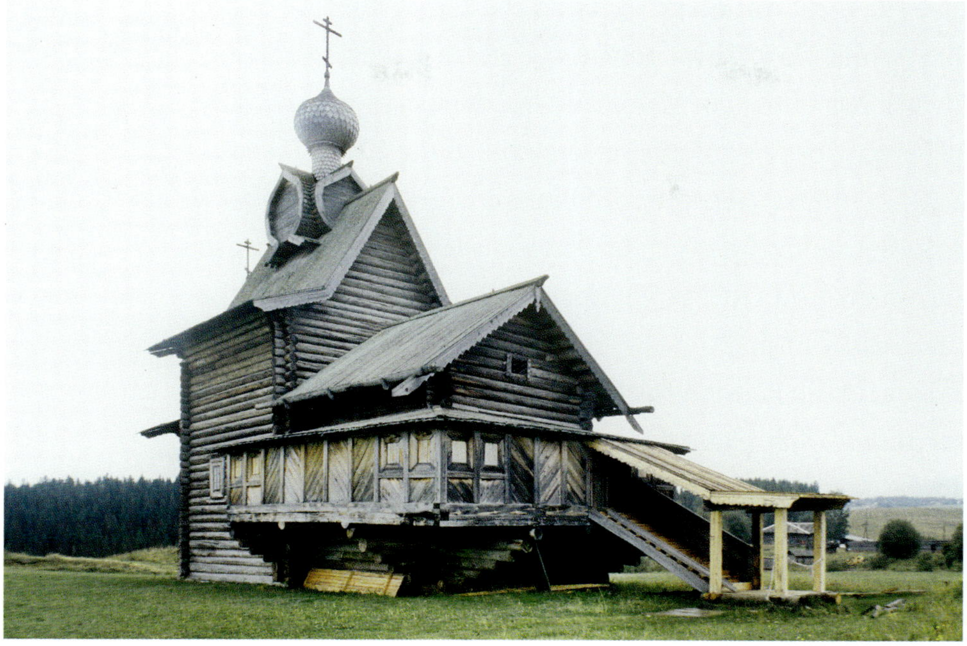

KHOKHLOVKA (near Perm, outdoor museum). Church of the Nativity of the Virgin from Tokhtarevo village, southwest view. Traditional in its basic design, this 1694 structure is notable for its height and steeply pitched roof. August 22, 1999.

KHOKHLOVKA. Church of the Transfiguration (1702–6) from Yanidor village, northwest view. August 22, 1999.

the aid of captions and archival photographs. Some of the most delightful structures at Khokhlovka are also the smallest—the hunter's hut (*pyvzen*) and the miniature elevated storage boxes, or caches, used to protect bounty from scavengers during extended forest hunts (see page 422).

The Ural Mountains have long been one of the most significant sources of the country's mineral wealth. In the seventeenth and eighteenth centuries the discovery of iron, copper, salt, and other valuable mineral deposits transformed remote mining outposts into thriving towns such as Yekaterinburg. Before the expansion of Russia's rail network into the Urals during the second half of the nineteenth century, one of the major challenges was delivering this bounty to Russia's major population centers. A partial solution to this transportation problem was provided by the region's ample

KHOKHLOVKA. Nikolsky Salt Barn. Built in the 1880s for the Ust-Borovsk salt refinery in Solikamsk. August 22, 1999.

KHOKHLOVKA. Hunter's forest hut (*pyvzen*). August 22, 1999.

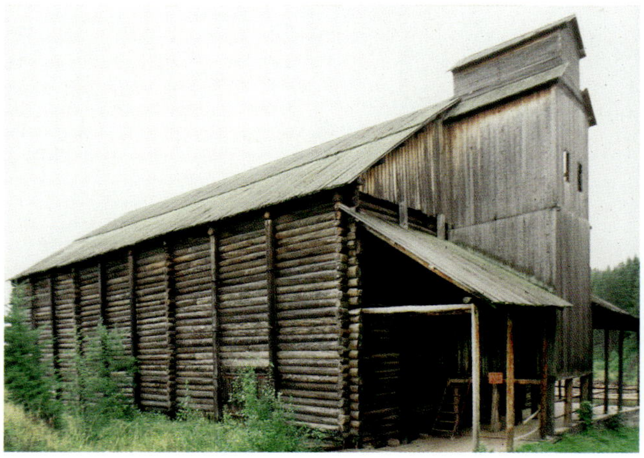

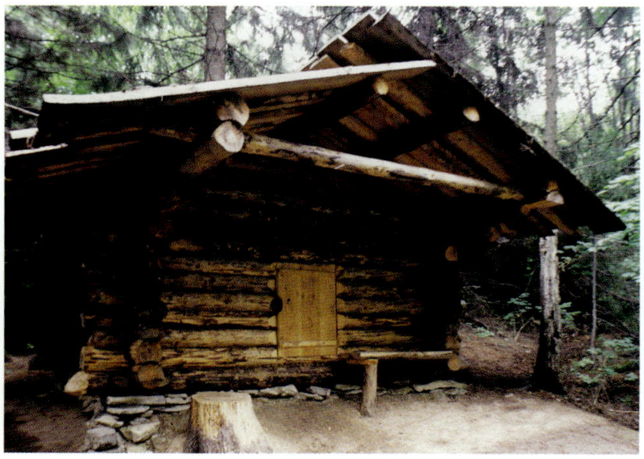

network of rivers. The most important river on the European side of the Urals is the Kama, which flows through the vast Perm Territory and enters the Volga River south of Kazan. Major mineral deposits—particularly potash—are still being processed along the left bank of the Kama at towns such as the Soviet-era industrial center of Berezniki.

Some 370 kilometers to the north of Perm is the city of Solikamsk (current population around 110,000), whose name means "salt on the Kama." Solikamsk was founded in 1430 when the Kalinnikov merchant family (from Vologda, in the Russian North) established a salt works there. To this day the economy of Solikamsk depends heavily on the mining of potassium and related salts. By the end of the seventeenth century Solikamsk also served as a major transit point to Siberia and China. The combination of salt refining, administration, and transportation of goods to market created the economic base necessary for major construction in Solikamsk, particularly of churches. Despite the losses suffered during the Soviet suppression of religion, Solikamsk has preserved many of the buildings of its historic center. During the reign of Catherine, the path of further mining and industrial development in the Urals shifted to the south, to the newer settlements of Perm and Yekaterinburg, which were served not by the sixteenth-century Babinov Road, but by the newly opened Siberian Route. Nonetheless, Solikamsk experienced modest growth in the latter part of the nineteenth century, development reflected in the form of large wooden houses with decorative fretwork from the turn of the twentieth century. Much of the town's economy was supported by the renovation in the 1870s of local salt works under the ownership of the Ryazantsev family. Salt continued to be produced at the former Ryazantsev salt refinery (under Soviet ownership) until 1972, and in 1999 I was able to photograph massive nineteenth-century log structures on the former territory—a rare surviving example of log industrial facilities in situ.

SOLIKAMSK. Wooden house, May First Street. This facade detail, with miniature rustication, vertical plank siding, and carved plaiting around the window, is a compendium of provincial inventiveness. August 24, 1999.

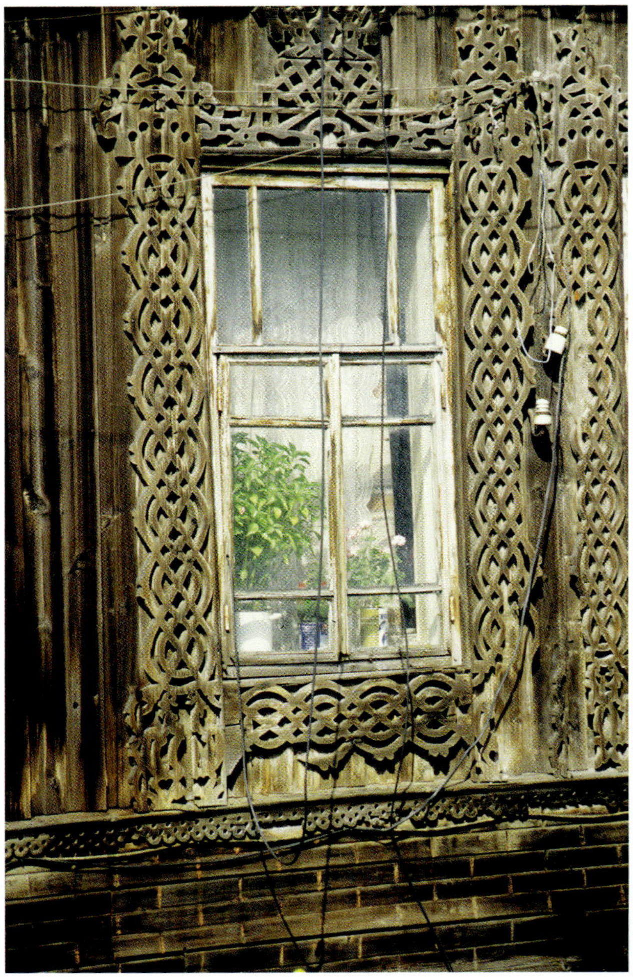

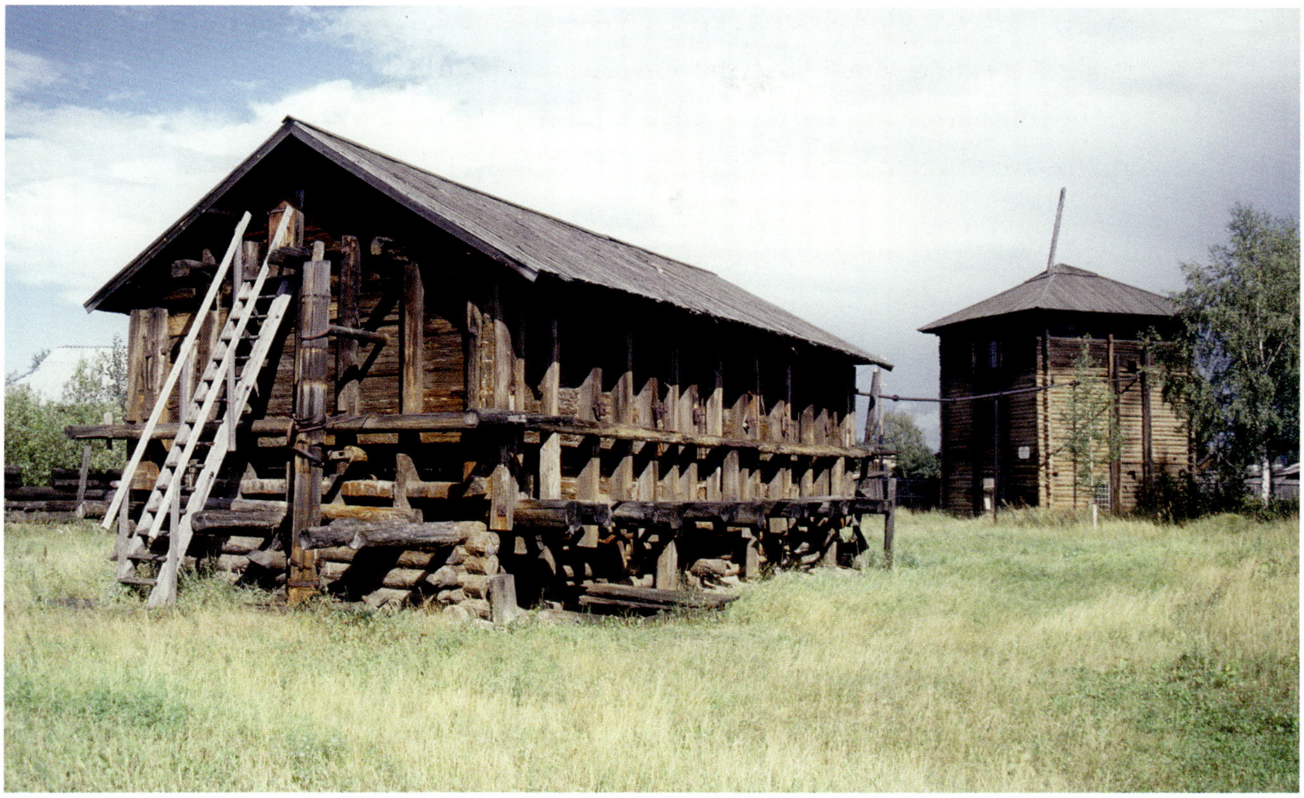

The path from Perm and Solikamsk on the Kama River to Cherdyn on the upper tributaries of the Kama traces a straight line parallel to the spine of the Urals just to the east. Cherdyn itself was settled perhaps as early as the ninth century, with Russians (and Orthodox missionaries) moving into the area by the fourteenth century. Not until the 1470s did the Cherdyn region come under the control of Moscow, and the area continued to be subjected to Nogai raids until the conquest of Kazan by Ivan the Terrible in 1552. Through the sixteenth century, Cherdyn was a gateway for Russian settlers crossing the Ural Mountains to the east. Situated on the right bank of the Kolva River, near its confluence with the Vishera, Cherdyn controlled river passage in several directions: to the north, via the Kolva River, to the Pechora basin; to the south, via the mighty Kama River, to the Volga and Moscow; and to the east, via the Vishera, to the Ob River basin and Siberia. At the turn of the seventeenth century a more direct Siberian route via Solikamsk undercut Cherdyn's strategic position. Nonetheless, it retained regional commercial significance, intensified in the late nineteenth century by gold prospecting in the Vishera River basin. This prosperity is beautifully reflected in its festively decorative houses, often wooden structures resting on brick ground floors.

SOLIKAMSK. Ryazantsev Salt Works, salt bin. Background: Resurrection brine pumping tower. Local salt magnates endowed brine pumping towers with religious names, perhaps with hopes of perpetuating the flow of white gold. August 12, 2000.

Surrounding Cherdyn are small towns and villages whose names are rich with consonants and churches: Vilgort, Kamgort, Pokcha, and Pyanteg, located on a bend in the Kama River some forty kilometers southwest of Cherdyn. Overlooking that river bend and perhaps designed to serve as a watchtower is the archaic Church of the Icon of the Smolensk Virgin (also known as the Epiphany Church), which lays claim to being the oldest surviving log structure in the western Urals. Built as early as the late sixteenth century (or perhaps 1617), the structure has an unusual hexagonal (instead of octagonal) form that suggests a possible derivation from hexagonal towers at log forts. With an advantageous location on the steep left bank of the Kama River, the church might also have served as a beacon. Studies of the interior and upper log structure suggest that the original design culminated not in the low-pitched roof currently visible, but in a high tent tower similar to those above other polygonal log churches from the sixteenth through the eighteenth centuries.

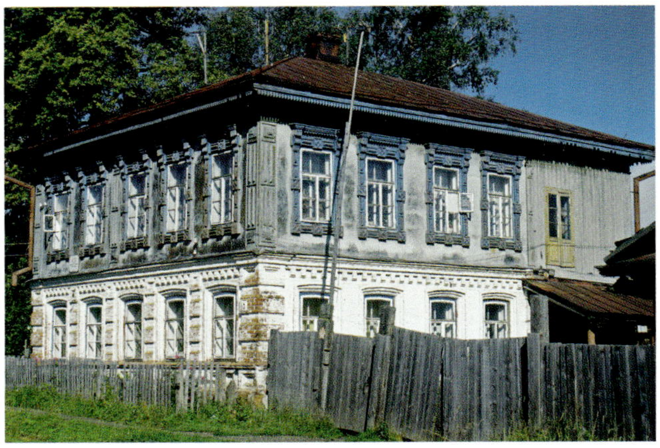

CHERDYN. Yaborov house. This beautifully proportioned late nineteenth-century house on a brick ground floor reflects the prosperity of local gold prospecting. August 13, 2000.

POKCHA. The florid decoration of this early twentieth-century house includes facade rustication and a saturated courtyard gate. August 14, 2000.

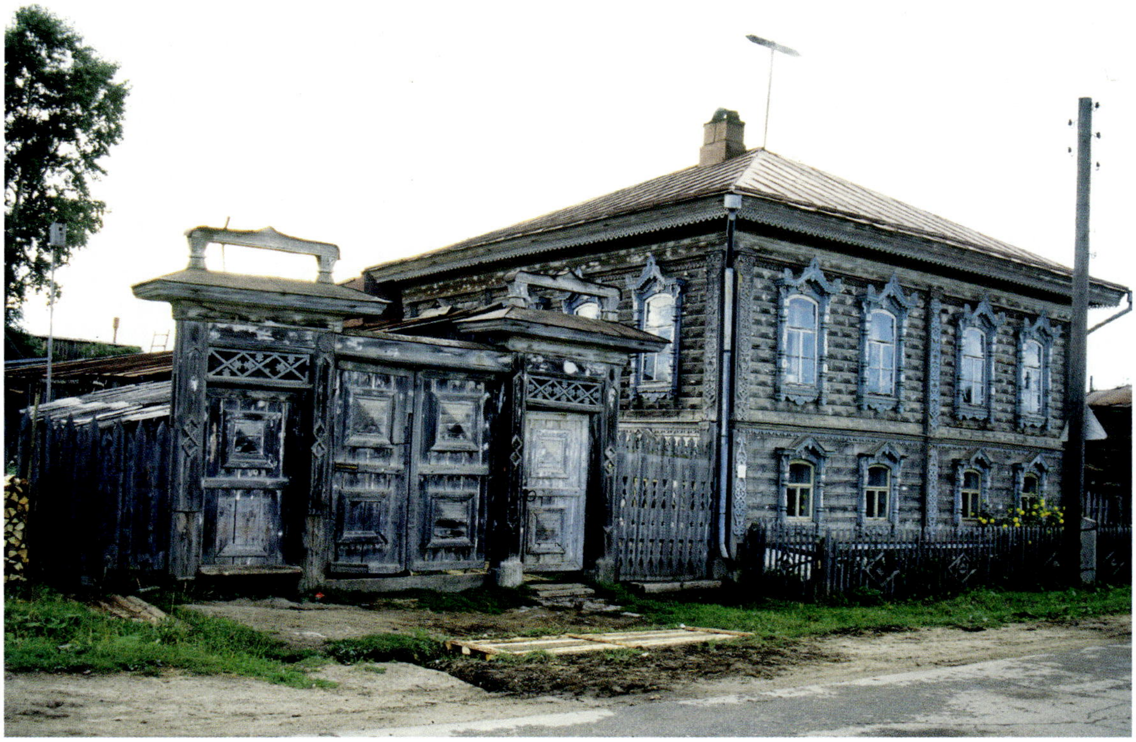

PYANTEG. Church of the Epiphany, northeast view. Considered the oldest surviving log structure in the western Urals. August 15, 2000.

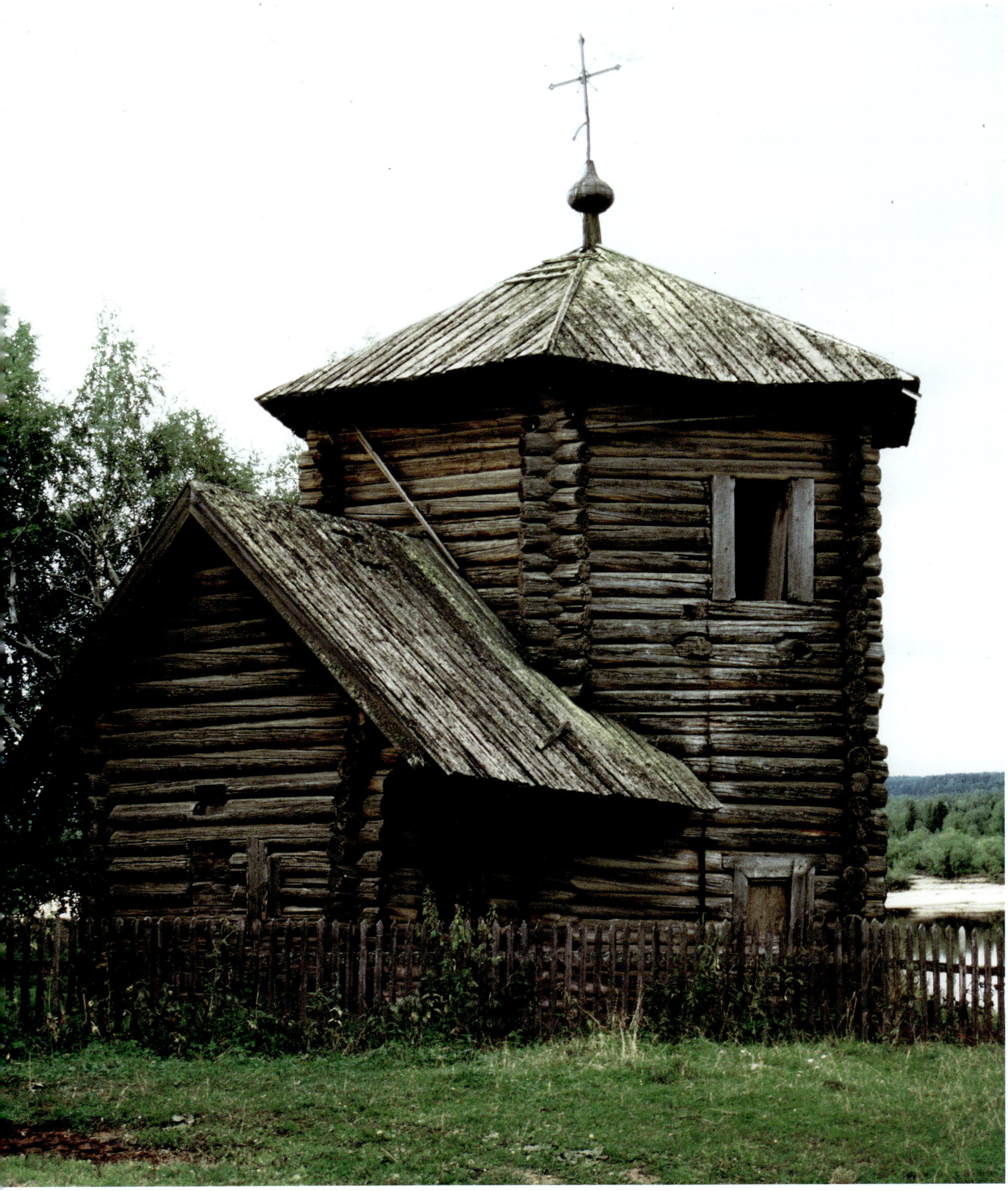

The Yekaterinburg Area

Yekaterinburg (current population 1,539,000) is a relatively recent creation, originating in the early 1720s through Peter the Great's quest to develop heavy industry and armaments for his expanding army. The modernization of Russian metal-working capabilities was a major part of the tsar's ambitious industrial strategy, and the rich mineral resources of the Urals led to the creation of numerous factory settlements and towns. Construction at the settlement began in 1721 under the guidance of Vasily Tatishchev, who also played a pivotal role in the development of Perm. Production at the first State Metals Factory on the Iset River began in 1723, and three years later the settlement was named in honor of Empress Catherine I, Peter the Great's second wife, who after his death reigned briefly between 1725 and 1727. In the eighteenth century, Yekaterinburg gained renown as a center for ornamental objects from semiprecious Urals stones, such as jasper, porphyry, and malachite. With the extension of the Moscow Road through Yekaterinburg in 1763, the factory town also flourished as a transportation center despite its considerable distance from a large river. With the construction of a rail network through the Urals and into Siberia, Yekaterinburg witnessed a rapid increase in the pace of development. The first rail link, to Perm, opened in 1878, and the next two decades witnessed new lines in several directions.

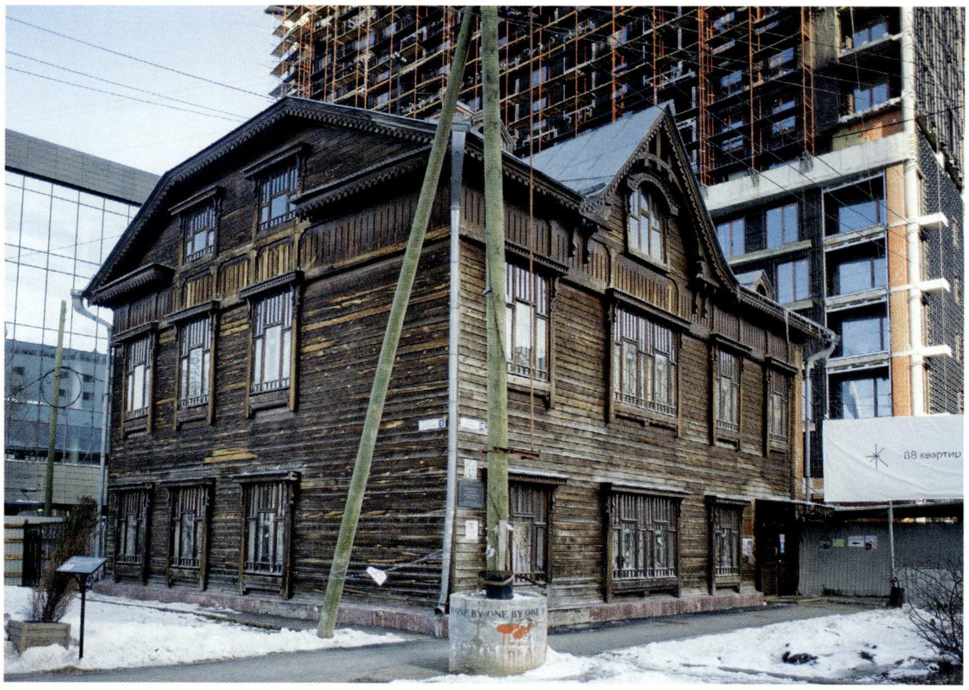

YEKATERINBURG. Kazantsev building. Superb early twentieth-century log commercial structure with *style moderne* detailing. April 2, 2017.

By the turn of the century its population was approaching fifty thousand, and while the center of town was characterized by masonry construction, the development of sawmills provided building materials for the city's largely wooden habitat. In the latter part of the twentieth century, that wooden environment retreated, as it had in Nizhny Novgorod, Kazan, and other cities. Isolated examples survive in central Yekaterinburg, including wooden houses built in the *style moderne*. An example of contemporary wooden religious architecture is the Chapel of Saints Elisabeth Feodorovna and Barbara of Alapaevsk, erected in 1992 on the site of the Ipatyev house, where Nicholas II and his family were killed on the night of July 16/17, 1918. (Saints Elisabeth and Barbara were among a group shot the following day near Alapaevsk, a mining town northeast of Yekaterinburg.) The chapel is now part of the grand complex of the Cathedral of all Saints Resplendent in the Russian Land. Other contemporary log shrines include the Ganina Yama memorial complex (formally known as the Monastery of the Holy Royal Martyrs) north of the city at the site of an abandoned mine shaft where the bodies of the royal victims were thrown.

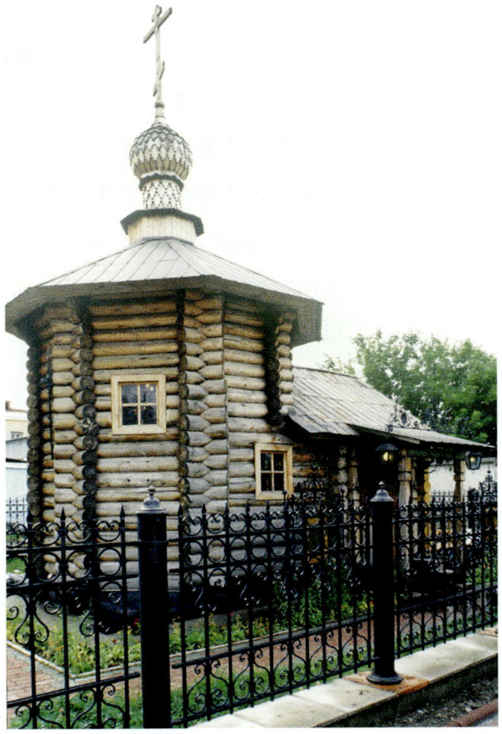

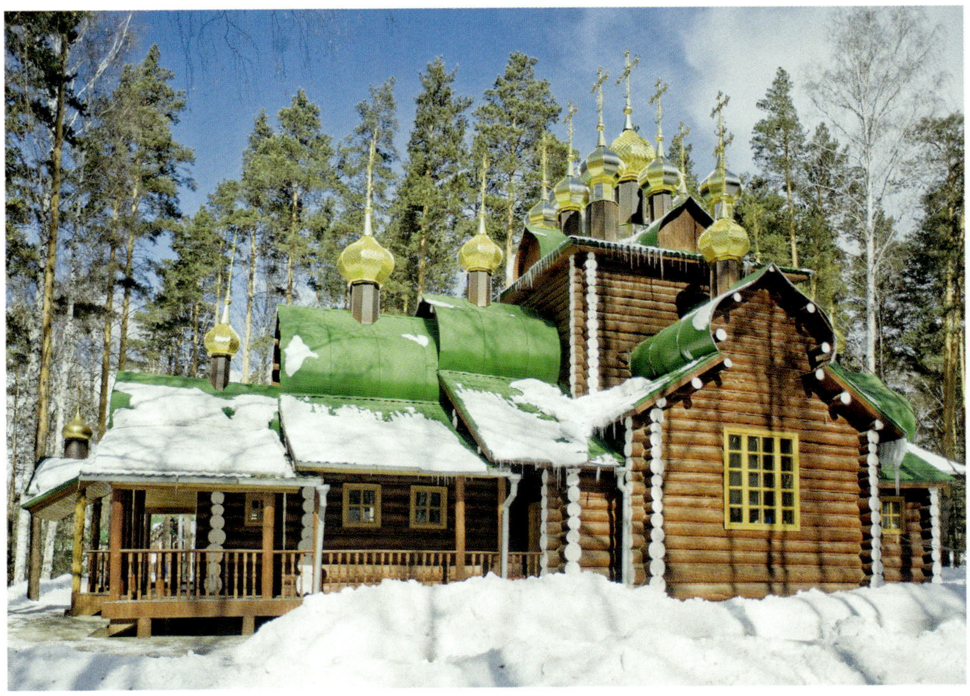

YEKATERINBURG. Chapel of Saints Elisabeth Feodorovna and Barbara of Alapaevsk, northeast view. Architect: Alexander Dolgov. August 2, 1999.

GANINA YAMA (near Yekaterinburg). Church of Saint Nicholas at Monastery of the Holy Royal Martyrs, south view. Built in 2002 by Natalya Akchurina, designer of most of the shrines at Ganina Yama. April 1, 2017.

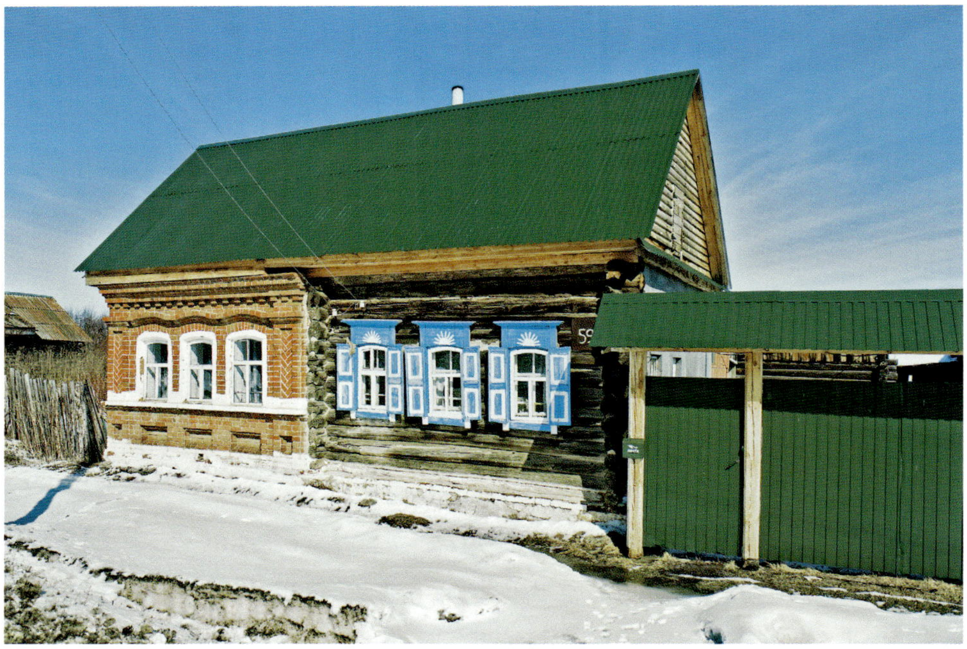

TROITSKOE (near Yekaterinburg). House, Lenin Street 59. The owners of this village property have the virtues of both brick and wood, with a late nineteenth-century brick core and subsequent log extension beneath a modern aluminum roof. April 2, 2017.

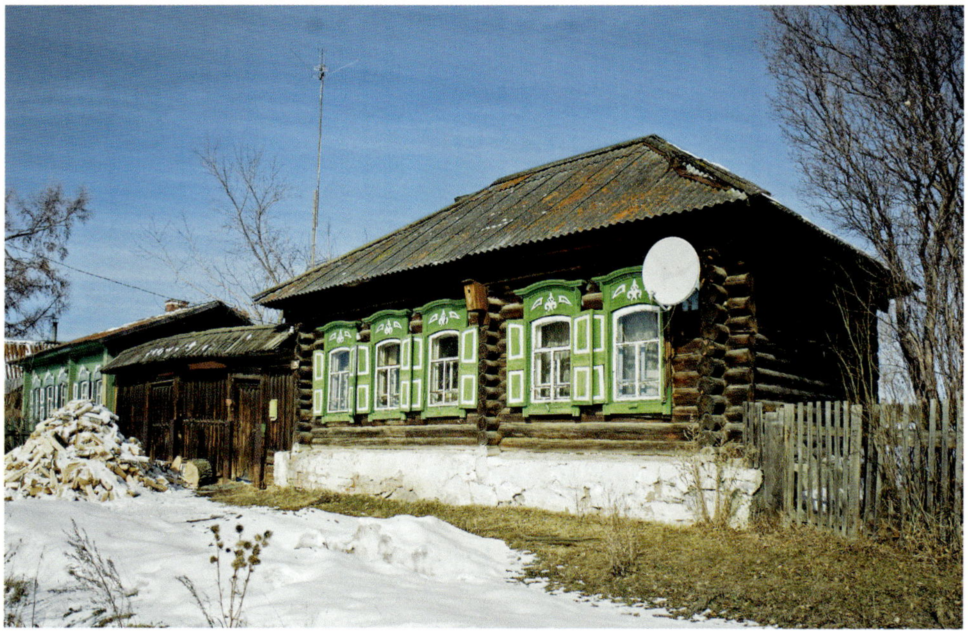

ISETSKOE (near Yekaterinburg). House, Lenin Street 3. Well-maintained five-wall structure with urbanizing elements. Facade displays decorative surrounds, a bird house, and a satellite dish. April 2, 2017.

The area beyond Yekaterinburg is dotted with historic settlements, including the eighteenth-century factory town of Nevyansk. The most visually dramatic is the town of Verkhoturye (pronounced "verkho-tUr-ye"), on the upper reaches of the Tura River some three hundred kilometers to the north of Yekaterinburg. Verkhoturye (its name means "upper Tura") played a critical role in extending Russian authority to the east during the seventeenth century. Although the Tura River, one thousand kilometers long, is not particularly large by Russian standards, it is a crucial link from the eastern watershed of the Urals to the great Siberian River networks. With the founding of Tobolsk in 1585, Russia had a strategic anchor in western Siberia at the confluence of the Tobol and Irtysh Rivers. In 1595 Tsar Feodor, son of Ivan the Terrible, announced a search for a more direct way across the Urals to the Tobol basin and into Siberia. The Tura, which flows into the Tobol River south of Tobolsk, proved the logical choice. Shortly thereafter Artemy Babinov, a free peasant from Solikamsk, blazed a trail across the Urals from Solikamsk to the Tura River. Within the remarkably short period of two years the almost three-hundred-kilometer path was improved to a state road that led to the fortified settlement of Verkhoturye, founded in 1598. In the same year a log church was built and dedicated to the Trinity. Shortly thereafter Verkhoturye was designated the primary customs point for passage to Siberia. This tight control on movement to and from Siberia allowed the state to maintain its revenues through taxes on goods such as fur pelts—most especially the highly valued sable. Throughout the seventeenth century Verkhoturye bustled with activity as salt, manufactured goods, and other essential items were shipped to new settlements in Siberia, while a flow of fur pelts made its way back toward Moscow. This "black gold" was so valuable that a separate fur treasury was created to guard and assess the pelts.

Despite its decline when the main route over the Urals to Siberia shifted southward to Yekaterinburg in the 1760s, Verkhoturye remained

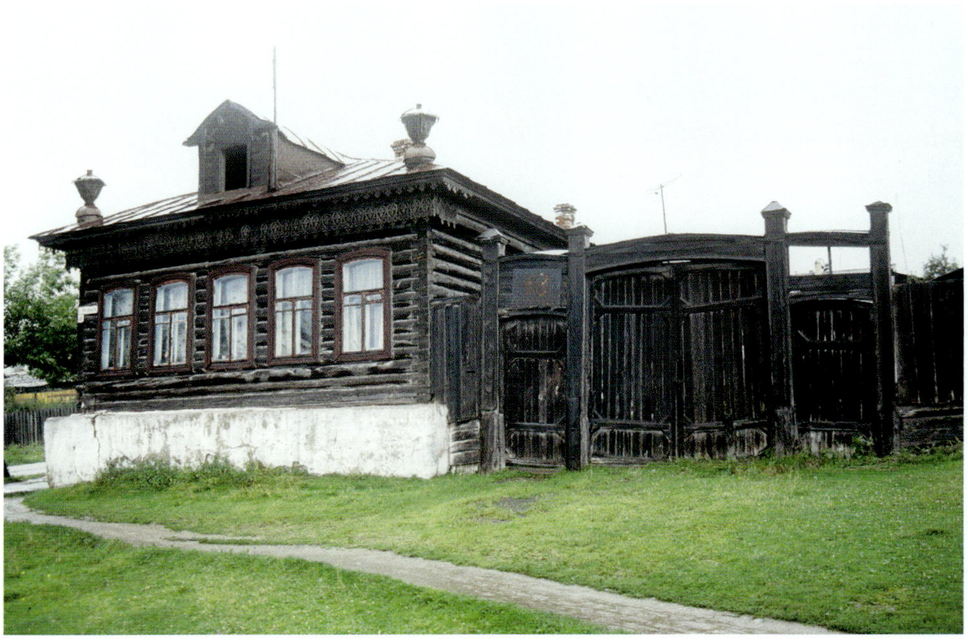

NEVYANSK. House, Engels Street 18. Excellent example of a factory town log dwelling with a painted metal roof graced with decorative urns. August 26, 1999.

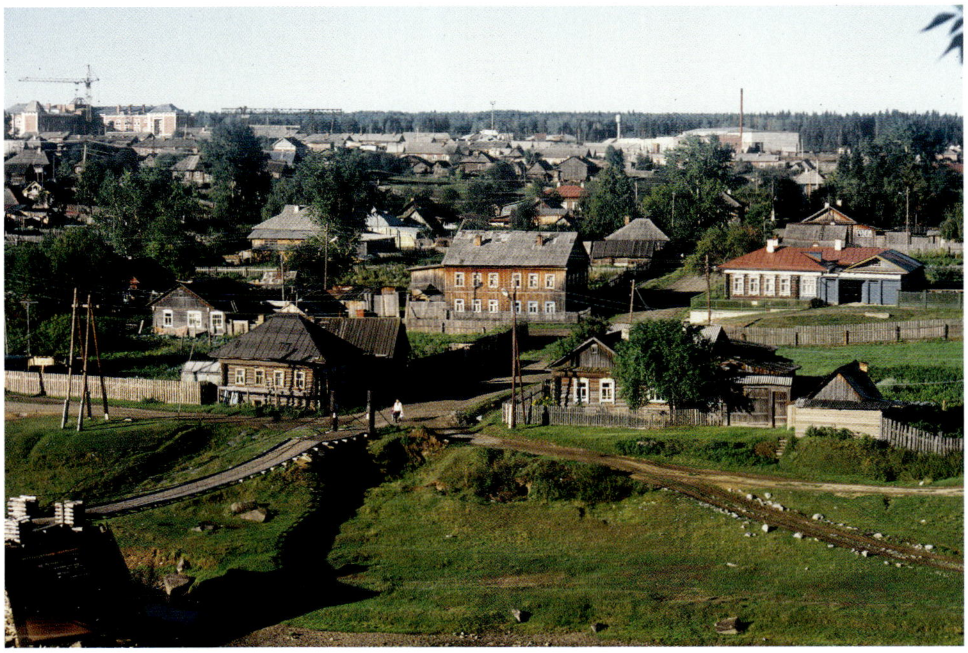

VERKHOTURYE. View from Trinity Rock toward west bank of Tura River. Although most of these wooden houses were built during the Soviet period, the view gives a sense of the wooden environment that characterized Russian provincial towns. August 27, 1999.

an important religious center, its churches and monasteries receiving numerous pilgrims visiting the relics of local saints. Although small in comparison with regional centers such as Yekaterinburg, Verkhoturye has well-preserved enclaves of nineteenth- and early twentieth-century wooden buildings with traditional exterior decoration, particularly on the right bank of the Tura.

The Southern Urals

Chelyabinsk (current population 1,182,000) is among those largely ignored workhorses that form the backbone of Russian heavy industry. Located on the Miass River just on the east flank of the Ural Mountains, the settlement was founded in the fall of 1736 as part of a chain of forts to protect supply lines from the granaries of western Siberia to the new Orenburg Territory on Russia's southern frontier. Cossack troops and settlers were moving into vast steppes roamed by Bashkir tribes, who responded with frequent attacks on Russian supply trains and outposts. By 1739 the Chelyabinsk fort already had a population of more than a thousand, mostly military. Although situated in a region rich in metals and towns that worked those metals, such as Zlatoust and Miass, Chelyabinsk remained a local market town for more than a century. Its modest claim to fame was its capture

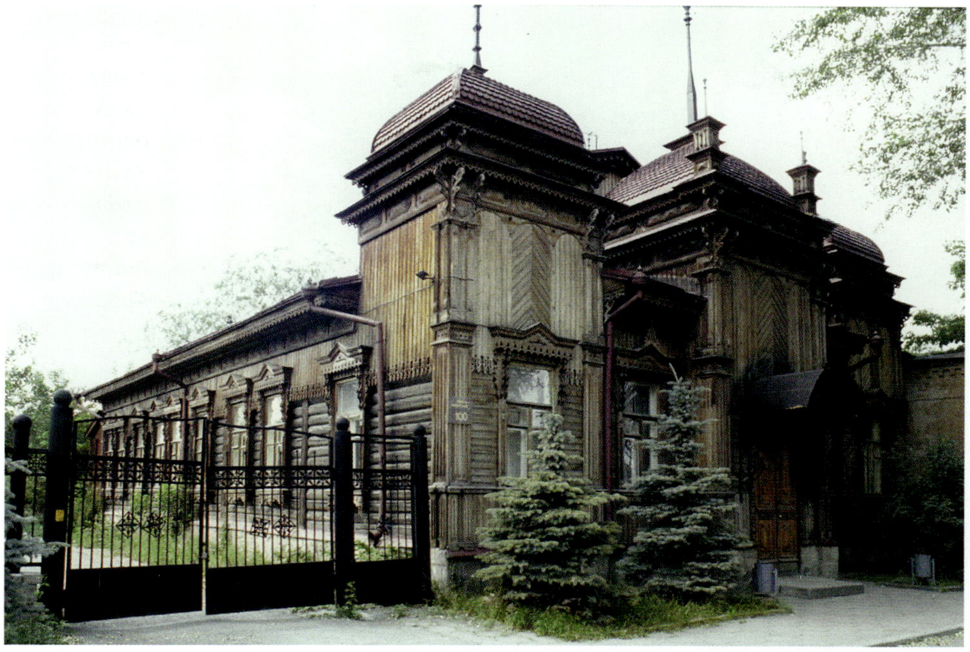

CHELYABINSK. House, Red Army Street 100. This early twentieth-century mansion shows an unusual combination of Beaux Arts and *style moderne* with flanking towers and decorative siding. A fascinating compendium of ornament. July 12, 2003.

for two months in 1774 by forces allied with the renowned rebel Emelyan Pugachev.

That changed in the 1890s with the construction of the Trans-Siberian Railroad, which made Chelyabinsk a major junction in the southern Urals and a gateway to the east. Lured by agricultural reforms and promises of rich lands in Siberia, thousands of peasant families passed through special resettlement centers in Chelyabinsk, where they received rudimentary care and supplies for the trip to Siberia, cast as a land of opportunity. By 1897 the town had twenty thousand inhabitants but a much larger commercial significance enabled by the railroad. The transfer to Chelyabinsk of the main eastern customs point meant that the trade in Chinese tea was now processed in the town's tea sorting plants. And the region's agriculture gained through the railroad an exponentially larger market that led to the construction of tall, modern grain elevators of reinforced concrete. The territory around Chelyabinsk marks a transition from the forest zone to the north to what is known as a "forest-steppe" zone. Nonetheless, logs and milled timber for housing could readily be transported by rail to supplement local sources. If the town's commercial district consisted mostly of brick structures, houses continued to be built largely of wood for reasons of habit, affordability, and comfort. A few examples still stand, but more have survived in smaller towns near the border of Kazakhstan, such as Kyshtym, Kasli, Miass, and Troitsk.

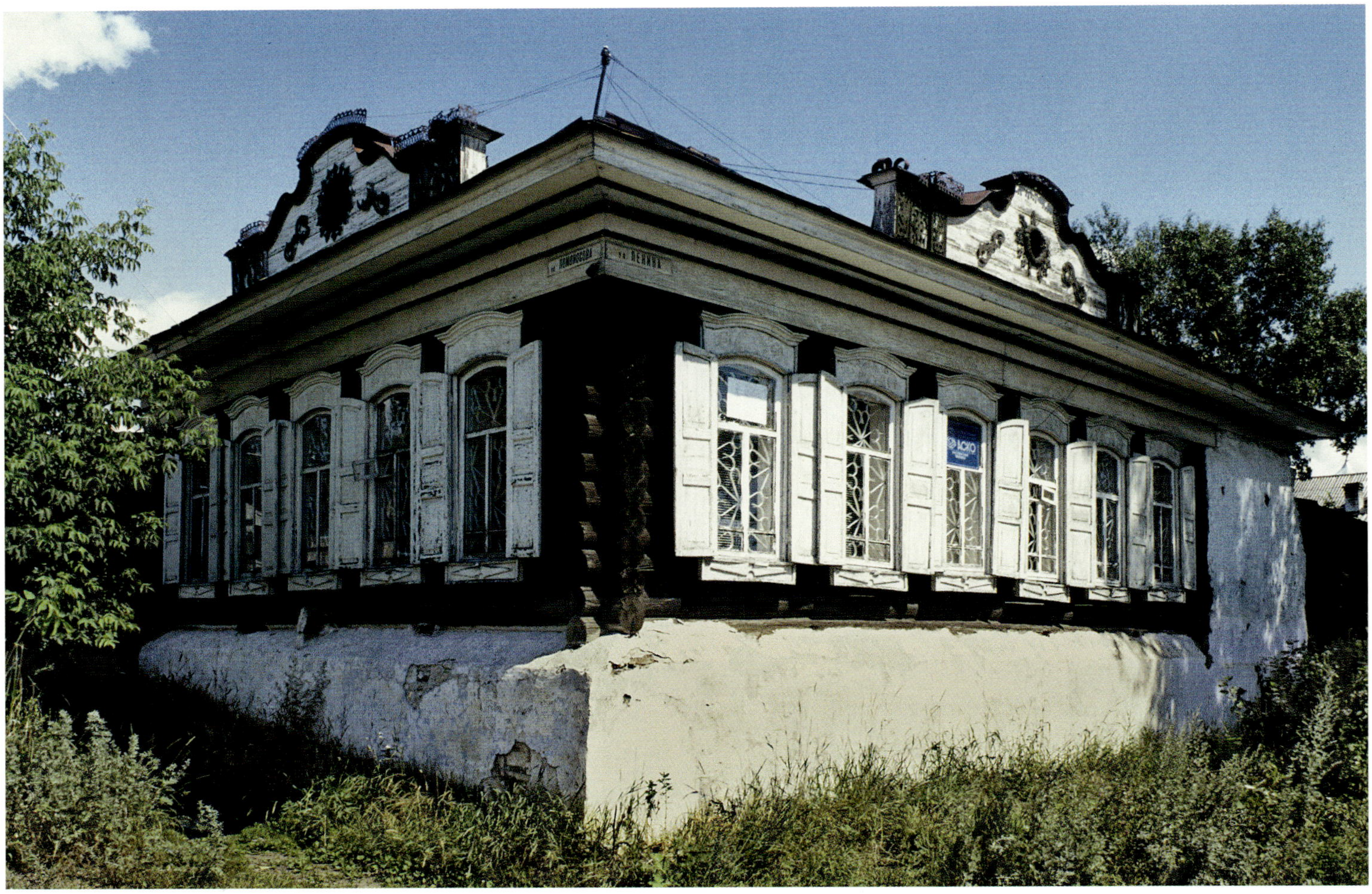

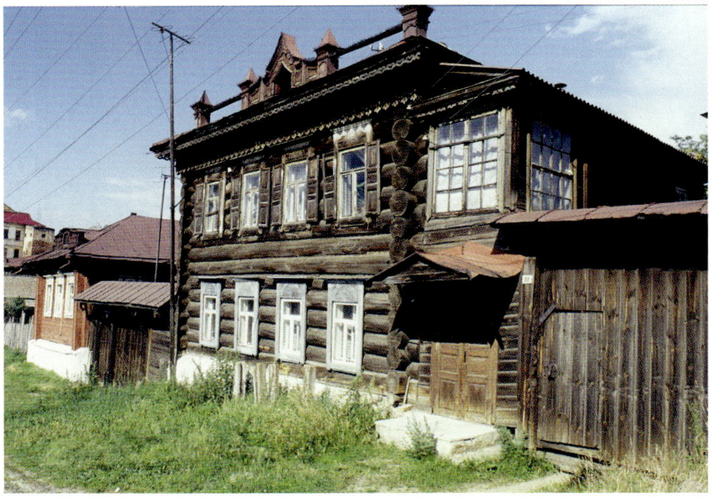

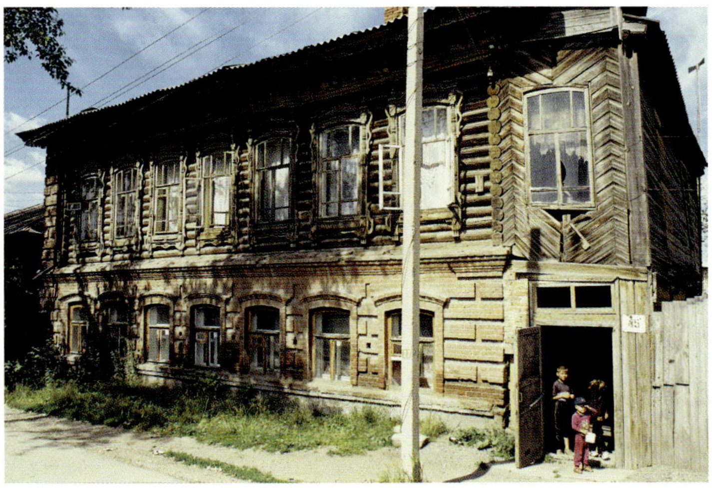

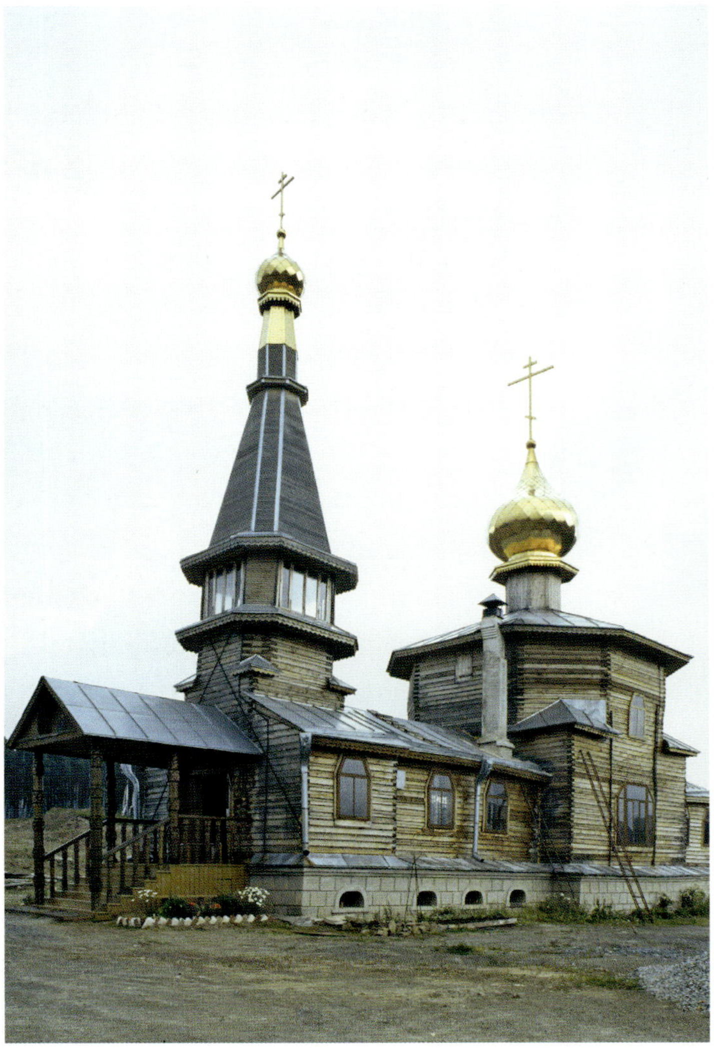

KASLI. House, Lenin and Lomonosov Streets. Resting on masonry, this log structure is designed for a severe climate but with maximum double-glazed window space. July 14, 2003.

KYSHTYM. House, Soviet Street 37. This early twentieth-century multi-family dwelling is notable for its cornice flourish. July 14, 2003.

MIASS. Apartment house, Pushkin Street 45. July 15, 2003.

ZLATOUST. Church of Saint George at Degtyarka, south-west view. Built in 1990s to a traditional linear plan. July 16, 2003.

VERKHNEURALSK. House, Soviet Street 43A. The decorative flourishes continue here on the brick base. July 17, 2003.

SYROSTAN. House, Lenin Street 42. Well-maintained five-wall Soviet dwelling with a high masonry cellar typical of this forest-steppe area. July 15, 2003.

TROITSK. House, Soviet Street 121. This fortress has a high brick half floor typical of the forest-steppe area near the Kazakh border. Note extended gate structure. July 19, 2003.

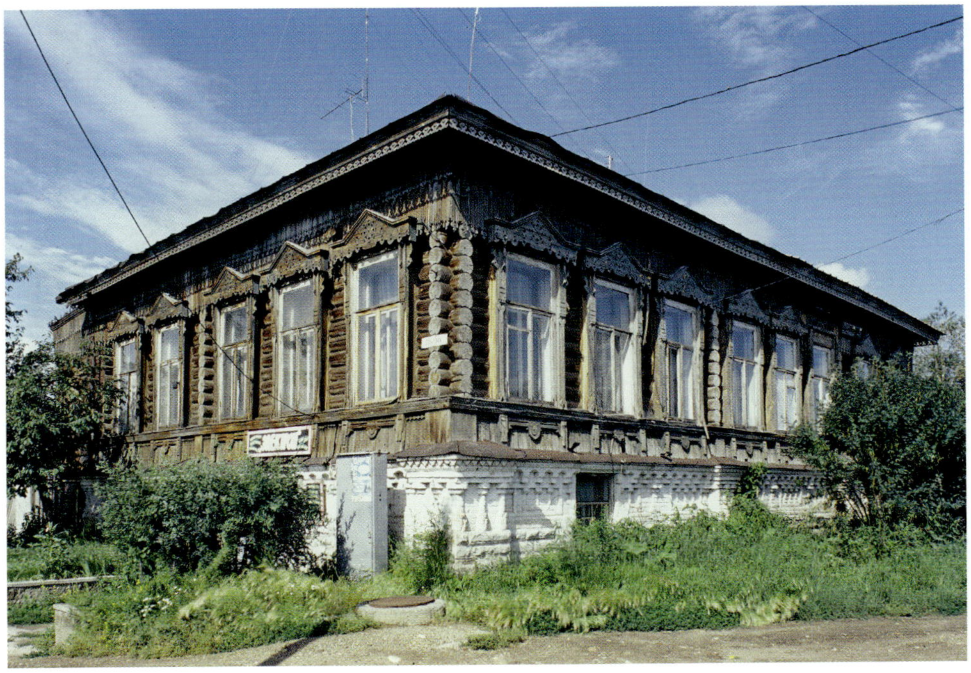

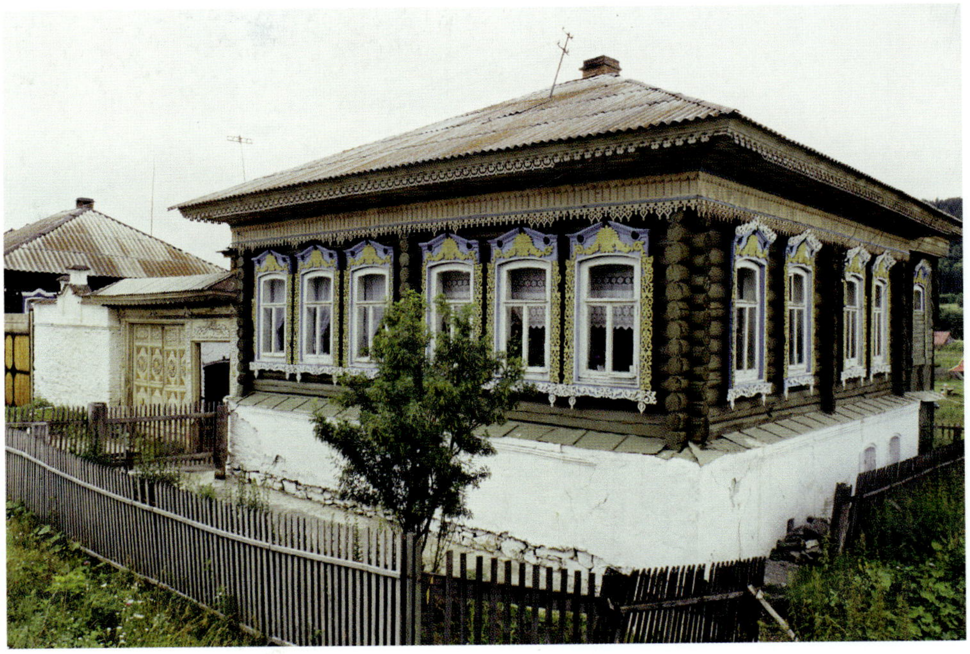

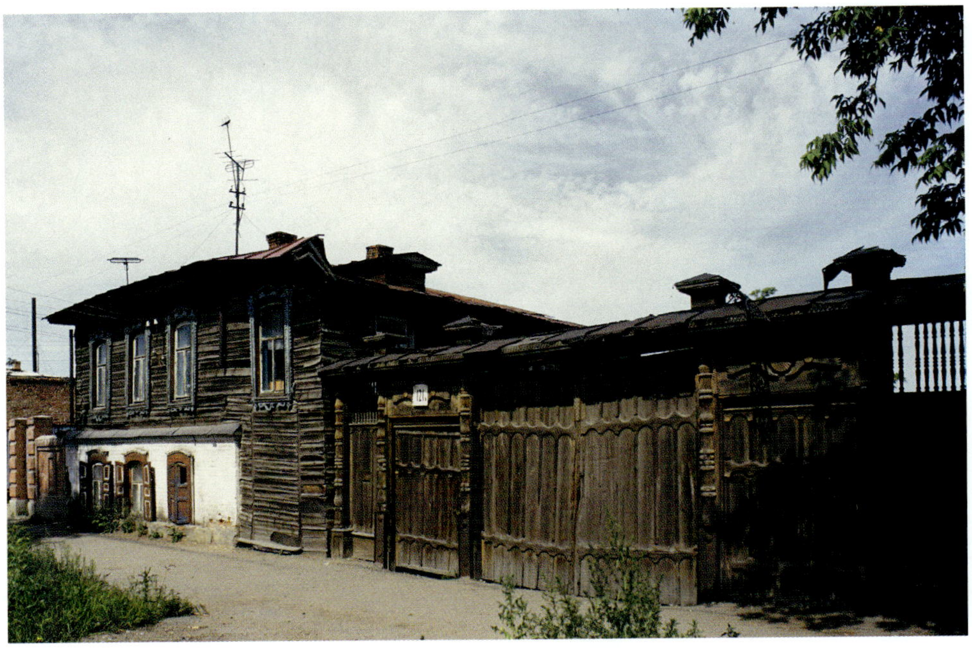

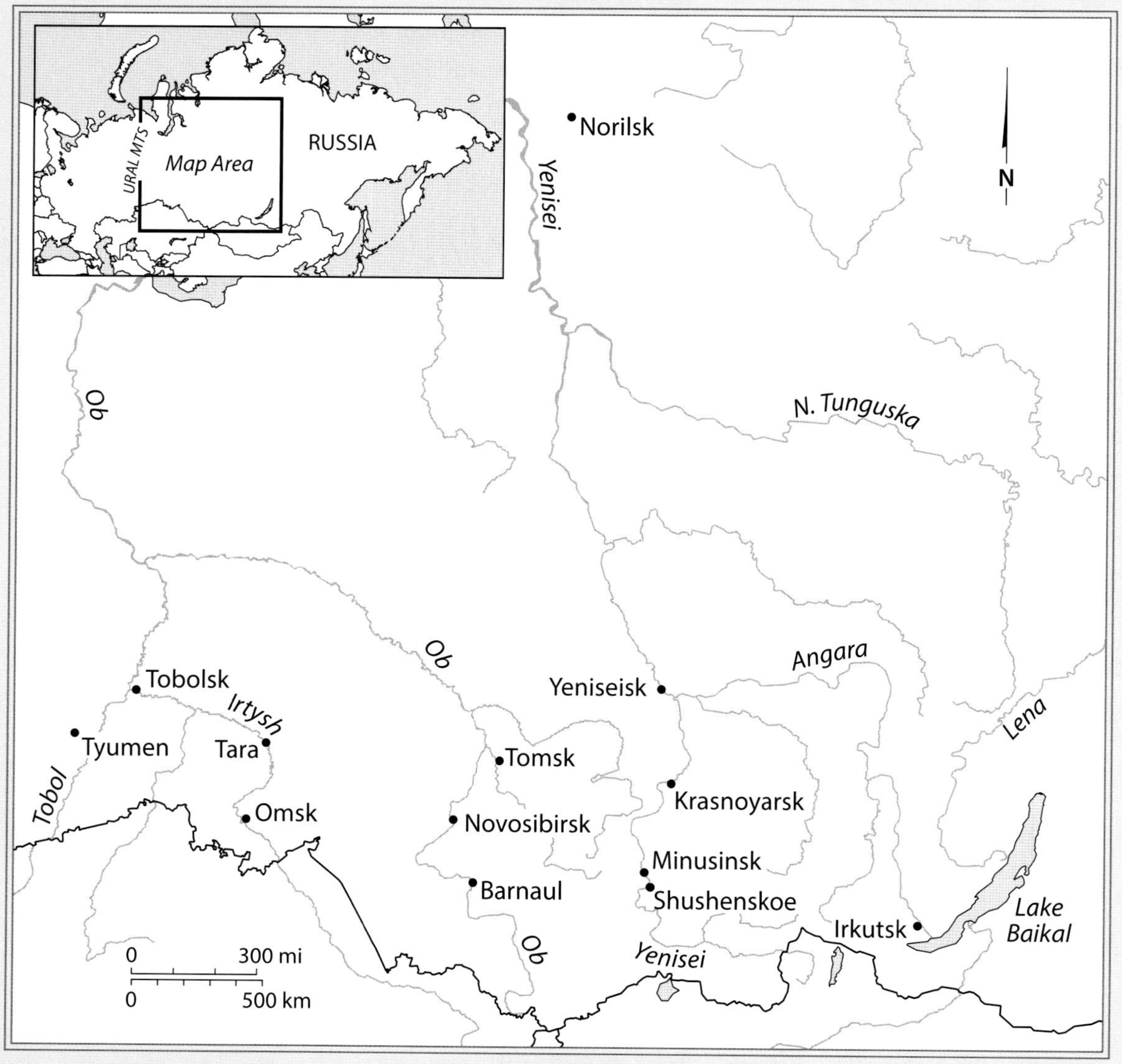

RUSSIA
URAL MTS
Map Area
N
Norilsk
Yenisei
Ob
N. Tunguska
Ob
Angara
Yeniseisk
Lena
Tobolsk
Irtysh
Tyumen
Tara
Tomsk
Tobol
Omsk
Krasnoyarsk
Novosibirsk
Minusinsk
Shushenskoe
Barnaul
Irkutsk
Lake Baikal
Ob
Yenisei
0
300 mi
0
500 km

Siberia.

CHAPTER SIX

Into Siberia

Siberia is one of the largest and most ancient land masses on the planet, so large that opinions diverge as to its geographical and administrative extent. At the maximum, it extends from the Asian face of the Urals to the Pacific Ocean in the east, and from the Arctic Ocean to the northern areas of Kazakhstan in the south. When Russian explorers and traders tentatively moved beyond the Urals in the sixteenth century, much of western Siberia was controlled by a Siberian Tatar khanate formed after the disintegration of the Golden Horde in the latter half of the fifteenth century. By the end of the seventeenth century, Russian presence was already established on the shores of the Pacific, a remarkable—by some measures, unsurpassed—feat of territorial expansion.

The Irtysh River Basin

Although Tyumen, some three hundred kilometers east of Yekaterinburg, is now the capital of the vast territory that bears its name, this region was for much of its history ruled from Tobolsk, with its citadel overlooking the high right bank of the Irtysh River. Of the many rivers that run through Siberia, none has more historical and emotional resonance than the Irtysh, a tributary of the mighty Ob River and a critical artery for Russian movement into Siberia. It was near the Irtysh that a hardy band of Cossacks, led by the legendary Yermak and supported by the Stroganovs from their citadel in Solvychegodsk, defeated the Tartar troops of Khan Kuchum in 1582. Although the precise dates are questioned by historians, it would appear that in the fall of 1581 Yermak captured Chingi-Tura (later Tyumen) but abandoned his conquest in order to proceed straight to Kashlyk, capital of Khan Kuchum, where there occurred the epochal battle memorialized in a painting by Ivan Surikov. Yermak was himself killed in a surprise raid in 1584, and his conquests remained temporarily unconsolidated after

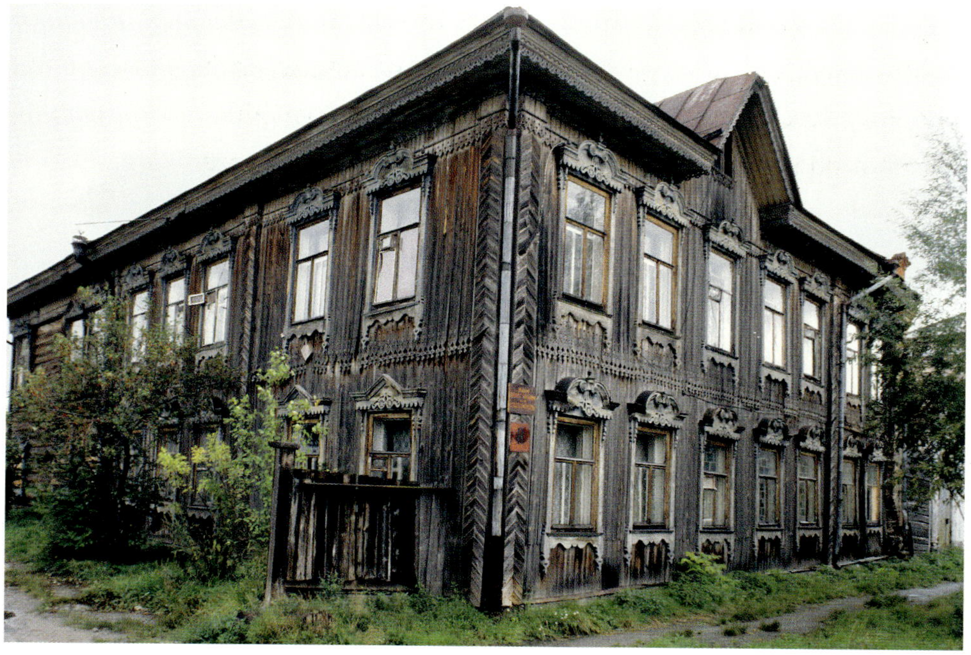

TOBOLSK. Apartment house, Mir (Peace) Street 8. An early twentieth-century remnant with decorative siding and neo-baroque window pediments. Demolished. September 2, 1999.

his death, but Boris Godunov was aware of the enormous significance of Siberia and launched an aggressive campaign to establish settlements. Tobolsk was founded in 1587 by the Cossack leader Daniel Chulkov at the confluence of the Tobol and Irtysh Rivers, near the site of Yermak's victory.

Tobolsk (population around 100,000) is sharply divided by the landscape into two sections: upper and lower. The lower part, being closer to the Irtysh River, was the most intensively developed in the eighteenth and nineteenth centuries. Here lived the merchants—some of them in grand mansions—as well as the tradesmen and craftsmen in a town largely built of wood. Tobolsk had large districts with large wooden houses, many with fanciful carved decorative details. With few resources available for maintenance, wooden Tobolsk is in rapid decline. A particularly grievous loss was the destruction by fire in November 1990 of the large wooden Tobolsk Drama Theater, opened to the public in 1899. As usual, discussions about rebuilding the landmark were undertaken soon after the fire, but to no avail.

Founded in 1586 on the site of an earlier Tatar settlement at the confluence of the Tura and Tyumenka Rivers, Tyumen was the first Russian town in Siberia. The area had been conquered by the Cossack leader Yermak only a few years before as the beginning step of an epochal Russian move across the Ural Mountains into the enormous north Asian land mass. Although its rivers were only tributaries of the Irtysh (itself a tributary of the great Ob River), Tyumen was well situated to use Siberia's water network. Like most early Russian towns in Siberia, Tyumen originally served as a fortified settlement for Cossacks and other troops, who in the seventeenth century protected newly developing trade routes, particularly with China. When the southern boundary of Moscow's Asian territory became more settled during the eighteenth century, Tyumen's importance increased for the development of transportation as well as small commercial and industrial enterprises. On a more lugubrious note, Tyumen's status as a transportation nexus involved it in the notorious exile system, which sent thousands of convicts and political exiles throughout the distant reaches of Siberia. As a regional administrative point for western Siberia, Tyumen also became a center of the Russian Orthodox Church.

The daunting vastness of Siberia's reaches gradually submitted in the nineteenth century to new forms of transportation. The first steamboat to ply a Siberian river was constructed here in 1838. The greatest impulse for economic growth came with the completion of a railroad from Yekaterinburg, on the east slope of the Ural Mountains. This line ultimately became an important segment of the Trans-Siberian Railroad, transporting the wealth of Siberia's forests, mines, and new grain farms, as well as leather and other products of local factories. Furthermore, at the turn of the twentieth century more than half a million settlers passed through the town en route to Siberia's rich agricultural lands.

Some remnants of Tyumen's past are being preserved. This is especially evident in the city's historic wooden houses, with elaborate framed

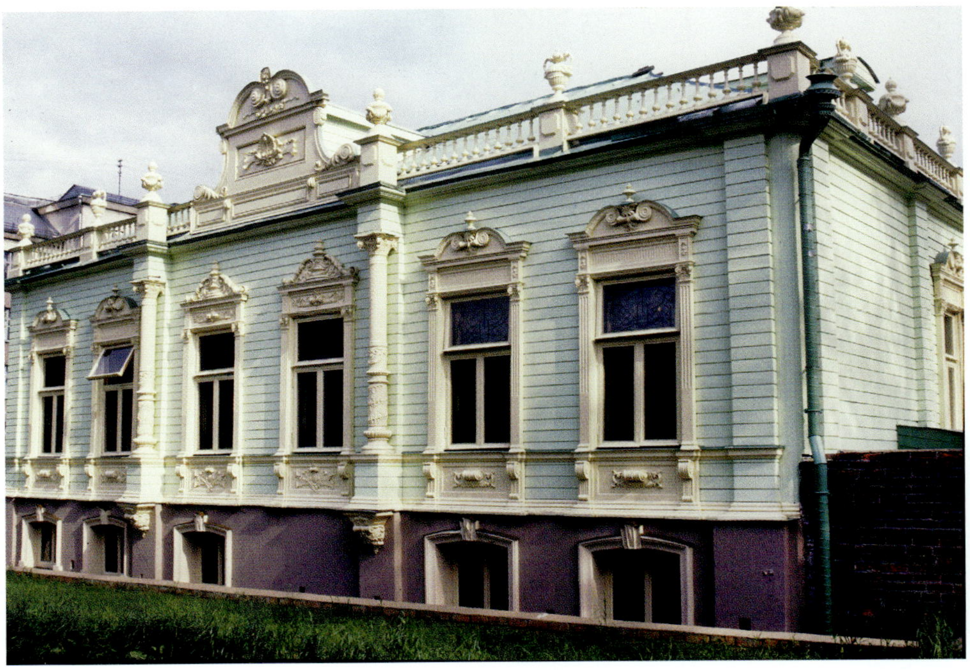

TYUMEN. Kolokolnikov house, corner of Republic Street 18 and Turgenev Street. Originally built in 1804 by the merchant Ivan Ikonnikov, this fine example of classically inspired wooden architecture was acquired in 1888 by the tea magnate Ivan Kolokolnikov, who modified the original design. Now part of a museum of merchant culture. August 29, 1999.

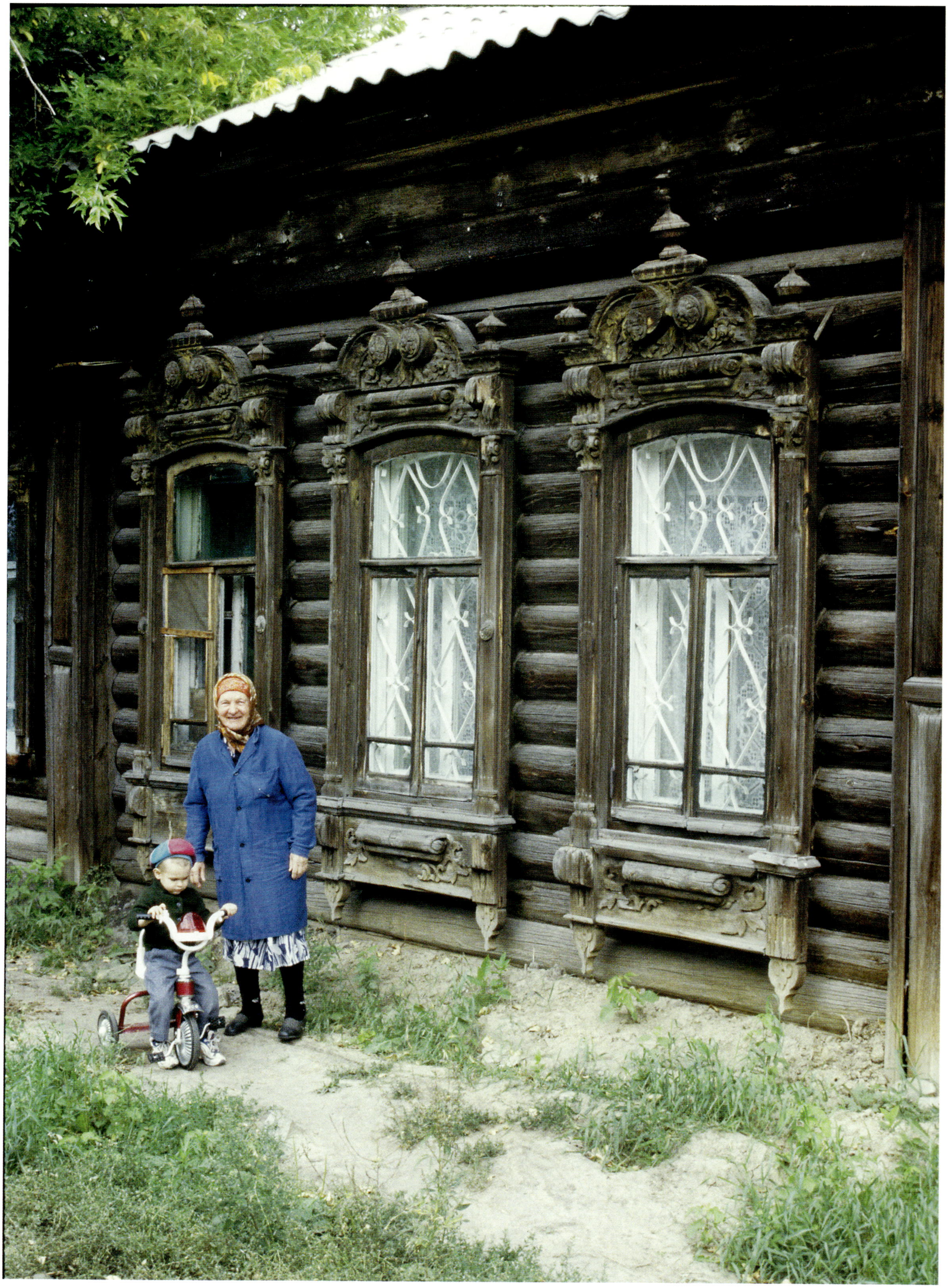

and carved window surrounds in a style specific to Tyumen. Many Siberian cities, such as Tomsk and Novosibirsk, have distinctive wooden houses with decorative windows, but Tyumen is unique in the massive quality of the window construction, which often includes carved panels below the sill as an additional decorative and protective device. Their double-glazed construction permitted rows of large windows in wooden houses even in this harsh climate, thus bringing maximum available light to interiors during the long Siberian winters.

Omsk (current population around 1,170,000) was founded in 1716 as a fort on the middle reaches of the Irtysh River. During the eighteenth century the primary purpose of this garrison town was to protect Russia's southern border and establish authority over the aboriginal steppe tribes. Although administratively subordinate to Tobolsk throughout the eighteenth century, Omsk gained increasing power in the nineteenth century. From 1808 until 1917, Omsk served as the headquarters of all Siberian Cossack troops, and in 1822 a separate Omsk Province was formed. This strong military presence also connected Omsk with the notorious Siberian exile system. The most famous of the fortress's exiles was the writer Fyodor Dostoevsky, condemned in 1849 for associating with the radicals in Saint Petersburg. In January 1850 Dostoevsky arrived under guard at the Omsk fort, and for the most part of three years (1850–54), he lived the harrowing existence of a convict sentenced to hard labor. During the latter part of the nineteenth century, Omsk began a period of heady expansion, as the town became a transportation center for Russia's boundless interior. Regular steamboat service along the Irtysh River to Tobolsk began in 1862. But it was the railroads that made Omsk a boomtown. In 1894–95 Omsk was linked by the Trans-Siberian Railroad to Chelyabinsk in the west and Novonikolaevsk (later Novosibirsk) in the east. In 1913 another rail line was completed from Omsk to Tyumen in what would become the new Siberian mainline.

By the beginning of the twentieth century, the population of Omsk had tripled to more than sixty thousand inhabitants. During this rapid development, wooden buildings remained a major part of the urban fabric, particularly for housing. Sometimes the log walls were clad with plank siding, and in other cases they were left exposed. To lessen the ever-present danger from fire, many of the buildings in Siberian towns had a wall of brick on the right side—the *brandmauer*, or "fire wall." An excellent example is the mansion, built in 1911 on what was then known as Duma (City Council) Street

TYUMEN. House, Turgenev Street 57. An example of massive, double-glazed windows with neo-baroque pediments typical of prosperous Tyumen at the turn of the twentieth century. Demolished(?) August 29, 1999.

for Alexander Solomonovich Kabalkin, a prominent member of the legal profession. The Kabalkin mansion displays an assured sense of design in which the unclad dark log walls contrast with the light color of simple window surrounds for an aesthetic effect. The left corner is punctuated with a bay turret that dominates the area. When I photographed this structure, the lots around it had been cleared, which gave an unobstructed view of the organic plasticity of the structure. This approach to design was intended to create a unified work of art from all perspectives, a characteristic of the *style moderne* (the Russian equivalent of Art Nouveau) that flourished at the turn of the twentieth century. The *style moderne* also appears in the exuberant decorative detailing of smaller houses with sweeping curvilinear flourishes throughout the main facade. An excellent example is the house at 48 Michurin Street with its Art Nouveau doorway and window surrounds crowned with dragon motifs in an imitation Nordic style (Norwegian stave churches). Unfortunately, the house and lot have been poorly maintained. The decoration of some wooden houses shows an eclectic mixture of *style moderne* with fretwork detailing. Window surrounds are often crowned with elaborate flourishes in carved wood. One of the most playful decorative expressions is the Philip Shtumfp house (Valikhanov Street 10), built at the turn of twentieth century for a prominent agronomist, entrepreneur, and civic activist. Its turrets, complicated roof line, and ornamental window surrounds hark back to a traditional folk style launched by the artist Ivan Ropet in the 1870s. Although part of the historic center—with its imposing early twentieth-century offices and shops—has been preserved and repurposed, the condition of wooden architecture has deteriorated since 1999.

A unique wooden monument in Omsk is the so-called Soldiers Synagogue (Marshal Zhukov Street 53), built in 1855 for a community of "cantonists," soldiers taken at an early age from Jewish communities during the reign of Nicholas I to serve in the army throughout the empire. At the end of a long period of schooling and service, they were allowed to remain in their place of service without restrictions that existed in the Pale of Settlement. In 1854 the Omsk community of 178 registered Jews chose a rabbi and gathered the funds to erect a beautiful wooden synagogue decorated in a Moorish style. Miraculously, the building has survived as a national landmark despite the difficulties imposed on the community during the Soviet period. Closed in the early 1920s, the building was long used as the House of Sanitary Education. Another synagogue, built in

OMSK. Alexander Kabalkin house, main and side facades. September 18, 1999

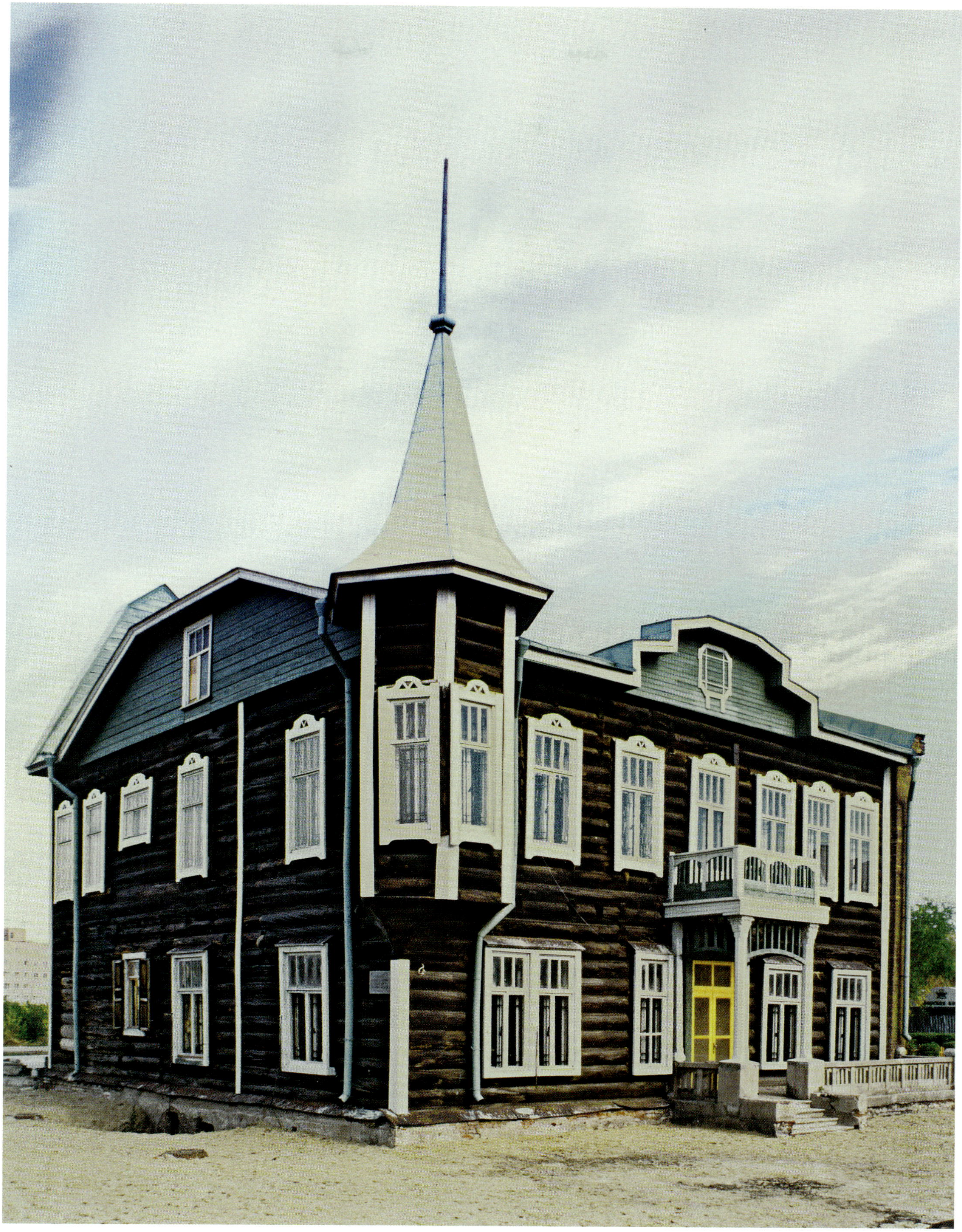

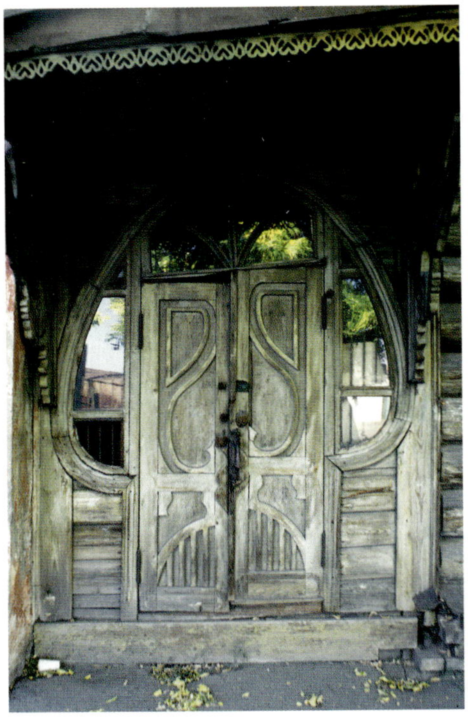

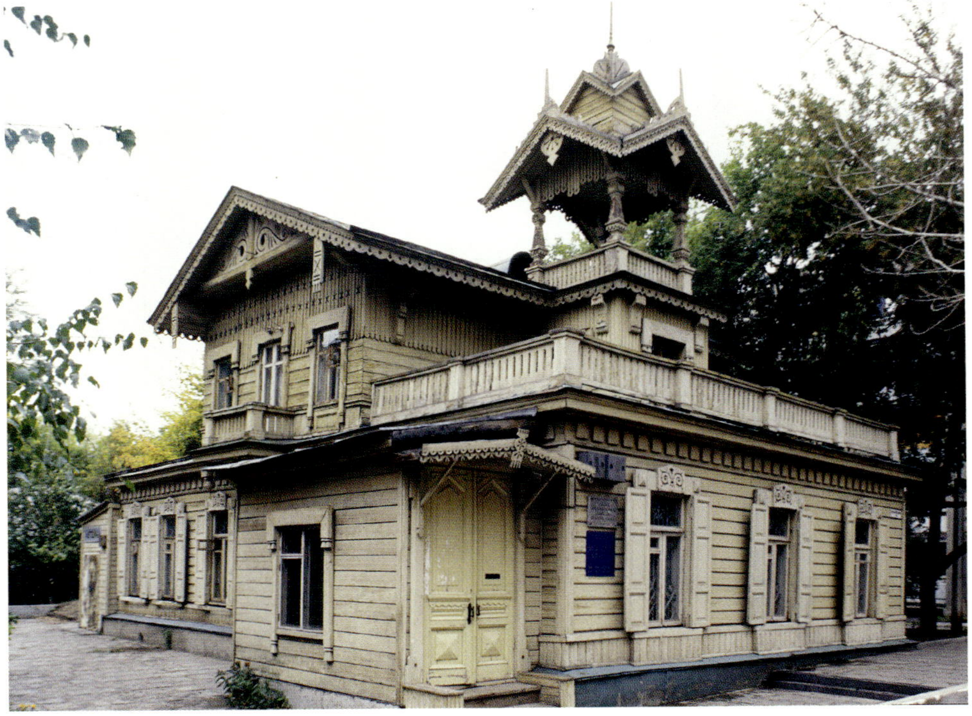

1873, served the Jewish community for some decades, but it was destroyed by fire and razed in the 1970s. This left the community without a formal place of worship until 1991, when the Soldiers Synagogue was returned as a house of worship to the Or Hadash ("New Light") community. Damaged by fire in 1995, the synagogue was carefully restored, using plank siding, with Moorish crowns for the upper windows and an ornamental cornice.

OMSK. House at Michurin Street 48. Entrance porch with *style moderne* doorway. September 18, 1999.

OMSK. Philip Shtumfp house. Festive example of Russian Revival style. September 19, 1999.

To the north of Omsk, along the Irtysh River, grain fields extend for dozens of kilometers on all sides. This is rich agricultural land, dotted by villages and small towns. Among the most interesting from a historical perspective is the town of Tara (current population 27,000), founded in 1594 as one of the earliest settlements to defend the route east. In August 1598 a detachment of Cossacks from Tara led by the *voevoda* (regional authority) Andrey Voeikov, defeated the remaining forces of Khan Kuchum, the main potentate of the Siberian Tatars, thus completing a campaign begun by Yermak. During the seventeenth century, before the founding of Omsk, Tara was the main Russian outpost on the upper reaches of the Irtysh River. The town with its stockade was swept by fire in 1669 and again in 1709. In 1722 the rebuilt town was gripped with an uprising of Old Believers, who were widespread in the area and refused to swear general allegiance to Peter the Great's heir, still unnamed. Both the revolt itself (with apocalyptic overtones) and its hideously savage suppression by government forces sent from Tobolsk suggest a collective psychosis that beggars description. The position of ruined Tara was further reduced by

OMSK. Soldiers Synagogue. Side facade with Moorish window detailing. September 18, 1999.

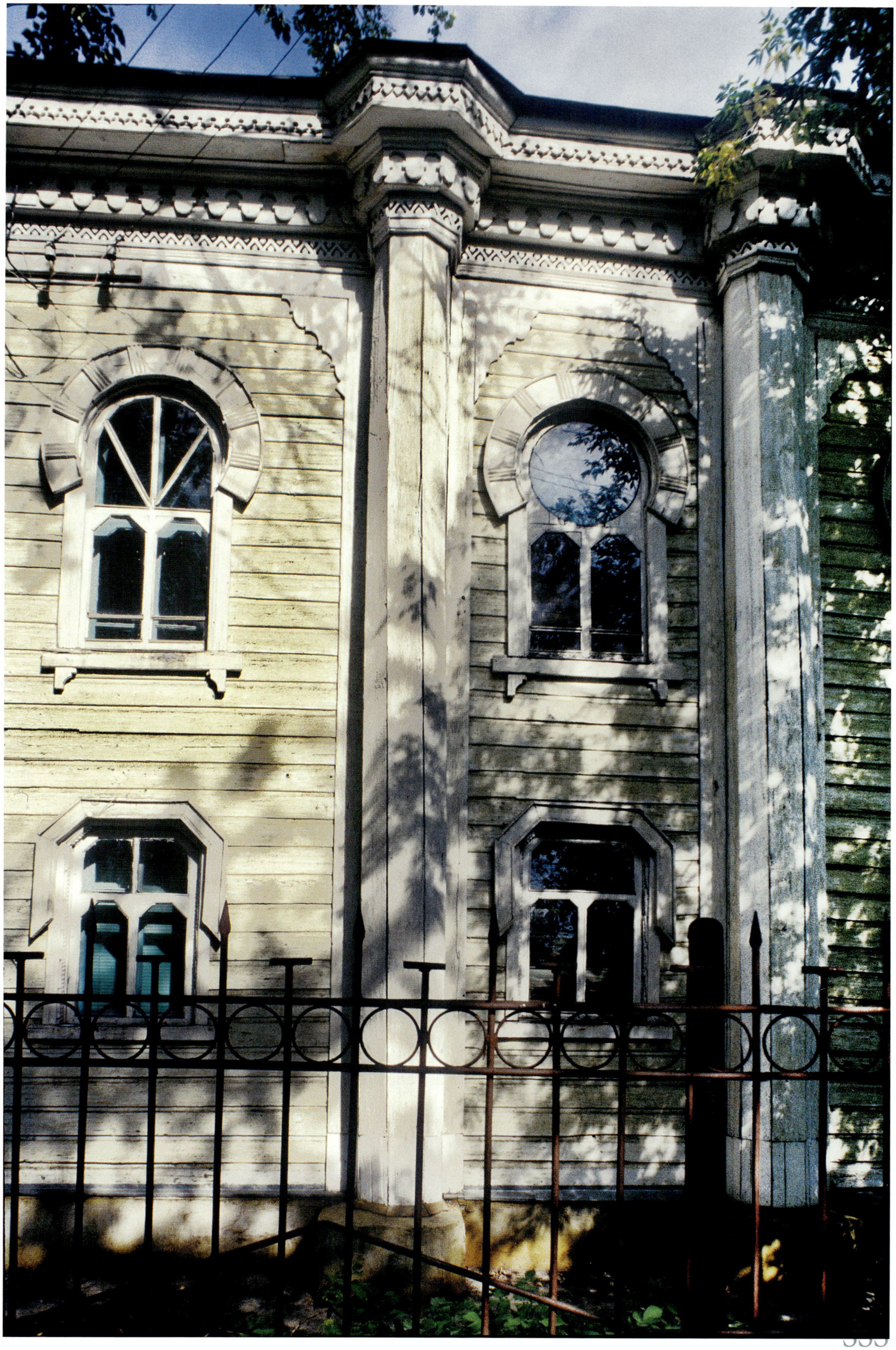

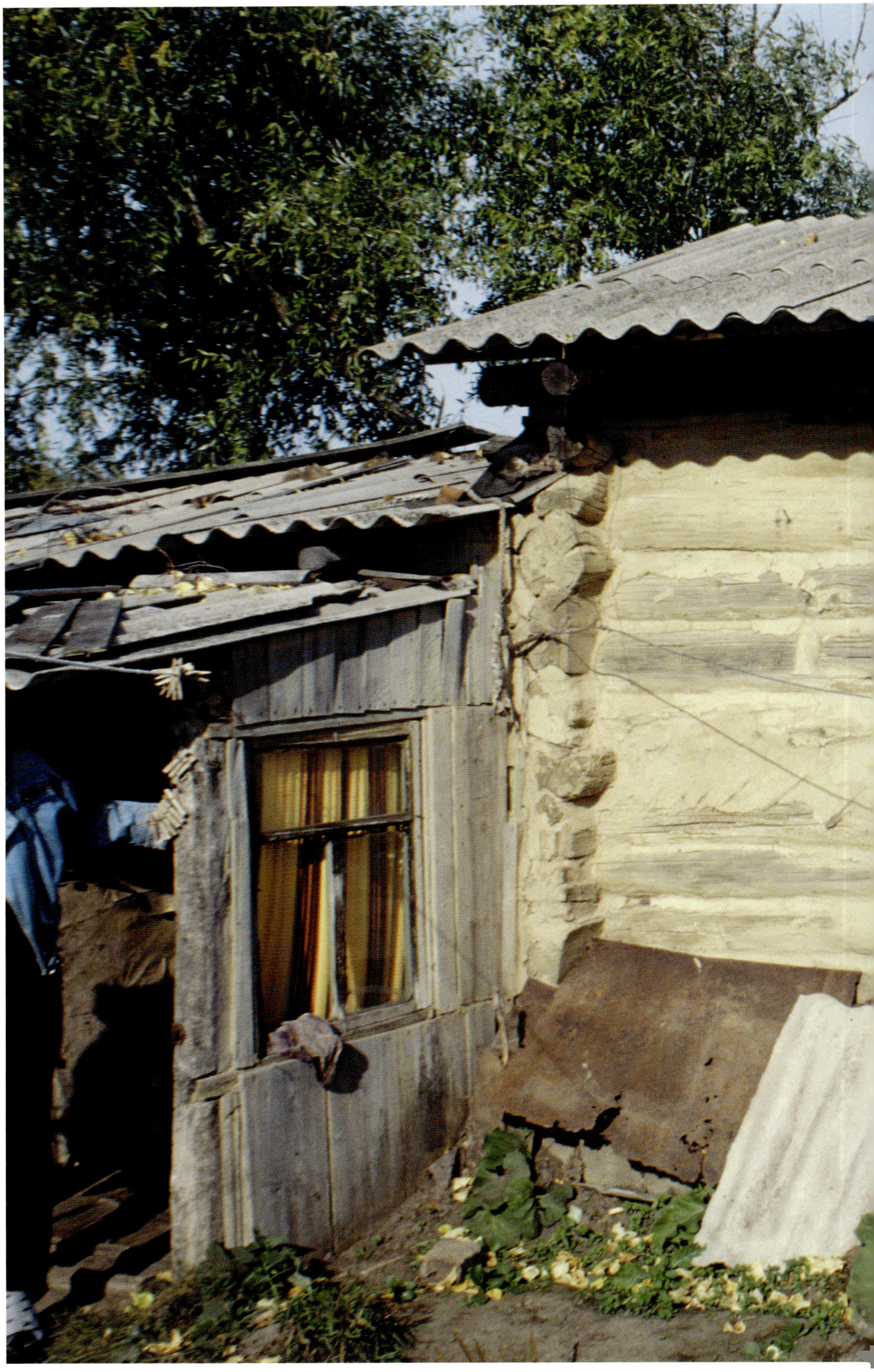

STAROKARASUK. Example of the most primitive type of Siberian log dwelling, with clay-chinked walls and scrap metal fragments protecting the base. A single decorative window proclaims the human spirit, as does the small young mother with her healthy infant. September 16, 1999.

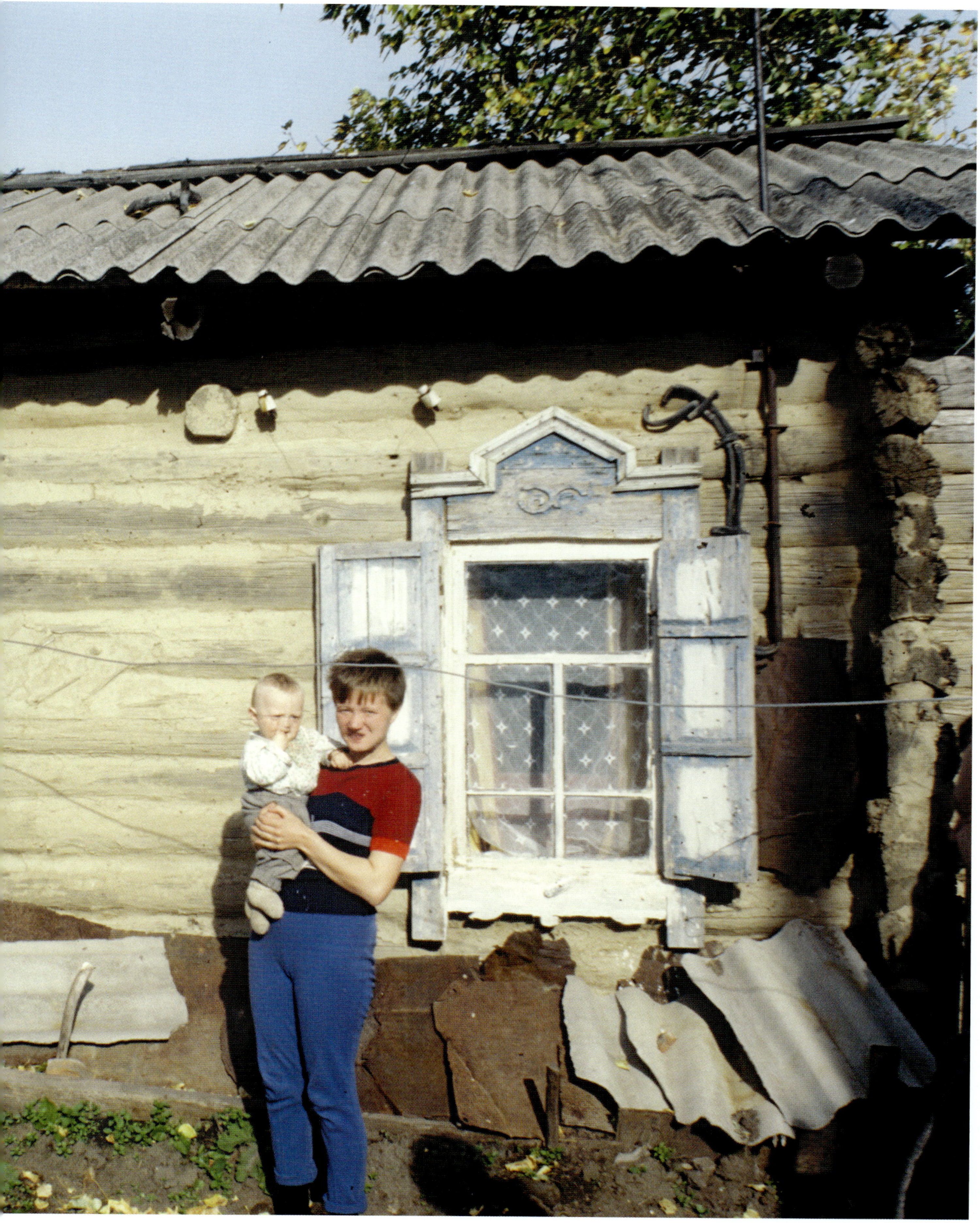

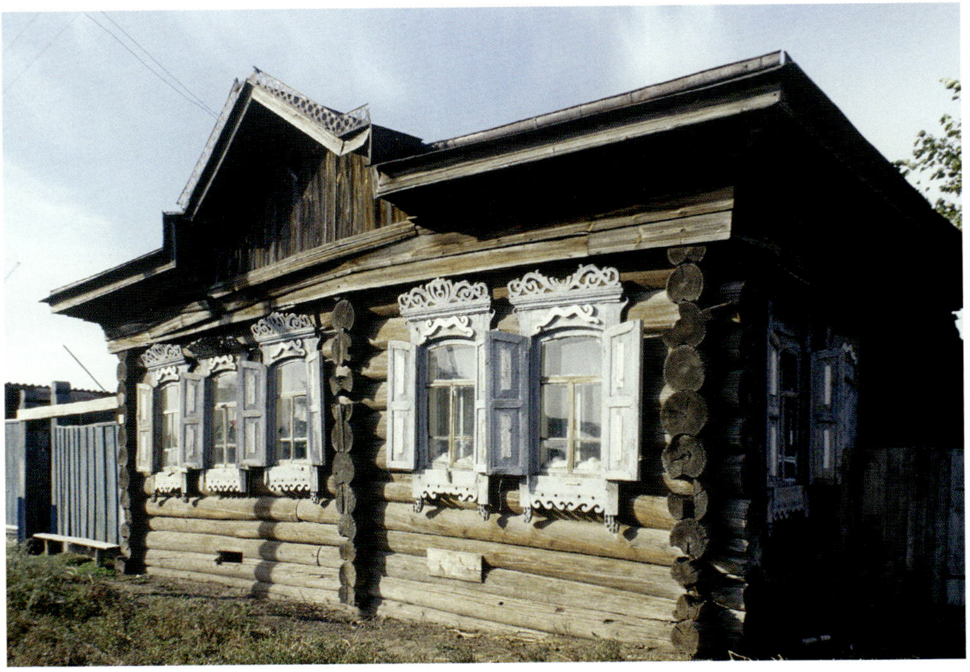

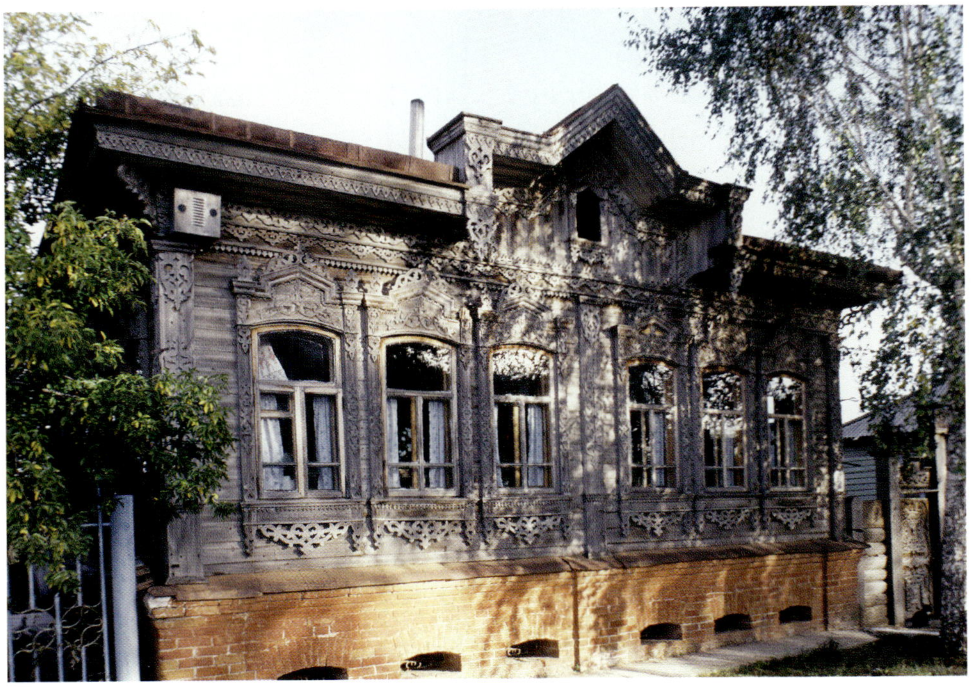

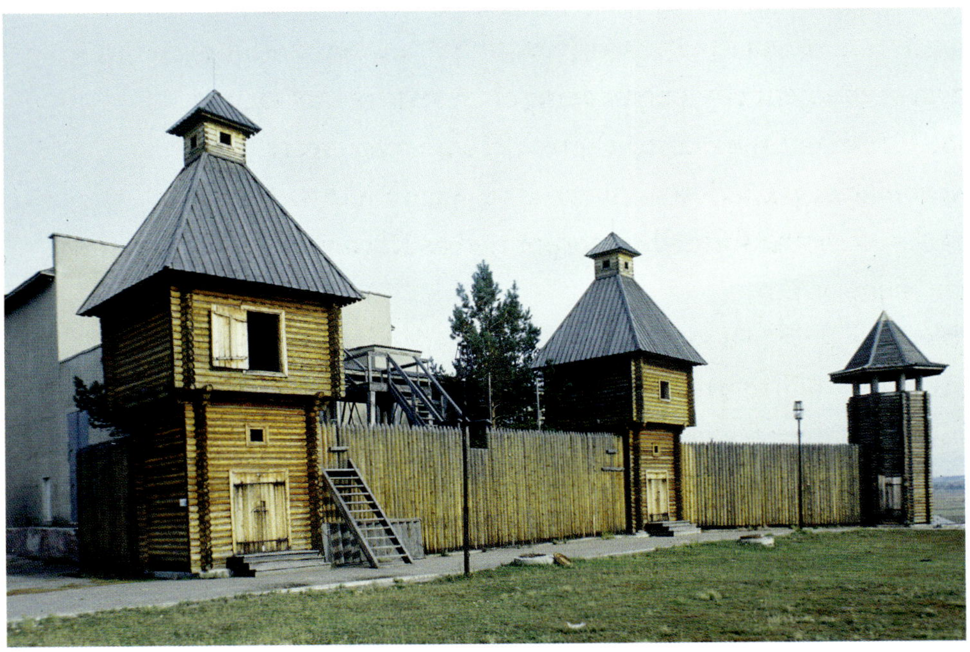

INGALI. Simple form of five-wall *izba* with primitive decorative flourishes. September 16, 1999.

BOLSHERECHYE. Well-maintained house on a brick base with facade fretwork. September 16, 1999.

TARA. Replica of seventeenth-century log stockade. September 17, 1999.

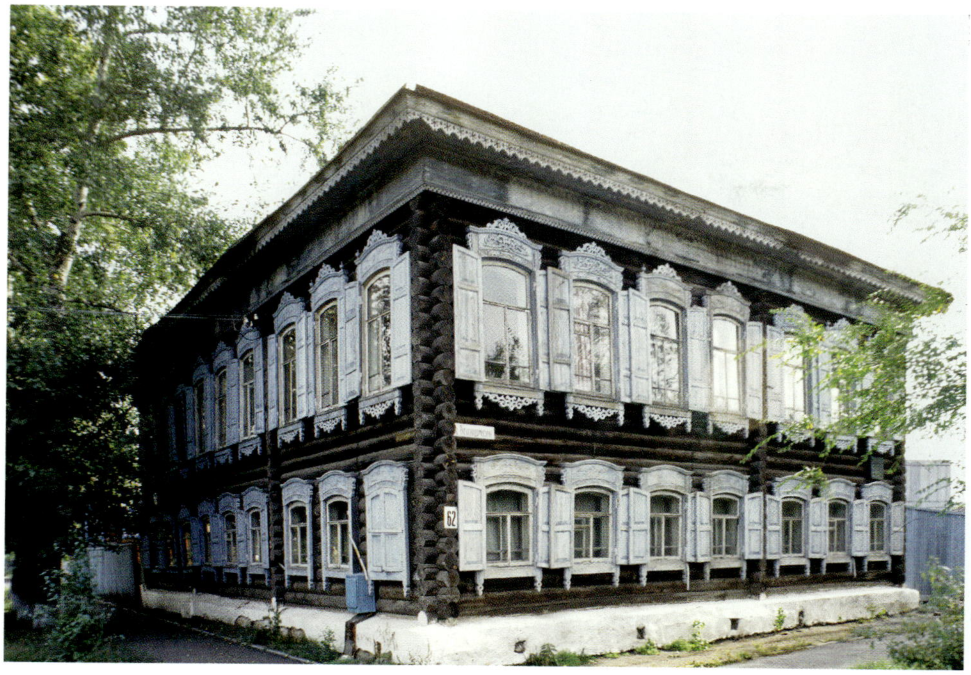

TARA. Apartment house, Alexandrovskaya Street 62. Built in the early twentieth century, the walls are saturated with massive, double-glazed window emplacements. September 17, 1999.

the establishment of Omsk on the new Siberian Road to the south. Tara's revived prosperity in the nineteenth century led to the construction of richly decorated wooden houses belonging to local merchants. A few still existed at the turn of this century, together with a partial re-creation of the town's seventeenth-century log stockade.

The Ob River Basin

As the Trans-Siberian train approaches Novosibirsk from the west, the landscape becomes rougher and more arid, marked by small ridges largely devoid of trees. Suddenly, at the very approaches to the city, there appears the broad channel of the Ob River, one of the three great Siberian rivers. Beyond rises the skyline of Novosibirsk. With a population of some 1,450,000 (currently ranked third in Russia), Novosibirsk has become Siberia's largest and most energetic city, outstripping older settlements such as Tomsk and Tobolsk. In effect, the intersection of rail with river created Novosibirsk—or Novonikolaevsk, as it was known at the turn of the twentieth century. In 1903 the town was formally incorporated as Novonikolaevsk, named after tsar Nicholas II.

The favorable linking of geography and the railroad led to the town's rapid growth, traces of which are evident in buildings from the early twentieth century, including festively decorated wooden houses of considerable size. For the first two decades of its existence, the settlement

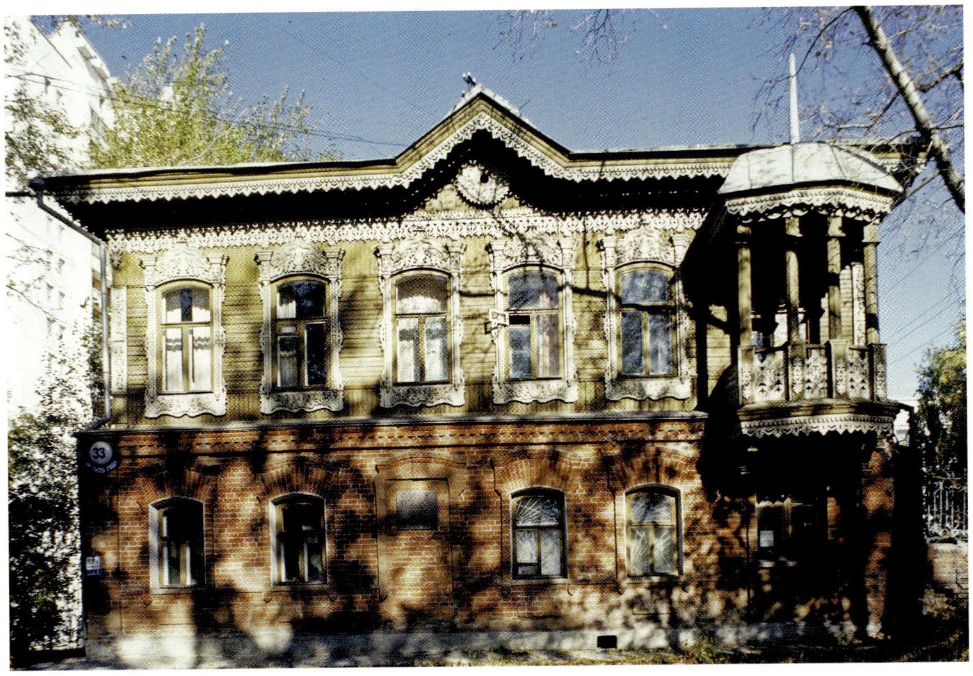

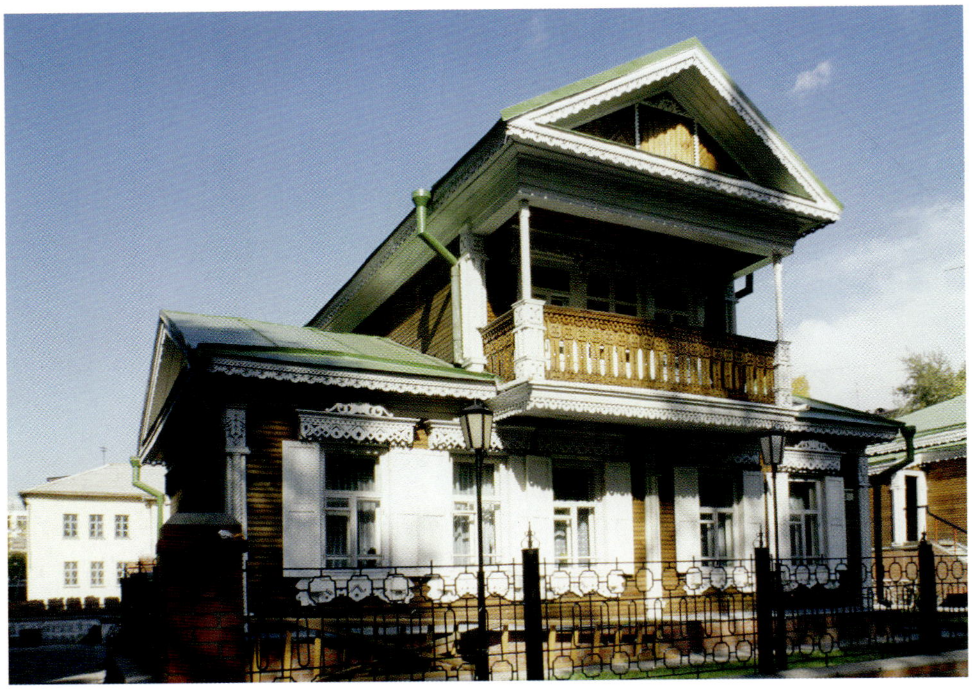

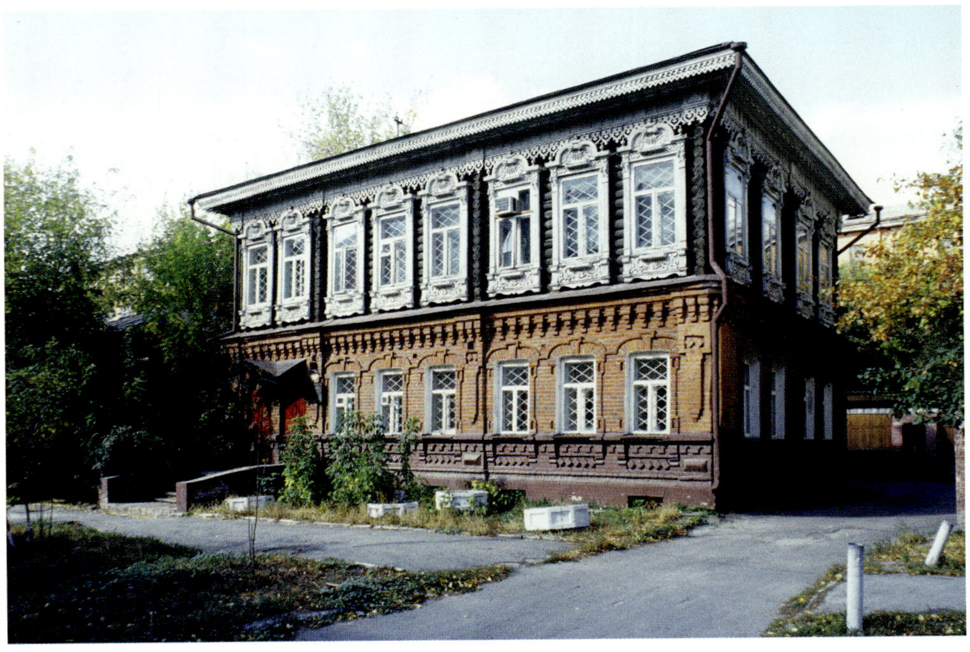

NOVOSIBIRSK. Roman Kopylov house. Built in 1901 for an entrepreneur who supported far right political causes, the house has a handsome brick ground floor and an elegant corner bay that serves as a veranda. September 21, 1999.

NOVOSIBIRSK. Alexey Runin house. Built in 1903 for a tea and sugar merchant, the ornamental house with large *mezonin* has been well maintained as a city landmark. September 21, 1999.

NOVOSIBIRSK. Yakov Istomin house. Built in 1903–5 for a merchant who also served as city council chair, this multifamily dwelling has a richly decorated brick ground floor and massive window embrasures with neo-baroque pediments. Repaired after a fire in 2004 that destroyed the adjacent, uninhabited wooden house. September 21, 1999.

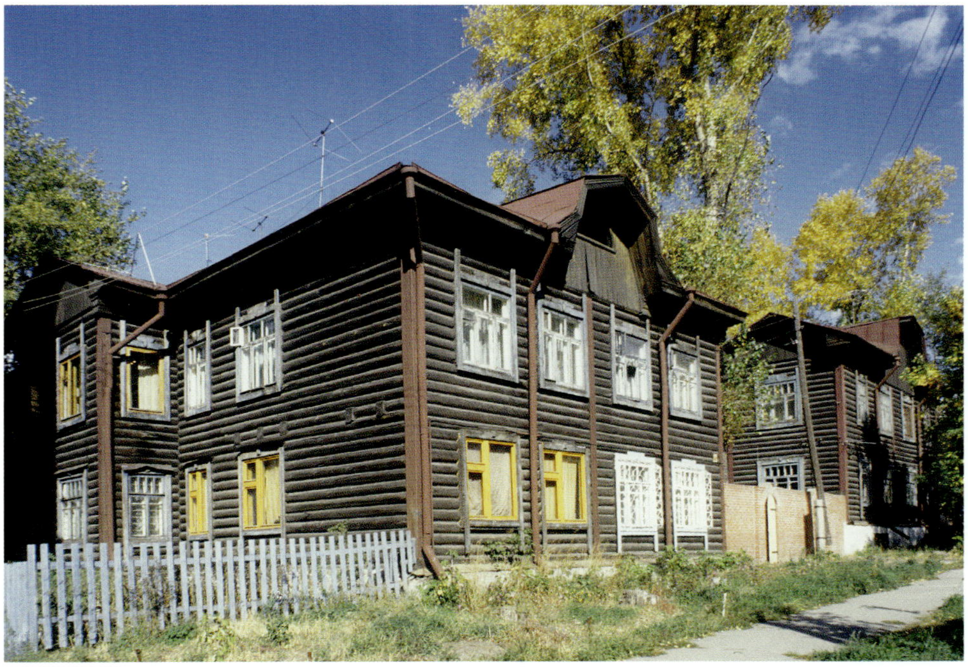

NOVOSIBIRSK. Workers' housing built in the early twentieth century in a "functionalist" variant of *style moderne*. September 21, 1999.

consisted almost entirely of log buildings. In 1926 the town was renamed Novosibirsk. Despite rapid industrial and administrative development throughout the Soviet period, several ornamented examples of wooden housing have survived, a reflection of the town's flourishing prerevolutionary merchant culture and a contemporary sense of enlightened civic pride.

Much of the intellectual energy of Novosibirsk comes from the nearby scientific satellite city of Akademgorodok, whose name means "academic town." Begun in 1957 as part of the Sputnik-era scientific boom, Akademgorodok eventually acquired international renown as an idyllic community devoted to the life of the mind. In addition to its research institutes, Akademgorodok also has an open-air museum of wooden architecture, its masterpiece being the reassembled log Church of the Miraculous Image of the Savior from the village of Zashiversk, located in the Indigirka River basin, some three thousand kilometers to the east in Yakutia (now known as the Republic of Sakha). Built around 1700, the Savior Church served the fort of Zashiversk for many decades until the entire population of the village died from an epidemic of smallpox in 1883. After such a devastating catastrophe, Zashiversk acquired the reputation of a haunted site and was avoided by travelers. Although most of its log buildings gradually fell into ruin, the church—built of rock-solid larch—and its bell tower continued to stand. The rediscovery of this "village of the dead" in the 1930s came as something of a sensation. In 1969–71 the Zashiversk site was carefully studied by a team of experts from the Siberian Division of the

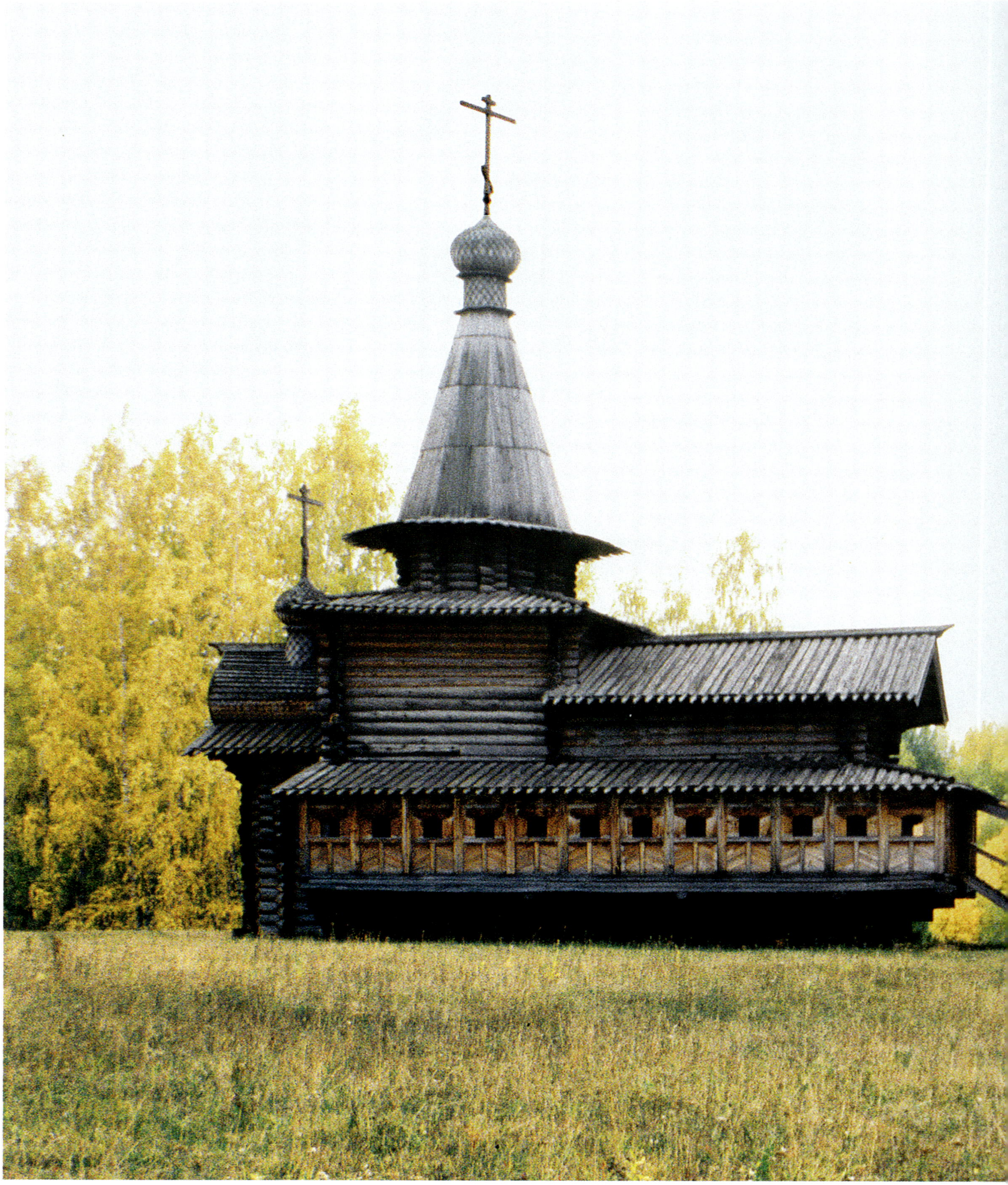

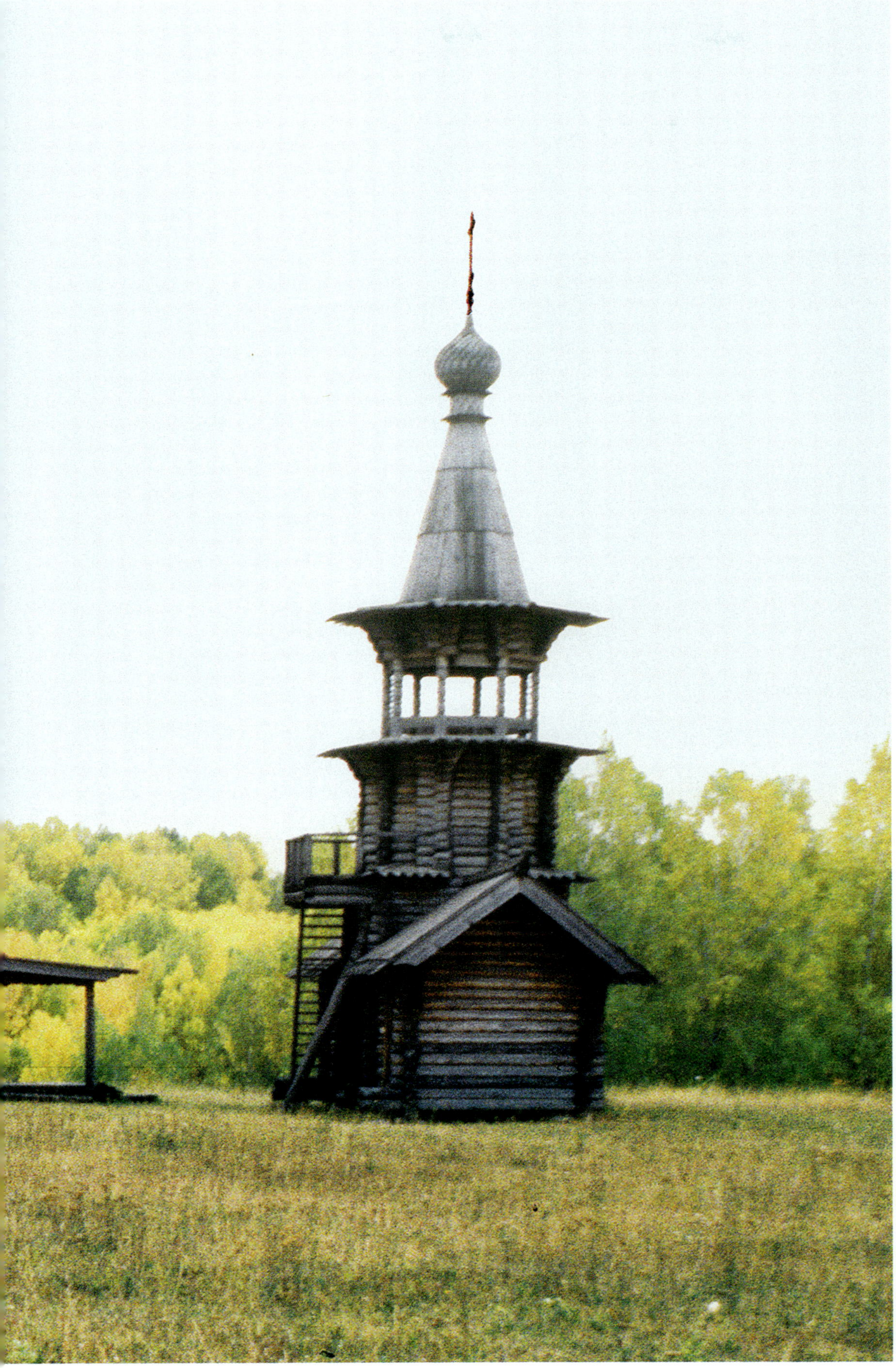

AKADEMGORODOK (near Novosibirsk). Church of the Miraculous Image of the Savior, north view with freestanding bell tower. Originally built in 1700 at the village of Zashiversk in what is now the Republic of Sakha (formerly Yakutia). September 20, 1999.

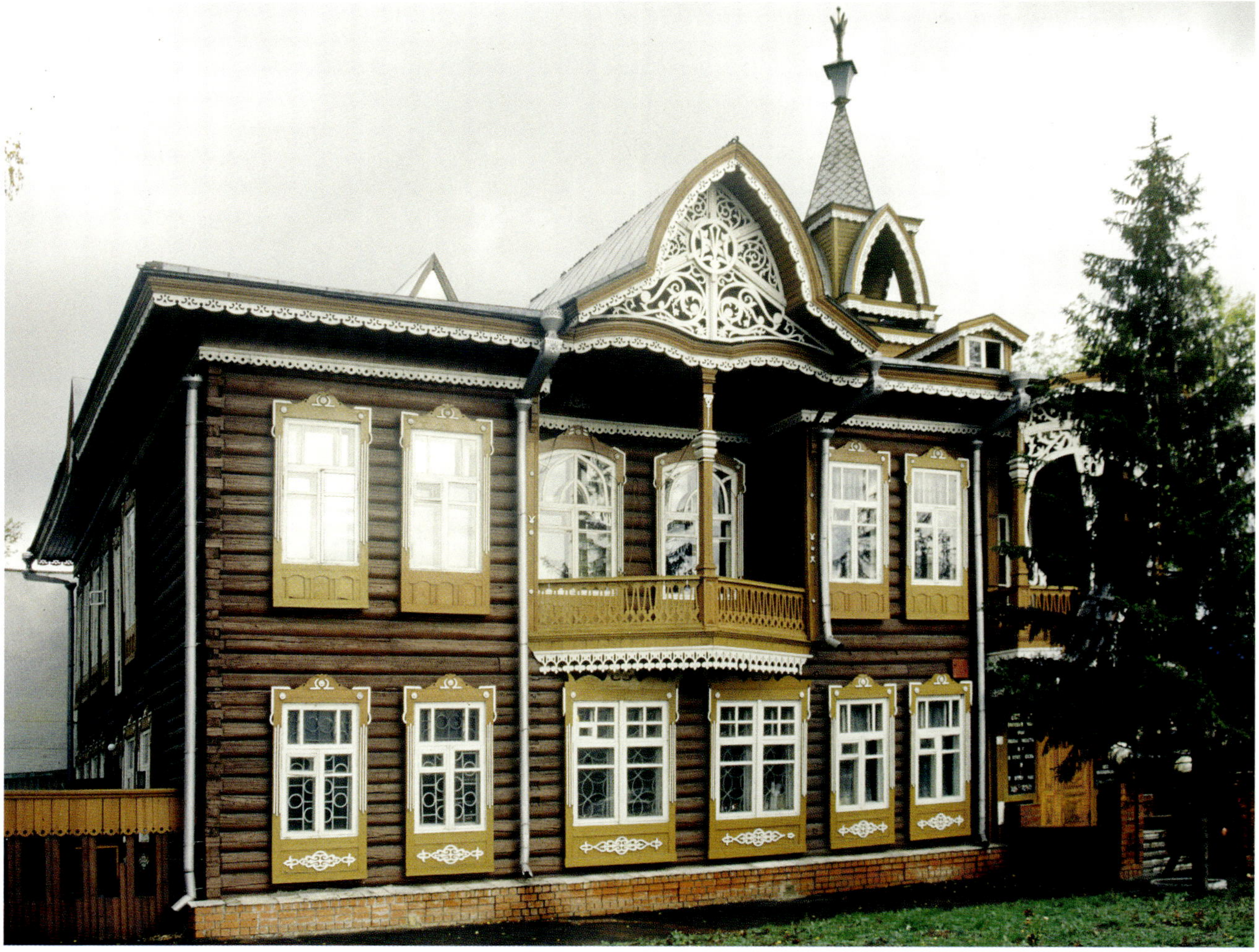

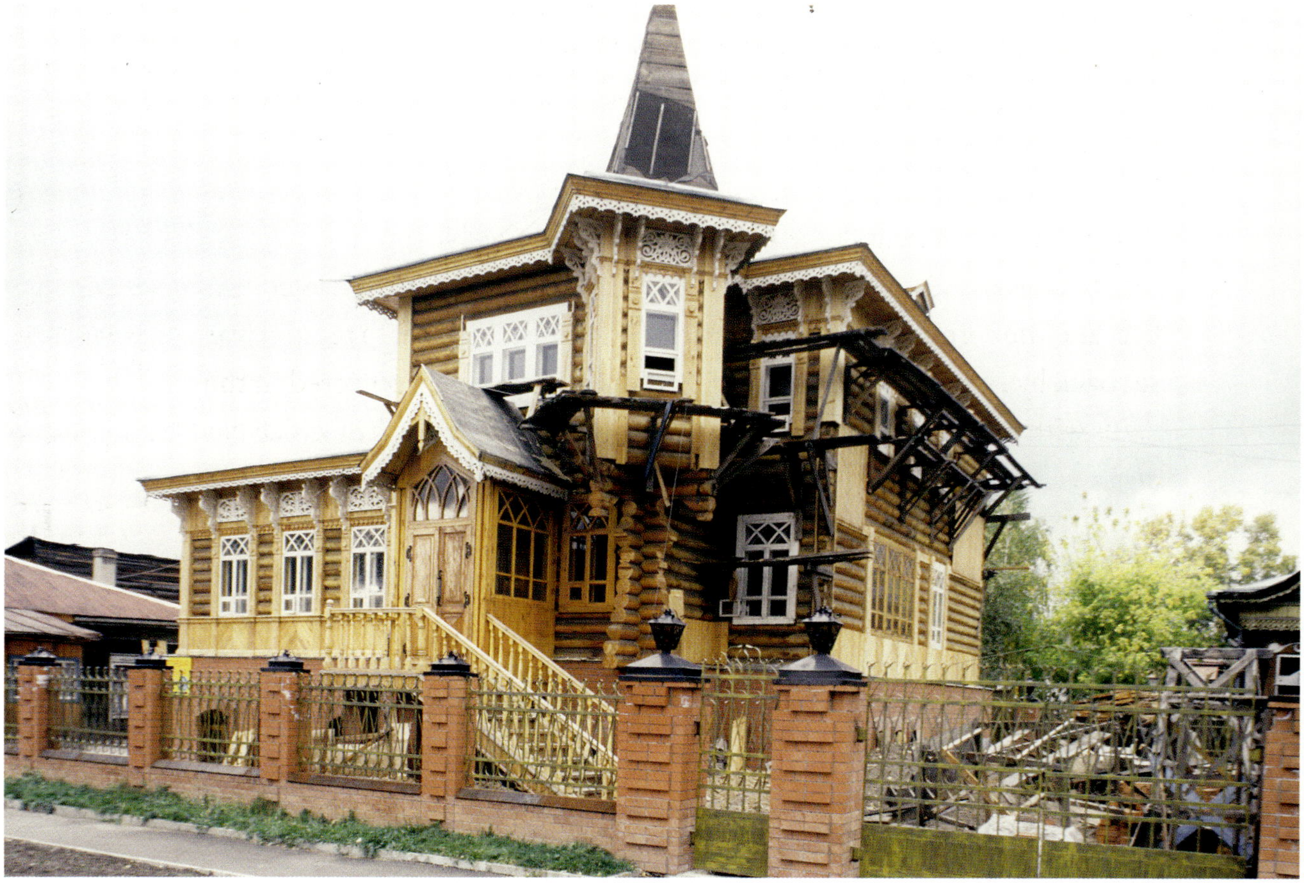

Academy of Sciences (based in Novosibirsk/Akademgorodok). In the mid-1970s the church and bell tower were dismantled for shipment to the Akademgorodok architectural museum, where they have now been reassembled. Thus, a tragedy in remote Yakutia preserved for posterity this small gem of a church, now on display in the center of Siberia.

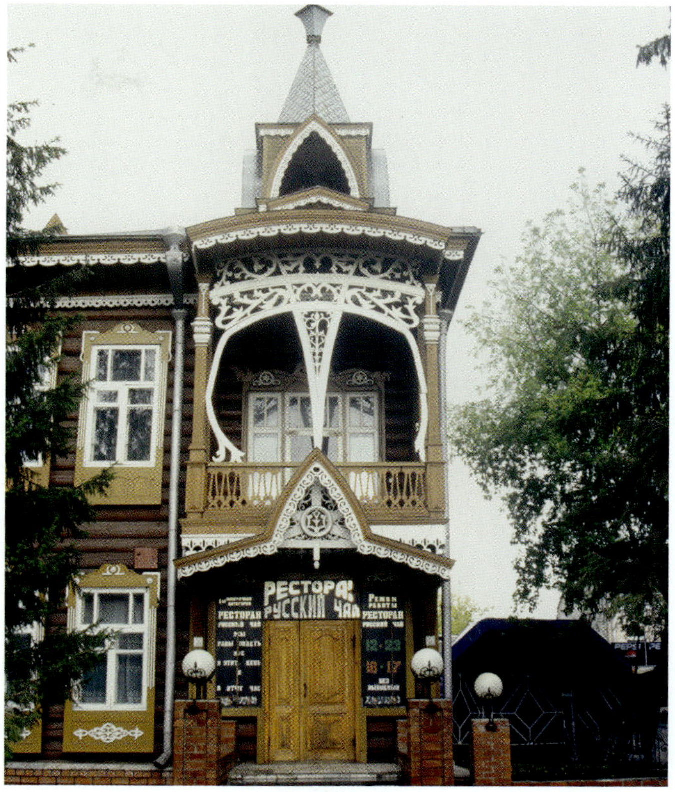

BARNAUL. Fyodor Shchadrin house. Built in 1914 for a merchant family, this flamboyant *style moderne* structure was severely damaged by fire in 1976 and "restored" (largely rebuilt) with changes to corner design to create a restaurant entrance. September 22, 1999.

BARNAUL. Nosovich house. Built in 1908 as a dwelling and studio in the Russian Revival style on a high brick base by the architect Ivan Nosovich. Moved to its present location in 1992. September 22, 1999.

BARNAUL. Fyodor Shchadrin house. View of balcony corner with 1970s restaurant entrance (instead of original hooded double window). September 22, 1999.

From Novosibirsk the Trans-Siberian races toward Krasnoyarsk, but along the way there are two major regional centers to the south and north of the mainline. To the south is Barnaul (current population 623,000), located on the upper reaches of the Ob River near the foothills of the majestic Altai Mountain range. The first Russian settlement occurred in 1730 when the prominent Tula entrepreneur Akinfy Demidov brought two hundred serfs with a plan to exploit the area's rich copper and silver resources. In 1739 work began on a copper and silver smelter, which ultimately provided a firm basis for the town's existence.

The renowned Demidov Silver Smelter closed in 1893, but the town already had other economic sources. Construction of a spur railroad from what was then Novonikolaevsk to Barnaul proved problematic and required building another great bridge across the Ob River, but the line finally opened in October 1915. The city's population reached sixty-one thousand the following year before several disasters struck. In May 1917 most of the largely wooden town burned to the ground in a catastrophic fire, and the complicated task of marshalling the resources to rebuild was set back by revolution and civil war. Barnaul eventually recovered in the 1920s with a heavy component of wooden construction, much of which has disappeared with urban redevelopment. Remarkably, a few outstanding examples of early twentieth-century wooden architecture survived—large mansions that were built slightly beyond the central district. Still standing during my visit in 1999, these structures represent some of the best examples of *style moderne* wooden architecture in Russia.

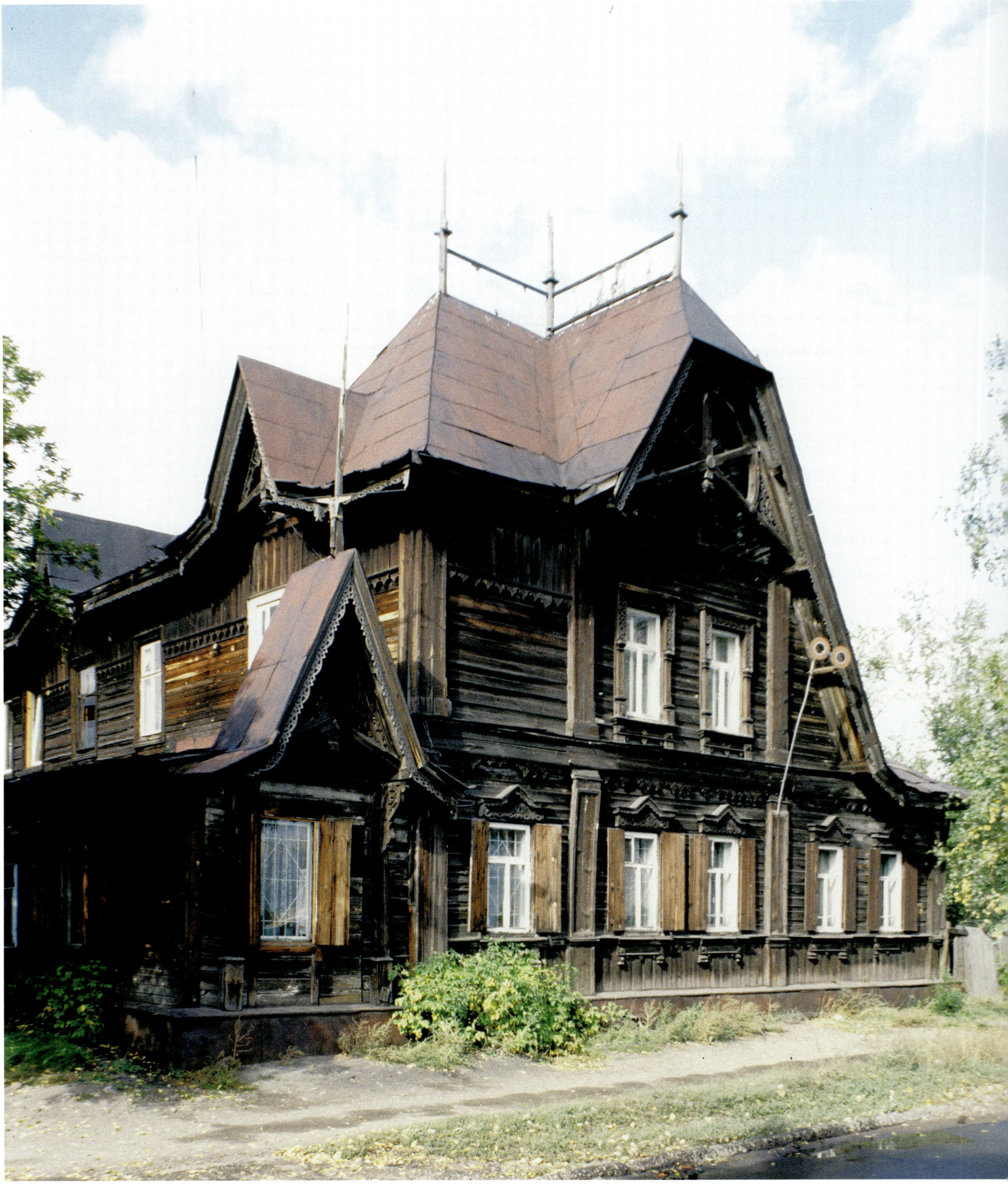

The Tomsk Area

Archeological evidence suggests that the Tomsk region, part of the Ob River basin in central Siberia, has been settled for at least four millennia. By the time detachments of Russian Cossacks arrived in 1598, the native inhabitants included the Khanty and Siberian Tatars, who in 1603 accepted the authority of Tsar Boris Godunov. In 1604 a fort was founded on the banks of the River Tom (a tributary of the Ob), and throughout the seventeenth century the Tomsk settlement served as a bulwark against the steppe tribes of Kalmyks and Kirgiz. With the expansion of Russian control to the south during the eighteenth century, the military significance of Tomsk was replaced by trade and transportation centered on caravans of tea from China. The expansion of the Moscow Road through Siberia in the middle of the eighteenth century provided further stimulus for growth that was reflected in the construction of masonry churches. In the 1830s the development of gold mines in the territory greatly increased the town's significance as a center of mining operations and administration. The Tomsk region also continued to serve as a place of political exile, as it had in the seventeenth and eighteenth centuries.

During the construction of the Trans-Siberian Railway at the end of the nineteenth century, Tomsk missed an opportunity when the Ministry of Transportation decided to place the Ob River railroad bridge to the

BARNAUL. Lesnevsky house. Built in 1906–7 of larch logs in the *style moderne* as a dwelling and studio by the architect Alexander Lesnevsky (who also served as mayor in 1913–16), this national landmark is now in a dilapidated state with a grim prognosis. September 22, 1999.

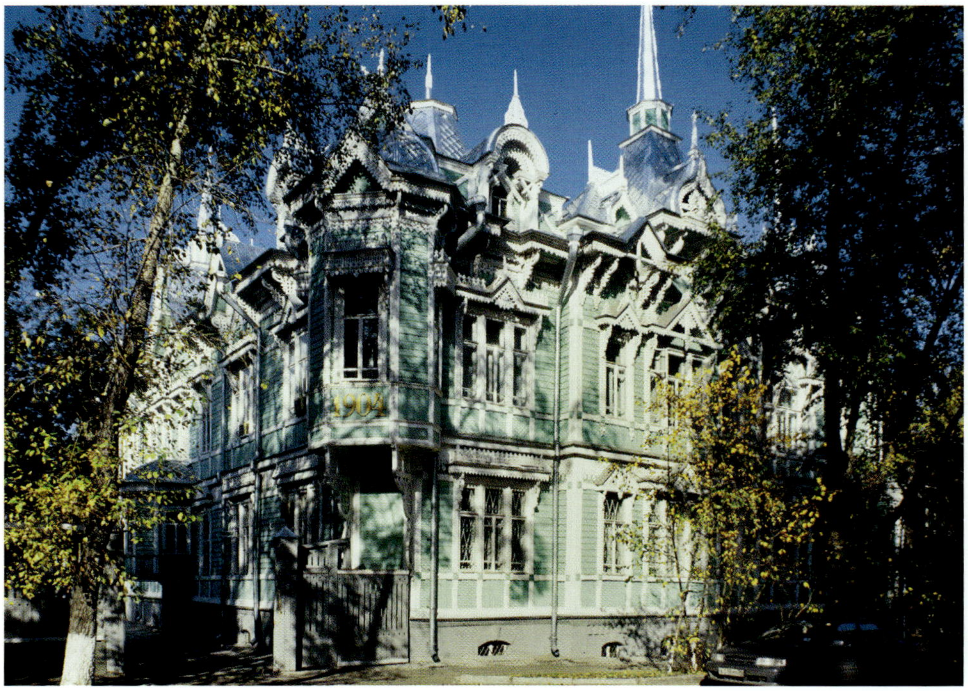

TOMSK. Khomich house, Belinsky Street 19. Built around 1904 by the architect Stanislav Khomich in a florid variant of the Russian Revival style, this magnificent landmark resembles what elsewhere might be called Carpenter Gothic style. September 24, 1999.

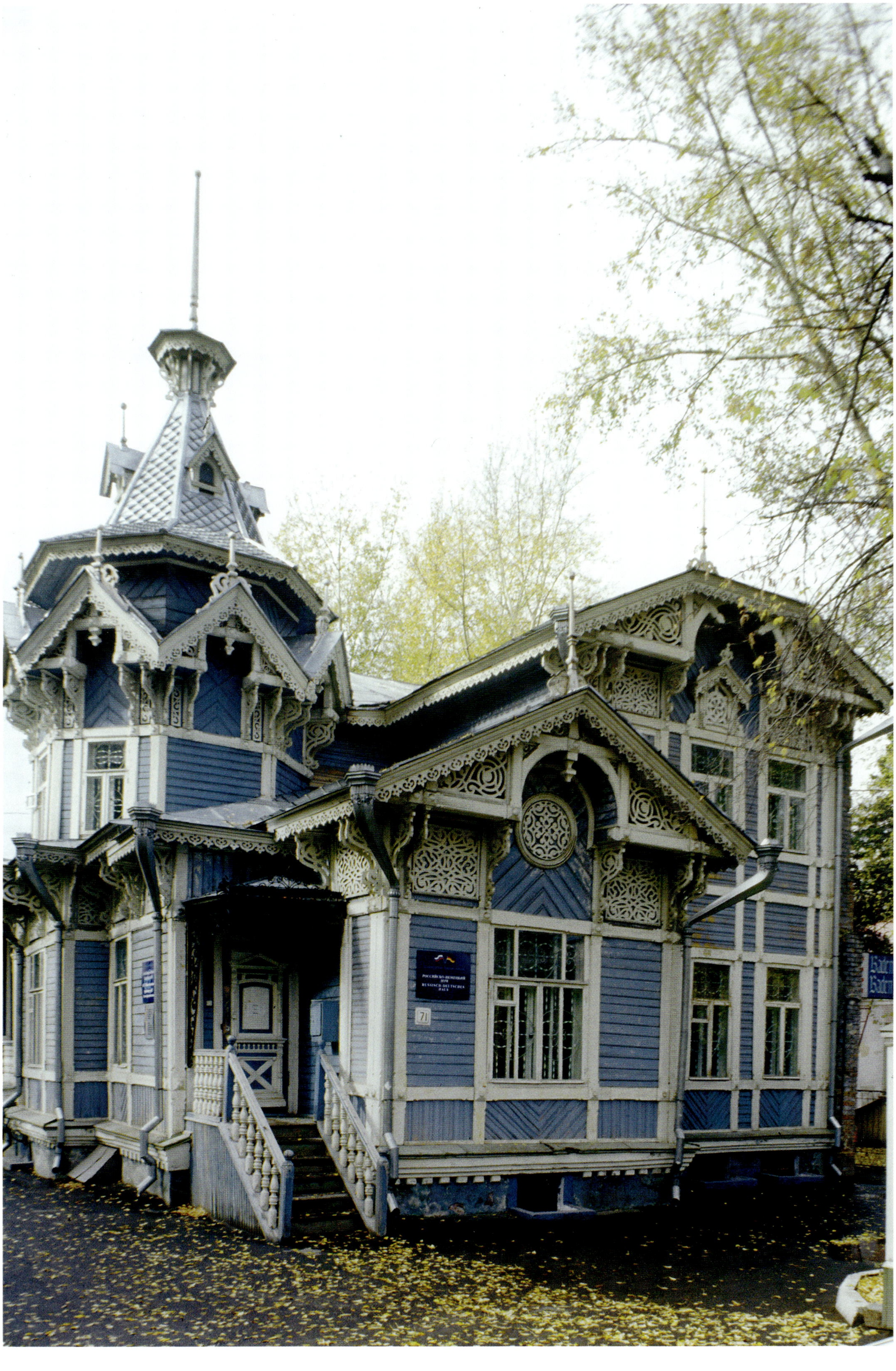
71

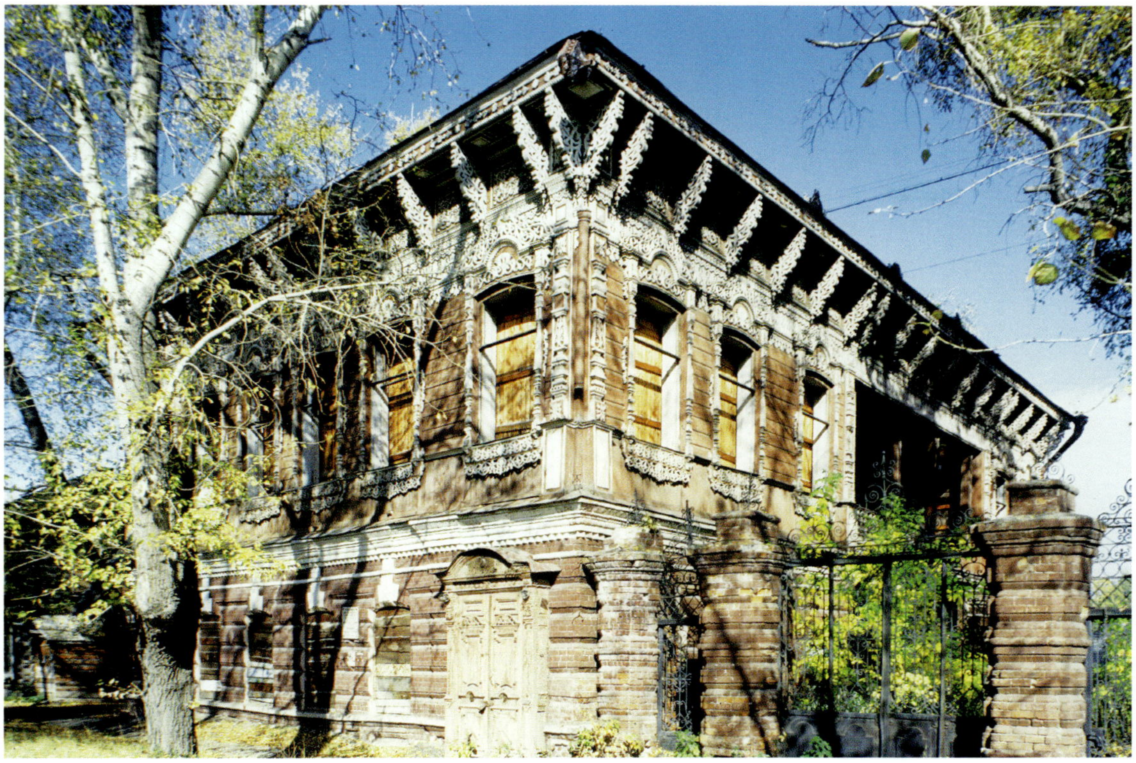

TOMSK. Yegor Golovanov house. Built in 1904 for a wealthy retail merchant, the project was supervised by Stanislav Khomich with obvious decorative similarities to his own house but with a more picturesque, asymmetrical form. Known locally as the "house with the tent tower." September 24, 1999.

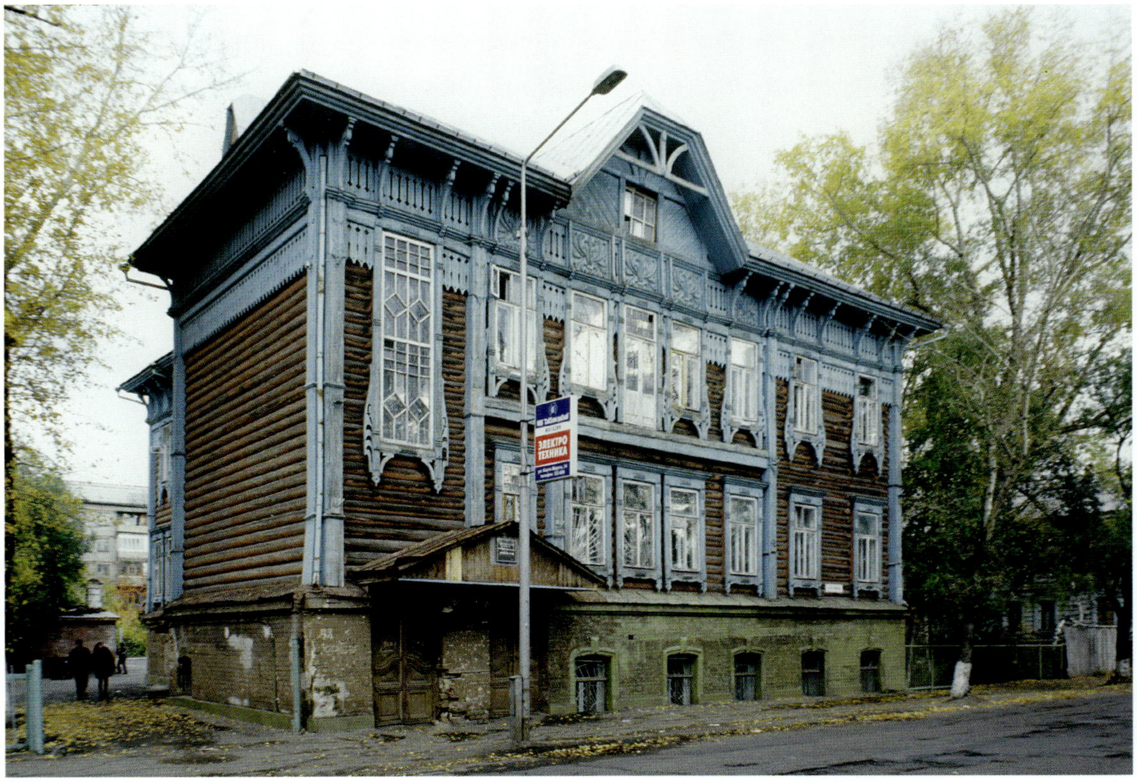

TOMSK. Apartment house, Shishkov Street 10. Built in 1904–5 with a brick rusticated ground floor and florid decorative detailing (e.g., cornice brackets). September 24, 1999

TOMSK. Apartment house, Karl Marx Street 17. Beautiful example of a basic early twentieth-century commercial structure with *style moderne* detailing. Demolished. September 25, 1999.

south, at Novonikolaevsk. Tomsk settled for a branch line constructed in 1896 through the small junction of Taiga (eighty kilometers south of the city), and that spur enabled Tomsk to remain a center of trade and agricultural development in central Siberia. The most distinctive part of the city's architectural heritage is displayed in its neighborhoods of elaborately decorated wooden houses, structures of solid logs often covered with

TOMSK. Kryachkov house. Built in 1910–11, this superb *style moderne* dwelling was intended by the architect Andrey Kryachkov to demonstrate the practicality of log structures in contemporary design with modern conveniences. Note the battered chimneys. September 27, 1999.

TOMSK. Known as the "House with Dragons," Red Army Street 68. Another theatrical example of *style moderne*, this house with its rich plasticity of form was built in 1917 by the architect Vikenty Orzheshko for a physician, Bistrzhitsky, both members of the local Polish diaspora. The dragon motif, which appears frequently in Siberian wooden *style moderne*, is likely a Nordic reference. September 26, 1999.

TOMSK. Courtyard gates attached to early twentieth-century house, Solianoy Lane 18. Ironically, many such festive ancillary structures have been destroyed because they limit access to fire-fighting equipment. September 26, 1999.

TOMSK. Gromov house. Built in 1908 for the merchant Alexander Gromov by Vikenty Orzheshko, this structure brilliantly emphasizes the properties of the log within the asymmetrical plasticity of *style moderne*. Note the complementary color of the abandoned Soviet telephone booth. September 26, 1999.

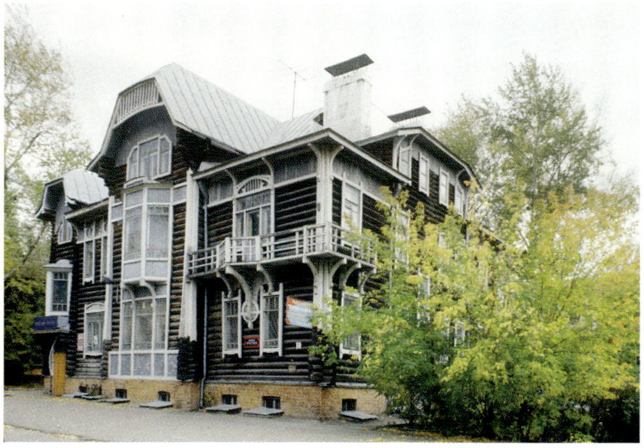

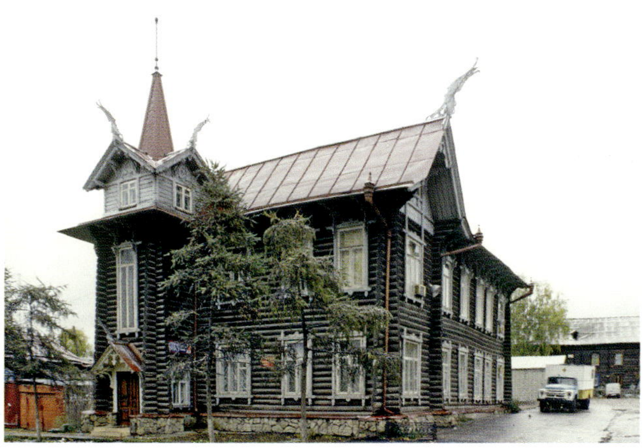

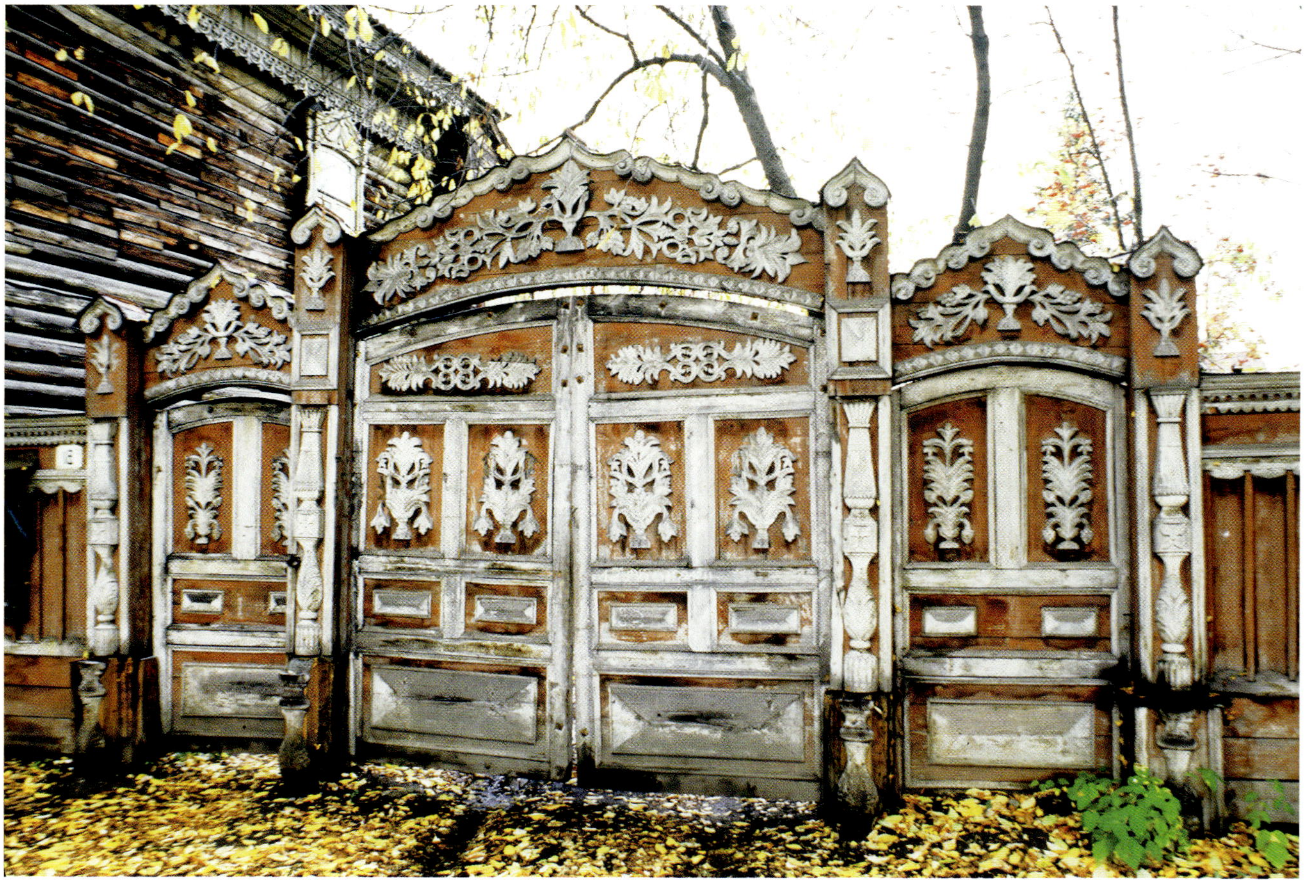

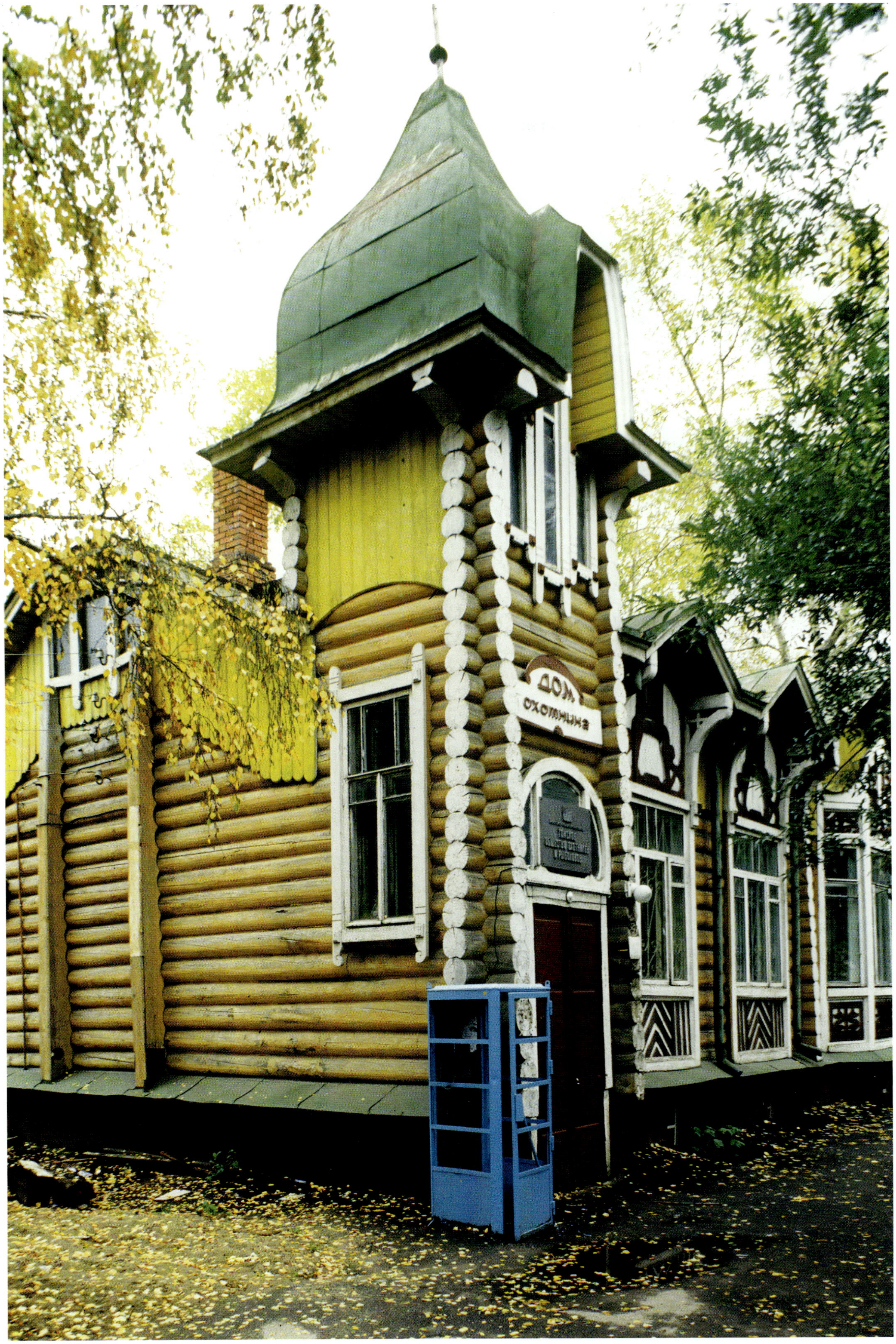
ДОМ
охотника

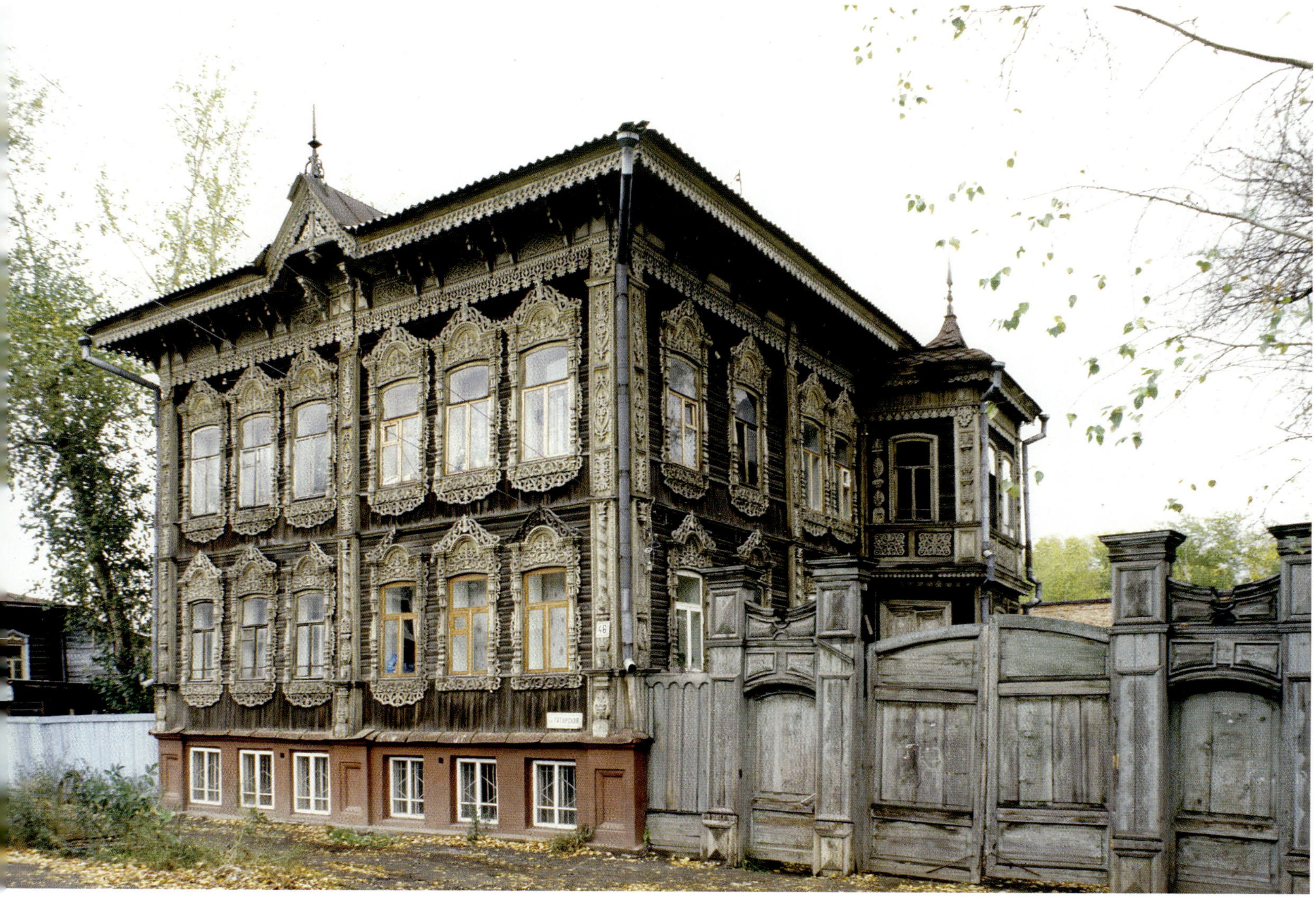

plank siding. It is no exaggeration to say that the "lacework" of Tomsk's wooden architectural ornament—particularly the window surrounds, or *nalichniki*—is unrivaled in Russia for its lavish detail and the extent of its preservation. Many of the best examples were built for merchants who lived in the Tatar Quarter. Public opinion and an enlightened administration have succeeded in preserving many early twentieth-century wooden buildings, but budget resources are rapidly dwindling and much has been destroyed by redevelopment.

A particularly impressive example of Tomsk architecture is the Old Believer Church of the Dormition, built of Siberian pine and consecrated in 1913. My visit in September 1999 coincided with a pastoral visit from Moscow of Metropolitan Alimpy (Gusev) (1929–2003), spiritual leader of the Russian Orthodox Old Believer Church. Not only were the parishioners very

TOMSK. Moskov house, Tatar Street 46. Built in 1902 for the Tatar horse trader Ahmedull Moskov, this proud structure on a brick cellar contains every decorative device imaginable. The courtyard gates have survived. September 26, 1999.

TOMSK. Old Believer Church of the Dormition, south view. September 27, 1999.

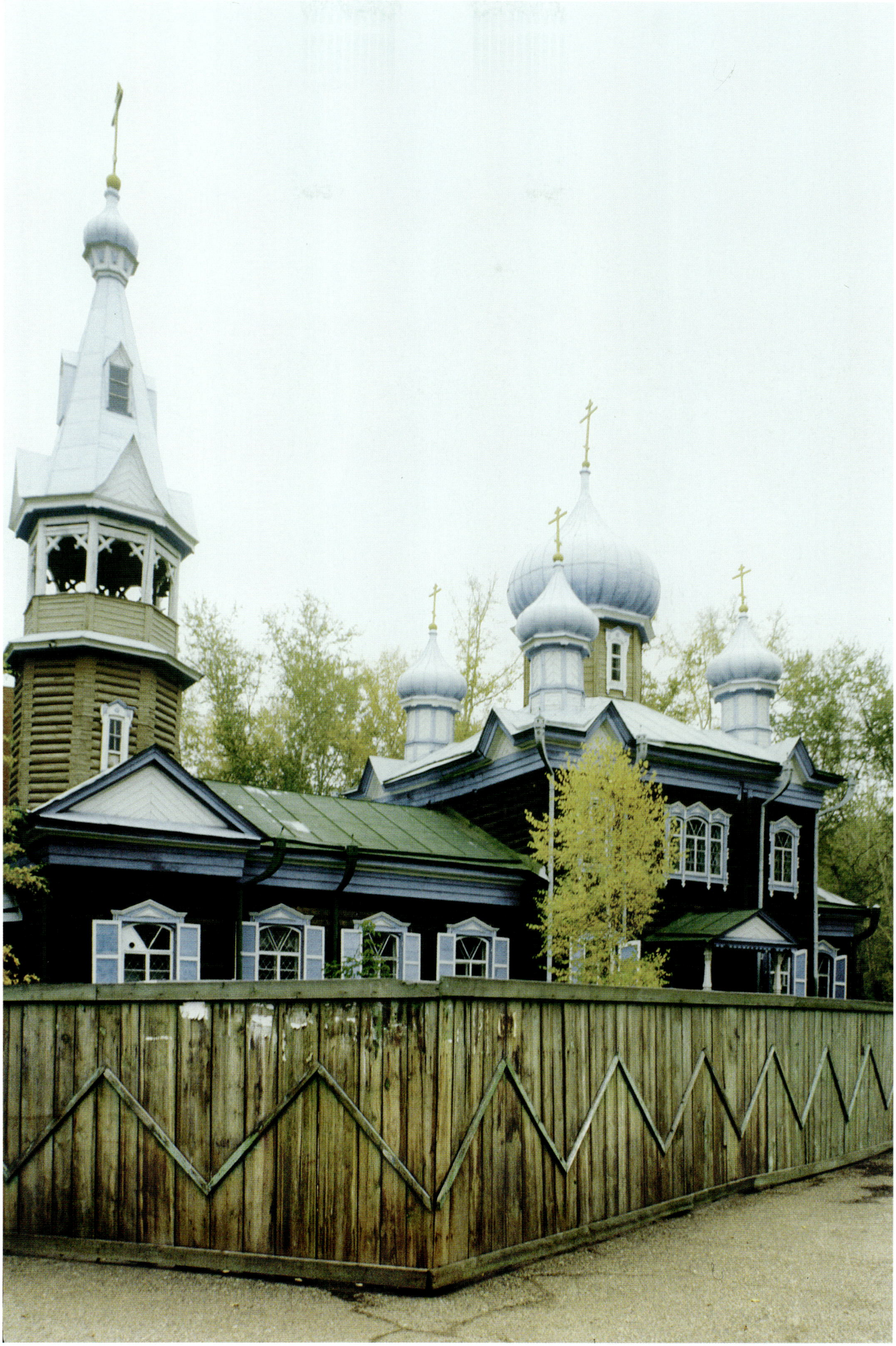

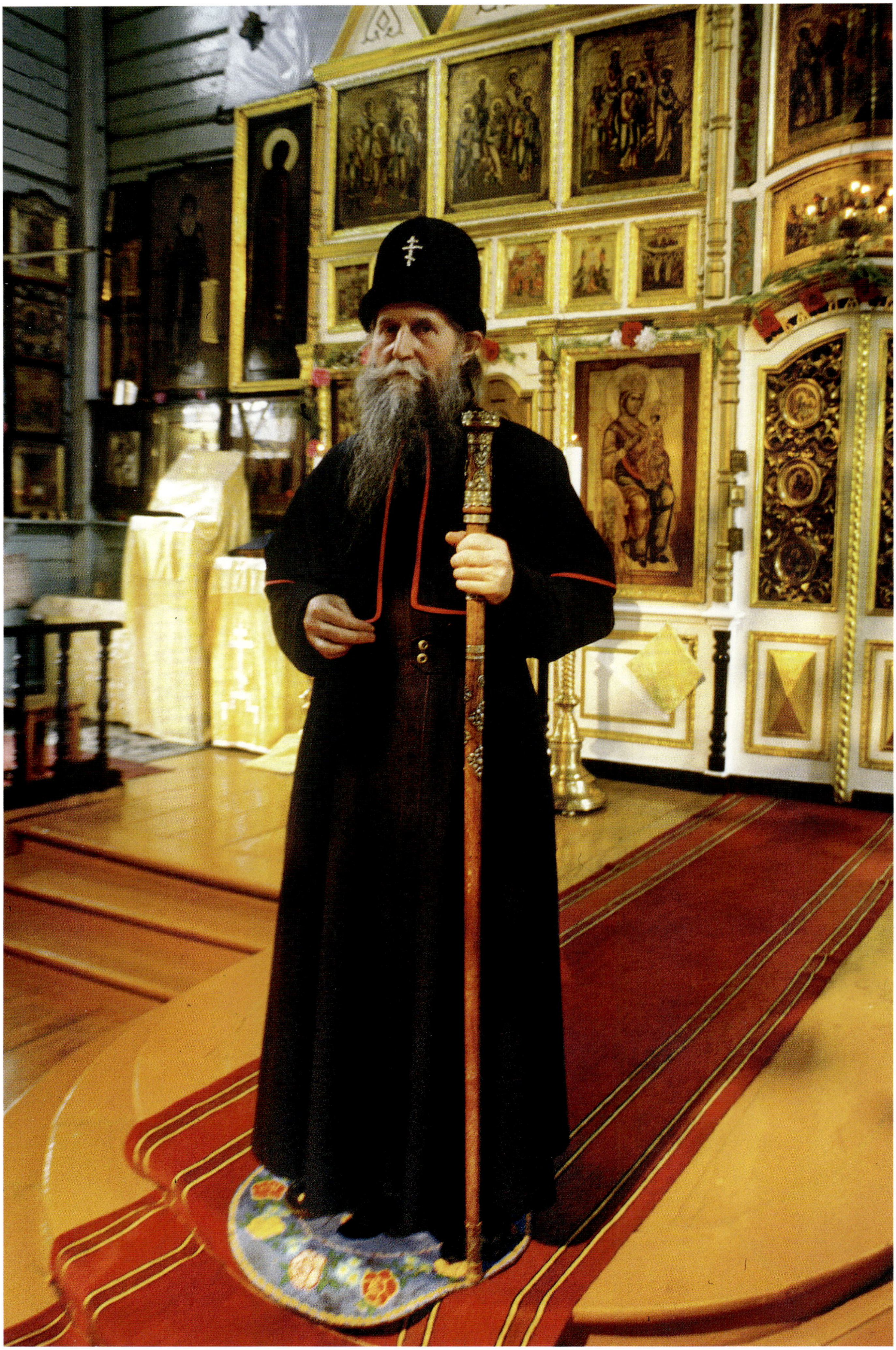

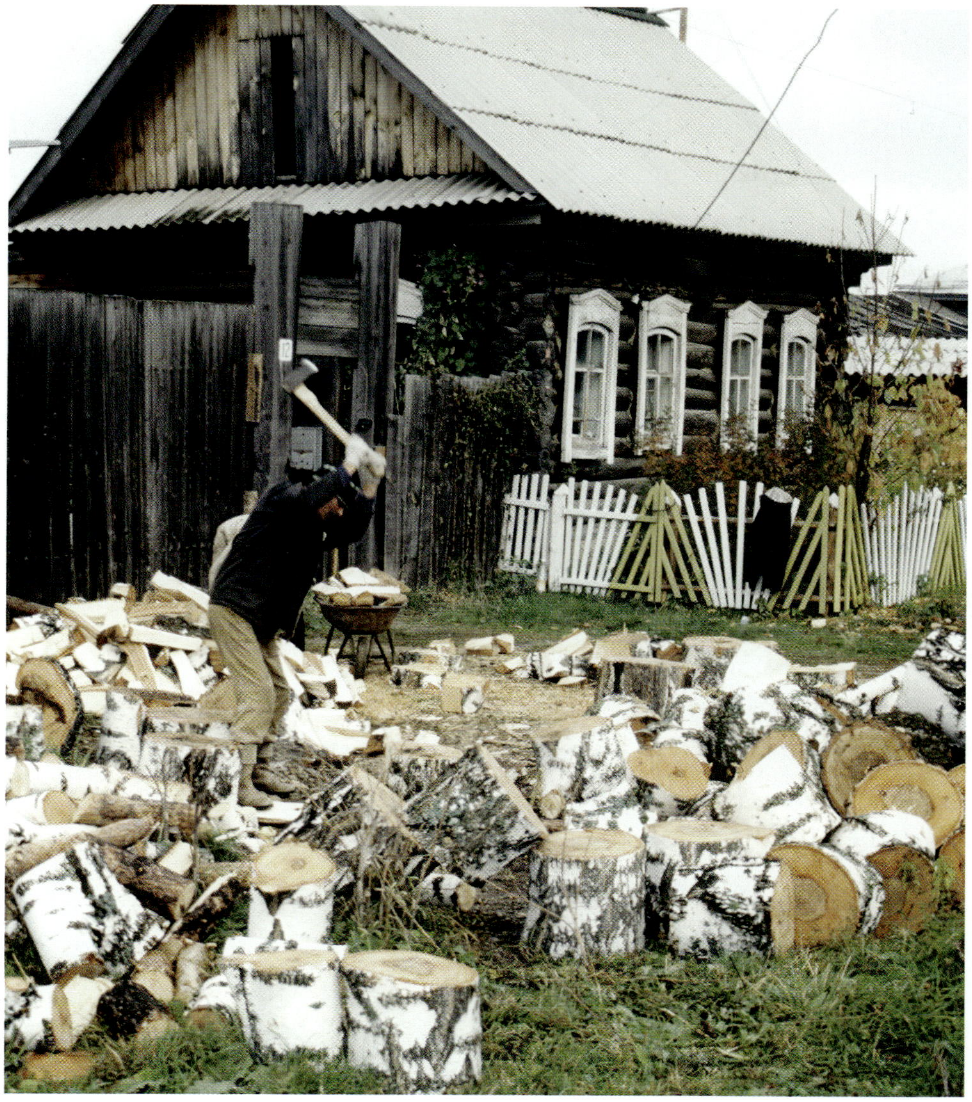

TOMSK. Old Believer Church of the Dormition. Interior with my historic portrait of Metropolitan Alimpy (Gusev), with the icon screen in the background. September 27, 1999.

BATURINO (Tomsk region). Soviet-era log house, Proletariat Street 12. Splitting birch sections into firewood. September 25, 1999.

welcoming, but I was asked to take the prelate's photograph. The moment was so unexpected that I had difficulty holding the camera steady, but the natural light was sufficient to capture his presence in austere robes, a figure out of the late seventeenth century when the split with the official church occurred (1660s). That portrait has become one of my most treasured works. A walk through the historic neighborhoods of Tomsk or a visit to villages to the north of the city reminds one how deeply Russian culture belongs to the forest.

Yenisei River Basin

From west to east Siberia is marked by three of the Northern Hemisphere's greatest rivers: the Ob, the Yenisei, and the Lena. During the Russian move east toward the Pacific in the early seventeenth century, the great challenge after the Ob River basin was reaching the Yenisei River. Together with its tributaries, the Yenisei not only opened a territory of natural wealth but also raised the possibility of expanded trade with China. As usual in the exploration of Siberia, the earliest land route was the most northerly, such as that from the fur-trapping haven of Mangazei, founded in 1601 on the Taz Bay (northeast of the mouth of the Ob). Yet reaching the Yenisei by this means tested the endurance even of the sturdy northerners from the White Sea area—the Pomors—who formed the early scouting and trading parties. Long portages through tundra—inhospitable at any time of year—sapped body and soul.

A more southerly route led from the Ob River along the Ket almost due east toward the Yenisei River. The Yenisei was not the only prize: The Angara tributary and the Lena River farther to the east were equally important in terms of access to fur pelts and other resources. Therefore, the logical site for a strategic outpost was slightly to the north of the confluence of the Yenisei and Angara. In the summer of 1619, a group of servicemen and Cossacks from Tobolsk founded a settlement on the left bank of the Yenisei, on a rise near the entry of the small Ket River into the Yenisei. The geographic importance of the site led in 1623 to Moscow's appointment of a *voevoda* for the new settlement, which henceforth became the administrative center for the boundless territory beyond the Yenisei River. In this capacity the town served as a transit point for an increasing number of exiles, including archpriest Avvakum, the spiritual leader of the Old Believers. As a gateway to eastern Siberia, the Yeniseisk fort launched several exploration parties. Among the explorers was Semyon Dezhnev, a Yeniseisk Cossack sent to

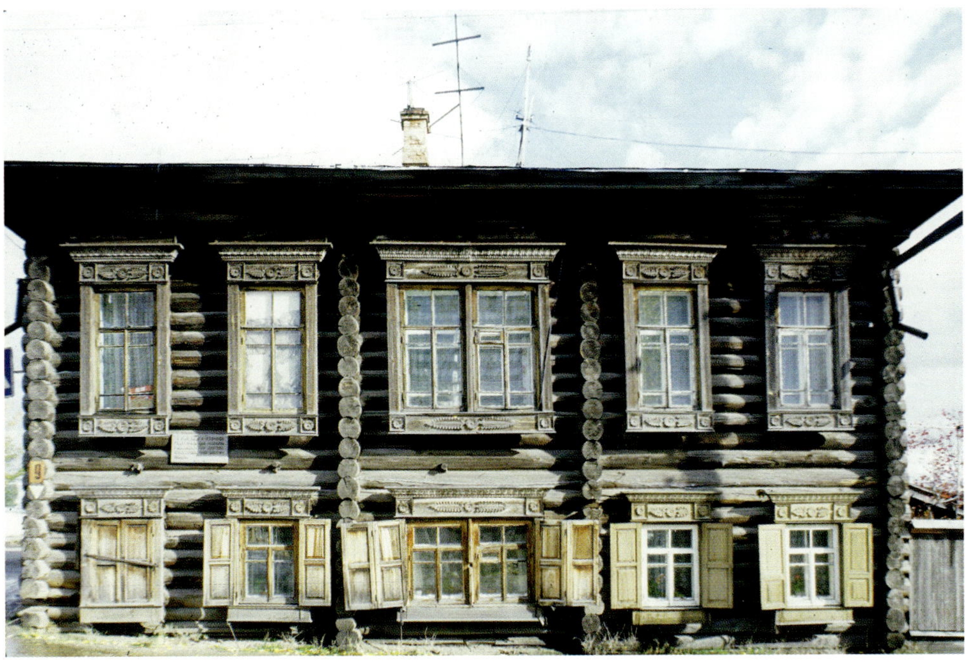

YENISEISK. House, Dudarev Street 9 and Worker Peasant Street 121. Built in the late nineteenth century, this weathered structure is the epitome of function combined with traditional carved decoration in Siberia. September 29, 1999.

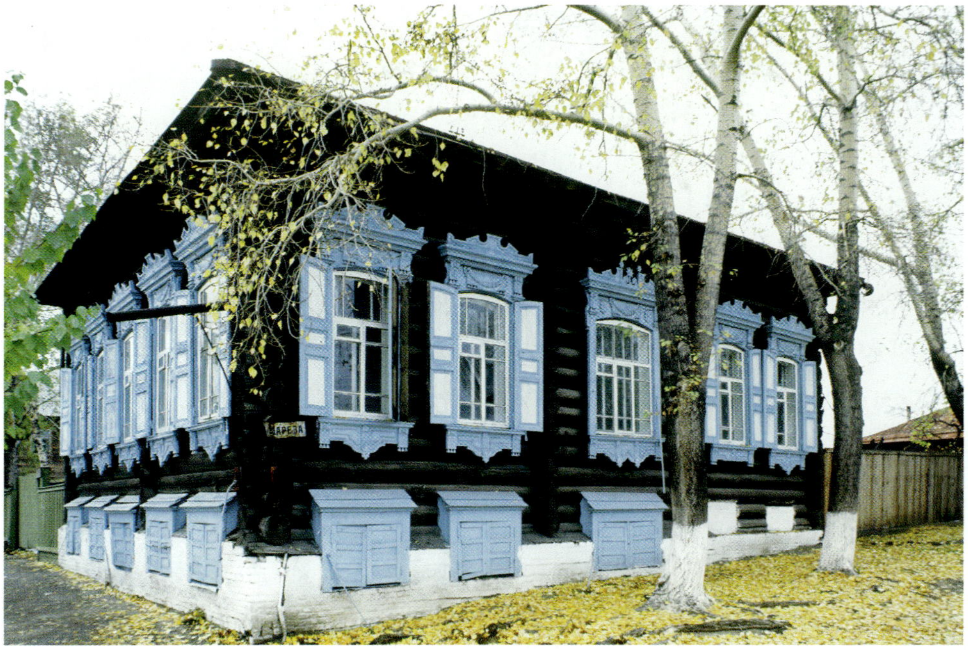

YENISEISK. House, Dudarev Street 14/11. Bright window frames on dark log walls over distinctive shuttered basement in this fine early twentieth-century dwelling. September 29, 1999.

remote Yakutsk in 1638. He subsequently led a group that is thought to have sailed through the strait between Russia and North America in 1648, sixty years before Vitus Bering. For another century Yeniseisk would thrive as a Siberian trading center. Important components of commerce included valuable sable furs, dubbed black gold, as well as fish from the region's abundant rivers. The Dormition Fair, held annually in August, attracted merchants from the distant reaches of Muscovy as well as Asia.

The regional administration has recently invested heavily in restoring damaged eighteenth-century churches and brick commercial buildings from the prerevolutionary period. But wooden structures have also benefited from the attempt to refurbish the town's appearance. Although many log dwellings seem consigned to decay and demolition, several are well preserved, particularly those brick half-cellar foundations—a distinctive local trait. Brightly painted decorative window surrounds and shutters further enliven the appearance of a bucolic town where cattle often graze along the grassy shoulders of streets.

Krasnoyarsk

The Siberian city of Krasnoyarsk (current population around 1,197,000) is the capital of one of Russia's largest administrative regions, stretching from the Tyva Republic in the south (on Mongolia's northwestern border) all the way to the Kara and Laptev Seas in the Arctic Ocean. Founded in 1628 as a frontier outpost on the southern reaches of the mighty Yenisei River, the town for the first century of its existence consisted of little more than a Cossack detachment. Its name is a Russian translation of the original site name ("red riverbank") in the Khakas language spoken by the native population. The area's rich natural resources eventually gave rise to industrial and crafts production during the eighteenth century, particularly after the subduing of southern steppe tribes and the opening of the Moscow Road (1735–41), a more even, southerly route that redirected settlement and transportation in Siberia. Copper smelting and ironworking factories were in operation by the 1750s. Throughout this period the territory along the Yenisei River was administered from the town of Yeniseisk, located some 340 kilometers to the north of Krasnoyarsk. In 1822 Krasnoyarsk was designated the administrative center of Yeniseisk Province.

Krasnoyarsk was transformed from a provincial garrison town into a major transportation center by the construction of the Trans-Siberian Railroad, begun in 1891. By 1895 it was connected by rail with European Russia, and subsequently with Irkutsk and the Far East. The conjunction of rail and river (the Yenisei) proved an enormous stimulus for the city's growth. Its economic activity sustained a merchant elite, prominent among whom was Gennady Yudin, a bibliophile who sold much of his valuable collection of books to the Library of Congress in 1907. Other prominent cultural figures included the painter Vasily Surikov (1848–1916),

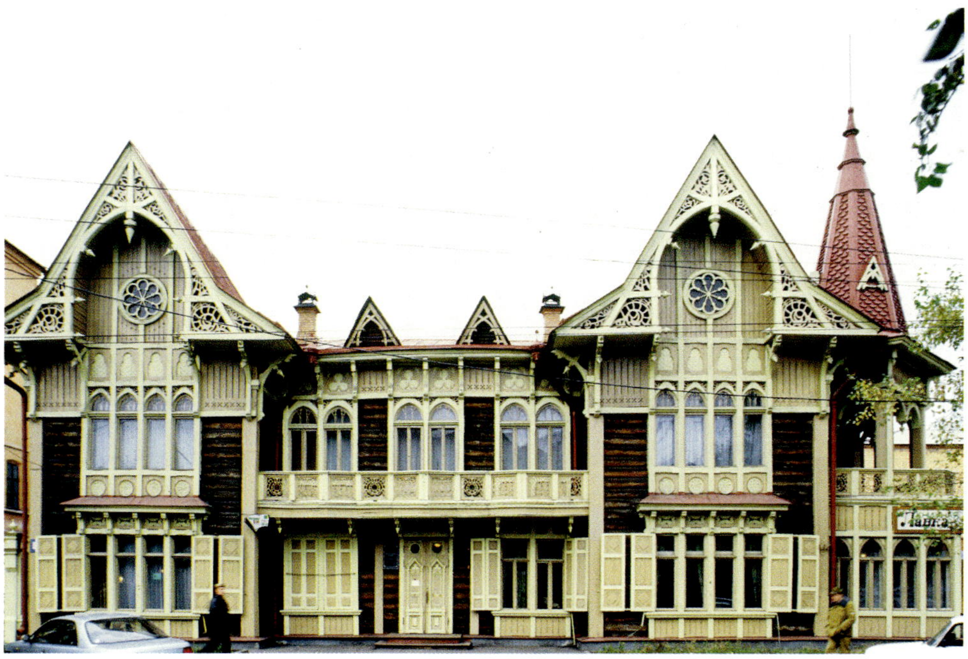

KRASNOYARSK. Elias Tsukerman apartment house. September 28, 1999.

whose house has been preserved as a museum. The brightest exercise in wooden architecture is the multipurpose building originally erected in 1894 for Elias Tsukerman, a Jewish exile from Odessa who acquired a local fortune in flour milling and brickmaking. In 1911 the house was rebuilt by the architect Vladimir Sokolovsky in a picturesque combination of *style moderne* with Gothic Revival. Plank siding added in 1913 enhanced the stunning display. Although a handful of these wooden landmarks will survive, swathes of modest wooden housing have been demolished for redevelopment in Krasnoyarsk.

In the area around Krasnoyarsk there are small settlements that seem to exist in another time, although they are situated near one of Siberia's most advanced industrial regions. One such is the village of Barabanovo, located near the left bank of the Yenisei River some sixty kilometers to the northwest of Krasnoyarsk. In a pattern typical of Siberia's early development, Barabanovo was founded in the mid-seventeenth century as a community of Cossacks, who combined farming skills with the hardiness needed for life on the Siberian frontier. They were joined by exiles and peasant settlers from the west of Russia, part of an early twentieth-century state policy encouraging land-poor peasants to populate the territory of Siberia. Its landmark is a mid-nineteenth-century wooden church dedicated to Saint Paraskeva Pyatnitsa, a third-century martyr and patron of commerce. Desperately in need of repair, the church is an excellent example of nineteenth-century parish architecture with significant wall paintings

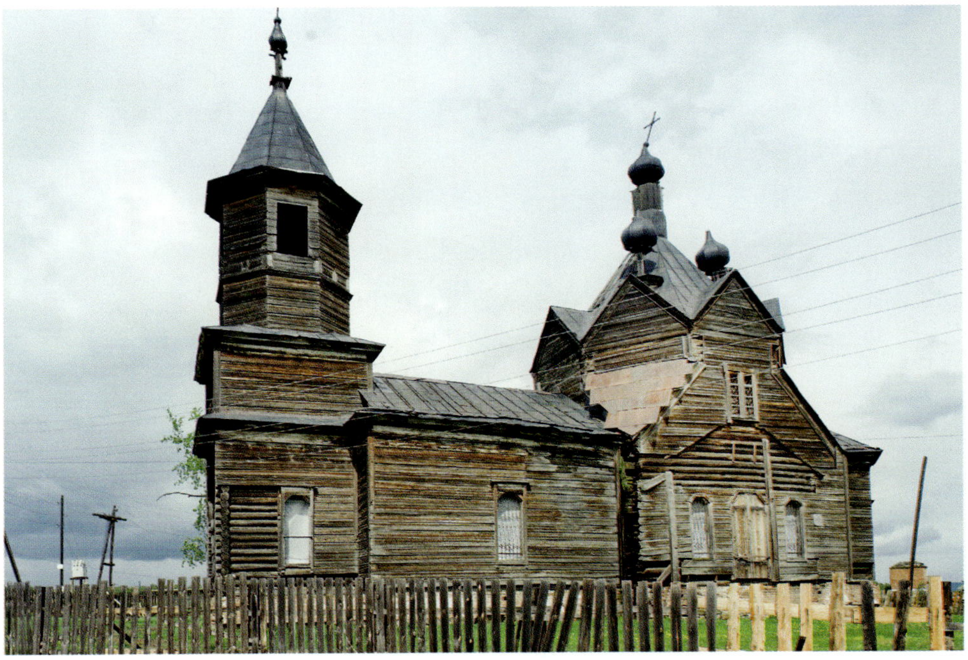

BARABANOVO (Krasnoyarsk region). Church of Saint Paraskeva Pyatnitsa, south view. This unusual structure merges a traditional linear design with an eight-gabled crown in an attempt to emulate an urban style. May 24, 2015.

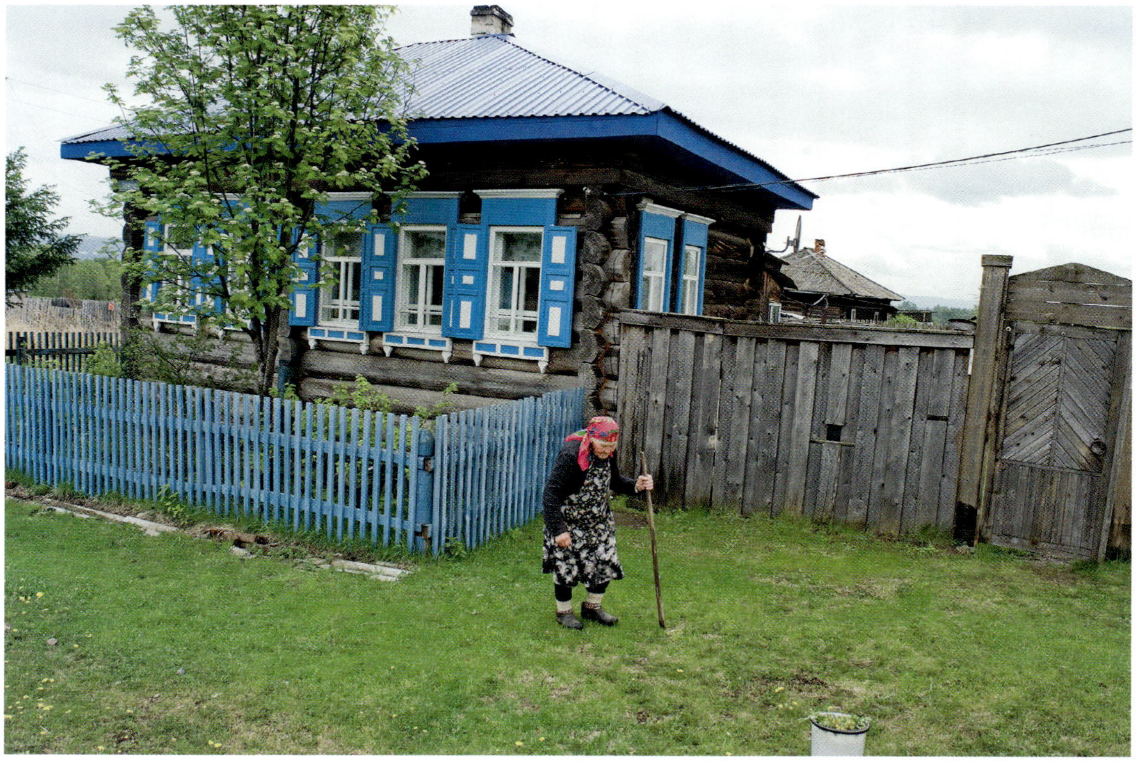

BARABANOVO. Miniature *izba* for retired schoolteacher Klavdia Korkunova, who is surveying her domain. May 24, 2015.

KUVARSHINO (Krasnoyarsk region). House with gate. So much of Siberia's peasant existence is evoked in this abandoned homestead from the turn of the twentieth century. May 24, 2015.

DIVNOGORSK (Krasnoyarsk region). Old Hermitage, with the Church of the Abalatsk Icon of the Virgin of the Sign, southeast view. Built in 1888, this austere structure summons the rigorous asceticism of Siberian monastic retreats and attracts local artists who advocate restoration of the grounds as an environmental park. May 20, 2015.

preserved on the interior. The village of Barabanovo also has traditional wooden houses that have been well preserved by their owners. Their dark log walls provide a background for painted shutters and decorative window surrounds (*nalichniki*).

One of the oldest Russian towns within the upper reaches of the Yenisei River, Minusinsk was founded by Cossacks in 1739 on the Minusa River (or Minusinka), a right tributary of the Yenisei. Minusinsk is located in a forest-steppe zone, where the dense northern forests gradually yield to open plains. Although the townscape is flat, the town is surrounded by hills, and the Yenisei is only six miles west of the town. Attracted by this fertile land, Russian settlers first came to the area in the early eighteenth century, but the proximity to China led to an uncertain border situation, initially regulated in 1727 by a border treaty between Russia and China. Territory north of the Sayan Range was considered Russian, but the threat of Chinese incursions remained, and in the middle of the century Cossack detachments were sent to guard the borders. During the eighteenth

OVSYANKA (Krasnoyarsk region). Church of Saint Inokenty, bishop of Irkutsk, southeast view. Situated near the Yenisei River, the church was built in 1998, and designed by architect Areg Demirkhanov, with the support of the Siberian writer Viktor Astafyev (1924–2001), whose house and museum are nearby. May 20, 2015.

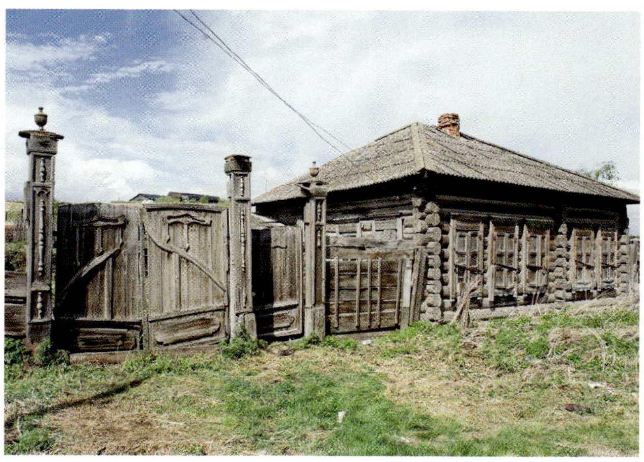

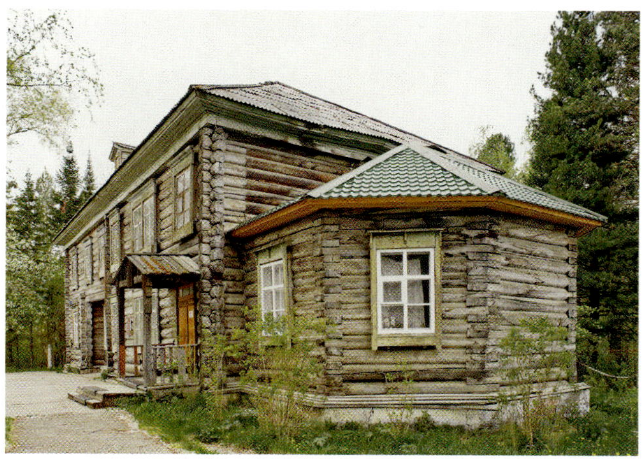

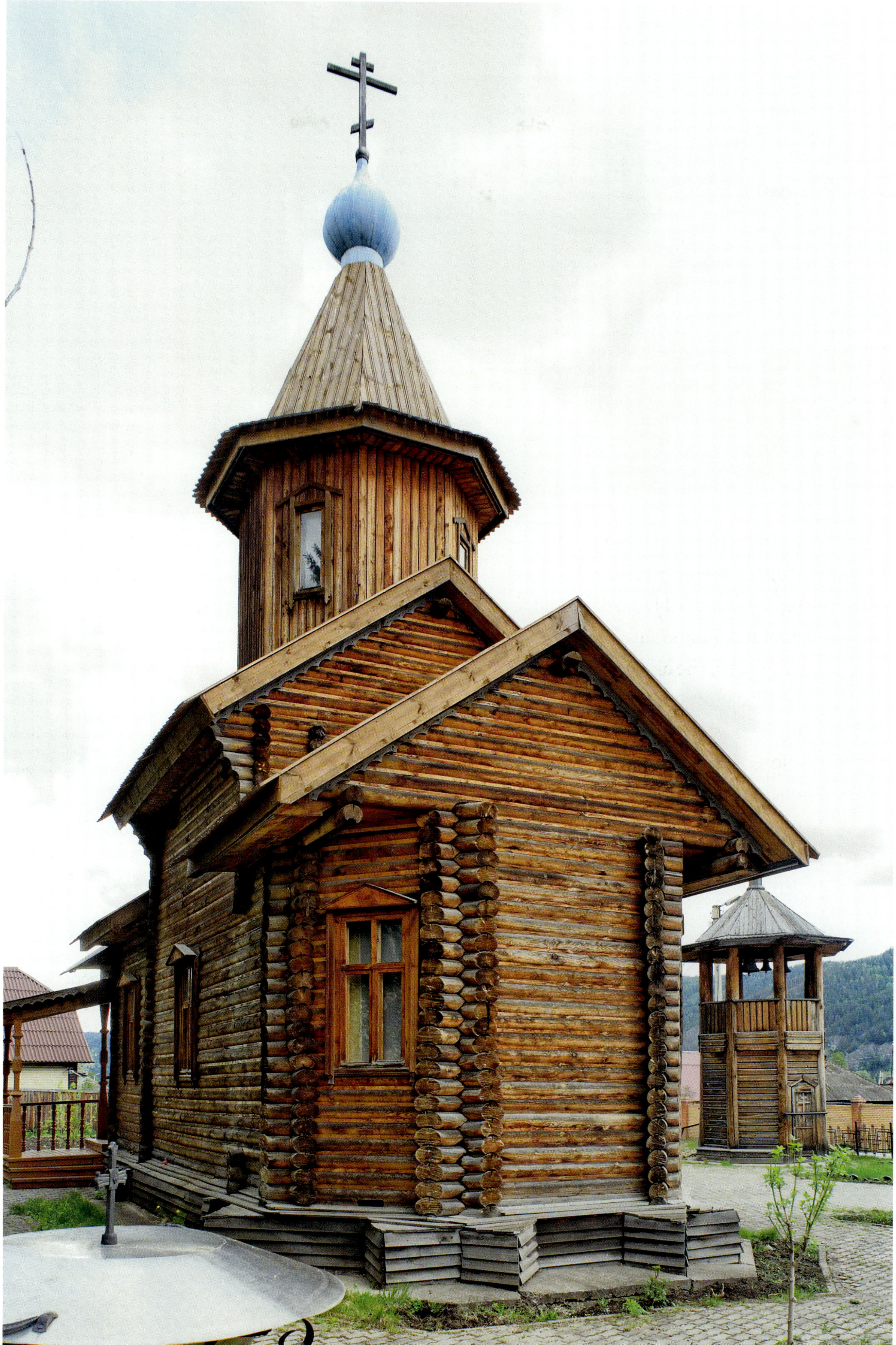

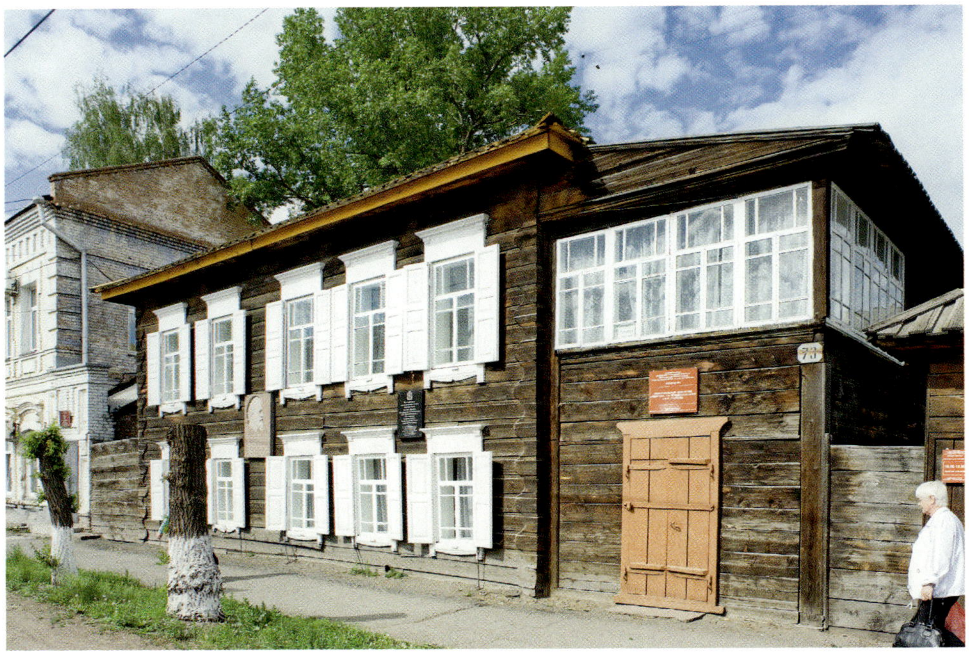

MINUSINSK. Fyodor Bragin house. May 25, 2015.

century Minusinsk slowly grew as a settlement linked to the area's copper and iron-working factories. Local growth was also stimulated by a policy, implemented in 1775–76, of resettling peasants from northern Siberian villages to the better land around Minusinsk and thus consolidating the Russian presence in the borderlands near China.

Like many remote Siberian towns, Minusinsk served as a place of exile for convicts as well as political dissidents, including certain prominent political thinkers during the latter part of the nineteenth century. This aspect of the town's history is memorialized in a spacious wooden house built in 1878 by the brothers Fyodor and Yefim Bragin, who had been exiled to Minusinsk from the Caucasus. The house and the structures in its courtyard now serve as a museum to nineteenth-century provincial life.

Among the Bragin guests was none other than Vladimir Lenin, exiled to the nearby village of Shushenskoe, where he lived in reasonable comfort until his release in February 1900. The entire village was subsequently preserved as a major Lenin shrine. Shushenskoe was established no later than the 1740s on the River Shush (pronounced shoosh) near its confluence with the much larger Yenisei. In the early nineteenth century the village became an administrative center with facilities for grain storage and a stockade containing a jail. Because of its official apparatus, the village became a place of exile for those who had served their terms in prison. Prominent exiles included two members of the 1825 Decembrist conspiracy as well as the radical intellectual Mikhail Petrushevsky, whose underground discus-

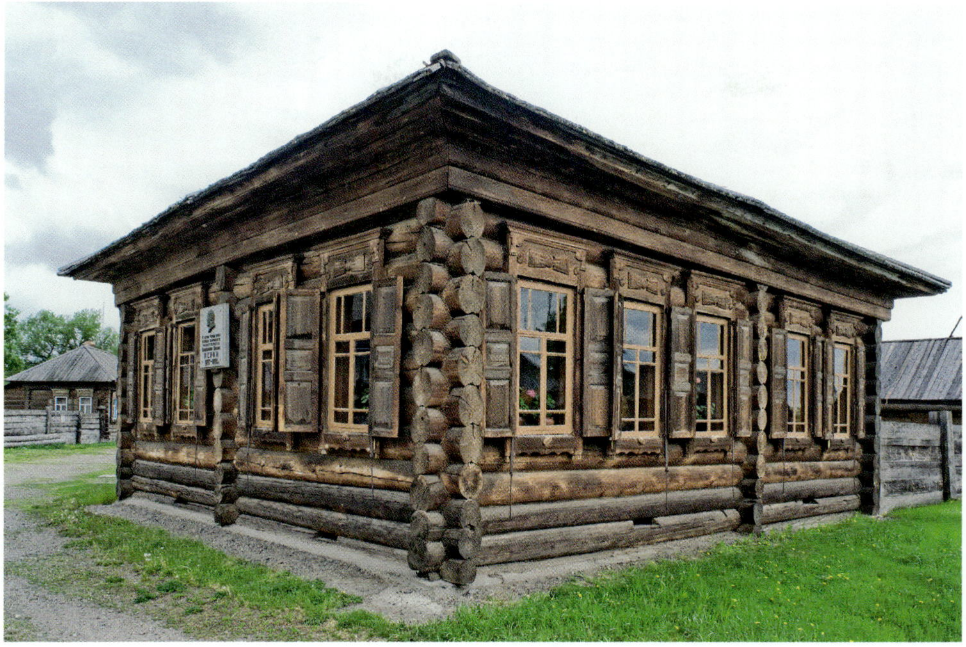

SHUSHENSKOE (Krasnoyarsk region, outdoor museum). Apollon Zyryanov *izba*. Vladimir Lenin lived here in 1897–98. May 26, 2015.

sion circle involved Fyodor Dostoevsky in the late 1840s. (Members of the group were arrested and condemned to death by firing squad, but their execution was commuted at the last moment.)

By far the most prominent of those exiles was Vladimir Ulyanov (Lenin), who arrived at Shushenskoe in May 1897. At that time, he was head of the Union of Struggle for the Liberation of the Working Class. For the first fourteen months (until July 1898) Lenin rented a spacious room from the prosperous peasant Apollon Zyryanov. The state provided the political exile with a monthly allowance of eight rubles, which for a village economy was quite ample for all basic needs—as Lenin's notes indicated. (Most peasants rarely used money since they raised their own food and bartered whenever possible.) Lenin's largest expense was books and journals, for which he paid with funds sent by relatives and royalties from his published articles.

Built in the 1840s, the house was bought by the village Soviet (council) in 1928 as part of a memorial to Lenin. The interior has been preserved to a rare degree due in no small measure to the donation by the Zyryanovs of several dozen items, including the bed from the time Lenin lived there. As typical for prosperous peasant households in Siberia, the backyard was divided by a fence into two parts: the "clean," which contained a grain barn, a shed for agricultural implements, and a bathhouse; and the "black," which contained the stables, smaller sheds, barns, and a well. After the sale of the house, the Zyryanovs moved to Minusinsk.

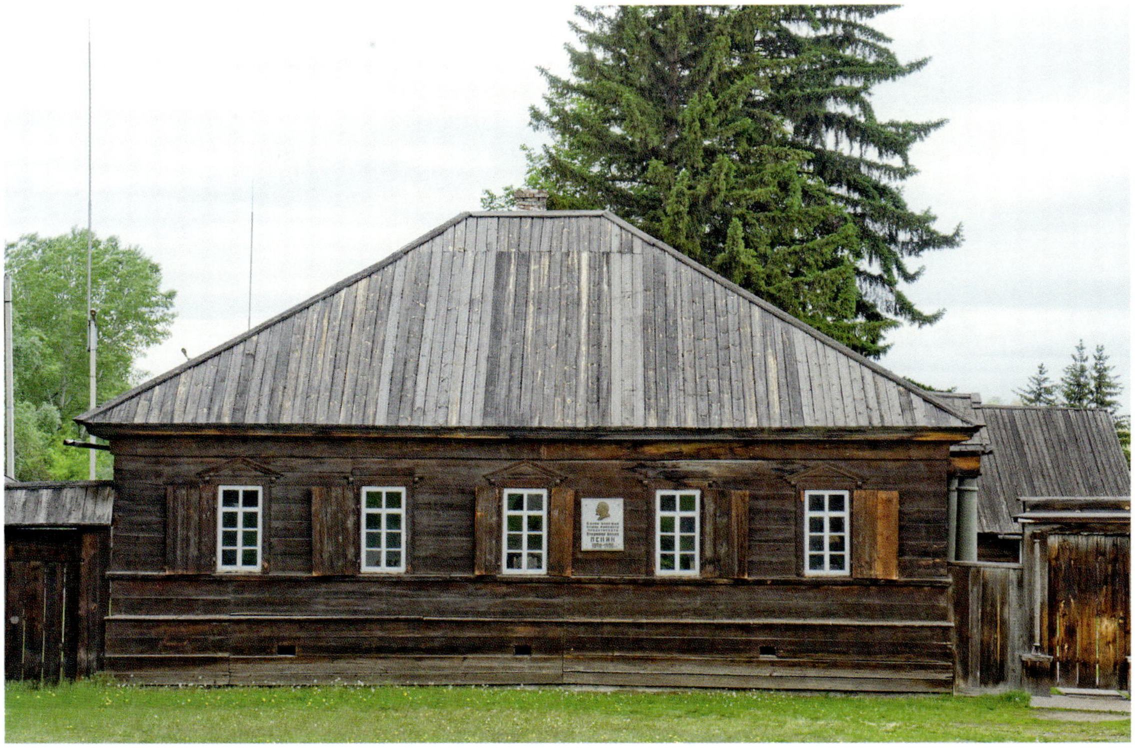

SHUSHENSKOE. Praskovya Petrova house, street view. Vladimir Lenin and Nadezhda Krupskaya lived here in 1898–1900. May 26, 2015.

In May 1898, Lenin's partner Nadezhda Krupskaya arrived in Shushenskoe. In order to be able to live together, the couple were married in July at the Church of Saints Peter and Paul (demolished in 1938), although both were atheists. After the wedding, they moved to a larger wooden house owned by Praskovya Petrova, widow of a prosperous peasant, where they lived until the conclusion of the period of exile in February 1900. The house had an enclosed yard fronted by the main entrance that was framed by a simple neoclassical portico—a highly unusual detail for a peasant dwelling, whatever the social level. As with the smaller Zyryanov house, the yard encompassed barns, sheds, and a bathhouse. The Petrova house had been purchased by the local Soviet in 1924, the year of Lenin's death, and in 1930 the council decided to create a formal museum to Lenin's exile at the Petrova house. In 1939 that museum was transferred to the Krasnoyarsk Regional Committee of the Communist Party as part of the national Lenin Museum network.

A new level of museum activity occurred in 1968 in preparation for the 1970 centennial of Lenin's birth. At that time the Central Committee declared the original village a memorial preserve dedicated to Lenin's exile. The preserve consisted of twenty-nine log houses, of which twenty-three

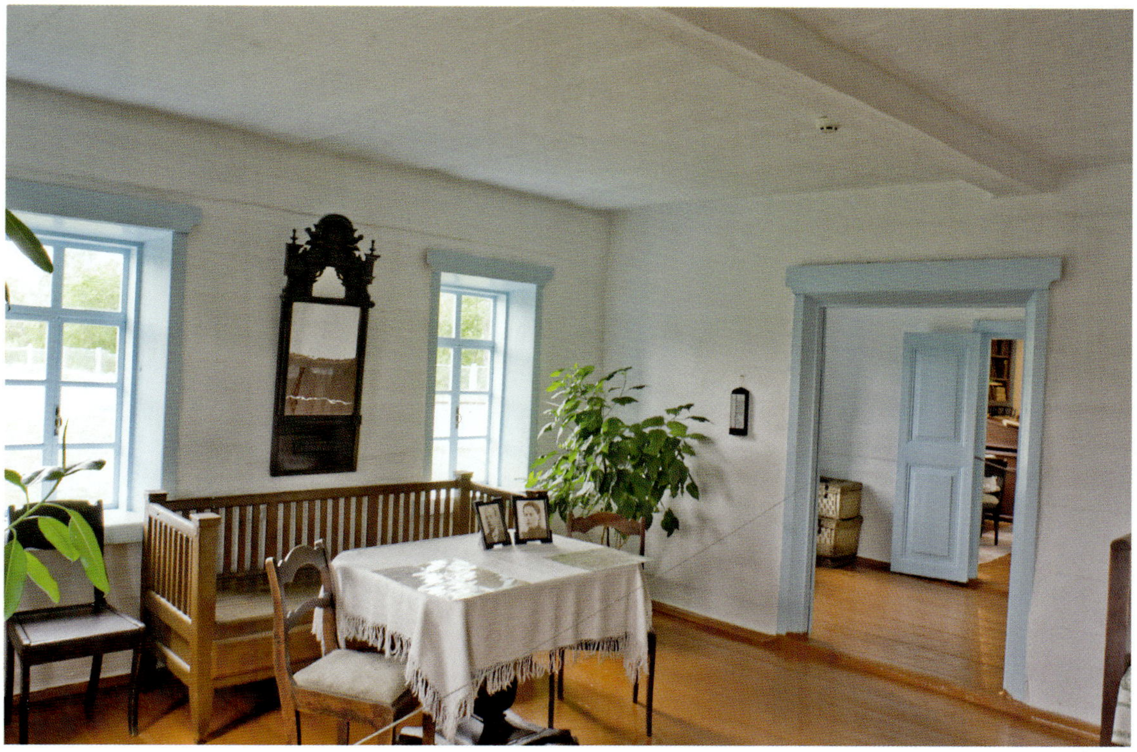

SHUSHENSKOE. Praskovya Petrova house, main room with view toward rooms rented by Vladimir Lenin. May 26, 2015.

were built no later than the end of the nineteenth century, when Lenin was there. Even considering refurbishments, this is a unique degree of preservation of an original village environment in Russia. Among the other buildings on display are log houses belonging to peasants who had resettled to the area throughout the nineteenth century. A few houses are identified by the occupation of the owners—beekeeper, fisher, cooper. Some of the houses are quite small, an indication of the poverty in which many settlers lived. The larger houses belonged to former exiles who took root and prospered (relatively speaking) as entrepreneurs. One house contained a dry goods store. And there is also the local administration building that fronts a reconstruction of the local jail within a stockade of vertical logs. And there is a small local tavern (*kabak*).

With the collapse of the Soviet Union and the closing of Communist Party financial support, the Shushenskoe museum complex faced an existential crisis. Fortunately, with the support of regional funding, the museum adroitly repurposed itself as a display of traditional Siberian folkways—without denying the presence of Lenin. (Many comrades throughout the world are still interested.) As part of the transformation, a new tourist complex was added to the north of museum territory with

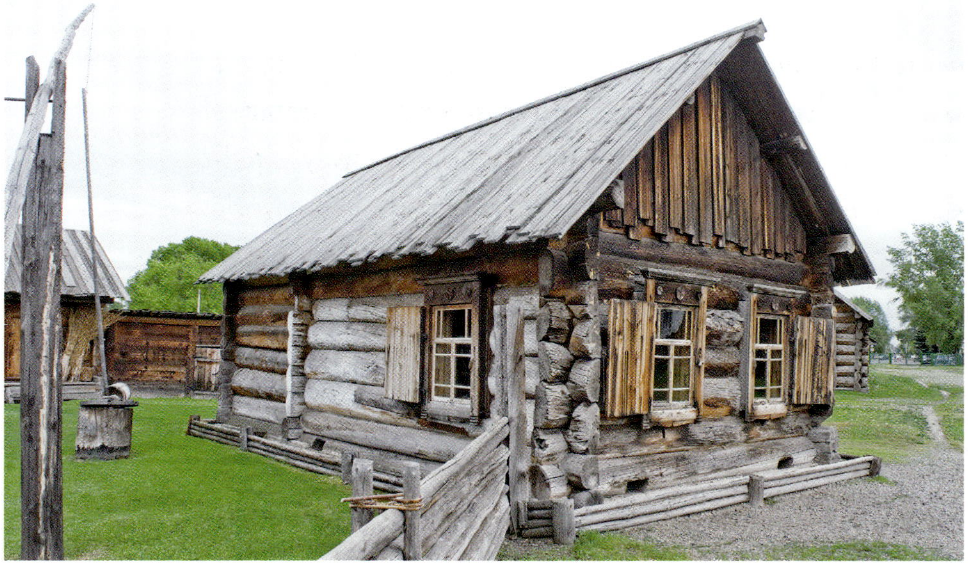

SHUSHENSKOE. P. Tvardovsky *izba*. Built in the late nineteenth century by the poorest category of peasant (*bednyak*, who in this case was a cobbler), the dwelling also had a few sheds around a yard that included a crane well, visible on the far left. May 26, 2015.

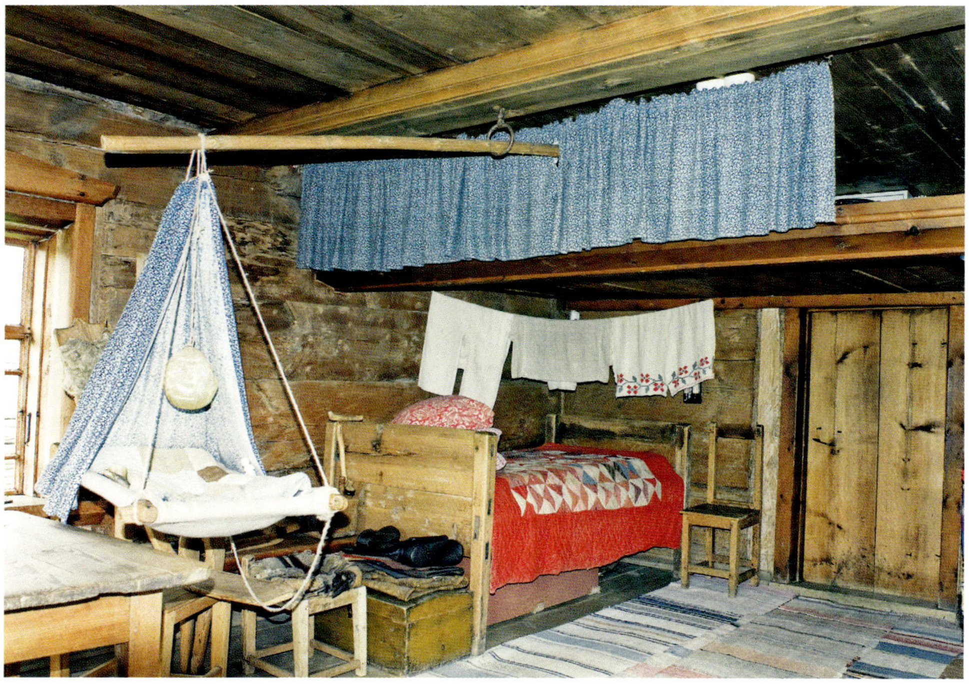

SHUSHENSKOE. P. Tvardovsky *izba*. The entire family lived in this one room, which had a sleeping ledge for children above the bed and a cradle suspended from a pole. May 26, 2015.

modern conveniences in a traditional shell, including housing in sanitized *izba* reconstructions from neighboring villages. Ironically, the biography of an urban Marxist revolutionary has assured a comprehensive preservation of a traditional, conservative rural past. At the same time, it must be noted that the fate of some who lived in Shushenkoe was anything but enviable after 1917, as there was civil war, dispossession, imprisonment, repression, and murder. Little is said of that at the museum.

The Angara River Basin

IRKUTSK

For a dramatic natural setting, few Russian cities can rival the Siberian metropolis of Irkutsk. Located on the banks of the Angara River (a tributary of the Yenisei), Irkutsk is a major point on the Trans-Siberian Railway and the gateway to sacred Lake Baikal, the deepest body of fresh water in the world. Russian settlements had existed in the Irkutsk area from the early part of the seventeenth century. A log fort was eventually constructed in 1661 at the confluence of the Angara and Irkut Rivers. The original purpose of the settlement was to establish Russian authority with the region's aboriginal Buryats. In 1686 it gained the status of town and shortly thereafter began sending caravans to China, which became a source of trade and cultural influence for Irkutsk. By the beginning of the eighteenth century, Irkutsk was becoming the administrative and commercial center of a large territory in central and eastern Siberia. Much of its population was involved in entrepreneurial activity, and its merchants assumed an increasingly important role in guiding the city in the absence of an established local nobility.

Until the Soviet era, housing in Irkutsk was largely built of wood. Among the earliest surviving examples of wooden houses are those belonging to Prince Sergey Volkonsky (1788–1865) and Prince Sergey Trubetskoy (1790–1860), members of the noble elite who were exiled to Siberia for their role in an uprising against tsarist authority in December 1825. After ten

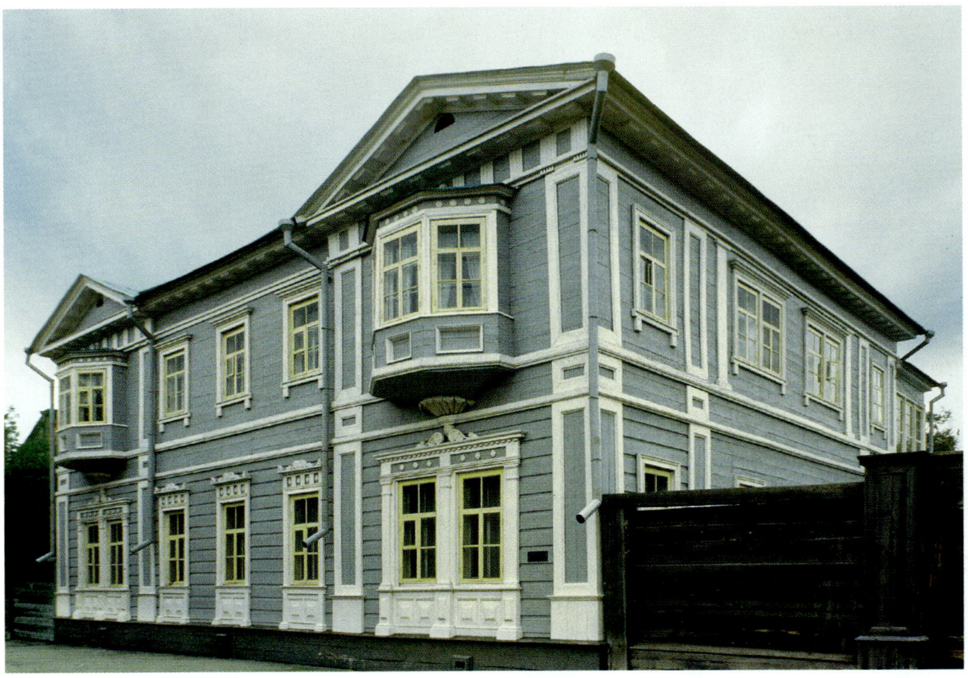

IRKUTSK. Sergey Volkonsky house. Originally built in the village of Urik (the Volkonsky place of exile from 1837), the structure was taken apart and moved with the family in 1845 to a lot in Irkutsk, where it was reassembled. Enlarged for a family of six, the house was urbanized with neoclassical detailing and plank siding painted gray with white trim. September 2, 2000.

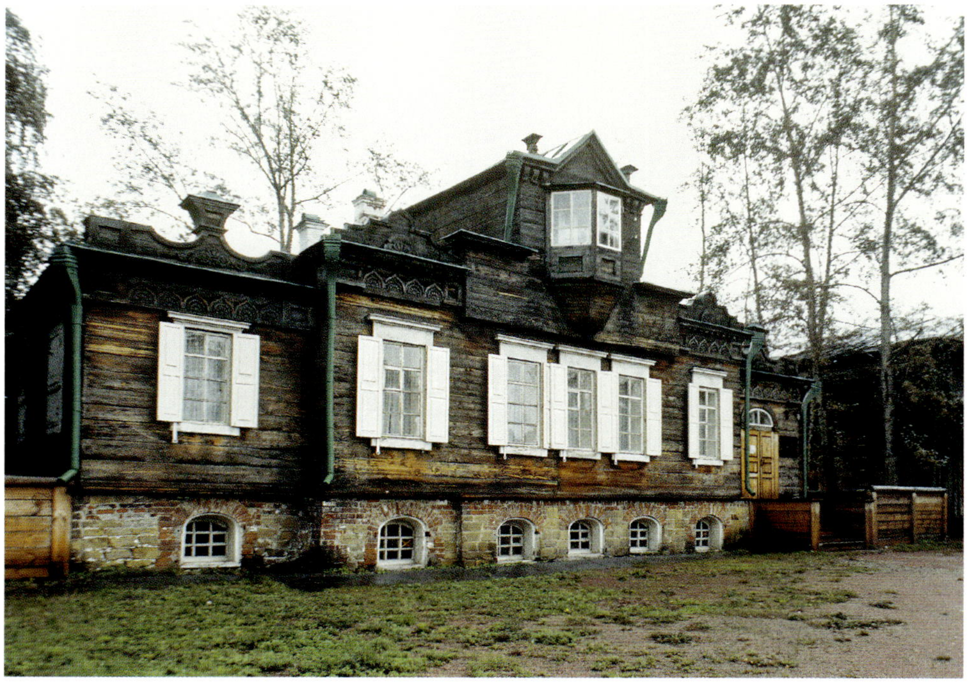

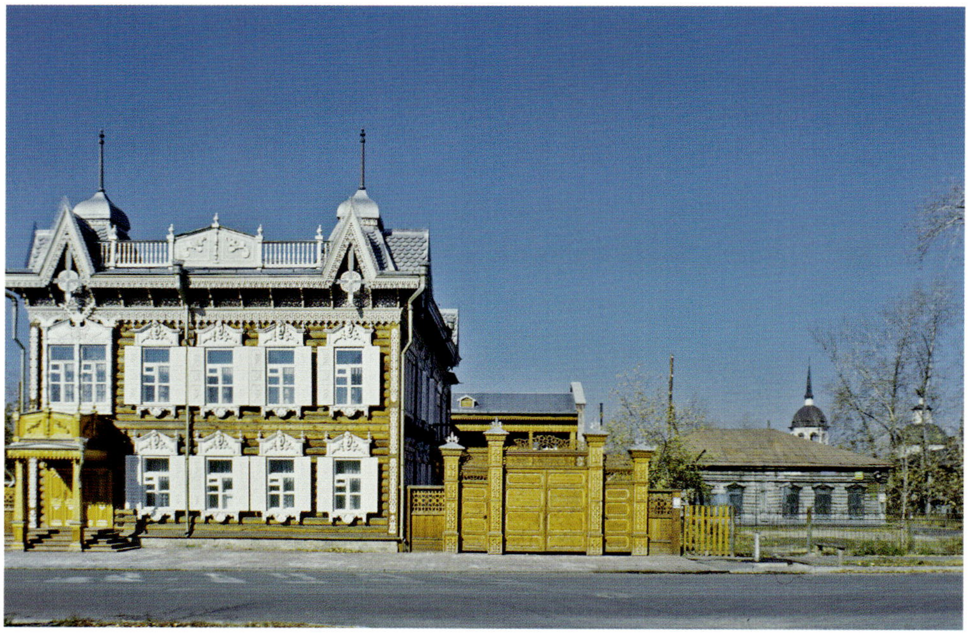

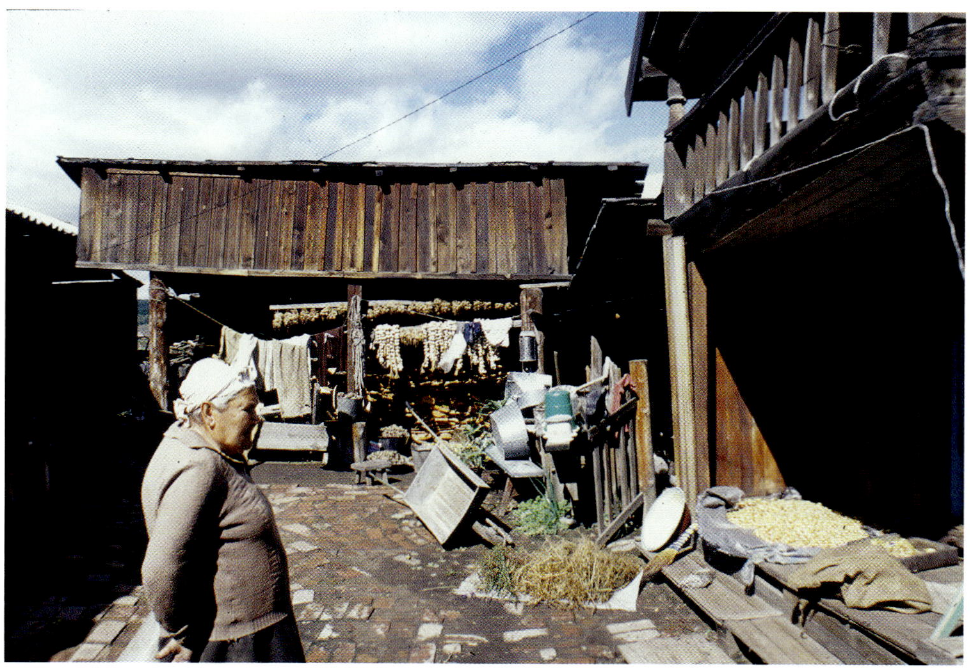

IRKUTSK. Sergey Trubetskoy house. Although the house was owned by the Trubetskoy family and was built presumably at some point between 1847 and 1854, it is not clear whether (or when) the prince lived in this peculiar structure. September 2, 2000.

IRKUTSK. Apollos Shastin house. Completed for a wealthy merchant by 1911, the house is an exuberant display of decorative excess, with carved and fretwork elements on every possible space. Restored in 1997–99. October 3, 1999.

UST-KUDA. *Izba*-enclosed yard (late nineteenth century) with winter preparations underway, including drying onions and garlic braids. September 1, 2000.

USOLYE-SIBIRSKOE. House, Lenin Street 41. Typical factory town *izba* from late nineteenth century with painted shuttered windows and iron roof. September 3, 2000.

BELSK. Tower built in 1691 at the Belsk Fort (*ostrog*), which was manned by Don Cossacks who defended a strategic road from Irkutsk toward the Chinese border. This is the only *ostrog* tower to survive at its original location. September 3, 2000.

BRATSK. Northwest tower built in early 1630s at the Bratsk Fort (*ostrog*) on the Angara River, a critical point protecting Russian settlements in the direction of Irkutsk. Disassembled in 1958 with completion of the Bratsk Reservoir and moved in 1959 to the Kolomenskoe outdoor museum in Moscow. August 31, 2014.

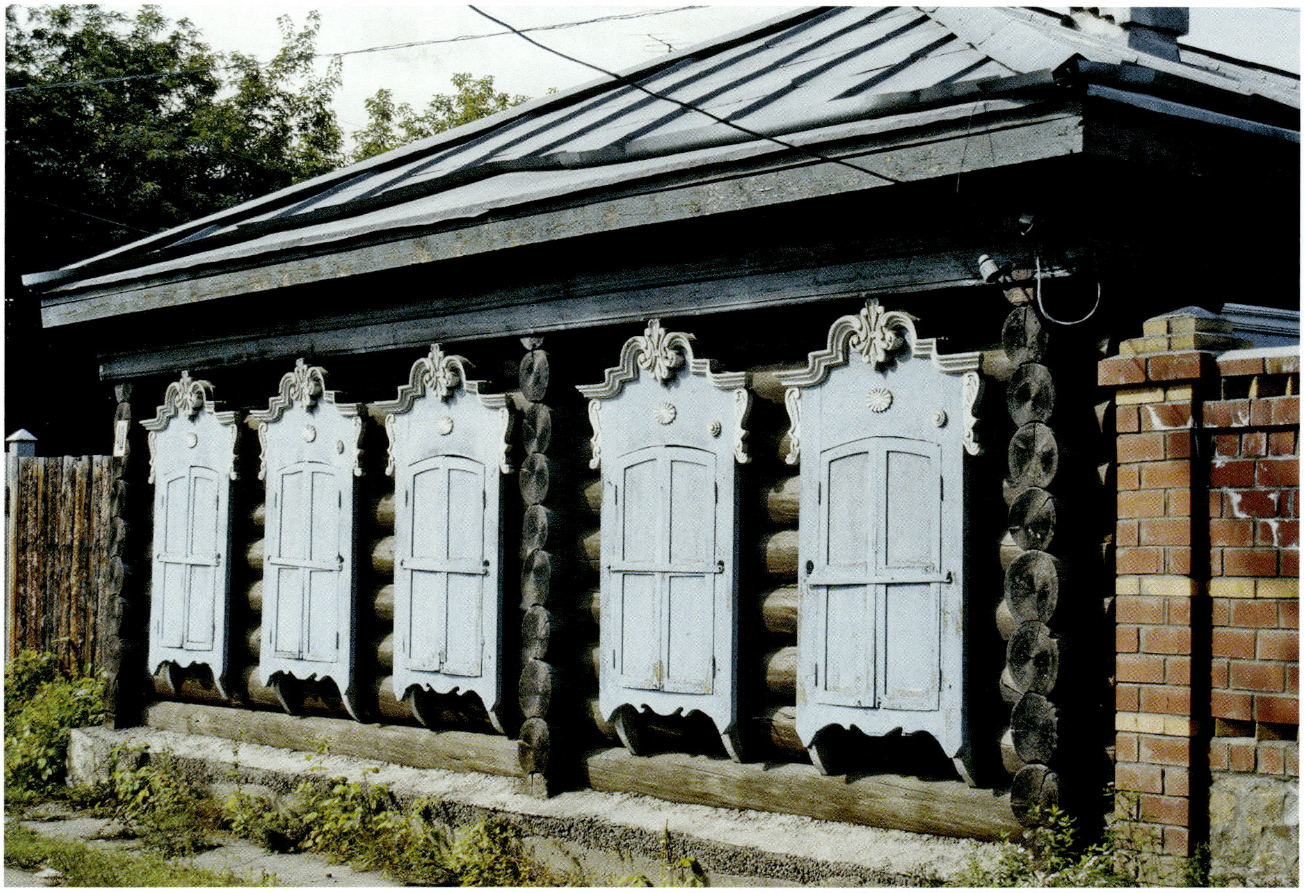

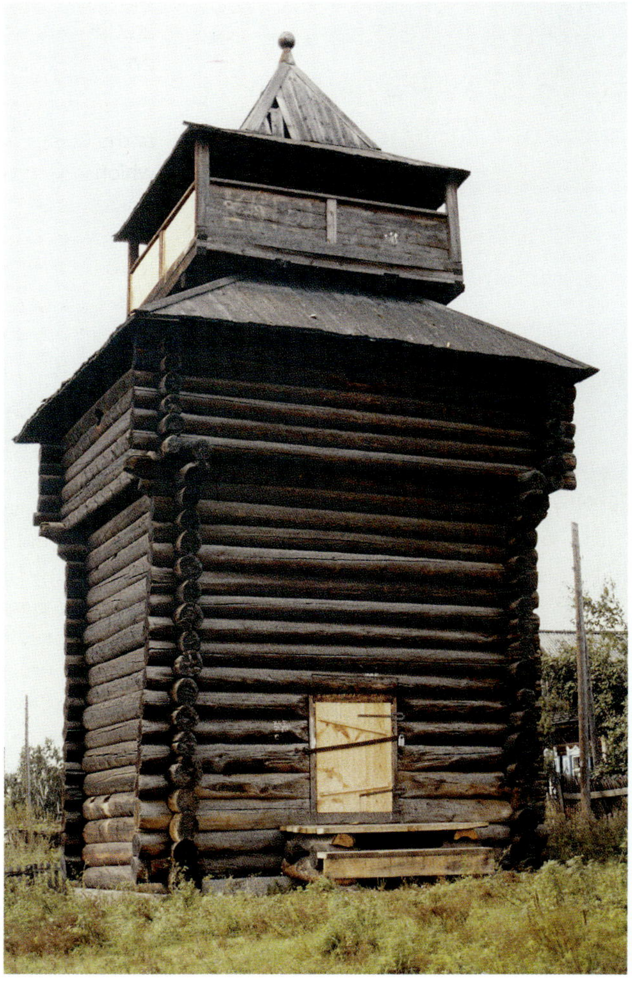

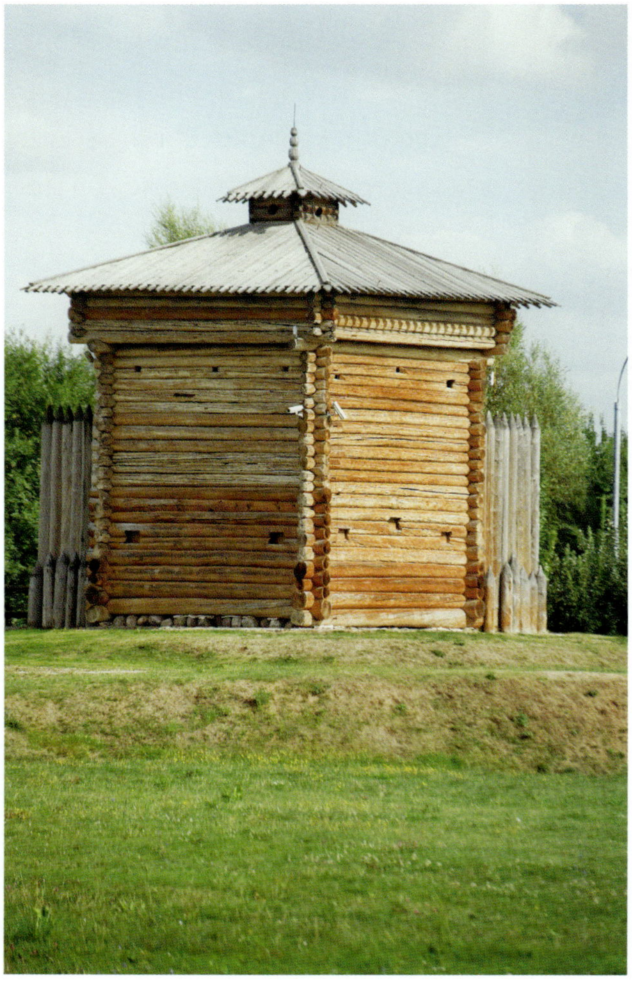

years of penal labor in mines, both were allowed to live with their families in exile villages and eventually to move to Irkutsk in 1845. Later examples of wooden houses in Irkutsk show a more ornate merchant style with elaborately carved decorations comparable to examples in other Siberian cities, such as Tomsk and Chita.

A catastrophic fire in 1879 destroyed much of Irkutsk, including masonry buildings and wooden houses. Nonetheless, the town quickly rebounded on the strength of gold mining and growing trade, both domestic and foreign. In 1898 the Trans-Siberian Railroad reached Irkutsk with a concomitant stimulus to regional trade and communication. During this period Irkutsk was transformed by an eclectic array of commercial buildings and theaters, but most of its housing was built of wood, frequently with a brick side wall as a fire break. Today, the central part of Irkutsk (population 611,000) has preserved the ambiance created during the commercial and building expansion at the beginning of the twentieth century. Although much of its wooden architecture has been demolished, some of the remnants have been restored. Historic villages surrounding Irkutsk, such as Ust-Kuda and Belsk (on the Belaya River), also have surviving examples of homesteads.

TALTSY

One of the most appealing outdoor museums of traditional culture in Siberia is Taltsy, located in a forest grove midway between Irkutsk and the village of Listvyanka, on the southwest shore of Lake Baikal. A Russian settlement at the site, located on steep cliffs above the Angara River near its confluence of the Taltsinka River, can be dated to the eighteenth century. Construction of the Ust-Ilim Hydroelectric Station elsewhere on the Angara River threatened one of Siberia's most important wooden historical monuments, the seventeenth-century Ilim Fort, with its impressive Savior Gate Tower (1667) and portions of the fort walls, as well as the small Church of the Kazan Icon of the Virgin (1679). In 1966 the regional administration authorized measures to save the Ilim monuments by creating a museum park near Irkutsk. The Taltsy site was recommended, and Galina Oranskaya (1913–86), a Moscow-trained architect and preservation specialist who became the guiding light of historic preservation in Irkutsk, led the restoration. Construction work at the museum site began in 1970, with years spent in finding and reconstructing traditional log structures from the Irkutsk Territory. The museum opened in 1980.

Taltsy consists of several sectors. The largest is the Angara-Ilim sector, where the centerpiece is formed by the seventeenth-century log structures from the Ilim area. The Ilim Fort (*ostrog*) arose in the summer of 1630, when twenty-eight Cossacks led by ataman Ivan Galkin made their way up the Angara to fertile lands at the mouth of the Ilim River. Their winter camp (*zimovye*) was replaced by a log fort the following year. The early forts succumbed to the fires that plagued Russia's wooden villages, but portions of a third fort, built in 1667, endured for three centuries. The Ilim Fort consisted of a rectangular stockade wall with vertical logs pointed at the top. The wall was anchored by eight log towers, including four on the corners. Three of the towers had gates, above which were small projecting chapels. Only the Savior Gate Tower—restored in 1984—has survived from 1667, but a section of the west wall has been reconstructed. The small Church of the Kazan Icon of the Virgin, generally assumed to have been built in 1679, was situated near the Savior Gate Tower and served both as a place of worship and an additional defensive structure. The small structure was frequently modified over the centuries, but the core remained and has been restored to what is considered its likely original appearance. The Taltsy museum also includes Church of the Trinity, built in 1914 in the remote village of Dyadino and moved to the museum park in 1990 to serve as background for a joint Russian-Japanese film entitled *Dreams of Russia*.

Beyond the Ilim monuments is a recreational village similar to those that arose around the early forts and then served as administrative

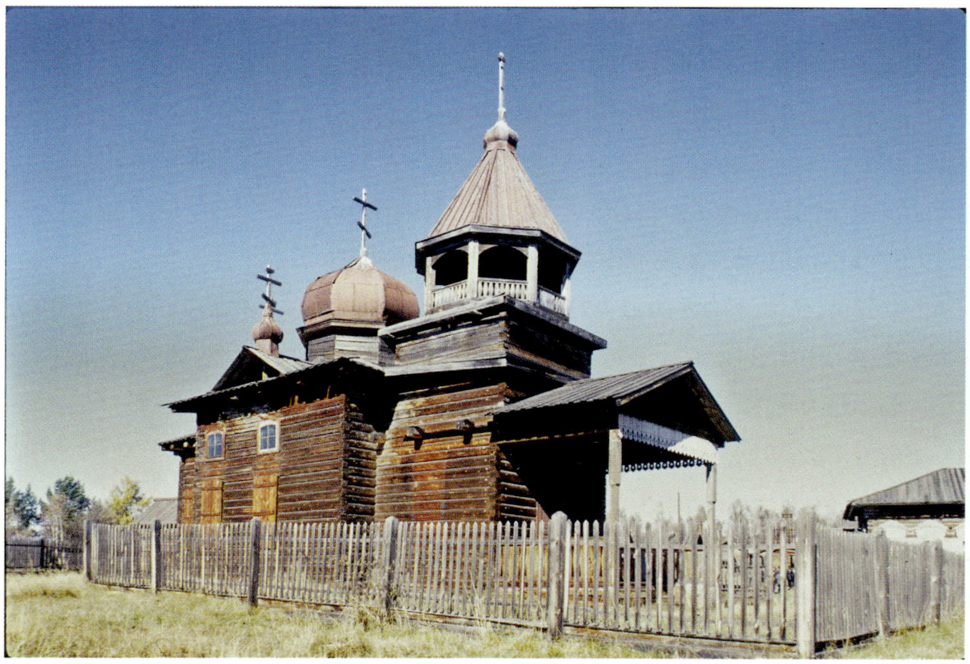

TALTSY. Church of the Trinity, northwest view. Built in 1914 to a basic linear plan at the village of Dyadino, the church was moved to Taltsy in 1990. October 2, 1999.

TALTSY (Irkutsk region, outdoor museum). Church of Kazan Icon of the Virgin, southwest view. Originally built in 1679(?) at Ilim Fort. Background: Savior Gate Tower over south gate and wall of Ilim Fort (*ostrog*). October 2, 1999.

centers for the surrounding district (*volost*). It has a one-room parish school (1885) from Keul village in the Ilim area, as well as a *volost* administration building, a roadhouse, and a communal grain storehouse. Of particular interest are the re-creations of peasant homesteads from the late eighteenth century, the nineteenth century, and the turn of the twentieth century. The majority of peasants in the Irkutsk Territory were of the middle level economically and thus could afford livestock, an array of agricultural implements, and some store-bought goods. One of the museum's early examples of a homestead comes from Antonova village (Bratsk region) and was built at the turn of the nineteenth century by a certain Moskovsky. It is known that he served as a "town Cossack," a group that performed various police and administrative duties—as opposed to "line Cossacks," who guarded the border areas. The housing displays include a type of homestead arranged around enclosed courtyards, with one wall of the house facing the street, a gateway, and barns and sheds arranged around two or three separate yards, including one where livestock were kept. Such homesteads existed throughout the area when the museum was being formed and still exist in some villages. Some of the dwellings are known as "linked" houses. A family would begin with a single log house and then, as the family grew, build a twin structure connected by a passageway.

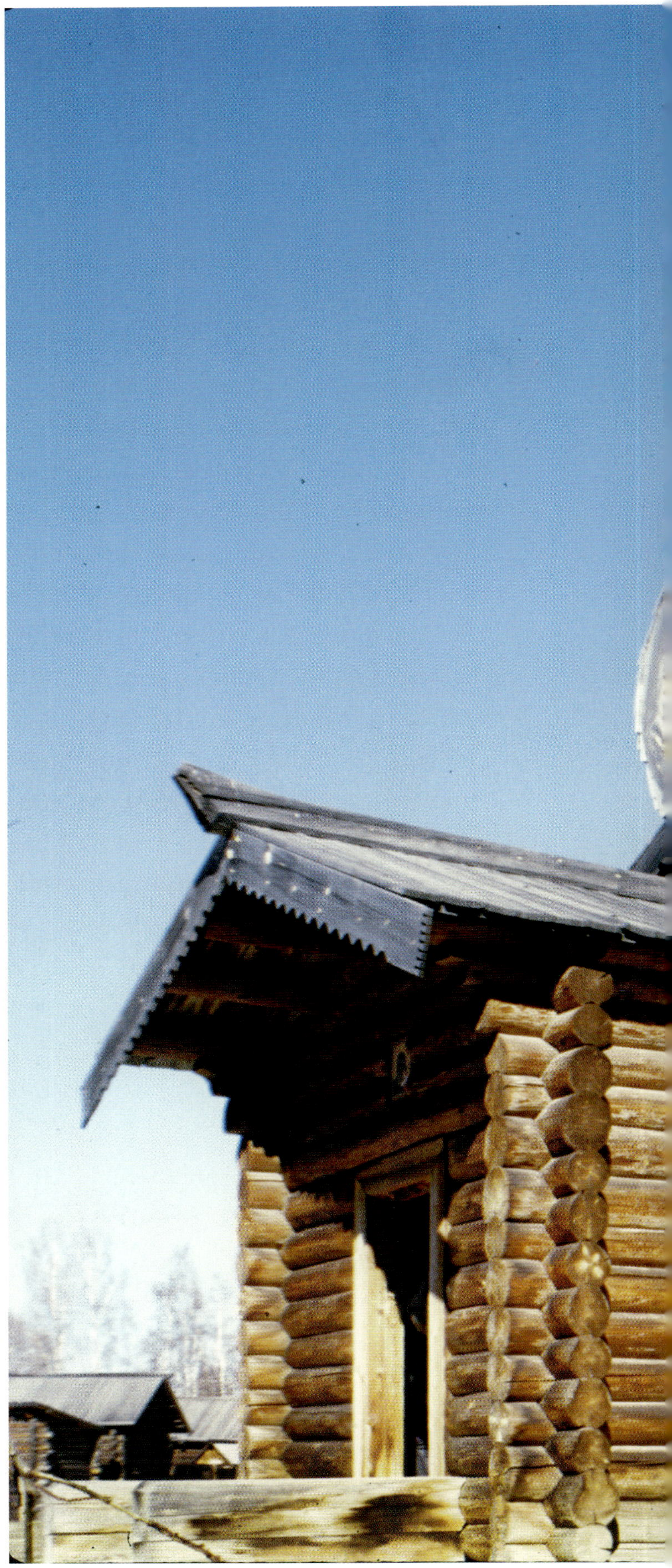

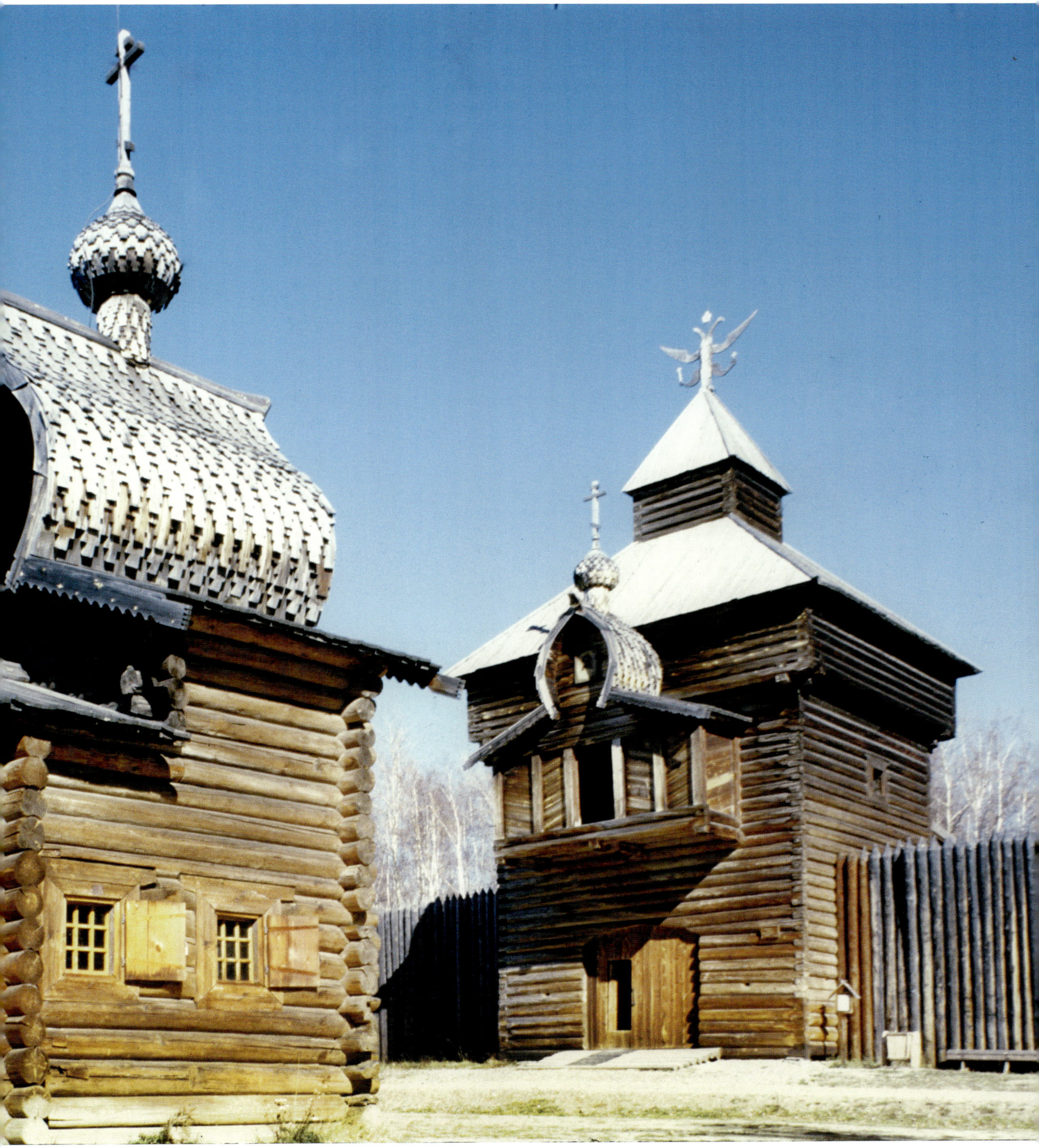

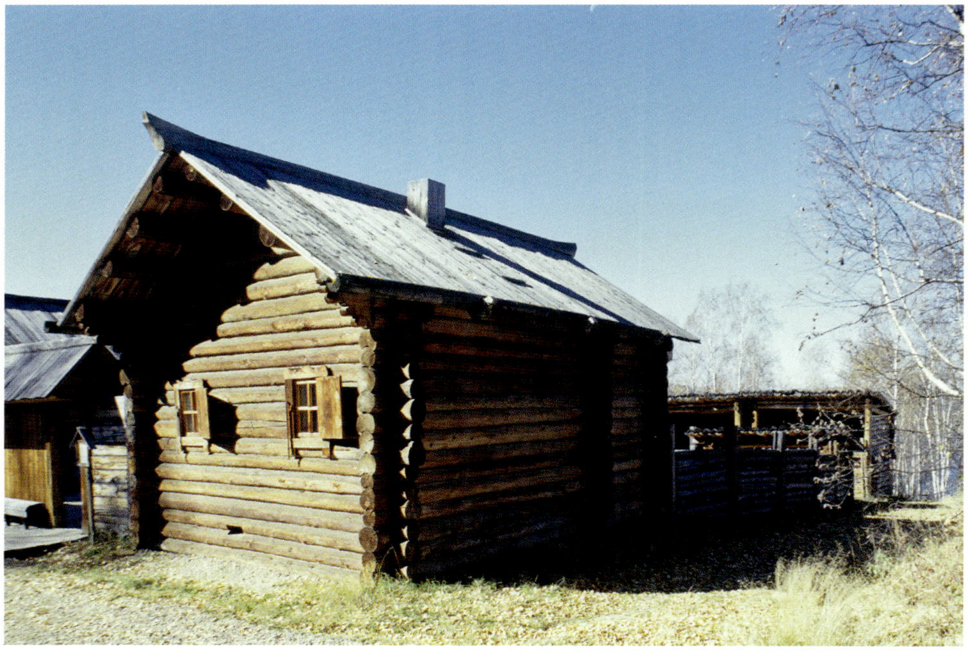

TALTSY. House and yard barns at Moskovsky farmstead from Antonova village (Bratsk region). October 2, 1999.

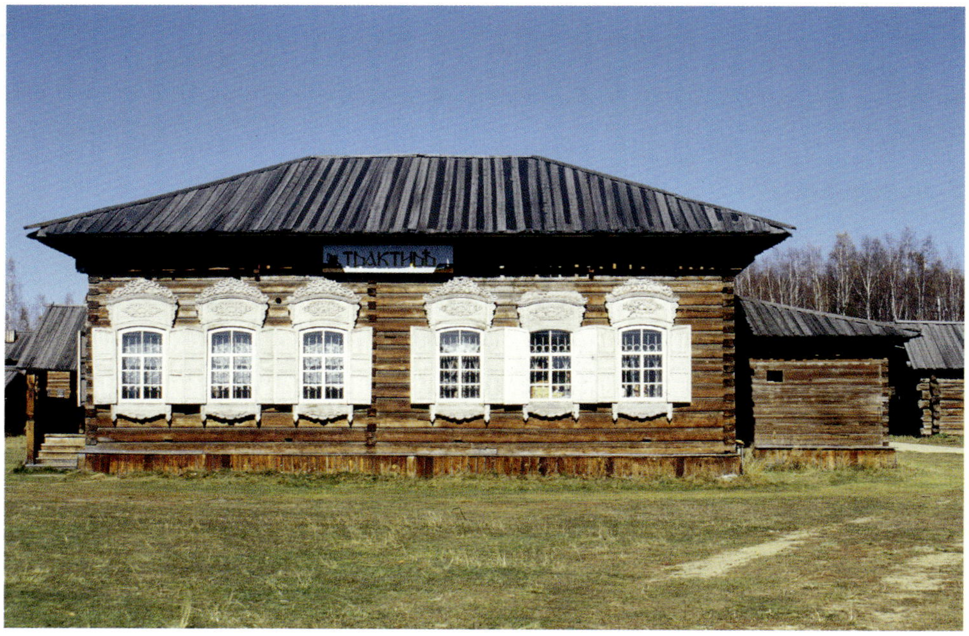

TALTSY. Post house built in late nineteenth century in lower Angara River area as part of system of waystations along the Siberian Highway (*trakt*). October 2, 1999.

The other large sector at Taltsy displays traditional structures of the Indigenous Buryat people, one population of which lives in the Irkutsk Territory to the west of Lake Baikal. Before the Russian appearance in the seventeenth century, the Buryats were herders who frequently moved to favorable grazing lands. In the eighteenth and nineteenth centuries they developed a more settled existence but continued to build wooden yurts, often covered with turf roofs. The museum has a display of log yurts brought from the encampment of Alagui near the village of Buguldeika.

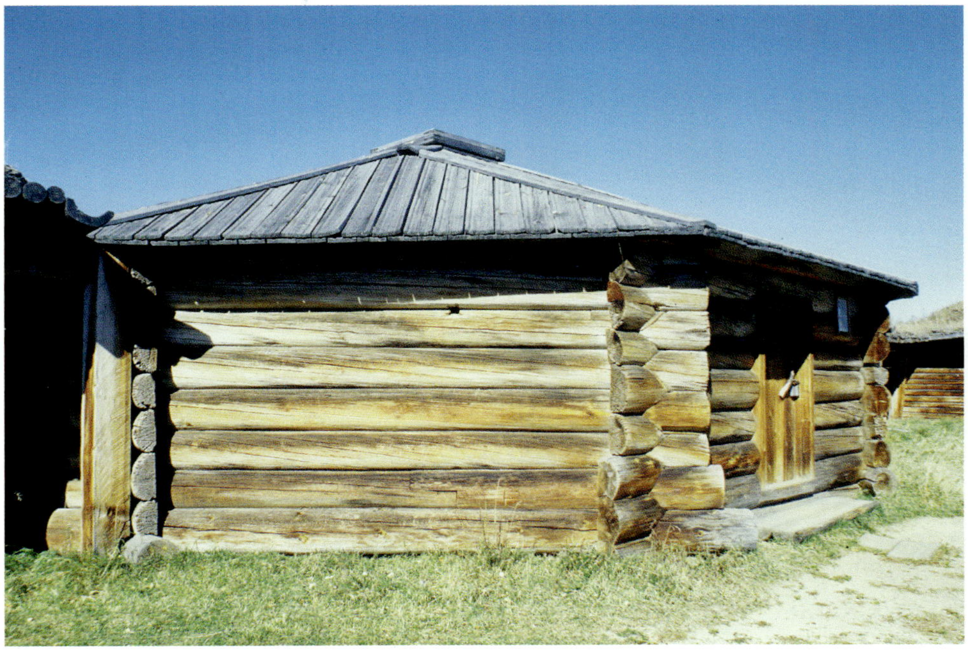

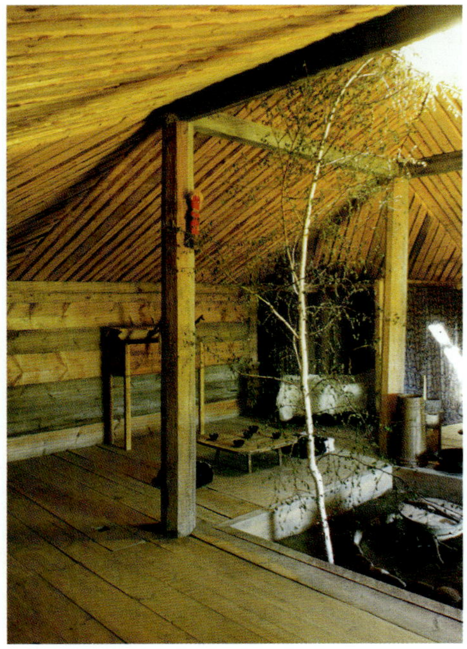

TALTSY. Buryat yurt with wooden roof brought from the encampment of Alagui near the village of Buguldeika. October 2, 1999.

TALTSY. Buryat yurt with wooden roof. Interior with hearth in center. October 2, 1999.

The interiors are a single space with posts supporting a roof tilted upward to release smoke from the hearth in the center. The display also has log sheds typical of summer encampments. At the bottom of the park by the Angara River is a display of a fishing camp.

Beyond Taltsy, Lake Baikal beckons with seemingly endless vistas. The small port of Listvyanka has a wooden Church of Saint Nicholas, originally built in 1846 with funds provided by the merchant Ksefont Serebryakov and subsequently moved twice to a more advantageous, protected location. The town also had several traditional wooden houses at the time of my visits at the turn of this century, but the development of tourism has resulted in overbuilding at scenic locations. There are, however, better preserved locations within the national park created along the original Trans-Siberian line on the south shore of Lake Baikal.

The Far North

NORILSK

During its history Russia has witnessed the creation of special towns whose existence was considered a state priority. The largest such site is Saint Petersburg, built by order of Tsar Peter in a remote, sparsely inhabited part of northwestern Russia. But none of these state settlements arose in more

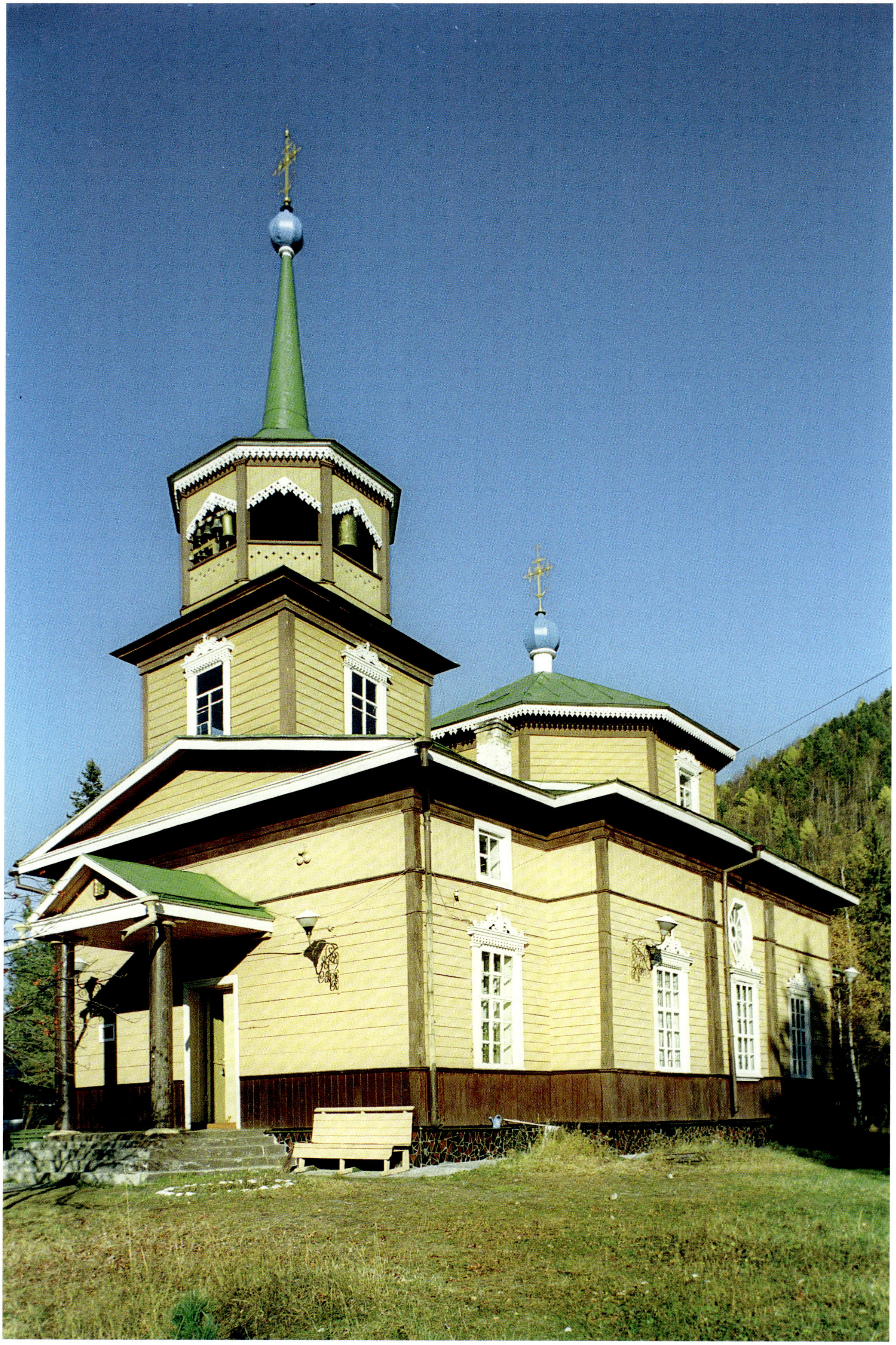

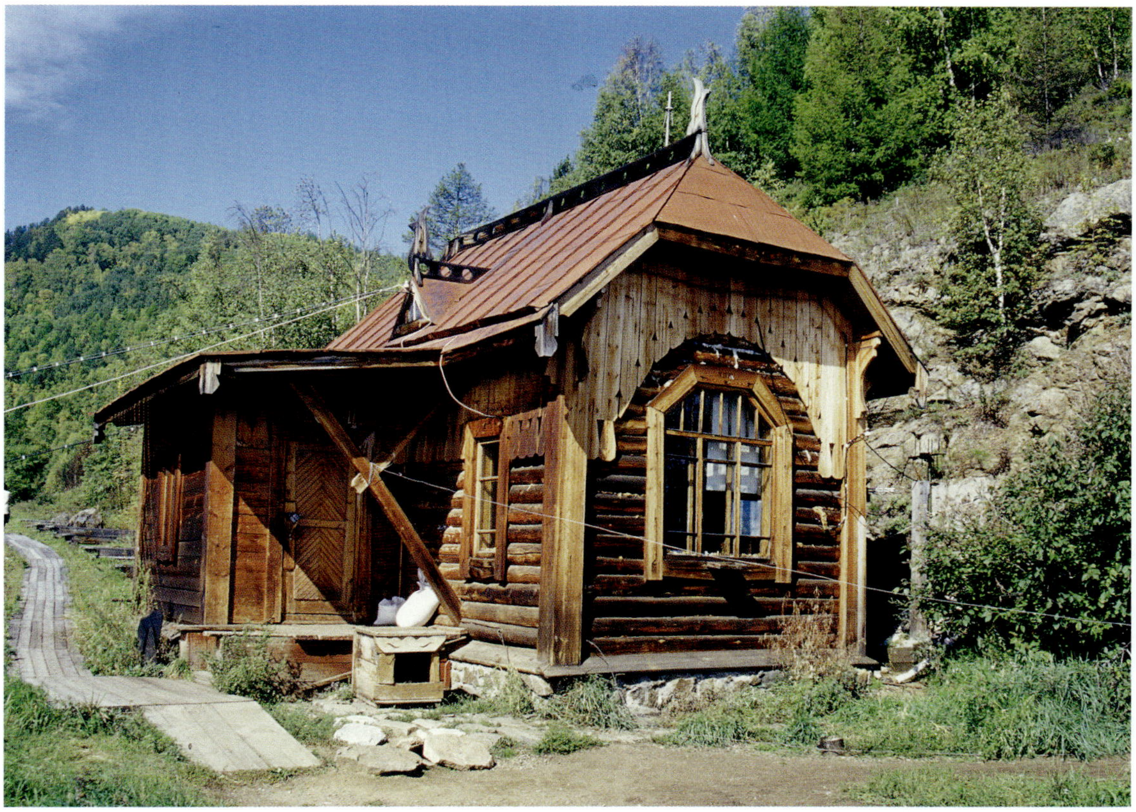

LISTVYANKA. Church of Saint Nicholas, southwest view. October 4, 1999.

CIRCUM-BAIKAL RAILWAY. Watchman's house at Elektrosvyaz Station. September 6, 2000.

difficult conditions than Norilsk, now a city of some 176,000 inhabitants in the far northern Arctic part of Krasnoyarsk Territory. Norilsk owes its existence to an unusually rich concentration of valuable mineral elements, most notably nickel. The area's mineral wealth was known to the Russians at least by the early seventeenth century, and over the next two centuries the territory to the northeast of the Taz River was occasionally explored, particularly the area around the long estuary of the Yenisei. Scientific exploration of the region resumed in the early 1920s when Nikolay Urvantsev (1893–1985) undertook explorations at the base of the Taymyr Peninsula where he found not only rich coal deposits but also ore containing nickel, copper, and platinum, all in the area of the Norilskaya River.

In June 1935 the Soviet Council of Commissars ordered the rapid development of a nickel extraction plant at the base of Shmidt Mountain. As a strategic priority for Soviet heavy industry, the project was placed under the control of the NKVD (People's Commissariat of Internal Affairs), which created a labor camp complex known as Norillag. By 1939 the Norilsk plant had produced an intermediate product known as "matte" (a nickel sulfide aggregate), and by mid-1942 Norilsk achieved production of refined nickel through a labor-intensive and noxious reduction process. Production of copper began the following year, but nickel was especially valued for its use in tank armor and airplane construction. The existence of Norillag was

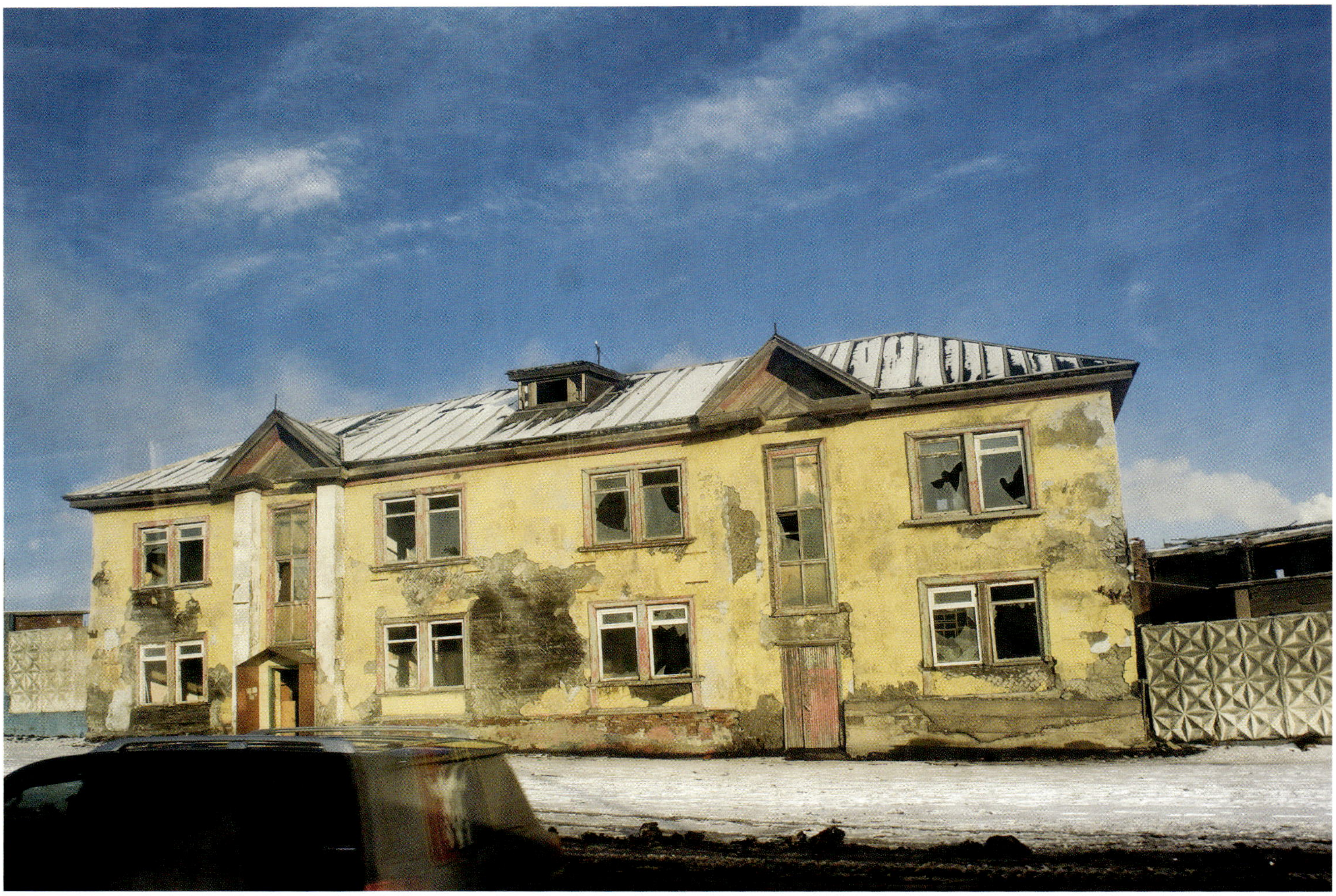

formally terminated only in the fall of 1956, but the strategic importance of the metal extraction ensured that Norilsk and its factories would continue to expand. In 1966 new ore sources were opened to the northeast of Norilsk at Talnakh, which was developed as a satellite town for Norilsk.

In the 1990s work began on the Norilsk Golgotha memorial complex, devoted to the memory of the many who died at Norillag. The memorial is located on the site of a mass grave at the base of Shmidt Mountain overlooking Norilsk and its factories. Visitors enter the memorial, which includes a chapel and several monuments, through a log gate containing bells that are rung in memory of the dead. Like Komsomolsk, Norilsk was intended entirely for industrialized masonry construction as soon as technical conditions permitted, but Norilsk and Dudinka still have wooden structures that remind of a grim, often deadly history. Talnakh now has a log Church of the Trinity, built in 2005–8.

NORILSK. Stuccoed wooden barracks, nickel factory, October Street 21. Abandoned. September 30, 2014.

NORILSK. Norilsk Golgotha memorial. Wooden gateway with bells. September 30, 2014.

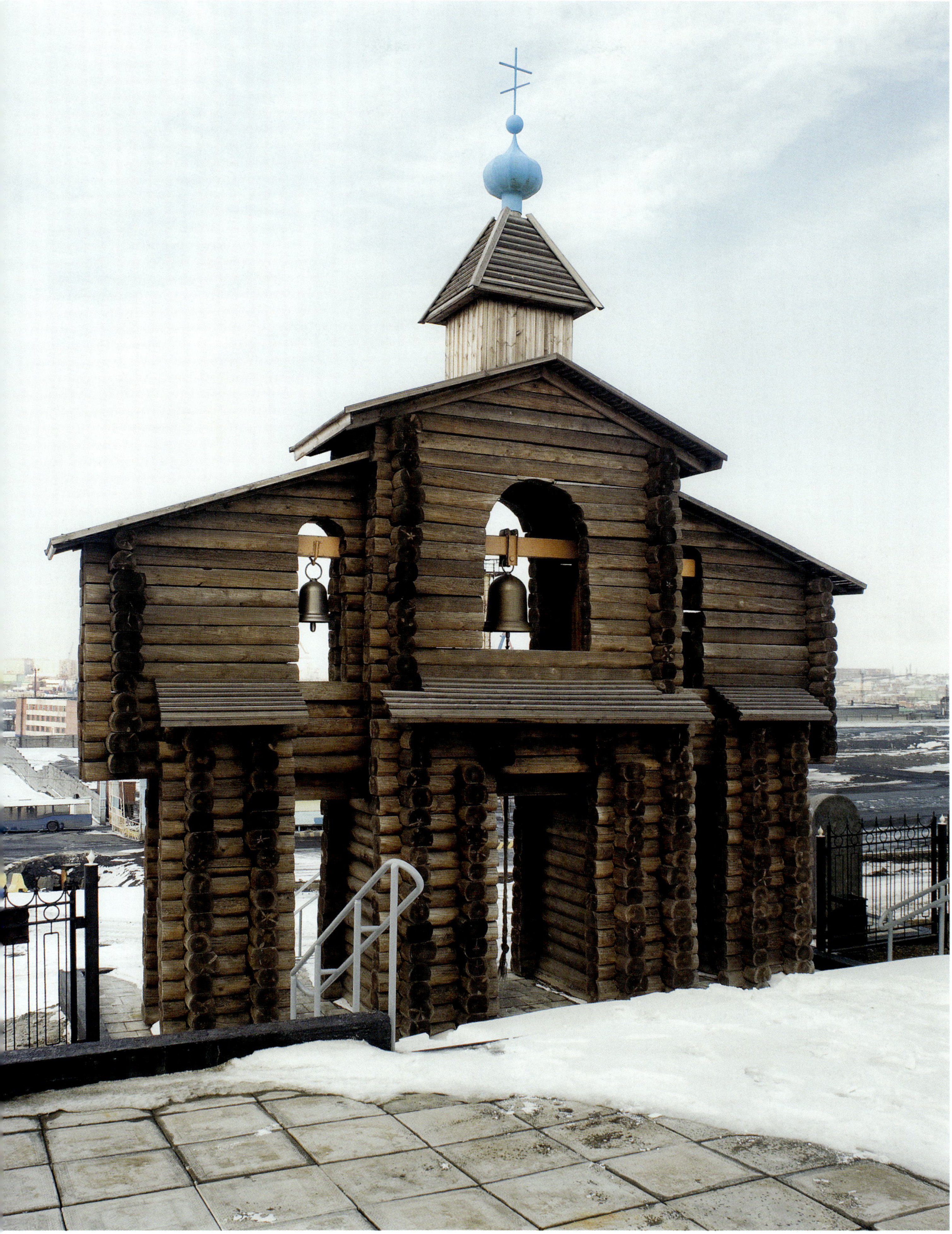

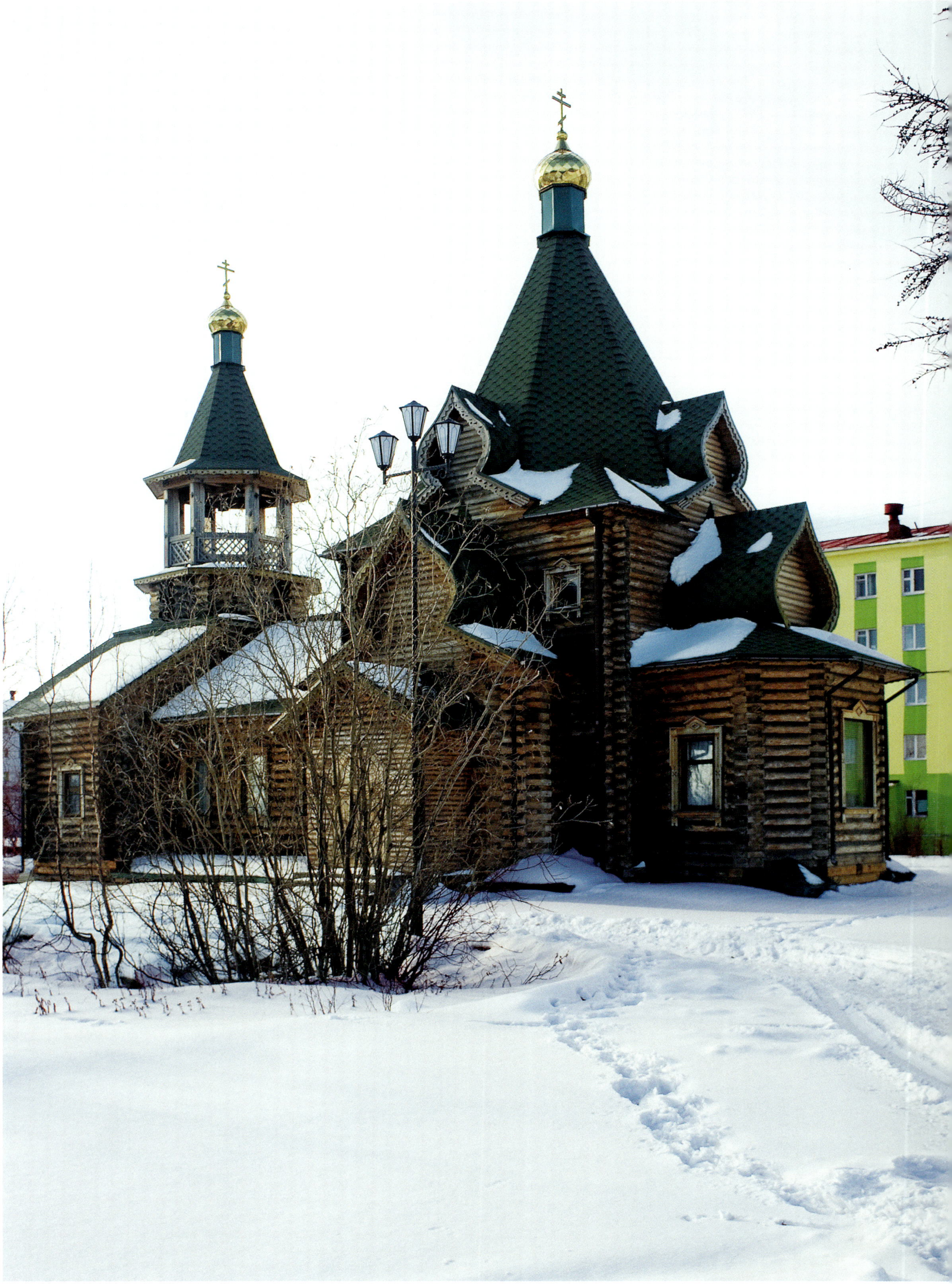

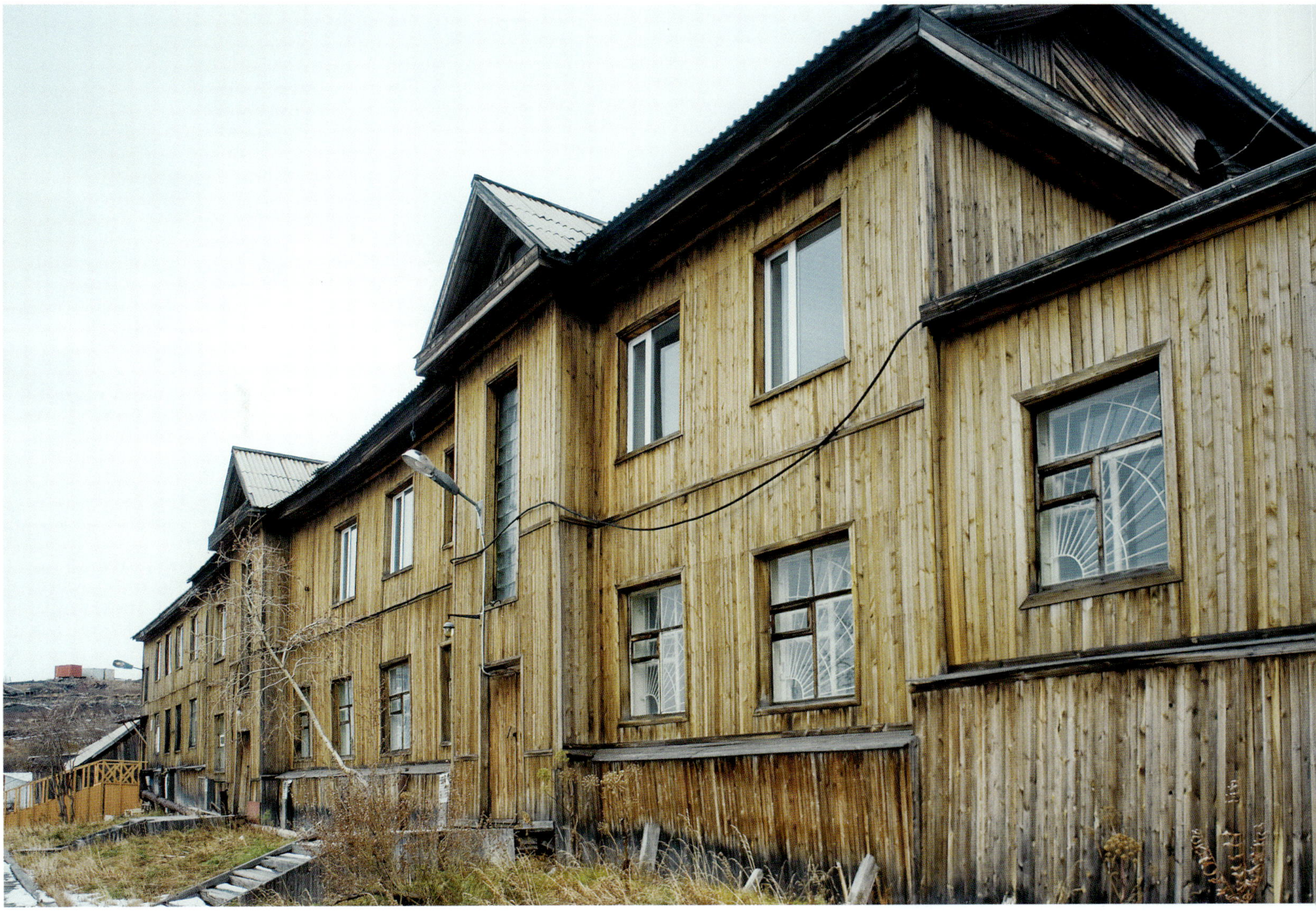

TALNAKH (Norilsk). Church of the Trinity, southeast view. A sensitive contemporary interpretation of traditional church design. September 30, 2014.

DUDINKA. Administrative building (1940s?) with plank siding at Yenisei River landing. October 2, 2014.

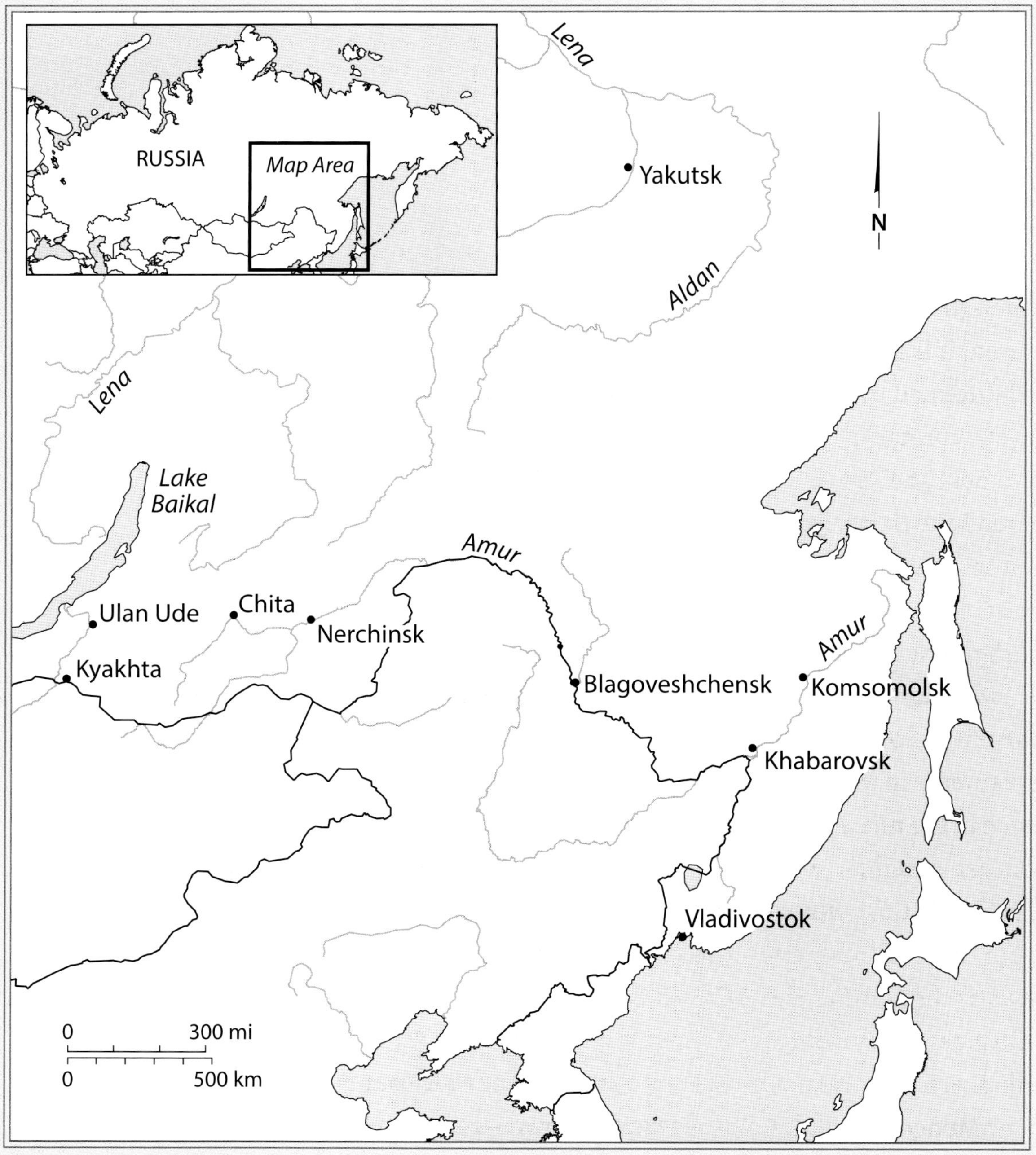
RUSSIA
Map Area
Lena
Yakutsk
N
Aldan
Lena
Lake
Baikal
Amur
Ulan Ude
Chita
Nerchinsk
Kyakhta
Blagoveshchensk
Amur
Komsomolsk
Khabarovsk
Vladivostok
0
300 mi
0
500 km

The Far East.

CHAPTER SEVEN

The Far East

Buryatia

Although the Russian Far East is commonly considered an extension of Siberia, it is administratively a separate region whose geography is generally defined by river basins that empty into the Pacific. That, at least, is the interpretation preferred in presenting the vast geographic sweep of this book. The Republic of Buryatia, situated beyond the eastern shores of sacred Lake Baikal (see map 7.1), is home to a mixture of Russians and Indigenous peoples, primarily Buryats, who have rich cultures of their own. The capital of Buryatia, Ulan-Ude, is located some one hundred kilometers southeast of Lake Baikal and has about 370,000 inhabitants. The city takes its name from the Uda River, a tributary of the Selenga, which is the primary river flowing into Baikal from the east. The appearance of Russian settlements in the area (known as Transbaikal or, more broadly, Dauriya) began in the middle of the seventeenth century, when Cossacks and other explorers sought new trading routes to China, as well as valuable furs such as sable. Within this vast territory rivers assumed vital importance as a means of transportation. Therefore, a small fort was established in the 1660s at the confluence of the Uda and Selenga Rivers. Originally called Udinskoe, the settlement became an administrative center of the Transbaikal region and a major point on the lucrative trade route from Irkutsk to the Mongolian border. By the 1780s the town—renamed Verkhneudinsk ("Upper Udinsk")—had two annual trade fairs, in late winter and midsummer. Like other provincial centers during the reign of Catherine the Great, Verkhneudinsk was provided with an ordered city plan, approved in 1793. Most of merchant Verkhneudinsk consisted of log houses, with or without plank siding and decorated with carved window surrounds. Fortunately, a number of these houses remain in the central districts of the city, while other examples of the region's wooden architecture are displayed at the Trans-Baikal Ethnographic Museum ("Verkhnyaya Berezovka") on the outskirts of Ulan-Ude. The architecture ranges from urban houses to Indigenous Buryat yurts and an Old Believer village homestead with a brightly painted yard gate. Also shown are a log church and a small polychrome Buddhist temple.

The importance of Buddhism in its relation to local cultural traditions is impressively displayed in the city's Museum of the History of Buryatia. Buddhism is also an active presence in contemporary Buryatia. As the Tibetan form of Buddhism spread among the Buryats during the eighteenth century, there appeared early examples of the

ULAN-UDE. N. A. Buturin house, corner of Cathedral and Communist Streets. Early twentieth-century dwelling with fretwork and corner dormer. September 11, 2000.

VERKHNYAYA BEREZOVKA (Ulan-Ude). Old Believer Church of Saint Nicholas, south view. Originally built around 1905 at Nikolsk village (Mukhoshibirsk region), the church was reassembled at the museum in 1971. September 11, 2000.

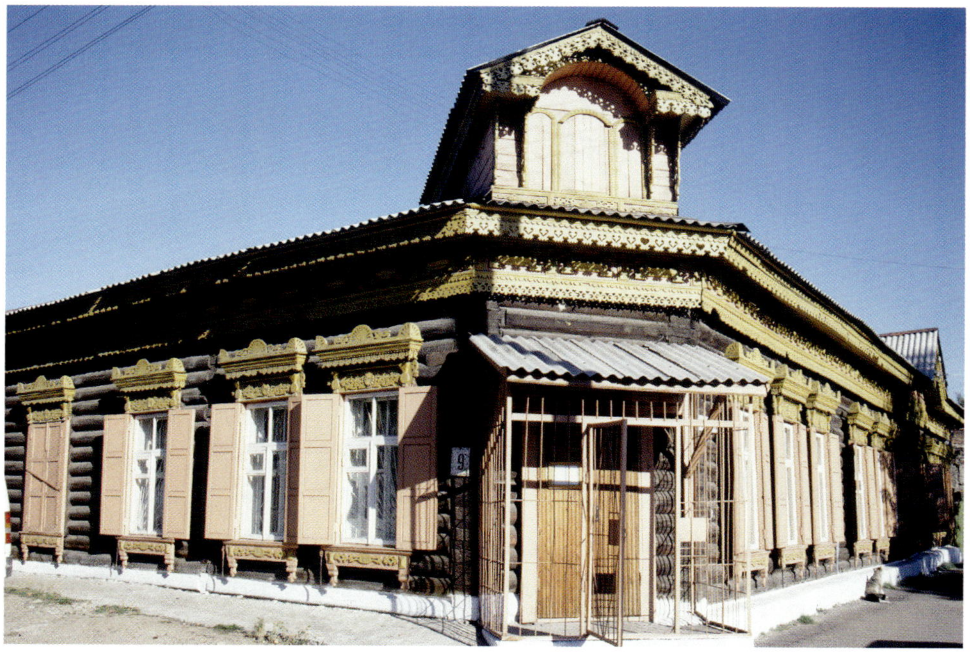

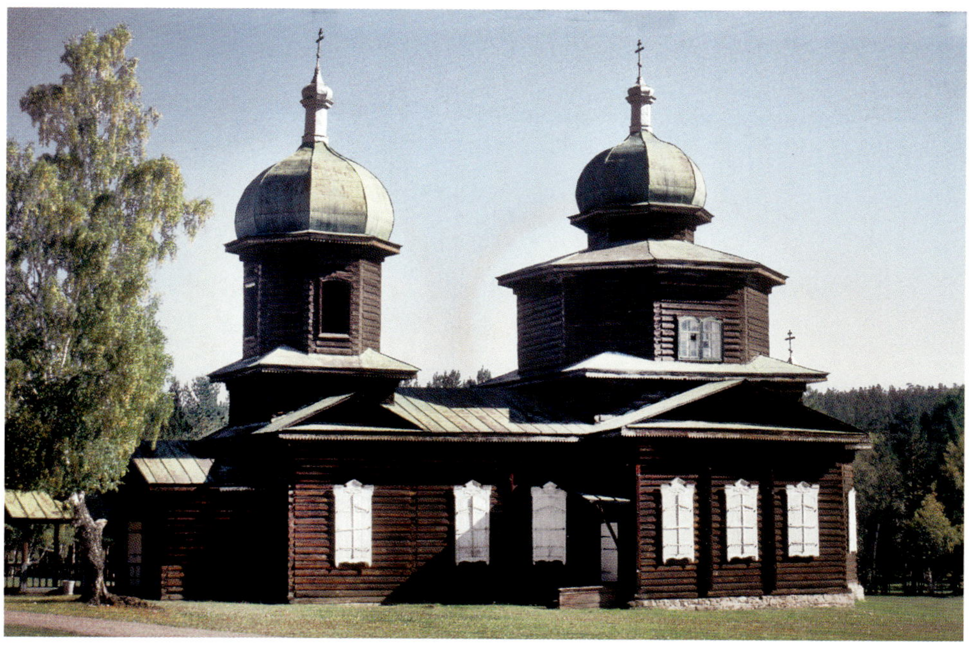

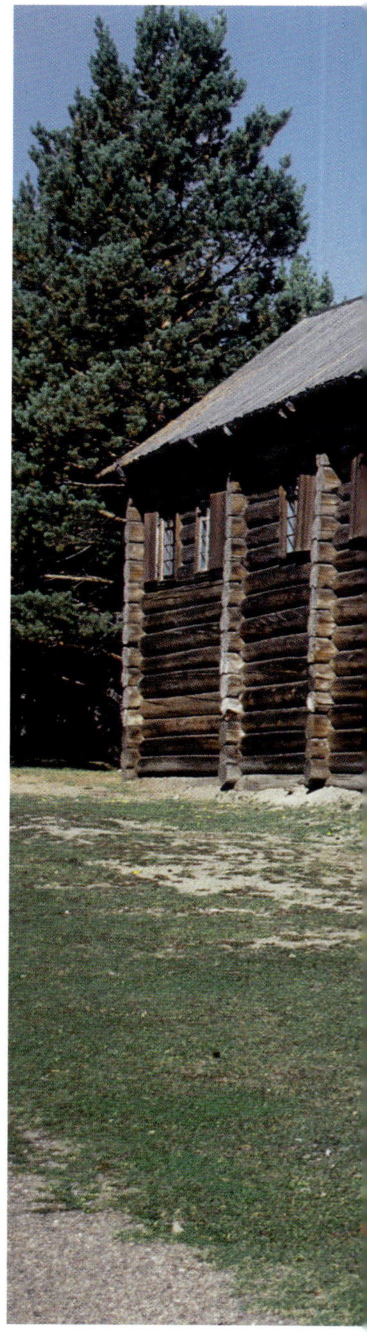

Buddhist monastery (*datsan*, from the Tibetan "court of meetings"). By the middle of the nineteenth century, thirty-four of these institutions existed among Buryat clans in the Transbaikal area. Today the most active Buddhist center in Buryatia is the Ivolginsk *datsan*, located some twenty kilometers to the south of Ulan-Ude near the Ivolga River. Founded in 1946, after the destruction or closure of Buddhist monastic communities in the 1920s and 1930s, the Ivolginsk *datsan* follows regional Buddhist principles in the structure and decoration of its temples, shrines, and libraries. The main temple (*tsokchen dugan*)

VERKHNYAYA BEREZOVKA. Borisov house. This stout two-story dwelling was built in the latter half of the nineteenth century for a prosperous Old Believer peasant merchant in the village of Kuytun (Tarbagataisk region). Attached to it is a riotously painted courtyard gate created in 1906 for an Old Believer homestead in Novaya Bran village (Zaigraevsk region). September 11, 2000.

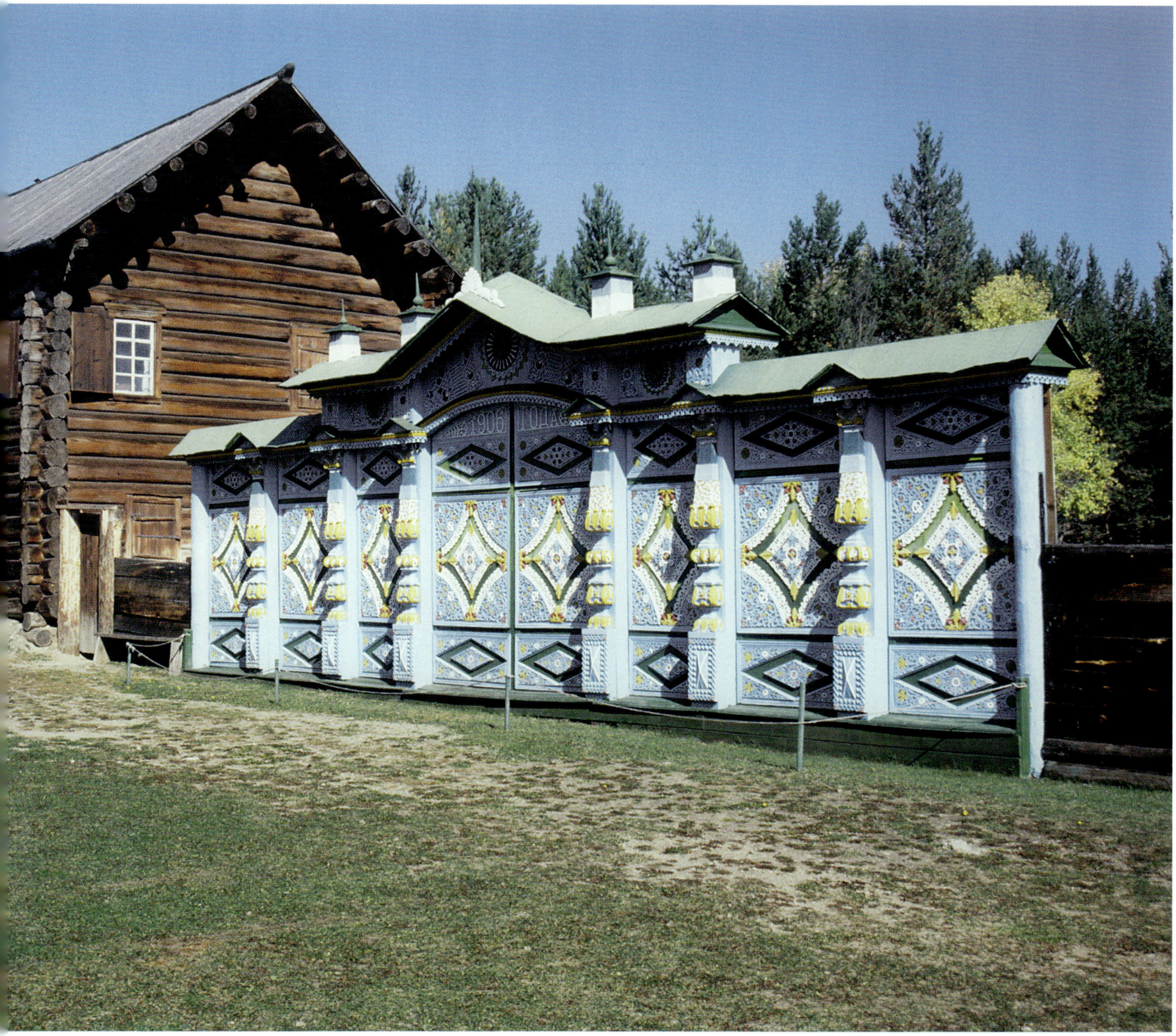

was built of engineering brick in the late 1940s, but the traditional multileveled upper structure is of wood, and the interior is framed by wooden elements decorated in a riot of bright polychrome. The monastery's other buildings are for the most part built of wood, also brightly painted. Within this sacred compound, Buddhist art and ritual merge with the dramatic landscape of Buryatia. Although grievously damaged during the Stalinist campaign against religion, there are other monuments of Buddhist architecture in the region, including the Tamchinsky Datsan at Gusinoe Ozero (Goose Lake), itself a remarkable body of cerulean water nestled among the hills in the southern part of Buryatia.

One of the most dramatically picturesque areas in Buryatia is located to the south along the border with Mongolia. The dry, clear air provides endless vistas of plains with sparse cover giving way to rolling hills with pine forests. The main hub of activity in this area is the town of Kyakhta, for centuries the main border crossing for trade between Russia and China. Located 140 miles south by road from Ulan-Ude, Kyakhta was originally an agglomeration of two—indeed, three—settlements dating from the early eighteenth century to regulate trade and customs between Russia

VERKHNYAYA IVOLGA (near Ulan-Ude). Ivolginsk Datsan (Buddhist lamasery). Choira Dugan temple, built in the mid-twentieth century. September 8, 2000.

GUSINOOZERSK. Tamchinsk Datsan. Dugan Ayusha temple, early twentieth century. September 8, 2000.

NOVOSELENGINSK. Massive, unadorned two-story merchant dwelling built in the nineteenth century. September 8, 2000.

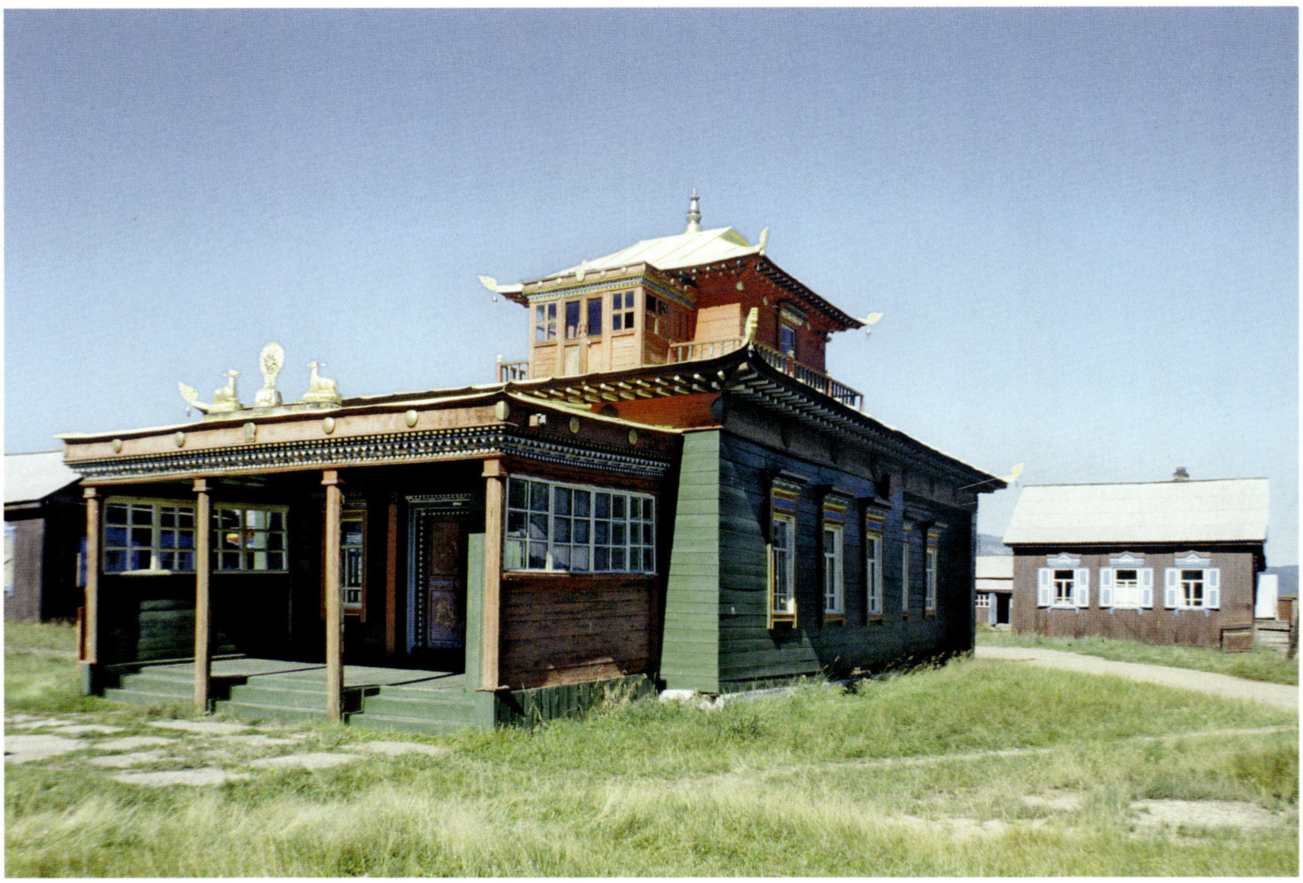

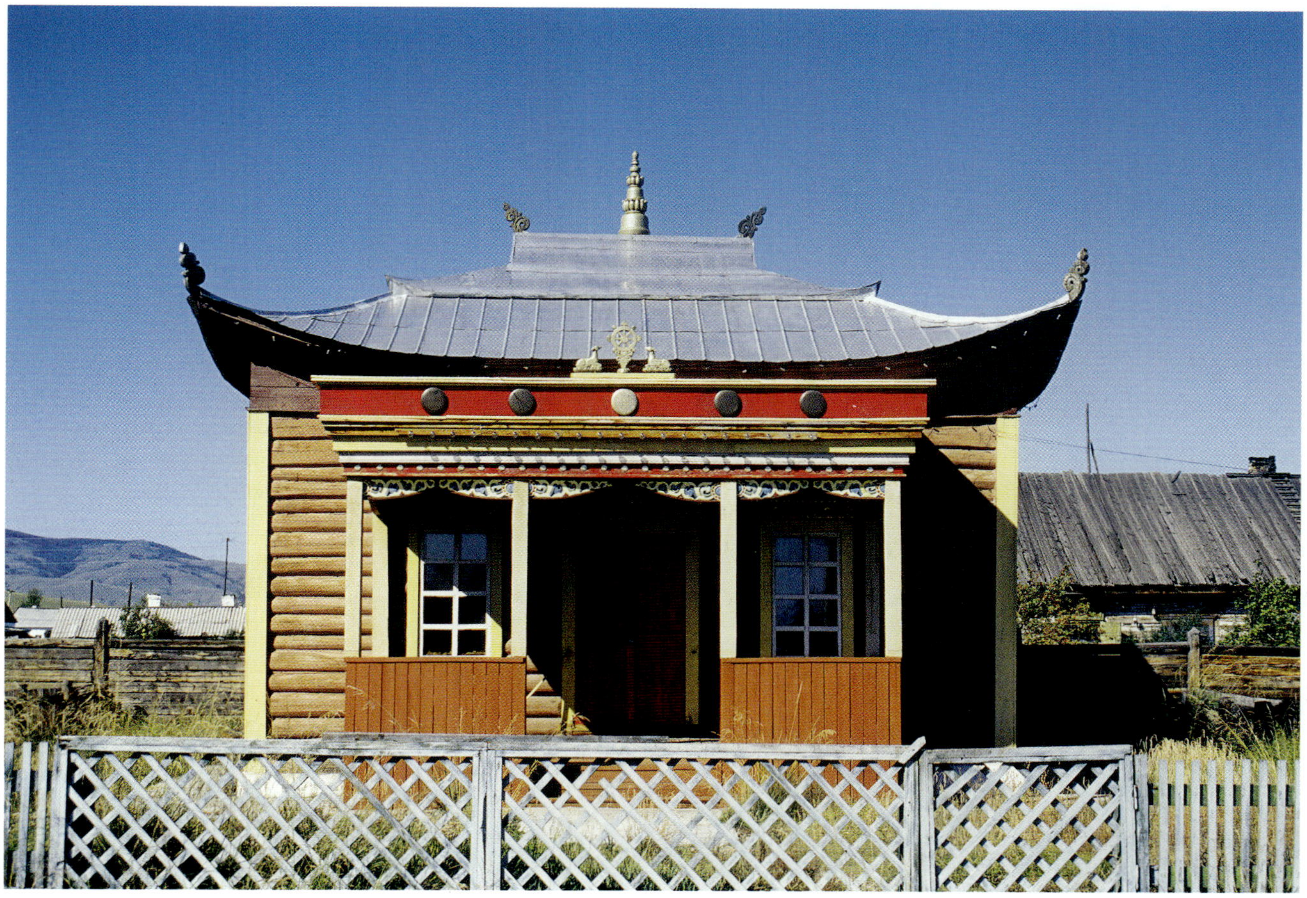

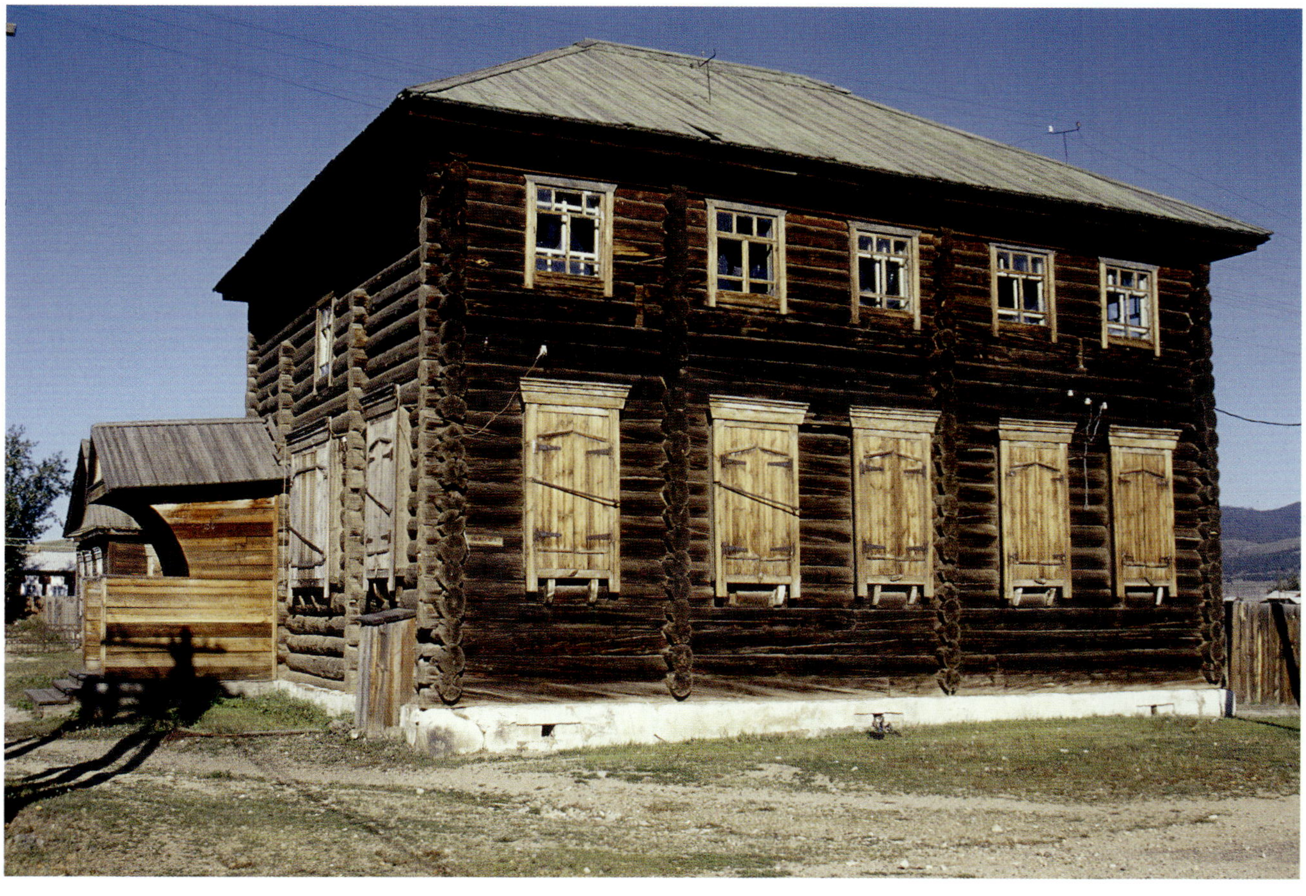

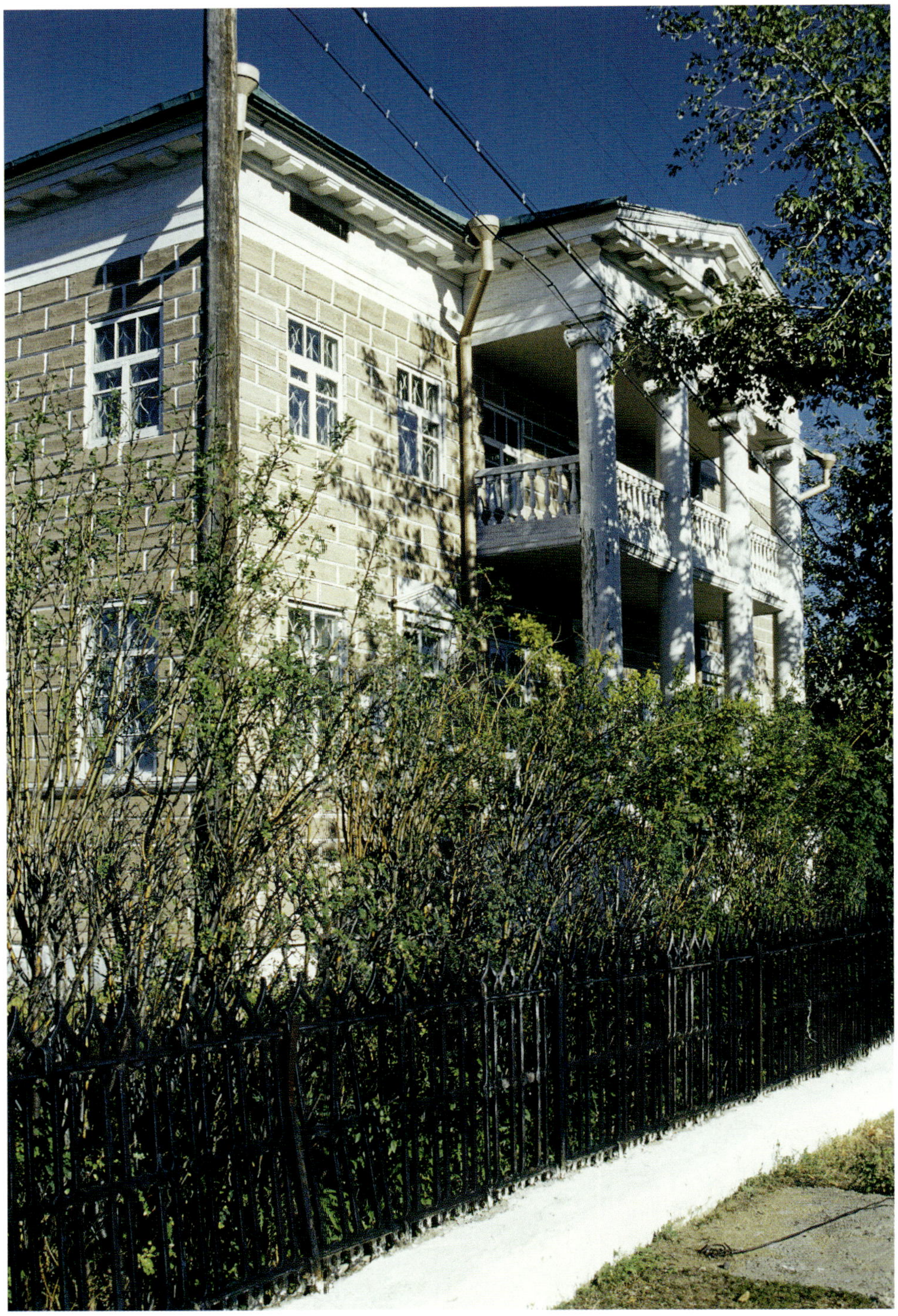

NOVOSELENGINSK. Dmitry Startsev house. Built probably in the early 1840s in the manner of a noble estate house (with two-story portico and plank facade rustication) for Startsev, a wealthy merchant who befriended and supported the brothers Nikolay and Mikhail Bestuzhev, exiled for their participation in the Decembrist uprising and resettled in Selenginsk in 1839. It is possible that the house was designed by Nikolay Bestuzhev, who endowed a nearby merchant house (see preceding figure) with the trappings of noble culture. September 8, 2000.

and China. Situated by the small Kyakhta River, the settlement was on the direct caravan route between the Siberian center of Irkutsk and the Qing (or Manchu) capital of Beijing. While the Trinity Fort (1727) fulfilled administrative and security functions, trade was handled by the adjacent settlement of Kyakhtinskaya Sloboda (Kyakhta Quarter), also founded in 1727. Here Russian merchants gathered to export fur, leather, hides, and

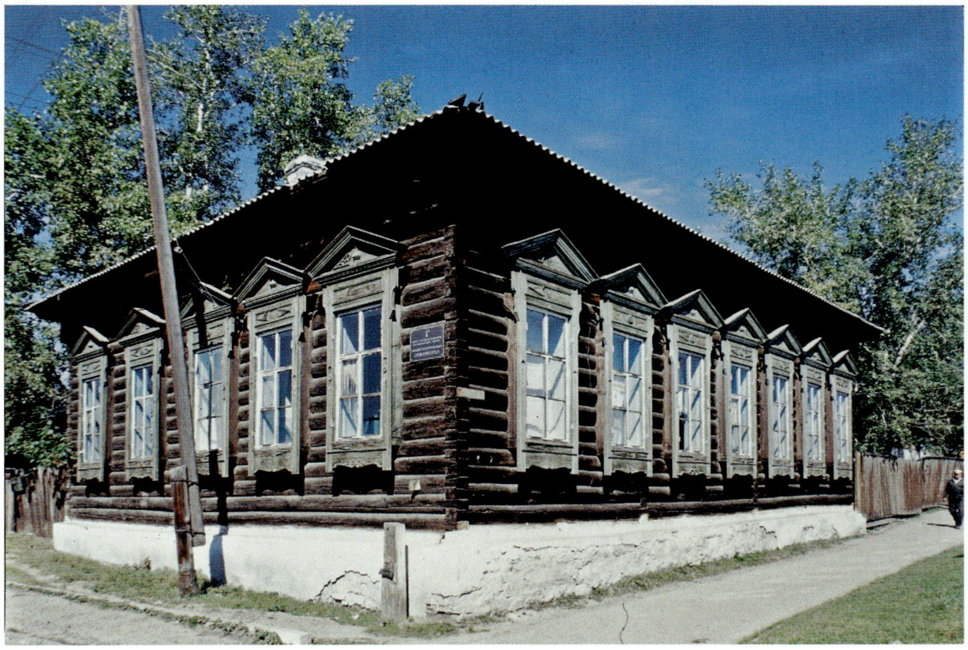

KYAKHTA. Former office of Russo-Asiatic Bank (turn of twentieth century). September 9, 2000.

cattle and to import a variety of Chinese goods, including silk and some porcelain, but with special emphasis on spices such as ginger and rhubarb, highly valued for medicinal properties. Chinese merchants gathered across the border in a third settlement, known as Maimachin—a generic Chinese term meaning "trading center." By the late eighteenth century, the most significant import was tea. For almost a century Kyakhta provided tea not only to the enormous Russian market but also to much of Europe. With the opening of Chinese ports to English ships in the mid-nineteenth century

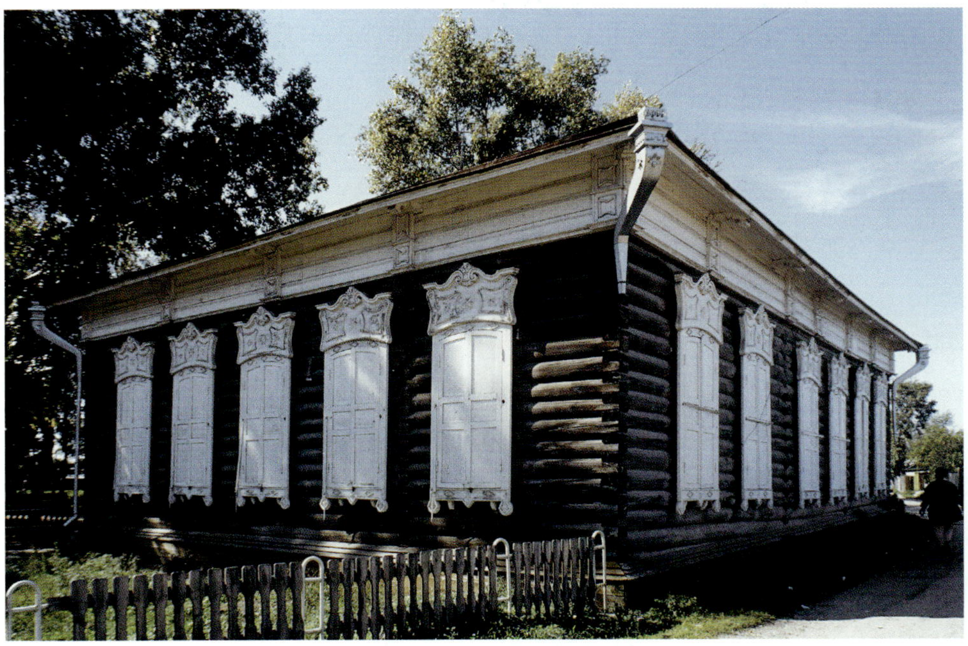

KABANSK. Mark Eidelman house. Built in the late nineteenth century for a pillar of the local Jewish community. September 10, 2000.

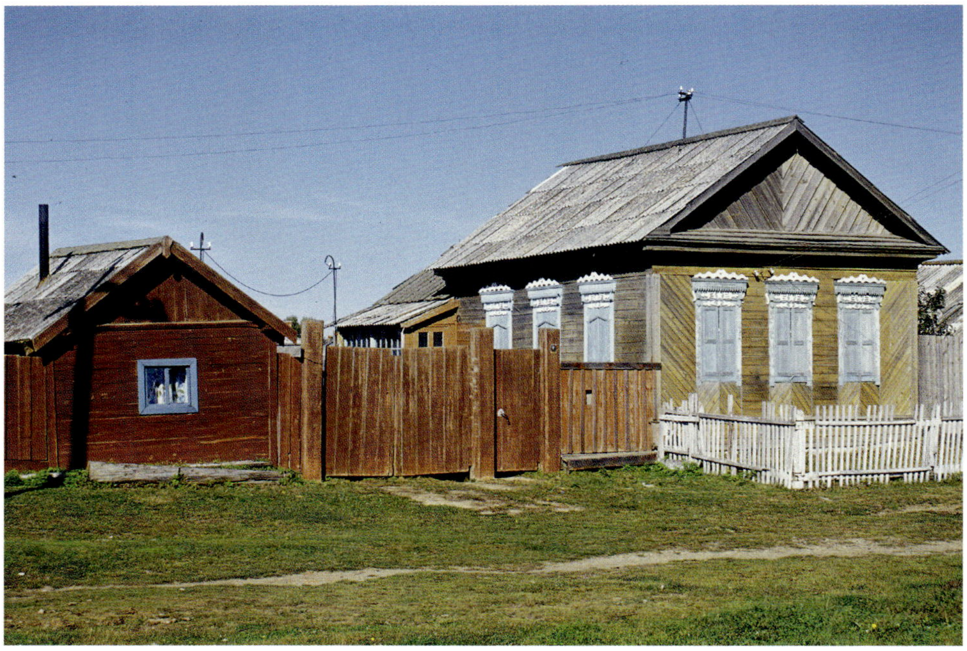

POSOLSKOE. House with courtyard gate in fishing village on eastern shore of Lake Baikal. September 10, 2000.

and the subsequent building of the Suez Canal, Kyakhta's importance to the tea trade waned.

During the first century of Kyakhta's existence, all its structures were built of logs, and wooden architecture predominated well into the Soviet period. Perhaps the greatest charm of Kyakhta is its individual houses, which to this day are primarily of wood. With a minimum of maintenance, they have been relatively well preserved in the area's dry climate. The houses rest on masonry foundations, some of which are high enough to accommodate a ground floor with small windows. Much care was given to architectural decoration, with special attention to window shutters and surrounds.

The Amur River Basin

Chita (current population 334,000; capital of what is now known as Transbaikal region) seems to have arisen overnight with the coming of the Trans-Siberian Railway in 1900, yet its founding can be dated more than two centuries earlier. Located at the confluence of the Chita and Ingoda Rivers, the site of contemporary Chita attracted the attention of the Siberian pathfinder Peter Beketov, who made a small winter camp on the Ingoda in 1653. The first permanent settlement, established in the late 1670s, grew slowly under harsh conditions. Although a few Cossacks, trappers, and

CHITA. Church of Archangel Michael, southeast view. September 14, 2000.

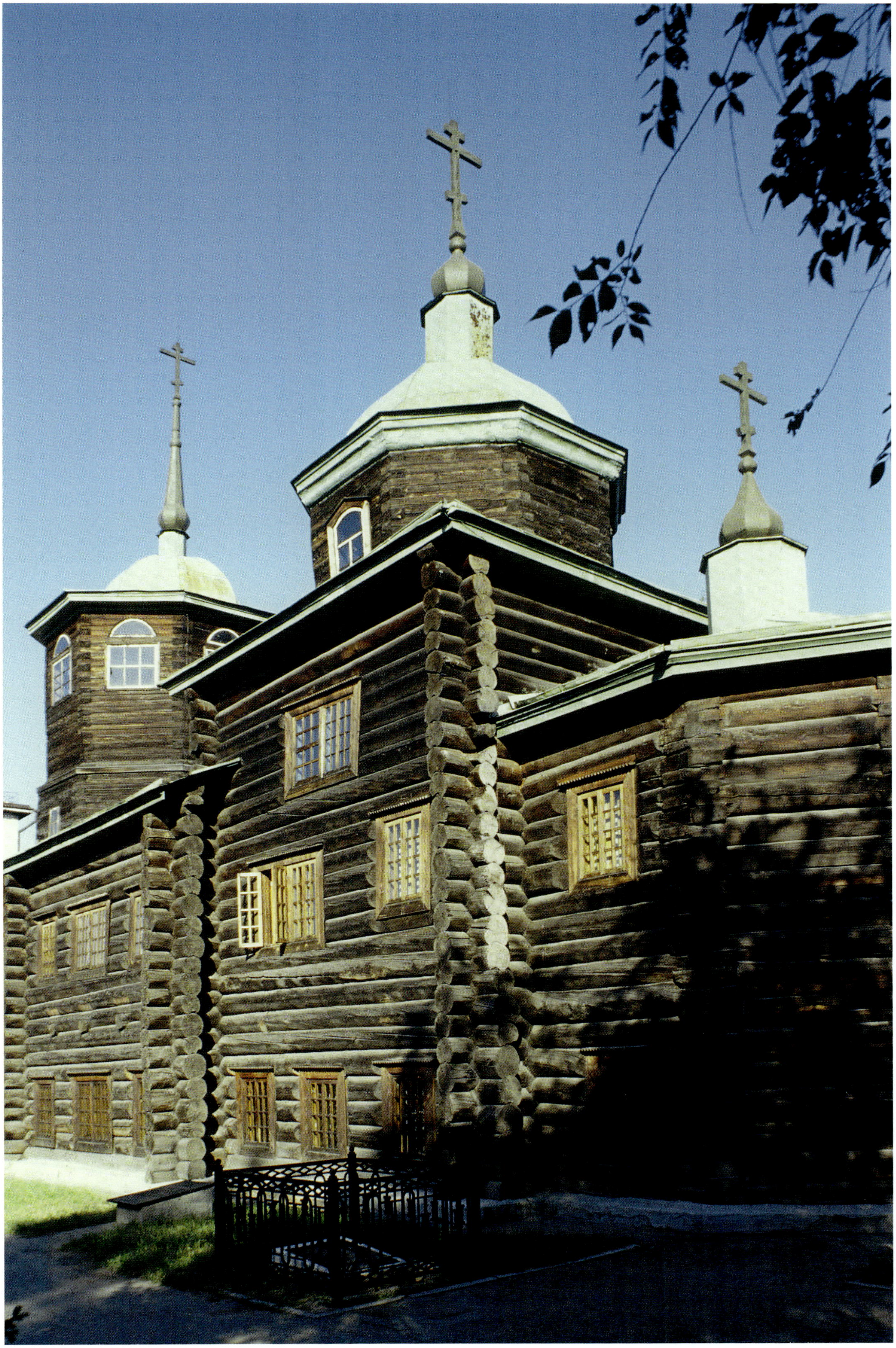

fishermen were resettled to the fort in the 1690s, their presence did little to stimulate development.

Chita's one landmark from the eighteenth century, the log Church of Archangel Michael, was originally built in 1705, shortly after the Chita settlement was elevated to the status of "fort" (*ostrog*). After a fire the church was rebuilt in the 1770s. Its patron was one Evgeny Gurkin, a merchant from distant Solvychegodsk in the north of European Russia. The Archangel Michael Church is an example of traditional wooden Orthodox architecture, with an octagonal bell tower in the west. The central structure culminates in an octagonal drum and low dome. The church's excellent state of preservation owes much to its reputation as "the church of the Decembrists," a reference to the Chita exile of some two dozen participants in the failed uprising against Nicholas I in December 1825. During the nineteenth century Chita was identified with Siberian exile culture, particularly after 1851, when Chita became the administrative center of the Transbaikal Territory and headquarters of the Transbaikal Cossack troops. In his book *Siberia and the Exile System*, the American writer George Kennan described meetings in the fall of 1885 with Chita's political exiles.

With the arrival of the Trans-Siberian Railway in Chita in 1900, the town experienced a substantial increase in building, further accelerated by the completion of the Chinese Eastern Railway in 1903. The latter railroad, negotiated as part of an 1896 defense treaty with the Chinese, allowed the Russians transit across Manchuria and thus much shorter access to Vladivostok and surrounding territories along the Ussuri River. As the nearest major settlement to the junction between the Chinese Eastern Railway and the still uncompleted Trans-Siberian Railway, Chita seemed poised to play a commanding role for a Russian presence in the Far East. If the population of Chita in 1900 was approximately twelve thousand, the population in 1913 was seventy-three thousand, an extraordinary rate of growth driven by railroad expansion. Photographs of the town in the early twentieth century show large buildings arising from streets of dark Siberian muck. Most of the substantial commercial structures were of brick, but much housing continued to be of wood. One of the best-preserved examples is the Ignatiev house, built in 1899 by the merchant Dmitry Ignatiev and inherited by his wife Maria in 1911. This large log structure was erected on a masonry foundation and clad in plank siding imitating rusticated stone and painted dark green. The right facade of the house was a brick firewall. The main facade is enlivened by a polygonal bay window, and

CHITA. Dmitry Ignatiev house (1899). Right: corner of Maria Ignatiev building (Russo-Chinese Bank). September 14, 2000.

CHITA. Mikhail Timokhovich house. Built in 1910 by its owner, the *style moderne* house is delightfully eccentric in its "Sea Kingdom" decoration. September 14, 2000.

the roof is crowned by a turret and dome in what might loosely be called Second Empire style. Although the original furnishings have disappeared, the preservation of the house is due to reasonable use by a series of offices including, on the second floor, the Center for the Preservation of Cultural

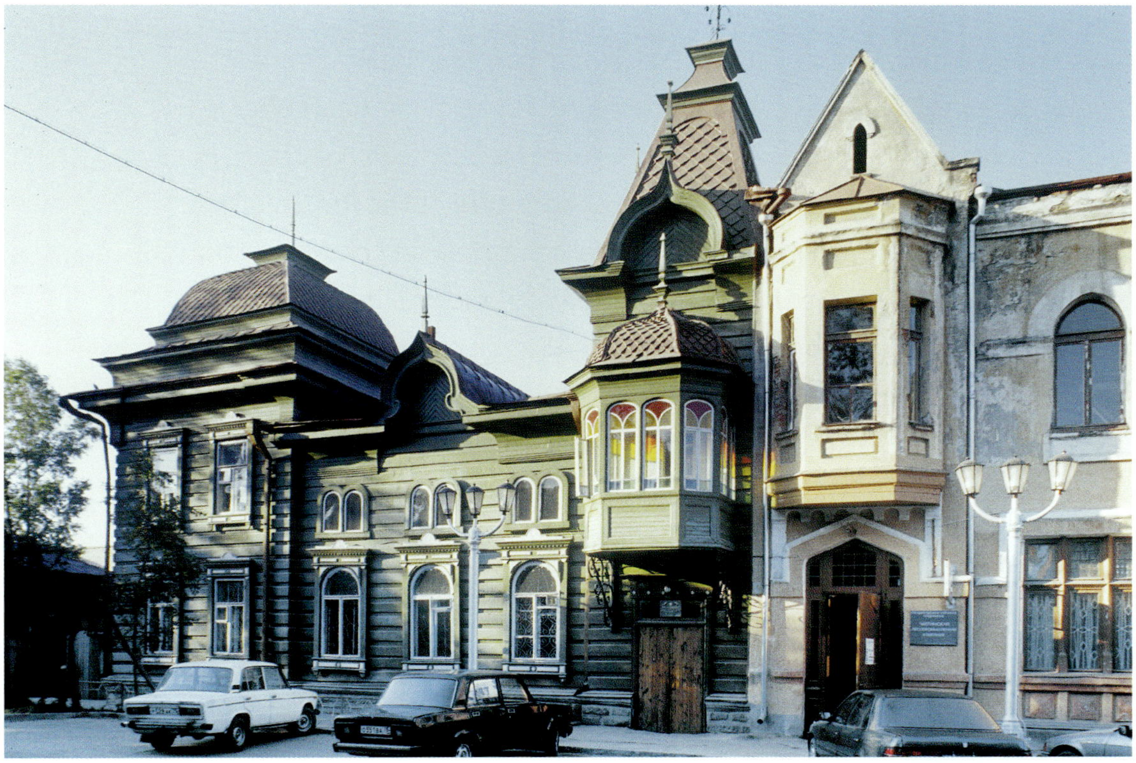

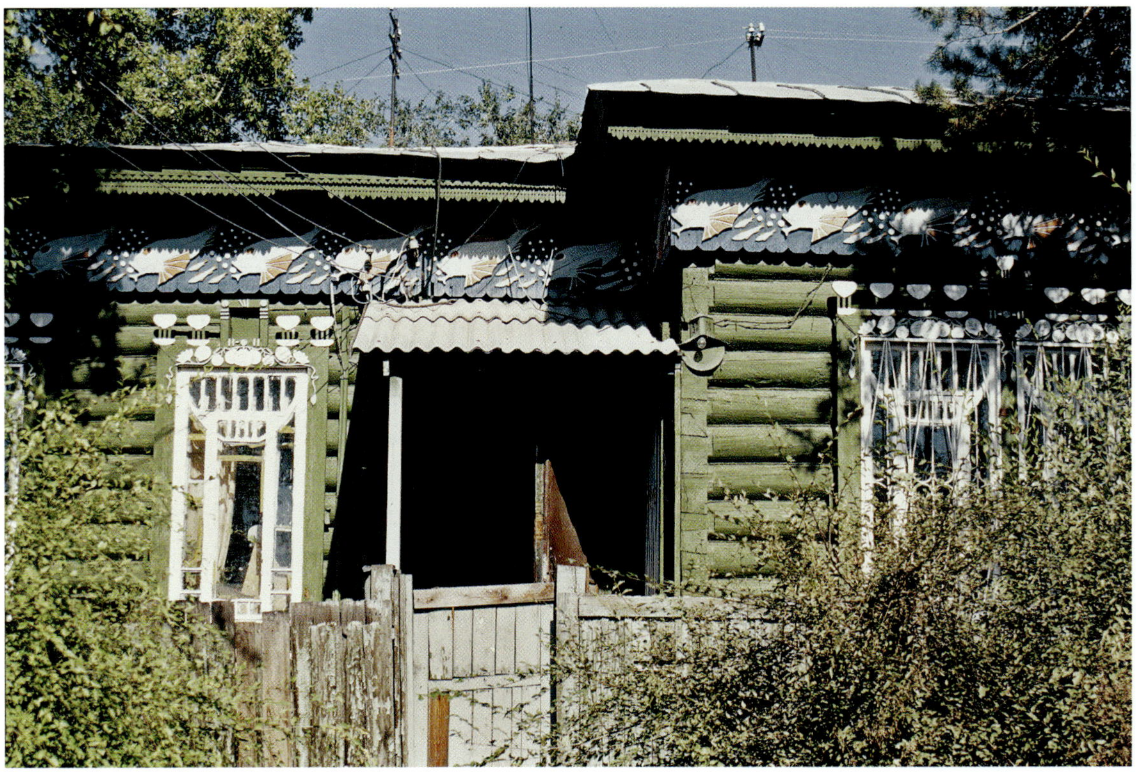

Heritage Objects. I still have fond memories of sleeping on that second floor. My generous hosts, the Zherebtsovs, who managed the preservation office, wanted to place me in a hotel, but after a quick inspection of the options, my sense of smell convinced me of the superiority of a sleeping bag on the floor of the Ignatiev mansion—yet another blessed memory of a night spent in a spacious wooden structure.

Russian settlements in the Far East have had widely divergent fates. Some become major cities, and others settle into provincial obscurity after moments of historical fame. A prime example of the latter is Nerchinsk, located near the Shilka River, a tributary of the Amur in the Transbaikal Territory. Among historians, Nerchinsk is associated with a late seventeenth-century treaty that defined the border between Russia and China. As the Russian Empire expanded in the nineteenth century, Nerchinsk lost its strategic significance. Bypassed by the Trans-Siberian Railway, Nerchinsk became another provincial river landing with limited importance for transportation and commerce. Yet this modest backwater settlement was linked to the ancestors of Vasily (Wassily) Kandinsky and appeared in the travel letters of Anton Chekhov.

The original settlement arose from Moscow's attempt to define its border with China in the mid-seventeenth century. By the beginning of 1654 Cossacks had built a rudimentary fort near the confluence of the Shilka and Nercha Rivers, but Russian presence remained vulnerable. With the signing of the Treaty of Nerchinsk on August 29, 1689, Russian envoys had made the best of a difficult situation. By virtue of a favorable location near the Shilka River, Nerchinsk became a center for administration and trade with the Manchu Empire. In 1812 Nerchinsk was relocated to ground north of the confluence of the Nercha and Shilka Rivers to escape periodic floods. After the suppression of the Decembrist uprising in 1825, Nerchinsk and the Nerchinsk silver mines (distant from the town) gained notoriety as a territory of exile. Like Irkutsk, Nerchinsk gained from the education and culture of the Decembrist exiles, most of whom were gradually allowed to resettle in more favorable conditions.

With the reforms of the reign of Alexander II, the economic development of Siberia accelerated, and Nerchinsk benefited accordingly. Commerce in the Nerchinsk area was represented by the Kandinsky family, which began with the fur trade in the eighteenth century and then moved into the tea trade with connections to the regional center of Kyakhta. The family patriarch, Khrisanf Petrovich Kandinsky (1774–1850s), had a grandson

NERCHINSK. Jewish house and store, Soviet Street 12. September 12, 2000.

AGINSKOE. Tsugol Datsan. Tsogchen Dugan (main temple). Smaller Buryat temples were built of wood (see above), while the main temple was of brick with lavish wood fittings for the superstructure and interior. September 13, 2000.

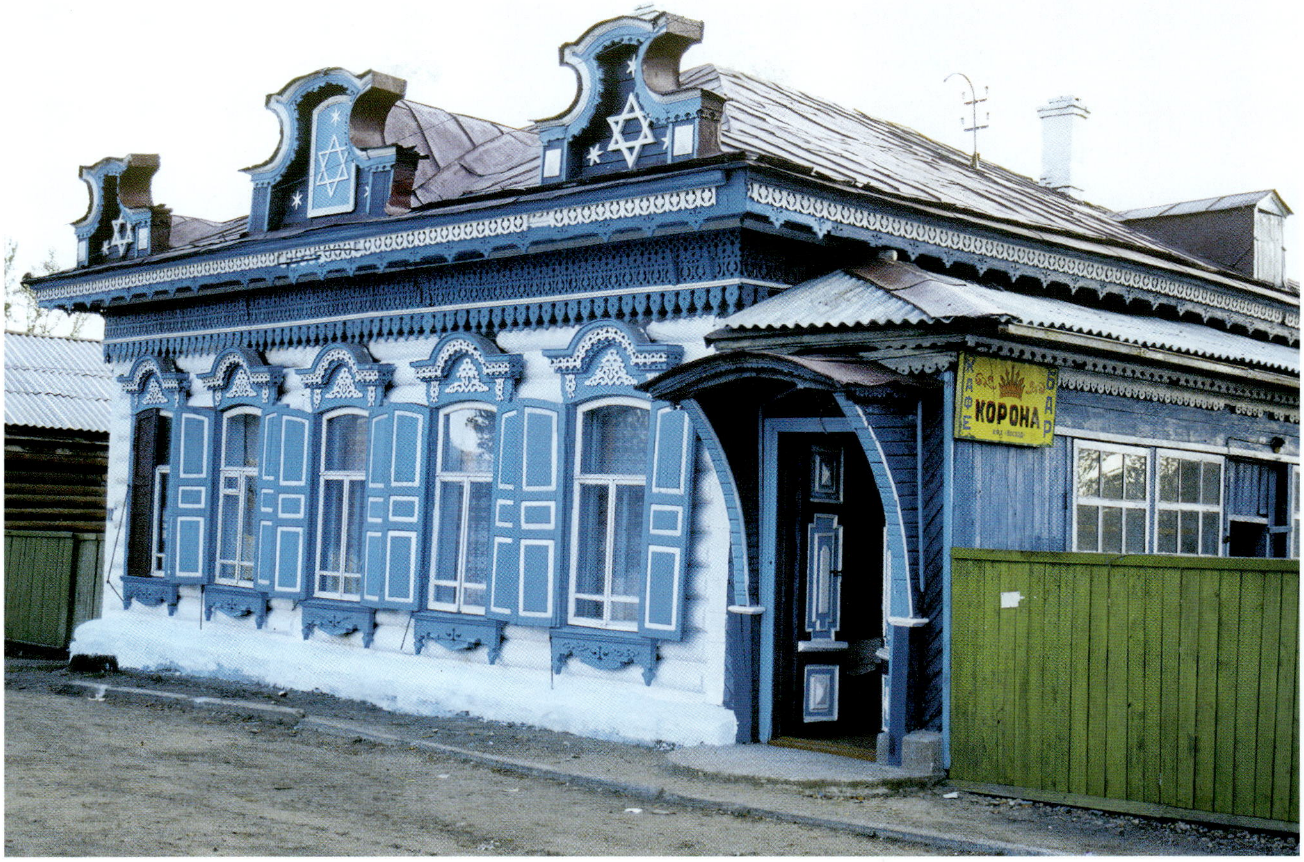
КАФЕ
КОРОНА
БАР

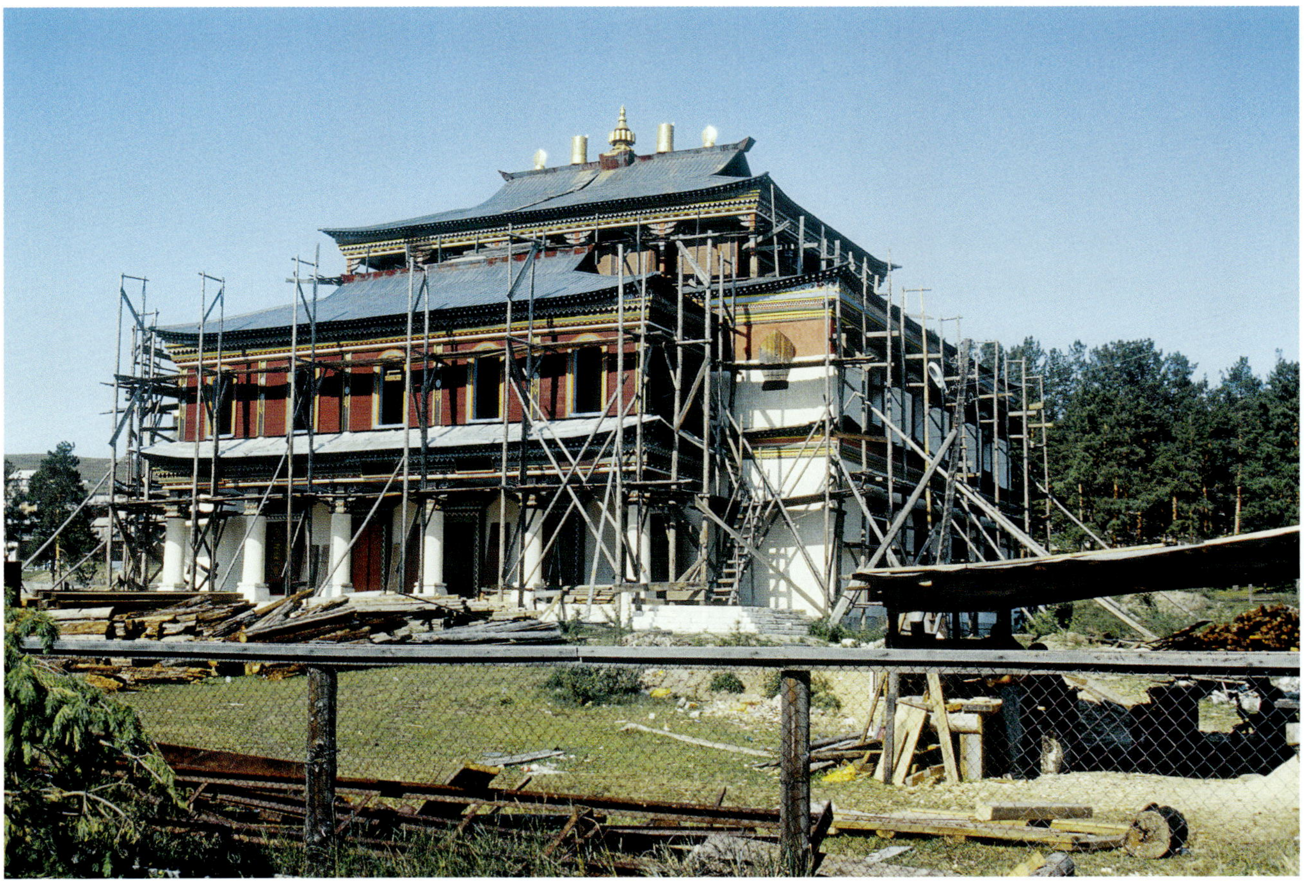

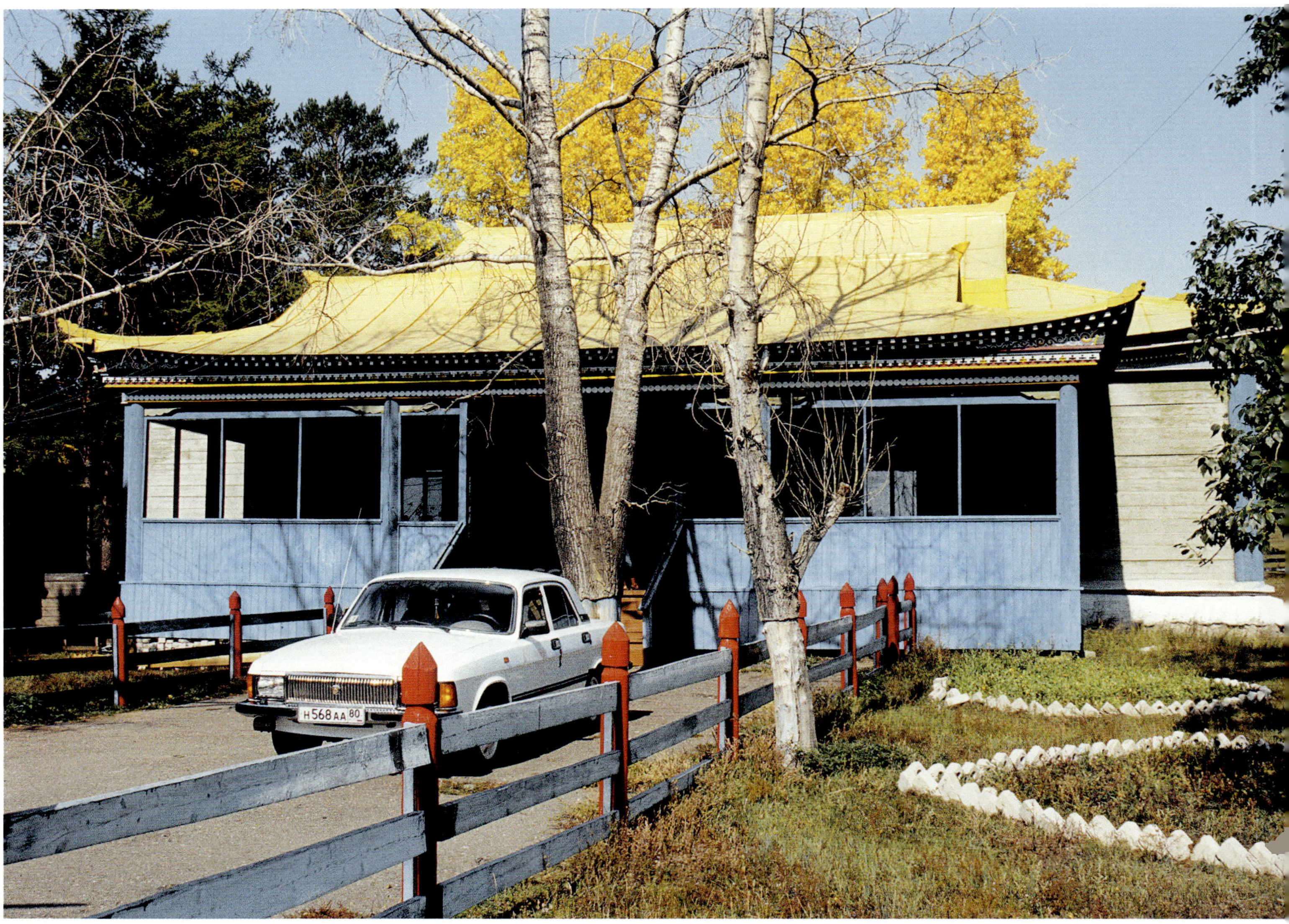

named Vasily (1832–1926), who was the father of the great artist. By the time of Wassily Kandinsky's birth, in 1866, that branch of the family had moved to Moscow. Although the painter never visited his ancestral homeland, it is tempting to see the spiritual influence of Siberia in mystical aspects of his work.

While the tea trade waned in Nerchinsk, the town's location near a major river network sustained a level of prosperity. Historic Nerchinsk consists primarily of wooden dwellings, usually of one story with ornamental carving typical of Siberia. In some cases, the dwellings were connected to a store. Of special interest is the store with a Star of David on the facade, a reflection of the Jewish presence in communities of Siberia and the Far East. The area between Chita and Nerchinsk also includes the Aginsk Autonomous Territory, known for its centers of Buddhist culture, such as the large Tsugol Datsan (lamasery) at Aginskoe.

AGINSKOE. Buryat house. Built of logs, this private dwelling has a distinctive flared, stepped roof and cornice decorated in the manner of a temple. September 12, 2000.

SHILKA STATION (Transbaikal region). Church of Saints Peter and Paul, southwest view. Completed in 1908 for a local parish of railroad workers, the structure exemplified a design for Trans-Siberian station churches, built of logs with painted siding for economy and aesthetic purposes. September 12, 2000.

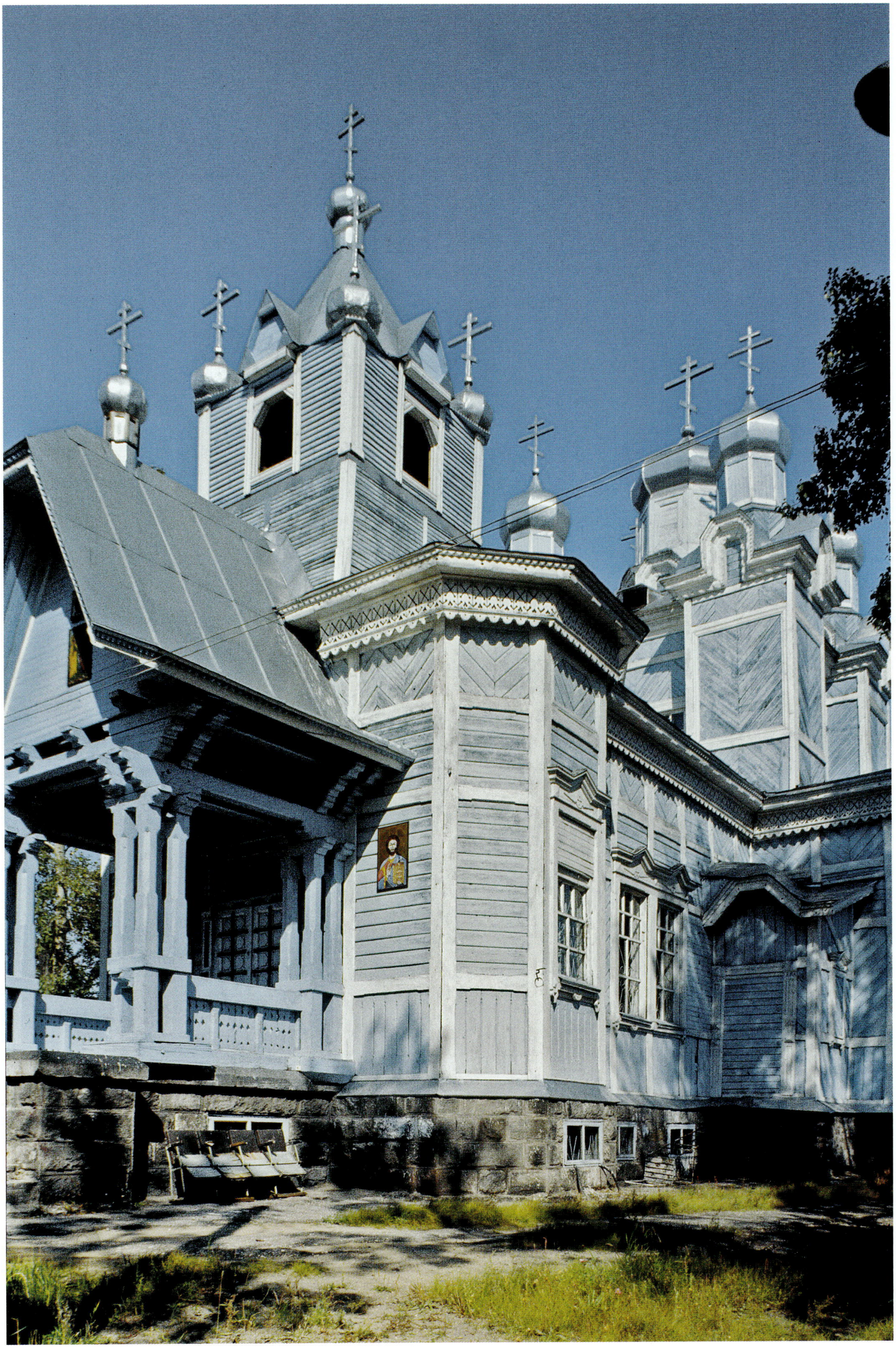

Khabarovsk

Founded in 1858—two years earlier than Vladivostok some eighth hundred kilometers to the south—Khabarovsk has become a major center of culture and trade in the Far East. Indeed, Khabarovsk is a city of two great strategic rivers: the Amur, which flows eastward along the northern Manchurian border; and the Ussuri, which flows northward some nine hundred kilometers from its origins in the southern Sikhote-Alin Mountains, not far from the Sea of Japan. The confluence of these two rivers near Khabarovsk, and the state boundaries defined by their merger, have created one of the most important geopolitical zones in northern Asia.

Russian Cossacks and explorers had attempted to gain control of the north bank of the Amur as early as the 1640s. Yet following the prolonged siege by Manchu forces of the Russian Albazin Fort on the Amur in 1685–86, Russia was compelled by the Treaty of Nerchinsk (1689) to abandon the area north of the Amur and retreat west of the Argun River. Not until the mid-nineteenth century did substantial Russian forces return to the area under the leadership of Governor-General Nikolay Muravyov, given the title "Amursky" for his role in acquiring territory for the Russian Empire. China, weakened by the Taiping Rebellion and the Second Opium War, recognized the Russian presence by the Treaty of Aigun (1858), which ceded to Russia territory north of the Amur and east of the Ussuri. These treaties negotiated with the Qing Dynasty were ratified by the Convention of Peking in 1860.

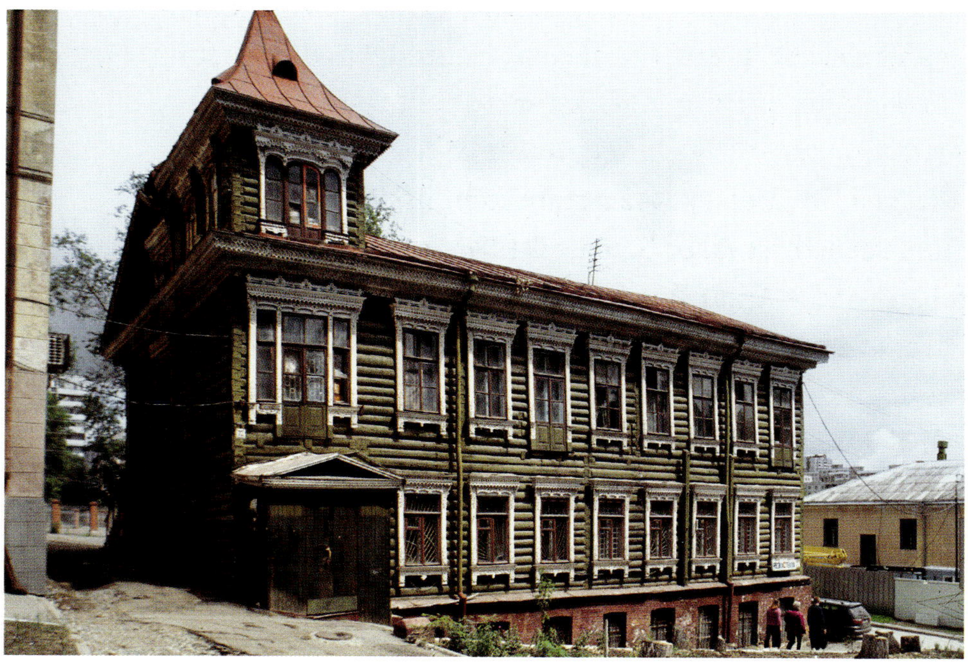

KHABAROVSK. Semyon Tabolov and Alexander Bitarov commercial building. Completed in 1911 for two entrepreneurs with links to the local Polish diaspora, the structure shows the remarkable durability of wood when properly maintained. In addition to retail space, the building housed the Grand Hotel on the first floor and the upscale restaurant London. Restored in 2005. June 2, 2002.

Khabarovsk, like Vladivostok, arose as a consequence of the Treaty of Aigun. The first Russian settlement was established in May 1858 by a detachment of Siberian troops under the command of Captain Yakov Dyachenko. The post was initially named Khabarovka in homage to the renowned seventeenth-century Cossack leader Yerofey Khabarov, who explored these parts. The settlement rapidly expanded and by 1864 already had a formal plan for growth on hilly terrain along the left bank of the Amur. A telegraph line to Vladivostok began operating in 1868, and a proper river port was completed in 1874. By the end of 1880 Khabarovsk had gained more than four thousand inhabitants and official status as a town. With the development of river trading routes, entrepreneurs were quick to settle in the young town, which offered considerable potential for commerce with China. Progress in transportation also led to increased government authority. In 1884 Khabarovsk became the administrative center of a vast area from the Amur River to the Pacific.

Komsomolsk on the Amur

Founded in 1932, Komsomolsk-on-Amur is located on a wind-swept, marshy basin of the lower Amur River, midway on its path north to the Sea of Okhotsk. In 1930 the Soviet government and its Central Executive Committee declared the development of the Far East territory a state priority. Soviet control over this vast, sparsely inhabited region seemed tenuous. The Trans-Siberian Railway had spurred rapid development in new eastern settlements, such as Khabarovsk and Vladivostok, but these areas remained vulnerably close to international borders throughout the first half of the twentieth century. In view of the tense geopolitical situation in Asia, the Soviet strategy was to create a new, reasonably secure industrial anchor in the Far East. In January 1932 a state commission headed by prominent Communist activist Yakov Gamarnik (1894–1937) found a location on the left bank of the Amur River at the small Russian village of Permskoy. The river's width at this point was suitable for the creation of a shipyard, a development priority set forth as early as 1931. While the Amur River provided a major transportation route, the new site was also buffered by some four hundred kilometers from the regional center of Khabarovsk, located on the Manchurian border at the confluence of the Amur and Ussuri Rivers. In February 1932 the site was accepted by the Soviet government,

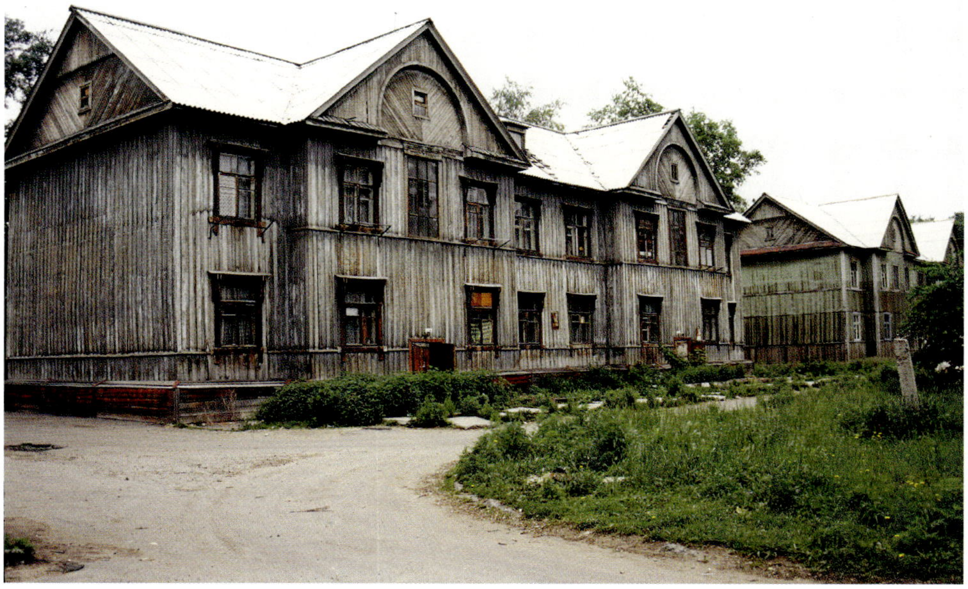

KOMSOMOLSK-ON-AMUR. Standardized wooden apartment house, Zaporozhskaya Street 10. Built in the late 1930s when economy and speed were a premium for housing workers, these log structures with plank siding continued to function decades later. June 11, 2002.

which also confirmed construction of an aviation plant at Dzyomgi. In the spring a national call went out to the Komsomol (Communist Union of Youth) network, and by April more than six thousand volunteers arrived in Khabarovsk. Fanatic idealism overcame extreme difficulties, and the town, officially designated as Komsomolsk in December 1932, held on. In May 1935 the first temporary dock wharf was completed, and construction began on the aviation plant, aided throughout by the labor of Gulag prisoners. Although masonry construction methods were ultimately applied throughout Komsomolsk, a few of the early wooden structures were still standing at the time of my visit at the beginning of this century. Standardized in construction, they are echoes of a turbulent past.

Vladivostok

Vladivostok ("rule the east") is the final point on the Trans-Siberian Railway, the point where Russia ends on the brink of the Pacific Ocean. The settlement began in July 1860, when a small group of soldiers erected buildings on the Golden Horn Bay at a site designated in 1859 by Count Nikolay Muravyov-Amursky (1809–81). He had been the driving figure in Russia's acquisition of large territories along the Amur and Ussuri Rivers following treaties negotiated with the Qing Dynasty and ratified by the Convention of Peking in 1860. As governor-general of Eastern Siberia,

Muravyov-Amursky succeeded in consolidating the new gains using army posts and creating Amur Cossack units from Siberian peasants.

The establishment of an active port at Vladivostok was an essential part of Muravyov's strategy. The town's first thoroughfare was named American Street after the corvette *America*, on which Muravyov sailed into Golden Horn Bay in 1859. In 1873 the street was renamed Svetlanskaya—the name it bears to this day—in honor of the visit of Grand Duke Alexey Alexandrovich on the naval vessel *Svetlana*. (The grand duke was quite the traveler: In 1872 he made a much-publicized trip to America, including New Orleans, where he presided over the Mardi Gras krewe of Rex.) Chinese comprised a substantial portion of the town's population in its early decades. The labor and skills of the Chinese—and to a lesser extent the Koreans and Japanese—were essential to the growth of Vladivostok, where Russian settlers were difficult to attract. In 1888 Vladivostok replaced Khabarovsk as the administrative center of the Eastern Siberian Province.

Eventually, the lure of commerce and opportunities created by railroad construction and port development led to a substantial increase in the city's size. By 1897 Vladivostok had a rail link to Khabarovsk, located 760 kilometers to the north at the confluence of the Ussuri and Amur Rivers, and in 1903 Vladivostok was connected to Moscow via the Trans-Siberian Railway. By that time its population was more than thirty thousand. With a current population just under six hundred thousand, Vladivostok has

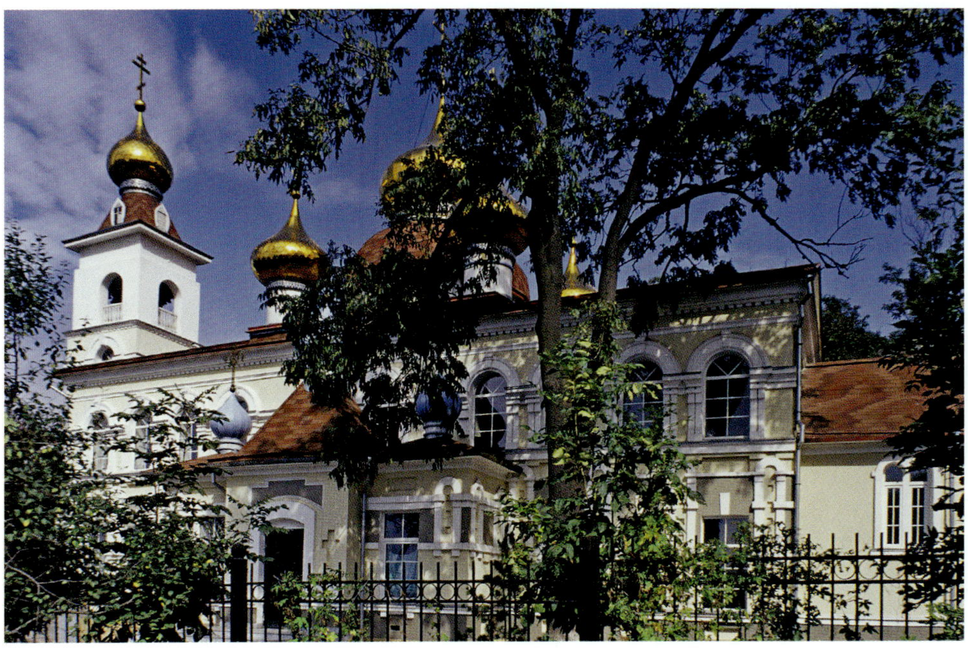

VLADIVOSTOK. Cathedral of Saint Nicholas, south view. Completed in 1907 and originally consecrated in 1908 to the Icon of the Virgin, "Joy to All Who Grieve," the church was intended as a memorial to Russian losses in the Russo-Japanese War. Returned to the parish in 1976, the shrine was converted to the eparchial cathedral with the establishment of the Vladivostok Eparchy in 1991. September 25, 2000.

undergone major redevelopment, and only a few wooden buildings remain, including, notably, the main cathedral, dedicated to Saint Nicholas.

The Lena River

Yakutsk—located on the left, or west, bank of the Lena River—is one of the most distant of Russia's cities, a strategic outpost in a region of permafrost and intense cold. It is the capital of the Republic of Sakha—also known as Yakutia—the largest territorial division in the Russian Federation. From Moscow it is almost five thousand kilometers by air and more than eight thousand kilometers by land. Arriving by plane, one is greeted with an unforgettable, awe-inspiring view of the vastness of the Lena. Despite the isolation of Yakutsk and the severity of its climate, there are many reasons to explain the city's steady growth: diamonds, gold, oil, just to name a few. With its suburbs, Yakutsk now has almost three hundred thousand inhabitants, or roughly a third of the Sakha Republic's population. The Yakuts, who now number almost half a million, are a Turkic people who migrated to their current lands from the Lake Baikal region. Indigenous Yakut culture has traditionally been based on the spiritual authority of the shaman. Yakut culture possesses a distinctive crafts tradition and a remarkably beautiful musical heritage, particularly in song.

Yakutsk is officially considered to have originated with a fort established in September 1632 by Peter Beketov, who had been given command of thirty Cossacks in Yeniseisk, the capital of east Siberia. Moscow's representative in Yeniseisk ordered Beketov to establish a Russian presence on the Lena River, the next great Siberian waterway to the east of the Yenisei River. The small outpost that Beketov built on the Lena was rapidly expanded, particularly since early relations with the Yakuts were turbulent. Heavy Russian demands for tribute payments in furs led to discontent and brutally suppressed uprisings in the 1630s and again in 1642. The year 1632 is considered as the founding date not only of the city but also of Sakha/Yakutia as a territory. In fact, Beketov's original fort was situated some sixty kilometers south of the current site of Yakutsk. Ten years after its founding the settlement was relocated to its current site in the Tuimaada Valley, and the new fort was considerably expanded during the following decades. By the late eighteenth century, the fort was no longer necessary, and only one late seventeenth-century log tower was preserved

YAKUTSK. Yakutsk Fort (*ostrog*), original late seventeenth-century tower with attached upper chapel. Three months after I photographed it on May 27, 2002, this unique historic monument burned (August 22, 2002).

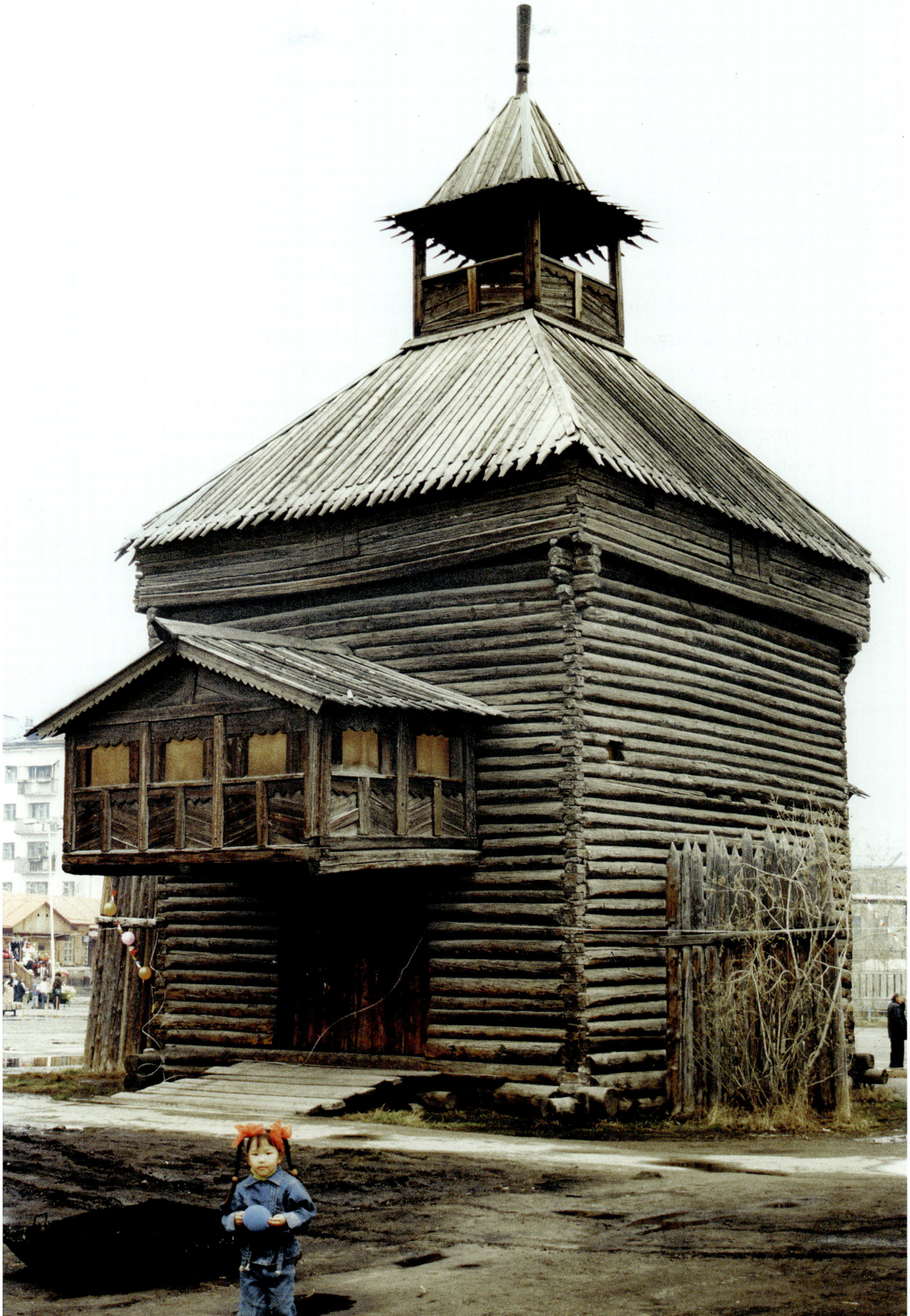

in 1912. That tower was restored in 1981 by Alexander Opolovnikov and survived until August 22, 2002 (three months after my photograph), when it burned—perhaps arson by two disgruntled park employees dismissed for chronic drunkenness. A replica of the tower now stands on the site.

During the tsarist regime, Yakutsk served as the administrative center of a vast territory and as the headquarters of the Yakutsk Cossacks. The Russian Orthodox Church also had a strong presence, and by the nineteenth century many Yakuts had converted to Russian Orthodoxy. Like settlements throughout Siberia, Yakutsk had a grim reputation as a place of exile for political prisoners, including many of Polish nationality. To this day there is a Roman Catholic mission supported in part by residents of Polish descent. In the early twentieth century Yakutsk experienced significant progress, primarily under the capable governorship of Ivan Kraft, son of a Polish exile. Between 1907 and 1913 Kraft oversaw improvements both in the town and in the surrounding agriculture. Most of the town's historic architecture dates from the turn of the twentieth century: banks, churches, and administrative buildings, as well as houses, and much of this of wood, including early Soviet apartment buildings and schools. These log structures proved durable, but they need constant maintenance, particularly at the foundation level, because of the periodic melting of the upper layer of permafrost. Predictably, there is waning interest in the effort involved for such maintenance, and many of the individual wooden dwellings are being abandoned.

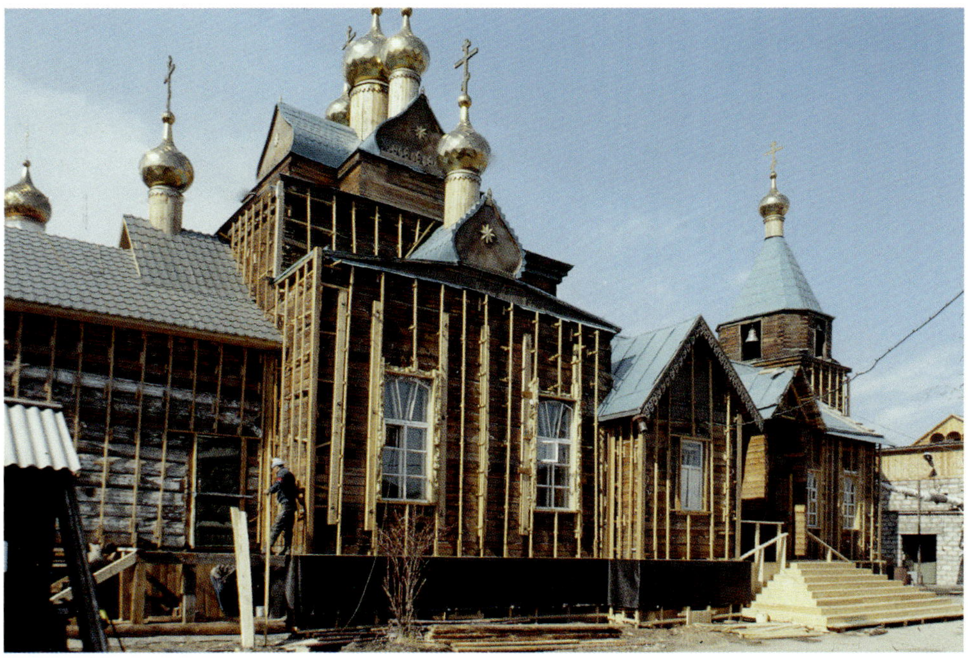

YAKUTSK. Church of the Intercession, Intercession Convent. Originally built in 1980 and dedicated to Saint Nicholas, the shrine underwent major repairs in the 1990s and was reconsecrated in 1998 for the Intercession Convent, founded in 1996. My view uniquely shows the process of placing plank siding on a log structure. May 28, 2002.

YAKUTSK. Fyodor Romanov house. Built in the late nineteenth century by the merchant Fyodor Romanov with rooms rented to, among others, political exiles, the house became known for an armed standoff in February 1904 between fifty-six exiles and local troops. When the house was stormed, one exile and two soldiers were killed. May 28, 2002.

YAKUTSK. Former Russo-Asiatic Bank. Built in 1909 by local architect Klimenty Leshevich in the *style moderne*. Restored in 2005. May 25, 2002.

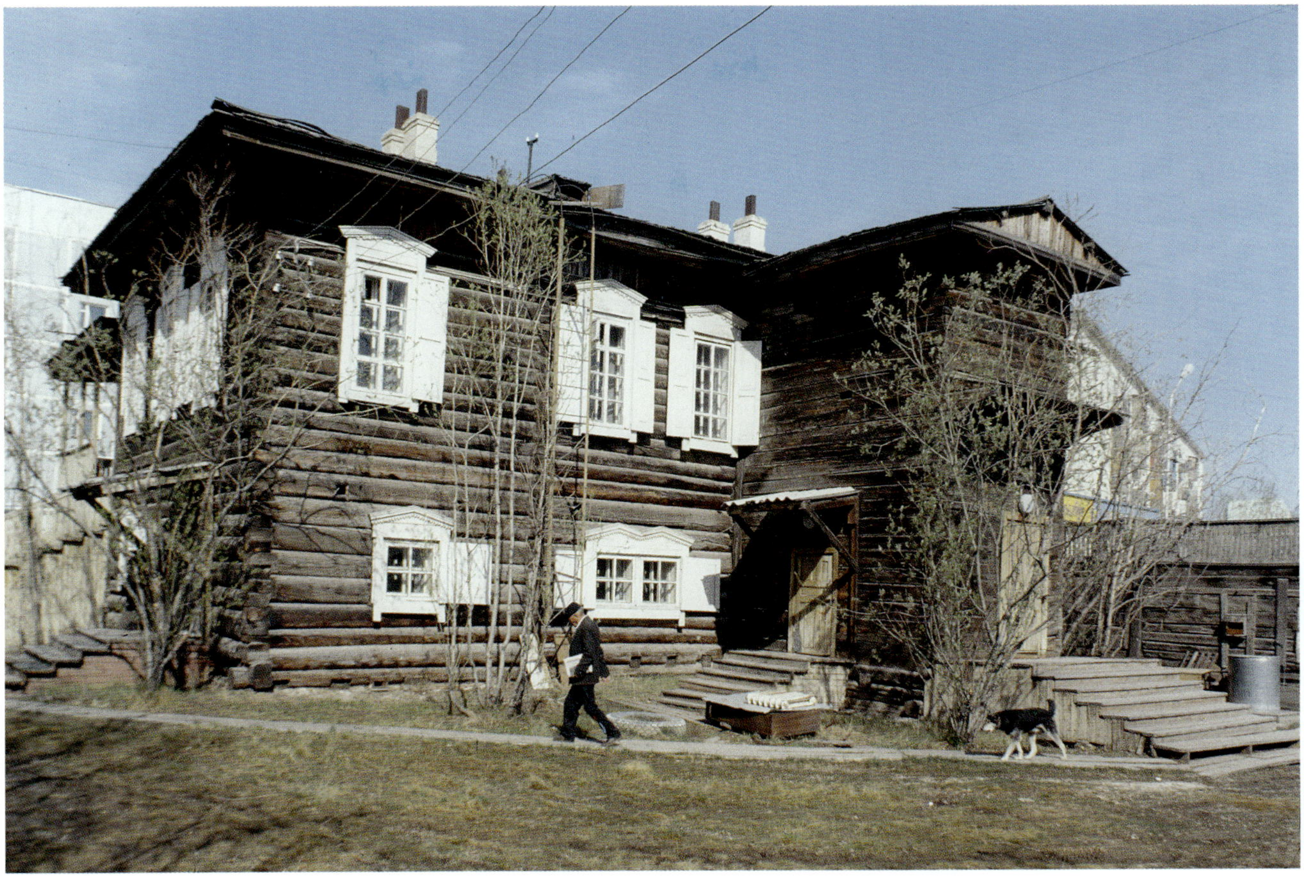

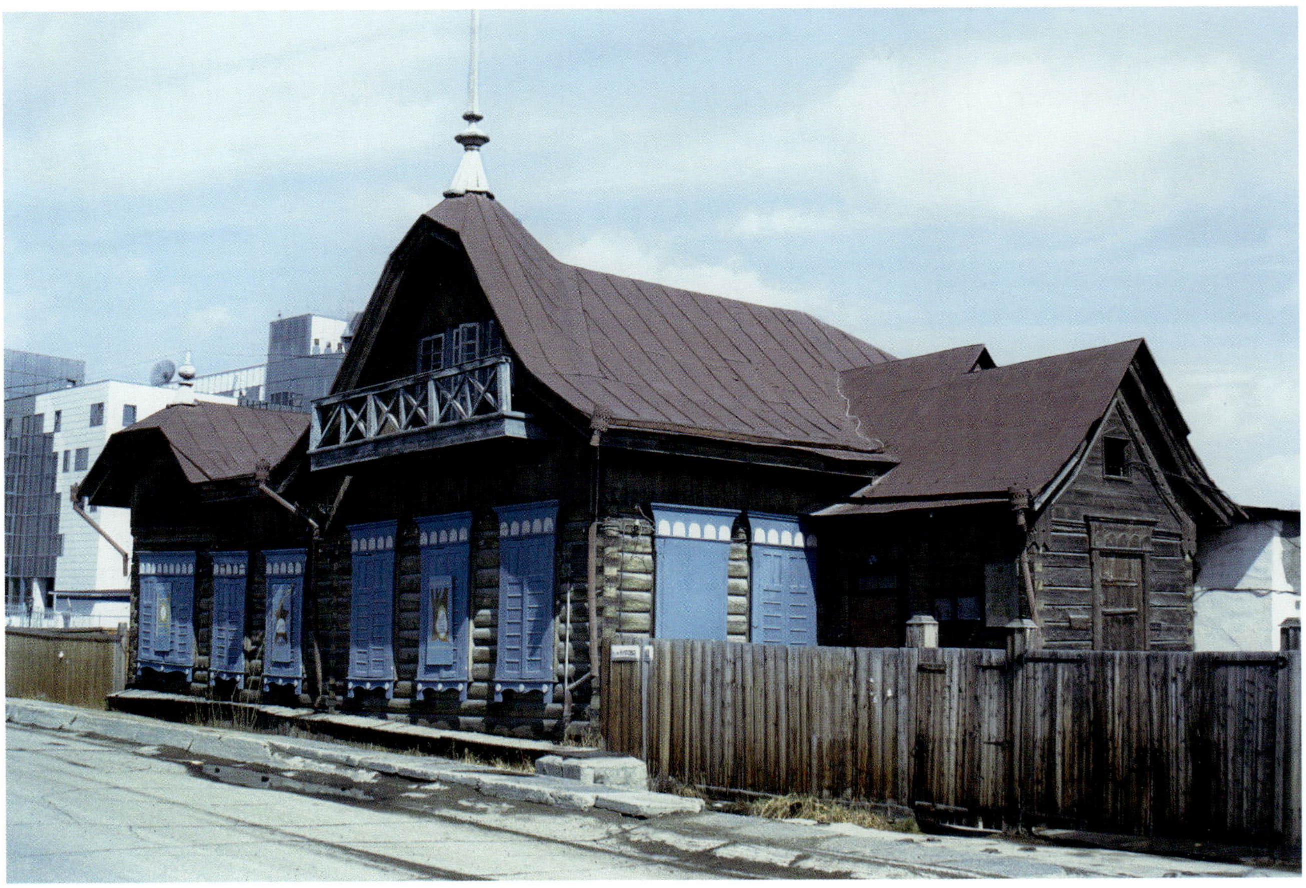

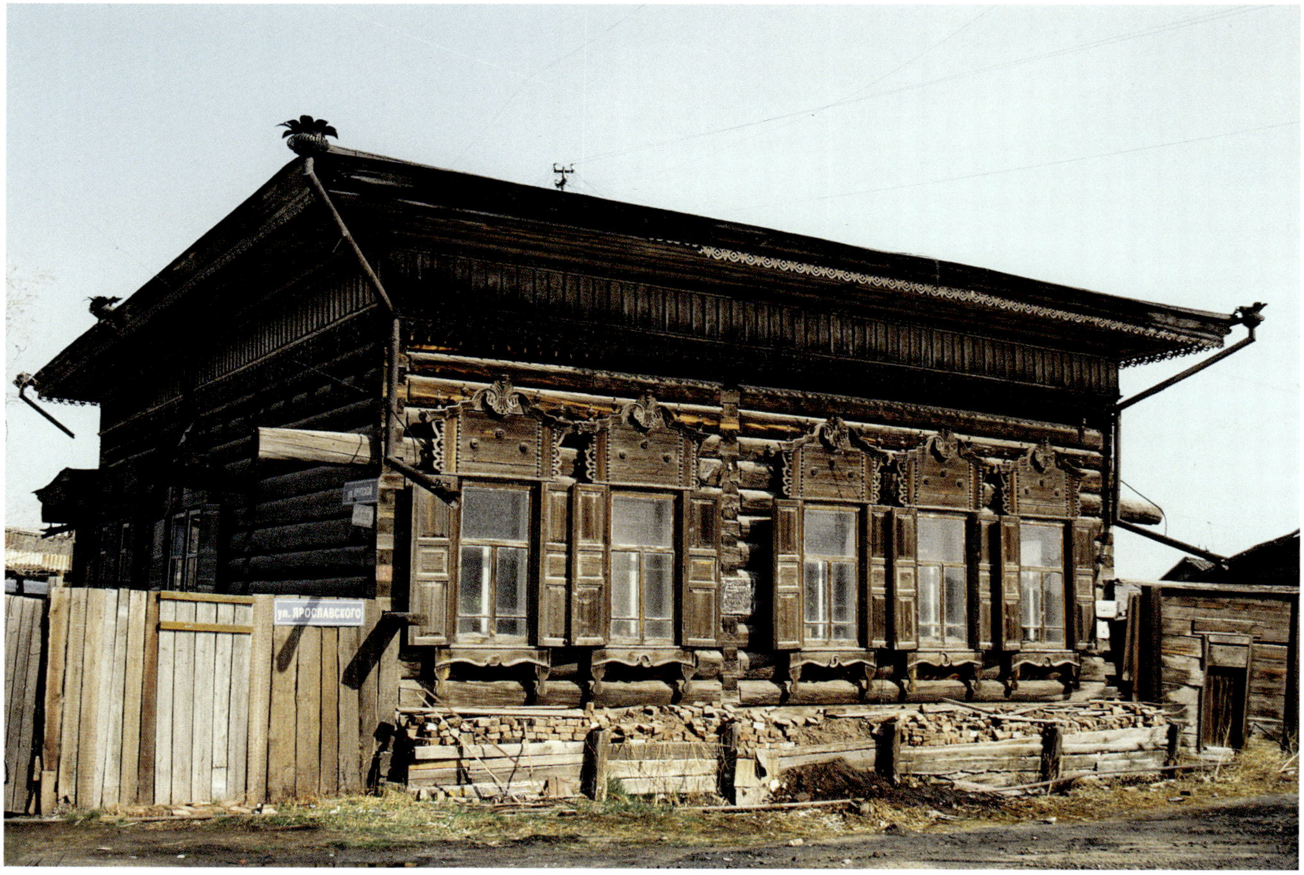
ул. ЯРОСЛАВСКОГО

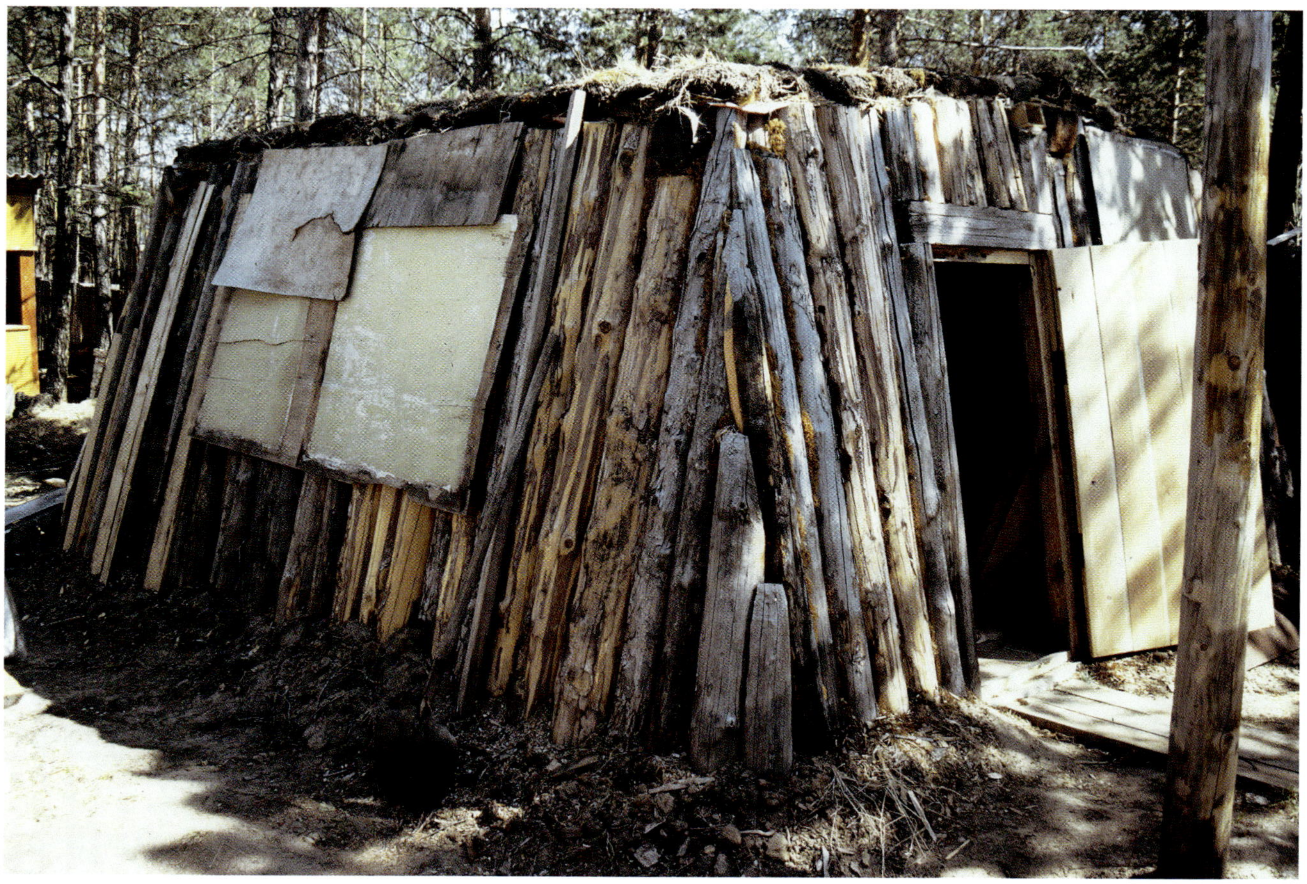

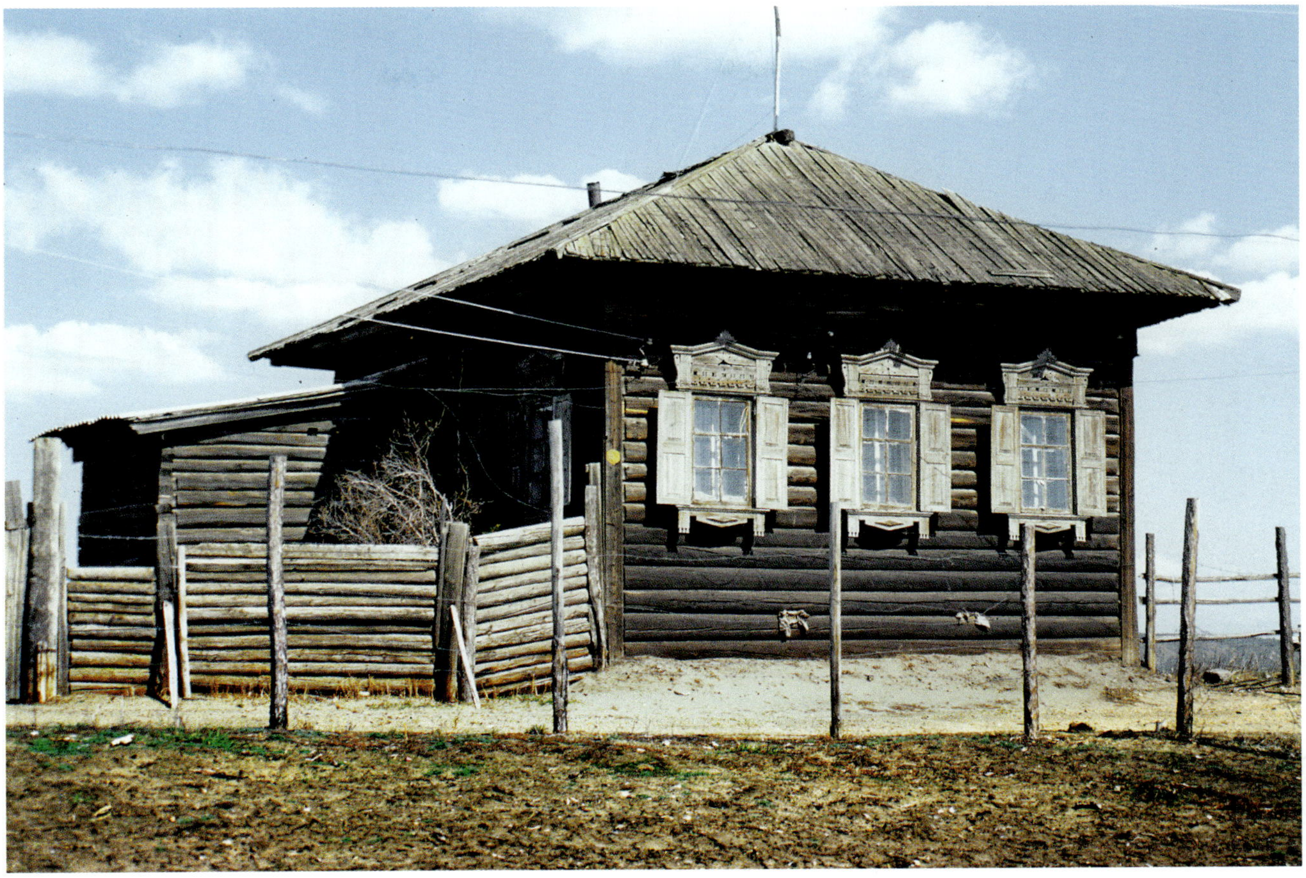

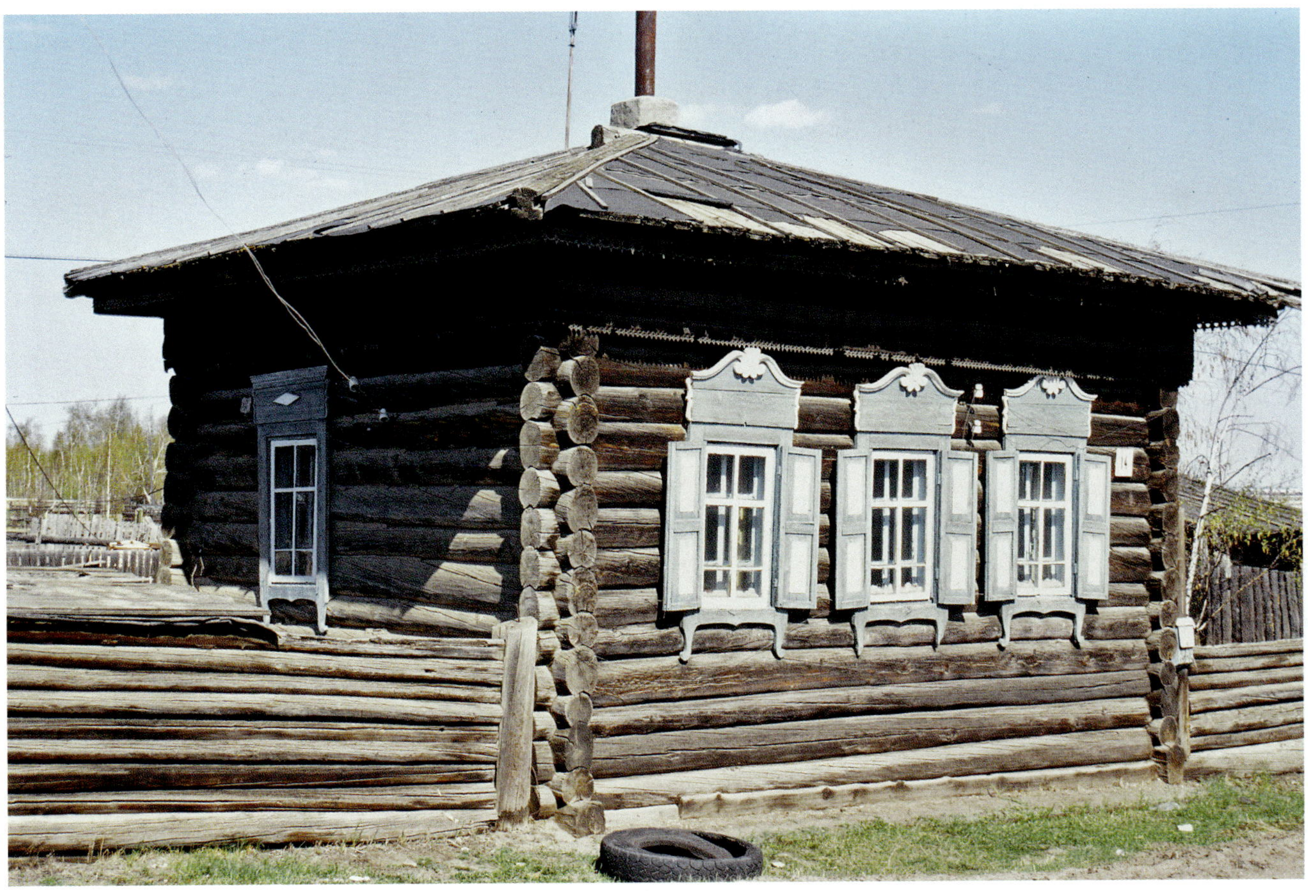

Previous pages:

YAKUTSK. Prokopy Lepchikov house. Built in the late nineteenth century, the house was one of the best examples of craftsmanship in the design of a merchant dwelling. Now threatened with collapse. May 25, 2002.

YAKUTSK. Yakovlev household. Traditional Yakut winter dwelling (*urasa*). May 26, 2002.

US-KHATYN. Molchanov house. This small *izba* with enclosed yard is typical for villages south of Yakutsk near the main road to Irkutsk. Peasants here often worked as carters. May 26, 2002.

VLADIMIROVKA. *Izba* with typical three decorated windows and enclosed yard. This is survival mode at its most basic in wooden architecture. May 26, 2002.

Conclusion
What Will Remain?

The preceding chapters and photographs have described the many ways in which the inhabitants of Russia—be they Russian or Buryat or any other ethnicity—have used the Eurasian boreal forests to create a distinctive environment for survival. For something like a millennium, the country's building heritage has in many ways been defined by log structures—and they are log structures no matter what the cladding. Yet these traditions are rapidly being erased in their original settings and consigned to outdoor museums if they are preserved at all. It is possible that Russia will join other countries, such as Finland, Sweden, and Canada, in new technologies to create multistoried apartment and office buildings of wood, an ecologically friendly and less costly construction material in comparison with concrete and steel. But whatever the practical applications of these new approaches, their design is unlikely to signify "Russia." Imagine a wooden tower with ten stories of decorative window surrounds.

The traditional *izba* was designed for survival, not prosperity. In an environment of unremitting harshness (and not just of climate), the wooden house could readily be rebuilt on the ashes of burned villages and the unmarked graves of slaughtered inhabitants. Too often, log houses and barns were the combustible material for punitive expeditions, most notably during the Great Fatherland War (as Russians refer to World War II) on the Eastern front, but also during the Russian Civil War, as anarchy descended into pathological savagery from Ukraine to eastern Siberia. Even in areas not touched by military campaigns and social upheaval, such as collectivization, log houses were usually abandoned after a period of decades, usually due to demographic shifts from villages to urban areas. Some of my most unexpected discoveries were wooden *izba* interiors covered with decades-old newspapers and chromolithographs. (In the United States, one could see a similar practice of wall covering in 1930s Farm Security

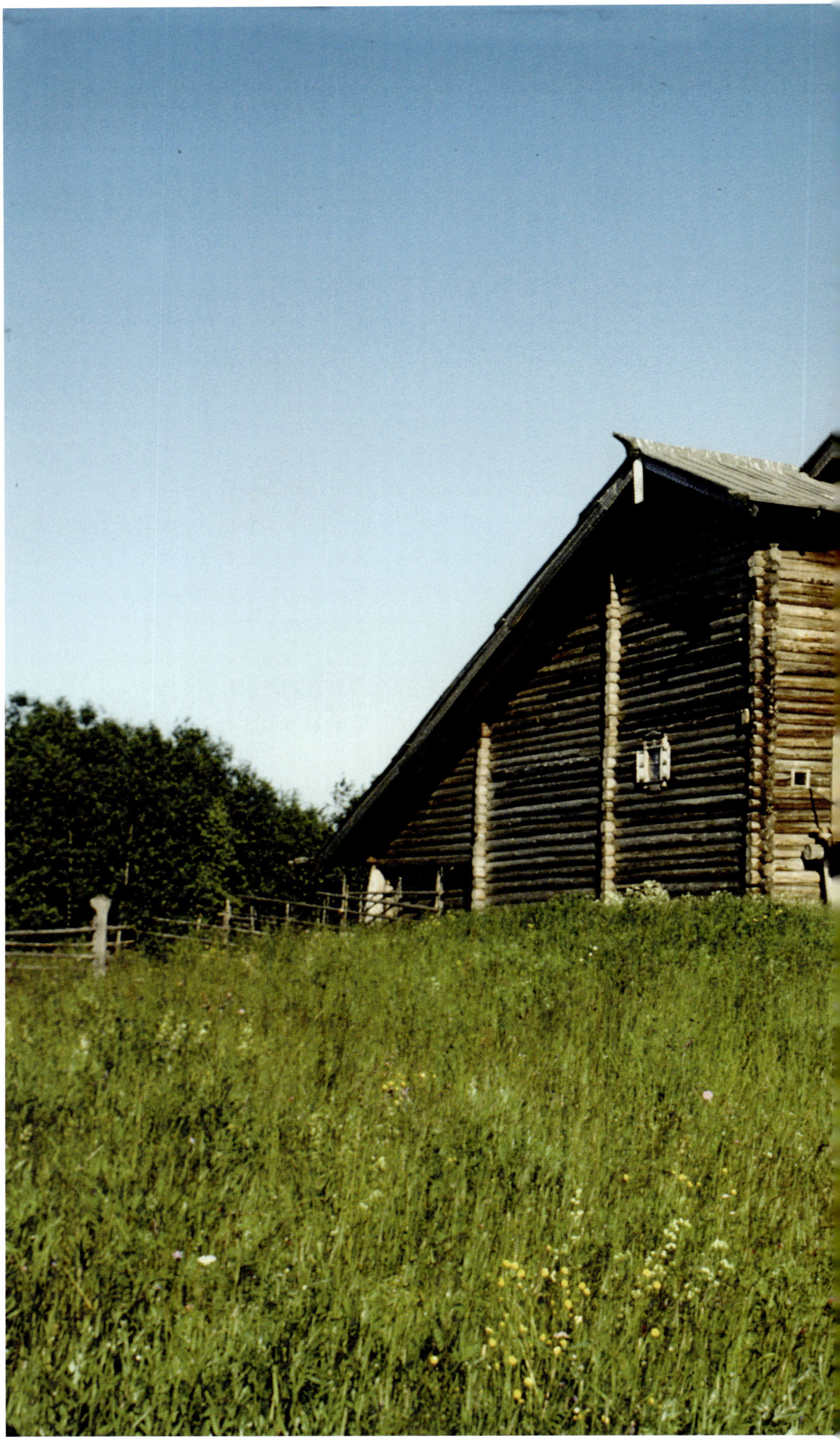

KIZHI ISLAND. Sergin house, northwest view. Built during the late nineteenth century in Munozero village for a prosperous extended peasant family, this massive log dwelling has two stories of living space with a large barn attached at the back and extending from the north facade (left). In the summer the family moved to the top story beneath the roof, where two gables (west and south facades) contain decorative balconies. August 6, 1991.

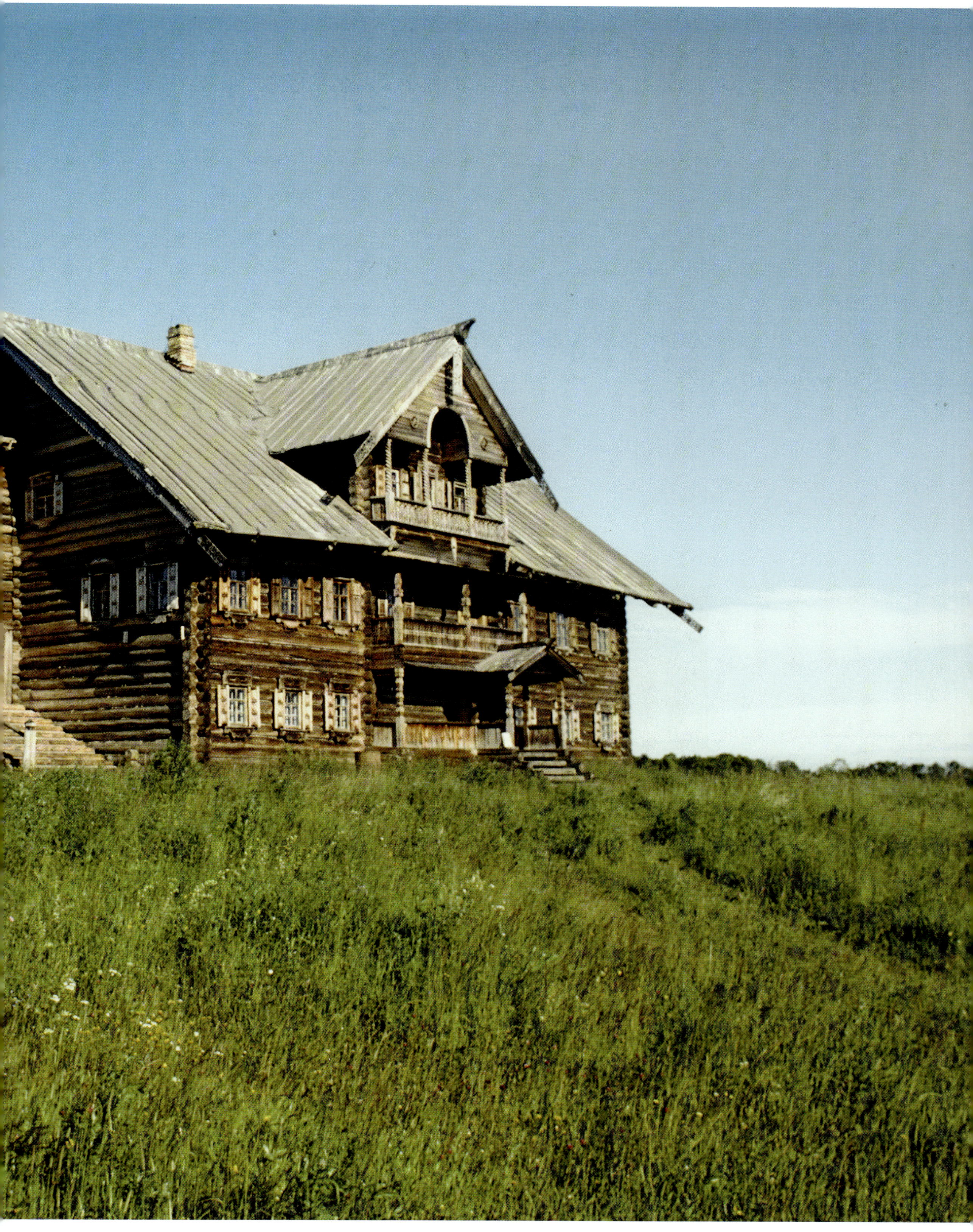

Administration photographs of the interiors of wooden dwellings that reflected conditions of widespread poverty.)

Villages with excellent examples of the traditional wooden *izba* still exist, prerevolutionary wooden houses still stand in provincial towns (the smaller, the better), and modest Soviet-era cottages abound along roadways and outlying town streets. Nonetheless, wooden structures, evocative of the forest and solid in construction, will succumb to indifference and the northern elements unless properly maintained. As the decades pass, open-air museums of wooden architecture increasingly represent the surviving tribute—or epitaph—to a vanished peasant culture that sustained Russia for centuries.

General Bibliography

Alekseeva, T. V., ed. *Russkoe iskusstvo barokko*. Moscow: Nauka, 1977.

Amirkhanov, L. I., E. A. Balashov, and V. A. Dorogin. *Istoriia Sestroretska i ego okrestnostei*. Saint Petersburg: Ostrov, 2006.

Arenzon, E. R. "Ot Kireeva do Abramtseva. K biografii Savvy Ivanovicha Mamontova." *Panorama iskusstv* 6 (1986): 359–82.

Ashchepkov, E. A. *Russkoe dereviannoe zodchestvo*. Moscow: Gos. izdatel'stvo arkhitektury i gradostroitelstva, 1950.

Ashchepkov, E. A. *Russkoe narodnoe zodchestvo v vostochnoi Sibiri*. Moscow: Gos. izdatel'stvo literatury po stroitel'stvu i arkhitekture, 1953.

Ashchepkov, E. A. *Russkoe narodnoe zodchestvo v zapadnoi Sibiri*. Moscow: Izdatel'stvo Akademii arkhitektury SSSR, 1950.

Baiburin, A. K. *Zhilishche v obriadakh i predstavleniiakh vostochnykh slavian*. Leningrad: Nauka, 1983.

Baiburova, R. M. "Zal i gostinaia usadebnogo doma russkogo klassitsizma." In *Pamiatniki russkoi arkhitektury i monumental'nogo iskusstva*, edited by V. P. Vygolov et al., 113–14. Moscow: Nauka, 1983.

Baikova, T. N. *Na zemle blagoslovennoi: Istoriko-kraevedcheskoe izdanie*. Kostroma: Kostromaizdat, 2014.

Baranov, D. A., et al. *Russkaia izba: Illiustrirovannaia entsiklopediia*. Saint Petersburg: Iskusstvo-SPB, 2001.

Barashkov, Iurii. *Nostal'giaa po dereviannomu gorodu*. Moscow: Kripto-Logos, 1992.

Beliaev, L., and T. Panova. *Dvorets Tsaria Alekseia Mikhailovicha XVII veka: Istoriko-khudozhestvennaia rekonstruktsiia*. Moscow: MGOMZ, 2011.

Bode, A. B., ed. *Dereviannoe zodchestvo: Novye materialy i otkrytiia*. Vol. 3. Moscow: Kolo, 2013.

Bode, A. B., ed. *Russkoe dereviannoe zodchesto: Proizvedeniia narodnykh masterov i vekovye Traditsii*. Moscow: Severnyi palomnik, 2012.

Borisova, Elena. *Russkaia arkhitektura vtoroi poloviny XIX veka*. Moscow: Nauka, 1979.

Brumfield, William Craft. *Architecture at the End of the Earth: Photographing the Russian North*. Durham, NC: Duke University Press, 2015.

Brumfield, William Craft. *Belozersk*. Moscow: Tri kvadrata, 2011.

Brumfield, William Craft. *Buriatiia: Arkhitekturnoe nasledie v fotografiiakh/Buriatiia: Architectural Heritage in Photographs*. Moscow: Tri kvadrata, 2008.

Brumfield, William Craft. *Cherepovets: Arkhitekturnoe nasledie cherepovetskogo kraia/Cherepovets: Architectural Heritage of the Cherepovets Region*. Moscow: Tri kvadrata, 2017.

Brumfield, William Craft. *Chita: Arkhitekturnoe nasledie v fotografiiakh/Chita: Architectural Heritage in Photographs*. Moscow: Tri kvadrata, 2008.

Brumfield, William Craft. *Chukhlomskii krai: Arkhitekturnoe nasledie v fotografiiakh/Chukhlomskii Region: Architectural Heritage in Photographs*. Moscow: Tri kvadrata, 2016.

Brumfield, William Craft. *A History of Russian Architecture*. Cambridge: Cambridge University Press, 1993.

Brumfield, William Craft. *Irkutsk: Arkhitekturnoe nasledie v fotografiiakh/Irkutsk: Architectural Heritage in Photographs*. Moscow: Tri kvadrata, 2006.

Brumfield, William Craft. *Kirillov: Ferapontovo*. Moscow: Tri kvadrata, 2009.

Brumfield, William Craft. *The Origins of Modernism in Russian Architecture*. Berkeley: University of California Press, 1991.

Brumfield, William Craft. *Smolensk: Arkhitekturnoe nasledie v fotografiiakh/Smolensk: Architectural Heritage in Photographs*. Moscow: Tri kvadrata, 2014.

Brumfield, William Craft. *Solikamsk: Arkhitekturnoe nasledie v fotografiiakh/Solikamsk: Architectural Heritage in Photographs*. Moscow: Tri kvadrata, 2007.

Brumfield, William Craft. *Suzdal': Arkhitekturnoe nasledie v fotografiiakh/Suzdal: Architectural Heritage in Photographs*. Moscow: Tri kvadrata, 2009.

Brumfield, William Craft. *Tobol'sk: Arkhitekturnoe nasledie v fotografiiakh/Tobolsk: Architectural Heritage in Photographs*. Moscow: Tri kvadrata, 2006.

Brumfield, William Craft. *Torzhok: Arkhitekturnoe nasledie v fotografiiakh/ Torzhok: Architectural Heritage in Photographs*. Moscow: Tri kvadrata, 2010.

Brumfield, William Craft. *Tot'ma: Arkhitekturnoe nasledie v fotografiiakh/Totma: Architectural Heritage in Photographs*. Moscow: Tri kvadrata, 2005.

Brumfield, William Craft. *Usol'e: Zemlia Stroganovykh na Kame*. Moscow: Tri kvadrata, 2013.

Brumfield, William Craft. *Velikii Ustiug*. Moscow: Tri kvadrata, 2007.

Brumfield, William Craft. *Vologda*. Moscow: Tri kvadrata, 2012.

Bubnov, E. N. *Russkoe dereviannoe zodchestvo Urala*. Moscow: Stroiizdat, 1988.

Diaghilev, Sergey. "Neskol'ko slov o S. V. Maliutine." *Mir Iskusstva* 4 (1903): 157–60.

Glozman, I. M., ed. *Kuskovo; Ostankino; Arkhangel'skoe*. Moscow: Iskusstvo, 1976.

Golubev, Alexey. "'A Wonderful Song of Wood': Heritage Architecture and the Search for Historical Authenticity in North Russia." *Rethinking Marxism* 29, no. 1 (2017): 142–72.

Khodakovsky, Evgeny. *Dereviannaia tserkovnaia arkhitektura Russkogo Severa XIX-nachala XX veka: Letopis' khramostroitel'stva*. Saint Petersburg: "Kolo," 2020.

Khodakovsky, Evgeny. *Wooden Church Architecture of the Russian North*. New York: Routledge, 2016.

Kirichenko, E. I. "Arkhitektor I. P. Ropet." *Arkhitekturnoe nasledstvo* 20 (1972): 85–93.

Korobko, M. Iu. *Usad'ba Uzkoe*. Moscow: Veche, 2013.

Lepskaia, L. A., et al. *Ostankinskii dvorets-muzei: Tvorchestvo krepostnykh*. Leningrad: Khudozhnik RSFSR, 1982.

Liubomirov, L. G. "Iz istorii lesopil'nogo proizvodstva v Rossii v XVII, XVIII i nachale XIX vv." *Istoricheskie Zapiski* 10 (1941): 222–49.

Liushin, D. "Dereviannyi dom g-na Porokhovshchikova." *Zodchii*, no. 2 (1872): 16.

Makovetskii, I. V. *Arkhitektura russkogo narodnogo zhilishche: Sever i Verkhnee Povolzh'e*. Moscow: Izdatel'stvo Akademii nauk SSSR, 1962.

Milchik, M. I., Ushakov, Iu. S. *Dereviannaia arkhitektura russkogo Severa: Stranitsy istorii*. Leningrad: Stroiizdat, 1981.

Opolovnikov, A. V. *Pamiatniki dereviannogo zodchestva Karelo-Finskoi SSR*. Moscow: Stroiizdat, 1955.

Opolovnikov, A. V. *Restavratsiia pamiatnikov narodnogo zodchestva*. Moscow: Stroiizdat, 1974.

Opolovnikov, A. V. *Sokrovishche Russkogo Severa*. Moscow: Stroiizdat, 1989.

Orfinskii, V. P., and I. E. Grishina. *Tipologiia dereviannogo kul'tovogo zodchestva Russkogo Severa*. Petrozavodsk: Izdatel'stvo Petrozavodskogo gos. Universiteta, 2004.

Popov, Alexander. *Konstruktsii russkikh dereviannykh sooruzhenii XVII–XVIII vekov: Materialy vystavki*. Ferapontovo: Muzei fresok Dionisii, 2007.

Reinbot A., ed. *Motivy russkoi arkhitektury*. 7 vols. Saint Petersburg: A. Reinbot, 1874–80.

Rudchenko, V. M., G. K. Smirnov, P. N. Sharmin, and E. G. Shcheboleva. *Pamiatniki arkhitektury Kostromskoi oblasti: Katalog*. Vol. 6. Kostroma: Komitet po delam kul'tury i iskusstva Administratsii Kostromskoi oblasti, 2004.

Samoilov, V. S. *Stroitel'stvo dereviannogo doma*. Moscow: Adelant, 2006.

Shinaev, S. Ia. *Dereviannoe zodchestvo: Tolkovyi slovar terminov i poniatii*. Moscow: Spetsproektrestavratsiia, 1992.

Snegirev, Iurii. "Kto v tereme zhivet?" *Rossiiskaia Gazeta Nedelia*, March 24, 2016, 8–9.

Sternin, G. Iu. "Abramtsevo: Ot 'usad'by' k 'dacha.'" In *Russkaia khudozhestvennaia kul'tura vtoroi poloviny XIX-nachala XX veka*, edited by G. Iu. Sternin, 187–88. Moscow: Sovetskii khudozhnik, 1984.

Tydman, L. V. "Kuskovo." In *Kuskovo; Ostankino; Arkhangel'skoe*, edited by I. M. Gozman, 15–74. Moscow: Iskusstvo, 1976.

Tydman, L. V. "Rabota arkhitektora K. I. Blanka v Kuskove (Zakazchik i arkhitektor v XVIII v.)." In *Russkoe iskusstvo barokko*, edited by T. V. Alekseeva, 216–25. Moscow: Nauka, 1977.

Ushakov, Iu. S. *Dereviannaia arkhitektura russkogo Severa (narodnye traditsii i sovremennye Problemy)*. Leningrad: Znanie RSFSR, 1974.

Vergunov, A. P, V. A. Gorokhov, P. I. Lapin, and L. N. Andreev. *Russkie sady i parky*. Moscow: Nauka, 1988.

Vygolov, V. P., A. I. Vlasiuk, and V. I. Pluzhnikov, eds. *Pamiatniki russkoi arkhitektury i monumental'nogo iskusstva*. Moscow: Nauka, 1985.

Zabello, S. Ia., V. N. Ivanov, and P. N. Maksimov. *Russkoe dereviannoe zodchestvo*. Moscow: Izdatel'stvo Akademii arkhitektury, 1942.

Index of Places

Page numbers in italics indicate illustrations.

General Index

Overleaf:

KHOKHLOVKA. Hunter's cache, used to protect game from scavengers. August 22, 1999.

KIZHI ISLAND. Church of the Transfiguration of the Savior, west view from Lake Onega. August 6, 1991.

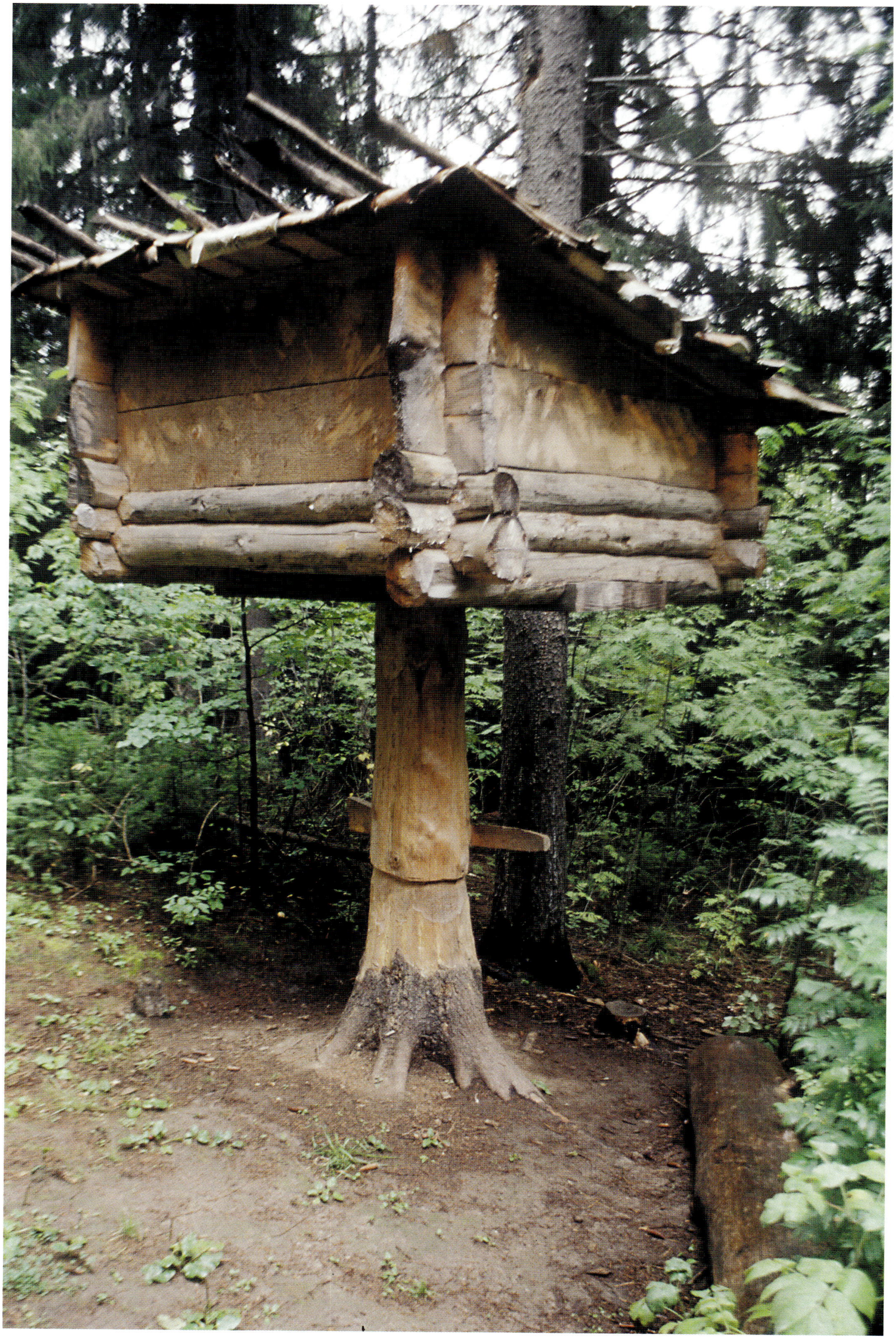

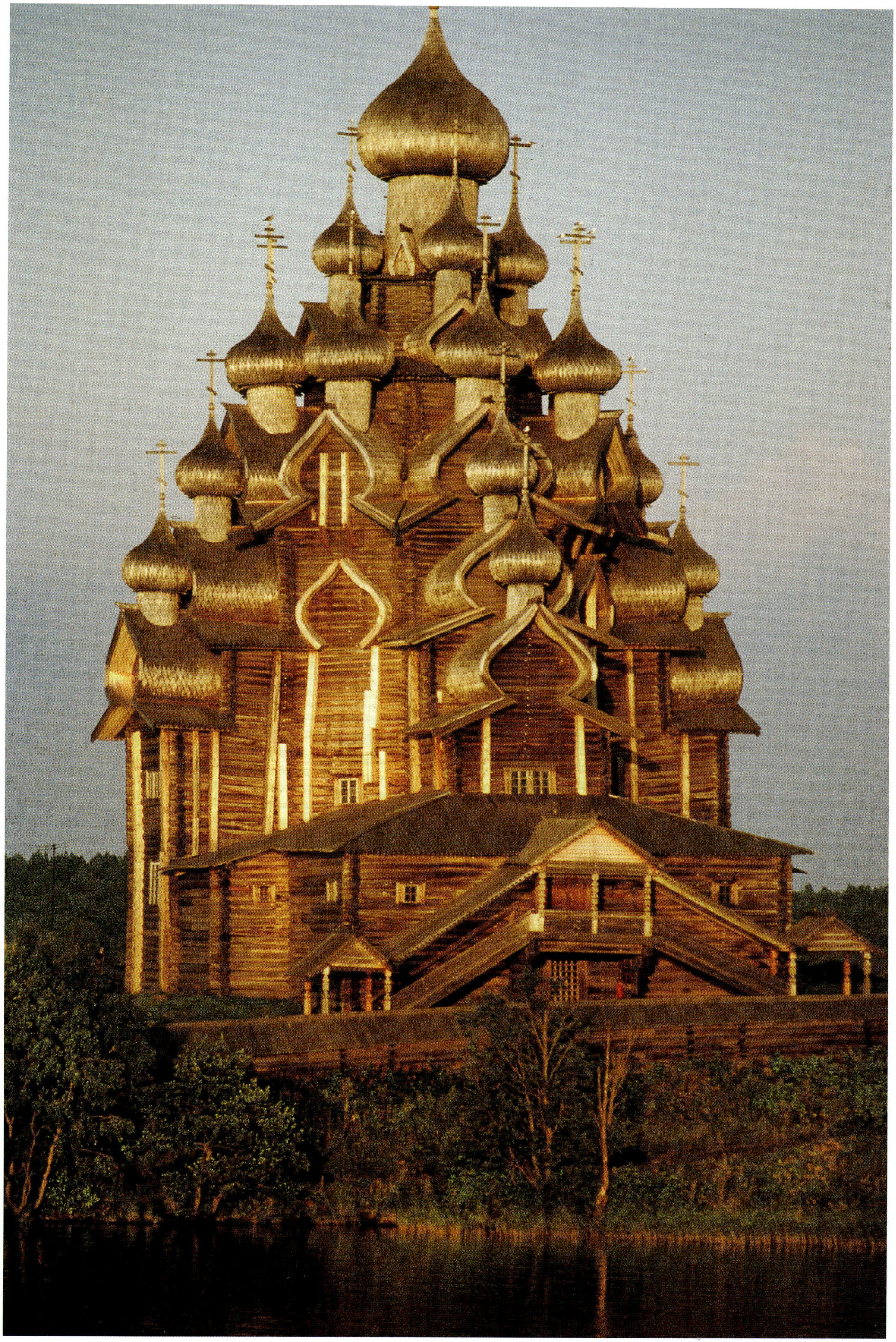